GIVE ME LIBERTY!

AN AMERICAN HISTORY

★

Fifth Edition

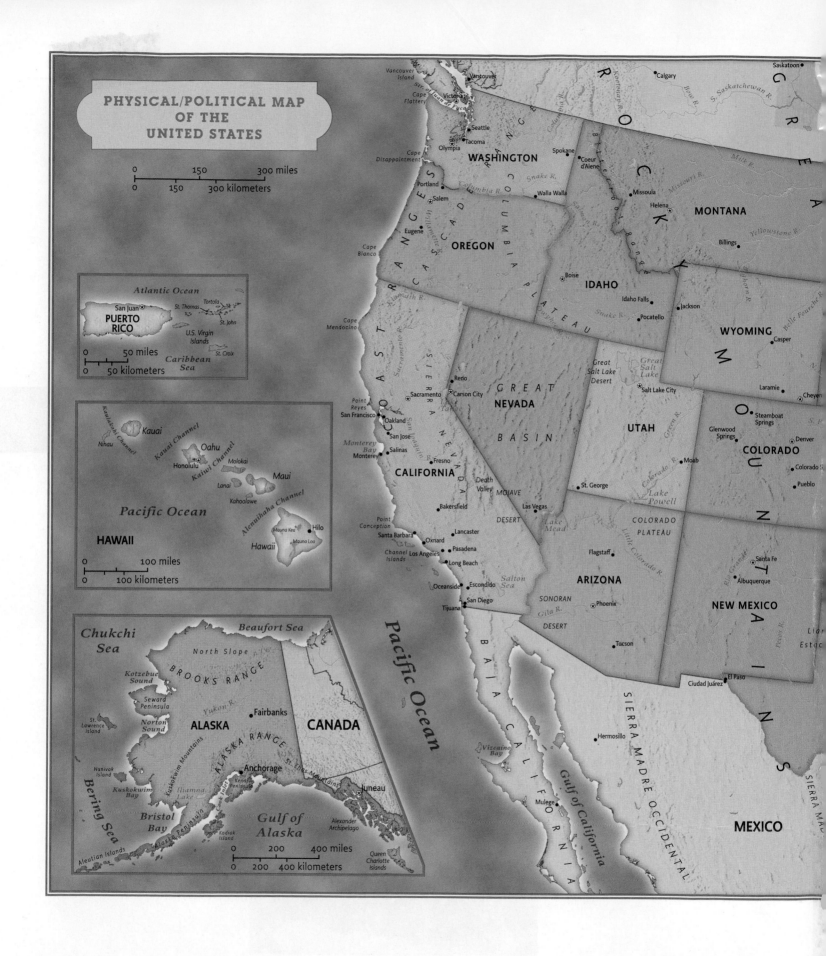

PHYSICAL/POLITICAL MAP OF THE UNITED STATES

0   150   300 miles
0   150   300 kilometers

PUERTO RICO

Atlantic Ocean
San Juan · St. Thomas · Tortola
St. John
U.S. Virgin Islands
St. Croix
Caribbean Sea

0   50 miles
0   50 kilometers

HAWAII

Kauai
Nihau
Kauai Channel
Oahu
Honolulu · Kaiwi Channel
Molokai
Lanai
Maui
Kahoolawe
Alenuihaha Channel
Pacific Ocean
Mauna Kea
Hawaii
Mauna Loa
Hilo

0   100 miles
0   100 kilometers

ALASKA

Chukchi Sea
Beaufort Sea
North Slope
BROOKS RANGE
Kotzebue Sound
Seward Peninsula
Yukon R.
Fairbanks
St. Lawrence Island
Norton Sound
ALASKA RANGE
CANADA
Nunivak Island
Kuskokwim Mountains
St. Elias Mountains
Anchorage
Juneau
Kuskokwim Bay
Iliamna Lake
Cook Inlet
Kenai Peninsula
Bristol Bay
Bering Sea
Alaska Peninsula
Kodiak Island
Gulf of Alaska
Alexander Archipelago
Aleutian Islands
Queen Charlotte Islands

0   200   400 miles
0   200   400 kilometers

Vancouver Island
Vancouver
Cape Flattery
Str. of Juan de Fuca
Victoria
Calgary
Bow R.
Saskatoon
S. Saskatchewan R.
Seattle
Tacoma
Olympia
Cape Disappointment
WASHINGTON
Spokane
Coeur d'Alene
Columbia R.
Snake R.
Milk R.
R O C K Y
Portland
Salem
Walla Walla
Missoula
Missouri R.
Helena
MONTANA
Yellowstone R.
Billings
Eugene
CASCADE RANGE
OREGON
COLUMBIA PLATEAU
Salmon R.
Bitterroot Range
Boise
IDAHO
Snake R.
Belle Fourche R.
Cape Blanco
Idaho Falls
Jackson
Pocatello
WYOMING
Casper
Cape Mendocino
Klamath R.
Sacramento R.
GREAT
Great Salt Lake Desert
Great Salt Lake
Salt Lake City
Laramie
Cheyenne
Reno
SIERRA NEVADA
Sacramento
Carson City
NEVADA
BASIN
UTAH
Green R.
Steamboat Springs
M O U N T A I N S
San Francisco
Point Reyes
Oakland
San Jose
Salinas
Monterey Bay
Monterey
San Joaquin R.
Fresno
CALIFORNIA
Death Valley
MOJAVE
DESERT
Lake Mead
St. George
Colorado R.
Lake Powell
COLORADO PLATEAU
Little Colorado R.
Glenwood Springs
Moab
Denver
COLORADO
Colorado S.
Pueblo
Bakersfield
Las Vegas
Flagstaff
Point Conception
Santa Barbara
Oxnard
Lancaster
Pasadena
Los Angeles
Long Beach
Channel Islands
Salton Sea
ARIZONA
Phoenix
Santa Fe
Albuquerque
NEW MEXICO
Oceanside
Escondido
San Diego
Tijuana
SONORAN DESERT
Gila R.
Tucson
El Paso
Ciudad Juárez
Rio Grande
Llano Estacado
Pecos R.
SIERRA MADRE OCCIDENTAL
Pacific Ocean
BAJA CALIFORNIA
Vizcaino Bay
Gulf of California
Hermosillo
Mulege
MEXICO
SIERRA MADRE

GIVE ME LIBERTY!

AN AMERICAN HISTORY

★

Fifth Edition

Volume 1: To 1877

ERIC FONER

W · W · NORTON & COMPANY
NEW YORK · LONDON

For my mother, Liza Foner (1909–2005), an accomplished artist who lived through most of the twentieth century and into the twenty-first

W. W. Norton & Company has been independent since its founding in 1923, when William Warder Norton and Mary D. Herter Norton first published lectures delivered at the People's Institute, the adult education division of New York City's Cooper Union. The firm soon expanded its program beyond the Institute, publishing books by celebrated academics from America and abroad. By midcentury, the two major pillars of Norton's publishing program—trade books and college texts—were firmly established. In the 1950s, the Norton family transferred control of the company to its employees, and today—with a staff of four hundred and a comparable number of trade, college, and professional titles published each year—W. W. Norton & Company stands as the largest and oldest publishing house owned wholly by its employees.

Editor: Steve Forman
Associate Editor: Scott Sugarman
Project Editor: Jennifer Barnhardt
Editorial Assistants: Travis Carr, Kelly Rafey
Managing Editor, College: Marian Johnson
Managing Editor, College Digital Media: Kim Yi
Production Manager: Sean Mintus
Media Editor: Laura Wilk
Media Project Editor: Rachel Mayer
Media Associate Editor: Michelle Smith
Media Assistant Editor: Chris Hillyer
Marketing Manager, History: Sarah England Bartley
Associate Design Director: Hope Miller Goodell
Designer: Chin-Yee Lai
Photo Editor: Stephanie Romeo
Permissions Manager: Megan Schindel
Permissions Specialist: Bethany Salminen
Composition: Jouve
Illustrations: Mapping Specialists, Ltd.
Manufacturing: Transcontinental

Permission to use copyrighted material is included on page A-83.

The Library of Congress has cataloged the Full Edition as follows:

Names: Foner, Eric, 1943- author.
Title: Give me liberty!: an American history / Eric Foner.
Description: Fifth edition. | New York: W. W. Norton & Company, 2016 |
 Includes bibliographical references and index.
Identifiers: LCCN 2016018497 | ISBN 9780393283167 (hardcover)
Subjects: LCSH: United States—History. | United States—Politics and
 government. | Democracy—United States—History. | Liberty—History.
Classification: LCC E178 .F66 2016 | DDC 973—dc23 LC record available at
 https://lccn.loc.gov/2016018497

ISBN this edition: 978-0-393-28312-9

W. W. Norton & Company, Inc., 500 Fifth Avenue, New York, NY 10110-0017
wwnorton.com
W. W. Norton & Company Ltd., 15 Carlisle Street, London W1D 3BS

3 4 5 6 7 8 9 0

ABOUT THE AUTHOR

ERIC FONER is DeWitt Clinton Professor of History at Columbia University, where he earned his B.A. and Ph.D. In his teaching and scholarship, he focuses on the Civil War and Reconstruction, slavery, and nineteenth-century America. Professor Foner's publications include *Free Soil, Free Labor, Free Men: The Ideology of the Republican Party before the Civil War*; *Tom Paine and Revolutionary America*; *Nothing but Freedom: Emancipation and Its Legacy*; *Reconstruction: America's Unfinished Revolution, 1863–1877*; *The Story of American Freedom*; and *Forever Free: The Story of Emancipation and Reconstruction*. His history of Reconstruction won the *Los Angeles Times* Book Award for History, the Bancroft Prize, and the Parkman Prize. He has served as president of the Organization of American Historians and the American Historical Association. In 2006 he received the Presidential Award for Outstanding Teaching from Columbia University. His most recent books are *The Fiery Trial: Abraham Lincoln and American Slavery*, winner of the Bancroft and Lincoln Prizes and the Pulitzer Prize for History, and *Gateway to Freedom: The Hidden History of the Underground Railroad*, winner of the New York Historical Society Book Prize.

CONTENTS

ABOUT THE AUTHOR ... vii
LIST OF MAPS, TABLES, AND FIGURES ... xix
PREFACE ... xxi
ACKNOWLEDGMENTS ... xxvii

PART 1: AMERICAN COLONIES TO 1763
1. A NEW WORLD ... 4

THE FIRST AMERICANS ... 6

The Settling of the Americas ... 6 ★ Indian Societies of the Americas ... 8 ★ Mound Builders of the Mississippi River Valley ... 9 ★ Western Indians ... 10 ★ Indians of Eastern North America ... 10 ★ Native American Religion ... 12 ★ Land and Property ... 12 ★ Gender Relations ... 14 ★ European Views of the Indians ... 14

INDIAN FREEDOM, EUROPEAN FREEDOM ... 15

Indian Freedom ... 15 ★ Christian Liberty ... 16 ★ Freedom and Authority ... 17 ★ Liberty and Liberties ... 17

THE EXPANSION OF EUROPE ... 18

Chinese and Portuguese Navigation ... 18 ★ Portugal and West Africa ... 19 ★ Freedom and Slavery in Africa ... 20 ★ The Voyages of Columbus ... 20

CONTACT ... 21

Columbus in the New World ... 21 ★ Exploration and Conquest ... 23 ★ The Demographic Disaster ... 24

THE SPANISH EMPIRE ... 24

Governing Spanish America ... 25 ★ Colonists in Spanish America ... 25 ★ Colonists and Indians ... 26 ★ Justifications for Conquest ... 27 ★ Spreading the Faith ... 28 ★ Las Casas's Complaint ... 29 ★ Reforming the Empire ... 29 ★ Exploring North America ... 30 ★ Spanish Florida ... 32 ★ Spain in the Southwest ... 33 ★ The Pueblo Revolt ... 33

THE FRENCH AND DUTCH EMPIRES ... 35

French Colonization ... 35

Voices of Freedom: *From* Bartolomé de las Casas, *History of the Indies* (1528), and *From* "Declaration of Josephe" (December 19, 1681) ... 36

New France and the Indians ... 38 ★ The Dutch Empire ... 39 ★ Dutch Freedom ... 41 ★ Freedom in New Netherland ... 41 ★ The Dutch and Religious Toleration ... 41 ★ Settling New Netherland ... 43 ★ New Netherland and the Indians ... 43 ★ Borderlands and Empire in Early America ... 44

REVIEW ... 47

2. BEGINNINGS OF ENGLISH AMERICA, 1607-1660 ... 48

ENGLAND AND THE NEW WORLD ... 50

Unifying the English Nation ... 50 ★ England and Ireland ... 50 ★ England and North America ... 51 ★ Spreading Protestantism ... 51 ★ The Social Crisis ... 52 ★ Masterless Men ... 53

THE COMING OF THE ENGLISH ... 54

English Emigrants ... 54 ★ Indentured Servants ... 54 ★ Land and Liberty ... 55 ★ Englishmen and Indians ... 55 ★ The Transformation of Indian Life ... 57 ★ Changes in the Land ... 57

SETTLING THE CHESAPEAKE ... 58

The Jamestown Colony ... 58 ★ From Company to Society ... 58 ★ Powhatan and Pocahontas ... 59 ★ The Uprising of 1622 ... 60 ★ A Tobacco Colony ... 61 ★ Women and the Family ... 61 ★ The Maryland Experiment ... 63 ★ Religion in Maryland ... 63

THE NEW ENGLAND WAY ... 64

The Rise of Puritanism ... 64 ★ Moral Liberty ... 65 ★ The Pilgrims at Plymouth ... 66 ★ The Great Migration ... 67 ★ The Puritan Family ... 67 ★ Government and Society in Massachusetts ... 68 ★ Church and State in Puritan Massachusetts ... 69

NEW ENGLANDERS DIVIDED ... 70

Roger Williams ... 70 ★ Rhode Island and Connecticut ... 71 ★ The Trial of Anne Hutchinson ... 71 ★ Puritans and Indians ... 73

Voices of Freedom: *From* "The Trial of Anne Hutchinson" (1637), and *From* John Winthrop, Speech to the Massachusetts General Court (July 3, 1645) ... 74

The Pequot War ... 76 ★ The New England Economy ... 76 ★ The Merchant Elite ... 77 ★ The Half-Way Covenant ... 78

RELIGION, POLITICS, AND FREEDOM ... 79

The Rights of Englishmen ... 79 ★ The English Civil War ... 80 ★ England's Debate over Freedom ... 80 ★ English Liberty ... 81 ★ The Civil War and English America ... 81 ★ The Crisis in Maryland ... 82 ★ Cromwell and the Empire ... 83

REVIEW ... 85

3. CREATING ANGLO-AMERICA, 1660-1750 ... 86

GLOBAL COMPETITION AND THE EXPANSION OF ENGLAND'S EMPIRE ... 88

The Mercantilist System ... 88 ★ The Conquest of New Netherland ... 88 ★ New York and the Rights of Englishmen and Englishwomen ... 90 ★ New York and the Indians ... 90 ★ The Charter of Liberties ... 91 ★ The Founding of Carolina ... 91 ★ The Holy Experiment ... 92 ★ Quaker Liberty ... 93 ★ Land in Pennsylvania ... 94

ORIGINS OF AMERICAN SLAVERY ... 94

Englishmen and Africans ... 94 ★ Slavery in History ... 95 ★ Slavery in the West Indies ... 96 ★ Slavery and the Law ... 98 ★ The Rise of Chesapeake Slavery ... 99 ★ Bacon's Rebellion: Land and Labor in Virginia ... 99 ★ The End of the Rebellion, and Its Consequences ... 100 ★ A Slave Society ... 100 ★ Notions of Freedom ... 101

COLONIES IN CRISIS ... 101

The Glorious Revolution ... 102 ★ The Glorious Revolution in America ... 103 ★ The Maryland Uprising ... 103 ★ Leisler's Rebellion ... 104 ★ Changes in New England ... 104 ★ The Prosecution of Witches ... 105 ★ The Salem Witch Trials ... 105

THE GROWTH OF COLONIAL AMERICA ... 106

A Diverse Population ... 107 ★ Attracting Settlers ... 107 ★ The German Migration ... 109 ★ Religious Diversity ... 109 ★ Indian Life in Transition ... 111

Voices of Freedom: From Letter by a Swiss-German Immigrant to Pennsylvania (August 23, 1769), and From Memorial against Non-English Immigration (December 1727) ... 112

Regional Diversity ... 114 ★ The Consumer Revolution ... 115 ★ Colonial Cities ... 115 ★ Colonial Artisans ... 116 ★ An Atlantic World ... 116

SOCIAL CLASSES IN THE COLONIES ... 117

The Colonial Elite ... 117 ★ Anglicization ... 118 ★ The South Carolina Aristocracy ... 119 ★ Poverty in the Colonies ... 120 ★ The Middle Ranks ... 121 ★ Women and the Household Economy ... 122 ★ North America at Mid-Century ... 123

REVIEW ... 125

4. SLAVERY, FREEDOM, AND THE STRUGGLE FOR EMPIRE, TO 1763 ... 126

SLAVERY AND EMPIRE ... 128

Atlantic Trade ... 128 ★ Africa and the Slave Trade ... 130 ★ The Middle Passage ... 130 ★ Chesapeake Slavery ... 132 ★ Freedom and Slavery in the Chesapeake ... 133 ★ Indian Slavery in Early Carolina ... 134 ★ The Rice Kingdom ... 134 ★ The Georgia Experiment ... 135 ★ Slavery in the North ... 135

SLAVE CULTURES AND SLAVE RESISTANCE ... 136

Becoming African-American ... 136 ★ African Religion in Colonial America ... 137 ★ African-American Cultures ... 138 ★ Resistance to Slavery ... 138 ★ The Crisis of 1739–1741 ... 139

AN EMPIRE OF FREEDOM ... 140

British Patriotism ... 140 ★ The British Constitution ... 140 ★ Republican Liberty ... 141 ★ Liberal Freedom ... 142

THE PUBLIC SPHERE ... 143

The Right to Vote ... 143 ★ Political Cultures ... 144 ★ Colonial Government ... 145 ★ The Rise of the Assemblies ... 145 ★ Politics in

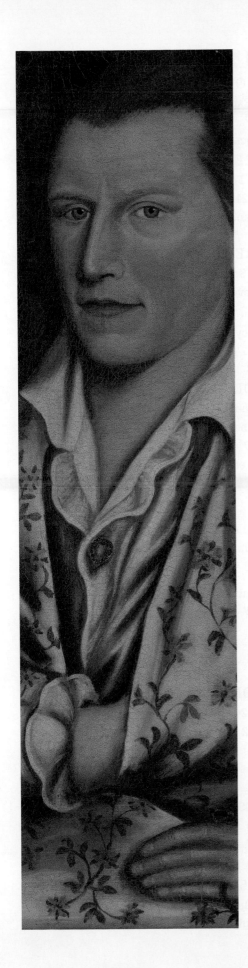

Public ... 146 ★ The Colonial Press ... 146 ★ Freedom of Expression and Its Limits ... 147 ★ The Trial of Zenger ... 148 ★ The American Enlightenment ... 148

THE GREAT AWAKENING ... 149

Religious Revivals ... 149 ★ The Preaching of Whitefield ... 150 ★ The Awakening's Impact ... 151

IMPERIAL RIVALRIES ... 151

Spanish North America ... 151 ★ The Spanish in California ... 154 ★ The French Empire ... 155

BATTLE FOR THE CONTINENT ... 156

The Middle Ground ... 156 ★ The Seven Years' War ... 157 ★ A World Transformed ... 158 ★ Pontiac's Rebellion ... 159 ★ The Proclamation Line ... 159 ★ Pennsylvania and the Indians ... 161

Voices of Freedom: *From* Scarouyady, Speech to Pennsylvania Provincial Council (1756), and *From* Pontiac, Speeches (1762 and 1763) ... 162

Colonial Identities ... 164

REVIEW ... 166

PART 2: A NEW NATION, 1763–1840
5. THE AMERICAN REVOLUTION, 1763–1783 ... 170

THE CRISIS BEGINS ... 171

Consolidating the Empire ... 172 ★ Taxing the Colonies ... 173 ★ The Stamp Act Crisis ... 173 ★ Taxation and Representation ... 174 ★ Liberty and Resistance ... 175 ★ Politics in the Streets ... 176 ★ The Regulators ... 177 ★ The Tenant Uprising ... 177

THE ROAD TO REVOLUTION ... 178

The Townshend Crisis ... 178 ★ Homespun Virtue ... 178 ★ The Boston Massacre ... 179 ★ Wilkes and Liberty ... 180 ★ The Tea Act ... 181 ★ The Intolerable Acts ... 181

THE COMING OF INDEPENDENCE ... 182

The Continental Congress ... 182 ★ The Continental Association ... 182 ★ The Sweets of Liberty ... 183 ★ The Outbreak of War ... 184 ★ Independence? ... 185 ★ *Common Sense* ... 186 ★ Paine's Impact ... 187 ★ The Declaration of Independence ... 187

Voices of Freedom: *From* Samuel Seabury, *An Alarm to the Legislature of the Province in New-York* (1775), and *From* Thomas Paine, *Common Sense* (1776) ... 188

The Declaration and American Freedom ... 190 ★ An Asylum for Mankind ... 191 ★ The Global Declaration of Independence ... 191

SECURING INDEPENDENCE ... 193

The Balance of Power ... 193 ★ Blacks in the Revolution ... 194 ★ The First Years of the War ... 194 ★ The Battle of Saratoga ... 195 ★ The War in the South ... 197 ★ Victory at Last ... 199

REVIEW ... 203

6. THE REVOLUTION WITHIN ... 204

DEMOCRATIZING FREEDOM ... 206

The Dream of Equality ... 206 ★ Expanding the Political Nation ... 206 ★ The Revolution in Pennsylvania ... 207 ★ The New Constitutions ... 208 ★ The Right to Vote ... 209 ★ Democratizing Government ... 209

TOWARD RELIGIOUS TOLERATION ... 210

Catholic Americans ... 211 ★ The Founders and Religion ... 211 ★ Separating Church and State ... 212 ★ Jefferson and Religious Liberty ... 213 ★ The Revolution and the Churches ... 214 ★ Christian Republicanism ... 214

DEFINING ECONOMIC FREEDOM ... 215

Toward Free Labor ... 215 ★ The Soul of a Republic ... 216 ★ The Politics of Inflation ... 217 ★ The Debate over Free Trade ... 217

THE LIMITS OF LIBERTY ... 218

Colonial Loyalists ... 218 ★ The Loyalists' Plight ... 219 ★ The Revolution as a Borderlands Conflict ... 219 ★ The Indians' Revolution ... 221 ★ White Freedom, Indian Freedom ... 222

SLAVERY AND THE REVOLUTION ... 223

The Language of Slavery and Freedom ... 224 ★ Obstacles to Abolition ... 224 ★ The Cause of General Liberty ... 225 ★ Petitions for Freedom ... 225 ★ British Emancipators ... 227 ★ Voluntary Emancipations ... 227 ★ Abolition in the North ... 228 ★ Free Black Communities ... 228

DAUGHTERS OF LIBERTY ... 229

Revolutionary Women ... 229

Voices of Freedom: *From* Abigail Adams to John Adams, Braintree, Mass. (March 31, 1776), and *From* Petitions of Slaves to the Massachusetts Legislature (1773 and 1777) ... 230

Gender and Politics ... 232 ★ Republican Motherhood ... 233 ★ The Arduous Struggle for Liberty ... 234

REVIEW ... 237

7. FOUNDING A NATION, 1783–1791 ... 238

AMERICA UNDER THE CONFEDERATION ... 240

The Articles of Confederation ... 240 ★ Congress and the West ... 242 ★ Settlers and the West ... 242 ★ The Land Ordinances ... 243 ★ The Confederation's Weaknesses ... 245 ★ Shays's Rebellion ... 246 ★ Nationalists of the 1780s ... 247

A NEW CONSTITUTION ... 247

The Structure of Government ... 248 ★ The Limits of Democracy ... 249 ★ The Division and Separation of Powers ... 250 ★ The Debate over Slavery ... 251 ★ Slavery in the Constitution ... 251 ★ The Final Document ... 253

THE RATIFICATION DEBATE AND THE ORIGIN OF THE BILL OF RIGHTS ... 254

The Federalist ... 254 ★ "Extend the Sphere" ... 255 ★ The Anti-Federalists ... 256 ★ The Bill of Rights ... 258

Voices of Freedom: *From* David Ramsay, *The History of the American Revolution* (1789), and *From* James Winthrop, Anti-Federalist Essay Signed "Agrippa" (1787) ... 260

"WE THE PEOPLE" ... 263

National Identity ... 263 ★ Indians in the New Nation ... 263 ★ Blacks and the Republic ... 266 ★ Jefferson, Slavery, and Race ... 268 ★ Principles of Freedom ... 269

REVIEW ... 271

8. SECURING THE REPUBLIC, 1791–1815 ... 272

POLITICS IN AN AGE OF PASSION ... 273

Hamilton's Program ... 274 ★ The Emergence of Opposition ... 274 ★ The Jefferson–Hamilton Bargain ... 275 ★ The Impact of the French Revolution ... 276 ★ Political Parties ... 277 ★ The Whiskey Rebellion ... 278 ★ The Republican Party ... 279 ★ An Expanding Public Sphere ... 279 ★ The Democratic-Republican Societies ... 280 ★ The Rights of Women ... 280 ★ Women and the Republic ... 281

Voices of Freedom: *From* Judith Sargent Murray, "On the Equality of the Sexes" (1790), and *From* Address of the Democratic-Republican Society of Pennsylvania (December 18, 1794) ... 282

THE ADAMS PRESIDENCY ... 284

The Election of 1796 ... 284 ★ The "Reign of Witches" ... 285 ★ The Virginia and Kentucky Resolutions ... 286 ★ The "Revolution of 1800" ... 287 ★ Slavery and Politics ... 288 ★ The Haitian Revolution ... 288 ★ Gabriel's Rebellion ... 289

JEFFERSON IN POWER ... 290

Judicial Review ... 291 ★ The Louisiana Purchase ... 291 ★ Lewis and Clark ... 293 ★ Incorporating Louisiana ... 294 ★ The Barbary Wars ... 294 ★ The Embargo ... 295 ★ Madison and Pressure for War ... 296

THE "SECOND WAR OF INDEPENDENCE" ... 297

The Indian Response ... 297 ★ Tecumseh's Vision ... 298 ★ The War of 1812 ... 298 ★ The War's Aftermath ... 302 ★ The War of 1812 and the Canadian Borderland ... 302 ★ The End of the Federalist Party ... 303

REVIEW ... 305

9. THE MARKET REVOLUTION, 1800–1840 ... 306

A NEW ECONOMY ... 308

Roads and Steamboats ... 309 ★ The Erie Canal ... 309 ★ Railroads and the Telegraph ... 311 ★ The Rise of the West ... 312 ★ An Internal Borderland ... 315 ★ The Cotton Kingdom ... 316 ★ The Unfree Westward Movement ... 318

MARKET SOCIETY ... 318

Commercial Farmers ... 318 ★ The Growth of Cities ... 319 ★ The Factory System ... 321 ★ The Industrial Worker ... 323 ★ The "Mill Girls" ... 324 ★

The Growth of Immigration ... 324 ★ Irish and German Newcomers ... 325
★ The Rise of Nativism ... 326 ★ The Transformation of Law ... 328

THE FREE INDIVIDUAL ... 329

The West and Freedom ... 329 ★ The Transcendentalists ... 330 ★
Individualism ... 330

Voices of Freedom: From Recollections of Harriet L. Noble (1824), and
From "Factory Life as It Is, by an Operative" (1845) ... 332

The Second Great Awakening ... 334 ★ The Awakening's Impact ... 335 ★
The Emergence of Mormonism ... 336

THE LIMITS OF PROSPERITY ... 337

Liberty and Prosperity ... 337 ★ Race and Opportunity ... 338 ★ The Cult
of Domesticity ... 339 ★ Women and Work ... 340 ★ The Early Labor
Movement ... 341 ★ The "Liberty of Living" ... 342

REVIEW ... 345

10. DEMOCRACY IN AMERICA, 1815–1840 ... 346

THE TRIUMPH OF DEMOCRACY ... 348

Property and Democracy ... 348 ★ The Dorr War ... 348 ★ Tocqueville on
Democracy ... 349 ★ The Information Revolution ... 350 ★ The Limits of
Democracy ... 351 ★ A Racial Democracy ... 352 ★ Race and Class ... 352

NATIONALISM AND ITS DISCONTENTS ... 353

The American System ... 353 ★ Banks and Money ... 355 ★ The Panic of
1819 ... 355 ★ The Politics of the Panic ... 356 ★ The Missouri
Controversy ... 356 ★ The Slavery Question ... 358

NATION, SECTION, AND PARTY ... 359

The United States and the Latin American Wars of Independence ... 359
★ The Monroe Doctrine ... 360 ★ The Election of 1824 ... 361

Voices of Freedom: From The Memorial of the Non-Freeholders of the
City of Richmond (1829), and From Appeal of Forty Thousand Citizens
Threatened with Disfranchisement (1838) ... 362

The Nationalism of John Quincy Adams ... 364 ★ "Liberty Is Power" ...
365 ★ Martin Van Buren and the Democratic Party ... 365 ★ The Election
of 1828 ... 366

THE AGE OF JACKSON ... 367

The Party System ... 367 ★ Democrats and Whigs ... 368 ★ Public and
Private Freedom ... 369 ★ Politics and Morality ... 370 ★ South Carolina
and Nullification ... 371 ★ Calhoun's Political Theory ... 371 ★ The
Nullification Crisis ... 373 ★ Indian Removal ... 374 ★ The Supreme Court
and the Indians ... 374

THE BANK WAR AND AFTER ... 378

Biddle's Bank ... 378 ★ The Pet Banks and the Economy ... 379 ★ The
Panic of 1837 ... 380 ★ Van Buren in Office ... 381 ★ The Election of
1840 ... 381 ★ His Accidency ... 382

REVIEW ... 384

Eng'd by H.B.Hall, Jr N.Y.

MARGARET FUL

PART 3: SLAVERY, FREEDOM, AND THE CRISIS OF THE UNION, 1840–1877

11. THE PECULIAR INSTITUTION ... 388

THE OLD SOUTH ... 390

Cotton Is King ... 390 ★ The Second Middle Passage ... 391 ★ Slavery and the Nation ... 391 ★ The Southern Economy ... 393 ★ Plain Folk of the Old South ... 394 ★ The Planter Class ... 395 ★ The Paternalist Ethos ... 396 ★ The Code of Honor ... 396 ★ The Proslavery Argument ... 397 ★ Abolition in the Americas ... 398 ★ Slavery and Liberty ... 399 ★ Slavery and Civilization ... 400

LIFE UNDER SLAVERY ... 400

Slaves and the Law ... 400 ★ Conditions of Slave Life ... 401 ★ Free Blacks in the Old South ... 402

Voices of Freedom: *From* Letter by Joseph Taper to Joseph Long (1840), and *From* "Slavery and the Bible" (1850) ... 404

The Upper and Lower South ... 406 ★ Slave Labor ... 407 ★ Gang Labor and Task Labor ... 407 ★ Slavery in the Cities ... 409 ★ Maintaining Order ... 409

SLAVE CULTURE ... 410

The Slave Family ... 411 ★ The Threat of Sale ... 411 ★ Gender Roles among Slaves ... 412 ★ Slave Religion ... 412 ★ The Gospel of Freedom ... 413 ★ The Desire for Liberty ... 413

RESISTANCE TO SLAVERY ... 415

Forms of Resistance ... 415 ★ Fugitive Slaves ... 415 ★ The Underground Railroad ... 417 ★ The *Amistad* ... 418 ★ Slave Revolts ... 418 ★ Nat Turner's Rebellion ... 419

REVIEW ... 423

12. AN AGE OF REFORM, 1820–1840 ... 424

THE REFORM IMPULSE ... 425

Utopian Communities ... 426 ★ The Shakers ... 426 ★ Oneida ... 427 ★ Worldly Communities ... 428 ★ The Owenites ... 429 ★ Religion and Reform ... 430 ★ The Temperance Movement ... 431 ★ Critics of Reform ... 431 ★ Reformers and Freedom ... 432 ★ The Invention of the Asylum ... 433 ★ The Common School ... 433

THE CRUSADE AGAINST SLAVERY ... 435

Colonization ... 435 ★ Blacks and Colonization ... 435 ★ Militant Abolitionism ... 436 ★ The Emergence of Garrison ... 437 ★ Spreading the Abolitionist Message ... 437 ★ Slavery and Moral Suasion ... 439 ★ Abolitionists and the Idea of Freedom ... 439 ★ A New Vision of America ... 440

BLACK AND WHITE ABOLITIONISM ... 441

Black Abolitionists ... 441 ★ Abolitionism and Race ... 442 ★ Slavery and American Freedom ... 443 ★ Gentlemen of Property and Standing ... 444 ★ Slavery and Civil Liberties ... 445

THE ORIGINS OF FEMINISM ... 446

The Rise of the Public Woman ... 446 ★ Women and Free Speech ... 447 ★ Women's Rights ... 447 ★ Feminism and Freedom ... 449 ★ Women and Work ... 449

Voices of Freedom: *From* Angelina Grimké, Letter in *The Liberator* (August 2, 1837), and *From* Catharine Beecher, *An Essay on Slavery and Abolitionism* (1837) ... 450

The Slavery of Sex ... 453 ★ "Social Freedom" ... 453 ★ The Abolitionist Schism ... 454

REVIEW ... 457

13. A HOUSE DIVIDED, 1840–1861 ... 458

FRUITS OF MANIFEST DESTINY ... 459

Continental Expansion ... 459 ★ The Mexican Frontier: New Mexico and California ... 460 ★ The Texas Revolt ... 461 ★ The Election of 1844 ... 463 ★ The Road to War ... 464 ★ The War and Its Critics ... 465 ★ Combat in Mexico ... 466 ★ The Texas Borderland ... 468 ★ Race and Manifest Destiny ... 469 ★ Gold-Rush California ... 469 ★ California and the Boundaries of Freedom ... 470 ★ Opening Japan ... 471

A DOSE OF ARSENIC ... 472

The Wilmot Proviso ... 473 ★ The Free Soil Appeal ... 473 ★ Crisis and Compromise ... 475 ★ The Great Debate ... 475 ★ The Fugitive Slave Issue ... 476 ★ Douglas and Popular Sovereignty ... 477 ★ The Kansas-Nebraska Act ... 478

THE RISE OF THE REPUBLICAN PARTY ... 480

The Northern Economy ... 480 ★ The Rise and Fall of the Know-Nothings ... 480 ★ The Free Labor Ideology ... 483 ★ Bleeding Kansas and the Election of 1856 ... 484

THE EMERGENCE OF LINCOLN ... 485

The Dred Scott Decision ... 485 ★ The Decision's Aftermath ... 486 ★ Lincoln and Slavery ... 486 ★ The Lincoln-Douglas Campaign ... 487 ★ John Brown at Harpers Ferry ... 489

Voices of Freedom: *From* The Lincoln-Douglas Debates (1858) ... 490

The Rise of Southern Nationalism ... 492 ★ The Democratic Split ... 493 ★ The Nomination of Lincoln ... 494 ★ The Election of 1860 ... 494

THE IMPENDING CRISIS ... 495

The Secession Movement ... 495 ★ The Secession Crisis ... 496 ★ And the War Came ... 497

REVIEW ... 501

14. A NEW BIRTH OF FREEDOM: THE CIVIL WAR, 1861–1865 ... 502

THE FIRST MODERN WAR ... 503

The Two Combatants ... 504 ★ The Technology of War ... 504 ★ The Public and the War ... 506 ★ Mobilizing Resources ... 507 ★ Military

Strategies ... 508 ★ The War Begins ... 508 ★ The War in the East, 1862 ... 509 ★ The War in the West ... 510

THE COMING OF EMANCIPATION ... 511

Slavery and the War ... 511 ★ The Unraveling of Slavery ... 513 ★ Steps toward Emancipation ... 513 ★ Lincoln's Decision ... 514 ★ The Emancipation Proclamation ... 516 ★ Enlisting Black Troops ... 517 ★ The Black Soldier ... 518

THE SECOND AMERICAN REVOLUTION ... 519

Liberty and Union ... 519 ★ Lincoln's Vision ... 520 ★ The War and American Religion ... 521 ★ Liberty in Wartime ... 522 ★ The North's Transformation ... 523 ★ Government and the Economy ... 523 ★ The West and the War ... 524

Voices of Freedom: *From* Frederick Douglass, "Men of Color, to Arms!" (1863), and *From* Abraham Lincoln, Address at Sanitary Fair, Baltimore (April 18, 1864) ... 526

A New Financial System ... 529 ★ Women and the War ... 530 ★ The Divided North ... 531

THE CONFEDERATE NATION ... 532

Leadership and Government ... 532 ★ The Inner Civil War ... 534 ★ Economic Problems ... 534 ★ Southern Unionists ... 535 ★ Women and the Confederacy ... 536 ★ Black Soldiers for the Confederacy ... 538

TURNING POINTS ... 538

Gettysburg and Vicksburg ... 538 ★ 1864 ... 539

REHEARSALS FOR RECONSTRUCTION AND THE END OF THE WAR ... 541

The Sea Islands Experiment ... 541 ★ Wartime Reconstruction in the West ... 542 ★ The Politics of Wartime Reconstruction ... 542 ★ Victory at Last ... 543 ★ The War and the World ... 545 ★ The War in American History ... 546

REVIEW ... 549

15. "WHAT IS FREEDOM?": RECONSTRUCTION, 1865–1877 ... 550

THE MEANING OF FREEDOM ... 552

Blacks and the Meaning of Freedom ... 552 ★ Families in Freedom ... 552 ★ Church and School ... 553 ★ Political Freedom ... 553 ★ Land, Labor, and Freedom ... 554 ★ Masters without Slaves ... 555 ★ The Free Labor Vision ... 556 ★ The Freedmen's Bureau ... 557 ★ The Failure of Land Reform ... 558 ★ Toward a New South ... 559 ★ The White Farmer ... 560 ★ The Urban South ... 561 ★ The Aftermath of Slavery ... 561

Voices of Freedom: *From* Petition of Committee in Behalf of the Freedmen to Andrew Johnson (1865), and *From* A Sharecropping Contract (1866) ... 562

THE MAKING OF RADICAL RECONSTRUCTION ... 564

Andrew Johnson ... 564 ★ The Failure of Presidential Reconstruction ... 565 ★ The Black Codes ... 565 ★ The Radical Republicans ... 566 ★ The Origins of Civil Rights ... 567 ★ The Fourteenth Amendment ... 568 ★ The Reconstruction Act ... 568 ★ Impeachment and the Election of Grant ... 569 ★ The Fifteenth Amendment ... 570 ★ The "Great Constitutional Revolution" ... 570 ★ Boundaries of Freedom ... 571 ★ The Rights of Women ... 572 ★ Feminists and Radicals ... 572

RADICAL RECONSTRUCTION IN THE SOUTH ... 574

"The Tocsin of Freedom" ... 574 ★ The Black Officeholder ... 575 ★ Carpetbaggers and Scalawags ... 576 ★ Southern Republicans in Power ... 577 ★ The Quest for Prosperity ... 578

THE OVERTHROW OF RECONSTRUCTION ... 579

Reconstruction's Opponents ... 579 ★ "A Reign of Terror" ... 579 ★ The Liberal Republicans ... 581 ★ The North's Retreat ... 582 ★ The Triumph of the Redeemers ... 584 ★ The Disputed Election and Bargain of 1877 ... 584 ★ The End of Reconstruction ... 585

REVIEW ... 587

APPENDIX

DOCUMENTS

The Declaration of Independence (1776) ... A-2 ★ The Constitution of the United States (1787) ... A-5 ★ *From* George Washington's Farewell Address (1796) ... A-16 ★ The Seneca Falls Declaration of Sentiments and Resolutions (1848) ... A-21 ★ *From* Frederick Douglass's "What, to the Slave, Is the Fourth of July?" Speech (1852) ... A-24 ★ The Gettysburg Address (1863) ... A-27 ★ Abraham Lincoln's Second Inaugural Address (1865) ... A-28 ★ The Populist Platform of 1892 ... A-29 ★ Franklin D. Roosevelt's First Inaugural Address (1933) ... A-32 ★ *From* The Program for the March on Washington for Jobs and Freedom (1963) ... A-35 ★ Ronald Reagan's First Inaugural Address (1981) ... A-36 ★ Barack Obama's First Inaugural Address (2009) ... A-39

TABLES AND FIGURES

Presidential Elections ... A-42 ★ Admission of States ... A-50 ★ Population of the United States ... A-51 ★ Historical Statistics of the United States: Labor Force—Selected Characteristics Expressed as a Percentage of the Labor Force, 1800–2010 ... A-52 ★ Immigration, by Origin ... A-52 ★ Unemployment Rate, 1890–2015 ... A-53 ★ Union Membership as a Percentage of Nonagricultural Employment, 1880–2015 ... A-53 ★ Voter Participation in Presidential Elections, 1824–2012 ... A-53 ★ Birthrate, 1820–2015 ... A-53

GLOSSARY ★ ... A-55
CREDITS ★ ... A-83
INDEX ★ ... A-87

MAPS

CHAPTER 1
The First Americans...7
Native Ways of Life, ca. 1500...11
The Old World on the Eve of American Colonization, ca. 1500...19
Voyages of Discovery...22
Early Spanish Conquests and Explorations in the New World...31
The New World—New France and New Netherland, ca. 1650...40

CHAPTER 2
English Settlement in the Chesapeake, ca. 1650...58
English Settlement in New England, ca. 1640...72

CHAPTER 3
Eastern North America in the Seventeenth and Early Eighteenth Centuries...89
European Settlement and Ethnic Diversity on the Atlantic Coast of North America, 1760...108

CHAPTER 4
Atlantic Trading Routes...129
The Slave Trade in the Atlantic World, 1460–1770...131
European Empires in North America, ca. 1750...153
Eastern North America after the Peace of Paris, 1763...160

CHAPTER 5
The Revolutionary War in the North, 1775–1781...196
The Revolutionary War in the South, 1775–1781...198
North America, 1783...201

CHAPTER 6
Loyalism in the American Revolution...220

CHAPTER 7
Western Lands, 1782–1802...241
Western Ordinances, 1784–1787...244
Ratification of the Constitution...262
Indian Tribes, 1795...264

CHAPTER 8
The Presidential Election of 1800...287
The Louisiana Purchase...293
The War of 1812...301

CHAPTER 9
The Market Revolution: Roads and Canals, 1840...310
The Market Revolution: Western Settlement, 1800–1820...313
Travel Times from New York City in 1800 and 1830...314
The Market Revolution: The Spread of Cotton Cultivation, 1820–1840...317

Major Cities, 1840...320
Cotton Mills, 1820s...322

CHAPTER 10
The Missouri Compromise, 1820...357
The Americas, 1830...360
The Presidential Election of 1824...364
The Presidential Election of 1828...366
Indian Removals, 1830–1840...375
The Presidential Election of 1840...382

CHAPTER 11
Slave Population, 1860...392
Size of Slaveholdings, 1860...397
Distribution of Free Blacks, 1860...403
Major Crops of the South, 1860...408
Slave Resistance in the Nineteenth-Century Atlantic World...416

CHAPTER 12
Utopian Communities, Mid-Nineteenth Century...428

CHAPTER 13
The Trans-Mississippi West, 1830s–1840s...462
The Mexican War, 1846–1848...467
Gold-Rush California...470
Continental Expansion through 1853...474
The Compromise of 1850...477
The Kansas-Nebraska Act, 1854...479
The Railroad Network, 1850s...481
The Presidential Election of 1856...485
The Presidential Election of 1860...494

CHAPTER 14
The Secession of Southern States, 1860–1861...505
The Civil War in the East, 1861–1862...510
The Civil War in the West, 1861–1862...512
The Emancipation Proclamation...515
The Civil War in the Western Territories, 1862–1864...528
The Civil War, 1863...537
The Civil War, Late 1864–1865...544

CHAPTER 15
The Barrow Plantation...555
Sharecropping in the South, 1880...559
The Presidential Election of 1868...570
Reconstruction in the South, 1867–1877...583
The Presidential Election of 1876...584

TABLES AND FIGURES

CHAPTER 1
Table 1.1 Estimated Regional Populations: The Americas, ca. 1500...24
Table 1.2 Estimated Regional Populations: The World, ca. 1500...25

CHAPTER 3
Table 3.1 Origins and Status of Migrants to British North American Colonies, 1700–1775...107

CHAPTER 4
Table 4.1 Slave Population as Percentage of Total Population of Original Thirteen Colonies, 1770...135

CHAPTER 7
Table 7.1 Total Population and Black Population of the United States, 1790...267

CHAPTER 9
Table 9.1 Population Growth of Selected Western States, 1800–1850...316

Table 9.2 Total Number of Immigrants by Five-Year Period...325
Figure 9.1 Sources of Immigration, 1850...326

CHAPTER 11
Table 11.1 Growth of the Slave Population...393
Table 11.2 Slaveholding, 1850...394
Table 11.3 Free Black Population, 1860...406

CHAPTER 14
Figure 14.1 Resources for War: Union versus Confederacy...506

PREFACE

Give Me Liberty! An American History is a survey of American history from the earliest days of European exploration and conquest of the New World to the first decades of the twenty-first century. It offers students a clear, concise narrative whose central theme is the changing contours of American freedom.

I am extremely gratified by the response to the first four editions of Give Me Liberty!, which have been used in survey courses at many hundreds of two- and four-year colleges and universities throughout the country. The comments I have received from instructors and students encourage me to think that Give Me Liberty! has worked well in their classrooms. Their comments have also included many valuable suggestions for revisions, which I greatly appreciate. These have ranged from corrections of typographical and factual errors to thoughts about subjects that needed more extensive treatment. In making revisions for this Fifth Edition, I have tried to take these suggestions into account. I have also incorporated the findings and insights of new scholarship that has appeared since the original edition was written.

The most significant changes in this Fifth Edition reflect my desire to integrate the history of the American West and especially the regions known as borderlands more fully into the narrative. In recent years these aspects of American history have been thriving areas of research and scholarship. Of course earlier editions of Give Me Liberty! have discussed these subjects, but in this edition their treatment has been deepened

and expanded. I have also added notable works in these areas to many chapter bibliographies and lists of websites.

The definition of the West has changed enormously in the course of American history. In the colonial period, the area beyond the Appalachians—present-day Kentucky, Tennessee, and western Pennsylvania and New York—constituted the West. In the first half of the nineteenth century, the term referred to Ohio, Michigan, Alabama, and Mississippi. After the Civil War, the West came to mean the area beyond the Mississippi River. Today, it is sometimes used to refer mainly to the Pacific coast. But whatever its geographic locale, the West has been as much an idea as a place—an area beyond the frontier of settlement that promised newcomers new kinds of freedom, sometimes at the expense of the freedom of others, such as native inhabitants and migrant laborers. In this edition we follow Americans as they constructed their Wests, and debated the kinds of freedom they would enjoy there.

Borderlands is a more complex idea that has influenced much recent historical scholarship. Borders are lines dividing one country, region, or state from another. Crossing them often means becoming subject to different laws and customs, and enjoying different degrees of freedom. Borderlands are regions that exist on both sides of borders. They are fluid areas where people of different cultural and social backgrounds converge. At various points in American history, shifting borders have opened new opportunities and closed off others in the borderlands. Families living for decades or centuries in a region have suddenly found themselves divided by a newly created border but still living in a borderland that transcends the new division. This happened to Mexicans in modern-day California, Arizona, and New Mexico, for example, in 1848, when the treaty ending the Mexican-American War transferred the land that would become those states from Mexico to the United States.

Borderlands exist within the United States as well as at the boundaries with other countries. For example, in the period before the Civil War, the region straddling the Ohio River contained cultural commonalities that in some ways overrode the division there between free and slave states. The borderlands idea also challenges simple accounts of national development in which empires and colonies pave the way for territorial expansion and a future transcontinental nation. It enables us, for example, to move beyond the categories of conquest and subjugation in understanding how Native Americans and Europeans interacted over the early centuries of contact. This approach also provides a way of understanding how the people of Mexico and the United States interact today in the borderland region of the American Southwest, where many families have members on both sides of the boundary between the two countries.

Small changes relating to these themes may be found throughout the book. The major additions seeking to illuminate the history of the West and of borderlands are as follows:

Chapter 1 now introduces the idea of borderlands with a discussion of the areas where European empires and Indian groups interacted and where authority was fluid and fragile. Chapter 4 contains expanded treatment of the part of the Spanish empire now comprising the borderlands United States (Arizona, California, New Mexico, Texas, and Florida) and how Spain endeavored, with limited success, to consolidate its authority in these regions. In Chapter 6, a new subsection, "The American Revolution as a Borderlands Conflict," examines the impact on both Americans and Canadians of the creation, because of American independence, of a new national boundary separating what once had been two parts of the British empire. Chapter 8 continues this theme with a discussion of the borderlands aspects of the War of 1812. Chapter 9 discusses how a common culture came into being along the Ohio River in the early nineteenth century despite the existence of slavery on one side and free labor on the other. Chapter 13 expands the treatment of Texan independence from Mexico by discussing its impact on both Anglo and Mexican residents of this borderland region. Chapter 14 contains a new examination of the Civil War in the American West.

In Chapter 16, I have expanded the section on the industrial west with new discussions of logging and mining, and added a new subsection on the dissemination of a mythical image of the Wild West in the late nineteenth century. Chapter 17 contains an expanded discussion of Chinese immigrants in the West and the battle over exclusion and citizenship, a debate that centered on what kind of population should be allowed to inhabit the West and enjoy the opportunities the region offered. Chapter 18 examines Progressivism, countering conventional narratives that emphasize the origins of Progressive political reforms in eastern cities by relating how many, from woman suffrage to the initiative, referendum, and recall, emerged in Oregon, California, and other western states. Chapter 20 expands the treatment of western agriculture in the 1920s by highlighting the acceleration of agricultural mechanization in the region and the agricultural depression that preceded the general economic collapse of 1929 and after. In Chapter 22 we see the new employment opportunities for Mexican-American women in the war production factories that opened in the West. In Chapter 26, there is a new subsection on conservatism in the West and the Sagebrush Rebellion of the 1970s and 1980s. Chapter 27 returns to the borderlands theme by discussing the consequences of the creation, in the 1990s, of a free trade zone connecting the two sides of the Mexican-American border. And Chapters 27 and 28 now include expanded discussions of the southwestern borderland as a site of an acrimonious battle over immigration—legal and undocumented—involving the federal and state governments, private vigilantes, and continuing waves of people trying to cross into the United States. The contested borderland now extends many miles into the United States north of the boundary between the two nations, and southward well into Mexico and even Central America.

I have also added a number of new selections to Voices of Freedom, the paired excerpts from primary documents in each chapter. Some of the new documents reflect the stronger emphasis on the West and borderlands; others seek to sharpen the juxtaposition of divergent concepts of freedom at particular moments in American history. And this edition contains many new images—paintings, broadsides, photographs, and others—related to these themes.

Americans have always had a divided attitude toward history. On the one hand, they tend to be remarkably future-oriented, dismissing events of even the recent past as "ancient history" and sometimes seeing history as a burden to be overcome, a prison from which to escape. On the other hand, like many other peoples, Americans have always looked to history for a sense of personal or group identity and of national cohesiveness. This is why so many Americans devote time and energy to tracing their family trees and why they visit historical museums and National Park Service historical sites in ever-increasing numbers. My hope is that this book will convince readers with all degrees of interest that history does matter to them.

The novelist and essayist James Baldwin once observed that history "does not refer merely, or even principally, to the past. On the contrary, the great force of history comes from the fact that we carry it within us, . . . [that] history is literally present in all that we do." As Baldwin recognized, the force of history is evident in our own world. Especially in a political democracy like the United States, whose government is designed to rest on the consent of informed citizens, knowledge of the past is essential—not only for those of us whose profession is the teaching and writing of history, but for everyone. History, to be sure, does not offer simple lessons or immediate answers to current questions. Knowing the history of immigration to the United States, and all of the tensions, turmoil, and aspirations associated with it, for example, does not tell us what current immigration policy ought to be. But without that knowledge, we have no way of understanding which approaches have worked and which have not—essential information for the formulation of future public policy.

History, it has been said, is what the present chooses to remember about the past. Rather than a fixed collection of facts, or a group of interpretations that cannot be challenged, our understanding of history is constantly changing. There is nothing unusual in the fact that each generation rewrites history to meet its own needs, or that scholars disagree among themselves on basic questions like the causes of the Civil War or the reasons for the Great Depression. Precisely because each generation asks different questions of the past, each generation formulates different answers. The past thirty years have witnessed a remarkable expansion of the scope of historical study. The experiences of groups neglected by earlier scholars, including women, African-Americans, working people, and others, have received unprecedented attention from historians. New subfields—social history, cultural history, and family history among them—have taken their place alongside traditional political and diplomatic history.

Give Me Liberty! draws on this voluminous historical literature to present an up-to-date and inclusive account of the American past, paying due attention to the experience of diverse groups of Americans while in no way neglecting the events and processes Americans have experienced in common. It devotes serious attention to political, social, cultural, and economic history, and to their interconnections. The narrative brings together major events and prominent leaders with the many groups of ordinary people who make up American society. *Give Me Liberty!* has a rich cast of characters, from Thomas Jefferson to campaigners for woman suffrage, from Franklin D. Roosevelt to former slaves seeking to breathe meaning into emancipation during and after the Civil War.

Aimed at an audience of undergraduate students with little or no detailed knowledge of American history, *Give Me Liberty!* guides readers through the complexities of the subject without overwhelming them with excessive detail. The unifying theme of freedom that runs through the text gives shape to the narrative and integrates the numerous strands that make up the American experience. This approach builds on that of my earlier book, *The Story of American Freedom* (1998), although *Give Me Liberty!* places events and personalities in the foreground and is more geared to the structure of the introductory survey course.

Freedom, and the battles to define its meaning, have long been central to my own scholarship and undergraduate teaching, which focuses on the nineteenth century and especially the era of the Civil War and Reconstruction (1850–1877). This was a time when the future of slavery tore the nation apart and emancipation produced a national debate over what rights the former slaves, and all Americans, should enjoy as free citizens. I have found that attention to clashing definitions of freedom and the struggles of different groups to achieve freedom as they understood it offers a way of making sense of the bitter battles and vast transformations of that pivotal era. I believe that the same is true for American history as a whole.

No idea is more fundamental to Americans' sense of themselves as individuals and as a nation than freedom. The central term in our political language, freedom—or liberty, with which it is almost always used interchangeably—is deeply embedded in the record of our history and the language of everyday life. The Declaration of Independence lists liberty among mankind's inalienable rights; the Constitution announces its purpose as securing liberty's blessings. The United States fought the Civil War to bring about a new birth of freedom, World War II for the Four Freedoms, and the Cold War to defend the Free World. Americans' love of liberty has been represented by liberty poles, liberty caps, and statues of liberty, and acted out by burning stamps and burning draft cards, by running away from slavery, and by demonstrating for the right to vote. "Every man in the street, white, black, red, or yellow," wrote the educator and statesman Ralph Bunche in 1940, "knows that this is 'the land of the free' . . . 'the cradle of liberty.' "

The very universality of the idea of freedom, however, can be misleading. Freedom is not a fixed, timeless category with a single unchanging definition. Indeed, the history of the United States is, in part, a story of debates, disagreements, and struggles over freedom. Crises like the American Revolution, the Civil War, and the Cold War have permanently transformed the idea of freedom. So too have demands by various groups of Americans to enjoy greater freedom. The meaning of freedom has been constructed not only in congressional debates and political treatises, but on plantations and picket lines, in parlors and even bedrooms.

Over the course of our history, American freedom has been both a reality and a mythic ideal—a living truth for millions of Americans, a cruel mockery for others. For some, freedom has been what some scholars call a "habit of the heart," an ideal so taken for granted that it is lived out but rarely analyzed. For others, freedom is not a birthright but a distant goal that has inspired great sacrifice.

Give Me Liberty! draws attention to three dimensions of freedom that have been critical in American history: (1) the *meanings* of freedom; (2) the *social conditions* that make freedom possible; and (3) the *boundaries* of freedom that determine who is entitled to enjoy freedom and who is not. All have changed over time.

In the era of the American Revolution, for example, freedom was primarily a set of rights enjoyed in public activity—the right of a community to be governed by laws to which its representatives had consented and of individuals to engage in religious worship without governmental interference. In the nineteenth century, freedom came to be closely identified with each person's opportunity to develop to the fullest his or her innate talents. In the twentieth, the "ability to choose," in both public and private life, became perhaps the dominant understanding of freedom. This development was encouraged by the explosive growth of the consumer marketplace (a development that receives considerable attention in *Give Me Liberty!*), which offered Americans an unprecedented array of goods with which to satisfy their needs and desires. During the 1960s, a crucial chapter in the history of American freedom, the idea of personal freedom was extended into virtually every realm, from attire and "lifestyle" to

INVICTA.

relations between the sexes. Thus, over time, more and more areas of life have been drawn into Americans' debates about the meaning of freedom.

A second important dimension of freedom focuses on the social conditions necessary to allow freedom to flourish. What kinds of economic institutions and relationships best encourage individual freedom? In the colonial era and for more than a century after independence, the answer centered on economic autonomy, enshrined in the glorification of the independent small producer—the farmer, skilled craftsman, or shopkeeper—who did not have to depend on another person for his livelihood. As the industrial economy matured, new conceptions of economic freedom came to the fore: "liberty of contract" in the Gilded Age, "industrial freedom" (a say in corporate decision-making) in the Progressive era, economic security during the New Deal, and, more recently, the ability to enjoy mass consumption within a market economy.

The boundaries of freedom, the third dimension of this theme, have inspired some of the most intense struggles in American history. Although founded on the premise that liberty is an entitlement of all humanity, the United States for much of its history deprived many of its own people of freedom. Non-whites have rarely enjoyed the same access to freedom as white Americans. The belief in equal opportunity as the birthright of all Americans has coexisted with persistent efforts to limit freedom by race, gender, and class and in other ways.

Less obvious, perhaps, is the fact that one person's freedom has frequently been linked to another's servitude. In the colonial era and nineteenth century, expanding freedom for many Americans rested on the lack of freedom—slavery, indentured servitude, the subordinate position of women—for others. By the same token, it has been through battles at the boundaries—the efforts of racial minorities, women, and others to secure greater freedom—that the meaning and experience of freedom have been deepened and the concept extended into new realms.

Time and again in American history, freedom has been transformed by the demands of excluded groups for inclusion. The idea of freedom as a universal birthright owes much both to abolitionists who sought to extend the blessings of liberty to blacks and to immigrant groups who insisted on full recognition as American citizens. The principle of equal protection of the law without regard to race, which became a central element of American freedom, arose from the antislavery struggle and the Civil War and was reinvigorated by the civil rights revolution of the 1960s, which called itself the "freedom movement." The battle for the right of free speech by labor radicals and birth-control advocates in the first part of the twentieth century helped to make civil liberties an essential element of freedom for all Americans.

Although concentrating on events within the United States, *Give Me Liberty!* also situates American history in the context of developments in other parts of the world. Many of the forces that shaped American history, including the international migration of peoples, the development of slavery, the spread of democracy, and the expansion of capitalism, were worldwide processes not confined to the United States. Today, American ideas, culture, and economic and military power exert unprecedented influence throughout the world. But beginning with the earliest days of settlement, when European empires competed to colonize North America and enrich themselves from its trade, American history cannot be understood in isolation from its global setting.

Freedom is the oldest of clichés and the most modern of aspirations. At various times in our history, it has served as the rallying cry of the powerless and as a justification of the status quo. Freedom helps to bind our culture together and exposes the contradictions between what America claims to be and what it sometimes has been. American history is not a narrative of continual progress toward greater and greater freedom. As the abolitionist Thomas Wentworth Higginson noted after the Civil War, "revolutions may go backward." Though freedom can be achieved, it may also be taken away. This happened, for example, when the equal rights granted to former slaves immediately after the Civil War were essentially nullified during the era of segregation. As was said in the eighteenth century, the price of freedom is eternal vigilance.

In the early twenty-first century, freedom continues to play a central role in American political and social life and thought. It is invoked by individuals and groups of all kinds, from critics of economic globalization to those who seek to secure American freedom at home and export it abroad. I hope that *Give Me Liberty!* will offer beginning students a clear account of the course of American history, and of its central theme, freedom, which today remains as varied, contentious, and ever-changing as America itself.

ACKNOWLEDGMENTS

All works of history are, to a considerable extent, collaborative books, in that every writer builds on the research and writing of previous scholars. This is especially true of a textbook that covers the entire American experience, over more than five centuries. My greatest debt is to the innumerable historians on whose work I have drawn in preparing this volume. The Suggested Reading list at the end of each chapter offers only a brief introduction to the vast body of historical scholarship that has influenced and informed this book. More specifically, however, I wish to thank the following scholars, who generously read portions of this work and offered valuable comments, criticisms, and suggestions:

Joel Benson, Northwest Missouri State University
Lori Bramson, Clark College
Tonia Compton, Columbia College
Adam Costanzo, Texas A&M University
Carl Creasman Jr., Valencia College
Blake Ellis, Lone Star College–CyFair
Carla Falkner, Northeast Mississippi Community College
Van Forsyth, Clark College
Aram Goudsouzian, University of Memphis
Michael Harkins, Harper College
Sandra Harvey, Lone Star College–CyFair
Robert Hines, Palo Alto College
Traci Hodgson, Chemeketa Community College
Tamora Hoskisson, Salt Lake Community College
William Jackson, Salt Lake Community College
Alfred H. Jones, State College of Florida
David Kiracofe, Tidewater Community College

Brad Lookingbill, Columbia College

Jennifer Macias, Salt Lake Community College

Thomas Massey, Cape Fear Community College

Derek Maxfield, Genesee Community College

Marianne McKnight, Salt Lake Community College

Jonson Miller, Drexel University

Ted Moore, Salt Lake Community College

Robert Pierce, Foothills College

Ernst Pinjing, Minot State University

Harvey N. Plaunt, El Paso Community College

Steve Porter, University of Cincinnati

John Putman, San Diego State University

R. Lynn Rainard, Tidewater Community College

Nicole Ribianszky, Georgia Gwinnett College

Nancy Marie Robertson, Indiana University—Purdue University Indianapolis

John Shaw, Portland Community College

Danielle Swiontek, Santa Barbara Community College

Richard Trimble, Ocean County College

Alan Vangroll, Central Texas College

Eddie Weller, San Jacinto College

Andrew Wiese, San Diego State University

Matthew Zembo, Hudson Valley Community College

I am particularly grateful to my colleagues in the Columbia University Department of History: Pablo Piccato, for his advice on Latin American history; Evan Haefeli and Ellen Baker, who read and made many suggestions for improvements in their areas of expertise (colonial America and the history of the West, respectively); and Sarah Phillips, who offered advice on treating the history of the environment.

I am also deeply indebted to the graduate students at Columbia University's Department of History who helped with this project. For this edition, Michael "Mookie" Kideckel offered invaluable assistance in gathering material related to borderlands and Western history. For previous editions, Theresa Ventura assisted in locating material for new sections placing American history in a global context, April Holm did the same for new coverage of the history of American religion and debates over religious freedom, James Delbourgo conducted research for the chapters on the colonial era, and Beverly Gage did the same for the twentieth century. In addition, Daniel Freund provided all-around research assistance. Victoria Cain did a superb job of locating images. I also want to thank my colleagues Elizabeth Blackmar and Alan Brinkley for offering advice and encouragement throughout the writing of this book. I am also grateful to students who, while using the textbook, pointed out to me errors or omissions that I have corrected in this edition: Jordan Farr, Chris Jendry, Rafi Metz, Samuel Phillips-Cooper, Richard Sereyko, and David Whittle.

Many thanks to Joshua Brown, director of the American Social History Project, whose website, History Matters, lists innumerable online resources for the study of American history. Thanks also to the instructors who helped build our robust digital resource and ancillary package. The new InQuizitive for History was developed by Tonia M. Compton (Columbia College), Matt Zembo (Hudson Valley Community College), Jodie Steeley (Merced Community College District), Bill Polasky (Stillman Valley High School), and Ken Adler (Spring Valley High School). Our new History Skills Tutorials were created by Geri Hastings. The Coursepack was thoroughly updated by Beth Hunter (University of Alabama at Birmingham). Allison Faber (Texas A&M University) and Ben Williams (Texas A&M University) revised the Lecture PowerPoint slides. And our Test Bank and Instructor's Manual was revised to include new questions authored by Robert O'Brien (Lone Star College–CyFair) and Tamora M. Hoskisson (Salt Lake Community College).

At W. W. Norton & Company, Steve Forman was an ideal editor—patient, encouraging, and always ready to offer sage advice. I would also like to thank Steve's editorial assistants, Travis Carr and Kelly Rafey, and associate editor, Scott Sugarman, for their indispensable and always cheerful help on all aspects of the project; Ellen Lohman and Bob Byrne for their careful copyediting and proofreading work; Stephanie Romeo and Fay Torresyap for their resourceful attention to the illustrations program; Hope Miller Goodell and Chin-Yee Lai for their refinements of the book design; Leah Clark, Tiani Kennedy, and Debra Morton-Hoyt for splendid work on the covers for the Fifth Edition; Jennifer Barnhardt for keeping the many threads of the project aligned and then tying them together; Sean Mintus for his efficiency and care in book production; Laura Wilk for orchestrating the rich media package that accompanies the textbook; Sarah England Bartley, Steve Dunn, and Mike Wright for their alert reads of the U.S. survey market and their hard work in helping establish *Give Me Liberty!* within it; and Drake McFeely, Roby Harrington, and Julia Reidhead for maintaining Norton as an independent, employee-owned publisher dedicated to excellence in its work.

Many students may have heard stories of how publishing companies alter the language and content of textbooks in an attempt to maximize sales and avoid alienating any potential reader. In this case, I can honestly say that W. W. Norton allowed me a free hand in writing the book and, apart from the usual editorial corrections, did not try to influence its content at all. For this I thank them, while I accept full responsibility for the interpretations presented and for any errors the book may contain. Since no book of this length can be entirely free of mistakes, I welcome readers to send me corrections at ef17@columbia.edu.

My greatest debt, as always, is to my family—my wife, Lynn Garafola, for her good-natured support while I was preoccupied by a project that consumed more than its fair share of my time and energy, and my daughter, Daria, who while a ninth and tenth grader read every chapter as it was written and offered invaluable suggestions about improving the book's clarity, logic, and grammar.

Eric Foner
New York City
July 2016

GIVE ME LIBERTY! DIGITAL RESOURCES FOR STUDENTS AND INSTRUCTORS

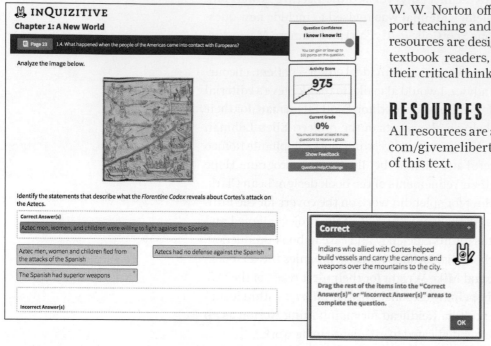

W. W. Norton offers a robust digital package to support teaching and learning with *Give Me Liberty!* These resources are designed to make students more effective textbook readers, while at the same time developing their critical thinking and history skills.

RESOURCES FOR STUDENTS

All resources are available through digital.wwnorton.com/givemeliberty5v1 with the access card at the front of this text.

NORTON INQUIZITIVE FOR HISTORY

Norton InQuizitive for history is an adaptive quizzing tool that improves students' understanding of the themes and objectives from each chapter, while honing their critical-analysis skills with primary source, image, and map analysis questions. Students receive personalized quiz questions with detailed, guiding feedback on the topics in which they need the most help, while the engaging, gamelike elements motivate them as they learn.

HISTORY SKILLS TUTORIALS

The History Skills Tutorials feature three modules—Images, Documents, and Maps—to support students' development of the key skills needed for the history course. These tutorials feature videos of Eric Foner modeling the analysis process, followed by interactive questions that will challenge students to apply what they have learned.

STUDENT SITE

The free and easy-to-use Student Site offers additional resources for students to use outside of class. Resources include interactive iMaps from each chapter, author videos, and a comprehensive Online Reader with a collection of historical longer works, primary sources, novellas, and biographies.

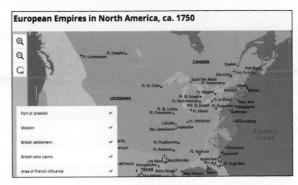

EBOOK

Free and included with new copies of the text, the **Norton Ebook Reader** provides an enhanced reading experience that works on all computers and mobile devices. Features include intuitive highlighting, note-taking, and bookmarking as well as pop-up definitions and enlargeable maps and art. Direct links to InQuizitive also appear in each chapter. Instructors can focus student reading by sharing notes with their classes, including embedded images and video. Reports on student and class-wide access and time on task allow instructors to monitor student reading and engagement.

RESOURCES FOR INSTRUCTORS

All resources are available through www.wwnorton .com/instructors.

NORTON COURSEPACKS

Easily add high-quality digital media to your online, hybrid, or lecture course—all at no cost to students. Norton's Coursepacks work within your existing Learning Management System and are ready to use and easy to customize. The coursepack offers a diverse collection of assignable and assessable resources: **Primary Source Exercises, Guided Reading Exercises, Review Quizzes, U.S. History Tours powered by Google Earth, Flashcards, Map Exercises**, and all of the resources from the **Student Site.**

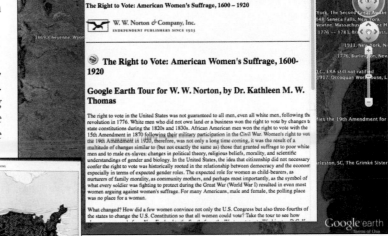

NORTON AMERICAN HISTORY DIGITAL ARCHIVE

The Digital Archive offers roughly 2,000 additional primary source images, audio, and video files spanning American history that can be used in assignments and lecture presentations.

TEST BANK

The Test Bank is authored by Robert O'Brien, Lone Star College–CyFair, and Tamora M. Hoskisson, Salt Lake Community College, and contains more than 4,000 multiple-choice, true/false, short-answer, and essay questions.

INSTRUCTOR'S MANUAL

The Instructor's Manual contains detailed Chapter Summaries, Chapter Outlines, Suggested Discussion Questions, and Supplemental Web, Visual, and Print Resources.

LECTURE AND ART POWERPOINT SLIDES

The Lecture PowerPoint sets authored by Allison Faber, Texas A&M University, and Ben Williams, Texas A&M University, combine chapter review, art, and maps.

GIVE ME LIBERTY!

AN AMERICAN HISTORY

Fifth Edition

T he colonial period of American history was a time of enormous change, as the people of four continents—North America, South America, Europe, and Africa—were suddenly and unexpectedly thrown into contact with one another. The period also initiated a new era in the history of freedom. It was not, however, a desire for freedom that drove early European explorations of North and South America. Contact between Europe and the Americas began as a by-product of the quest for a sea route for trade with Asia. But it quickly became a contest for power between rival empires, who moved to conquer, colonize, and exploit the resources of the New World.

At the time of European contact, the Western Hemisphere was home to tens of millions of people. Within the present borders of the United States there existed Indian societies based on agriculture, hunting, or fishing, with their own languages, religious practices, and forms of government. All experienced wrenching changes after Europeans arrived, including incorporation into the world market and epidemics of disease that devastated many native groups.

The colonies that eventually came to form the United States originated in very different ways. Virginia, the first permanent colony to be established, was created by a private company that sought to earn profits through exploration for gold and the development of transatlantic trade. Individual proprietors— well-connected Englishmen given large grants of land by the king—established Maryland and Pennsylvania. New York, which had been founded by the Dutch, came into British hands as the result of a war. Religious groups seeking escape from persecution in England and hoping to establish communities rooted in their understanding of the principles of the Bible founded colonies in New England.

In the seventeenth century, all the British colonies experienced wrenching social conflicts as groups within them battled for control. Relations with Indians remained tense and sometimes violent. Religious and political divisions in England, which experienced a civil war in the 1640s and the ouster of the king in 1688, reverberated in the colonies. So did wars between European powers, which spilled over into North America. Nonetheless, after difficult beginnings, Britain's mainland colonies experienced years of remarkable growth in population and economic activity. By the eighteenth century, the non-Indian population of Britain's North American colonies had far outstripped that of the colonies of France and Spain.

In every colony in British America, well-to-do landowners and merchants dominated economic and political life. Nonetheless, emigration to the colonies offered numerous settlers opportunities they had not enjoyed at home, including access to land, the freedom to worship as they pleased, and the right to vote. Every British colony had an elected assembly that shared power with a governor, who was usually appointed from London. Even this limited degree of self-government contrasted sharply with the lack of representative institutions in the Spanish and French empires. All these circumstances drew thousands of English emigrants to North America in the seventeenth century, and thousands more from Ireland, Scotland, and the European continent in the eighteenth century.

Yet the conditions that allowed colonists to enjoy such freedoms were made possible by lack of freedom for millions of others. For the native inhabitants of the Western Hemisphere, European colonization brought the spread of devastating epidemics and either dispossession from the land or forced labor for the colonizers. Millions of Africans were uprooted from their homes and transported to the New World to labor on the plantations of Brazil, the Caribbean, and England's North American colonies. Even among European immigrants, the majority arrived not as completely free individuals but as indentured servants who owed a prearranged number of years of labor to those who paid their passage.

In colonial America, many modern ideas of freedom did not exist, or existed in very different forms than today. Equality before the law was unknown—women, non-whites, and propertyless men enjoyed far fewer rights than landowning white male citizens. Economic freedom, today widely identified with participation in an unregulated market, meant independence—owning land or a shop and not relying on another person for a livelihood. Most colonies had official churches, and many colonists who sought religious liberty for themselves refused to extend it to others. Speaking or writing critically of public authorities could land a person in jail.

Nonetheless, ideas about freedom played a major role in justifying European colonization. The Spanish and French claimed to be liberating Native Americans by bringing them advanced civilization and Roman Catholicism. England insisted that true freedom for Indians meant adopting English ways, including Protestantism. Moreover, the expansion of England's empire occurred at a time when freedom came to be seen as the defining characteristic of the English nation. Slavery existed in every New World colony. In many, it became the basis of economic life. Yet most Britons, including colonists, prided themselves on enjoying "British liberty," a common set of rights that included protection from the arbitrary exercise of governmental power.

Thus, freedom and lack of freedom expanded together in the colonies of British North America that would eventually form the United States.

CHAPTER 1

A
NEW WORLD

★

"The discovery of America," the British writer Adam Smith announced in his celebrated work *The Wealth of Nations* (1776), was one of "the two greatest and most important events recorded in the history of mankind." Historians no longer use the word "discovery" to describe the European exploration, conquest, and colonization of a hemisphere already home to millions of people. But there can be no doubt that when Christopher Columbus made landfall in the West Indian islands in 1492, he set in motion some of the most pivotal developments in human history. Immense changes soon followed in both the Old and New Worlds; the consequences of these changes are still with us today.

The peoples of the American continents and Europe, previously unaware of each other's existence, were thrown into continuous interaction. Crops new to each hemisphere crossed the Atlantic, reshaping diets and transforming the natural environment. Because of their long isolation, the inhabitants of North and South America had developed no immunity to the germs that also accompanied the colonizers. As a result, they suffered a series of devastating epidemics, the greatest population catastrophe in human history. Within a decade of Columbus's voyage, a fourth continent—Africa—found itself drawn into the new Atlantic system of trade and population movement. In Africa, Europeans found a supply of unfree labor that enabled them to exploit the fertile lands of the Western Hemisphere. Indeed, of approximately 10 million men, women, and children who crossed from the Old World to the New between 1492 and 1820, the vast majority, about 7.7 million, were African slaves.

From the vantage point of 1776, the year the United States declared itself an independent nation, it seemed to Adam Smith that the "discovery" of America had produced both great "benefits" and great "misfortunes." To the nations of western Europe, the development of American colonies brought an era of "splendor and glory." The emergence of the Atlantic as the world's major avenue for trade and population movement, Smith noted, enabled millions of Europeans to increase the "enjoyments" of life. To the "natives" of the Americas, however, Smith went on, the years since 1492 had been ones of "dreadful misfortunes" and "every sort of injustice." And for millions of Africans, the settlement of America meant a descent into the abyss of slavery.

Long before Columbus sailed, Europeans had dreamed of a land of abundance, riches, and ease beyond the western horizon. Once the "discovery" of this New World had taken place, they invented an America of the imagination, projecting onto it their hopes for a better life. Here, many believed, would arise unparalleled opportunities for riches, or at least liberation from poverty. Europeans envisioned America as a religious refuge, a society of equals, a source of power and glory. They searched the New World for golden cities and fountains of eternal youth. Some sought to establish ideal communities based on the lives of the early Christian saints or other blueprints for social justice.

Some of these dreams of riches and opportunity would indeed be fulfilled. To many European settlers, America offered a far greater chance to own land and worship as they pleased than existed in Europe, with its rigid, unequal

FOCUS QUESTIONS

What were the major patterns of Native American life in North America before Europeans arrived? –*p. 6*

How did Indian and European ideas of freedom differ on the eve of contact? –*p. 15*

What impelled European explorers to look west across the Atlantic? –*p. 18*

What happened when the peoples of the Americas came in contact with Europeans? –*p. 21*

What were the chief features of the Spanish empire in America? –*p. 24*

What were the chief features of the French and Dutch empires in North America? –*p. 35*

Painted around 1725, *Genealogy of the Inca Rulers and Their Spanish Successors from Manco Capac, the First Inca King, to Ferdinand VI of Spain*, depicts Spanish conquistadors and rulers as direct successors of Inca kings. The unknown artist aimed both to assimilate the pre-conquest history of the Americas into Spanish history and to legitimate Spain's colonial rule over the former Inca empire.

7000 BC	Agriculture developed in Mexico and Andes
900–1200 AD	Hopi and Zuni tribes build planned towns
1200	Cahokia city-empire along the Mississippi
1400s	Iroquois League established
1434	Portuguese explore sub-Saharan African Coast
1487	Bartolomeu Dias reaches the Cape of Good Hope
1492	*Reconquista* of Spain
	Columbus's first voyage to the Americas
1498	Vasco da Gama sails to the Indian Ocean
1500	Pedro Cabral claims Brazil for Portugal
1502	First African slaves transported to Caribbean islands
1517	Martin Luther's *Ninety-Five Theses*
1519	Hernán Cortés arrives in Mexico
1528	Las Casas's *History of the Indies*
1530s	Pizarro's conquest of Peru
1542	Spain promulgates the New Laws
1608	Champlain establishes Quebec
1609	Hudson claims New Netherland
1610	Santa Fe established
1680	Pueblo Revolt

social order and official churches. Yet the conditions that enabled millions of settlers to take control of their own destinies were made possible by the debasement of millions of others. The New World became the site of many forms of unfree labor, including indentured servitude, forced labor, and one of the most brutal and unjust systems ever devised by man, plantation slavery. The conquest and settlement of the Western Hemisphere opened new chapters in the long histories of both freedom and slavery.

There was a vast human diversity among the peoples thrown into contact with one another in the New World. Exploration and settlement took place in an era of almost constant warfare among European nations, each racked by internal religious, political, and regional conflicts. Native Americans and Africans consisted of numerous groups with their own languages and cultures. They were as likely to fight one another as to unite against the European newcomers. All these peoples were changed by their integration into the new Atlantic economy. The complex interactions of Europeans, American Indians, and Africans would shape American history during the colonial era.

THE FIRST AMERICANS

The Settling of the Americas

The residents of the Americas were no more a single group than Europeans or Africans. They spoke hundreds of different languages and lived in numerous kinds of societies. Most, however, were descended from bands of hunters and fishers who had crossed the Bering Strait via a land bridge at various times between 15,000 and 60,000 years ago—the exact dates are hotly debated by archaeologists. Others may have arrived by sea from Asia or Pacific islands. Around 14,000 years ago, when glaciers began to melt at the end of the last Ice Age, the land link became submerged under water, separating the Western Hemisphere from Asia.

History in North and South America did not begin with the coming of Europeans. The New World was new to Europeans but an ancient homeland to those who already lived there. The hemisphere had witnessed many changes during its human history. First, the early inhabitants and their descendants spread across the two continents, reaching the tip of South America perhaps 11,000 years ago. As the climate warmed, they faced a food crisis as the immense animals they hunted, including woolly mammoths and giant bison, became extinct. Around 9,000 years ago, at the same time that agriculture was being developed in the Near East, it also emerged in modern-day Mexico and the Andes, and then spread to other parts of the Americas, making settled civilizations possible. Throughout the hemisphere, maize (corn), squash, and beans formed the basis of agriculture. The absence of livestock in the Western Hemisphere, however, limited farming by preventing the plowing of fields and the application of natural fertilizer.

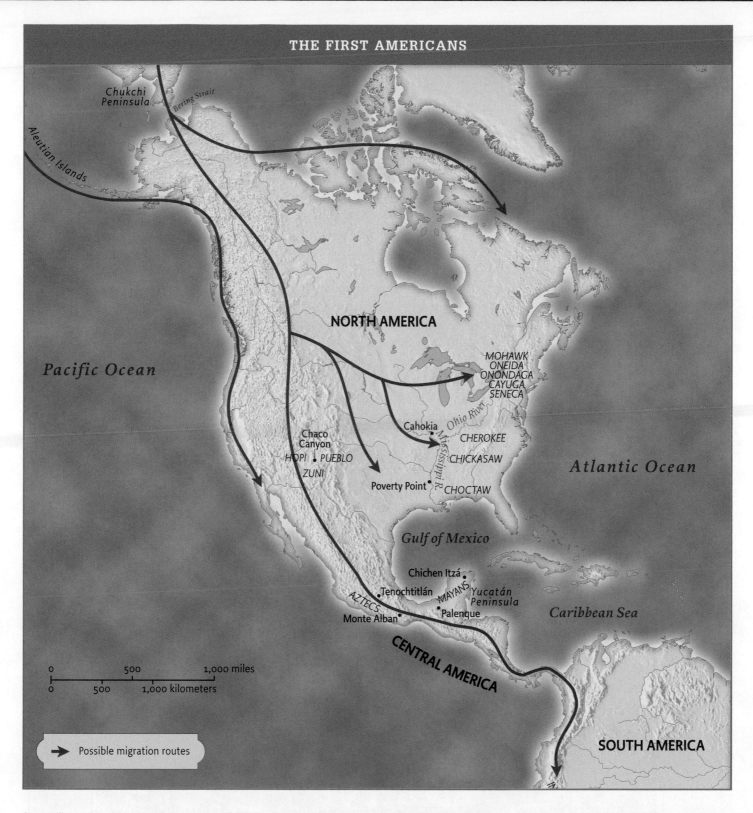

THE FIRST AMERICANS

Chukchi Peninsula

Bering Strait

Aleutian Islands

Pacific Ocean

NORTH AMERICA

MOHAWK
ONEIDA
ONONDAGA
CAYUGA
SENECA

Ohio River

Cahokia

CHEROKEE

Chaco Canyon

HOPI · PUEBLO

CHICKASAW

Atlantic Ocean

ZUNI

Mississippi R.

Poverty Point

CHOCTAW

Gulf of Mexico

Chichen Itzá

Tenochtitlán

MAYANS

Yucatán Peninsula

AZTECS

Palenque

Caribbean Sea

Monte Alban

CENTRAL AMERICA

SOUTH AMERICA

| 0 | 500 | 1,000 miles |
| 0 | 500 | 1,000 kilometers |

➤ Possible migration routes

A map illustrating the probable routes by which the first Americans settled the Western Hemisphere at various times between 15,000 and 60,000 years ago.

Indian Societies of the Americas

North and South America were hardly an empty wilderness when Europeans arrived. The hemisphere contained cities, roads, irrigation systems, extensive trade networks, and large structures such as pyramid-temples, whose beauty still inspires wonder. With a population close to 250,000, **Tenochtitlán**, the capital of the **Aztec** empire in what is now Mexico, was one of the world's largest cities. Its great temple, splendid royal palace, and a central market comparable to that of European capitals made the city seem "like an enchanted vision," according to one of the first Europeans to encounter it. Farther south lay the Inca kingdom, centered in modern-day Peru. Its population of perhaps 12 million was linked by a complex system of roads and bridges that extended 2,000 miles along the Andes mountain chain.

> *Roads, irrigation systems, and trade networks*

When Europeans arrived, a wide variety of native peoples lived within the present borders of the United States. Indian civilizations in North America had not developed the scale, grandeur, or centralized organization of the Aztec and Inca societies to their south. North American Indians lacked the technologies Europeans had mastered, such as metal tools and machines, gunpowder, and the scientific knowledge necessary for long-distance navigation. No society north of Mexico had achieved literacy (although some made maps on bark and animal hides). They also lacked wheeled vehicles, since they had no domestic animals like horses or oxen to pull them. Their "backwardness" became a central justification for European conquest. But, over time, Indian societies had perfected

This world map, produced in 1507 by the German mapmaker Martin Waldseemüller, was the first to depict the full Western Hemisphere and the first to include the name "America" (on the lower part of South America) for part of the New World. It also seems to indicate the Pacific Ocean, but no European encountered that ocean until the Spanish explorer Balboa in 1513.

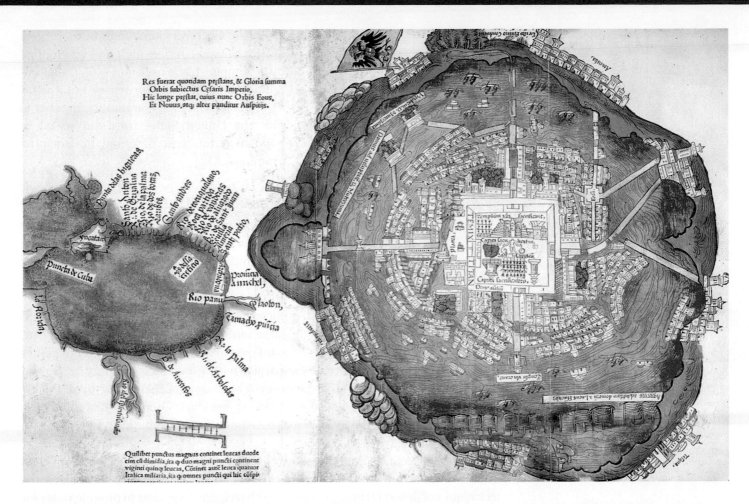

techniques of farming, hunting, and fishing, developed structures of political power and religious belief, and engaged in far-reaching networks of trade and communication.

Map of the Aztec capital Tenochtitlán and the Gulf of Mexico, probably produced by a Spanish conquistador and published in 1524 in an edition of the letters of Hernán Cortés. The map shows the city's complex system of canals, bridges, and dams, with the Great Temple at the center. Gardens and a zoo are also visible.

Mound Builders of the Mississippi River Valley

Remarkable physical remains still exist from some of the early civilizations in North America. Around 3,500 years ago, before Egyptians built the pyramids, Native Americans constructed a large community centered on a series of giant semicircular mounds on a bluff overlooking the Mississippi River in present-day Louisiana. Known today as Poverty Point, it was a commercial and governmental center whose residents established trade routes throughout the Mississippi and Ohio River valleys. Archaeologists have found there copper from present-day Minnesota and Canada, and flint mined in Indiana.

More than a thousand years before Columbus sailed, Indians of the Ohio River valley, called "mound builders" by eighteenth-century settlers who encountered the large earthen burial mounds they created, had traded across half the continent. After their decline, another culture flourished in the Mississippi River valley, centered on the city of Cahokia near present-day St. Louis, a fortified community with between 10,000 and 30,000 inhabitants in the year 1200. Its

Cahokia

residents, too, built giant mounds, the largest of which stood 100 feet high and was topped by a temple. Little is known of Cahokia's political and economic structure. But it stood as the largest settled community in what is now the United States until surpassed in population by New York and Philadelphia around 1800.

A modern aerial photograph of the ruins of Pueblo Bonita, in Chaco Canyon in present-day New Mexico. The rectangular structures are the foundations of dwellings, and the circular ones are *kivas*, or places of religious worship.

Western Indians

In the arid northeastern area of present-day Arizona, the Hopi and Zuni and their ancestors engaged in settled village life for over 3,000 years. During the peak of the region's culture, between the years 900 and 1200, these peoples built great planned towns with large multiple-family dwellings in local canyons, constructed dams and canals to gather and distribute water, and conducted trade with groups as far away as central Mexico and the Mississippi River valley. The largest of their structures, Pueblo Bonita, in Chaco Canyon, New Mexico, stood five stories high and had more than 600 rooms. Not until the 1880s was a dwelling of comparable size constructed in the United States.

After the decline of these communities, probably because of drought, survivors moved to the south and east, where they established villages and perfected the techniques of desert farming, complete with irrigation systems to provide water for crops of corn, beans, and cotton. These were the people Spanish explorers called the Pueblo Indians (because they lived in small villages, or *pueblos*, when the Spanish first encountered them in the sixteenth century).

On the Pacific coast, another densely populated region, hundreds of distinct groups resided in independent villages and lived primarily by fishing, hunting sea mammals, and gathering wild plants and nuts. As many as 25 million salmon swam up the Columbia River each year, providing Indians with abundant food. On the Great Plains, with its herds of buffalo—descendants of the prehistoric giant bison—many Indians were hunters (who tracked animals on foot before the arrival of horses with the Spanish), but others lived in agricultural communities.

Cliff dwellings in Cañon de Chelly, in the area of modern-day Arizona, built sometime between 300 and 1300 and photographed in 1873.

Indians of Eastern North America

In eastern North America, hundreds of tribes inhabited towns and villages scattered from the Gulf of Mexico to present-day Canada. They lived on corn, squash, and beans, supplemented by fishing and hunting deer, turkeys, and other animals. Indian trade routes crisscrossed the eastern part of the continent. Tribes frequently warred with one another to obtain goods, seize captives, or take revenge for the killing of relatives. They conducted diplomacy and made peace. Little in the way of centralized authority existed until, in the fifteenth century, various leagues or confederations emerged in an effort to bring order to local regions. In the Southeast, the

NATIVE WAYS OF LIFE, ca. 1500

TLINGIT
INUIT
Hudson Bay
INUIT
TSHIMSHIAN
KWAKIUTLS
NOOTKIN   SHUSWAP
thinly populated
CREE
MICMAC
PENOBSCOT
ABENAKI
KOOTENAY
BLACKFEET
ASSINIBOINE   CHIPPEWA
ALGONQUIAN
SKAGIT
CHEYENNE
L. Superior
WALLA WALLA
FLATHEAD
SIOUX
CHIPPEWA
CHINOOK
NEZ PERCE
CHIPPEWA
L. Huron
HURON
WAMPANOAG
CAYUSE
HIDATSA
L. Michigan
MENOMINEE   OTTAWA
L. Ontario
MOHEGAN
PEQUOT
TILLAMOOK
MANDAN   SIOUX
NEUTRAL   IROQUOIS
NARRAGANSETT
KLAMATH
KIOWA   ARAPAHO
WINNEBAGO
L. Erie   SUSQUEHANNOCK
POMO   MODOC
thinly populated
PAWNEE   IOWA
POTAWATOMI   ERIE   MOSOPELEA
MAIDU
SHOSHONE
SAUK
COSTANO
KICKAPOO   SHAWNEE
PAMLICO
UTE
ILLINOIS
KASKASKIA
CHEROKEE   TUSCARORA
CHEMEHUEVI   SOUTHERN
WICHITA
CHUMASH   PAIUTE
COMANCHE
CHICKASAW
CREEK   YAMASEE
Atlantic Ocean
LUISENO   SERRANO
HOPI   ZUNI   TEWA
CADDO
CAHUILLA
MESCALERO
CHOCTAW   TIMUCUA
DIEGUENO
NATCHEZ   APALACHEE
JUMANO
CONCHO
KABANKAWA   CALUSA
YACHI
LAGUERNO
Gulf of Mexico
COAHUILTEC
Pacific Ocean

0   250   500 miles
0   250   500 kilometers

ARAWAK

Ways of Life in North America, AD 1515

Arctic hunter-gatherers	Non-horticultural rancherian peoples	Marginal horticultural hunters
Subarctic hunter-fisher-gatherers	Rancherian peoples with low-intensity horticulture	River-based horticultural chiefdoms
Northwest coast marine economy	Rancherian peoples with intensive horticulture	Orchard-growing alligator hunters
Plains hunter-gatherers	Pueblos with intensive horticulture	Tidewater horticulturalists
Plains horticulturalists	Seacoast foragers	Fishers and wild-rice gatherers

The native population of North America at the time of first contact with Europeans consisted of numerous tribes with their own languages, religious beliefs, and economic and social structures. This map suggests the numerous ways of life existing at the time.

The Village of Secoton, by John White, an English artist who spent a year on the Outer Banks of North Carolina in 1585–1586 as part of an expedition sponsored by Sir Walter Raleigh. A central street links houses surrounded by fields of corn. In the lower part, dancing Indians take part in a religious ceremony.

Rituals

Choctaw, Cherokee, and Chickasaw each united dozens of towns in loose alliances. In present-day New York and Pennsylvania, five Iroquois peoples—the Mohawk, Oneida, Cayuga, Seneca, and Onondaga—formed a **Great League of Peace**, bringing a period of stability to the area. Each year a Great Council, with representatives from the five groupings, met to coordinate behavior toward outsiders.

The most striking feature of Native American society at the time Europeans arrived was its sheer diversity. Each group had its own political system and set of religious beliefs, and North America was home to literally hundreds of mutually unintelligible languages. Indians had no sense of "America" as a continent or hemisphere. They did not think of themselves as a single unified people, an idea invented by Europeans and only many years later adopted by Indians themselves. Indian identity centered on the immediate social group—a tribe, village, chiefdom, or confederacy. When Europeans first arrived, many Indians saw them as simply one group among many. Their first thought was how to use the newcomers to enhance their standing in relation to other native peoples, rather than to unite against them. The sharp dichotomy between Indians and "white" persons did not emerge until later in the colonial era.

Native American Religion

Nonetheless, the diverse Indian societies of North America did share certain common characteristics. Their lives were steeped in religious ceremonies often directly related to farming and hunting. Spiritual power, they believed, suffused the world, and sacred spirits could be found in all kinds of living and inanimate things—animals, plants, trees, water, and wind—an idea known as "animism." Through religious ceremonies, they aimed to harness the aid of powerful supernatural forces to serve the interests of man. In some tribes, hunters performed rituals to placate the spirits of animals they had killed. Other religious ceremonies sought to engage the spiritual power of nature to secure abundant crops or fend off evil spirits. Indian villages also held elaborate religious rites, participation in which helped to define the boundaries of community membership. In all Indian societies, those who seemed to possess special abilities to invoke supernatural powers—shamans, medicine men, and other religious leaders—held positions of respect and authority.

Indian religion did not pose a sharp distinction between the natural and the supernatural, or secular and religious activities. In some respects, however, Indian religion was not that different from popular spiritual beliefs in Europe. Most Indians held that a single Creator stood atop the spiritual hierarchy. Nonetheless, nearly all Europeans arriving in the New World quickly concluded that Indians were in dire need of being converted to a true, Christian faith.

Land and Property

Equally alien in European eyes were Indian attitudes toward property. Numerous land systems existed among Native Americans. Generally, however, village leaders assigned plots of land to individual families to use for a season or more, and tribes claimed specific areas for hunting. Unclaimed land remained free for anyone to use. Families "owned" the right to use land, but they did not own the land itself. Indians saw land, the basis of economic life for both hunting and farming societies, as a common resource, not an economic commodity. In the nineteenth century, the

Indian leader Black Hawk would explain why, in his view, land could not be bought and sold: "The Great Spirit gave it to his children to live upon, and cultivate as far as necessary for their subsistence; and so long as they occupy and cultivate it, they have a right to the soil." Few if any Indian societies were familiar with the idea of a fenced-off piece of land belonging forever to a single individual or family. There was no market in real estate before the coming of Europeans.

Land as a common resource

Nor were Indians devoted to the accumulation of wealth and material goods. Especially east of the Mississippi River, where villages moved every few years when soil or game became depleted, acquiring numerous possessions made little sense. However, status certainly mattered in Indian societies. Tribal leaders tended to come from a small number of families, and chiefs lived more splendidly than average members of society. But their reputation often rested on their willingness to share goods with others rather than hoarding them for themselves.

A few Indian societies had rigid social distinctions. Among the Natchez, descendants of the mound-building Mississippian culture, a chief, or "Great Sun," occupied the top of the social order, with nobles, or "lesser suns," below him, and below them, the common people. In general, however, wealth mattered far less in Indian society than in European society at the time. Generosity was among the most valued social qualities, and gift giving was essential to Indian society. Trade, for example, meant more than a commercial transaction—it was accompanied by elaborate ceremonies of gift exchange. Although Indians had no experience of the wealth enjoyed at the top of European society, under normal circumstances no one in Indian societies went hungry or experienced the extreme inequalities of Europe. "There are no beggars among them," reported the English colonial leader Roger Williams of New England's Indians.

Gift giving

A Catawba map illustrates the differences between Indian and European conceptions of landed property. The map depicts not possession of a specific territory, but trade and diplomatic connections between various native groups and with the colony of Virginia, represented by the rectangle on the lower right. The map, inscribed on deerskin, was originally presented by Indian chiefs to Governor Francis Nicholson of South Carolina in 1721. This copy, the only version that survives, was made by the governor for the authorities in London. It added English labels that conveyed what the Indians had related orally with the gift.

Gender Relations

The system of gender relations in most Indian societies also differed markedly from that of Europe. Membership in a family defined women's lives, but they openly engaged in premarital sexual relations and could even choose to divorce their husbands. Most, although not all, Indian societies were matrilineal—that is, centered on clans or kinship groups in which children became members of the mother's family, not the father's. Tribal leaders were almost always men, but women played an important role in certain religious ceremonies, and female elders often helped to select male village leaders and took part in tribal meetings. Under English law, a married man controlled the family's property and a wife had no independent legal identity. In contrast, Indian women owned dwellings and tools, and a husband generally moved to live with the family of his wife. In Indian societies, men contributed to the community's well-being and demonstrated their masculinity by success in hunting or, in the Pacific Northwest, by catching fish with nets and harpoons. Because men were frequently away on the hunt, women took responsibility not only for household duties but for most agricultural work as well. Among the Pueblo of the Southwest, however, where there was less hunting than in the East, men were the primary cultivators.

Matrilineal societies

European Views of the Indians

Europeans tended to view Indians in extreme terms. They were regarded either as "noble savages," gentle, friendly, and superior in some ways to Europeans, or as uncivilized barbarians. Giovanni da Verrazano, a Florentine navigator who sailed up and down the eastern coast of North America in 1524, described Indians he encountered as "beautiful of stature and build." (For their part, many Indians, whose diet was probably more nutritious than that of most Europeans, initially found the newcomers weak and ugly.)

Indians fishing, in a 1585 drawing by John White. The canoe is filled with fish, while two men harpoon others in the background. Among the wildlife illustrated are hammerhead sharks and catfish.

Over time, however, negative images of Indians came to overshadow positive ones. Early European descriptions of North American Indians as barbaric centered on three areas—religion, land use, and gender relations. Whatever their country of origin, European newcomers concluded that Indians lacked genuine religion, or in fact worshiped the devil. Their shamans and herb healers were called "witch doctors," their numerous ceremonies and rituals at best a form of superstition, their belief in a world alive with spiritual power a worship of "false gods." Christianity presented no obstacle to the commercial use of the land, and indeed in some ways encouraged it, since true religion was thought to promote the progress of civilization. Whereas the Indians saw nature as a world of spirits and souls, the Europeans viewed it as a collection of potential commodities, a source of economic opportunity.

Europeans invoked the Indians' distinctive pattern of land use and ideas about property to answer the awkward question raised by a British minister at an early stage of England's colonization: "By what right or warrant can we enter into the land of these Savages, take away their rightful inheritance from them, and plant ourselves in their places?" While the Spanish claimed title to land in America by right of conquest and papal authority, the English, French, and Dutch came to rely on the idea that Indians had not actually "used" the land and thus had no claim to it. Despite the Indians' highly developed agriculture and well-established towns, Europeans frequently described them as nomads without settled communities. The land was thus deemed to be a vacant wilderness ready to be claimed by newcomers who would cultivate and improve it. European settlers believed that mixing one's labor with the earth, which Indians supposedly had failed to do, gave one title to the soil.

In the Indians' gender division of labor and matrilineal family structures, Europeans saw weak men and mistreated women. Hunting and fishing, the primary occupations of Indian men, were considered leisure activities in much of Europe, not "real" work. Because Indian women worked in the fields, Europeans often described them as lacking freedom. They were "not much better than slaves," in the words of one English commentator. Europeans considered Indian men "unmanly"—too weak to exercise authority within their families and restrain their wives' open sexuality, and so lazy that they forced their wives to do most of the productive labor. Throughout North America, Europeans promoted the ideas that women should confine themselves to household work and that men ought to exercise greater authority within their families. Europeans insisted that by subduing the Indians, they were actually bringing them freedom—the freedom of true religion, private property, and the liberation of both men and women from uncivilized and unchristian gender roles.

A seventeenth-century engraving by a French Jesuit priest illustrates many Europeans' view of Indian religion. A demon hovers over an Iroquois longhouse, suggesting that Indians worship the devil.

European view of Indian gender roles

INDIAN FREEDOM, EUROPEAN FREEDOM

Indian Freedom

And what of liberty as the native inhabitants of the New World understood it? Many Europeans saw Indians as embodying freedom. The Iroquois, wrote one colonial official, held "such absolute notions of liberty that they allow of no kind of superiority of one over another, and banish all servitude from their territories." But

Indian women planting crops while men break the sod. An engraving by Theodor de Bry, based on a painting by Jacques Le Moyne de Morgues. Morgues was part of an expedition of French Huguenots to Florida in 1564; he escaped when the Spanish destroyed the outpost in the following year.

most colonizers quickly concluded that the notion of "freedom" was alien to Indian societies. Early English and French dictionaries of Indian languages contained no entry for "freedom" or *liberté*. Nor, wrote one early trader, did Indians have "words to express despotic power, arbitrary kings, oppressed or obedient subjects."

Indeed, Europeans considered Indians barbaric in part because they did not appear to live under established governments or fixed laws, and had no respect for authority. "They are born, live, and die in a liberty without restraint," wrote one religious missionary. In a sense, they were *too* free, lacking the order and discipline that Europeans considered the hallmarks of civilization. When Giovanni da Verrazano described the Indians as living in "absolute freedom," he did not intend this as a compliment.

The familiar modern understanding of freedom as personal independence, often based on ownership of private property, had little meaning in most Indian societies. But Indians certainly had their own ideas of freedom. While the buying and selling of slaves was unknown, small-scale slavery existed in some Indian societies. So too did the idea of personal liberty as the opposite of being held as a slave. Indians would bitterly resent the efforts of some Europeans to reduce them to slavery.

Although individuals were expected to think for themselves and did not always have to go along with collective decision making, Indian men and women judged one another according to their ability to live up to widely understood ideas of appropriate behavior. Far more important than individual autonomy were kinship ties, the ability to follow one's spiritual values, and the well-being and security of one's community. In Indian culture, group autonomy and self-determination, and the mutual obligations that came with a sense of belonging and connectedness, took precedence over individual freedom. Ironically, the coming of Europeans, armed with their own language of liberty, would make freedom a preoccupation of American Indians, as part and parcel of the very process by which they were reduced to dependence on the colonizers.

Christian Liberty

On the eve of colonization, Europeans held numerous ideas of freedom. Some were as old as the city-states of ancient Greece, others arose during the political struggles of the early modern era. Some laid the foundations for modern conceptions of freedom, others are quite unfamiliar today. Freedom was not a single idea but a collection of distinct rights and privileges, many enjoyed by only a small portion of the population.

One conception common throughout Europe was that freedom was less a political or social status than a moral or spiritual condition. Freedom meant abandoning the life of sin to embrace the teachings of Christ. "Where the Spirit of the Lord is," declares the New Testament, "there is liberty." In this definition, servitude and freedom were mutually reinforcing, not contradictory states, since those who accepted the teachings of Christ simultaneously became "free from sin" and "servants to God."

Freedom as a spiritual condition

"Christian liberty" had no connection to later ideas of religious toleration, a notion that scarcely existed anywhere on the eve of colonization. Every nation in

Europe had an established church that decreed what forms of religious worship and belief were acceptable. Dissenters faced persecution by the state as well as condemnation by church authorities. Religious uniformity was thought to be essential to public order; the modern idea that a person's religious beliefs and practices are a matter of private choice, not legal obligation, was almost unknown. The religious wars that racked Europe in the sixteenth and seventeenth centuries centered on which religion would predominate in a kingdom or region, not the right of individuals to choose which church in which to worship.

Freedom and Authority

In its secular form, the equating of liberty with obedience to a higher authority suggested that freedom meant obedience to law. Aristotle had described the law as liberty's "salvation," not its enemy. The identification of freedom with the rule of law did not, however, mean that all subjects of the crown enjoyed the same degree of freedom. Early modern European societies were extremely hierarchical, with marked gradations of social status ranging from the king and hereditary aristocracy down to the urban and rural poor. Inequality was built into virtually every social relationship. The king claimed to rule by the authority of God. Persons of high rank demanded deference from those below them.

Within families, men exercised authority over their wives and children. According to the widespread legal doctrine known as "coverture," when a woman married she surrendered her legal identity, which became "covered" by that of her husband. She could not own property or sign contracts in her own name, control her wages if she worked, write a separate will, or, except in the rarest of circumstances, go to court seeking a divorce. The husband conducted business and testified in court for the entire family. He had the exclusive right to his wife's "company," including domestic labor and sexual relations.

Everywhere in Europe, family life depended on male dominance and female submission. Indeed, political writers of the sixteenth century explicitly compared the king's authority over his subjects with the husband's over his family. Both were ordained by God. To justify this argument, they referred to a passage in the New Testament: "As the man is the head of the woman, so is Christ the head of the Church." Neither kind of authority could be challenged without threatening the fabric of social order.

Liberty and Liberties

In this hierarchical society, liberty came from knowing one's social place and fulfilling the duties appropriate to one's rank. Most men lacked the freedom that came with economic independence. Property qualifications and other restrictions limited the electorate to a minuscule part of the adult male population. The law required strict obedience of employees, and breaches of labor contracts carried criminal penalties.

European ideas of freedom still bore the imprint of the Middle Ages, when "liberties" meant formal, specific privileges such as self-government, exemption from taxation, or the right to practice a particular trade, granted to individuals or groups by contract, royal decree, or purchase. One legal dictionary defined a liberty

The title page of *The Great Voyage to the Country of the Hurons*, published in Paris in 1632 by Gabriel Sagard, one of the first missionaries to New France, includes images of Native Americans and Catholic friars. Father Sagard also produced a dictionary of the Huron language.

Hierarchy in society

as "a privilege . . . by which men may enjoy some benefit beyond the ordinary subject." Only those who enjoyed the "freedom of the city," for example, could engage in certain economic activities. Numerous modern civil liberties did not exist. The law decreed acceptable forms of religious worship. The government regularly suppressed publications it did not like, and criticism of authority could lead to imprisonment. Personal independence was reserved for a small part of the population, and this was one reason why authorities found "masterless men"—those without regular jobs or otherwise outside the control of their social superiors—so threatening. Nonetheless, every European country that colonized the New World claimed to be spreading freedom—for its own population and for Native Americans.

THE EXPANSION OF EUROPE

It is fitting that the second epochal event that Adam Smith linked to Columbus's voyage of 1492 was the discovery by Portuguese navigators of a sea route from Europe to Asia around the southern tip of Africa. The European conquest of America began as an offshoot of the quest for a sea route to India, China, and the islands of the East Indies, the source of the silk, tea, spices, porcelain, and other luxury goods on which international trade in the early modern era centered. For centuries, this commerce had been conducted across land, from China and South Asia to the Middle East and the Mediterranean region. Profit and piety—the desire to eliminate Islamic middlemen and win control of the lucrative trade for Christian western Europe—combined to inspire the quest for a direct route to Asia.

Chinese and Portuguese Navigation

At the beginning of the fifteenth century, one might have predicted that China would establish the world's first global empire. Between 1405 and 1433, Admiral Zheng He led seven large naval expeditions in the Indian Ocean. The first convoy consisted of 62 ships that were larger than those of any European nation, along with 225 support vessels and more than 25,000 men. On his sixth voyage, Zheng explored the coast of East Africa. China was already the world's most important trading economy, with trade routes dotting the Indian Ocean. Zheng's purpose was not discovery, but to impress other peoples with China's might. Had his ships continued westward, they could easily have reached North and South America. But as a wealthy land-based empire, China did not feel the need for overseas expansion, and after 1433 the government ended support for long-distance maritime expeditions. It fell to Portugal, situated on the western corner of the Iberian Peninsula, far removed from the overland route to Asia, to take advantage of new techniques of sailing and navigation to begin exploring the Atlantic.

The development of the **caravel**, a ship capable of long-distance travel, and of the compass and quadrant, devices that enabled sailors to determine their location and direction with greater accuracy than in the past, made it possible to sail down the coast of Africa and return to Portugal. Portuguese seafarers initially hoped to locate the source of gold that for centuries had been transported in caravans

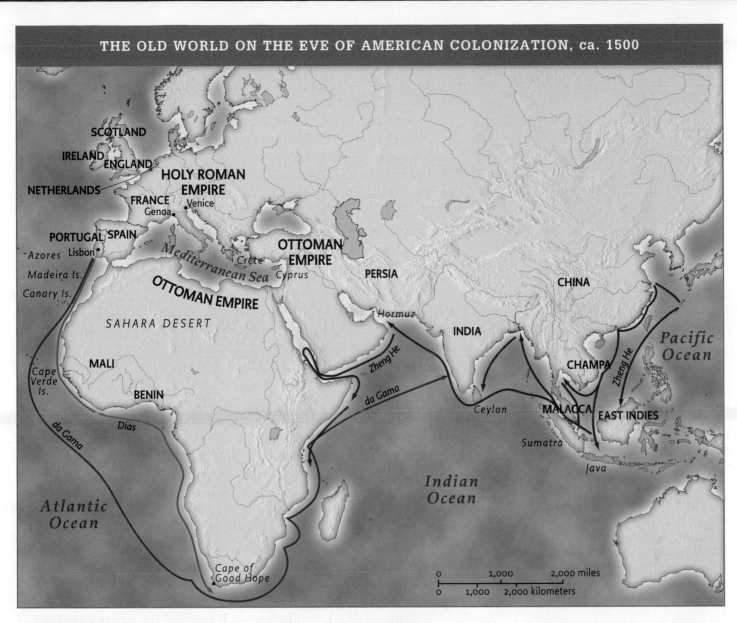

THE OLD WORLD ON THE EVE OF AMERICAN COLONIZATION, ca. 1500

across the Sahara Desert to North Africa and Europe. This commerce, which passed through the African kingdom of Mali on the southern edge of the Sahara, provided Europe with most of its gold. Around 1400, it rivaled trade with the East in economic importance. And like trade with Asia, it was controlled by Muslim merchants.

Portugal and West Africa

Until 1434, no European sailor had seen the coast of Africa below the Sahara, or the forest kingdoms south of Mali that contained the actual gold fields. But in that year, a Portuguese ship brought a sprig of rosemary from West Africa, proof that one could sail beyond the desert and return. Little by little, Portuguese ships moved farther down the coast. In 1485, they reached Benin, an imposing city whose craftsmen produced bronze sculptures that still inspire admiration for their artistic

In the fifteenth century, the world known to Europeans was limited to Europe, parts of Africa, and Asia. Explorers from Portugal sought to find a sea route to the East in order to circumvent the Italian city-states and Middle Eastern rulers who controlled the overland trade.

Sankore University in Timbuktu, in present-day Mali, was one of the great Islamic centers of learning in fourteenth-century Africa.

A detail from the *Cantino World Map* depicting the western coast of Africa at the beginning of the Atlantic slave trade. Created by an anonymous Portuguese mapmaker in 1502, the map included Europe, Africa, and a small part of the Western Hemisphere, described as "the islands lately discovered in the parts of India." It was smuggled out of Portugal by Alberto Cantino, a diplomat representing an Italian city-state.

beauty and superb casting techniques. The Portuguese established fortified trading posts on the western coast of Africa. The profits reaped by these Portuguese "factories"—so named because merchants were known as "factors"—inspired other European powers to follow in their footsteps.

Portugal also began to colonize Madeira, the Azores, and the Canary and Cape Verde Islands, which lie in the Atlantic off the African coast. Sugar plantations worked by Muslim captives and slaves from Slavic areas of eastern Europe had flourished in the Middle Ages on Mediterranean islands like Cyprus, Malta, and Crete. Now, the Portuguese established plantations on the Atlantic islands, eventually replacing the native populations with thousands of slaves shipped from Africa—an ominous precedent for the New World. Soon, the center of sugar production would shift again, to the Western Hemisphere.

Freedom and Slavery in Africa

Slavery in Africa long predated the coming of Europeans. Traditionally, African slaves tended to be criminals, debtors, and captives in war. They worked within the households of their owners and had well-defined rights, such as possessing property and marrying free persons. It was not uncommon for African slaves to acquire their freedom. Slavery was one of several forms of labor, not the basis of the economy as it would become in large parts of the New World. The coming of the Portuguese, soon followed by traders from other European nations, accelerated the buying and selling of slaves within Africa. At least 100,000 African slaves were transported to Spain and Portugal between 1450 and 1500. In 1502, the first African slaves were transported to islands in the Caribbean. The transatlantic slave trade, and its impact on Africa, will be discussed in Chapter 4.

Having reached West Africa, Portuguese mariners pushed their explorations ever southward along the coast. Bartholomeu Dias reached the Cape of Good Hope at the continent's southern tip in 1487. In 1498, Vasco da Gama sailed around it to India, demonstrating the feasibility of a sea route to the East. With a population of under 1 million, Portugal established a vast trading empire, with bases in India, southern China, and Indonesia. It replaced the Italian city-states as the major European commercial partner of the East. But six years before da Gama's voyage, Christopher Columbus had, he believed, discovered a new route to China and India by sailing west.

The Voyages of Columbus

A seasoned mariner and fearless explorer from Genoa, a major port in northern Italy, Columbus had for years sailed the Mediterranean and North Atlantic, studying ocean currents and wind patterns. Like nearly all navigators of the time, Columbus knew the earth was round. But he drastically underestimated its size. He believed that by sailing westward he could relatively quickly cross the Atlantic and reach Asia. No one in Europe knew that two giant continents lay 3,000 miles to the west. The Vikings, to be sure, had sailed from Greenland to Newfoundland around the year 1000 and established a settlement, Vinland, at a site now known as L'Anse aux Meadows. But this outpost was abandoned after a few years and had been forgotten, except in Norse legends.

For Columbus, as for other figures of the time, religious and commercial motives reinforced one another. A devout Catholic, he drew on the Bible for his estimate of the size of the globe. Along with developing trade with the East, he hoped to convert Asians to Christianity and enlist them in a crusade to redeem Jerusalem from Muslim control. Columbus sought financial support throughout Europe for the planned voyage. Most of Columbus's contemporaries, however, knew that he considerably underestimated the earth's size, which helps to explain why he had trouble gaining backers for his expedition. Eventually, King Ferdinand and Queen Isabella of Spain agreed to become sponsors. Their marriage in 1469 had united the warring kingdoms of Aragon and Castile. In 1492, they completed the *reconquista*—the "reconquest" of Spain from the Moors, African Muslims who had occupied part of the Iberian Peninsula for centuries. To ensure its religious unification, Ferdinand and Isabella ordered all Muslims and Jews to convert to Catholicism or leave the country. Along with the crown, much of Columbus's financing came from bankers and merchants of Spain and the Italian city-states, who desperately desired to circumvent the Muslim stranglehold on eastern trade. Columbus set sail with royal letters of introduction to Asian rulers, authorizing him to negotiate trade agreements.

> Columbus's sponsors

CONTACT

Columbus in the New World

On October 12, 1492, after only thirty-three days of sailing from the Canary Islands, where he had stopped to resupply his three ships, Columbus and his expedition arrived at the Bahamas. His exact landing site remains in dispute, but it was probably San Salvador, a tiny spot of land known today as Watling Island. Soon afterward, he encountered the far larger islands of Hispaniola (today the site of Haiti and the Dominican Republic) and Cuba. When one of his ships ran aground, he abandoned it and left thirty-eight men behind on Hispaniola. But he found room to bring ten inhabitants of the island back to Spain for conversion to Christianity.

In the following year, 1493, European colonization of the New World began. Columbus returned with seventeen ships and more than 1,000 men to explore the area and establish a Spanish outpost. Columbus's settlement on the island of Hispaniola, which he named La Isabella, failed, but in 1502 another Spanish explorer, Nicolás de Ovando, arrived with 2,500 men and established a permanent base, the first center of the Spanish empire in America. Before he died in 1506, Columbus made two more voyages to the New World, in 1498 and 1502. He went to his grave believing that he had discovered a westward route to Asia. The explorations of another Italian, Amerigo Vespucci, along the coast of South America between 1499 and 1502 made plain that a continent entirely unknown to Europeans had been encountered. The New World would come to bear not Columbus's name but one

Columbus's Landfall, an engraving from *La lettera dell'isole* (Letter from the Islands). This 1493 pamphlet reproduced, in the form of a poem, Columbus's first letter describing his voyage of the previous year. Under the watchful eye of King Ferdinand of Spain, Columbus and his men land on a Caribbean island, while local Indians flee.

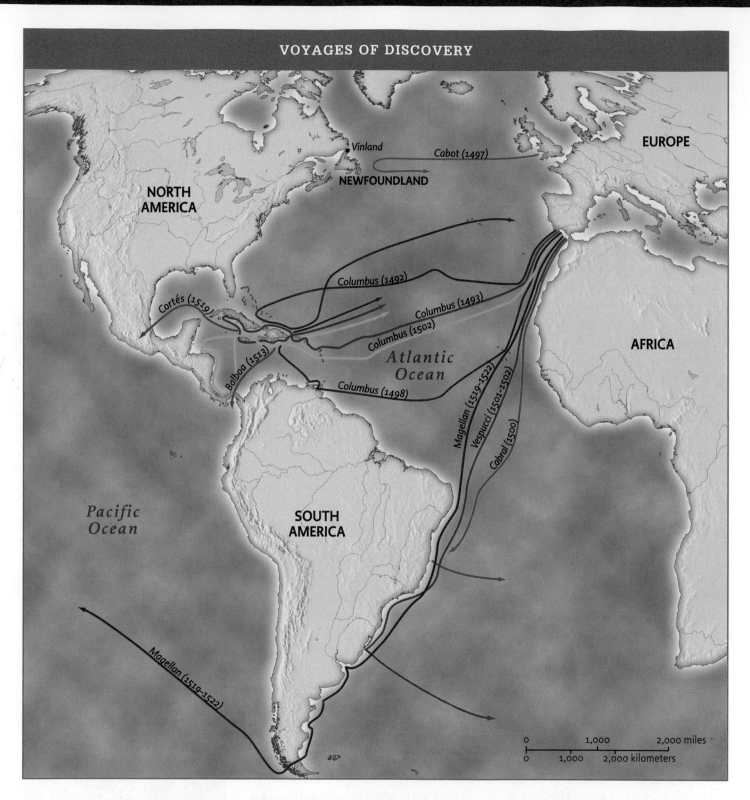

VOYAGES OF DISCOVERY

EUROPE

Vinland

Cabot (1497)

NORTH AMERICA

NEWFOUNDLAND

Cortés (1519)

Columbus (1492)

Columbus (1493)

Columbus (1502)

AFRICA

Balboa (1513)

Atlantic Ocean

Columbus (1498)

Magellan (1519–1522)

Vespucci (1501–1502)

Cabral (1500)

Pacific Ocean

SOUTH AMERICA

Magellan (1519–1522)

| 0 | 1,000 | 2,000 miles |
| 0 | 1,000 | 2,000 kilometers |

Christopher Columbus's first Atlantic crossing, in 1492, was soon followed by voyages of discovery by English, Portuguese, Spanish, and Italian explorers.

based on Vespucci's—America. Vespucci also realized that the native inhabitants were distinct peoples, not residents of the East Indies as Columbus had believed, although the name "Indians," applied to them by Columbus, has endured to this day.

Vespucci

Exploration and Conquest

The speed with which European exploration proceeded in the aftermath of Columbus's first voyage is remarkable. The technique of printing with movable type, invented in the 1430s by the German craftsman Johannes Gutenberg, had made possible the rapid spread of information in Europe, at least among the educated minority. News of Columbus's achievement traveled quickly. One writer hailed him as "a hero such as the ancients made gods of." Others were inspired to follow in his wake. John Cabot, a Genoese merchant who had settled in England, reached Newfoundland in 1497. Soon, scores of fishing boats from France, Spain, and England were active in the region. Pedro Cabral claimed Brazil for Portugal in 1500.

But the Spanish took the lead in exploration and conquest. Inspired by a search for wealth, national glory, and the desire to spread Catholicism, Spanish *conquistadores*, often accompanied by religious missionaries and carrying flags emblazoned with the sign of the cross, radiated outward from Hispaniola. In 1513, Vasco Núñez de Balboa trekked across the isthmus of Panama and became the first European to gaze upon the Pacific Ocean. Between 1519 and 1522, Ferdinand Magellan led the first expedition to sail around the world, encountering Pacific islands and peoples previously unknown to Europe. Magellan was killed in the Philippines, but his fleet completed the journey, correcting once and for all Columbus's erroneous assessment of the earth's size.

The first explorer to encounter a major American civilization was Hernán Cortés, who in 1519 arrived at Tenochtitlán, the nerve center of the Aztec empire, whose wealth and power rested on domination of numerous subordinate peoples nearby. The Aztecs were violent warriors who engaged in the ritual sacrifice of captives and others, sometimes thousands at a time. This practice thoroughly alienated their neighbors and reinforced the Spanish view of America's native inhabitants as barbarians, even though in Europe at this time thousands of men and women were burned at the stake as witches or religious heretics, and criminals were executed in public spectacles that attracted throngs of onlookers.

With only a few hundred European men, the daring Cortés conquered the Aztec city, relying on superior military technology such as iron weapons and gunpowder, as well as shrewdness in enlisting the aid of some of the Aztecs' subject peoples, who supplied him with thousands of warriors. His most powerful ally, however, was disease—a smallpox epidemic that devastated Aztec society. A few years later, Francisco Pizarro conquered the great Inca kingdom centered in modern-day Peru. Pizarro's tactics were typical of the conquistadores. He captured the Incan king,

Engravings, from the *Florentine Codex*, of the forces of Cortés marching on Tenochtitlán and assaulting the city with cannon fire. The difference in military technology between the Spanish and Aztecs is evident. Indians who allied with Cortés had helped him build vessels and carry them in pieces over mountains to the city. The codex (a volume formed by stitching together manuscript pages) was prepared under the supervision of a Spanish missionary in sixteenth-century Mexico.

TABLE 1.1 Estimated Regional Populations: The Americas, ca. 1500	
North America	3,800,000
Mexico	17,200,000
Central America	5,625,000
Hispaniola	1,000,000
The Caribbean	3,000,000
The Andes	15,700,000
South America	8,620,000
Total	54,945,000

A drawing from around 1700 shows an Indian suffering from smallpox. The Columbian Exchange—the flow of goods and people across the Atlantic—included animals, plants, technology, and diseases.

demanded and received a ransom, and then killed the king anyway. Soon, treasure fleets carrying cargoes of gold and silver from the mines of Mexico and Peru were traversing the Atlantic to enrich the Spanish crown.

The Demographic Disaster

The transatlantic flow of goods and people, sometimes called the **Columbian Exchange**, altered millions of years of evolution. Plants, animals, and cultures that had evolved independently on separate continents were now thrown together. Products introduced to Europe from the Americas included corn, tomatoes, potatoes, peanuts, tobacco, and cotton, while people from the Old World brought wheat, rice, sugarcane, horses, cattle, pigs, and sheep to the New. But Europeans also carried germs previously unknown in the Americas.

No one knows exactly how many people lived in the Americas at the time of Columbus's voyages—current estimates range between 50 and 90 million. By comparison, the European population in 1492 (including Russia) was around 90 million, the African population was around 40 million, and about 210 million lived in China and modern-day India. Most inhabitants of the New World lived in Central and South America. In 1492, the Indian population within what are now the borders of the United States was between 2 and 5 million.

Whatever their numbers, the Indian populations suffered a catastrophic decline because of contact with Europeans and their wars, enslavement, and especially diseases like smallpox, influenza, and measles. Never having encountered these diseases, Indians had not developed antibodies to fight them. The result was devastating. Many West Indian islands were all but depopulated. On Hispaniola, the native population, estimated at between 300,000 and 1 million in 1492, had nearly disappeared fifty years later. The population of Mexico would fall by more than 90 percent in the sixteenth century, from perhaps 20 million to less than 2 million. As for the area that now forms the United States, its Native American population fell continuously. It reached its lowest point around 1900, at only 250,000.

Overall, the death of perhaps 80 million people—close to one-fifth of humankind—in the first century and a half after contact with Europeans represents the greatest loss of life in human history. It was disease as much as military prowess and more-advanced technology that enabled Europeans to conquer the Americas.

THE SPANISH EMPIRE

By the middle of the sixteenth century, Spain had established an immense empire that reached from Europe to the Americas and Asia. The Atlantic and Pacific oceans, once barriers separating different parts of the world, now became highways for the exchange of goods and the movement of people. Spanish galleons carried gold and silver from Mexico and Peru eastward to Spain and westward to Manila in the Philippines and on to China.

The Spanish empire included the most populous parts of the New World and the regions richest in natural resources. Stretching from the Andes Mountains of

South America through present-day Mexico and the Caribbean and eventually into Florida and the southwestern United States, Spain's empire exceeded in size the Roman empire of the ancient world. Its center in North America was Mexico City, a magnificent capital built on the ruins of the Aztec city of Tenochtitlán that boasted churches, hospitals, monasteries, government buildings, and the New World's first university. Unlike the English and French New World empires, Spanish America was essentially an urban civilization, an "empire of towns." For centuries, its great cities, notably Mexico City, Quito, and Lima, far outshone any urban centers in North America and most of those in Europe.

Governing Spanish America

Spain's system of colonial government rivaled that of ancient Rome. Alarmed by the destructiveness of the conquistadores, the Spanish crown replaced them with a more stable system of government headed by lawyers and bureaucrats. At least in theory, the government of Spanish America reflected the absolutism of the newly unified nation at home. Authority originated with the king and flowed downward through the Council of the Indies—the main body in Spain for colonial administration—and then to viceroys in Mexico and Peru and other local officials in America. The Catholic Church also played a significant role in the administration of Spanish colonies, frequently exerting its authority on matters of faith, morals, and treatment of the Indians.

Successive kings kept elected assemblies out of Spain's New World empire. Royal officials were generally appointees from Spain, rather than *criollos*, or **creoles**, as persons born in the colonies of European ancestry were called. The imperial state was a real and continuous presence in Spanish America. But as its power declined in Europe beginning in the seventeenth century, the local elite came to enjoy more and more effective authority over colonial affairs. Given the vastness of the empire, local municipal councils, universities, merchant organizations, and craft guilds enjoyed considerable independence.

Colonists in Spanish America

Despite the decline in the native population, Spanish America remained populous enough that, with the exception of the West Indies and a few cities, large-scale importations of African slaves were unnecessary. Instead, the Spanish forced tens of thousands of Indians to work in gold and silver mines, which supplied the empire's wealth, and on large-scale farms, or **haciendas**, controlled by Spanish landlords. In Spanish America, unlike other New World empires, Indians performed most of the labor, and although the Spanish introduced livestock, wheat, and sugar, the main agricultural crops were the same ones grown before colonization—corn, beans, and squash.

"The maxim of the conqueror must be to settle," said one Spanish official. The government barred non-Spaniards from emigrating to its American domains, as well as non-Christian

TABLE 1.2 Estimated Regional Populations: The World, ca. 1500	
India	110,000,000
China	103,000,000
Other Asia	55,400,000
Western Europe	57,200,000
The Americas	54,000,000
Russia and Eastern Europe	34,000,000
Sub-Saharan Africa	38,300,000
Japan	15,400,000
World Total	467,300,000

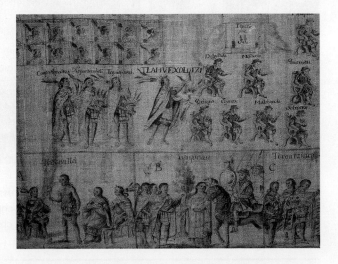

An image from the *Tlaxcala Codex*, which chronicles events in a region of central Mexico in the sixteenth century. Aztec warriors dressed in eagle and jaguar costumes dance before Spanish officials and priests.

Spaniards, including Jews and Moors. But the opportunity for social advancement drew numerous colonists from Spain—225,000 in the sixteenth century and a total of 750,000 in the three centuries of Spain's colonial rule. Eventually, a significant number came in families, but at first the large majority were young, single men, many of them laborers, craftsmen, and soldiers. Many also came as government officials, priests, professionals, and minor aristocrats, all ready to direct the manual work of Indians, since living without having to labor was a sign of noble status. The most successful of these colonists enjoyed lives of luxury similar to those of the upper classes at home.

Colonists and Indians

Although persons of European birth, called *peninsulares*, stood atop the social hierarchy, they never constituted more than a tiny proportion of the population of Spanish America. Unlike in the later British empire, Indian inhabitants always outnumbered European colonists and their descendants in Spanish America, and large areas remained effectively under Indian control for many years. Like the later French empire and unlike the English, Spanish authorities granted Indians certain rights within colonial society and looked forward to their eventual assimilation.

The Spanish crown ordered wives of colonists to join them in America and demanded that single men marry. But with the population of Spanish women remaining low, the intermixing of the colonial and Indian peoples soon began. As early as 1514, the Spanish government formally approved of such marriages, partly as a way of bringing Christianity to the native population. By 1600, **mestizos** (persons of mixed origin) made up a large part of the urban population of Spanish America. In the century that followed, *mestizos* repopulated the Valley of Mexico, where disease had decimated the original inhabitants. Over time, Spanish America evolved into a hybrid culture, part Spanish, part Indian, and in some areas part African, but with a single official faith, language, and governmental system. In

Young Woman with a Harpsichord, a colorful painting from Mexico in the early 1700s, depicts an upper-class woman. Her dress, jewelry, fan, the cross around her neck, and the musical instrument all emphasize that while she lives in the colonies, she embodies the latest in European fashion and culture.

Four Racial Groups, taken from a series of paintings by the eighteenth-century Mexican artist Andrés de Islas, illustrates the racial mixing that took place in the Spanish empire and some of the new vocabulary invented to describe it. *First:* The offspring of a Spaniard and Indian is a *mestizo*. *Second:* A Spaniard and a *mestiza* produce a *castizo*. *Third:* The child of an Indian and a *mestiza* is a *coyote*. *Fourth:* And the child of an Indian man and African woman is a *chino*.

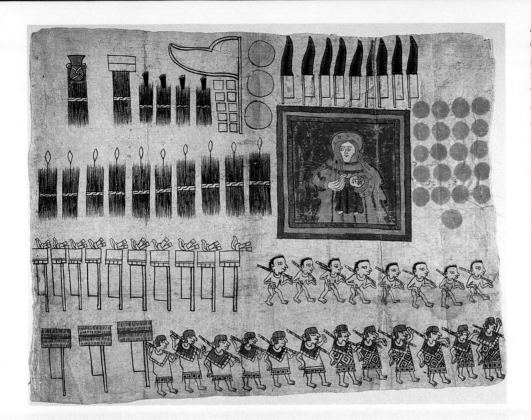

An illustration from the *Huexotzinco Codex* (1531) depicts Mexicans providing products and services as taxes to the Spanish conquerors. The banner of the Virgin Mary and baby Jesus reflects the early spread of Christianity. The people of Huexotzinco, a town near Mexico City, had aided Hernán Cortés in his conquest of the Aztec empire. The codex was part of a successful lawsuit, endorsed by Cortés, in which the Indians challenged excessive taxation by colonial officials.

1531, a poor Indian, Juan Diego, reported seeing a vision of the Virgin Mary, looking very much like a dark-skinned Indian, near a Mexican village. Miracles began to be reported, and a shrine was built in her honor. The Virgin of Guadalupe would come to be revered by millions as a symbol of the mixing of Indian and Spanish cultures, and later of the modern nation of Mexico.

The Virgin of Guadalupe

Justifications for Conquest

What allowed one nation, the seventeenth-century Dutch legal thinker Hugo Grotius wondered, to claim possession of lands that "belonged to someone else"? This question rarely occurred to most of the Europeans who crossed the Atlantic in the wake of Columbus's voyage, or to rulers in the Old World. They had immense confidence in the superiority of their own cultures to those they encountered in America. They expected these societies to abandon their own beliefs and traditions and embrace those of the newcomers. Failure to do so reinforced the conviction that these people were uncivilized "heathens" (non-Christians).

Europeans brought with them not only a long history of using violence to subdue their internal and external foes but also missionary zeal to spread the benefits of their own civilization to others, while reaping the rewards of empire. Spain was no exception. The establishment of its empire in America took place in the wake of Spain's own territorial unification, the rise of a powerful royal government, and the enforcement of religious orthodoxy by the expulsion of Muslims and Jews in 1492. To further legitimize Spain's claim to rule the New World, a year after Columbus's first voyage Pope Alexander VI divided the non-Christian world between Spain and Portugal. The line was subsequently adjusted to give Portugal control of Brazil, with the remainder of the Western Hemisphere falling under Spanish authority.

Religious motivation

The Virgin of Guadalupe, a symbol of Mexican culture, in an image from 1770. She is portrayed as the protector of the Indians.

Converting Indians

Spreading the Faith

Not surprisingly, the pope justified this pronouncement by requiring Spain and Portugal to spread Catholicism among the native inhabitants of the Americas. The missionary element of colonization, already familiar because of the long holy war against Islam within Spain itself, was powerfully reinforced in the sixteenth century, when the Protestant Reformation divided the Catholic Church. In 1517, Martin Luther, a German priest, posted his *Ninety-Five Theses*, which accused the church of worldliness and corruption. Luther wanted to cleanse the church of abuses such as the sale of indulgences (official dispensations forgiving sins). He insisted that all believers should read the Bible for themselves, rather than relying on priests to interpret it for them. His call for reform led to the rise of new Protestant churches independent of Rome and plunged Europe into more than a century of religious and political strife.

Spain, the most powerful bastion of orthodox Catholicism, redoubled its efforts to convert the Indians to the "true faith." National glory and religious mission went hand in hand. Convinced of the superiority of Catholicism to all other religions, Spain insisted that the primary goal of colonization was to save the Indians from heathenism and prevent them from falling under the sway of Protestantism. The aim was neither to exterminate nor to remove the Indians, but to transform them into obedient, Christian subjects of the crown. Indeed, lacking the later concept of "race" as an unchanging, inborn set of qualities and abilities, many Spanish writers insisted that Indians could in time be "brought up" to the level of European civilization. Of course, this meant not only the destruction of existing Indian political structures but also a transformation of their economic and spiritual lives. Religious orders established missions throughout the empire, and over time millions of Indians were converted to Catholicism.

On the other hand, Spanish rule, especially in its initial period, witnessed a disastrous fall in Indian population, not only because of epidemics but also because of the brutal conditions of labor to which Indians were subjected. The

A benign view of Spanish colonization. This engraving from a 1621 book depicts Spanish missionaries bringing Christianity to New World natives while priests do construction work. A fortified colonial town is visible in the background.

conquistadores and subsequent governors, who required conquered peoples to acknowledge the Catholic Church and provide gold and silver, saw no contradiction between serving God and enriching themselves. Others, however, did.

Las Casas's Complaint

As early as 1537, Pope Paul III, who hoped to see Indians become devout subjects of Catholic monarchs, outlawed their enslavement (an edict never extended to apply to Africans). His decree declared Indians to be "truly men," who must not be "treated as dumb beasts." Fifteen years later, the Dominican priest **Bartolomé de Las Casas** published an account of the decimation of the Indian population with the compelling title *A Very Brief Account of the Destruction of the Indies*. Las Casas's father had sailed on Columbus's second voyage, and he himself had participated in the conquest of Cuba. But in 1514 Las Casas freed his own Indian slaves and began to preach against the injustices of Spanish rule.

Las Casas's writings denounced Spain for causing the death of millions of innocent people. He narrated in shocking detail the "strange cruelties" carried out by "the Christians," including the burning alive of men, women, and children and the imposition of forced labor. The Indians, he wrote, had been "totally deprived of their freedom and were put in the harshest, fiercest, most terrible servitude and captivity." Long before the idea was common, Las Casas insisted that Indians were rational beings, not barbarians, and that Spain had no grounds on which to deprive them of their lands and liberty. "The entire human race is one," he proclaimed, and while he continued to believe that Spain had a right to rule in America, largely on religious grounds, he called for Indians to enjoy "all guarantees of liberty and justice" from the moment they became subjects of Spain. "Nothing is certainly more precious in human affairs, nothing more esteemed," he wrote, "than freedom." Yet Las Casas also suggested that importing slaves from Africa would help to protect the Indians from exploitation.

> *Spain's "strange cruelties"*

Spanish conquistadores murdering Indians at Cuzco, in Peru. The Dutch-born engraver Theodor de Bry and his sons illustrated ten volumes about New World exploration published between 1590 and 1618. A Protestant, de Bry created vivid images that helped to spread the Black Legend of Spain as a uniquely cruel colonizer.

Reforming the Empire

Like other Spaniards, Las Casas believed that the main justification for empire was converting the Indians to Christianity. Spanish cruelty, he feared, undermined this effort. Largely because of Las Casas's efforts, Spain in 1542 promulgated the New Laws, commanding that Indians no longer be enslaved. In 1550, Spain abolished the *encomienda* system, under which the first settlers had been granted authority over conquered Indian lands with the right to extract forced labor from the native inhabitants. In its place, the government established the ***repartimiento* system**, whereby residents of Indian villages remained legally free and entitled to wages, but were still required to perform a fixed amount of labor each year. The Indians were not slaves—they had access to land, were paid wages, and could not be bought and sold. But since the requirement that they

A view of San Carlos Borromeo de Carmelo, or Mission Carmel, in 1786, two years after the death of Father Junipero Serra, depicts Native Americans lined up to welcome a French scientific expedition. Sketched by a French explorer, this is the earliest known image of California.

Resivimiento del Conde dela ʃ̃i̇ Ruo in la minⱬion del Carmelo de Monteres

Indian labor

work for the Spanish remained the essence of the system, it still allowed for many abuses by Spanish landlords and by priests who required Indians to toil on mission lands as part of the conversion process. Indeed, a long struggle ensued among settlers, missionaries, and colonial authorities for control of Indian labor. Each party proclaimed itself a humane overlord and denounced the others for exploiting the native population.

By the end of the sixteenth century, work in the Spanish empire consisted largely of forced wage labor by native inhabitants and slave labor by Africans on the West Indian islands and a few parts of the mainland. Like all empires, Spain's always remained highly exploitative. Over time, the initial brutal treatment of Indians improved somewhat. The Spanish established their domination not just through violence and disease but by bringing education, medical care, and European goods, and because many Indians embraced Christianity. But Las Casas's writings, translated almost immediately into several European languages, contributed to the spread of the **Black Legend**—the image of Spain as a uniquely brutal and exploitative colonizer. This would provide a potent justification for other European powers to challenge Spain's predominance in the New World. Influenced by Las Casas, the eighteenth-century French historian Guillaume Thomas Raynal would write of Columbus's arrival in the New World, "Tell me, reader, whether these were civilized people landing among savages, or savages among civilized people?"

Exploring North America

New colonies

While the Spanish empire centered on Mexico, Peru, and the West Indies, the hope of finding a new kingdom of gold soon led Spanish explorers into new territory. In 1508, Spain established the first permanent colony in what is now the United States.

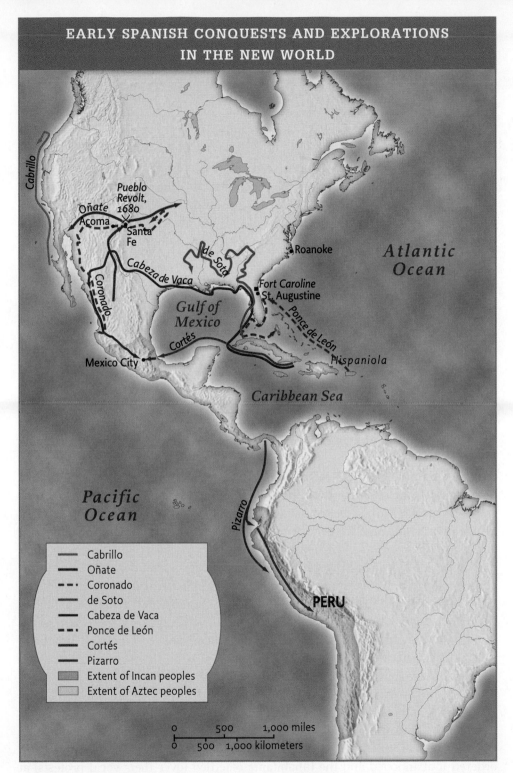

By around 1600, New Spain had become a vast empire stretching from the modern-day American Southwest through Mexico and Central America and into the former Inca kingdom in South America. This map shows early Spanish exploration, especially in the present-day United States.

That first colony was not, as many people believe, at Jamestown, Virginia, or St. Augustine, Florida, but on the island of Puerto Rico, now a U.S. "commonwealth." Unlike many other European settlements that followed it, Puerto Rico had gold; Juan Ponce de León, who led the colony, sent a considerable amount to Spain, while keeping some for himself. In 1513, Ponce embarked for Florida, in search of wealth, slaves, and a fountain of eternal youth, only to be repelled by local Indians. In 1528, another expedition seeking plunder in Florida embarked from Spain, but after a series of storms only a handful of men reached the Gulf Coast. For seven years they traversed the Southwest until a few survivors arrived in Mexico in 1536. One, Álvar Núñez Cabeza de Vaca, wrote an account of his adventures, including tales told by native inhabitants (possibly to persuade the newcomers to move on) of the seven golden cities of Cibola, somewhere over the horizon.

Exploring the West

In the late 1530s and 1540s, Juan Rodriguez Cabrillo explored the Pacific coast as far north as present-day Oregon, and expeditions led by Hernando de Soto, Cabeza de Vaca, Francisco Vásquez de Coronado, and others marched through the Gulf region and the Southwest, fruitlessly searching for another Mexico or Peru. Coronado explored much of the interior of the continent, reaching as far north as the Great Plains, and became the first European to encounter the immense herds of buffalo that roamed the West. These expeditions, really mobile communities with hundreds of adventurers, priests, potential settlers, slaves, and livestock, spread disease and devastation among Indian communities. De Soto's was particularly brutal. His men tortured, raped, and enslaved countless Indians and transmitted deadly diseases. When Europeans in the seventeenth century returned to colonize the area traversed by de Soto's party, little remained of the societies he had encountered. Where large towns had existed, explorers found only herds of grazing bison.

Spanish Florida

Nonetheless, these explorations established Spain's claim to a large part of what is now the American South and Southwest. The first region to be colonized within the present-day United States was Florida. Spain hoped to establish a military base there to combat pirates who threatened the treasure fleet that each year sailed from Havana for Europe loaded with gold and silver from Mexico and Peru. Spain also wanted to forestall French incursions in the area. In 1565, Philip II of Spain authorized the nobleman Pedro Menéndez de Avilés to lead a colonizing expedition to Florida. Menéndez destroyed a small outpost at Fort Caroline, which a group of Huguenots (French Protestants) had established in 1562 near present-day Jacksonville. Menéndez and his men massacred the 500 colonists and went on to establish Spanish forts on St. Simons Island, Georgia, and at St. Augustine, Florida. The latter remains the oldest site in the continental United States continuously inhabited by European settlers and their descendants.

Military base

Forts and missions

Spanish expeditions soon established forts from present-day Miami into South Carolina, and Spanish religious missionaries set up outposts in Florida and on the Sea Islands, hoping to convert the local Indians to Christianity. In 1566, 500 Spanish colonists landed near modern-day Port Royal, South Carolina, and established the settlement of Santa Elena. It survived until 1587, when the government in Spain ordered it abandoned and the inhabitants resettled (over their vocal protests) at St. Augustine, to protect them from English naval raids. Most of the forts fell into disuse, and many of the missions were destroyed by local Guale Indians in an uprising that began in 1597. The Indians explained their revolt by noting that the

Religious oppression

and technologies they introduced. Some natives welcomed them as a counterbalance to the depredations of soldiers and settlers and accepted baptism, even as they continued to practice their old religion, adding Jesus, Mary, and the Catholic saints to their already rich spiritual pantheon. But as the Inquisition—the persecution of non-Catholics—became more and more intense in Spain, so did the friars' efforts to stamp out traditional religious ceremonies in New Mexico. By burning Indian idols, masks, and other sacred objects, the missionaries alienated far more Indians than they converted. A prolonged drought that began around 1660 and the authorities' inability to protect the villages and missions from attacks by marauding Navajo and Apache Indians added to local discontent.

The Pueblo peoples had long been divided among themselves. The Spanish assumed that the Indians could never unite against the colonizers. In August 1680, they were proven wrong.

Little is known about the life of Popé, who became the main organizer of an uprising that aimed to drive the Spanish from the colony and restore the Indians' traditional autonomy. A religious leader born around 1630 in San Juan Pueblo, Popé first appears in the historical record in 1675, when he was one of forty-seven Pueblo Indians arrested for "sorcery"—that is, practicing their traditional religion. Four of the prisoners were hanged, and the rest, including Popé, were brought to Santa Fe to be publicly whipped. After this humiliation, Popé returned home and began holding secret meetings in Pueblo communities.

Under Popé's leadership, New Mexico's Indians joined in a coordinated uprising. Ironically, because the Pueblos spoke six different languages, Spanish became the revolt's "lingua franca" (a common means of communication among persons of different linguistic backgrounds). Some 2,000 warriors destroyed isolated farms and missions, killing 400 colonists, including 21 Franciscan missionaries. They then surrounded Santa Fe. The Spanish resisted fiercely but eventually had no choice but to abandon the town. Most of the Spanish survivors, accompanied by several hundred Christian Indians, made their way south out of New Mexico. Within a few weeks, a century of colonization in the area had been destroyed. From their own point of view, the Pueblo Indians had triumphantly reestablished the freedom lost through Spanish conquest.

The **Pueblo Revolt** was the most complete victory for Native Americans over Europeans and the only wholesale expulsion of settlers in the history of North America. According to a royal attorney who interviewed the Spanish survivors in Mexico City, the revolt arose from the "many oppressions" the Indians had suffered. The victorious Pueblos turned with a vengeance on all symbols of European culture, uprooting fruit trees, destroying cattle, burning churches and images of Christ and the Virgin Mary, and wading into rivers to wash away their Catholic baptisms. They rebuilt their places of worship, called "kivas," and resumed sacred dances the friars had banned. "The God of the Spaniards," they shouted, "is dead."

Cooperation among the Pueblo peoples, however, soon evaporated. By the end of the 1680s, warfare had broken out among several villages, even as Apache and Navajo raids continued. Popé died around 1690. In 1692, the Spanish launched an invasion that reconquered New Mexico. Some communities welcomed them back

nthony and the Infant Jesus, painted
tanned buffalo hide by a Franciscan
t in New Mexico in the early eigh-
:h century. This was not long after
Spanish reconquered the area, from
h they had been driven by the Pueblo
lt.

missionaries had sought to eliminate "our dances, banquets, feasts, celebrations, and wars. . . . They persecute our old people by calling them witches." The missions were soon rebuilt, only to be devastated again a century later, this time by English and Indian forces from South Carolina. In general, Florida failed to attract settlers, remaining an isolated military settlement, in effect a fortified outpost of Cuba. As late as 1763, Spanish Florida had only 4,000 inhabitants of European descent.

Spain in the Southwest

Spain took even longer to begin the colonization of the American Southwest. Although Coronado and others made incursions into the area in the sixteenth century, their explorations were widely considered failures, since they had discovered neither gold nor advanced civilizations whose populations could be put to work for the Spanish empire. Spain then neglected the area for another half-century. It was not until 1598 that Juan de Oñate led a group of 400 soldiers, colonists, and missionaries north from Mexico to establish a permanent settlement. While searching for fabled deposits of precious metals, Oñate's nephew and fourteen soldiers were killed by inhabitants of Acoma, the "sky city" located on a high bluff in present-day New Mexico.

Oñate decided to teach the local Indians a lesson. After a two-day siege, his forces scaled the seemingly impregnable heights and destroyed Acoma, killing more than 800 of its 1,500 or so inhabitants, including 300 women. Of the 600 Indians captured, the women and children were consigned to servitude in Spanish families, while adult men were punished by the cutting off of one foot. Not until the 1640s was Acoma, which had been inhabited since the thirteenth century, rebuilt. Oñate's message was plain—any Indians who resisted Spanish authority would be crushed. But his method of rule, coupled with his failure to locate gold, alarmed authorities in Mexico City. In 1606, Oñate was ordered home and punished for his treatment of New Mexico's Indians. In 1610, Spain established the capital of New Mexico at Santa Fe, the first permanent European settlement in the Southwest.

Acoma, the "sky city
1904.

The Pueblo Revolt

In 1680, New Mexico's small and vulnerable colonist population numbered fewer than 3,000. Most were *mestizos* (persons of mixed Spanish and Indian origin), since few European settlers came to the region. Relations between the Pueblo Indians and colonial authorities had deteriorated throughout the seventeenth century, as governors, settlers, and missionaries sought to exploit the labor of an Indian population that declined from about 60,000 in 1600 to some 17,000 eighty years later. Franciscan friars worked relentlessly to convert Indians to Catholicism, often using intimidation and violence. Their spiritual dedication and personal courage impressed many Indians, however, as did the European goods

as a source of military protection. But Spain had learned a lesson. In the eighteenth century, colonial authorities adopted a more tolerant attitude toward traditional religious practices and made fewer demands on Indian labor.

THE FRENCH AND DUTCH EMPIRES

If the Black Legend inspired a sense of superiority among Spain's European rivals, the precious metals that poured from the New World into the Spanish treasury aroused the desire to try to match Spain's success. The establishment of Spain's American empire transformed the balance of power in the world economy. The Atlantic replaced the overland route to Asia as the major axis of global trade. During the seventeenth century, the French, Dutch, and English established colonies in North America. England's mainland colonies, to be discussed in the next chapter, consisted of agricultural settlements with growing populations whose hunger for land produced incessant conflict with native peoples. New France and New Netherland were primarily commercial ventures that never attracted large numbers of colonists. More dependent on Indians as trading partners and military allies, these French and Dutch settlements allowed Native Americans greater freedom than the English.

Shifts in global trade

French Colonization

The first of Spain's major European rivals to embark on New World explorations was France. The French initially aimed to find gold and to locate a Northwest Passage—a sea route connecting the Atlantic to the Pacific. But early French explorers were soon disappointed, and North America came to seem little more than a barrier to be crossed, not a promising site for settlement or exploitation. For most of the sixteenth century, only explorers, fishermen, pirates preying on Spanish shipping farther south, and, as time went on, fur traders visited the eastern coast of North America. French efforts to establish settlements in Newfoundland and Nova Scotia failed, beset by native resistance and inadequate planning and financing. Not until the seventeenth century would France, as well as England and the Netherlands, establish permanent settlements in North America.

Northwest Passage

The explorer Samuel de Champlain, sponsored by a French fur-trading company, founded Quebec in 1608. In 1673, the Jesuit priest Jacques Marquette and the fur trader Louis Joliet located the Mississippi River, and by 1681 René-Robert Cavelier, Sieur de La Salle, had descended to the Gulf of Mexico, claiming the entire Mississippi River valley for France. New France eventually formed a giant arc along the St. Lawrence, Mississippi, and Ohio rivers.

Until 1663, when the population of European origin was fewer than 3,000, French Canada was ruled by the Company of New France through a governor-general appointed in Paris. There was no representative assembly. In that year, the French government established a new company. It granted land along the St. Lawrence River to well-connected nobles and army officers who would transport colonists to take their place in a feudal society. But most of the **indentured servants**

The Company of New France

VOICES OF FREEDOM

From BARTOLOMÉ DE LAS CASAS, HISTORY OF THE INDIES (1528)

Las Casas was the Dominican priest who condemned the treatment of Indians in the Spanish empire. His widely disseminated *History of the Indies* helped to establish the Black Legend of Spanish cruelty.

———————

The Indians [of Hispaniola] were totally deprived of their freedom and were put in the harshest, fiercest, most horrible servitude and captivity which no one who has not seen it can understand. Even beasts enjoy more freedom when they are allowed to graze in the fields. But our Spaniards gave no such opportunity to Indians and truly considered them perpetual slaves, since the Indians had not the free will to dispose of their persons but instead were disposed of according to Spanish greed and cruelty, not as men in captivity but as beasts tied to a rope to prevent free movement. When they were allowed to go home, they often found it deserted and had no other recourse than to go out into the woods to find food and to die. When they fell ill, which was very frequently because they are a delicate people unaccustomed to such work, the Spaniards did not believe them and pitilessly called them lazy dogs and kicked and beat them; and when illness was apparent they sent them home as useless. . . . They would go then, falling into the first stream and dying there in desperation; others would hold on longer but very few ever made it home. I sometimes came upon dead bodies on my way, and upon others who were gasping and moaning in their death agony, repeating "Hungry, hungry." And this was the freedom, the good treatment and the Christianity the Indians received.

About eight years passed under [Spanish rule] and this disorder had time to grow; no one gave it a thought and the multitude of people who originally lived on the island . . . was consumed at such a rate that in these eight years 90 per cent had perished. From here this sweeping plague went to San Juan, Jamaica, Cuba and the continent, spreading destruction over the whole hemisphere.

From "DECLARATION OF JOSEPHE"
(DECEMBER 19, 1681)

Josephe was a Spanish-speaking Indian questioned by a royal attorney in Mexico City investigating the Pueblo Revolt. The revolt of the Indian population, in 1680, temporarily drove Spanish settlers from present-day New Mexico.

Asked what causes or motives the said Indian rebels had for renouncing the law of God and obedience to his Majesty, and for committing so many of crimes, [he answered] the causes they have were alleged ill treatment and injuries received from [Spanish authorities], because they beat them, took away what they had, and made them work without pay. Thus he replies.

Asked if he has learned if it has come to his notice during the time that he has been here the reason why the apostates burned the images, churches, and things pertaining to divine worship, making a mockery and a trophy of them, killing the priests and doing the other things they did, he said that he knows and had heard it generally stated that while they were besieging the villa the rebellious traitors burned the church and shouted in loud voices, "Now the God of the Spaniards, who was their father, is dead, and Santa Maria, who was their mother, and the saints, who were pieces of rotten wood," saying that only their own god lived. Thus they ordered all the temples and images, crosses and rosaries burned, and their function

being over, they all went to bathe in the rivers, saying that they thereby washed away the water of baptism. For their churches, they placed on the four sides and in the center of the plaza some small circular enclosures of stone where they went to offer flour, feathers, and the seed of maguey [a local plant], maize, and tobacco, and performed other superstitious rites, giving the children to understand that they must all do this in the future. The captains and the chiefs ordered that the names of Jesus and Mary should nowhere be uttered. . . . He has seen many houses of idolatry which they have built, dancing the dance of the cachina [part of a traditional Indian religious ceremony], which this declarant has also danced. Thus he replies to the question.

QUESTIONS

1. *Why does Las Casas, after describing the ill treatment of Indians, write, "And this was the freedom, the good treatment and the Christianity the Indians received"?*

2. *What role did religion play in the Pueblo Revolt?*

3. *What ideas of freedom are apparent in the two documents?*

returned home after their contracts expired. More than 80 percent of the migrants were men. Apart from nuns, fewer than 1,800 women (compared with more than 12,000 men) emigrated to French Canada in the seventeenth century. And during the entire colonial period, only about 250 complete families did so.

Settlement in New France

By 1700, the number of white inhabitants of New France had risen to only 19,000. With a far larger population than England, France sent many fewer emigrants to the Western Hemisphere. The government at home feared that significant emigration would undermine France's role as a European great power and might compromise its effort to establish trade and good relations with the Indians. Unfavorable reports about America circulated widely in France. Canada was widely depicted as an icebox, a land of savage Indians, a dumping ground for criminals. Most French who left their homes during these years preferred to settle in the Netherlands, Spain, or the West Indies. The revocation in 1685 of the Edict of Nantes, which had extended religious toleration to French Protestants, led well over 100,000 Huguenots to flee their country. But they were not welcome in New France, which the crown desired to remain an outpost of Catholicism.

New France and the Indians

Alliances with Indians

The viability of New France, with its small white population and emphasis on the fur trade rather than agricultural settlement, depended on friendly relations with local Indians. The French prided themselves on adopting a more humane policy than their imperial rivals. "Only our nation," declared one French writer, "knows the secret of winning the Indians' affection." Lacking the need for Indian labor of the Spanish and the voracious appetite for land of the English colonies, and relying on Indians to supply furs to trading posts, the French worked out a complex series of military, commercial, and diplomatic connections, the most enduring alliances between Indians and settlers in colonial North America. Samuel de Champlain,

This engraving, which appears in Samuel de Champlain's 1613 account of his voyages, is the only likeness of the explorer from his own time. Champlain, wearing European armor and brandishing an arquebus (an advanced weapon of the period), stands at the center of this pitched battle between his Indian allies and the hostile Iroquois.

the intrepid explorer who dominated the early history of New France, insisted on religious toleration for all Christians and denied that Native Americans were intellectually or culturally inferior to Europeans—two positions that were unusual for his time. Although he occasionally engaged in wars with local Indians, he dreamed of creating a colony based on mutual respect between diverse peoples. The Jesuits, a missionary religious order, did seek, with some success, to convert Indians to Catholicism. But unlike Spanish missionaries in early New Mexico, they allowed Christian Indians to retain a high degree of independence and much of their traditional social structure, and they did not seek to suppress all traditional religious practices.

Jesuits

Like other colonists throughout North America, however, the French brought striking changes in Indian life. Contact with Europeans was inevitably followed by the spread of disease. Participation in the fur trade drew natives into the burgeoning Atlantic economy, introducing new goods and transforming hunting from a search for food into a quest for marketable commodities. Indians were soon swept into the rivalries among European empires, and Europeans into conflicts among Indians. As early as 1615, the Huron of present-day southern Ontario and upper New York State forged a trading alliance with the French, and many converted to Catholicism. In the 1640s, however, after being severely weakened by a smallpox epidemic, the tribe was virtually destroyed in a series of attacks by Iroquois armed by the Dutch.

As in the Spanish empire, New France witnessed considerable cultural exchange and intermixing between colonial and native populations. On the "middle ground" of the upper Great Lakes region in French America, Indians and whites encountered each other for many years on a basis of relative equality. And *métis*, or children of marriages between Indian women and French traders and officials, became guides, traders, and interpreters. Like the Spanish, the French seemed willing to accept Indians as part of colonial society. They encouraged Indians to adopt the European division of labor between men and women, and to speak French. Indians who converted to Catholicism were promised full citizenship. In fact, however, it was far rarer for natives to adopt French ways than for French settlers to become attracted to the "free" life of the Indians.

The middle ground

The Dutch Empire

In 1609, Henry Hudson, an Englishman employed by the Dutch East India Company, sailed into New York Harbor searching for a Northwest Passage to Asia. Hudson and his crew became the first Europeans to sail up the river that now bears his name. Hudson did not find a route to Asia, but he did encounter abundant fur-bearing animals and Native Americans more than willing to trade furs for European goods. He claimed the area for the Netherlands, and his voyage planted the seeds for what would eventually become a great metropolis, New York City. By 1614, Dutch traders had established an outpost at Fort Orange, near present-day Albany. Ten years later, the Dutch West India Company, which had been awarded a monopoly of Dutch trade with America, settled colonists on Manhattan Island.

Henry Hudson

These ventures formed one small part in the rise of the Dutch overseas empire. In the early seventeenth century, the Netherlands dominated international

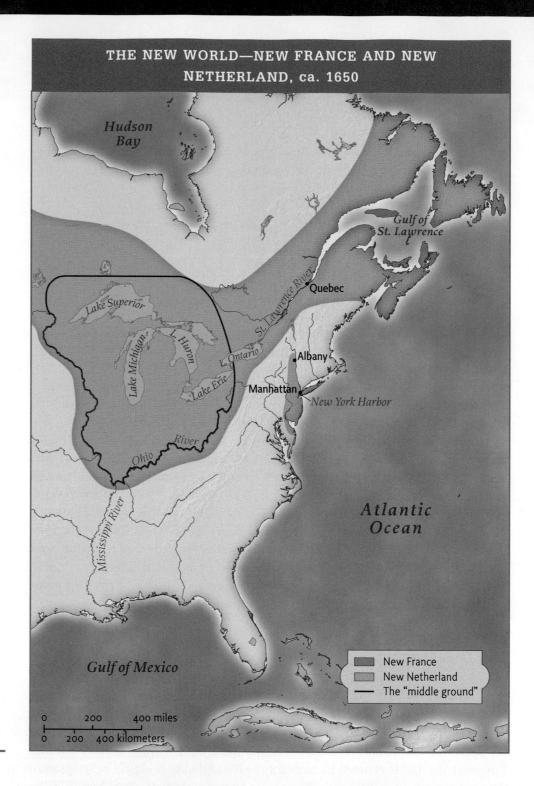

THE NEW WORLD—NEW FRANCE AND NEW NETHERLAND, ca. 1650

Hudson Bay

Gulf of St. Lawrence

Lake Superior

St. Lawrence River

Quebec

L. Huron

Lake Michigan

L. Ontario

Albany

Lake Erie

Manhattan

New York Harbor

Ohio River

Atlantic Ocean

Mississippi River

Gulf of Mexico

New France
New Netherland
The "middle ground"

0   200   400 miles
0   200   400 kilometers

New France and New Netherland.

Dutch trade

commerce, and Amsterdam was Europe's foremost shipping and banking center. The small nation had entered a golden age of rapidly accumulating wealth and stunning achievements in painting, philosophy, and the sciences. The Dutch invented the joint stock company, a way of pooling financial resources and sharing the risk of maritime voyages, which proved central to the development of modern capitalism. With a population of only 2 million, the Netherlands established a far-flung empire that reached from Indonesia to South Africa and the Caribbean and temporarily wrested control of Brazil from Portugal.

Dutch Freedom

The Dutch prided themselves on their devotion to liberty. Indeed, in the early seventeenth century they enjoyed two freedoms not recognized elsewhere in Europe—freedom of the press and of private religious practice. Even though there was an established church, the Dutch Reformed, individuals could hold whatever religious beliefs they wished. Amsterdam had become a haven for persecuted Protestants from all over Europe, including French Huguenots, German Calvinists, and those, like the Pilgrims, who desired to separate from the Church of England. Jews, especially those fleeing from Spain, also found refuge there. Other emigrants came to the Netherlands in the hope of sharing in the country's prosperity. During the seventeenth century, the nation attracted about half a million migrants from elsewhere in Europe. Many of these newcomers helped to populate the Dutch overseas empire.

Religious freedom

Freedom in New Netherland

Despite the Dutch reputation for cherishing freedom, New Netherland was hardly governed democratically. New Amsterdam, the main population center, was essentially a fortified military outpost controlled by appointees of the West India Company. Although the governor called on prominent citizens for advice from time to time, neither an elected assembly nor a town council, the basic unit of government at home, was established.

In other ways, however, the colonists enjoyed more liberty, especially in religious matters, than their counterparts elsewhere in North America. Even their slaves possessed rights. The Dutch dominated the Atlantic slave trade in the early seventeenth century, and they introduced slaves into New Netherland as a matter of course. By 1650, the colony's 500 slaves outnumbered those in the Chesapeake. Some enjoyed "half-freedom"—they were required to pay an annual fee to the company and work for it when called upon, but they were given land to support their families. Settlers employed slaves on family farms or for household or craft labor, not on large plantations as in the West Indies.

Women in the Dutch settlement enjoyed far more independence than in other colonies. According to Dutch law, married women retained their separate legal identity. They could go to court, borrow money, and own property. Men were used to sharing property with their wives. Their wills generally left their possessions to their widows and daughters as well as sons. Margaret Hardenbroeck, the widow of a New Amsterdam merchant, expanded her husband's business and became one of the town's richest residents after his death in 1661.

Women's rights

The Dutch and Religious Toleration

New Netherland attracted a remarkably diverse population. As early as the 1630s, at least eighteen languages were said to be spoken in New Amsterdam, whose

A view of New Amsterdam from 1651 illustrates the tiny size of the outpost.

Limits of religious toleration

Governor Stuyvesant

residents included not only Dutch settlers but also Africans, Belgians, English, French, Germans, Irish, and Scandinavians. Of course, these settlers adhered to a wide variety of religions.

The Dutch long prided themselves on being uniquely tolerant in religious matters compared to other European nations and their empires. It would be wrong, however, to attribute modern ideas of religious freedom to either the Dutch government and company at home or the rulers of New Netherland. Both Holland and New Netherland had an official religion, the Dutch Reformed Church, one of the Protestant national churches to emerge from the Reformation. The Dutch commitment to freedom of conscience extended to religious devotion exercised in private, not public worship in nonestablished churches. It did not reflect a willing acceptance of religious diversity.

The West India Company's officials in the colony, particularly Governor Petrus Stuyvesant, were expected to be staunch defenders of the Dutch Reformed Church. When Jews, Quakers, Lutherans, and others demanded the right to practice their religion openly, Stuyvesant adamantly refused, seeing such diversity as a threat to a godly, prosperous order. Under Stuyvesant, the colony was more restrictive in its religious policies than the Dutch government at home. Twenty-three Jews arrived in New Amsterdam in 1654 from Brazil and the Caribbean. Referring to them as "members of a deceitful race," Stuyvesant ordered the newcomers to leave. But the company overruled him, noting that Jews at home had invested "a large amount of capital" in its shares.

As a result of Stuyvesant's policies, challenges arose to the limits on religious toleration. One, known as the Flushing Remonstrance, was a 1657 petition by a group of English settlers protesting the governor's order barring Quakers from living in the town of Flushing, on Long Island. Although later seen as a landmark of religious liberty, the Remonstrance had little impact at the time. Stuyvesant ordered several signers arrested for defying his authority.

Nonetheless, it is true that the Dutch dealt with religious pluralism in ways quite different from the practices common in other New World empires. Religious dissent was tolerated—often grudgingly, as in the case of Catholics—as long as it did not involve open and public worship. No one in New Netherland was forced to attend the official church, nor was anyone executed for holding the wrong religious beliefs (as would happen in Puritan New England around the time of the Flushing Remonstrance).

Settling New Netherland

In an attempt to attract settlers to North America, the Dutch West India Company promised colonists not only the right to practice their religion freely (in private) but also cheap livestock and free land after six years of labor. Eventually, it even surrendered its monopoly of the fur trade, opening this profitable commerce to all comers. Many settlers, Stuyvesant complained, had been lured by "an imaginary liberty" and did not display much respect for the company's authority.

In 1629, the company adopted a plan of "Freedoms and Exemptions," offering large estates to *patroons*—shareholders who agreed to transport tenants for agricultural labor. The patroon was required to purchase a title to the land from Indians, but otherwise his "freedoms" were like those of a medieval lord, including the right to 10 percent of his tenants' annual income and complete authority over law enforcement within his domain. Only one patroonship became a going concern, that of Kiliaen van Rensselaer, who acquired some 700,000 acres in the Hudson Valley. His family's autocratic rule over the tenants, as well as its efforts to extend its domain to include lands settled by New Englanders who claimed that they owned their farms, would inspire sporadic uprisings into the mid-nineteenth century.

During the seventeenth century, the Netherlands sent 1 million people overseas (many of them recent immigrants who were not in fact Dutch) to populate and govern their far-flung colonies. Very few, however, made North America their destination. By the mid-1660s, the European population of New Netherland numbered only 9,000. New Netherland remained a tiny backwater in the Dutch empire. So did an even smaller outpost near present-day Wilmington, Delaware, established in 1638 by a group of Dutch merchants. To circumvent the West India Company's trade monopoly, they claimed to be operating under the Swedish flag and called their settlement New Sweden. Only 300 settlers were living there when New Netherland seized the colony in 1655.

New Netherland and the Indians

The Dutch came to North America to trade, not to conquer. They were less interested in settling the land than in exacting profits from it. Mindful of the Black Legend of Spanish cruelty, the Dutch determined to treat the native inhabitants more humanely. Having won their own independence from Spain after the longest and bloodiest war of sixteenth-century Europe, many Dutch identified with American Indians as fellow victims of Spanish oppression.

From the beginning, Dutch authorities recognized Indian sovereignty over the land and forbade settlement in any area until it had been purchased. But they also required tribes to make payments to colonial authorities. Near the coast, where most newcomers settled, New Netherland was hardly free of conflict with the Indians. The expansionist ambitions of Governor William Kieft, who in the 1640s

Patroons

The seal of New Netherland, adopted by the Dutch West India Company in 1630, suggests the centrality of the fur trade to the colony's prospects. Surrounding the beaver is wampum, a string of beads used by Indians in religious rituals and as currency.

- Knaut, Andrew L. *The Pueblo Revolt of 1680: Conquest and Resistance in Seventeenth-Century New Mexico* (1997). A recent account of the largest revolt of native peoples.

- Mann, Charles C. *1491: New Revelations of the Americas before Columbus* (2005). A comprehensive portrait of life in the Western Hemisphere before the arrival of Europeans.

- Parry, J. H. *The Age of Reconnaissance* (1981). A global history of the era of European exploration and colonization.

- Richter, Daniel K. *Facing East from Indian Country* (2001). Examines the era of exploration and settlement as viewed through the experience of Native Americans.

- ———. *The Ordeal of the Longhouse: The Peoples of the Iroquois League in the Era of European Colonization* (1992). Describes life among one of the most important Indian groups before and after the arrival of Europeans.

- Witgen, Michael. *An Infinity of Nations: How the Native New World Shaped Early North America* (2012). An imaginative account of how native peoples and Europeans interacted in the Great Lakes region.

WEBSITES

- American Indians and the Natural World: http://carnegiemnh.org/online/indians/index.html

- Archive of Early American Images: www.brown.edu/academics/libraries/john-carter-brown/jcb-online/image-collections/archive-early-american-images

- Cahokia Mounds: http://cahokiamounds.org

- Exploring the Early Americas: www.loc.gov/exhibits/earlyamericas/

- France in America: http://international.loc.gov/intldl/fiahtml

- Jamestown, Quebec, Santa Fe: Three North American Beginnings: http://americanhistory.si.edu/jamestown-quebec-santafe/en/introduction

CHAPTER REVIEW AND ONLINE RESOURCES

REVIEW QUESTIONS

1. Describe why the "discovery" of America was one of the "most important events recorded in the history of mankind," according to Adam Smith.

2. Describe the different global economies that Europeans participated in or created during the European age of expansion.

3. One of the most striking features of Indian societies at the time of the encounter with Europeans was their diversity. Support this statement with several examples.

4. Compare and contrast European values and ways of life with those of the Indians. Consider addressing religion, views about ownership of land, gender relations, and notions of freedom.

5. What were the main factors fueling the European age of expansion?

6. Compare the different economic and political systems of Spain, Portugal, the Netherlands, and France in the age of expansion.

7. Compare the political, economic, and religious motivations behind the French and Dutch empires with those of New Spain.

8. Describe how the idea of the "Black Legend" affected subsequent policies and practices of Spain as well as those of the Netherlands and France.

9. How would European settlers explain their superiority to Native Americans and justify both the conquest of Native lands and terminating their freedom?

KEY TERMS

Tenochtitlán (p. 8)

Aztec (p. 8)

Great League of Peace (p. 12)

caravel (p. 18)

reconquista (p. 21)

conquistadores (p. 23)

Columbian Exchange (p. 24)

creoles (p. 25)

hacienda (p. 25)

mestizos (p. 26)

Ninety-Five Theses (p. 28)

Bartolomé de Las Casas (p. 29)

repartimiento system (p. 29)

Black Legend (p. 30)

Pueblo Revolt (p. 34)

indentured servants (p. 35)

métis (p. 39)

borderland (p. 44)

Go to INQUIZITIVE

To see what you know—and learn what you've missed—with personalized feedback along the way.

Visit the *Give Me Liberty!* **Student Site** for primary source documents and images, interactive maps, author videos featuring Eric Foner, and more.

CHAPTER 2

BEGINNINGS OF
ENGLISH AMERICA

★

1607–1660

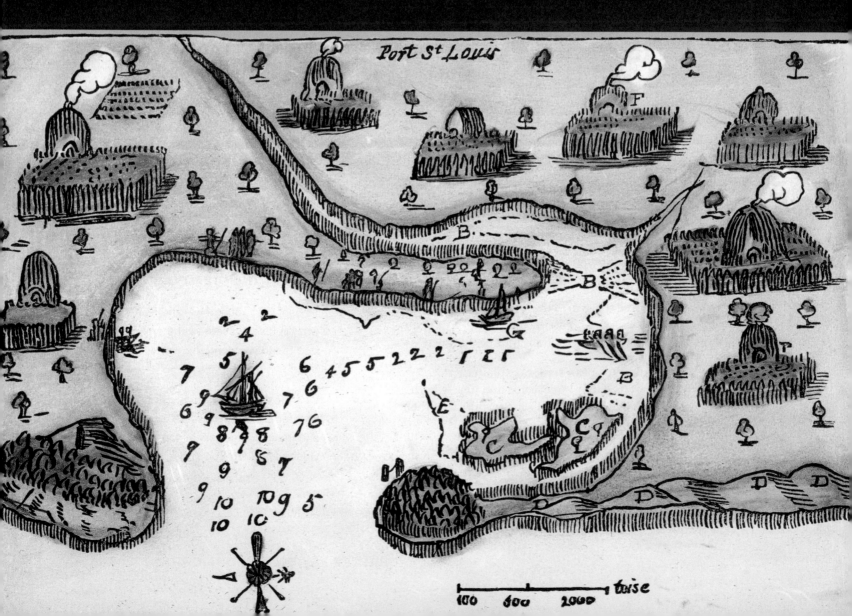

Port St Louis

toise
100   500   2000

On April 26, 1607, three small ships carrying colonists from England sailed out of the morning mist at what is now called Cape Henry into the mouth of Chesapeake Bay. After exploring the area for a little over two weeks, they chose a site sixty miles inland on the James River for their settlement, hoping to protect themselves from marauding Spanish warships. Here they established Jamestown (named for the king of England) as the capital of the colony of Virginia (named for his predecessor, Elizabeth I, the "virgin queen"). But despite these bows to royal authority, the voyage was sponsored not by the English government, which in 1607 was hard-pressed for funds, but by the **Virginia Company**, a private business organization whose shareholders included merchants, aristocrats, and members of Parliament, and to which the queen had given her blessing before her death in 1603.

When the three ships returned home, 104 settlers remained in Virginia. All were men, for the Virginia Company had more interest in searching for gold and in other ways of exploiting the area's natural resources than in establishing a functioning society. Nevertheless, Jamestown became the first permanent English settlement in the area that is now the United States. The settlers were the first of tens of thousands of Europeans who crossed the Atlantic during the seventeenth century to live and work in North America. They led the way for new empires that mobilized labor and economic resources, reshaped societies throughout the Atlantic world, and shifted the balance of power at home from Spain and Portugal to the nations of northwestern Europe.

The founding of Jamestown took place at a time of heightened European involvement in North America. Interest in colonization was spurred by national and religious rivalries and the growth of a merchant class eager to invest in overseas expansion and to seize for itself a greater share of world trade. As noted in Chapter 1, it was quickly followed by the founding of Quebec by France in 1608, and Henry Hudson's exploration in 1609 of the river that today bears his name, leading to the founding of the Dutch colony of New Netherland. In 1610, the Spanish established Santa Fe as the capital of New Mexico. More than a century after the voyages of Columbus, the European penetration of North America had finally begun in earnest. It occurred from many directions at once—from east to west at the Atlantic coast, north to south along the St. Lawrence and Mississippi rivers, and south to north in what is now the American Southwest.

English North America in the seventeenth century was a place where entrepreneurs sought to make fortunes, religious minorities hoped to worship without governmental interference and to create societies based on biblical teachings, and aristocrats dreamed of re-creating a vanished world of feudalism. Those who drew up blueprints for settlement expected to reproduce the social structure with which they were familiar, with all its hierarchy and inequality. The lower orders would occupy the same less-than-fully-free status as in England, subject to laws regulating their labor and depriving them of a role in politics. But for ordinary men and women, emigration offered an escape from lives of deprivation and inequality. "No man," wrote John Smith, an early leader of Jamestown, "will go from [England] to

FOCUS QUESTIONS

What were the main contours of English colonization in the seventeenth century? –p. 50

What obstacles did the English settlers in the Chesapeake overcome? –p. 54

How did Virginia and Maryland develop in their early years? –p. 58

What made the English settlement of New England distinctive? –p. 64

What were the main sources of discord in early New England? –p. 70

How did the English Civil War affect the colonies in America? –p. 79

Samuel de Champlain's 1605 sketch of Plymouth Harbor, made when he was exploring the coast of modern-day New England in search of a site for a French settlement, shows the area dotted with wigwams and fields of corn, squash, and beans. By the time the Pilgrims arrived in 1620, epidemics had destroyed this thriving Indian community.

1215	Magna Carta
1584	Hakluyt's *A Discourse Concerning Western Planting*
1585	Roanoke Island settlement
1607	Jamestown established
1619	First Africans arrive in Virginia
1619	House of Burgesses convenes
1620	Pilgrims found Plymouth
1622	Uprising led by Opechanca-nough against Virginia
1624	Virginia becomes first royal colony
1630s	Great Migration to New England
1630	Massachusetts Bay Colony founded
1632	Maryland founded
1636	Roger Williams banished from Massachusetts to Rhode Island
1637	Anne Hutchinson placed on trial in Massachusetts
1636–1637	Pequot War
1639	Fundamental Orders of Connecticut
1641	Body of Liberties
1642–1651	English Civil War
1649	Maryland adopts an Act Concerning Religion
1662	Puritans' Half-Way Covenant
1691	Virginia outlaws English-Indian marriages

have less freedom" in America. The charter of the Virginia Company, granted by James I in 1606, promised that colonists would enjoy "all liberties" of those residing in "our realm of England." The settlers of English America came to enjoy greater rights than colonists of other empires, including the power to choose members of elected assemblies, protections of the common law such as the right to trial by jury, and access to land, the key to economic independence. In some colonies, though by no means all, colonists enjoyed considerably more religious freedom than existed in Europe.

Many degrees of freedom coexisted in seventeenth-century North America, from the slave, stripped completely of liberty, to the independent land-owner, who enjoyed a full range of rights. During a lifetime, a person might well occupy more than one place on this spectrum. The settlers' success, how-ever, rested on depriving Native Americans of their land and, in some colonies, on importing large numbers of African slaves as laborers. Freedom and lack of freedom expanded together in seventeenth-century America.

ENGLAND AND THE NEW WORLD

Unifying the English Nation

Although John Cabot, sailing from England in 1497, had been the first European since the Vikings to encounter the North American continent, English exploration and colonization would wait for many years. As the case of Spain suggests, early empire building was, in large part, an extension of the consolidation of national power in Europe. But during the sixteenth century, England was a second-rate power racked by internal disunity. Henry VII, who assumed the throne in 1485, had to unify the kingdom after a long period of civil war. His son and successor, Henry VIII, launched the Reformation in England. When the pope refused to annul his marriage to Catherine of Aragon, Henry severed the nation from the Catholic Church. In its place he established the Church of England, or **Anglican Church**, with himself at the head. Decades of religious strife followed. Under Henry's son Edward VI, who became king at the age of ten in 1547, the regents who governed the country persecuted Catholics. When Edward died in 1553, his half sister Mary became queen. Mary temporarily restored Catholicism as the state religion and executed a number of Protestants. Her rule was so unpopular that reconciliation with Rome became impossible. Mary's successor, Elizabeth I (reigned 1558–1603), restored the Anglican ascendancy and executed more than 100 Catholic priests.

England and Ireland

England's long struggle to conquer and pacify Ireland, which lasted well into the seventeenth century, absorbed money and energy that might have been directed toward the New World. In subduing Ireland, whose Catholic population was deemed a threat to the stability of Protestant rule in England, the government employed a variety of approaches, including military conquest, the slaughter of civilians, the seizure of land and introduction of English economic practices, and the dispatch of large numbers of settlers. Rather than seeking to absorb the Irish into English society, the English excluded the native population from a territory of settlement known as the Pale, where the colonists created their own social order.

Just as the "reconquest" of Spain from the Moors established patterns that would be repeated in Spanish New World colonization, the methods used in Ireland anticipated policies England would undertake in America. Some sixteenth-century English writers directly compared the allegedly barbaric "wild Irish" with American Indians. Like the Indians, the Irish supposedly confused liberty and license. They refused to respect English authority and resisted conversion to English Protestantism. The early English colonies in North America and the West Indies were known as "plantations" (that is, communities "planted" from abroad among an alien population); the same term was originally used to describe Protestant settlements in Ireland.

England and North America

Not until the reign of Elizabeth I did the English turn their attention to North America, although sailors and adventurers still showed more interest in raiding Spanish cities and treasure fleets in the Caribbean than establishing settlements. The government granted charters (grants of exclusive rights and privileges) to Sir Humphrey Gilbert and Sir Walter Raleigh, authorizing them to establish colonies in North America at their own expense.

With little or no support from the crown, both ventures failed. Gilbert, who had earned a reputation for brutality in the Irish wars by murdering civilians and burning their crops, established a short-lived settlement on Newfoundland in 1582. Three years later, Raleigh dispatched a fleet of five ships with some 100 colonists (many of them his personal servants) to set up a base on Roanoke Island, off the North Carolina coast, partly to facilitate continuing raids on Spanish shipping. But the colonists, mostly young men under military leadership, abandoned the venture in 1586 and returned to England. A second group of 100 settlers, composed of families who hoped to establish a permanent colony, was dispatched that year. Their fate remains a mystery. When a ship bearing supplies arrived in 1590, the sailors found the **Roanoke colony** abandoned, with the inhabitants evidently having moved to live among the Indians. The word "Croatoan," the Indian name for a nearby island or tribe, had been carved on a tree. Raleigh, by now nearly bankrupt, lost his enthusiasm for colonization. To establish a successful colony, it seemed clear, would require more planning and economic resources than any individual could provide.

Spreading Protestantism

As in the case of Spain, national glory, profit, and religious mission merged in early English thinking about the New World. The Reformation heightened the English government's sense of Catholic Spain as its mortal enemy (a belief reinforced in 1588

Mary I, the queen who tried to restore Catholicism in England, as painted in 1554 by Antonis Mor, a Dutch artist who made numerous portraits of European royalty. He depicts her as a women of firm determination. During her brief reign (1553–1558), nearly three hundred Protestants were burned at the stake.

The Armada Portrait of Queen Elizabeth I, by the artist George Gower, commemorates the defeat of the Spanish Armada in 1588 and appears to link it with English colonization of the New World. England's victorious navy is visible through the window, while the queen's hand rests on a globe, with her fingers pointing to the coast of North America.

An engraving by Theodor de Bry depicts colonists hunting and fishing in Virginia. Promotional images such as this emphasized the abundance of the New World and suggested that colonists could live familiar lives there.

when a Spanish naval armada unsuccessfully attempted to invade the British Isles). Just as Spain justified its empire in part by claiming to convert Indians to Catholicism, England expressed its imperial ambitions in terms of an obligation to liberate the New World from the tyranny of the pope. The very first justification James I offered for the English settlement of Virginia was "propagating of the Christian religion [by which he meant Protestantism] to such people as yet live in darkness and miserable ignorance of the true knowledge and worship of God." By the late sixteenth century, anti-Catholicism had become deeply ingrained in English popular culture. English translations of Bartolomé de Las Casas's writings appeared during Elizabeth's reign. One, using a common Protestant term for the Catholic Church, bore the title, "Popery Truly Displayed."

Although atrocities were hardly confined to any one nation—as England's own conduct in Ireland demonstrated—the idea that the empire of Catholic Spain was uniquely murderous and tyrannical enabled the English to describe their own imperial ambitions in the language of freedom. In *A Discourse Concerning Western Planting*, written in 1584 at the request of Sir Walter Raleigh, the Protestant minister and scholar Richard Hakluyt listed twenty-three reasons why Queen Elizabeth I should support the establishment of colonies. Among them was the idea that English settlements would strike a blow against Spain's empire and therefore form part of a divine mission to rescue the New World and its inhabitants from the influence of Catholicism and tyranny. "Tied as slaves" under Spanish rule, he wrote, the Indians of the New World were "crying out to us . . . to come and help." They would welcome English settlers and "revolt clean from the Spaniard," crying "with one voice, Liberta, Liberta, as desirous of liberty and freedom." England would repeat much of Spain's behavior in the New World. But the English always believed that they were unique. In their case, empire and freedom would go hand in hand.

Empire and freedom

But bringing freedom to Indians was hardly the only argument Hakluyt marshaled as England prepared to step onto the world stage. National power and glory were never far from the minds of the era's propagandists of empire. Through colonization, Hakluyt and other writers argued, England, a relatively minor power in Europe at the end of the sixteenth century, could come to rival the wealth and standing of great nations like Spain and France.

The Social Crisis

Equally important, America could be a refuge for England's "surplus" population, benefiting mother country and emigrants alike. The late sixteenth century was a time of social crisis in England, with economic growth unable to keep pace with the needs of a population that grew from 3 million in 1550 to about 4 million in 1600. For many years, English peasants had enjoyed a secure hold on their plots of land. But in the sixteenth and seventeenth centuries, landlords sought profits by raising sheep for the expanding trade in wool and introducing more modern farming practices such as crop rotation. They evicted small farmers and fenced in "commons" previously open to all.

While many landlords, farmers, and town merchants benefited from the **enclosure movement**, as this process was called, thousands of persons were uprooted from the land. Many flooded into England's cities, where wages fell dramatically. Others, denounced by authorities as rogues, vagabonds, and vagrants, wandered the roads in search of work. Their situation grew worse as prices throughout Europe rose, buoyed by the influx of gold and silver from the mines of Latin America into Spain. A pioneering study of English society conducted at the end of the seventeenth century estimated that half the population lived at or below the poverty line. The cost of poor relief fell mainly on local communities. "All our towns," wrote the Puritan leader John Winthrop in 1629, shortly before leaving England for Massachusetts, "complain of the burden of poor people and strive by all means to rid any such as they have." England, he added somberly, "grows weary of her inhabitants."

The government struggled to deal with this social crisis. Under Henry VIII, those without jobs could be whipped, branded, forced into the army, or hanged. During Elizabeth's reign, a law authorized justices of the peace to regulate hours and wages and put the unemployed to work. "Vagrants" were required to accept any job offered to them and could be punished if they sought to change employment. Another solution was to encourage the unruly poor to leave for the New World. Richard Hakluyt wrote of the advantages of settling in America "such needy people of our country who now trouble the commonwealth and . . . commit outrageous offenses." As colonists, they could become productive citizens, contributing to the nation's wealth.

> Responses to poverty

Masterless Men

As early as 1516, when Thomas More published *Utopia*, a novel set on an imaginary island in the Western Hemisphere, the image of America as a place where settlers could escape from the economic inequalities of Europe had been circulating in England. This ideal coincided with the goals of ordinary Englishmen. Although authorities saw wandering or unemployed "masterless men" as a danger to society and tried to force them to accept jobs, popular attitudes viewed economic dependence as itself a form of servitude. Working for wages was widely associated with servility and loss of liberty. Only those who controlled their own labor could be regarded as truly free. Indeed, popular tales and ballads romanticized the very vagabonds, highwaymen, and even beggars denounced by the propertied and powerful, since despite their poverty they at least enjoyed freedom from wage work.

The image of the New World as a unique place of opportunity, where the English laboring classes could regain economic independence by acquiring land and where even criminals would enjoy a second chance, was deeply rooted from the earliest days of settlement. John Smith had scarcely landed in Virginia in 1607 when he wrote that in America "every man may be the master and owner of his own labor and land." In 1623, the royal letter approving the recruitment of emigrants to New England promised that any settler could easily become "lord of 200 acres of land"—an amount far beyond the reach of most Englishmen. The main lure for emigrants from England to the New World was not so much riches in gold and

William Hogarth's well-known engraving *Gin Lane* (1751) offers a satiric glimpse of lower-class life in London. Hogarth was particularly concerned about the abuse of alcohol. A drunken woman allows her baby to fall from her arms while, on the left, a man and his wife pawn their coats, tools, and cooking utensils for money for liquor.

silver as the promise of independence that followed from owning land. Economic freedom and the possibility of passing it on to one's children attracted the largest number of English colonists.

THE COMING OF THE ENGLISH

English Emigrants

Dangers of emmigration

Seventeenth-century North America was an unstable and dangerous environment. Diseases decimated Indian and settler populations alike. Colonies were racked by religious, political, and economic tensions and drawn into imperial wars and conflict with Indians. They remained dependent on the mother country for protection and economic assistance. Without sustained immigration, most settlements would have collapsed. With a population of between 4 million and 5 million, about half that of Spain and a quarter of that of France, England produced a far larger number of men, women, and children willing to brave the dangers of emigration to the New World. In large part, this was because economic conditions in England were so bad.

Between 1607 and 1700, more than half a million people left England. North America was not the destination of the majority of these emigrants. Approximately 180,000 settled in Ireland, and about the same number migrated to the West Indies, where the introduction of sugar cultivation promised riches for those who could obtain land. Nonetheless, the population of England's mainland colonies quickly outstripped that of their rivals. The Chesapeake area, where the tobacco-producing colonies of Virginia and Maryland developed a constant demand for cheap labor, received about 120,000 settlers, most of whom landed before 1660. New England attracted 21,000 emigrants, nearly all of them arriving before 1640. In the second part of the seventeenth century, the Middle Colonies (New York, New Jersey, and Pennsylvania) attracted about 23,000 settlers. Although the arrivals to New England and the Middle Colonies included many families, the majority of newcomers were young, single men from the bottom rungs of English society, who had little to lose by emigrating. Many had already moved from place to place in England. Colonial settlement was in many ways an extension of the migration at home of an increasingly mobile English population.

Indentured Servants

Settlers who could pay for their own passage—government officials, clergymen, merchants, artisans, landowning farmers, and members of the lesser nobility—arrived in America as free persons. Most quickly acquired land. In the seventeenth century, however, nearly two-thirds of English settlers came as indentured servants, who voluntarily surrendered their freedom for a specified time (usually five to seven years) in exchange for passage to America.

Like slaves, servants could be bought and sold, could not marry without the permission of their owner, were subject to physical punishment, and saw their obligation to labor enforced by the courts. To ensure uninterrupted work by female servants, the law lengthened the term of their indenture if they became pregnant. "Many Negroes are better used," complained Elizabeth Sprigs, an indentured

A pamphlet published in 1609 promoting emigration to Virginia.

servant in Maryland who described being forced to work "day and night . . . then tied up and whipped." But, unlike slaves, servants could look forward to a release from bondage. Assuming they survived their period of labor, servants would receive a payment known as "freedom dues" and become free members of society.

For most of the seventeenth century, however, indentured servitude was not a guaranteed route to economic autonomy. Given the high death rate, many servants did not live to the end of their terms. Freedom dues were sometimes so meager that they did not enable recipients to acquire land. Many servants found the reality of life in the New World less appealing than they had anticipated. Employers constantly complained of servants running away, not working diligently, or being unruly, all manifestations of what one commentator called their "fondness for freedom."

Land and Liberty

Access to land played many roles in seventeenth-century America. Land, English settlers believed, was the basis of liberty. Owning land gave men control over their own labor and, in most colonies, the right to vote. The promise of immediate access to land lured free settlers, and freedom dues that included land persuaded potential immigrants to sign contracts as indentured servants. Land in America also became a way for the king to reward relatives and allies. Each colony was launched with a huge grant of land from the crown, either to a company or to a private individual known as a proprietor. Some grants, if taken literally, stretched from the Atlantic Ocean to the Pacific.

Land was a source of wealth and power for colonial officials and their favorites, who acquired enormous estates. Without labor, however, land would have little value. Since emigrants did not come to America intending to work the land of others (except temporarily in the case of indentured servants), the very abundance of "free" land eventually led many property owners to turn to slaves as a workforce.

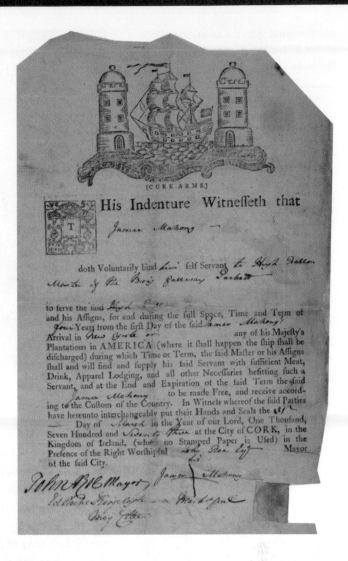

An indenture (a contract for labor for a period of years) signed by James Mahoney, who emigrated from Ireland to North America in 1723.

Englishmen and Indians

Land in North America, of course, was already occupied. And the arrival of English settlers presented the native inhabitants of eastern North America with the greatest crisis in their history. Unlike the Spanish, English colonists did not call themselves "conquerors" (*conquistadores*). They wanted land, not dominion over the existing population. The Chesapeake and New England attracted more settlers than New Mexico, Florida, and New France combined, thus placing far greater pressure on Indian landholdings and provoking more frequent wars. The English were chiefly interested in displacing the Indians and settling on their land, not intermarrying with them, organizing their labor, or making them subjects of the crown. The

The English and Indian land

Another drawing by the artist John White shows an Indian village surrounded by a stockade.

marriage between John Rolfe and Pocahontas, the daughter of Virginia's leading chief, discussed below, is well known but almost unique. No such mixed marriage took place in seventeenth-century Massachusetts and only two more occurred in Virginia before the legislature outlawed the practice in 1691. The English exchanged goods with the native population, and Indians often traveled through colonial settlements. Fur traders on the frontiers of settlement sometimes married Indian women, partly as a way of gaining access to native societies and the kin networks essential to economic relationships. Most English settlers, however, remained obstinately separate from their Indian neighbors.

Purchasing land

Despite their insistence that Indians had no real claim to the land since they did not cultivate or improve it, most colonial authorities in practice recognized Indians' title based on occupancy. They acquired land by purchase, often in treaties forced upon Indians after they had suffered military defeat. Colonial courts recorded numerous sales of Indian land to governments or individual settlers. To keep the peace, some colonial governments tried to prevent the private seizure or purchase of Indian lands, or they declared certain areas off-limits to settlers. But these measures were rarely enforced and ultimately proved ineffective. New settlers and freed servants sought land for themselves, and those who established families in America needed land for their children.

Recurrent warfare between colonists and Indians

The seventeenth century was marked by recurrent warfare between colonists and Indians. These conflicts generated a strong feeling of superiority among the colonists and left them intent on maintaining the real and imagined boundaries separating the two peoples. In the initial stages of settlement, English colonists often established towns on sites Indians had cleared, planted Indian crops, and adopted Indian technology such as snowshoes and canoes, which were valuable for travel in the American wilderness. But over time the English displaced the original inhabitants more thoroughly than any other European empire.

The Transformation of Indian Life

The coming of English settlers profoundly affected Indian societies. Like the other colonial empires, the English used native people as guides, trading partners, and allies in wars and for other purposes. Many eastern Indians initially welcomed the newcomers, or at least their goods, which they appreciated for their practical advantages. Items like woven cloth, metal kettles, iron axes, fishhooks, hoes, and guns were quickly integrated into Indian life. Indians also displayed a great desire for goods like colorful glass beads and copper ornaments that could be incorporated into their religious ceremonies.

European goods

As Indians became integrated into the Atlantic economy, subtle changes took place in Indian life. European metal goods changed their farming, hunting, and cooking practices. Men devoted more time to hunting beaver for fur trading. Older skills deteriorated as the use of European products expanded, and alcohol became increasingly common and disruptive. Indians learned to bargain effectively and to supply items that Europeans desired. Later observers would describe this trade as one in which Indians exchanged valuable commodities like furs and animal skins for worthless European trinkets. In fact, both Europeans and Indians gave up goods they had in abundance in exchange for items in short supply in their own society. But as the colonists achieved military superiority over the Indians, the profits of trade mostly flowed to colonial and European merchants. Growing connections with Europeans stimulated warfare among Indian tribes, and the overhunting of beaver and deer forced some groups to encroach on territory claimed by others. And newcomers from Europe brought epidemics that decimated Indian populations.

The only known contemporary portrait of a New England Indian, this 1681 painting by an unknown artist was long thought to represent Ninigret II, a leader of the Narragansetts of Rhode Island. It has been more recently identified as Robin Cassacinamon, an influential Pequot leader and friend of John Winthrop II, a governor of colonial Connecticut, who originally owned the painting. Apart from the wampum beads around his neck, everything the Indian wears is of English manufacture.

Changes in the Land

Traders, religious missionaries, and colonial authorities all sought to reshape Indian society and culture. But as settlers spread over the land, they threatened Indians' ways of life more completely than any company of soldiers or group of bureaucrats. As settlers fenced in more and more land and introduced new crops and livestock, the natural environment changed in ways that undermined traditional Indian agriculture and hunting. Pigs and cattle roamed freely, trampling Indian cornfields and gardens. The need for wood to build and heat homes and export to England depleted forests on which Indians relied for hunting. The rapid expansion of the fur trade diminished the population of beaver and other animals. "Since you are here strangers, and come into our country," one group of Indians told early settlers in the Chesapeake, "you should rather conform yourselves to the customs of our country, than impose yours on us." But it was the Indians whose lives were most powerfully altered by the changes set in motion in 1607 when English colonists landed at Jamestown.

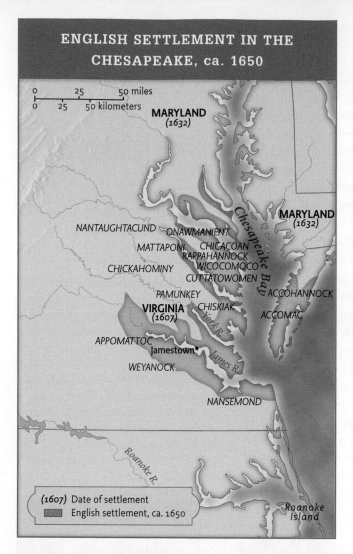

ENGLISH SETTLEMENT IN THE CHESAPEAKE, ca. 1650

MARYLAND
(1632)

NANTAUGHTACUND
ONAWMANIENT
MATTAPONI
CHICACOAN
RAPPAHANNOCK
CHICKAHOMINY
WICOCOMOCO
CUTTATOWOMEN
PAMUNKEY
VIRGINIA
(1607)
CHISKIAK
APPOMATTOC
Jamestown
WEYANOCK
NANSEMOND

Chesapeake Bay

MARYLAND
(1632)

ACCOHANNOCK
ACCOMAC

York R.
James R.
Roanoke R.
Roanoke Island

(1607) Date of settlement
English settlement, ca. 1650

By 1650, English settlement in the Chesapeake had spread well beyond the initial colony at Jamestown, as tobacco planters sought fertile land near navigable waterways.

SETTLING THE CHESAPEAKE

The Jamestown Colony

The early history of Jamestown was, to say the least, not promising. The colony's leadership changed repeatedly, its inhabitants suffered an extraordinarily high death rate, and, with the company seeking a quick profit, supplies from England proved inadequate. The hopes of locating riches such as the Spanish had found in Mexico were quickly dashed. "Silver and gold they have none," one Spanish observer commented, their local resources were "not much to be regarded," and they had "no commerce with any nation." The first settlers were "a quarrelsome band of gentlemen and servants." They included few farmers and laborers and numerous sons of English gentry and high-status craftsmen (jewelers, stonecutters, and the like), who preferred to prospect for gold rather than farm. They "would rather starve than work," declared **John Smith**, one of the colony's first leaders.

Jamestown lay beside a swamp containing malaria-carrying mosquitoes, and the garbage settlers dumped into the local river bred germs that caused dysentery and typhoid fever. Disease and lack of food took a heavy toll. By the end of the first year, the original population of 104 had fallen by half. New arrivals (including the first two women, who landed in 1608) brought the numbers up to 400 in 1609, but by 1610, after a winter long remembered as the "starving time," only 65 settlers remained alive. At one point, the survivors abandoned Jamestown and sailed for England, only to be intercepted and persuaded to return to Virginia by ships carrying a new governor, 250 colonists, and supplies. By 1616, about 80 percent of the immigrants who had arrived in the first decade were dead.

Only rigorous military discipline held the colony together. John Smith was a forceful man whose career before coming to America included a period fighting the Turks in Hungary, where he was captured and for a time enslaved. He imposed a regime of forced labor on company lands. "He that will not work, shall not eat," Smith declared. Smith's autocratic mode of governing alienated many of the colonists. After being injured in an accidental gunpowder explosion in 1609, he was forced to return to England. But his immediate successors continued his iron rule.

From Company to Society

The Virginia Company slowly realized that for the colony to survive it would have to abandon the search for gold, grow its own food, and find a marketable commodity. It would also have to attract more settlers. With this end in view, it announced new policies in 1618 that powerfully shaped Virginia's development as a functioning society rather than an outpost of London-based investors. Instead of retaining all the land for itself, the company introduced the **headright system**, awarding fifty acres of land to any colonist who paid for his own or another's passage. Thus, anyone who brought in a sizable number of servants would immediately acquire a large estate. In place of the governor's militaristic regime, a "charter of grants and liberties" was issued, including the establishment of a **House of Burgesses**. When it convened in 1619, this became the first elected assembly in colonial America.

The House of Burgesses was hardly a model of democracy—only freemen could vote, and the company and its appointed governor retained the right to nullify any measure the body adopted. But its creation established a political precedent that all English colonies would eventually follow. Also in 1619, the first twenty blacks arrived in Virginia on a Dutch vessel. The full significance of these two events would not be apparent until years later. But they laid the foundation for a society that would one day be dominated economically and politically by slaveowning planters.

Powhatan and Pocahontas

When the English arrived at Jamestown, they landed in an area inhabited by some 15,000 to 25,000 Indians living in numerous small agricultural villages. Most acknowledged the rule of Wahunsonacock, a shrewd and forceful leader who had recently consolidated his authority over the region and collected tribute from some thirty subordinate tribes. Called Powhatan by the settlers after the Indian word for both his tribe and his title of paramount chief, he quickly realized the advantages of trade with the newcomers. For its part, mindful of Las Casas's condemnation of Spanish behavior, the Virginia Company instructed its colonists to treat local Indians kindly and to try to convert them to Christianity. Realizing that the colonists depended on the Indians for food, John Smith tried to stop settlers from seizing produce from nearby villages, lest the Indians cut off all trade.

In the first two years of Jamestown's existence, relations with Indians were mostly peaceful and based on a fairly equal give-and-take. At one point, Smith was captured by the Indians and threatened with execution by Powhatan, only to be rescued by Pocahontas, reputedly the favorite among his many children by dozens of wives. The incident has come down in legend (most recently a popular animated film) as an example of a rebellious, love-struck teenager defying her father. In fact, it was probably part of an elaborate ceremony designed by Powhatan to demonstrate his power over the colonists and incorporate them into his realm. Pocahontas subsequently became an intermediary between the two peoples, bringing food and messages to Jamestown.

John Smith's return to England raised tensions between the two groups, and a period of sporadic conflict began in 1610, with the English massacring villagers indiscriminately and destroying Indian crops. Pocahontas herself was captured and held as a hostage by the settlers in 1613. While confined to Jamestown, she converted to Christianity. As part of the restoration of peace in 1614, she married

A portrait of John Smith, the leader of the early Virginia colony, engraved on a 1624 map of New England.

The only portrait of Pocahontas during her lifetime was engraved by Simon van de Passe in England in 1616. After converting to Christianity, Pocahontas took the name Rebecca.

the English colonist John Rolfe. Two years later, she accompanied her husband to England, where she caused a sensation in the court of James I as a symbol of Anglo-Indian harmony and missionary success. But she succumbed to disease in 1617. Her father died the following year.

The Uprising of 1622

Once it became clear that the English were interested in establishing a permanent and constantly expanding colony, not a trading post, conflict with local Indians was inevitable. The peace that began in 1614 ended abruptly in 1622 when Powhatan's brother and successor, Opechancanough, led a brilliantly planned surprise attack that in a single day wiped out one-quarter of Virginia's settler population of 1,200. The surviving 900 colonists organized themselves into military bands, which then massacred scores of Indians and devastated their villages. A spokesman for the Virginia Company explained the reason behind the Indian assault: "The daily fear that . . . in time we by our growing continually upon them would dispossess them of this country." But by going to war, declared Governor Francis Wyatt, the Indians had forfeited any claim to the land. Virginia's policy, he continued, must now be nothing less than the "expulsion of the savages to gain the free range of the country."

Powhatan, the most prominent Indian leader in the original area of English settlement in Virginia. This image, showing Powhatan and his court, was engraved on John Smith's map of Virginia and included in Smith's *General History of Virginia*, published in 1624.

Indians remained a significant presence in Virginia, and trade continued throughout the century. But the unsuccessful **Uprising of 1622** fundamentally shifted the balance of power in the colony. The settlers' supremacy was reinforced in 1644 when a last desperate rebellion led by Opechancanough, now said to be 100 years old, was crushed after causing the deaths of some 500 colonists. Virginia forced a treaty on the surviving coastal Indians, who now numbered fewer than 2,000, that acknowledged their subordination to the government at Jamestown and required them to move to tribal reservations to the west and not enter areas of European settlement without permission. This policy of separation followed the precedent already established in Ireland. Settlers spreading inland into the Virginia countryside continued to seize Indian lands.

The destruction caused by the uprising of 1622 was the last in a series of blows suffered by the Virginia Company. Two years later, it surrendered its charter and Virginia became the first royal colony, its governor now appointed by the crown. Virginia had failed to accomplish any of its goals for either the company or the settlers. Investors had not turned a profit, and although the company had sent 6,000 settlers to Virginia, its white population numbered only 1,200 when the king assumed control. Preoccupied with affairs at home, the government in London for years paid little attention to Virginia. Henceforth, the local elite, not a faraway company, controlled the colony's development. And that elite was growing rapidly in wealth and power thanks to the cultivation of a crop introduced from the West Indies by John Rolfe—tobacco.

A Tobacco Colony

King James I considered tobacco "harmful to the brain and dangerous to the lungs" and issued a spirited warning against its use. But increasing numbers of Europeans enjoyed smoking and believed the tobacco plant had medicinal benefits. As a commodity with an ever-expanding mass market in Europe, tobacco became Virginia's substitute for gold. It enriched an emerging class of tobacco planters, as well as members of the colonial government who assigned good land to themselves. The crown profited from customs duties (taxes on tobacco that entered or left the kingdom). By 1624, more than 200,000 pounds were being grown, producing startling profits for landowners. Forty years later, the crop totaled 15 million pounds, and it doubled again by the 1680s. The spread of tobacco farming produced a dispersed society with few towns and little social unity. It inspired a get-rich-quick attitude and a frenzied scramble for land and labor. By the middle of the seventeenth century, a new influx of immigrants with ample financial resources—sons of merchants and English gentlemen—had taken advantage of the headright system and governmental connections to acquire large estates along navigable rivers. They established themselves as the colony's social and political elite.

The expansion of tobacco cultivation also led to an increased demand for field labor, met for most of the seventeenth century by young, male indentured servants. Despite harsh conditions of work in the tobacco fields, a persistently high death rate, and laws mandating punishments from whipping to an extension of service for those who ran away or were unruly, the abundance of land continued to attract migrants. Of the 120,000 English immigrants who entered the Chesapeake region during the seventeenth century, three-quarters came as servants. Virginia's white society increasingly came to resemble that of England, with a wealthy landed gentry at the top; a group of small farmers, mostly former indentured servants who had managed to acquire land, in the middle; and an army of poor laborers—servants and landless former indentured servants—at the bottom. By 1700, the region's white population had grown to nearly 90,000.

Women and the Family

Virginia, however, lacked one essential element of English society—stable family life. The colony avidly promoted the immigration of women, including several dozen "tobacco brides" who arrived in 1620 and 1621 for arranged marriages. But given the demand for male servants to work in the tobacco fields, men in the Chesapeake outnumbered women for most of the seventeenth century by four or five to one. The vast majority of women who emigrated to

Theodor de Bry's engraving of the 1622 Indian uprising in Virginia depicts the Indians massacring defenseless colonists (who are shown unarmed although many in fact owned guns).

An advertisement for tobacco includes images of slaves handling barrels and tobacco plants.

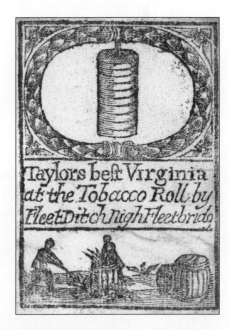

Englishmen smoking tobacco. European demand for tobacco enriched Virginia planters, British merchants, and the English government, and spurred an ever-increasing demand for field labor.

the region came as indentured servants. Since they usually had to complete their terms of service before marrying, they did not begin to form families until their mid-twenties. The high death rate, unequal ratio between the sexes, and late age of marriage for those who found partners retarded population growth and produced a society with large numbers of single men, widows, and orphans. Although patriarchal ideals remained intact in Virginia, in practice the traditional authority of husbands and fathers was weakened. Because of their own low life expectancy, fathers found it difficult to supervise the careers and marriages of their children.

Slow population growth

In the colonies as in England, a married woman possessed certain rights before the law, including a claim to **dower rights** of one-third of her husband's property in the event that he died before she did. When the widow died, however, the property passed to the husband's male heirs. (English law was far less generous than in Spain, where a woman could hold independently any property inherited from her parents, and a man and wife owned jointly all the wealth accumulated during a marriage.)

Social conditions in the colonies, however, opened the door to roles women rarely assumed in England. Widows and the few women who never married took advantage of their legal status as *feme sole* (a "woman alone," who enjoyed an independent legal identity denied to married women) to make contracts and conduct business. Margaret Brent, who emigrated to the Chesapeake in 1638, acquired land, managed her own plantation, and acted as a lawyer in court. Some widows were chosen to administer their husbands' estates or were willed their husbands' property outright, rather than receiving only the one-third "dower rights." But because most women came to Virginia as indentured servants, they could look forward only to a life of hard labor in the tobacco fields and early death. Servants were frequently subjected to sexual abuse by their masters. Those who married often found themselves in poverty when their husbands died.

Women's lives

The Maryland Experiment

Although it began under very different sponsorship and remained much smaller than Virginia during the seventeenth century, the second Chesapeake colony, Maryland, followed a similar course of development. As in Virginia, tobacco came to dominate the economy and tobacco planters the society. But in other ways, Maryland's history was strikingly different.

Maryland was established in 1632 as a proprietary colony, that is, a grant of land and governmental authority to a single individual. This was Cecilius Calvert, the son of a recently deceased favorite of King Charles I. The charter made Calvert proprietor of the colony and granted him "full, free, and absolute power," including control of trade and the right to initiate all legislation, with an elected assembly confined to approving or disapproving his proposals. Calvert imagined Maryland as a feudal domain. Land would be laid out in manors with the owners paying "quitrents" to the proprietor. Calvert disliked representative institutions and believed ordinary people should not meddle in governmental affairs. On the other hand, the charter also guaranteed to colonists "all privileges, franchises, and liberties" of Englishmen. While these were not spelled out, they undoubtedly included the idea of a government limited by the law. Here was a recipe for conflict, and Maryland had more than its share during the seventeenth century.

>> *Proprietary colony*

Religion in Maryland

Further aggravating instability in the colony was the fact that Calvert, a Catholic, envisioned Maryland as a refuge for his persecuted coreligionists, especially the

Processing tobacco was as labor-intensive as caring for the plant in the fields. Here scantily clad slaves and female indentured servants work with the crop after it has been harvested.

younger sons of Catholic gentry who had few economic or political prospects in England. In Maryland, he hoped, Protestants and Catholics could live in a harmony unknown in Europe. The first group of 130 colonists included a number of Catholic gentlemen and two priests. Most appointed officials were also Catholic, including relatives of the proprietor, as were those to whom he awarded the choicest land grants. But Protestants always formed a majority of the settlers. Most, as in Virginia, came as indentured servants, but others took advantage of Maryland's generous headright system to acquire land by transporting workers to the colony.

As in Virginia, the death rate remained very high. In one county, half the marriages during the seventeenth century lasted fewer than eight years before one partner died. Almost 70 percent of male settlers in Maryland died before reaching the age of fifty, and half the children born in the colony did not live to adulthood. But at least initially, Maryland seems to have offered servants greater opportunity for landownership than Virginia. Unlike in the older colony, freedom dues in Maryland included fifty acres of land. As tobacco planters engrossed the best land later in the century, however, the prospects for landless men diminished.

THE NEW ENGLAND WAY

The Rise of Puritanism

The first book printed in the English mainland colonies, *The Whole Book of Psalmes Faithfully Translated into English Metre* was published in Cambridge, Massachusetts, in 1640. Worshipers used it to sing psalms (religious songs from the Bible, sung in Massachusetts unaccompanied by music, which Puritan churches banned).

As Virginia and Maryland evolved toward societies dominated by a small aristocracy ruling over numerous bound laborers, a very different social order emerged in seventeenth-century New England. The early history of that region is intimately connected to the religious movement known as "Puritanism," which arose in England late in the sixteenth century. The term was initially coined by opponents to ridicule those not satisfied with the progress of the Protestant Reformation in England, who called themselves not Puritans but "godly" or "true Protestants." Puritanism came to define a set of religious principles and a view of how society should be organized. **Puritans** differed among themselves on many issues. But all shared the conviction that the Church of England retained too many elements of Catholicism in its religious rituals and doctrines. Puritans saw elaborate church ceremonies, the rule that priests could not marry, and ornate church decorations as vestiges of "popery." Many rejected the Catholic structure of religious authority descending from a pope or king to archbishops, bishops, and priests. Only independent local congregations, they believed, should choose clergymen and determine modes of worship. These Puritans were called "Congregationalists." All Puritans shared many of the beliefs of the Church of England and the society as a whole, including a hatred of Catholicism and a pride in England's greatness as a champion of liberty. But they believed that neither the church nor the nation was living up to its ideals.

Puritans considered religious belief a complex and demanding matter and urged believers to seek the truth by reading the Bible and listening to sermons by educated ministers, rather than devoting themselves to sacraments administered by priests and to what Puritans considered formulaic prayers. The sermon was the central rite of Puritan practice. In the course of a lifetime, according to one estimate, the average Puritan listened to some 7,000 sermons. In their religious beliefs, Puritans followed the ideas of the French-born Swiss theologian John Calvin. The world, Calvin taught, was divided between the elect and the damned. All persons sought salvation, but whether one was among the elect destined to be saved had already been determined by God. His will, ultimately, was unknowable, and nothing one did on earth—including prayers, good works, and offerings—would make any difference. But while there were no guarantees of salvation, worldly success—leading a good life, prospering economically—might well be indications of God's grace. Idleness and immoral behavior were sure signs of damnation.

Moral Liberty

Puritanism, however, was not simply a set of ideas but a state of mind, a zealousness in pursuing the true faith that alienated many who held differing religious views. A minority of Puritans (such as those who settled in Plymouth Colony) became separatists, abandoning the Church of England entirely to form their own independent churches. Most, however, hoped to purify the church from within. But in the 1620s and 1630s, as Charles I seemed to be moving toward a restoration of Catholic ceremonies and the Church of England dismissed Puritan ministers and censored their writings, many Puritans decided to emigrate. They departed England not so much because of persecution, but because they feared that "Popish" practices had grown to such "an intolerable height," as one minister complained, that "the consciences of God's saints . . . could no longer bear them." By the same token, Puritans blamed many of England's social problems on the wandering poor, whom they considered indolent and ungodly. When Puritans emigrated to New England, they hoped to escape what they believed to be the religious and worldly corruptions of English society. They would establish a "city set upon a hill," a Bible Commonwealth whose influence would flow back across the Atlantic and rescue England from godlessness and social decay.

Like so many other emigrants to America, Puritans came in search of liberty, especially the right to worship and govern themselves in what they deemed a truly Christian manner. Freedom for Puritans was primarily a spiritual affair. It implied the opportunity and the responsibility to obey God's will through self-government and self-denial. It certainly did not mean unrestrained action, improper religious practices, or sinful behavior, of which, Puritans thought, there were far too many examples in England. In a 1645 speech to the Massachusetts legislature explaining the Puritan conception of freedom, **John Winthrop**, the colony's governor, distinguished sharply between two kinds of liberty. "Natural" liberty, or acting without restraint, suggested "a liberty to do evil." This was the false idea of freedom supposedly adopted by the Irish, Indians, and bad Christians generally. Genuine "moral" liberty—the Christian liberty described in Chapter 1—meant "a liberty to that only which is good." It was quite compatible with severe restraints on speech, religion, and personal behavior. True freedom, Winthrop insisted, depended on "subjection to authority," both religious and secular; otherwise, anarchy was sure to follow. To Puritans, liberty meant that

A portrait of John Winthrop, first governor of the Massachusetts Bay Colony, painted in the 1640s.

"City set upon a hill"

"Moral" liberty

the elect had a right to establish churches and govern society, not that others could challenge their beliefs or authority.

The Pilgrims at Plymouth

The first Puritans to emigrate to America were a group of separatists known as the **Pilgrims**. They had already fled to the Netherlands in 1608, believing that Satan had begun "to sow errors, heresies and discords" in England. A decade later, fearing that their children were being corrupted by being drawn into the surrounding culture, they decided to emigrate to Virginia. The expedition was financed by a group of English investors who hoped to establish a base for profitable trade. In September 1620, the *Mayflower*, carrying 150 settlers and crew (among them many non-Puritans), embarked from England. Blown off course, they landed not in Virginia but hundreds of miles to the north, on Cape Cod. Here the 102 who survived the journey established the colony of Plymouth. Before landing, the Pilgrim leaders drew up the **Mayflower Compact**, in which the adult men going ashore agreed to obey "just and equal laws" enacted by representatives of their own choosing. This was the first written frame of government in what is now the United States.

A century earlier, when Giovanni da Verrazano explored the Atlantic coast of North America, he encountered thickly settled villages and saw the smoke of innumerable Indian bonfires. By the time the Pilgrims landed, hundreds of European fishing vessels had operated off New England, landing to trade with Indians and bringing, as elsewhere, epidemics. The Pilgrims arrived in an area whose native population had recently been decimated by smallpox. They established Plymouth on the site of an abandoned Indian village whose fields had been cleared before the epidemic and were ready for cultivation. Nonetheless, the settlers arrived six weeks before winter without food or farm animals. Half died during the first winter. The colonists only survived through the help of local Indians, notably Squanto, who with twenty other Indians had been kidnapped and brought to Spain in 1614 by the English explorer Thomas Hunt, who planned to sell them as slaves. Rescued by a local priest, Squanto somehow made his way to London, where he learned English. He returned to Massachusetts in 1619 only to find that his people, the Patuxet, had succumbed to disease. He served as interpreter for the Pilgrims, taught them where to fish and how to plant corn, and helped in the forging of an alliance with Massasoit, a local chief. In the autumn of 1621, the Pilgrims invited their Indian allies to a harvest feast celebrating their survival, the first Thanksgiving in North America. (Feasts of Thanksgiving were a feature of Puritan religious practice, not something conducted in this one instance.)

The Pilgrims hoped to establish a society based on the lives of the early Christian saints. Their government rested on the principle of consent, and voting was not restricted to church members. All land was held in common until 1627, when it was divided among the settlers. Plymouth survived as an independent colony until 1691, but it was soon overshadowed by Massachusetts Bay to its north.

The Mayflower

In this engraving, Theodor de Bry depicts an encounter between an English explorer and the Wampanoag Indians on Cape Cod or Martha's Vineyard in 1602. The region's Indians had much experience with Europeans before the Pilgrims settled there.

The Great Migration

Chartered in 1629, the Massachusetts Bay Company was founded by a group of London merchants who hoped to further the Puritan cause and turn a profit through trade with the Indians. The first five ships sailed from England in 1629, and by 1642 some 21,000 Puritans had emigrated to Massachusetts. Long remembered as the **Great Migration**, this flow of population represented less than one-third of English emigration in the 1630s. Far more English settlers arrived in Ireland, the Chesapeake, and the Caribbean. After 1640, migration to New England virtually ceased, and in some years more colonists left the region than arrived. Nonetheless, the Great Migration established the basis for a stable and thriving society.

In many ways, the settling of New England was unique. Although servants represented about one-quarter of the Great Migration, most settlers arrived in Massachusetts in families. They came for many reasons, including the desire to escape religious persecution, anxiety about the future of England, and the prospect of economic betterment. Compared with colonists in Virginia and Maryland, they were older and more prosperous, and the number of men and women more equally balanced. Because of the even sex ratio and New England's healthier climate, the population grew rapidly, doubling every twenty-seven years. Although the region received only a small fraction of the century's migration, by 1700 New England's white population of 91,000 outnumbered that of both the Chesapeake and the West Indies. Nearly all were descendants of those who crossed the Atlantic during the Great Migration.

Seal of the Massachusetts Bay Colony. The Indian's scanty attire suggests a lack of civilization. His statement "Come Over and Help Us," based on an incident in the Bible, illustrates the English conviction that they were liberating the native population, rather than exploiting them as other empires had.

The Puritan Family

While the imbalance between male and female migrants made it difficult for patriarchal family patterns fully to take root in the Chesapeake until the end of the seventeenth century, they emerged very quickly in New England. Whatever their differences with other Englishmen on religious matters, Puritans shared with the larger society a belief in male authority within the household as well as an adherence to the common-law tradition that severely limited married women's legal and economic rights. Puritans in America carefully emulated the family structure of England, insisting that the obedience of women, children, and servants to men's will was the foundation of social stability. The father's authority was all the more vital because in a farming society without large numbers of slaves or servants, control over the labor of one's family was essential to a man's economic success.

Male authority

To be sure, Puritans deemed women to be the spiritual equals of men, and women were allowed to become full church members. Although all ministers were men, the Puritan belief in the ability of believers to interpret the Bible opened the door for some women to claim positions of religious leadership. The ideal Puritan marriage was based on reciprocal affection and companionship, and divorce was legal. Yet within the household, the husband's authority was virtually absolute. Indeed, a man's position as head of his family was thought to replicate God's authority in spiritual matters and the authority of the government in the secular realm. Magistrates sometimes intervened to protect wives from physical abuse,

The Savage Family, a 1779 painting by the New England artist Edward Savage, depicts several generations of a typically numerous Puritan family.

but they also enforced the power of fathers over their children and husbands over their wives. Moderate physical "correction" was considered appropriate for women who violated their husbands' sense of proper behavior.

Their responsibilities as wives and mothers defined women's lives. In his 1645 speech on liberty, John Winthrop noted that a woman achieved genuine freedom by fulfilling her prescribed social role and embracing "subjection to her husband's authority." The family was the foundation of strong communities, and unmarried adults seemed a danger to the social fabric. An early law of Plymouth declared that "no single person be suffered to live of himself." The typical New England woman married at twenty-two, a younger age than her English counterpart, and gave birth seven times. Because New England was a far healthier environment than the Chesapeake, more children survived infancy. Thus, much of a woman's adult life was devoted to bearing and rearing children.

Government and Society in Massachusetts

In a sermon aboard the *Arabella*, on which he sailed for Massachusetts in 1630, John Winthrop spoke of the settlers binding themselves together "in the bond of brotherly affection" in order to promote the glory of God and their own "common good." Puritans feared excessive individualism and lack of social unity. Unlike the dispersed plantation-centered society of the Chesapeake, the leaders of Massachusetts organized the colony in self-governing towns. Groups of settlers received a land grant from the colony's government and then subdivided it, with residents awarded house lots in a central area and land on the outskirts for farming. Much land remained in commons, either for collective use or to be divided among later settlers or the sons of the town's founders. Each town had its own Congregational Church. Each, according to a law of 1647, was required to establish a school, since the ability to read the Bible was central to Puritan belief. To train an educated ministry, Harvard College was established in 1636 (nearly a century after the Royal University of Mexico, founded in 1551), and two years later the first printing press in English America was established in Cambridge.

The government of Massachusetts reflected the Puritans' religious and social vision. Wishing to rule the colony without outside interference and to prevent non-Puritans from influencing decision making, the shareholders of the Massachusetts Bay Company emigrated to America, taking the charter with them and transforming a commercial document into a form of government. At first, the eight shareholders chose the men who ruled the colony. In 1634, a group of deputies elected by freemen (landowning church members) was added to form a single ruling body, the General Court. Ten years later, company officers and elected deputies were divided into two legislative houses. Unlike Virginia, whose governors were

The New England town ▸

The Massachusetts Bay Charter ▸

appointed first by a faraway company and after 1624 by the crown, or Maryland, where authority rested with a single proprietor, the freemen of Massachusetts elected their governor.

The principle of consent was central to Puritanism. Church government was decentralized—each congregation, as one minister put it, had "complete liberty to stand alone." Churches were formed by voluntary agreement among members, who elected the minister. No important church decision was made without the agreement of the male members. Towns governed themselves, and local officials, delegates to the General Court, and the colonial governor were all elected. Puritans, however, were hardly believers in equality. Church membership, a status that carried great prestige and power, was a restrictive category. Anyone could worship at a church, or, as the Puritans preferred to call it, meeting house, but to be a full member required demonstrating that one had experienced divine grace and could be considered a "visible saint," usually by testifying about a conversion experience. Although male property holders generally chose local officials, voting in colony-wide elections was limited to men who had been accepted as full church members. As time went on, this meant that a smaller and smaller percentage of the population controlled the government. Puritan democracy was for those within the circle of church membership; those outside the boundary occupied a secondary place in the Bible Commonwealth.

An embroidered banner depicting the main building at Harvard, the first college established in the English colonies. It was probably made by a Massachusetts woman for a husband or son who attended Harvard.

Church and State in Puritan Massachusetts

Seventeenth-century New England was a hierarchical society in which socially prominent families were assigned the best land and the most desirable seats in church. "Some must be rich and some poor, some high and eminent in power and dignity; others mean and in subjection," declared John Winthrop. This was part of God's plan, reinforced by man-made law and custom. The General Court forbade ordinary men and women from wearing "the garb of gentlemen." Ordinary settlers were addressed as "goodman" and "goodwife," while the better sort were called "gentleman" and "lady" or "master" and "mistress." When the General Court in 1641 issued a Body of Liberties outlining the rights and responsibilities of Massachusetts colonists, it adopted the traditional understanding of liberties as privileges that derived from one's place in the social order. Inequality was considered an expression of God's will, and while some liberties applied to all inhabitants, there were separate lists of rights for freemen, women, children, and servants. The Body of Liberties also allowed for slavery. The first African slave appears in the records of Massachusetts Bay in 1640.

The Body of Liberties

Massachusetts forbade ministers from holding office so as not to interfere with their spiritual responsibilities. But church and state were closely interconnected.

The law required each town to establish a church and to levy a tax to support the minister. There were no separate church courts, but the state enforced religious devotion. The Body of Liberties affirmed the rights of free speech and assembly and equal protection of the law for all within the colony, but the laws of Massachusetts prescribed the death penalty for, among other things, worshiping "any god, but the lord god," practicing witchcraft, or committing blasphemy.

Like many others in the seventeenth century, Puritans believed that religious uniformity was essential to social order. They did not believe in religious toleration—there was one truth, and their faith embodied it. Religious liberty meant the liberty to practice this truth. The purpose of the Puritan experiment was to complete the Reformation and, they hoped, spread it back to England. Religious dissent might fatally undermine these goals. But the principle of autonomy for local congregations soon clashed with the desire for religious uniformity.

Church and state

NEW ENGLANDERS DIVIDED

The Puritans exalted individual judgment—hence their insistence on reading the Bible. The very first item printed in English America was a broadside, *The Oath of a Freeman* (1638), explaining the rights and duties of the citizens of Massachusetts and emphasizing that men should vote according to their "own conscience . . . without respect of persons, or favor of any men." Yet modern ideas of individualism, privacy, and personal freedom would have struck Puritans as quite strange. They considered too much emphasis on the "self" dangerous to social harmony and community stability. In the closely knit towns of New England, residents carefully monitored one another's behavior and chastised or expelled those who violated communal norms. In the Puritan view, as one colonist put it, the main freedom possessed by dissenters was the "liberty to keep away from us." Towns banished individuals for such offenses as criticizing the church or government, complaining about the colony in letters home to England, or, in the case of one individual, Abigail Gifford, for being "a very burdensome woman." Tolerance of difference was not high on the list of Puritan values.

Roger Williams, New England's most prominent advocate of religious toleration.

Roger Williams

Differences of opinion about how to organize a Bible Commonwealth, however, emerged almost from the founding of Massachusetts. With its emphasis on individual interpretation of the Bible, Puritanism contained the seeds of its own fragmentation. The first sustained criticism of the existing order came from the young minister Roger Williams, who arrived in Massachusetts in 1631 and soon began to insist that its congregations withdraw from the Church of England and that church and state be separated. "Soul liberty," Williams believed, required that individuals be allowed to follow their consciences wherever they led. To most Puritans, the social fabric was held together by certain religious truths, which could not be questioned. To Williams, any law-abiding citizen should be allowed to practice whatever form of religion he chose. For the government to "molest any person, Jew or Gentile, for either professing doctrine or practicing worship" violated the principle that genuine religious faith is voluntary.

Williams and religious liberty

Williams aimed to strengthen religion, not weaken it. The embrace of government, he insisted, corrupted the purity of Christian faith and drew believers into endless religious wars like those that wracked Europe. To leaders like John Winthrop, the outspoken minister's attack on the religious-political establishment of Massachusetts was bad enough, but Williams compounded the offense by rejecting the conviction that Puritans were an elect people on a divine mission to spread the true faith. Williams denied that God had singled out any group as special favorites.

Rhode Island and Connecticut

Banished from Massachusetts in 1636, Williams and his followers moved south, where they established the colony of Rhode Island, which eventually received a charter from London. In a world in which the right of individuals to participate in religious activities without governmental interference barely existed, Rhode Island became a beacon of religious freedom. It had no established church, no religious qualifications for voting until the eighteenth century, and no requirement that citizens attend church. It became a haven for **Dissenters** (Protestants who belonged to denominations other than the established church) and Jews persecuted in other colonies. Rhode Island's frame of government was also more democratic. The assembly was elected twice a year, the governor annually, and town meetings were held more frequently than elsewhere in New England.

Religious freedom in Rhode Island

Religious disagreements in Massachusetts generated other colonies as well. In 1636, the minister Thomas Hooker established a settlement at Hartford. Its system of government, embodied in the Fundamental Orders of 1639, was modeled on that of Massachusetts—with the significant exception that men did not have to be church members to vote. Quite different was the colony of New Haven, founded in 1638 by emigrants who wanted an even closer connection between church and state. In 1662, Hartford and New Haven received a royal charter that united them as the colony of Connecticut.

The Trial of Anne Hutchinson

More threatening to the Puritan establishment, both because of her gender and because she attracted a large and influential following, was Anne Hutchinson. A midwife and the daughter of a clergyman, Hutchinson, wrote John Winthrop, was "a woman of a ready wit and bold spirit." She arrived in Massachusetts with her husband in 1634 to join their minister, John Cotton, who had been expelled from his pulpit in England by church authorities. Hutchinson began holding meetings in her home, where she led discussions of religious issues among men and women, including a number of prominent merchants and public officials. In Hutchinson's view, salvation was God's direct gift to the elect and could not be earned by good works, devotional practices, or other human effort. Most Puritans shared this belief. What set Hutchinson apart was her charge that nearly all the ministers in Massachusetts were guilty of faulty preaching for distinguishing "saints" from the damned on the basis of activities such as church attendance and moral behavior rather than an inner state of grace.

Hutchinson's criticisms of Puritan leaders

ENGLISH SETTLEMENT IN NEW ENGLAND, ca. 1640

MAINE

Lake Champlain

MOHAWK

NEW HAMPSHIRE

ABENAKI

Portland

MAHICAN

York

Exeter

Atlantic Ocean

PENNACOOK · Gloucester

POCUMTUK

Salem
MASSACHUSETT
Cambridge · Boston

MASSACHUSETTS
(1629–1630)

Massachusetts Bay

Weymouth

NIPMUCK

POKANOKET

Springfield

Provincetown

NARRAGANSETT

Plymouth
PLYMOUTH
(1620)

Cape Cod Bay · Cape Cod

Windsor

Providence
(1636)

Hartford

RHODE ISLAND
(1636–1643)

Sandwich

CONNECTICUT
(1636–1662)

WAMPANOAG

Barnstable

Portsmouth

MOHEGAN
Pequot War,
1636–1637 ✕ Mystic

Newport

Edgartown

Nantucket

New Haven
(1638)

Martha's Vineyard

Stratford

Stamford

Long Island Sound

DELAWARE

Easthampton

Long Island

New Amsterdam

(1620) Date of settlement
☐ Massachusetts
☐ Plymouth
☐ Rhode Island
☐ Connecticut
☐ New Haven

0   25   50 miles
0   25   50 kilometers

By the mid-seventeenth century, English settlement in New England had spread well inland and up and down the Atlantic coast.

Hutchinson's trial

In Massachusetts, where most Puritans found the idea of religious pluralism deeply troubling and church and state reinforced each other, both ministers and magistrates were intent on suppressing any views that challenged their own leadership. Their critics denounced Cotton and Hutchinson for Antinomianism (a term for putting one's own judgment or faith above both human law and the teachings of the church). In 1637, she was placed on trial before a civil court for sedition (expressing opinions dangerous to authority). Her position as a "public woman" made her defiance seem even more outrageous. Her meetings, said Governor Winthrop, were neither "comely in the sight of God nor fitting to your sex." A combative and articulate woman, Hutchinson ably debated interpretation of the Bible with her university-educated accusers. She more than held her own during her trial. But when she spoke of divine revelations, of God speaking to her directly rather than through ministers or the Bible, she violated

Puritan doctrine and sealed her own fate. Such a claim, the colony's leaders felt, posed a threat to the very existence of organized churches—and, indeed, to all authority. Hutchinson and a number of her followers were banished. Her family made its way to Rhode Island and then to Westchester, north of what is now New York City, where Hutchinson and most of her relatives perished during an Indian war.

Anne Hutchinson lived in New England for only eight years, but she left her mark on the region's religious culture. As in the case of Roger Williams, her career showed how the Puritan belief in each individual's ability to interpret the Bible could easily lead to criticism of the religious and political establishment. It would take many years before religious toleration—which violated the Puritans' understanding of "moral liberty" and social harmony—came to Massachusetts.

Significance of Anne Hutchinson

Puritans and Indians

Along with disruptive religious controversies, New England, like other colonies, had to deal with the difficult problem of relations with Indians. The native population of New England numbered perhaps 100,000 when the Puritans arrived. But because of recent epidemics, the migrants encountered fewer Indians near the coast than in other parts of eastern North America. In areas of European settlement, colonists quickly outnumbered the native population. Some settlers, notably Roger Williams, sought to treat the Indians with justice. Williams learned complex Indian languages, and he insisted that the king had no right to grant land already belonging to someone else. No town, said Williams, should be established before its site had been purchased. While John Winthrop believed uncultivated land could legitimately be taken by the colonists, he also recognized the benefits of buying land rather than simply seizing it. But he insisted that such purchases (usually completed after towns had already been settled) must carry with them Indian agreement to submit to English authority and pay tribute to the colonists.

Treating Indians with justice

To New England's leaders, the Indians represented both savagery and temptation. In Puritan eyes, they resembled Catholics, with their false gods and deceptive rituals. They enjoyed freedom, but of the wrong kind—what Winthrop condemned as undisciplined "natural liberty" rather than the "moral liberty" of the civilized Christian. Always concerned that sinful persons might prefer a life of ease to hard work, Puritans feared that Indian society might prove attractive to colonists who lacked the proper moral fiber. In 1642, the Connecticut General Court set a penalty of three years at hard labor for any colonist who abandoned "godly society" to live with the Indians. To counteract the attraction of Indian life, the leaders of New England also encouraged the publication of **captivity narratives** by those captured by Indians. The most popular was *The Sovereignty and Goodness of God* by Mary Rowlandson, who had emigrated with her parents as a child in 1639 and was seized along with a group of other settlers and held for three months until ransomed during an Indian war in the 1670s. Rowlandson acknowledged that she had been well treated and suffered "not the least abuse or unchastity," but her book's overriding theme was her determination to return to Christian society.

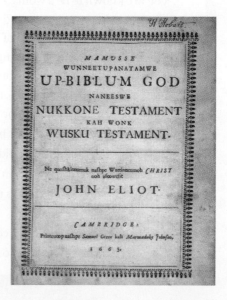

The title page of a translation of the Bible into the Massachusett Indian language, published by John Eliot in 1663.

VOICES OF FREEDOM

From "THE TRIAL OF ANNE HUTCHINSON" (1637)

A midwife and the daughter of a clergyman, Anne Hutchinson began holding religious meetings in her home in Massachusetts in 1634. She attracted followers who believed that most ministers were not adhering strictly enough to Puritan theology. In 1637 she was placed on trial for sedition. In her defense, she claimed to be inspired by a direct revelation from God, a violation of Puritan beliefs. The examination of Hutchinson by Governor John Winthrop and Deputy Governor Thomas Dudley is a classic example of the clash between established power and individual conscience.

GOV. JOHN WINTHROP: Mrs. Hutchinson, you are called here as one of those that have troubled the peace of the commonwealth and the churches here; you are known to be a woman that hath had a great share in the promoting and divulging of those opinions that are the cause of this trouble, . . . and you have maintained a meeting and an assembly in your house that hath been condemned by the general assembly as a thing not tolerable nor comely in the sight of God nor fitting for your sex . . . .

MRS. ANNE HUTCHINSON: What have I said or done?

GOV. JOHN WINTHROP: [Y]ou did harbor and countenance those that are parties in this faction. . . .

MRS. ANNE HUTCHINSON: That's matter of conscience, Sir.

GOV. JOHN WINTHROP: Your conscience you must keep, or it must be kept for you.

* * *

GOV. JOHN WINTHROP: Your course is not to be suffered for. Besides we find such a course as this to be greatly prejudicial to the state. . . . And besides that it will not well stand with the commonwealth that families should be neglected for so many neighbors and dames and so much time spent. We see no rule of God for this. We see not that any should have authority to set up any other exercises besides what authority hath already set up . . . .

MRS. ANNE HUTCHINSON: I bless the Lord, he hath let me see which was the clear ministry and which the wrong. . . . Now if you do condemn me for speaking what in my conscience I know to be truth I must commit myself unto the Lord.

MR. NOWEL (ASSISTANT TO THE COURT): How do you know that was the spirit?

MRS. ANNE HUTCHINSON: How did Abraham know that it was God that bid him offer his son, being a breach of the sixth commandment?

DEP. GOV. THOMAS DUDLEY: By an immediate voice.

MRS. ANNE HUTCHINSON: So to me by an immediate revelation.

DEP. GOV. THOMAS DUDLEY: How! an immediate revelation.

* * *

GOV. JOHN WINTHROP: Mrs. Hutchinson, the sentence of the court you hear is that you are banished from out of our jurisdiction as being a woman not fit for our society, and are to be imprisoned till the court shall send you away.

From JOHN WINTHROP,
SPEECH TO THE MASSACHUSETTS GENERAL COURT
(JULY 3, 1645)

John Winthrop, governor of the Massachusetts Bay Colony, describes two very different definitions of liberty in this speech.

The great questions that have troubled the country, are about the authority of the magistrates and the liberty of the people. . . . Concerning liberty, I observe a great mistake in the country about that. There is a twofold liberty, natural (I mean as our nature is now corrupt) and civil or federal. The first is common to man with beasts and other creatures. By this, man, as he stands in relation to man simply, hath liberty to do what he lists; it is a liberty to do evil as well as to [do] good. This liberty is incompatible and inconsistent with authority, and cannot endure the least restraint of the most just authority. The exercise and maintaining of this liberty makes men grow more evil, and in time to be worse than brute beasts. . . . This is that great enemy of truth and peace, that wild beast, which all the ordinances of God are bent against, to restrain and subdue it.

The other kind of liberty I call civil or federal, it may also be termed moral. . . . This liberty is the proper end and object of authority, and cannot subsist without it; and it is a liberty to that only which is good, just, and honest. . . . This liberty is maintained and exercised in a way of subjection to authority; it is of the same kind of liberty wherewith Christ hath made us free. The woman's own choice makes . . . a man her husband; yet being so chosen, he is her lord, and she is to be subject to him, yet in a way of liberty, not of bondage; and a true wife accounts her subjection her honor and freedom, and would not think her condition safe and free, but in her subjection to her husband's authority. Such is the liberty of the church under the authority of Christ.

QUESTIONS

1. *To what extent does Hutchinson's being a woman play a part in the accusations against her?*

2. *Why does Winthrop consider "natural" liberty dangerous?*

3. *How do Hutchinson and Winthrop differ in their understanding of religious liberty?*

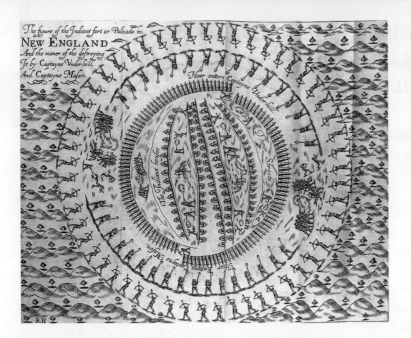

An engraving from John Underhill's *News from America*, published in London in 1638, shows the destruction of the Pequot village on the Mystic River in 1637. The colonial forces, firing guns, are aided by Indian allies with bows and arrows.

Massacre at Mystic

Puritans announced that they intended to bring Christian faith to the Indians, but they did nothing in the first two decades of settlement to accomplish this. They generally saw Indians as an obstacle to be pushed aside.

The Pequot War

Indians in New England lacked a paramount chief like Powhatan in Virginia. Coastal Indian tribes, their numbers severely reduced by disease, initially sought to forge alliances with the newcomers to enhance their own position against inland rivals. But as the white population expanded and new towns proliferated, conflict with the region's Indians became unavoidable. The turning point came in 1637 when a fur trader was killed by Pequots—a powerful tribe who controlled southern New England's fur trade and exacted tribute from other Indians. A force of Connecticut and Massachusetts soldiers, augmented by Narragansett allies, surrounded the main Pequot fortified village at Mystic and set it ablaze, killing those who tried to escape. Over 500 men, women, and children lost their lives in the massacre. By the end of the **Pequot War** a few months later, most of the Pequots had been exterminated or sold into Caribbean slavery. The treaty that restored peace decreed that their name be wiped from the historical record.

The destruction of one of the region's most powerful Indian groups not only opened the Connecticut River valley to rapid white settlement but also persuaded other Indians that the newcomers possessed a power that could not be resisted. The colonists' ferocity shocked their Indian allies, who considered European military practices barbaric. A few Puritans agreed. "It was a fearful sight to see them frying in the fire," the Pilgrim leader William Bradford wrote of the raid on Mystic. But to most Puritans, including Bradford, the defeat of a "barbarous nation" by "the sword of the Lord" offered further proof that they were on a sacred mission and that Indians were unworthy of sharing New England with the visible saints of the church.

The New England Economy

The leaders of the New England colonies prided themselves on the idea that religion was the primary motivation for emigration. "We all came into these parts of America," proclaimed an official document of the 1640s, "with one and the same end and aim, namely, to advance the kingdom of our Lord Jesus Christ and to enjoy the liberties of the Gospel in purity with peace." But economic motives were hardly unimportant. One promotional pamphlet of the 1620s spoke of New England as a place "where religion and profit jump together."

Most Puritans came to America from East Anglia, an internationally renowned cloth-producing region. One of the most economically advanced areas of England, East Anglia in the 1620s and 1630s was suffering from a series of poor harvests and the dislocations caused by a decline in the cloth trade. A majority of the emigrants from this area were weavers, tailors, or farmers. But while they were leaving a depressed region, they were relatively well-off. Most came from the middle ranks of society and paid for their family's passage rather than indenturing themselves to labor. They sought in New England not only religious liberty but also economic advancement—if not riches, then at least a "competency," the economic independence that came with secure landownership or craft status. When one preacher proclaimed that the "main end" of settlement was to honor God, a man in the congregation cried out, "Sir, you are mistaken . . . our main end was to catch fish." But to Puritans no contradiction existed between piety and profit so long as one did not forget the needs of the larger community. Success in one's calling might be taken as a sign of divine grace.

Lacking a marketable staple like sugar or tobacco, New Englanders turned to fishing and timber for exports. But the economy centered on family farms producing food for their own use and a small marketable surplus. Although the Body of Liberties of 1641, as noted above, made provision for slavery in the Bible Commonwealth, there were very few slaves in seventeenth-century New England. Nor were indentured servants as central to the economy as in the Chesapeake. Most households relied on the labor of their own members, including women in the home and children in the fields. Sons remained unmarried into their mid-twenties, when they could expect to receive land from their fathers, from local authorities, or by moving to a new town. Indeed, while religious divisions spawned new settlements, the desire for land among younger families and newcomers was the major motive for New England's expansion. In Sudbury, Massachusetts, for example, one resident proposed in 1651 that every adult man be awarded an equal parcel of land. When a town meeting rejected the idea, a group of young men received a grant from the General Court to establish their own town farther west.

The Merchant Elite

Per capita wealth in New England lagged far behind that of the Chesapeake, but it was much more equally distributed. A majority of New England families achieved the goal of owning their own land, the foundation for a comfortable independence. Nonetheless, as in the Chesapeake, economic development produced a measure of social inequality. On completing their terms, indentured servants rarely achieved full church membership or received grants of land. Most became disenfranchised wage earners.

New England gradually assumed a growing role within the British empire based on trade. As early as the 1640s, New England merchants shipped and marketed the staples of other colonies to markets in Europe and Africa. They engaged in a particularly profitable trade with the West Indies, whose growing slave plantations they supplied with fish, timber, and agricultural produce gathered at home. Especially in Boston, a powerful class of merchants arose who challenged some key

"Competency"

A self-portrait from around 1680, painted by Thomas Smith. A sailor who came to New England from Bermuda around 1650, Smith acquired considerable wealth, as evidenced by his fashionable clothing. The background depicts a naval battle involving Dutch and English ships (possibly a reference to their joint attack on a North African port in 1670). In the foreground is a poem with Smith's initials. This is the earliest-known American self-portrait.

enjoy security of person and property. These rights were embodied in the common law, whose provisions, such as habeas corpus (a protection against being imprisoned without a legal charge), the right to face one's accuser, and trial by jury came to apply to all free subjects of the English crown. And as serfdom slowly disappeared, the number of Englishmen considered "freeborn," and therefore entitled to these rights, expanded enormously.

The English Civil War

English freedom

At the beginning of the seventeenth century, when English emigrants began arriving in the New World, "freedom" still played only a minor role in England's political debates. But the political upheavals of that century elevated the notion of "English freedom" to a central place. The struggle for political supremacy between Parliament and the Stuart monarchs James I and Charles I culminated in the English Civil War of the 1640s and early 1650s. This long-running battle arose from religious disputes about how fully the Church of England should distance its doctrines and forms of worship from Catholicism. Conflict also developed over the respective powers of the king and Parliament, a debate that produced numerous invocations of the idea of the "freeborn Englishman" and led to a great expansion of the concept of English freedom.

Parliament vs. monarchy

The leaders of the House of Commons (the elective body that, along with the hereditary aristocrats of the House of Lords, made up the English Parliament) accused the Stuart kings of endangering liberty by imposing taxes without parliamentary consent, imprisoning political foes, and leading the nation back toward Catholicism. Civil war broke out in 1642, resulting in a victory for the forces of Parliament. In 1649, Charles I was beheaded, the monarchy abolished, and England declared "a Commonwealth and Free State"—a nation governed by the will of the people. Oliver Cromwell, the head of the victorious Parliamentary army, ruled for almost a decade after the execution of the king. In 1660, the monarchy was restored and Charles II assumed the throne. But by then, the breakdown of authority had stimulated intense discussions of liberty, authority, and what it meant to be a "freeborn Englishman."

England's Debate over Freedom

The idea of freedom suddenly took on new and expanded meanings between 1640 and 1660. The writer John Milton, who in 1649 called London "the mansion-house of liberty," called for freedom of speech and of the press. New religious sects sprang up, demanding the end of public financing and special privileges for the Anglican Church and religious toleration for all Protestants. The Levellers, history's first

The Levellers

democratic political movement, proposed a written constitution, the Agreement of the People, which began by proclaiming "at how high a rate we value our just freedom." At a time when "democracy" was still widely seen as the equivalent of anarchy and disorder, the document proposed to abolish the monarchy and House of Lords and to greatly expand the right to vote. "The poorest he that lives in England hath a life to live as the greatest he," declared the Leveller Thomas Rainsborough, and therefore "any man that is born in England . . . ought to have his voice in election." Rainsborough even condemned slavery.

The Levellers offered a glimpse of the modern definition of freedom as a universal entitlement in a society based on equal rights, not a function of social class.

Another new group, the Diggers, went even further, hoping to give freedom an economic underpinning through the common ownership of land. Previous discussion of freedom, declared Gerard Winstanley, the Diggers' leader, had been misguided: "You are like men in a mist, seeking for freedom and know not what it is." True freedom applied equally "to the poor as well as the rich"; all were entitled to "a comfortable livelihood in this their own land." Even before the restoration of the monarchy, the Levellers, Diggers, and other radical movements spawned by the English Civil War had been crushed or driven underground. But some of the ideas of liberty that flourished during the 1640s and 1650s would be carried to America by English emigrants.

English Liberty

These struggles elevated the notion of "English liberty" to a central place in Anglo-American political culture. It became a major building block in the assertive sense of nationhood then being consolidated in England. The medieval idea of liberties as a collection of limited entitlements enjoyed by specific groups did not suddenly disappear. But it was increasingly overshadowed by a more general definition of freedom grounded in the common rights of all individuals within the English realm. All Englishmen were governed by a king, but "he rules over free men," according to the law, unlike the autocratic monarchs of France, Spain, Russia, and other countries.

The belief in freedom as the common heritage of all Englishmen and the conception of the British empire as the world's guardian of liberty helped to legitimize English colonization in the Western Hemisphere and to cast its imperial wars against Catholic France and Spain as struggles between freedom and tyranny.

The Civil War and English America

These struggles, accompanied by vigorous discussions of the rights of freeborn Englishmen, inevitably reverberated in England's colonies, dividing them from one another and internally. Most New Englanders sided with Parliament in the Civil War of the 1640s. Some returned to England to join the Parliamentary army or take up pulpits to help create a godly commonwealth at home. But Puritan leaders were increasingly uncomfortable as the idea of religious toleration for Protestants gained favor in England. It was the revolutionary Parliament that in 1644 granted Roger Williams his charter for the Rhode Island colony he had founded after being banished from Massachusetts.

Meanwhile, a number of followers of Anne Hutchinson became Quakers, one of the sects that sprang up in England during the Civil War. Quakers held that the spirit of God dwelled within every individual, not just the elect, and that this "inner light," rather than the Bible or teachings of the clergy, offered the surest guidance in spiritual matters. When Quakers appeared in Massachusetts, colonial officials had them whipped, fined, and banished. In 1659 and 1660, four Quakers who returned from exile were hanged, including Mary Dyer, a former disciple of Hutchinson.

The frontispiece of *Leviathan*, by Thomas Hobbes. Written during the English Civil War and published in 1651, two years after the execution of King Charles I, *Leviathan* argues that the only effective form of government is an absolute monarchy. Hobbes designed this image himself to illustrate his thesis. The king wields the sword of justice in one hand and the staff of an archbishop in the other—he combines the powers of church and state. His person is composed of his people; he is literally a body politic. Beneath him is a peaceful, orderly country, and beneath that, images of threats to public order, both secular and religious, against which the king must guard.

SUGGESTED READING

BOOKS

- Anderson, Virginia. *Creatures of Empire: How Domestic Animals Transformed Early America* (2006). Shows how livestock brought by English settlers helped to transform the colonial landscape and provoked conflict with Native Americans.

- Banner, Stuart. *How the Indians Lost Their Land: Law and Power on the Frontier* (2005). Argues that most Indian land came into settlers' hands by legal processes rather than conquest.

- Bonomi, Patricia. *Under the Cope of Heaven: Religion, Society, and Politics in Colonial America* (1986). Traces the interrelationship of religion and politics and the rise of religious diversity in the colonies.

- Brown, Kathleen. *Good Wives, Nasty Wenches, and Anxious Patriarchs: Gender, Race, and Power in Colonial Virginia* (1996). A pioneering study of gender relations and their impact on Virginia society.

- Cronon, William. *Changes in the Land: Colonists and the Ecology of New England* (1983). A pathbreaking examination of how English colonization affected the natural environment in New England.

- Gleach, Frederic W. *Powhatan's World and Colonial Virginia: A Conflict of Cultures* (1997). A study of Indian culture and the impact of European colonization upon it.

- Hill, Christopher. *The Century of Revolution* (1961). A survey stressing the causes and consequences of the English Civil War.

- Horn, James. *Adapting to a New World: English Society in the Seventeenth-Century Chesapeake* (1994). A detailed examination of the lives of early settlers in England and later in Virginia.

- Morgan, Edmund S. *The Puritan Family* (1944). An early examination of family life and gender relations in colonial America.

- Noll, Mark. *The Old Religion in a New World: The History of North American Christianity* (2001). Relates how the transplantation of European religions to America changed religious institutions and practices.

- Pestana, Carla G. *The English Atlantic in an Age of Revolution, 1640–1661* (2001). Analyzes how the English Civil War reverberated in the American colonies.

- Philbrick, Nathaniel. *Mayflower* (2006). An account of one of the most celebrated voyages of the colonial era, and the early history of the Plymouth colony.

- Price, David A. *Love and Hate in Jamestown: John Smith, Pocahontas, and the Start of a New Nation* (2003). Presents the legend and reality of John Smith, Pocahontas, and early Virginia.

- Taylor, Alan. *American Colonies* (2001). A comprehensive survey of the history of North American colonies from their beginnings to 1763.

- Winship, Michael. *Making Heretics: Militant Protestantism and Free Grace in Massachusetts, 1636–1641* (2002). The most recent account of Anne Hutchinson and the Antinomian controversy.

WEBSITES

- The Plymouth Colony Archive Project: www.histarch.illinois.edu/plymouth

- Virtual Jamestown: www.virtualjamestown.org

CHAPTER REVIEW AND ONLINE RESOURCES

REVIEW QUESTIONS

1. Compare and contrast settlement patterns, treatment of Indians, and religion of the Spanish and English in the Americas.

2. For English settlers, land was the basis of independence and liberty. Explain the reasoning behind that concept and how it differed from the Indians' conception of land.

3. Describe the factors promoting and limiting religious freedom in the New England and Chesapeake colonies.

4. Describe who chose to emigrate to North America from England in the seventeenth century and explain their reasons.

5. In what ways did the economy, government, and household structure differ in New England and the Chesapeake colonies?

6. The English believed that, unlike the Spanish, their motives for colonization were pure, and that the growth of empire and freedom would always go hand in hand. How did the expansion of the British empire affect the freedoms of Native Americans, the Irish, and even many English citizens?

7. Considering politics, social tensions, and debates over the meaning of liberty, how do the events and aftermath of the English Civil War demonstrate that the English colonies in North America were part of a larger Atlantic community?

8. How did the tobacco economy draw the Chesapeake colonies into the greater Atlantic world?

KEY TERMS

Virginia Company (p. 49)

Anglican Church (p. 50)

Roanoke colony (p. 51)

enclosure movement (p. 52)

John Smith (p. 58)

headright system (p. 59)

House of Burgesses (p. 59)

Uprising of 1622 (p. 60)

dower rights (p. 62)

Puritans (p. 64)

John Winthrop (p. 65)

Pilgrims (p. 66)

Mayflower Compact (p. 66)

Great Migration (p. 67)

Dissenters (p. 71)

captivity narratives (p. 73)

Pequot War (p. 76)

Half-Way Covenant (p. 78)

English liberty (p. 79)

Act Concerning Religion (or Maryland Toleration Act) (p. 82)

Go to 🐇 INQUIZITIVE

To see what you know—and learn what you've missed—with personalized feedback along the way.

Visit the *Give Me Liberty!* **Student Site** for primary source documents and images, interactive maps, author videos featuring Eric Foner, and more.

1651	First Navigation Act issued by Parliament
1664	English seize New Netherland, which becomes New York
1670	First English settlers arrive in Carolina
1675	Lords of Trade established
1675–1676	King Philip's War
1676	Bacon's Rebellion
1677	Covenant Chain alliance
1681	William Penn granted Pennsylvania
1682	Charter of Liberty drafted by Penn
1683	Charter of Liberties and Privileges drafted by New York assembly
1686–1689	Dominion of New England
1688	Glorious Revolution in England
1689	Parliament enacts a Bill of Rights
	Maryland Protestant Association revolts
	Leisler's Rebellion
	Parliament passes Toleration Act
1691	Plymouth colony absorbed into Massachusetts
1692	Salem witch trials
1705	Virginia passes Slave Code
1715–1717	Yamasee uprising
1737	Walking Purchase

GLOBAL COMPETITION AND THE EXPANSION OF ENGLAND'S EMPIRE

The Mercantilist System

As the New World became a battleground in European nations' endless contests for wealth and power, England moved to seize control of Atlantic trade, solidify its hold on North America's eastern coast, and exert greater control over its empire. By the middle of the seventeenth century, it was apparent that the colonies could be an important source of wealth for the mother country. According to the prevailing theory known as **mercantilism**, the government should regulate economic activity so as to promote national power. It should encourage manufacturing and commerce by special bounties, monopolies, and other measures. Above all, trade should be controlled so that more gold and silver flowed into the country than left it. That is, exports of goods, which generated revenue from abroad, should exceed imports, which required paying foreigners for their products. In the mercantilist outlook, the role of colonies was to serve the interests of the mother country by producing marketable raw materials and importing manufactured goods from home. "Foreign trade," declared an influential work written in 1664 by a London merchant, formed the basis of "England's treasure." Commerce, not territorial plunder, was the foundation of empire.

Under Oliver Cromwell, Parliament passed in 1651 the first **Navigation Act**, which aimed to wrest control of world trade from the Dutch, whose merchants profited from free trade with all parts of the world and all existing empires. Additional measures followed in 1660 and 1663. England's new economic policy, mercantilism, rested on the idea that England should monopolize the profits arising from the English empire.

According to the Navigation laws, certain "enumerated" goods—essentially, the most valuable colonial products, such as tobacco and sugar—had to be transported in English ships and sold initially in English ports, although they could then be re-exported to foreign markets. Similarly, most European goods imported into the colonies had to be shipped through England, where customs duties were paid. This enabled English merchants, manufacturers, shipbuilders, and sailors to reap the benefits of colonial trade, and the government to enjoy added income from taxes. As members of the empire, American colonies would profit as well, since their ships were considered English. Indeed, the Navigation Acts stimulated the rise of New England's shipbuilding industry.

The Conquest of New Netherland

The restoration of the English monarchy when Charles II assumed the throne in 1660 sparked a new period of colonial expansion. The government chartered new trading ventures, notably the Royal African Company, which was given a monopoly of the slave trade. Within a generation, the number of English colonies in North America doubled. First to come under English control was New Netherland, seized in 1664 during an Anglo-Dutch war that also saw England gain control of Dutch trading posts in Africa. Charles II awarded the colony to his younger brother

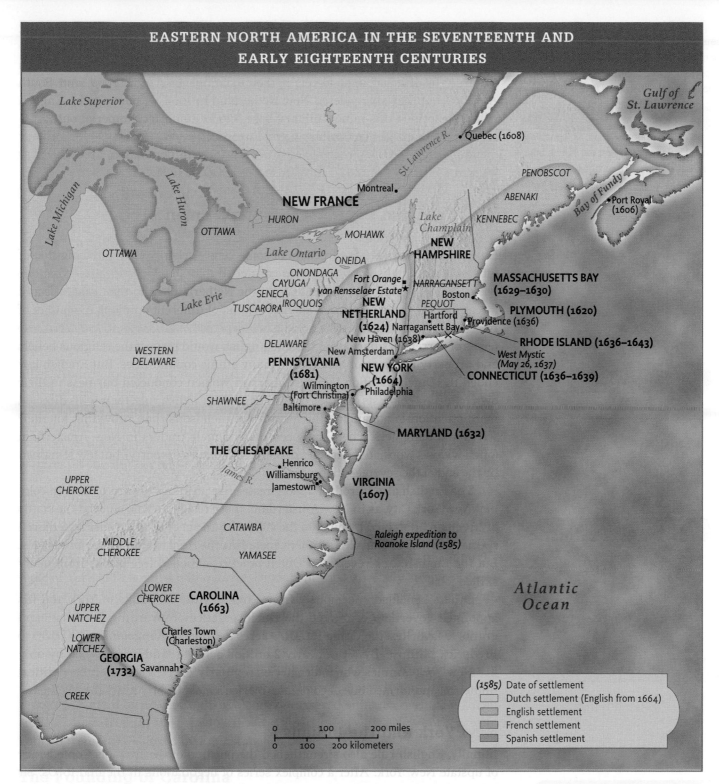

EASTERN NORTH AMERICA IN THE SEVENTEENTH AND EARLY EIGHTEENTH CENTURIES

Lake Superior

Gulf of St. Lawrence

Quebec (1608)

PENOBSCOT

Montreal

NEW FRANCE

Bay of Fundy

Port Royal (1606)

ABENAKI

Lake Huron

Lake Michigan

HURON

KENNEBEC

OTTAWA

MOHAWK

Lake Champlain

NEW HAMPSHIRE

OTTAWA

Lake Ontario

ONEIDA

ONONDAGA

CAYUGA

Fort Orange

NARRAGANSETT

MASSACHUSETTS BAY (1629–1630)

SENECA

van Rensselaer Estate ★

Boston

TUSCARORA

IROQUOIS

NEW NETHERLAND (1624)

PEQUOT

PLYMOUTH (1620)

Lake Erie

Hartford

Providence (1636)

Narragansett Bay

RHODE ISLAND (1636–1643)

WESTERN DELAWARE

DELAWARE

New Haven (1638)

New Amsterdam

West Mystic (May 26, 1637)

PENNSYLVANIA (1681)

NEW YORK (1664)

CONNECTICUT (1636–1639)

Wilmington (Fort Christina)

Philadelphia

SHAWNEE

Baltimore

MARYLAND (1632)

THE CHESAPEAKE

Henrico

UPPER CHEROKEE

James R.

Williamsburg

Jamestown

VIRGINIA (1607)

CATAWBA

MIDDLE CHEROKEE

Raleigh expedition to Roanoke Island (1585)

YAMASEE

Atlantic Ocean

LOWER CHEROKEE

CAROLINA (1663)

UPPER NATCHEZ

LOWER NATCHEZ

Charles Town (Charleston)

GEORGIA (1732)

Savannah

CREEK

(1585) Date of settlement
  Dutch settlement (English from 1664)
  English settlement
  French settlement
  Spanish settlement

0   100   200 miles
0   100   200 kilometers

By the early eighteenth century, numerous English colonies populated eastern North America, while the French had established their own presence to the north and west.

Indian slavery

found Carolina. In its early years, Carolina was the "colony of a colony." It began as an offshoot of the tiny island of Barbados. In the mid-seventeenth century, Barbados was the Caribbean's richest plantation economy, but a shortage of available land led wealthy planters to seek opportunities in Carolina for their sons. The early settlers of Carolina sought Indian allies by offering guns for deer hides and captives, a policy that unleashed widespread raiding among Indians for slaves to sell. The colonists also encouraged native allies to attack Indians in Spanish Florida; in one series of wars between 1704 and 1706 the Creek, Savannah, and Yamasee enslaved almost 10,000 Florida Indians, most of them shipped to other mainland colonies and the West Indies. Indeed, between 1670 and 1720, the number of Indian slaves exported from Charleston was larger than the number of African slaves imported. In 1715, the Yamasee and Creek, alarmed by the enormous debts they had incurred in trade with the settlers and by slave traders' raids into their territory, rebelled. The **Yamasee uprising** was crushed, and most of the remaining Indians were enslaved or driven out of the colony into Spanish Florida, from where they occasionally launched raids against English settlements.

The Fundamental Constitutions
of Carolina

The Fundamental Constitutions of Carolina, issued by the proprietors in 1669, proposed to establish a feudal society with a hereditary nobility (with strange titles like landgraves and caciques), serfs, and slaves. Needing to attract settlers quickly, however, the proprietors also provided for an elected assembly and religious toleration—by now recognized as essential to enticing migrants to North America. They also instituted a generous headright system, offering 150 acres for each member of an arriving family (in the case of indentured servants, of course, the land went to the employer) and 100 acres to male servants who completed their terms.

None of the baronies envisioned in the Fundamental Constitutions were actually established. Slavery, not feudalism, made Carolina an extremely hierarchical society. The proprietors instituted a rigorous legal code that promised slaveowners "absolute power and authority" over their human property and included imported slaves in the headright system. This allowed any persons who settled in Carolina and brought with them slaves, including planters from Barbados who resettled in the colony, instantly to acquire large new landholdings. In its early days, however, the economy centered on cattle raising and trade with local Indians, not agriculture. Carolina grew slowly until planters discovered the staple—rice—that would make them the wealthiest elite in English North America and their colony an epicenter of mainland slavery.

A portrait of William Penn, founder of Pennsylvania, by the British artist Francis Place.

The Holy Experiment

The last English colony to be established in the seventeenth century was Pennsylvania. The proprietor, William Penn, envisioned it as a place where those facing religious persecution in Europe could enjoy spiritual freedom, and colonists and Indians would coexist in harmony. Penn's late father had been a supporter and creditor of Charles II. To cancel his debt to the Penn family and bolster the English presence in North America, the king in 1681 granted Penn a vast tract of land south and west of New York, as well as the old Swedish-Dutch colony that became Delaware.

Th

Evi
the
nun
serv
Virg
the
shai
cour
At tl

was
(Thi
thro
slav
1667
relea
slave
tion
puni
freei
even
well
rary,
conv
mula
try a:

Bac

Virgi
plant
tions
thirt
wealt
lucra
plant
to ac
with
popu
to wo
tobac
of sm
remir
adult
peace
allow
coloni

A devout member of the **Society of Friends, or Quakers**, Penn was particularly concerned with establishing a refuge for his coreligionists, who faced increasing persecution in England. He had already assisted a group of English Quakers in purchasing half of what became the colony of New Jersey from Lord John Berkeley, who had received a land grant from the duke of York. Penn was largely responsible for the frame of government announced in 1677, the West Jersey Concessions, one of the most liberal of the era. Based on Quaker ideals, it created an elected assembly with a broad suffrage and established religious liberty. Penn hoped that West Jersey would become a society of small farmers, not large landowners.

Quaker Liberty

Like the Puritans, Penn considered his colony a "holy experiment," but of a different kind—"a free colony for all mankind that should go hither." He hoped that Pennsylvania could be governed according to Quaker principles, among them the equality of all persons (including women, blacks, and Indians) before God and the primacy of the individual conscience. To Quakers, liberty was a universal entitlement, not the possession of any single people—a position that would eventually make them the first group of whites to repudiate slavery. Penn also treated Indians with a consideration almost unique in the colonial experience, arranging to purchase land before reselling it to colonists and offering refuge to tribes driven out of other colonies by warfare. Sometimes, he even purchased the same land twice, when more than one Indian tribe claimed it. Since Quakers were pacifists who came to America unarmed and did not even organize a militia until the 1740s, peace with the native population was essential. Penn's Chain of Friendship appealed to the local Indians, promising protection from rival tribes who claimed domination over them.

Religious freedom was Penn's most fundamental principle. He condemned attempts to enforce "religious Uniformity" for depriving thousands of "free inhabitants" of England of the right to worship as they desired. His Charter of Liberty, approved by the assembly in 1682, offered "Christian liberty" to all who affirmed a belief in God and did not use their freedom to promote "licentiousness." There was no established church in Pennsylvania, and attendance at religious services was entirely voluntary, although Jews were barred from office by a required oath affirming belief in the divinity of Jesus Christ. At the same time, the Quakers upheld a strict code of personal morality. Penn's Frame of Government prohibited swearing, drunkenness, and adultery, as well as popular entertainments of the era such as "revels, bull-baiting, and cock-fighting." Private religious belief may not have been enforced by the government, but moral public behavior certainly was. Not religious uniformity but a virtuous citizenry would be the foundation of Penn's social order.

An early-eighteenth-century engraving depicts William Penn welcoming a German immigrant on the dock in Philadelphia. Penn sought to make migrants from all over Europe feel at home in Pennsylvania.

Penn and religious liberty

CHAPTER 4

SLAVERY, FREEDOM, AND THE STRUGGLE FOR EMPIRE

★

TO 1763

Sometime in the mid-1750s, Olaudah Equiano, the eleven-year-old son of a West African village chief, was kidnapped by slave traders. He soon found himself on a ship headed for Barbados. After a short stay on that Caribbean island, Equiano was sold to a plantation owner in Virginia and then purchased by a British sea captain, who renamed him Gustavus Vassa. He accompanied his owner on numerous voyages on Atlantic trading vessels. While still a slave, he enrolled in a school in England where he learned to read and write, and then enlisted in the Royal Navy. He fought in Canada under General James Wolfe in 1758 during the Seven Years' War. In 1763, however, Equiano was sold once again and returned to the Caribbean. Three years later, he was able to purchase his freedom. Equiano went on to live through shipwrecks, took part in an English colonizing venture in Central America, and even participated in an expedition to the Arctic Circle.

Equiano eventually settled in London, and in 1789 he published *The Interesting Narrative of the Life of Olaudah Equiano, or Gustavus Vassa, the African*, which he described as a "history of neither a saint, a hero, nor a tyrant," but of a victim of slavery who through luck or fate ended up more fortunate than most of his people. He condemned the idea that Africans were inferior to Europeans and therefore deserved to be slaves. He urged the European reader to recall that "his ancestors were once, like the Africans, uncivilized" and asked, "Did nature make them inferior . . . and should they too have been made slaves?" Persons of all races, he insisted, were capable of intellectual improvement. The book became the era's most widely read account by a slave of his own experiences. Equiano died in 1797.

Recent scholars have suggested that Equiano may actually have been born in the New World rather than Africa. In either case, while his rich variety of experience was no doubt unusual, his life illuminates broad patterns of eighteenth-century American history. As noted in the previous chapter, this was a period of sustained development for British North America. Compared to England and Scotland—united to create Great Britain by the Act of Union of 1707—the colonies were growing much more rapidly. Some contemporaries spoke of British America as a "rising empire" that would one day eclipse the mother country in population and wealth.

It would be wrong, however, to see the first three-quarters of the eighteenth century simply as a prelude to American independence. As Equiano's life illustrates, the Atlantic was more a bridge than a barrier between the Old and New Worlds. Ideas, people, and goods flowed back and forth across the ocean. Even as the colonies' populations became more diverse, they were increasingly integrated into the British empire. Their laws and political institutions were extensions of those of Britain, their ideas about society and culture reflected British values, their economies were geared to serving the empire's needs. As European powers jockeyed for advantage in North America, colonists were drawn into an almost continuous series of wars with France and its Indian allies, which reinforced their sense of identification with and dependence on Great Britain.

Equiano's life also underscores the greatest irony or contradiction in the history of the eighteenth century—the simultaneous expansion of freedom and slavery. This was the era when the idea of the "freeborn Englishman" became

FOCUS QUESTIONS

How did African slavery differ regionally in eighteenth-century North America? *–p. 128*

What factors led to distinct African-American cultures in the eighteenth century? *–p. 136*

What were the meanings of British liberty in the eighteenth century? *–p. 140*

What concepts and institutions dominated colonial politics in the eighteenth century? *–p. 143*

How did the Great Awakening challenge the religious and social structure of British North America? *–p. 149*

How did the Spanish and French empires in America develop in the eighteenth century? *–p. 151*

What was the impact of the Seven Years' War on imperial and Indian–white relations? *–p. 156*

Benjamin Latrobe's watercolor, *An Overseer Doing His Duty*, was sketched near Fredericksburg, Virginia, in 1798. The title is meant to be ironic: the well-dressed overseer relaxes while two female slaves work in the fields.

127

1689	Locke's *Two Treatises of Government* published
1707	Act of Union creating Great Britain
1712	Slave uprising in New York City
1718	French establish New Orleans
1720–1723	*Cato's Letters*
1727	Junto club founded
1728	*Pennsylvania Gazette* established
1730s	Beginnings of the Great Awakening
1732	Georgia colony founded
1735	John Peter Zenger tried for libel
1739	Stono Rebellion
1741	Rumors of slave revolt in New York
1749	Virginia awards land to the Ohio Company
1756–1763	Seven Years' War
1754	Albany Plan of Union proposed
1763	Pontiac's Rebellion
	Proclamation of 1763
1764	Paxton Boys march on Philadelphia
1769	Father Serra establishes first mission in California
1789	*The Interesting Narrative of the Life of Olaudah Equiano* published

powerfully entrenched in the outlook of both colonists and Britons. More than any other principle, liberty was seen as what made the British empire distinct. Yet the eighteenth century was also the height of the Atlantic slave trade, a commerce increasingly dominated by British merchants and ships. One of the most popular songs of the period included the refrain, "Britons never, never, never will be slaves." But during the eighteenth century, more than half the Africans shipped to the New World as slaves were carried on British vessels. Most were destined for the plantations of the West Indies and Brazil, but slaves also made up around 280,000 of the 585,000 persons who arrived in Britain's mainland colonies between 1700 and 1775. Although concentrated in the Chesapeake and areas farther south, slavery existed in every colony of British North America. And unlike Equiano, very few slaves were fortunate enough to gain their freedom.

SLAVERY AND EMPIRE

Of the estimated 10 million Africans transported to the New World between 1492 and 1820, more than half arrived between 1700 and 1800. The **Atlantic slave trade** would later be condemned by statesmen and general opinion as a crime against humanity. But in the eighteenth century, it was a regularized business in which European merchants, African traders, and American planters engaged in complex bargaining over human lives, all with the expectation of securing a profit. The slave trade was a vital part of world commerce. Every European empire in the New World utilized slave labor and battled for control of this lucrative trade. The *asiento*—an agreement whereby Spain subcontracted to a foreign power the right to provide slaves to Spanish America—was an important diplomatic prize. Britain's acquisition of the *asiento* from the Dutch in the Treaty of Utrecht of 1713 was a major step in its rise to commercial supremacy.

In the British empire of the eighteenth century, free laborers working for wages were atypical and slavery was the norm. Slave plantations contributed mightily to English economic development. The first mass consumer goods in international trade were produced by slaves—sugar, rice, coffee, and tobacco. The rising demand for these products fueled the rapid growth of the Atlantic slave trade.

Atlantic Trade

In the eighteenth century, the Caribbean remained the commercial focus of the British empire and the major producer of revenue for the crown. But slave-grown products from the mainland occupied a larger and larger part of Atlantic commerce. A series of triangular trading routes crisscrossed the Atlantic, carrying British manufactured goods to Africa and the colonies, colonial products to Europe, and slaves from Africa to the New World. Most colonial vessels, however, went back and forth between cities like New York, Charleston, and Savannah, and to ports in the Caribbean. Areas where slavery was only a minor institution also profited from slave labor. Merchants in New York, Massachusetts, and Rhode Island participated actively in the slave trade, shipping slaves from Africa to the Caribbean or southern

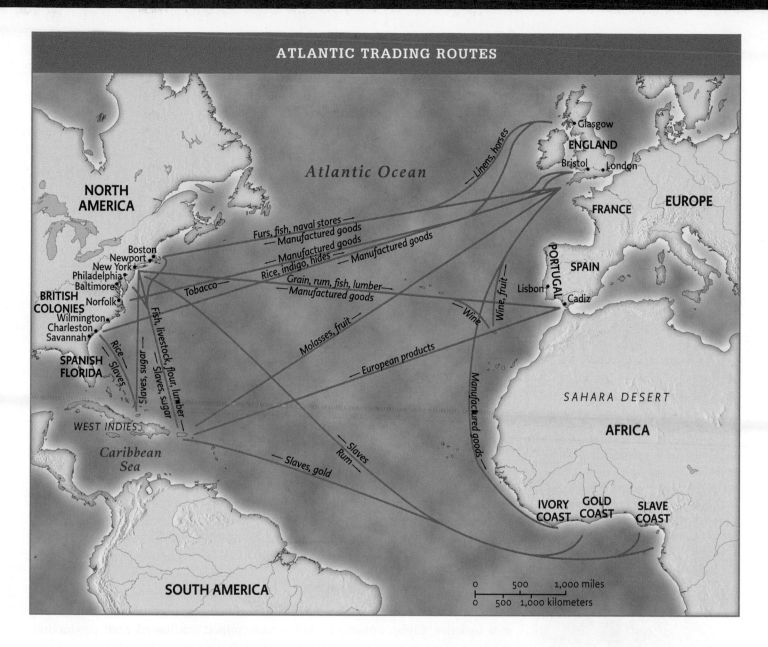

ATLANTIC TRADING ROUTES

A series of trading routes crisscrossed the Atlantic, bringing manufactured goods to Africa and Britain's American colonies, slaves to the New World, and colonial products to Europe.

colonies. The slave economies of the West Indies were the largest market for fish, grain, livestock, and lumber exported from New England and the Middle Colonies. Indeed, one historian writes, "The growth and prosperity of the emerging society of free colonial British America . . . were achieved as a result of slave labor." In Britain itself, the profits from slavery and the slave trade stimulated the rise of ports like Liverpool and Bristol and the growth of banking, shipbuilding, and insurance. They also helped to finance the early industrial revolution.

Overall, in the eighteenth century, Atlantic commerce consisted primarily of slaves, crops produced by slaves, and goods destined for slave societies. It should not be surprising that for large numbers of free colonists and Europeans, freedom meant in part the power and right to enslave others. And as slavery became more and more entrenched, so too, as the Quaker abolitionist John Woolman commented

A mid-eighteenth-century image of a woman going to church in Lima, Peru, accompanied by two slaves. Slavery existed throughout the Western Hemisphere.

The frontispiece of Olaudah Equiano's account of his life, the best-known narrative by an eighteenth-century slave. The portrait of Equiano in European dress and holding a Bible challenges stereotypes of blacks as "savages" incapable of becoming civilized.

in 1762, did "the idea of slavery being connected with the black color, and liberty with the white."

Africa and the Slave Trade

A few African societies, like Benin for a time, opted out of the Atlantic slave trade, hoping to avoid the disruptions it inevitably caused. But most African rulers took part, and they proved quite adept at playing the Europeans off against one another, collecting taxes from foreign merchants, and keeping the capture and sale of slaves under their own control. Few Europeans ventured inland from the coast. Traders remained in their "factories" and purchased slaves brought to them by African rulers and dealers.

The transatlantic slave trade made Africa a major market for European goods, especially textiles and guns. Both disrupted relationships within and among African societies. Cheap imported textiles undermined traditional craft production, while guns encouraged the further growth of slavery, since the only way to obtain European weapons was to supply slaves. By the eighteenth century, militarized states like Ashanti and Dahomey would arise in West Africa, with large armies using European firearms to prey on their neighbors in order to capture slaves. From a minor institution, slavery grew to become more and more central to West African society, a source of wealth for African merchants and of power for newly emerging African kingdoms. But the loss every year of tens of thousands of men and women in the prime of their lives to the slave trade weakened and distorted West Africa's society and economy.

The Middle Passage

For slaves, the voyage across the Atlantic—known as the **Middle Passage** because it was the second, or middle, leg in the triangular trading routes linking Europe, Africa,

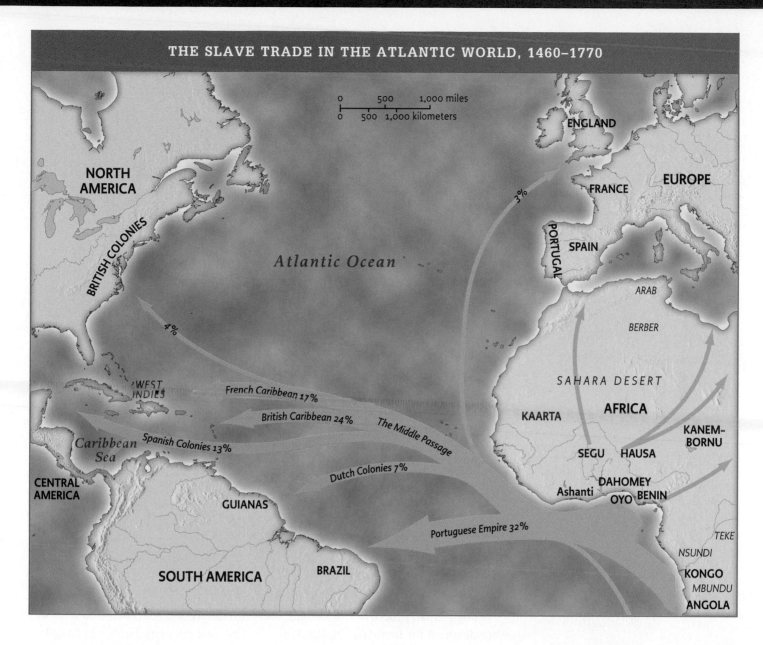

THE SLAVE TRADE IN THE ATLANTIC WORLD, 1460–1770

The Atlantic slave trade expanded rapidly in the eighteenth century. The mainland colonies received only a tiny proportion of the Africans brought to the New World, most of whom were transported to Brazil and the West Indies.

and America—was a harrowing experience. Since a slave could be sold in America for twenty to thirty times the price in Africa, men, women, and children were crammed aboard vessels as tightly as possible to maximize profits. "The height, sometimes, between decks," wrote one slave trader, "was only eighteen inches, so that the unfortunate human beings could not turn around, or even on their sides . . . and here they are usually chained to the decks by their necks and legs." Equiano, who later described "the shrieks of the women and the groans of the dying," survived the Middle Passage, but many Africans did not. Diseases like measles and smallpox spread rapidly, and about one slave in five perished before reaching the New World. Ship captains were known to throw the sick overboard in order to prevent the spread of epidemics. The crews on slave ships also suffered a high death rate.

This image, made by a sailor in 1769 for the ship's owner, a merchant in Nantes, France, depicts a slave-trading vessel, the *Marie-Séraphique*, anchored off the African coast, and the ship's interior. The cargo carried in barrels, generally guns, cloth, and metal goods, was to be traded for slaves. The third image from the left depicts the conditions under which slaves endured the Middle Passage across the Atlantic. The ship carried over 300 slaves. The broadside also included a calculation of the profit of the voyage.

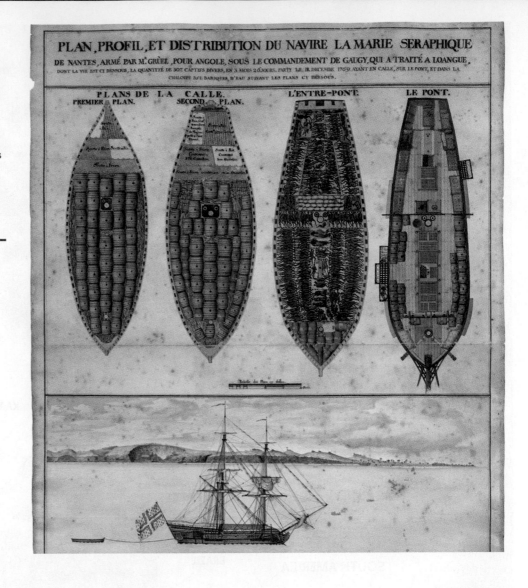

Only a small proportion (less than 5 percent) of slaves carried to the New World were destined for mainland North America. The vast majority landed in Brazil or the West Indies, where the high death rate on the sugar plantations led to a constant demand for new slave imports. As late as 1700, only about 20,000 Africans had been landed in Britain's colonies in North America. In the eighteenth century, however, their numbers increased steadily. Overall, the area that was to become the United States imported between 400,000 and 600,000 slaves. By 1770, due to the natural reproduction of the slave population, around one-fifth of the estimated 2.3 million persons (not including Indians) living in the English colonies of North America were Africans and their descendants.

Chesapeake Slavery

By the mid-eighteenth century, three distinct slave systems were well entrenched in Britain's mainland colonies: tobacco-based plantation slavery in the Chesapeake, rice-based plantation slavery in South Carolina and Georgia, and nonplantation

Slave population

slavery in New England and the Middle Colonies. The largest and oldest of these was the tobacco plantation system of the Chesapeake, where more than 270,000 slaves resided in 1770, nearly half of the region's population. On the eve of the Revolution, Virginia and Maryland were as closely tied to Britain as any other colonies and their economies were models of mercantilist policy (described in Chapter 3). They supplied the mother country with a valuable agricultural product, imported large amounts of British goods, and were closely linked in culture and political values to London. As we have seen, the period after 1680 witnessed a rapid shift from indentured servitude to slavery on the region's tobacco plantations. In the eighteenth century, the growing world demand for tobacco encouraged continued slave imports.

> *Ties to Britain*

As Virginia expanded westward, so did slavery. By the eve of the American Revolution, the center of gravity of slavery in the colony had shifted from the Tidewater (the region along the coast) to the Piedmont farther inland. Most Chesapeake slaves, male and female, worked in the fields, but thousands labored as teamsters, as boatmen, and in skilled crafts. Numerous slave women became cooks, seamstresses, dairy maids, and personal servants. The son of George Mason, one of Virginia's leading planters and statesmen, recorded that his father's slaves included "coopers, sawyers, blacksmiths, tanners, shoemakers, spinners, weavers, knitters, and even a distiller." Slavery was common on small farms as well as plantations; nearly half of Virginia's white families owned at least one slave in 1770.

> *Types of slave labor*

Slavery laid the foundation for the consolidation of the Chesapeake elite, a landed gentry that, in conjunction with merchants who handled the tobacco trade and lawyers who defended the interests of slaveholders, dominated the region's society and politics. Meanwhile, even as the consumer revolution improved the standard of living of lesser whites, their long-term economic prospects diminished. As slavery expanded, planters engrossed the best lands and wealth among the white population became more and more concentrated. Slavery transformed Chesapeake society into an elaborate hierarchy of degrees of freedom. At the top stood large planters, below them numerous lesser planters and landowning yeomen, and at the bottom a large population of convicts, indentured servants, tenant farmers (who made up half the white households in 1770), and, of course, the slaves.

Freedom and Slavery in the Chesapeake

With the consolidation of a slave society in the Chesapeake, planters filled the law books with measures enhancing the master's power over his human property and restricting blacks' access to freedom. Violence lay at the heart of the slave system. Even a planter like Landon Carter, who prided himself on his concern for the well-being of his slaves, noted casually in his diary, "They have been severely whipped day by day."

Race took on more and more importance as a line of social division. Whites increasingly considered free blacks dangerous and undesirable. Free blacks lost the right to employ white servants and to bear arms, were subjected to special taxes, and could be punished for striking a white person, regardless of the cause. In 1723, Virginia revoked the voting privileges of property-owning free blacks. When the Lords of Trade in London asked Virginia's governor to justify discriminating among "freemen, merely upon account of their complexion," he responded that "a distinction ought to be made between their offspring and the descendants of an Englishman, with whom they

Young Charles Calvert, a member of an aristocratic Maryland family, painted in 1761 by John Hesselius, who produced numerous portraits of prominent residents of the Chesapeake. The boy, obviously the son of wealthy parents, stands next to a young slave, a symbol of his family's wealth. Calvert holds drumsticks and the slave his drum, an allusion to a possible future military career.

never were to be accounted equal." Because Virginia law required that freed slaves be sent out of the colony, free blacks remained only a tiny part of the population—less than 4 percent in 1750. "Free" and "white" had become virtually identical.

Indian Slavery in Early Carolina

Sale of Indian slaves

Farther south, a different slave system, based on rice production, emerged in South Carolina and Georgia. The Barbadians who initially settled South Carolina in the 1670s were quite familiar with African slavery, but their first victims were members of the area's native population. The local Creek Indians initially welcomed the settlers and began selling them slaves, generally war captives and their families, most of whom were sold to the West Indies. They even launched wars against neighboring tribes specifically for the purpose of capturing and selling slaves. As the plantation system expanded, however, the Creeks became more and more concerned, not only because it led to encroachments on their land but also because they feared enslavement themselves. They were aware that only a handful of slaves worked in nearby Spanish Florida. The Creeks, one leader remarked in 1738, preferred to deal with the Spanish, who "enslave no one as the English do."

The Rice Kingdom

As in early Virginia, frontier conditions allowed leeway to South Carolina's small population of African-born slaves, who farmed, tended livestock, and were initially allowed to serve in the militia to fight the Spanish and Indians. And as in Virginia, the introduction of a marketable staple crop, in this case rice, led directly to economic development, the large-scale importation of slaves, and a growing divide between white and black. South Carolina was the first mainland colony to achieve a black majority. By the 1730s (by which time North Carolina had become a separate colony), two-thirds of its population was black. In the 1740s, another staple, indigo (a crop used in producing blue dye), was developed. Like rice, indigo required large-scale cultivation and was grown by slaves.

Ironically, it was Africans, familiar with the crop at home, who taught English settlers how to cultivate rice, which then became the foundation of South Carolina slavery and of the wealthiest slaveowning class on the North American mainland. Since rice production requires considerable capital investment to drain swamps and create irrigation systems, it is economically advantageous for rice plantations to be as large as possible. Thus, South Carolina planters owned far more land and slaves than their counterparts in Virginia. Moreover, since mosquitoes bearing malaria (a disease to which Africans had developed partial immunity) flourished in the watery rice fields, planters tended to leave plantations under the control of overseers and the slaves themselves.

In the Chesapeake, field slaves worked in groups under constant supervision. Under the "task" system that developed in eighteenth-century South Carolina, individual slaves were assigned daily jobs, the completion of which allowed them time for leisure or to cultivate crops of their own. In 1762, one rice district had a population of only 76 white males among 1,000 slaves. Fearful of the ever-increasing black population majority, South Carolina's legislature took steps to encourage the immigration of "poor Protestants," offering each newcomer a cash

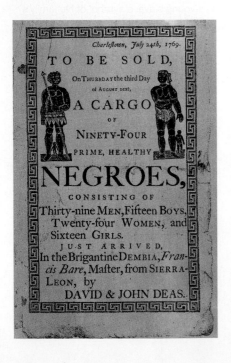

Slave Sale Broadside. This 1769 broadside advertises the sale of ninety-four slaves who had just arrived in Charleston from West Africa. Broadsides like this one were displayed prominently by slave traders to drum up business.

bounty and occasionally levying taxes on slave imports, only to see such restrictions overturned in London. By 1770, the number of South Carolina slaves had reached 75,000, well over half the colony's population.

The Georgia Experiment

Rice cultivation also spread into Georgia in the mid-eighteenth century. The colony was founded in 1732 by a group of philanthropists led by James Oglethorpe, a wealthy reformer whose causes included improved conditions for imprisoned debtors and the abolition of slavery. Oglethorpe hoped to establish a haven where the "worthy poor" of England could enjoy economic opportunity. The government in London supported the creation of Georgia to protect South Carolina against the Spanish and their Indian allies in Florida.

Initially, the proprietors banned the introduction of both liquor and slaves, leading to continual battles with settlers, who desired both. By the 1740s, Georgia offered the spectacle of colonists pleading for the "English liberty" of self-government so that they could enact laws introducing slavery. In 1751, the proprietors surrendered the colony to the crown. The colonists quickly won the right to an elected assembly, which met in Savannah, Georgia's main settlement. It repealed the ban on slavery (and liquor), as well as an early measure that had limited land holdings to 500 acres. Georgia became a miniature version of South Carolina. By 1770, as many as 15,000 slaves labored on its coastal rice plantations.

Founding of Georgia

Slavery in the North

Compared to the plantation regions, slavery was far less central to the economies of New England and the Middle Colonies, where small farms predominated. Slaves made up only a small percentage of these colonies' populations, and it was unusual for even rich families to own more than one or two slaves. Nonetheless, slavery was not entirely marginal to northern colonial life. Slaves worked as farm hands, in artisan shops, as stevedores loading and unloading ships, and as personal servants. With slaves so small a part of the population that they seemed to pose no threat to the white majority, laws were less harsh than in the South. In New England, where in 1770 the 15,000 slaves represented less than 3 percent of the region's population, slave marriages were recognized in law, the severe physical punishment of slaves was prohibited, and slaves could bring suits in court, testify against whites, and own property and pass it on to their children—rights unknown in the South.

Slavery had been present in New York from the earliest days of Dutch settlement. With white immigration lagging behind that of Pennsylvania, the colony's Hudson Valley landlords, small farmers, and craftsmen continued to employ considerable amounts of slave labor in the eighteenth century. As New York City's role in the slave trade expanded, so did slavery in the city. In 1746, its 2,440 slaves

TABLE 4.1 Slave Population as Percentage of Total Population of Original Thirteen Colonies, 1770

COLONY	SLAVE POPULATION	PERCENTAGE
Virginia	187,600	42%
South Carolina	75,168	61
North Carolina	69,600	35
Maryland	63,818	32
New York	19,062	12
Georgia	15,000	45
New Jersey	8,220	7
Connecticut	5,698	3
Pennsylvania	5,561	2
Massachusetts	4,754	2
Rhode Island	3,761	6
Delaware	1,836	5
New Hampshire	654	1

amounted to one-fifth of New York City's total population. Some 30 percent of its laborers were slaves, a proportion second only to Charleston among American cities. Most were domestic workers, but slaves worked in all sectors of the economy. In 1770, about 27,000 slaves lived in New York and New Jersey, 10 percent of their total population. Slavery was also a significant presence in Philadelphia, although the institution stagnated after 1750 as artisans and merchants relied increasingly on wage laborers, whose numbers were augmented by population growth and the completion of the terms of indentured servants. In an urban economy that expanded and contracted according to the ups and downs of international trade, many employers concluded that relying on wage labor, which could be hired and fired at will, made more economic sense than a long-term investment in slaves.

SLAVE CULTURES AND SLAVE RESISTANCE

Becoming African-American

The nearly 300,000 Africans brought to the mainland colonies during the eighteenth century were not a single people. They came from different cultures, spoke different languages, and practiced many religions. Eventually, an African-American people would emerge from the diverse peoples transported to the British colonies in the Middle Passage. Slavery threw together individuals who would never otherwise have encountered one another and who had never considered their color or residence on a single continent a source of identity or unity. Their bond was not kinship, language, or even "race," but slavery itself. The process of creating a cohesive culture and community took many years, and it proceeded at different rates in different regions. But by the nineteenth century, slaves no longer identified themselves as Ibo, Ashanti, Yoruba, and so on, but as African-Americans. In music, art, folklore, language, and religion, their cultural expressions emerged as a synthesis of African traditions, European elements, and new conditions in America.

For most of the eighteenth century, the majority of American slaves were African by birth. Advertisements seeking information about runaways often described them by African origin ("young Gambia Negro," "new Banbara Negro fellow") and spoke of their bearing on their bodies "country marks"—visible signs of ethnic identity in Africa. Indeed, during the eighteenth century, black life in the colonies was "re-Africanized" as the earlier Creoles (slaves born in the New World) came to be outnumbered by large-scale importations from Africa. Compared with the earliest generation of slaves, the newcomers worked harder, died earlier, and had less access to freedom. Charles Hansford, a white Virginia blacksmith, noted in a 1753 poem that he had frequently heard slaves speak of their desire to "reenjoy" life in Africa:

> I oft with pleasure have observ'd how they
> Their sultry country's worth strive to display
> In broken language, how they praise their case
> And happiness when in their native place . . .
> How would they dangers court and pains endure
> If to their country they could get secure!

A portrait of Ayuba Diallo, a Muslim merchant in Senegal who became a victim of the slave trade in 1731 and was transported to Maryland. He escaped in 1733 and with the help of wealthy patrons regained his freedom. Because of Diallo's unusual talents—he knew both English and Arabic and could relate the Koran from memory—he became a celebrity in England, which he visited in 1733. He sat for two portraits by the noted artist William Hoare. This is the earliest known painting of an African who experienced slavery in Britain's North American colonies. Diallo returned to his homeland in 1734.

Slave imports

African Religion in Colonial America

No experience was more wrenching for African slaves in the colonies than the transition from traditional religions to Christianity. Islam had spread across North Africa and the region of the Sahara Desert. The slaves who ended up in British North America, however, came from the forest regions of West Africa, where traditional religions continued to be practiced. Although these religions varied as much as those on other continents, they shared some elements, especially belief in the presence of spiritual forces in nature and a close relationship between the sacred and secular worlds. West Africans, like Europeans, Equiano wrote, believed in a single "Creator of all things," who "governs events" on earth, but otherwise their religious beliefs seemed more similar to those of Native Americans than to Christianity. In West African religions, there was no hard and fast distinction between the secular and spiritual worlds. Nature was suffused with spirits and the dead could influence the living: the spirits of departed "friends or relations always attend them and guard them from the bad spirits of their foes."

West African religions

Although some slaves came to the colonies familiar with Christianity or Islam, the majority of North American slaves practiced traditional African religions (which many Europeans deemed superstition or even witchcraft) well into the eighteenth century. When they did adopt Protestant religious practices, many slaves melded them with traditional beliefs, adding the Christian God to their own pantheon of lesser spirits, whom they continued to worship. A similar process occurred in slave societies like Brazil and Cuba, where African spirits merged with Catholic saints.

Melding of Christianity with traditional beliefs

The Old Plantation, a late-eighteenth-century watercolor, depicts slaves dancing in a plantation's slave quarters, perhaps at a wedding. The musical instruments and pottery are African in origin while much of the clothing is of European manufacture, indicating the mixing of African and white cultures among the era's slaves. The artist has recently been identified as John Rose, owner of a rice plantation near Beaufort, South Carolina.

This portrait of William Duguid, a Boston textile merchant, was painted in 1773 by Prince Demah Barnes. It depicts Duguid wearing imported clothing with an elaborate floral pattern. What makes the painting unique, however, is that Barnes was a slave whose owner, a Massachusetts merchant, encouraged what he called Barnes's "natural genius" and took him on a brief visit to London for training. Still a slave, Barnes enlisted in the Massachusetts militia in 1777 after his Loyalist owners fled the state. He died of smallpox in 1778.

Running away

African-American Cultures

By the mid-eighteenth century, the three slave systems in British North America had produced distinct African-American cultures. In the Chesapeake, because of a more healthful climate, the slave population began to reproduce itself by 1740, creating a more balanced sex ratio than in the seventeenth century and making possible the creation of family-centered slave communities. Because of the small size of most plantations and the large number of white **yeoman farmers**, slaves here were continuously exposed to white culture. They soon learned English, and many were swept up in the religious revivals known as the Great Awakening, discussed later in this chapter.

In South Carolina and Georgia, two very different black societies emerged. On the rice plantations, slaves lived in extremely harsh conditions and had a low birthrate throughout the eighteenth century, making rice production dependent on continued slave imports from Africa. The slaves seldom came into contact with whites and enjoyed far more autonomy than elsewhere in the colonies. The larger structures of their lives were established by slavery, but they were able to create an African-based culture. They constructed African-style houses, chose African names for their children, and spoke Gullah, a language that mixed various African roots and was unintelligible to most whites. Despite a continuing slave trade in which young, single males predominated, slaves slowly created families and communities that bridged generations. The experience of slaves who labored in Charleston and Savannah as servants and skilled workers was quite different. These assimilated more quickly into Euro-American culture, and sexual liaisons between white owners and slave women produced the beginnings of a class of free mulattos.

In the northern colonies, where slaves represented a smaller part of the population, dispersed in small holdings among the white population, a distinctive African-American culture developed more slowly. Living in close proximity to whites, they enjoyed more mobility and access to the mainstream of life than their counterparts farther south. But they had fewer opportunities to create stable family life or a cohesive community.

Resistance to Slavery

The common threads that linked these regional African-American cultures were the experience of slavery and the desire for freedom. Throughout the eighteenth century, blacks risked their lives in efforts to resist enslavement. Colonial newspapers, especially in the southern colonies, were filled with advertisements for runaway slaves. Most fugitives were young African men who had arrived recently. In South Carolina and Georgia, they fled to Florida, to uninhabited coastal and river swamps, or to Charleston and Savannah, where they could pass for free. In the Chesapeake and Middle Colonies, fugitive slaves tended to be familiar with white culture and therefore, as one advertisement put it, could "pretend to be free."

What Edward Trelawny, the colonial governor of Jamaica, called "a dangerous spirit of liberty" was widespread among the New World's slaves. The eighteenth century's first slave uprising occurred in New York City in 1712, when a group of slaves set fire to houses on the outskirts of the city and killed the first nine whites who arrived on the scene. Subsequently, eighteen conspirators were executed; some were tortured and burned alive in a public spectacle meant to intimidate the slave population. During the 1730s and 1740s, continuous warfare involving European empires and Indians opened the door to slave resistance. In 1731, a slave rebellion in Louisiana, where the French and Natchez Indians were at war, temporarily halted efforts to introduce the plantation system in that region. There were uprisings throughout the West Indies, including in the Virgin Islands, owned by Denmark, and on the French island of Guadeloupe. On Jamaica, a major British center of sugar production, communities of fugitive slaves known as "maroons" waged outright warfare against British authorities until a treaty of 1739 recognized their freedom, in exchange for which they agreed to return future escapees.

RUN AWAY

THE 18th Inftant at Night from the Subfcriber, in the City of New-York, four Negro Men, Viz. LESTER, about 40 Years of Age, had on a white Flannel Jacket and Drawers, Duck Trowfers and Home-fpun Shirt. CÆSAR, about 18 Years of Age, cloth-ed in the fame Manner. ISAAC, aged 17 Years cloathed in the fame Manner, except that his Breeches were Leather; and MINGO, 15 Years of Age, with the fame Clothing as the 2 firft, all of them of a middling Size, Whoever delivers either of the faid Negroes to the Subfcriber, fhall receive TWENTY SHILLINGS Reward for each befide all reafonable Charges. If any perfon can give Intelligence of their being harbour'd, a reward of TEN POUNDS will be paid upon conviction of the Offender. All Mafters of Veffels and others are forewarn'd not to Tranfport them from the City, as I am refolved to profecute as far as the Law will allow. WILLIAM BULL.

N. B. If the Negroes return, they fhall be pardon'd. - 88

An advertisement seeking the return of four runaway slaves from New York City. Note the careful description of the fugitives' clothing and the diversity of the names, presumably given by their owners—two common English names, one of African origin and one alluding to ancient Rome. The reward offered is a substantial amount of money in the colonial era.

The Crisis of 1739–1741

On the mainland, slaves seized the opportunity for rebellion offered by the War of Jenkins' Ear, which pitted England against Spain. In September 1739, a group of South Carolina slaves, most of them recently arrived from Kongo where some, it appears, had been soldiers, seized a store containing numerous weapons at the town of Stono. Beating drums to attract followers, the armed band marched southward toward Florida, burning houses and barns, killing whites they encountered, and shouting "Liberty." (Florida's Spanish rulers offered "Liberty and Protection" to fugitives from the British colonies.) The group eventually swelled to some 100 slaves. After a pitched battle with the colony's militia, the rebels were dispersed. The rebellion took the lives of more than two dozen whites and as many as 200 slaves, including many who had no connection to the rebellion. Some slaves managed to reach Florida, where in 1740 they were armed by the Spanish to help repel an attack on St. Augustine by a force from Georgia. The **Stono Rebellion** led to a severe tightening of the South Carolina slave code and the temporary imposition of a prohibitive tax on imported slaves.

The Stono Rebellion

In 1741, a panic (which some observers compared to the fear of witches in Salem in the 1690s) swept New York City. After a series of fires broke out, rumors spread that slaves, with some white allies, planned to burn part of the city, seize weapons, and either turn New York over to Spain or murder the white population. More than 150 blacks and 20 whites were arrested, and 34 alleged conspirators, including 4 white persons, were executed. Historians still disagree as to how extensive the plot was or whether it existed at all. But dramatic events like revolts, along with the constant stream of runaways, disproved the idea, voiced by the governor of South Carolina, that slaves had "no notion of liberty." In eighteenth-century America, dreams of freedom knew no racial boundary.

Panic in New York

AN EMPIRE OF FREEDOM

British Patriotism

Despite the centrality of slavery to its empire, eighteenth-century Great Britain prided itself on being the world's most advanced and freest nation. It was not only the era's greatest naval and commercial power but also the home of a complex governmental system with a powerful Parliament representing the interests of a self-confident landed aristocracy and merchant class. In London, the largest city in Europe with a population approaching 1 million by the end of the eighteenth century, Britain possessed a single political-cultural-economic capital. It enjoyed a common law, common language, and, with the exception of a small number of Jews, Catholics, and Africans, common devotion to Protestantism. For much of the eighteenth century, Britain found itself at war with France, which had replaced Spain as its major continental rival. This situation led to the development of a large military establishment, high taxes, and the creation of the Bank of England to help finance European and imperial conflicts. For both Britons and colonists, war helped to sharpen a sense of national identity against foreign foes.

British patriotic sentiment became more and more assertive as the eighteenth century progressed. Symbols of British identity proliferated: the songs "God Save the King" and "Rule, Britannia," and even the modern rules of cricket, the national sport. The rapidly expanding British economy formed another point of pride uniting Britons and colonists. Continental peoples, according to a popular saying, wore "wooden shoes"—that is, their standard of living was far below that of Britons. Especially in contrast to France, Britain saw itself as a realm of widespread prosperity, individual liberty, the rule of law, and the Protestant faith. Wealth, religion, and freedom went together. "There is no Popish nation," wrote the Massachusetts theologian Cotton Mather in 1710, "but what by embracing the Protestant Religion would . . . not only assert themselves into a glorious liberty, but also double their wealth immediately."

The British Constitution

Central to this sense of British identity was the concept of liberty. The fierce political struggles of the English Civil War and the Glorious Revolution bequeathed to eighteenth-century Britons an abiding conviction that liberty was their unique possession. They believed power and liberty to be natural antagonists. To mediate between them, advocates of British freedom celebrated the rule of law, the right to live under legislation to which one's representatives had consented, restraints on the arbitrary exercise of political authority, and rights like trial by jury enshrined in the common law. On both sides of the Atlantic, every political cause, it seemed, wrapped itself in the language of liberty and claimed to be defending the "rights of Englishmen." Continental writers dissatisfied with the lack of liberty in their own countries looked to Britain as a model. The House of Commons, House of Lords, and king each checked the power of the others. This structure, wrote the French political philosopher Baron Montesquieu, made Britain "the one nation in the world whose constitution has political liberty for its purpose." In its "balanced constitution" and the principle that no man, even the king, is above the law, Britons claimed to have devised the best means of preventing political tyranny. Until the 1770s, most

British power

British identity

British liberty

colonists believed themselves to be part of the freest political system mankind had ever known.

As the coexistence of slavery and liberty within the empire demonstrated, British freedom was anything but universal. It was closely identified with the Protestant religion and was invoked to contrast Britons with the "servile" subjects of Catholic countries. It viewed nearly every other nation on earth as "enslaved"—to popery, tyranny, or barbarism. One German military officer commented in 1743 on the British "contempt" of foreigners: "They [pride] themselves not only upon their being free themselves, but being the bulwarks of liberty all over Europe; and they vilify most of the Nations on the continent . . . for being slaves, as they call us." British liberty was fully compatible with wide gradations in personal rights. Yet in the minds of the free residents of Great Britain and its North American colonies, liberty was the bond of empire.

These ideas sank deep roots not only within the "political nation"—those who voted, held office, and engaged in structured political debate—but also far more broadly in British and colonial society. Laborers, sailors, and artisans spoke the language of British freedom as insistently as pamphleteers and parliamentarians. Although most white men in Britain and many in the colonies lacked the right to vote, they influenced public life in other ways, serving on juries, and taking to the streets to protest what they considered oppressive authority. Ordinary persons protested efforts by merchants to raise the cost of bread above the traditional "just price," and the Royal Navy's practice of "impressment"—kidnapping poor men on the streets for maritime service.

A 1770 engraving from the *Boston Gazette* by Paul Revere illustrates the association of British patriotism and liberty. Britannia sits with a liberty cap and her national shield, and releases a bird from a cage.

Protests against authority

Republican Liberty

Liberty was central to two sets of political ideas that flourished in the Anglo-American world. One is termed by scholars **republicanism** (although few in eighteenth-century England used the word, which literally meant a government without a king and conjured up memories of the beheading of Charles I). Republicanism celebrated active participation in public life by economically independent citizens as the essence of liberty. Republicans assumed that only property-owning citizens possessed "virtue"—defined in the eighteenth century not simply as a personal moral quality but as the willingness to subordinate self-interest to the pursuit of the public good. "Only a virtuous people are capable of freedom," wrote Benjamin Franklin.

In eighteenth-century Britain, this body of thought about freedom was most closely associated with a group of critics of the established political order known as the "Country Party" because much of their support arose from the landed gentry. In Britain, Country Party publicists like John Trenchard and Thomas Gordon, authors of *Cato's Letters*, published in the 1720s, had little impact. But their writings were eagerly devoured in the American colonies, whose elites were attracted to Trenchard and Gordon's emphasis on the political role of the independent

The "Country Party"

The Polling, by the renowned eighteenth-century British artist William Hogarth, satirizes the idea that British elections are decided by the reasoned deliberations of upstanding property owners. Inspired by a corrupt election of 1754, Hogarth depicts an election scene in which the maimed and dying are brought to the polls to cast ballots. At the center, lawyers argue over whether a man who has a hook for a hand can swear on the Bible.

landowner and their warnings against the constant tendency of political power to infringe upon liberty.

Liberal Freedom

The second set of eighteenth-century political ideas celebrating freedom came to be known as **liberalism** (although its meaning was quite different from what the word suggests today). Whereas republican liberty had a public and social quality, liberalism was essentially individual and private. The leading philosopher of liberty was John Locke, whose *Two Treatises of Government*, written around 1680, had limited influence in his own lifetime but became extremely well known in the next century. Government, he wrote, was formed by a mutual agreement among equals (the parties being male heads of households, not all persons). In this "social contract," men surrendered a part of their right to govern themselves in order to enjoy the benefits of the rule of law. They retained, however, their natural rights, whose existence predated the establishment of political authority. Protecting the security of life, liberty, and property required shielding a realm of private life and personal concerns—including family relations, religious preferences, and economic activity—from interference by the state. During the eighteenth century, Lockean ideas—individual rights, the consent of the governed, the right of rebellion against unjust or oppressive government—would become familiar on both sides of the Atlantic.

Like other Britons, Locke spoke of liberty as a universal right yet seemed to exclude many persons from its full benefits. While Locke was one of the first theorists to defend the property rights of women and even their access to divorce, and condemned slavery as a "vile and miserable estate of man," the free individual in liberal thought was essentially the propertied white man. Nonetheless,

Locke's Two Treatises of Government

by proclaiming that all individuals possess natural rights that no government may violate, Lockean liberalism opened the door to the poor, women, and even slaves to challenge limitations on their own freedom.

In the eighteenth century, these systems of thought overlapped and often reinforced each other. Both political outlooks could inspire a commitment to constitutional government and restraints on despotic power. Both emphasized the security of property as a foundation of freedom. Both traditions were transported to eighteenth-century America. Ideas about liberty imported from Britain to the colonies would eventually help to divide the empire.

THE PUBLIC SPHERE

Colonial politics for most of the eighteenth century was considerably less tempestuous than in the seventeenth, with its bitter struggles for power and frequent armed uprisings. Political stability in Britain coupled with the maturation of local elites in America made for more tranquil government. New York stood apart from this development. With its diverse population and bitter memories of Leisler's rebellion (see Chapter 3), New York continued to experience intense political strife among its many economic interests and ethnic groups. By the 1750s, semipermanent political parties competed vigorously for popular support in New York elections. But in most other colonies, although differences over policies of one kind or another were hardly absent, they rarely produced the civil disorder or political passions of the previous century.

The Right to Vote

In many respects, politics in eighteenth-century America had a more democratic quality than in Great Britain. Suffrage requirements varied from colony to colony, but as in Britain the linchpin of voting laws was the property qualification. Its purpose was to ensure that men who possessed an economic stake in society and the independence of judgment that supposedly went with it determined the policies of the government. The "foundation of liberty," the parliamentary leader Henry Ireton had declared during the English Civil War of the 1640s, "is that those who shall choose the lawmakers shall be men freed from dependence upon others." Slaves, servants, tenants, adult sons living in the homes of their parents, the poor, and women all lacked a "will of their own" and were therefore ineligible to vote. The wide distribution of property in the colonies, however, meant that a far higher percentage of the population enjoyed voting rights than in the Old World. It is estimated that between 50 and 80 percent of adult white men could vote in eighteenth-century colonial America, as opposed to fewer than 5 percent in Britain at the time.

Colonial politics, however, was hardly democratic in a modern sense. In a few instances—some towns in Massachusetts and on Long Island—propertied women, generally widows, cast ballots. But voting was almost everywhere considered a male prerogative. In some colonies, Jews, Catholics, and Protestant Dissenters like Baptists and Quakers could not vote. Propertied free blacks, who enjoyed the franchise in Virginia, South Carolina, and Georgia in the early days of settlement, lost

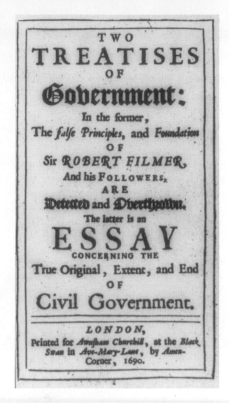

The title page of John Locke's *Two Treatises of Government*, which traced the origins of government to an original state of nature and insisted that political authorities must not abridge mankind's natural rights.

The British political philosopher John Locke, painted by Michael Dahl around 1696.

that right during the eighteenth century. In the northern colonies, while the law did not bar blacks from voting, local custom did. Native Americans were generally prohibited from voting.

Political Cultures

Despite the broad electorate among white men, "the people" existed only on election day. Between elections, members of colonial assemblies remained out of touch with their constituents. Strongly competitive elections were the norm only in the Middle Colonies. Elsewhere, many elections went uncontested, either because only one candidate presented himself or because the local culture stressed community harmony, as in many New England towns. Considerable power in colonial politics rested with those who held appointive, not elective, office. Governors and councils were appointed by the crown in the nine royal colonies and by the proprietors of Pennsylvania and Maryland. Only in Rhode Island and Connecticut were these offices elective. Moreover, laws passed by colonial assemblies could be vetoed by governors or in London. In New England, most town officers were elected, but local officials in other colonies were appointed by the governor or by powerful officials in London. The duke of Newcastle alone could appoint eighty-three colonial officials.

Property qualifications for officeholding were far higher than for voting. In South Carolina, for example, nearly every adult male could meet the voting qualification of fifty acres of land or payment of twenty shillings in taxes, but to sit in the assembly one had to own 500 acres of land and ten slaves or town property worth £1,000. As a result, throughout the eighteenth century nearly all of South Carolina's legislators were planters or wealthy merchants. Despite its boisterous and competitive politics, New York's diminutive assembly, with fewer than thirty members, was dominated by relatives and allies of the great landed families, especially the Livingstons and De Lanceys. Of seventy-two men who sat in the New York Assembly between 1750 and 1776, fifty-two were related to the families who owned the great Hudson River estates.

In some colonies, a majority of free men possessed the right to vote, but an ingrained tradition of "deference"—the assumption among ordinary people that wealth, education, and social prominence carried a right to public office—sharply limited effective choice in elections. Virginia politics, for example, combined political democracy for white men with the tradition that voters should choose among candidates from the gentry. Aspirants for public office actively sought to ingratiate themselves with ordinary voters, distributing food and liquor freely at the courthouse where balloting took place. In Thomas Jefferson's first campaign for the House of Burgesses in 1768, his expenses included hiring two men "for bringing up rum" to the polling place. Even in New England, with its larger number of elective positions, town leaders were generally the largest property holders and offices frequently passed from generation to generation in the same family.

Appointive office

This 1765 engraving depicting an election in Pennsylvania suggests the intensity of political debate in the Middle Colonies, as well as the social composition of the electorate. Those shown arguing outside the Old Court House in Philadelphia include physicians (with wigs and gold-topped canes), ministers, and lawyers. A line of men wait on the steps to vote.

Colonial Government

Preoccupied with events in Europe and imperial rivalries, successive British governments during the first half of the eighteenth century adopted a policy of **salutary neglect** toward the colonies, leaving them largely to govern themselves. With imperial authority so weak, the large landowners, merchants, and lawyers who dominated colonial assemblies increasingly claimed the right to control local politics.

Colonial assemblies

Convinced that they represented the will of the people, elected colonial assemblies used their control of finance to exert influence over appointed governors and councils. Although governors desired secure incomes for themselves and permanent revenue for their administrations (Robert Hunter of New York demanded a life salary), assemblies often authorized salaries only one year at a time and refused to levy taxes except in exchange for concessions on appointments, land policy, and other issues. Typically members of the British gentry who had suffered financial reversals and hoped to recoup their fortunes in America, governors learned that to rule effectively they would have to cooperate with the colonial elite.

The Rise of the Assemblies

In the seventeenth century, the governor was the focal point of political authority, and colonial assemblies were weak bodies that met infrequently. But in the eighteenth, as economic development enhanced the power of American elites, the assemblies they dominated became more and more assertive. Their leaders insisted that assemblies possessed the same rights and powers in local affairs as the House of Commons enjoyed in Britain. The most successful governors were those who accommodated the rising power of the assemblies and used their appointive powers and control of land grants to win allies among assembly members.

The most powerful assembly was Pennsylvania's, where a new charter, adopted in 1701, eliminated the governor's council, establishing the only unicameral (one-house) legislature in the colonies. Controlled until mid-century by an elite of Quaker merchants, the assembly wrested control of finance, appointments, and the militia from a series of governors representing the Penn family. Close behind in terms of power and legislative independence were the assemblies of New York, Virginia, South Carolina, and, especially, Massachusetts, which successfully resisted governors' demands for permanent salaries for appointed officials. Many of the conflicts between governors and elected assemblies stemmed from the colonies' economic growth. To deal with the scarcity of gold and silver coins, the only legal form of currency, some colonies printed paper money, although this was strongly opposed by the governors, authorities in London, and British merchants who did not wish to be paid in what they considered worthless paper. Numerous battles also took place over land policy (sometimes involving divergent attitudes toward the remaining Indian population) and the level of rents charged to farmers on land owned by the crown or proprietors.

Conflicts between governors and assemblies

In their negotiations and conflicts with royal governors, leaders of the assemblies drew on the writings of the English Country Party, whose emphasis on the constant tension between liberty and political power and the dangers of executive influence over the legislature made sense of their own experience. Of the European settlements in North America, only the British colonies possessed any considerable degree of popular participation in government. This fact reinforced the assemblies' claim to embody the rights of Englishmen and the principle of popular consent to government. They were defenders of "the people's liberty," in the words of one New York legislator.

Politics in Public

The public sphere

This language reverberated outside the relatively narrow world of elective and legislative politics. The "political nation" was dominated by the American gentry, whose members addressed each other in letters, speeches, newspaper articles, and pamphlets filled with Latin expressions and references to classical learning. But especially in colonial towns and cities, the eighteenth century witnessed a considerable expansion of the "public sphere"—the world of political organization and debate independent of the government, where an informed citizenry openly discussed questions that had previously been the preserve of officials.

In Boston, New York, and Philadelphia, clubs proliferated where literary, philosophical, scientific, and political issues were debated. Among the best known was the Junto, a "club for mutual improvement" founded by Benjamin Franklin in Philadelphia in 1727 for weekly discussion of political and economic questions. Beginning with only a dozen members, it eventually evolved into the much larger American Philosophical Society. Such groups were generally composed of men of property and commerce, but some drew ordinary citizens into discussions of public affairs. Colonial taverns and coffeehouses also became important sites not only for social conviviality but also for political debates. Philadelphia had a larger number of drinking establishments per capita than Paris. In Philadelphia, one clergyman commented, "the poorest laborer thinks himself entitled to deliver his sentiments in matters of religion or politics with as much freedom as the gentleman or scholar."

The Colonial Press

Neither the Spanish possessions of Florida and New Mexico nor New France possessed a printing press, although missionaries had established one in Mexico City in the 1530s. In British North America, however, the press expanded rapidly during the eighteenth century. So did the number of political broadsides and pamphlets published, especially at election time. Widespread literacy created an expanding market for printed materials. By the eve of the American Revolution, some three-quarters of the free adult male population in the colonies (and more than one-third of the women) could read and write, and a majority of American families owned at least one book. Philadelphia boasted no fewer than seventy-seven bookshops in the 1770s.

Circulating libraries appeared in many colonial cities and towns, making possible a wider dissemination of knowledge at a time when books were still expensive. The first, the Library Company of Philadelphia, was established by Benjamin Franklin in 1731. "So few were the readers at that time, and the majority of us so poor," Franklin recalled in his *Autobiography* (1791), that he could find only fifty persons, mostly "young tradesmen," anxious for self-improvement and willing to pay for the privilege of borrowing books. But reading, he added, soon "became fashionable." Libraries sprang up in other towns, and ordinary

Benjamin Franklin's quest for self-improvement, or, as he put it in his autobiography, "moral perfection," is illustrated in this "Temperance diagram," which charts his behavior each day of the week with regard to thirteen virtues. They are listed on the left by their first letters: temperance, silence, order, resolution, frugality, industry, sincerity, justice, moderation, cleanliness, tranquility, chastity, and humility. Franklin did not always adhere to these virtues.

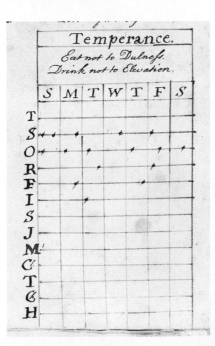

Americans came to be "better instructed and more intelligent than people of the same rank" abroad.

The first continuously published colonial newspaper, the *Boston News-Letter*, appeared in 1704 (a predecessor, *Publick Occurrences, Both Foreign and Domestick*, established in Boston in 1690, had been suppressed by authorities after a single issue for criticizing military cooperation with the Iroquois). There were thirteen colonial newspapers by 1740 and twenty-five in 1765, mostly weeklies with small circulations—an average of 600 sales per issue. Probably the best-edited newspaper was the *Pennsylvania Gazette*, established in 1728 in Philadelphia and purchased the following year by Benjamin Franklin, who had earlier worked as an apprentice printer on his brother's Boston periodical, the *New England Courant*. At its peak, the *Gazette* attracted 2,000 subscribers. Newspapers initially devoted most of their space to advertisements, religious affairs, and reports on British society and government. But by the 1730s, political commentary was widespread in the American press.

Freedom of Expression and Its Limits

The public sphere thrived on the free exchange of ideas. But free expression was not generally considered one of the ancient rights of Englishmen. The phrase "freedom of speech" originated in Britain during the sixteenth century in Parliament's struggle to achieve the privilege of unrestrained debate. A right of legislators, not ordinary citizens, it referred to the ability of members of Parliament to express their views without fear of reprisal, on the grounds that only in this way could they effectively represent the people. Outside of Parliament, free speech had no legal protection. A subject could be beheaded for accusing the king of failing to hold "true" religious beliefs, and language from swearing to criticism of the government exposed a person to criminal penalties.

Freedom of speech

As for freedom of the press, governments on both sides of the Atlantic viewed this as extremely dangerous, partly because they considered ordinary citizens prone to be misled by inflammatory printed materials. During the English Civil War of the 1640s, the Levellers had called for the adoption of a written constitution, an Agreement of the People, containing guarantees of religious liberty and freedom of the press. But until 1695, when a British law requiring the licensing of printed works before publication lapsed, no newspaper, book, or pamphlet could legally be printed without a government license. The instructions of colonial governors included a warning about the "great inconveniences that may arise by the liberty of printing." After 1695, the government could not censor newspapers, books, and pamphlets before they appeared in print, although it continued to try to manage the press by direct payments to publishers and individual journalists. Authors and publishers could still be prosecuted for "seditious libel"—a crime that included defaming government officials—or punished for contempt.

Freedom of the press

Elected assemblies, not governors, most frequently discouraged freedom of the press in colonial America. Dozens of publishers were hauled before assemblies and forced to apologize for comments regarding one or another member. If they refused, they were jailed. James Franklin, Benjamin's older brother, spent a month in prison in 1722 after publishing a piece satirizing public authorities in Massachusetts. Colonial newspapers vigorously defended freedom of the press as a

The first page of the *New-York Weekly Journal*, edited by John Peter Zenger, one of four issues ordered to be burned by local authorities.

Benjamin Franklin

central component of liberty, insisting that the citizenry had a right to monitor the workings of government and subject public officials to criticism. Many newspapers reprinted passages from *Cato's Letters* in which Trenchard and Gordon strongly opposed prosecutions for libel. "Without freedom of thought," they declared, "there can be no such thing as wisdom, and no such thing as public liberty, without freedom of speech." But since government printing contracts were crucial for economic success, few newspapers attacked colonial governments unless financially supported by an opposition faction.

The Trial of Zenger

The most famous colonial court case involving freedom of the press demonstrated that popular sentiment opposed prosecutions for criticism of public officials. This was the 1735 trial of John Peter Zenger, a German-born printer who had emigrated to New York as a youth. Financed by wealthy opponents of Governor William Cosby, Zenger's newspaper, the *Weekly Journal*, lambasted the governor for corruption, influence peddling, and "tyranny." New York's council ordered four issues burned and had Zenger himself arrested and tried for seditious libel. The judge instructed the jurors to consider only whether Zenger had actually published the offending words, not whether they were accurate. But Zenger's attorney, Andrew Hamilton, urged the jury to judge not the publisher but the governor. If they decided that Zenger's charges were correct, they must acquit him, and, Hamilton proclaimed, "every man who prefers freedom to a life of slavery will bless you."

Zenger was found not guilty. The case sent a warning to prosecutors that libel cases might be very difficult to win, especially in the superheated atmosphere of New York partisan politics. To be sure, had Zenger lambasted the assembly rather than the governor, he would in all likelihood have been lodged in jail without even the benefit of a trial. The law of libel remained on the books. But the outcome helped to promote the idea that the publication of truth should always be permitted, and it demonstrated that the idea of free expression was becoming ingrained in the popular imagination.

The American Enlightenment

During the eighteenth century, many educated Americans began to be influenced by the outlook of the European **Enlightenment**. This philosophical movement, which originated among French thinkers and soon spread to Britain, sought to apply the scientific method of careful investigation based on research and experiment to political and social life. Enlightenment ideas crisscrossed the Atlantic along with goods and people. Enlightenment thinkers insisted that every human institution, authority, and tradition be judged before the bar of reason. The self-educated Benjamin Franklin's wide range of activities—establishing a newspaper, debating club, and library; publishing the widely circulated *Poor Richard's Almanack*; and conducting experiments to demonstrate that lightning is a form of electricity—exemplified the Enlightenment spirit and made him probably the best-known American in the eighteenth-century world.

One inspiration for the American Enlightenment was a reaction against the bloody religious wars that wracked Europe in the seventeenth century. Enlightenment thinkers hoped that "reason," not religious enthusiasm, could govern human life. The criticism of social and political institutions based on tradition and hereditary privilege rather than the dictates of reason could also be applied to established churches. John Locke himself had published *The Reasonableness of Christianity* in 1695, which insisted that religious belief should rest on scientific evidence. During the eighteenth century, many prominent Americans moved toward the position called Arminianism, which taught that reason alone was capable of establishing the essentials of religion. Others adopted **Deism**, a belief that God essentially withdrew after creating the world, leaving it to function according to scientific laws without divine intervention. Belief in miracles, in the revealed truth of the Bible, and in the innate sinfulness of mankind were viewed by Arminians, Deists, and others as outdated superstitions that should be abandoned in the modern age.

In the seventeenth century, the English scientist Isaac Newton had revealed the natural laws that governed the physical universe. Here, Deists believed, was the purest evidence of God's handiwork. Many Protestants of all denominations could accept Newton's findings while remaining devout churchgoers (as Newton himself had). But Deists concluded that the best form of religious devotion was to study the workings of nature, rather than to worship in organized churches or appeal to divine grace for salvation. By the late colonial era, a small but influential group of leading Americans, including Benjamin Franklin and Thomas Jefferson, could be classified as Deists.

A 1762 portrait of Benjamin Franklin, done in London by the English artist Mason Chamberlain while Franklin was in the city as agent for the Pennsylvania Assembly. Franklin is depicted as a scientist making notes on his experiments, rather than as a politician. In the background, an electrical storm rages—a reference to Franklin's pioneering experiments that demonstrated the electrical nature of lightning and led to his election as a member of the Royal Society, Britain's premier scientific organization. Franklin also invented the lightning rod. The storm in the painting is destroying buildings that have not installed Franklin's invention.

THE GREAT AWAKENING

Like freedom of the press, religion was another realm where the actual experience of liberty outstripped its legal recognition. Religion remained central to eighteenth-century American life. Sermons, theological treatises, and copies of the Bible were by far the largest category of material produced by colonial printers. Religious disputes often generated more public attention than political issues. Yet many church leaders worried about lax religious observance as colonial economic growth led people to be more and more preoccupied with worldly affairs.

Religious Revivals

Many ministers were concerned that westward expansion, commercial development, the growth of Enlightenment rationalism, and lack of individual engagement in church services were undermining religious devotion. These fears helped to inspire the revivals that swept through the colonies beginning in the 1730s. Known as the **Great Awakening**, the revivals were less a coordinated movement than a series of local events united by a commitment to a "religion of the heart," a more emotional and personal Christianity than that offered by existing churches. The revivals redrew the religious landscape of the colonies.

The eighteenth century witnessed a revival of religious fundamentalism in many parts of the world, in part a response to the rationalism of the Enlightenment

Threats to religious devotion

CALIFORNIA

· San Francis
▪ Monterey
† San Luis
Santa▪   † Sa
Barbara   † S.
San Diego ▪

Pacific
Ocean

▪   Fort
†   Missi
▢   Britis
▨   Britis
▢   Area
▢   Area

Spain's hold
eliminating

Spain's
population.
slightly outr
Spanish wer
converting t
Mexico City
economy of
from the sur
in Europe m
commanders
continued to

An early draft, with corrections, of the Declaration of Independence, in Thomas Jefferson's handwriting. Note how the elimination of unnecessary words added to the document's power—"all men are created equal and independent" became "all men are created equal," and "inherent and inalienable" rights became "inalienable" (in the final version, this would be changed to "unalienable").

Jefferson's preamble

The Declaration's enduring impact came not from the complaints against George III but from Jefferson's preamble, especially the second paragraph, which begins, "We hold these truths to be self-evident, that all men are created equal, that they are endowed by their Creator with certain unalienable Rights, that among these are Life, Liberty, and the pursuit of Happiness." By "unalienable rights," Jefferson meant rights so basic, so rooted in human nature itself (or in what John Locke had called the state of nature), that no government could take them away.

Jefferson then went on to justify the breach with Britain. Government, he wrote, derives its powers from "the consent of the governed." When a government threatens its subjects' natural rights, the people have the authority "to alter or to abolish it." The Declaration of Independence is ultimately an assertion of the right of revolution.

The Declaration and American Freedom

The **Declaration of Independence** changed forever the meaning of American freedom. It completed the shift from the rights of Englishmen to the rights of mankind as the object of American independence. In Jefferson's language, "the Laws of Nature and of Nature's God," not the British constitution or the heritage of the freeborn Englishman, justified independence. No longer a set of specific rights, no longer a privilege to be enjoyed by a corporate body or people in certain social circumstances, liberty had become a universal entitlement.

Jefferson's argument (natural rights, the right to resist arbitrary authority, etc.) drew on the writings of John Locke, who, as explained in the previous chapter, saw government as resting on a "social contract," violation of which destroyed the legitimacy of authority. But when Jefferson substituted the "pursuit of happiness" for property in the familiar Lockean triad that opens the Declaration, he tied the new nation's star to an open-ended, democratic process whereby individuals develop their own potential and seek to realize their own life goals. Individual self-fulfillment, unimpeded by government, would become a central element of American freedom. Tradition would no longer rule the present, and Americans could shape their society as they saw fit.

America as a Symbol of Liberty, a 1775 engraving from the cover of the *Pennsylvania Magazine*, edited by Thomas Paine soon after his arrival in America. The shield displays the colony's coat of arms. The female figure holding a liberty cap is surrounded by weaponry of the patriotic struggle, including a cartridge box marked "liberty," hanging from a tree (*right*).

An Asylum for Mankind

A distinctive definition of nationality resting on American freedom was born in the Revolution. From the beginning, the idea of "American exceptionalism"—the belief that the United States has a special mission to serve as a refuge from tyranny, a symbol of freedom, and a model for the rest of the world—has occupied a central place in American nationalism. The new nation declared itself, in the words of Virginia leader James Madison, the "workshop of liberty to the Civilized World." Paine's remark in *Common Sense*, "we have it in our power to begin the world over again," and his description of the new nation as an "asylum for mankind" expressed a sense that the Revolution was an event of global historical importance. Countless sermons, political tracts, and newspaper articles of the time repeated this idea. Unburdened by the institutions—monarchy, aristocracy, hereditary privilege—that oppressed the peoples of the Old World, America and America alone was the place where the principle of universal freedom could take root. This was why Jefferson addressed the Declaration to "the opinions of mankind," not just the colonists themselves or Great Britain.

First to add his name to the Declaration of Independence was the Massachusetts merchant John Hancock, president of the Second Continental Congress, with a signature so large, he declared, according to legend, that King George III could read it without his spectacles.

American nationality

The Global Declaration of Independence

Even apart from the Declaration of Independence, 1776 was a momentous year in North America. Spain established Mission Dolores, the first European settlement at San Francisco, in an effort to block Russian advances on the Pacific coast. In San Diego, local Indians rebelled, unsuccessfully, against Spanish rule. The Lakota Sioux, migrating westward from Minnesota, settled in the Black Hills of North

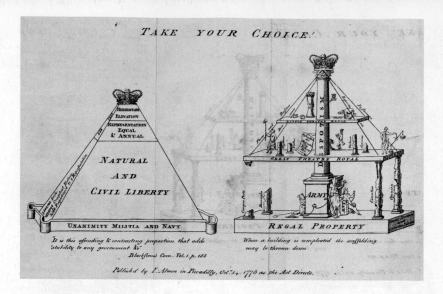

Inspired by the American Revolution, the British reformer John Cartwright published an appeal for the annual election of Parliament as essential to liberty in Britain. He included an engraving contrasting the principles of reform, on the left, with despotism, on the right.

Other declarations of independence

Dakota, their homeland for the next century. All these places and peoples would eventually become part of the United States, but, of course, no one knew this in 1776.

Meanwhile, the struggle for independence reverberated around the globe. The American colonists were less concerned with securing human rights for all mankind than with winning international recognition in their struggle for independence from Britain. But Jefferson hoped that this rebellion would become "the signal of arousing men to burst the chains . . . and to assume the blessings and security of self-government." And for more than two centuries, the Declaration has remained an inspiration not only to generations of Americans denied the enjoyment of their natural rights, but to colonial peoples around the world seeking independence. The Declaration quickly appeared in French and German translations, although not, at first, in Spanish, since the government feared it would inspire dangerous ideas among the peoples of Spain's American empire.

In the years since 1776, numerous anticolonial movements have modeled their own declarations of independence on America's. The first came in Flanders (part of today's Belgium, then part of the Austrian empire), where rebels in 1790 echoed Jefferson's words by declaring that their province "is and of rights ought to be, a Free and Independent State." Today, more than half the countries in the world, in places as far-flung as China (issued after the revolution of 1911) and Vietnam (1945), have such declarations. Many of these documents, like Jefferson's, listed grievances against an imperial power to justify revolution. Few of these documents, however, have affirmed the natural rights—life, liberty, and the pursuit of happiness—Jefferson invoked. Over time, the Declaration in a global context has become an assertion of the right of various groups to form independent states, rather than a list of the rights of citizens that their governments could not abridge.

But even more than the specific language of the Declaration, the principle that legitimate political authority rests on the will of "the people" has been adopted around the world. In 1780, even as the American War of Independence raged, a Jesuit-educated Indian of Peru took the name of the last Inca ruler, Túpac Amaru, and led an uprising against Spanish rule. By the time it was suppressed in 1783, some 10,000 Spanish and 100,000 Indians had perished. In the Dutch, French, and Spanish empires, where European governments had been trying to tighten their control much as the British had done in North America, local elites demanded greater autonomy, often drawing on the constitutional arguments of American patriots. The idea that "the people" possess rights was quickly internationalized. Slaves in the Caribbean, colonial subjects in India, and indigenous inhabitants of Latin America could all speak this language, to the dismay of those who exercised power over them.

SECURING INDEPENDENCE

The Balance of Power

Declaring Americans independent was one thing; winning independence another. The newly created American army confronted the greatest military power on earth. Viewing the Americans as traitors, Britain resolved to crush the rebellion. On the surface, the balance of power seemed heavily weighted in Britain's favor. It had a well-trained army (supplemented by hired soldiers from German states like Hesse), the world's most powerful navy, and experienced military commanders. The Americans had to rely on local militias and an inadequately equipped Continental army. Washington himself felt that militiamen were too "accustomed to unbounded freedom" to accept the "proper degree of subordination" necessary in soldiers. Moreover, many Americans were not enthusiastic about independence, and some actively supported the British.

On the other hand, many American soldiers did not lack military experience, having fought in the Seven Years' War or undergone intensive militia training in the early 1770s. They were fighting on their own soil for a cause that inspired devotion and sacrifice. During the eight years of war from 1775 to 1783, some 200,000 men bore arms in the American army (whose soldiers were volunteers) and militias (where service was required of every able-bodied man unless he provided a substitute). As the war progressed, enlistment waned among propertied Americans and the Continental army increasingly drew on young men with limited economic prospects—landless sons of farmers, indentured servants, laborers, and African-Americans. The patriots suffered dearly for the cause. Of the colonies' free white male population aged sixteen to forty-five, one in twenty died in the War of Independence, the equivalent of nearly 3 million deaths in today's population. But so long as the Americans maintained an army in the field, the idea of independence remained alive no matter how much territory the British occupied.

Despite British power, to conquer the thirteen colonies would be an enormous and expensive task, and it was not at all certain that the public at home wished to pay the additional taxes that a lengthy war would require. The British, moreover, made a string of serious mistakes. From the outset the British misjudged the degree of support for independence among the American population, as well as the capacity of American citizen-soldiers. "These people," admitted the British general Thomas Gage, "show a spirit and conduct against us that they never showed against the French [in the Seven Years' War], and everybody has judged them from their former appearance and behavior, which has led many into great mistakes." Moreover, European rivals, notably France, welcomed the prospect of a British defeat. If the Americans could forge an alliance with France, a world power second only to Britain, it would go a long way toward equalizing the balance of forces.

Military power

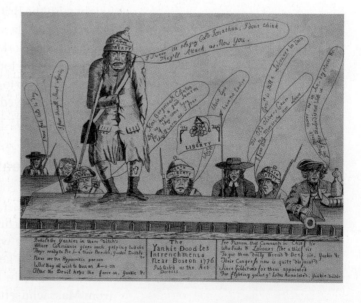

The Yankee Doodle Intrenchments near Boston, a 1776 British cartoon depicting the American revolutionaries as unimposing citizen soldiers egged on—according to the accompanying text—by a thieving commander and a reckless Puritan minister. The British greatly underestimated Americans' fighting ability in the War of Independence. One member of Parliament in 1775 claimed the colonists "were neither soldiers, nor could be made so," as they were naturally cowardly and "incapable of any sort of order or discipline."

American Foot Soldiers, Yorktown Campaign, a 1781 watercolor by a French officer, includes a black soldier from the First Rhode Island Regiment, an all-black unit of 250 men.

Blacks in the Revolution

At the war's outset, George Washington refused to accept black recruits. But he changed his mind after Lord Dunmore's 1775 proclamation, which offered freedom to slaves who joined the British cause. Some 5,000 blacks enlisted in state militias and the Continental army and navy. Since individuals drafted into the militia were allowed to provide a substitute, slaves suddenly gained considerable bargaining power. Not a few acquired their freedom by agreeing to serve in place of an owner or his son. In 1778, Rhode Island, with a higher proportion of slaves in its population than any other New England state, formed a black regiment and promised freedom to slaves who enlisted, while compensating the owners for their loss of property. Blacks who fought under George Washington and in other state militias did so in racially integrated companies (although invariably under white officers). They were the last black American soldiers to do so officially until the Korean War (except for the few black and white soldiers who fought alongside each other in irregular units at the end of World War II).

Except for South Carolina and Georgia, the southern colonies also enrolled free blacks and slaves to fight. They were not explicitly promised freedom, but many received it individually after the war ended. And in 1783, the Virginia legislature emancipated slaves who had "contributed towards the establishment of American liberty and independence" by serving in the army.

Fighting on the side of the British also offered opportunities for freedom. Before his forces were expelled from Virginia, 800 or more slaves had escaped from their owners to join Lord Dunmore's Ethiopian Regiment, wearing, according to legend, uniforms that bore the motto "Liberty to Slaves." During the war, blacks fought with the British in campaigns in New York, New Jersey, and South Carolina. Other escaped slaves served the Royal Army as spies, guided their troops through swamps, and worked as military cooks, laundresses, and construction workers. George Washington himself saw seventeen of his slaves flee to the British, some of whom signed up to fight the colonists. "There is not a man of them, but would leave us, if they believed they could make their escape," his cousin Lund Washington reported. "Liberty is sweet."

The First Years of the War

Had the British commander, Sir William Howe, prosecuted the war more vigorously at the outset, he might have nipped the rebellion in the bud by destroying Washington's army. But while Washington suffered numerous defeats in the first years of the war, he generally avoided direct confrontations with the British and managed to keep his army intact. Having abandoned Boston, Howe attacked New York City in the summer of 1776. Washington's army had likewise moved from Massachusetts to Brooklyn to defend the city. Howe pushed American forces

Dunmore's regiment

War in New York

back and almost cut off Washington's retreat across the East River. Washington managed to escape to Manhattan and then north to Peekskill, where he crossed the Hudson River to New Jersey. But the 3,000 men he had left behind at Fort Washington on Manhattan Island were captured by Howe.

Howe pursued the American army but never managed to inflict a decisive defeat. Demoralized by successive failures, however, many American soldiers simply went home. Once 28,000 men, Washington's army dwindled to fewer than 3,000. Indeed, Washington feared that without a decisive victory, it would melt away entirely. To restore morale and regain the initiative, he launched successful surprise attacks on **Hessian** soldiers at Trenton, New Jersey, on December 26, 1776, and on a British force at Princeton on January 3, 1777. Shortly before crossing the Delaware River to attack the Hessians, Washington had Thomas Paine's inspiring essay *The American Crisis* read to his troops. "These are the times that try men's souls," Paine wrote. "The summer soldier and the sunshine patriot will, in this crisis, shrink from the service of their country; but he that stands it *now*, deserves the love and thanks of man and woman."

> *Battles of New Jersey*

The Battle of Saratoga

In the summer of 1777, a second British army, led by General John Burgoyne, advanced south from Canada hoping to link up with Howe and isolate New England. But in July, Howe instead moved his forces from New York City to attack Philadelphia. In September, the Continental Congress fled to Lancaster, in central Pennsylvania, and Howe occupied the City of Brotherly Love. Not having been

> *Howe and Burgoyne*

Triumphant Entry of the Royal Troops into New York, an engraving showing the army of Sir William Howe occupying the city in 1776. New York City would remain in British hands for the duration of the War of Independence.

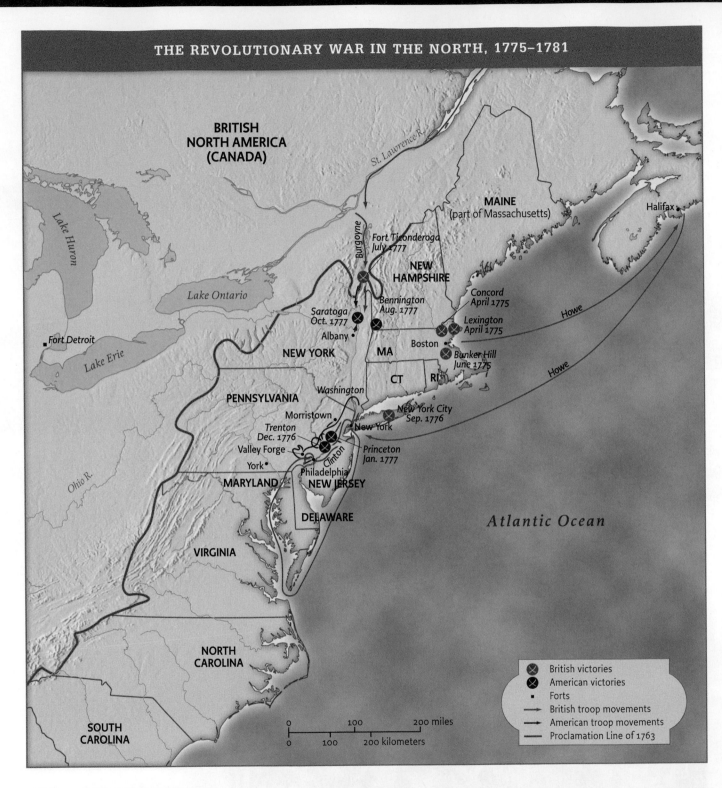

THE REVOLUTIONARY WAR IN THE NORTH, 1775–1781

BRITISH
NORTH AMERICA
(CANADA)

St. Lawrence R.

Lake Huron

Lake Ontario

MAINE
(part of Massachusetts)

Halifax

Burgoyne

Fort Ticonderoga
July 1777

NEW
HAMPSHIRE

Concord
April 1775

Bennington
Aug. 1777

Saratoga
Oct. 1777

Lexington
April 1775

Howe

Fort Detroit

Lake Erie

Albany

NEW YORK

MA

Boston

Bunker Hill
June 1775

Howe

CT

RI

Washington

PENNSYLVANIA

New York City
Sep. 1776

Morristown

Trenton
Dec. 1776

New York

Ohio R.

Valley Forge

Clinton

Princeton
Jan. 1777

York

Philadelphia

MARYLAND

NEW JERSEY

Atlantic Ocean

DELAWARE

VIRGINIA

NORTH
CAROLINA

⊗	British victories
⊗	American victories
■	Forts
→	British troop movements
→	American troop movements
—	Proclamation Line of 1763

SOUTH
CAROLINA

0   100   200 miles
0   100   200 kilometers

Key battles in the North during the War of Independence included Lexington and Concord, which began the armed conflict; the campaign in New York and New Jersey; and Saratoga, sometimes called the turning point of the war.

informed of Burgoyne's plans, Howe had unintentionally abandoned him. American forces blocked Burgoyne's way, surrounded his army, and on October 17, 1777, forced him to surrender at the **Battle of Saratoga**. The victory provided a significant boost to American morale.

During the winter of 1777–1778, the British army, now commanded by Sir Henry Clinton, was quartered in Philadelphia. (In the Revolution, as in most eighteenth-century wars, fighting came to a halt during the winter.) British officers took part in an elegant social life complete with balls and parties. Most notable was the great *Meschianza*, an extravaganza that included a regatta, a procession of medieval knights, and a jousting tournament. Meanwhile, Washington's army remained encamped at Valley Forge, where they suffered terribly from the frigid weather. Men who had other options simply went home. By the end of that difficult winter, recent immigrants and African-Americans made up half the soldiers at Valley Forge and most of the rest were landless or unskilled laborers.

But Saratoga helped to persuade the French that American victory was possible. In 1778, American diplomats led by Benjamin Franklin concluded a Treaty of Amity and Commerce in which France recognized the United States and agreed to supply military assistance. Still smarting from their defeat in the Seven Years' War, the French hoped to weaken Britain, their main European rival, and perhaps regain some of their lost influence and territory in the Western Hemisphere. Soon afterward, Spain also joined the war on the American side. French assistance would play a decisive part in the war's end. At the outset, however, the French fleet showed more interest in attacking British outposts in the West Indies than in directly aiding the Americans. And the Spanish confined themselves to regaining control of Florida, which they had lost to the British in the Seven Years' War. Nonetheless, French and Spanish entry transformed the War of Independence into a global conflict. By putting the British on the defensive in places ranging from Gibraltar to the West Indies, it greatly complicated their military prospects.

Alliance with France

The War in the South

In 1778, the focus of the war shifted to the South. Here the British hoped to exploit the social tensions between backcountry farmers and wealthy planters that had surfaced in the Regulator movements, to enlist the support of the numerous colonists in the region who remained loyal to the crown, and to disrupt the economy by encouraging slaves to escape. In December 1778, British forces occupied Savannah, Georgia. In May 1780, Clinton captured Charleston, South Carolina, and with it an American army of 5,000 men.

The year 1780 was arguably the low point of the struggle for independence. Congress was essentially bankrupt, and the army went months without being paid. The British seemed successful in playing upon social conflicts within the colonies, as thousands of southern Loyalists joined up with British forces (fourteen regiments from Savannah alone) and tens of thousands of slaves sought freedom by fleeing to British lines. In August, Lord Charles Cornwallis routed an American army at Camden, South Carolina. The following month one of

Setbacks in 1780

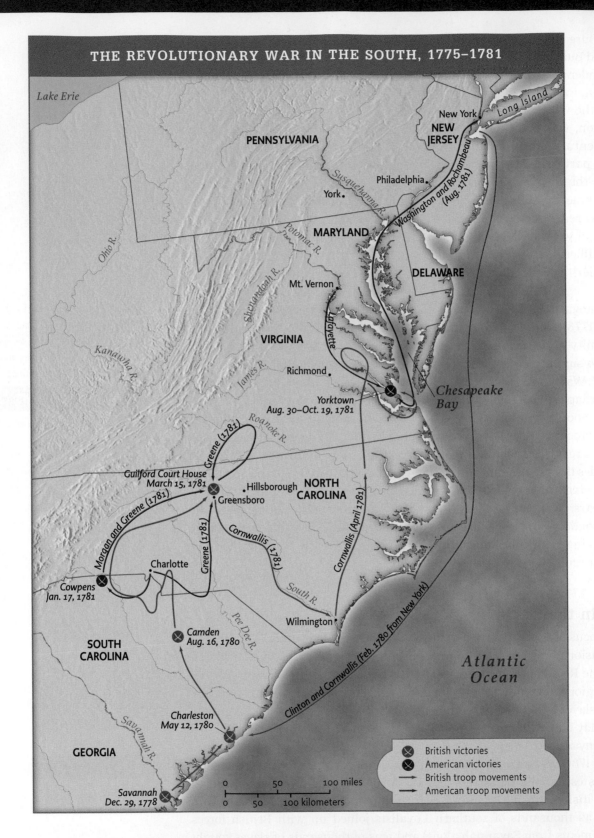

THE REVOLUTIONARY WAR IN THE SOUTH, 1775–1781

Lake Erie

Long Island

New York
NEW YORK

PENNSYLVANIA

NEW JERSEY

Philadelphia

York

Susquehanna R.

Washington and Rochambeau (Aug. 1781)

MARYLAND

Potomac R.

DELAWARE

Ohio R.

Mt. Vernon

Shenandoah R.

VIRGINIA

Lafayette

Kanawha R.

James R.

Richmond

Chesapeake Bay

Yorktown
Aug. 30–Oct. 19, 1781

Greene (1781)

Roanoke R.

Guilford Court House
March 15, 1781

Hillsborough

NORTH CAROLINA

Greensboro

Morgan and Greene (1781)

Greene (1781)

Cornwallis (April 1781)

Cornwallis (1781)

Charlotte

Cowpens
Jan. 17, 1781

South R.

Camden
Aug. 16, 1780

Pee Dee R.

SOUTH CAROLINA

Wilmington

Clinton and Cornwallis (Feb. 1780 from New York)

Atlantic Ocean

Savannah R.

Charleston
May 12, 1780

GEORGIA

Savannah
Dec. 29, 1778

⊗ British victories
⊗ American victories
→ British troop movements
→ American troop movements

0   50   100 miles
0   50   100 kilometers

After 1777, the focus of the War of Independence shifted to the South, where it culminated in 1781 with the British defeat at Yorktown.

Washington's ablest commanders, **Benedict Arnold**, defected and almost succeeded in turning over to the British the important fort at West Point on the Hudson River. On January 1, 1781, 1,500 disgruntled Pennsylvania soldiers stationed near Morristown, New Jersey, killed three officers and marched toward Philadelphia, where Congress was meeting. Their mutiny ended when the soldiers were promised discharges or bounties for reenlistment. Harsher treatment awaited a group of New Jersey soldiers who also mutinied. On Washington's orders, two of their leaders were executed.

But the British failed to turn these advantages into victory. British commanders were unable to consolidate their hold on the South. Wherever their forces went, American militias harassed them. Hit-and-run attacks by militiamen under Francis Marion, called the "swamp fox" because his men emerged from hiding places in swamps to strike swiftly and then disappear, eroded the British position in South Carolina. A bloody civil war engulfed North and South Carolina and Georgia, with patriot and Loyalist militias inflicting retribution on each other and plundering the farms of their opponents' supporters. The brutal treatment of civilians by British forces under Colonel Banastre Tarleton persuaded many Americans to join the patriot cause.

THE HORSE AMERICA, *throwing his Master.*

A British cartoon from 1779, *The Horse America Throwing His Master*, lampoons King George III for being unable to keep control of the colonies. In the background, a French officer carries a flag adorned with the fleur-de-lys, a symbol of that country, the colonists' ally. Powerful satirical attacks on public authorities, including the king, were commonplace in eighteenth-century Britain.

Victory at Last

In January 1781, American forces under Daniel Morgan dealt a crushing defeat to Tarleton at Cowpens, South Carolina. Two months later, at Guilford Courthouse, North Carolina, General Nathanael Greene, while conducting a

A 1781 French engraving showing the surrender of Lord Charles Cornwallis's army at Yorktown, ending the War of Independence. The French fleet sits just offshore.

This portrait of John Adams by the noted American artist John Singleton Copley was painted in London soon after the signing of the Treaty of Paris of 1783, which secured American independence. Adams, who helped to negotiate the treaty, points to a map and globe depicting the new nation. Copley hoped to display the painting in London but British audiences had no desire to see a work celebrating American independence.

campaign of strategic retreats, inflicted heavy losses on Cornwallis, the British commander in the South. Cornwallis moved into Virginia and encamped at Yorktown, located on a peninsula that juts into Chesapeake Bay. Brilliantly recognizing the opportunity to surround Cornwallis, Washington rushed his forces, augmented by French troops under the Marquis de Lafayette, to block a British escape by land. Meanwhile, a French fleet controlled the mouth of the Chesapeake, preventing supplies and reinforcements from reaching Cornwallis's army.

Imperial rivalries had helped to create the American colonies. Now, the rivalry of European empires helped to secure American independence. Taking land and sea forces together, more Frenchmen than Americans participated in the decisive **Battle of Yorktown**. On October 19, 1781, Cornwallis surrendered his army of 8,000 men. When the news reached London, public support for the war evaporated and peace negotiations soon began. Given its immense military prowess, Britain abandoned the struggle rather quickly. Many in Britain felt the West Indies were more valuable economically than the mainland colonies. In any event, British merchants expected to continue to dominate trade with the United States, and did so for many years.

Two years later, in September 1783, American and British negotiators concluded the **Treaty of Paris**. The American delegation—John Adams, Benjamin Franklin, and John Jay—achieved one of the greatest diplomatic triumphs in the country's history. They not only won recognition of American independence but also gained control of the entire region between Canada and Florida east of the Mississippi River and the right of Americans to fish in Atlantic waters off of Canada (a matter of considerable importance to New Englanders). At British insistence, the Americans agreed that colonists who had remained loyal to the mother country would not suffer persecution and that Loyalists' property that had been seized by local and state governments would be restored.

Until independence, the thirteen colonies had formed part of Britain's American empire, along with Canada and the West Indies. But Canada rebuffed repeated calls to join the War of Independence, and leaders of the West Indies, fearful of slave uprisings, also remained loyal to the crown. With the Treaty of Paris, the United States of America became the Western Hemisphere's first independent nation. Its boundaries reflected not so much the long-standing unity of a geographical region, but the circumstances of its birth.

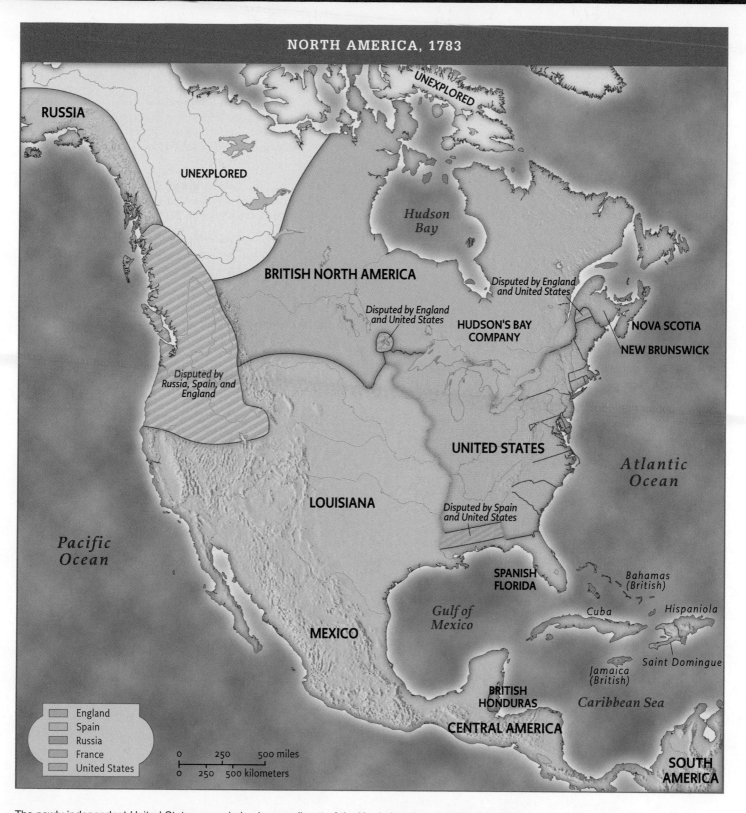

NORTH AMERICA, 1783

RUSSIA

UNEXPLORED

UNEXPLORED

Hudson Bay

BRITISH NORTH AMERICA

Disputed by England and United States

Disputed by England and United States

HUDSON'S BAY COMPANY

NOVA SCOTIA

NEW BRUNSWICK

Disputed by Russia, Spain, and England

UNITED STATES

Atlantic Ocean

LOUISIANA

Disputed by Spain and United States

Pacific Ocean

SPANISH FLORIDA

Bahamas (British)

Gulf of Mexico

Cuba

Hispaniola

MEXICO

Saint Domingue

Jamaica (British)

BRITISH HONDURAS

Caribbean Sea

CENTRAL AMERICA

SOUTH AMERICA

England
Spain
Russia
France
United States

0   250   500 miles
0   250   500 kilometers

The newly independent United States occupied only a small part of the North American continent in 1783.

SUGGESTED READING

BOOKS

- Armitage, David. *The Declaration of Independence: A Global History* (2007). Traces the international impact of the Declaration of Independence in the years since it was written.

- Bailyn, Bernard. *The Ideological Origins of the American Revolution* (1967; 2nd. ed., 1992). A classic study of the ideas that shaped the movement for independence.

- Bloch, Ruth. *Visionary Republic: Millennial Themes in American Thought, 1756–1800* (1988). Explores how the religious vision of a more perfect society contributed to the coming of the Revolution.

- Breen, T. H. *Marketplace of Revolution: How Consumer Politics Shaped American Independence* (2004). An examination of how the colonists' very dependence on British consumer goods led them to resent interference with trade.

- Countryman, Edward. *The American Revolution* (rev. ed., 2002). A brief summary of the Revolution's causes, conduct, and consequences.

- Ferling, John. *Independence: The Struggle to Set America Free* (2011). A recent history of the Revolution, covering its military, political, and social aspects.

- Foner, Eric. *Tom Paine and Revolutionary America* (1976). Examines the ideas of the era's greatest pamphleteer of revolution and how they contributed to the struggle for independence.

- Gross, Robert. *The Minutemen and Their World* (1976). A social history of the militia of Concord, Massachusetts, where the War of Independence began.

- Maier, Pauline. *American Scripture: Making the Declaration of Independence* (1997). The most detailed study of the writing of the Declaration and of previous calls for independence within the colonies.

- Nash, Gary. *The Urban Crucible: Social Change, Political Consciousness, and the Origins of the American Revolution* (1979). Explores how the social history of American cities contributed to the coming of the Revolution.

- Neimeyer, Charles. *America Goes to War: A Social History of the Continental Army* (1995). A history of Washington's army that stresses the role of nonelite Americans in the fighting and the impact of military service on the soldiers.

- Raphael, Ray. *A People's History of the American Revolution* (2001). A study of grassroots resistance to Britain before and during the War of Independence.

- Saunt, Claudio. *West of the Revolution: An Uncommon History of 1776* (2014). An account of events in North America among Indians, Spanish colonists, and others in the year of the Declaration of Independence.

- Taylor, Alan. *American Revolutions: A Continental History, 1750–1804* (2016). An excellent new history of the Revolution as a continental event.

- Withington, Anne. *Toward a More Perfect Union: Virtue and the Formation of American Republics* (1991). Considers how the boycotts of British goods promoted the idea of America's superior virtue, contributing to the movement for independence.

WEBSITES

- The American Revolution and Its Era: Maps and Charts of North America and the West Indies: http://memory.loc.gov/ammem/gmdhtml/armhtml/armhome.html

- The Coming of the American Revolution: www.masshist.org/revolution/

- Declaring Independence: www.loc.gov/exhibits/declara/declara1.html

CHAPTER REVIEW AND ONLINE RESOURCES

REVIEW QUESTIONS

1. What was the ideal of "homespun virtue," and how did it appeal to different groups in the colonies?

2. Patrick Henry proclaimed that he was not a Virginian, but rather an American. What unified the colonists and what divided them at the time of the Revolution?

3. Discuss the ramifications of using slaves in the British and Continental armies. Why did the British authorize the use of slaves? Why did the Americans? How did the slaves benefit?

4. Why did the colonists reach the conclusion that membership in the empire threatened their freedoms, rather than guaranteed them?

5. How did new ideas of liberty contribute to tensions between the social classes in the American colonies?

6. Why did people in other countries believe that the American Revolution (or the Declaration of Independence) was important to them or their own countries?

7. Summarize the difference of opinion between British officials and colonial leaders over the issues of taxation and representation.

8. How did the actions of the British authorities help to unite the American colonists during the 1760s and 1770s?

KEY TERMS

Stamp Act (p. 171)

virtual representation (p. 173)

writs of assistance (p. 173)

Sugar Act (p. 173)

"no taxation without representation" (p. 175)

Committee of Correspondence (p. 175)

Sons of Liberty (p. 176)

Regulators (p. 177)

Townshend Acts (p. 178)

Boston Massacre (p. 179)

Crispus Attucks (p. 179)

Boston Tea Party (p. 181)

Intolerable Acts (p. 181)

Continental Congress (p. 182)

Battles of Lexington and Concord (p. 184)

Battle of Bunker Hill (p. 185)

Continental army (p. 185)

Lord Dunmore's proclamation (p. 185)

Common Sense (p. 186)

Declaration of Independence (p. 190)

Hessians (p. 195)

Battle of Saratoga (p. 197)

Benedict Arnold (p. 199)

Battle of Yorktown (p. 200)

Treaty of Paris (p. 200)

Go to 🐰 INQUIZITIVE

To see what you know—and learn what you've missed—with personalized feedback along the way.

Visit the *Give Me Liberty!* **Student Site** for primary source documents and images, interactive maps, author videos featuring Eric Foner, and more.

DEMOCRATIZING FREEDOM

1700 Samuel Sewall's *The Selling of Joseph*, first antislavery tract in America

1770s Freedom petitions presented by slaves to New England courts and legislatures

1776 Adam Smith's *The Wealth of Nations*

John Adams's *Thoughts on Government*

1777 Vermont state constitution bans slavery

1779 Thomas Jefferson writes Bill for Establishing Religious Freedom

Philipsburg Proclamation

1780 Ladies' Association of Philadelphia founded

1782 Deborah Sampson enlists in Continental army

The Dream of Equality

The American Revolution took place at three levels simultaneously. It was a struggle for national independence, a phase in a century-long global battle among European empires, and a conflict over what kind of nation an independent America should be.

With its wide distribution of property, lack of a legally established hereditary aristocracy, and established churches far less powerful than in Britain, colonial America was a society with deep democratic potential. But it took the struggle for independence to transform it into a nation that celebrated equality and opportunity. The Revolution unleashed public debates and political and social struggles that enlarged the scope of freedom and challenged inherited structures of power within America. In rejecting the crown and the principle of hereditary aristocracy, many Americans also rejected the society of privilege, patronage, and fixed status that these institutions embodied. To be sure, the men who led the Revolution from start to finish were by and large members of the American elite. The lower classes did not rise to power as a result of independence. Nonetheless, the idea of liberty became a revolutionary rallying cry, a standard by which to judge and challenge homegrown institutions as well as imperial ones.

Jefferson's seemingly straightforward assertion in the Declaration of Independence that "all men are created equal" announced a radical principle whose full implications no one could anticipate. In both Britain and its colonies, a well-ordered society was widely thought to depend on obedience to authority—the power of rulers over their subjects, husbands over wives, parents over children, employers over servants and apprentices, slaveholders over slaves. Inequality had been fundamental to the colonial social order; the Revolution challenged it in many ways. Henceforth, American freedom would be forever linked with the idea of equality—equality before the law, equality in political rights, equality of economic opportunity, and, for some, equality of condition. "Whenever I use the words *freedom* or *rights*," wrote Thomas Paine, "I desire to be understood to mean a perfect equality of them. . . . The floor of Freedom is as level as water."

Expanding the Political Nation

With liberty and equality as their rallying cries, previously marginalized groups advanced their demands. Long-accepted relations of dependency and restrictions on freedom suddenly appeared illegitimate—a process not intended by most of the leading patriots. In political, social, and religious life, Americans challenged the previous domination by a privileged few. In the end, the Revolution did not undo the obedience to which male heads of household were entitled from their wives and children, and, at least in the southern states, their slaves. For free men, however, the democratization of freedom was dramatic. Nowhere was this more evident than in challenges to the traditional limitation of political participation to those who owned property.

Abigail Adams, a portrait by Gilbert Stuart, painted over several years beginning in 1800. Stuart told a friend that, as a young woman, Adams must have been a "perfect Venus."

In the political thought of the eighteenth century, "democracy" had several meanings. One, derived from the writings of Aristotle, defined democracy as a system in which the entire people governed directly. However, this was thought to mean mob rule. Another definition viewed democracy as the condition of primitive societies, which was not appropriate for the complex modern world. Yet another understanding revolved less around the structure of government than the principle that a government served the interests of the people rather than an elite. In the wake of the American Revolution, the term came into wider use to express the popular aspirations for greater equality inspired by the struggle for independence.

"We are all, from the cobbler up to the senator, become politicians," declared a Boston letter writer in 1774. Throughout the colonies, election campaigns became freewheeling debates on the fundamentals of government. Universal male suffrage, religious toleration, and even the abolition of slavery were discussed not only by the educated elite but by artisans, small farmers, and laborers, now emerging as a self-conscious element in politics. In many colonies-turned-states, the militia, composed largely of members of the "lower orders," became a "school of political democracy." Its members demanded the right to elect all their officers and to vote for public officials whether or not they met age and property qualifications. They thereby established the tradition that service in the army enabled excluded groups to stake a claim to full citizenship.

A pewter mug made by William Will, an important craftsman in Philadelphia, in the late 1770s. It depicts Captain Peter Ickes, a Pennsylvania militia officer, with the popular slogan "Liberty or Death."

The Revolution in Pennsylvania

The Revolution's radical potential was more evident in Pennsylvania than in any other state. Elsewhere, the established leadership either embraced independence by the spring of 1776 or split into pro-British and pro-independence factions (in New York, for example, the Livingstons and their supporters ended up as patriots, the De Lanceys as Loyalists). But in Pennsylvania nearly the entire prewar elite opposed independence, fearing that severing the tie with Britain would lead to rule by the "rabble" and to attacks on property.

The vacuum of political leadership opened the door for the rise of a new pro-independence grouping, based on the artisan and lower-class communities of Philadelphia, and organized in extralegal committees and the local militia. Their leaders included Thomas Paine (the author of *Common Sense*), Benjamin Rush (a local physician), Timothy Matlack (the son of a local brewer), and Thomas Young (who had already been involved in the Sons of Liberty in Albany and Boston). As a group, these were men of modest wealth who stood outside the merchant elite, had little political influence before 1776, and believed strongly in democratic reform. They formed a temporary alliance with supporters of independence in the Second Continental Congress (then meeting in Philadelphia), who disapproved of their strong belief in equality but hoped to move Pennsylvania toward a break with Britain.

Pro-independence leaders

As the public sphere expanded far beyond its previous boundaries, equality became the rallying cry of Pennsylvania's radicals. They particularly attacked property qualifications for voting. "God gave mankind freedom by nature,"

Americans have frequently defined the idea of freedom in relation to its opposite, which in the eighteenth century meant the highly unequal societies of the Old World. This engraving, *The Coronation of Louis XVI of France*, reveals the splendor of the royal court but also illustrates the world of fixed, unequal classes and social privilege repudiated by American revolutionaries.

declared the anonymous author of the pamphlet *The People the Best Governors*, "and made every man equal to his neighbors." The people, therefore, were "the best guardians of their own liberties," and every free man should be eligible to vote and hold office. In June 1776, a broadside (a printed sheet posted in public places) warned citizens to distrust "great and over-grown rich men" who were inclined "to be framing distinctions in society." Three months after independence, Pennsylvania adopted a new state constitution that sought to institutionalize democracy by concentrating power in a one-house legislature elected annually by all men over age twenty-one who paid taxes. It abolished the office of governor, dispensed with property qualifications for officeholding, and provided that schools with low fees be established in every county. It also included clauses guaranteeing "freedom of speech, and of writing," and religious liberty.

The New Constitutions

Like Pennsylvania, every state adopted a new constitution in the aftermath of independence. Nearly all Americans now agreed that their governments must be republics, meaning that their authority rested on the consent of the governed, and that there would be no king or hereditary aristocracy. The essence of a **republic**, Paine wrote, was not the "particular form" of government, but its object: the "public good." But as to how a republican government should be structured so as to promote the public good, there was much disagreement.

New state constitutions

Pennsylvania's new constitution reflected the belief that since the people had a single set of interests, a single legislative house was sufficient to represent it. In part to counteract what he saw as Pennsylvania's excessive radicalism, John Adams in 1776 published *Thoughts on Government*, which insisted that the new constitutions should create balanced governments whose structure would reflect the division of society between the wealthy (represented in the upper house) and ordinary men (who would control the lower). A powerful governor and judiciary would ensure that neither class infringed on the liberty of the other. Adams's call for

Balanced governments

two-house legislatures was followed by every state except Pennsylvania, Georgia, and Vermont. But only his own state, Massachusetts, gave the governor an effective veto over laws passed by the legislature. Americans had long resented efforts by appointed governors to challenge the power of colonial assemblies. They preferred power to rest with the legislature.

The Right to Vote

The issue of requirements for voting and officeholding proved far more contentious. Conservative patriots struggled valiantly to reassert the rationale for the old voting restrictions. It was ridiculous, wrote one pamphleteer, to think that "every silly clown and illiterate mechanic [artisan]" deserved a voice in government. To John Adams, as conservative on the internal affairs of America as he had been radical on independence, freedom and equality were opposites. Men without property, he believed, had no "judgment of their own," and the removal of property qualifications, therefore, would "confound and destroy all distinctions, and prostrate all ranks to one common level."

Voting restrictions

The provisions of the new state constitutions reflected the balance of power between advocates of internal change and those who feared excessive democracy. The least democratization occurred in the southern states, whose highly deferential political traditions enabled the landed gentry to retain their control of political affairs. In Virginia and South Carolina, the new constitutions retained property qualifications for voting and authorized the gentry-dominated legislature to choose the governor. Maryland combined a low property qualification for voting with high requirements for officeholding, including £5,000—a fortune—for the governor.

The most democratic new constitutions moved much of the way toward the idea of voting as an entitlement rather than a privilege, but they generally stopped short of universal **suffrage**, even for free men. Vermont's constitution of 1777 was the only one to sever voting completely from financial considerations, eliminating not only property qualifications but also the requirement that voters pay taxes. Pennsylvania's constitution no longer required ownership of property, but it retained the taxpaying qualification. As a result, it enfranchised nearly all of the state's free male population but left a small number, mainly paupers and domestic servants, still barred from voting. Nonetheless, even with the taxpaying requirement, it represented a dramatic departure from the colonial practice of restricting the suffrage to those who could claim to be economically independent. It elevated "personal liberty," in the words of one essayist, to a position more important than property ownership in defining the boundaries of the political nation.

John Dickinson's copy of the Pennsylvania constitution of 1776, with handwritten proposals for changes. Dickinson, one of the more conservative advocates of independence, felt the new state constitution was far too democratic. He crossed out a provision that all "free men" should be eligible to hold office, and another declaring the people not bound by laws that did not promote "the common good."

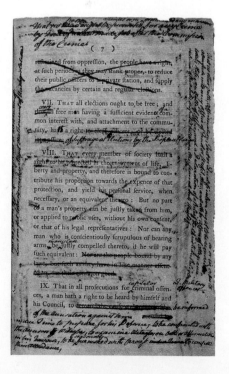

Democratizing Government

Overall, the Revolution led to a great expansion of the right to vote. By the 1780s, with the exceptions of Virginia, Maryland, and New York, a large majority of the adult white male population could meet voting requirements. New Jersey's new state constitution, of 1776, granted the suffrage to all "inhabitants" who met a property qualification. Until the state added the word "male" (along with "white") in 1807, property-owning women, mostly widows, did cast ballots. The new constitutions also expanded the number of legislative seats, with the result that numerous men of

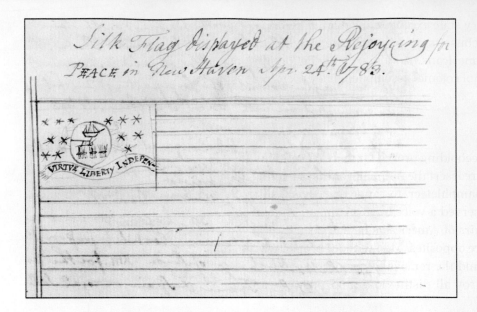

Ezra Stiles, the president of Yale College, drew this sketch of a flag in his diary on April 24, 1783, shortly after Congress ratified the Treaty of Paris. Thirteen stars surround the coat of arms of Pennsylvania. The banner text illustrates the linkage among virtue, liberty, and American independence.

lesser property assumed political office. The debate over the suffrage would, of course, continue for many decades. For white men, the process of democratization did not run its course until the Age of Jackson; for women and non-whites, it would take much longer.

Even during the Revolution, however, in the popular language of politics, if not in law, freedom and an individual's right to vote had become interchangeable. "The suffrage," declared a 1776 petition of disenfranchised North Carolinians, was "a right essential to and inseparable from freedom." Without it, Americans could not enjoy "equal liberty." A proposed new constitution for Massachusetts was rejected by a majority of the towns in 1778, partly because it contained a property qualification for voting. "All men were born equally free and independent," declared the town of Lenox. How could they defend their "life and liberty and property" without a voice in electing public officials? A new draft, which retained a substantial requirement for voting in state elections but allowed virtually all men to vote for town officers, was approved in 1780. And every state except South Carolina provided for annual legislative elections, to ensure that representatives remained closely accountable to the people. Henceforth, political freedom would mean not only, as in the past, a people's right to be ruled by their chosen representatives but also an individual's right to political participation.

TOWARD RELIGIOUS TOLERATION

As remarkable as the expansion of political freedom was the Revolution's impact on American religion. Religious toleration, declared one Virginia patriot, was part of "the common cause of Freedom." In Britain, Dissenters—Protestants who belonged to other denominations than the Anglican Church—had long invoked the language of liberty in seeking repeal of the laws that imposed various disabilities on non-Anglicans. (Few, however, included Catholics in their ringing calls for religious freedom.) We have already seen that Rhode Island and Pennsylvania had long made a practice of toleration. But freedom of worship before the Revolution arose more from the reality of religious pluralism than from a well-developed theory of religious liberty. Apart from Rhode Island, New England had little homegrown experience of religious pluralism. Indeed, authorities in England had occasionally pressed the region's rulers to become more tolerant. Before the Revolution, most colonies supported religious institutions with public funds and discriminated in voting and officeholding against Catholics, Jews, and even Dissenting Protestants. On the very eve of independence, Baptists who refused to pay taxes to support local

Religious pluralism

Congregational ministers were still being jailed in Massachusetts. "While our country are pleading so high for liberty," the victims complained, "yet they are denying of it to their neighbors."

Catholic Americans

The War of Independence weakened the deep tradition of American anti-Catholicism. The First Continental Congress denounced the Quebec Act of 1774, which, as noted in the previous chapter, allowed Canadian Catholics to worship freely, as part of a plot to establish "popery" in North America. But a year later, when the Second Continental Congress decided on an ill-fated invasion of Canada, it invited the inhabitants of Quebec to join in the struggle against Britain, assuring them that Protestants and Catholics could readily cooperate. In 1778, the United States formed an alliance with France, a Catholic nation. Benedict Arnold justified his treason, in part, by saying that an alliance with "the enemy of the protestant faith" was too much for him to bear. But the indispensable assistance provided by France to American victory strengthened the idea that Catholics had a role to play in the newly independent nation. This represented a marked departure from the traditional notion that the full rights of Englishmen only applied to Protestants. When America's first Roman Catholic bishop, John Carroll of Maryland, visited Boston in 1791, he received a cordial welcome.

Anti-Catholicism weakened

The Founders and Religion

The end of British rule immediately threw into question the privileged position enjoyed by the Anglican Church in many colonies. In Virginia, for example, backcountry Scotch-Irish Presbyterian farmers demanded relief from taxes supporting the official Anglican Church. "The free exercise of our rights of conscience," one patriotic meeting resolved, formed an essential part of "our liberties."

Many of the leaders of the Revolution considered it essential for the new nation to shield itself from the unruly passions and violent conflicts that religious differences had inspired during the past three centuries. Men like Thomas

Prospect of the City of New-York

1 Fort George	6 The Prison.	11 Old Dutch Church	16 Quaker's Meeting
2 Trinity Church	7 New Brick Meeting	12 Jew's Synagogue	17 Calvinist Church
3 Presbyter. Meeting	8 King's College	13 Lutherian Church	18 Anabaptist Meeting
4 North D. Church	9 St. Paul's Church	14 The French Church	19 Moravian Meeting
5 St. George's Chapel	10 N.Dutch Cal.Church	15 New Scot's Meeting	20 N. Lutheran Church
			21 Methodist Meeting

A 1771 image of New York City lists some of the numerous churches visible from the New Jersey shore, illustrating the diversity of religions practiced in the city.

View from Bushongo Tavern, an engraving from *The Columbian Magazine*, 1788, depicts the landscape of York County, Pennsylvania, exemplifying the kind of rural independence many Americans thought essential to freedom.

The lack of freedom inherent in apprenticeship and servitude increasingly came to be seen as incompatible with republican citizenship. Ebenezer Fox, a young apprentice on a Massachusetts farm, later recalled how he and other youths "made a direct application of the doctrines we heard daily, in relation to the oppression of the mother country, to our own circumstance. . . . I thought that I was doing myself a great injustice by remaining in bondage, when I ought to go free." Fox became one of many apprentices during the Revolution who decided to run away—or, as he put it, to "liberate myself." On the eve of the battles of Lexington and Concord in 1775, Fox and a friend set off for Rhode Island. After briefly working as a sailor, Fox, still a teenager, joined the Continental army.

In 1784, a group of "respectable" New Yorkers released a newly arrived shipload of indentured servants on the grounds that their status was "contrary to . . . the idea of liberty this country has so happily established." By 1800, indentured servitude had all but disappeared from the United States. This development sharpened the distinction between freedom and slavery, and between a northern economy relying on what would come to be called "free labor" (that is, working for wages or owning a farm or shop) and a southern economy ever more heavily dependent on the labor of slaves.

Sharpened distinction between freedom and slavery

The Soul of a Republic

Social conditions of freedom

Americans of the revolutionary generation were preoccupied with the social conditions of freedom. Could a republic survive with a sizable dependent class of citizens? "A general and tolerably equal distribution of landed property," proclaimed the educator and newspaper editor Noah Webster, "is the whole basis of national freedom." "Equality," he added, was "the very soul of a republic." Even a conservative like John Adams, who distrusted the era's democratic upsurge, hoped that every member of society could acquire land, "so that the multitude may be possessed of small estates" and the new nation could avoid the emergence of fixed and unequal social classes. At the Revolution's radical edge, some patriots believed that government had a responsibility to limit accumulations of property in the name of equality. To most free Americans, however, "equality" meant equal opportunity, rather than equality of condition. Many leaders of the Revolution nevertheless assumed that in the exceptional circumstances of the New World, with its vast areas of available land and large population of independent farmers and artisans, the natural workings of society would produce justice, liberty, and equality.

Like many other Americans of his generation, Thomas Jefferson believed that to lack economic resources was to lack freedom. His proudest achievements included laws passed by Virginia abolishing entail (the limitation of inheritance to a specified line of heirs to keep an estate within a family) and primogeniture (the practice of passing a family's land entirely to the eldest son). These measures, he believed, would help to prevent the rise of a "future aristocracy." To the same end, Jefferson proposed to award fifty acres of land to "every person of full age" who did not already possess it, another way government could enhance the liberty of its subjects. Of course, the land Jefferson hoped would secure American liberty would have to come from Indians.

> *Equal opportunity rather than equality of condition*

> *Abolishing entail and primogeniture*

The Politics of Inflation

The Revolution thrust to the forefront of politics debates over whether local or national authorities should take steps to bolster household independence and protect Americans' livelihoods by limiting price increases. Economic dislocations sharpened the controversy. To finance the war, Congress issued hundreds of millions of dollars in paper money. Coupled with wartime disruption of agriculture and trade and the hoarding of goods by some Americans hoping to profit from shortages, this produced an enormous **inflation** as prices rapidly rose. The country, charged a letter to a Philadelphia newspaper in 1778, had been "reduced to the brink of ruin by the infamous practices of monopolizers."

Between 1776 and 1779, more than thirty incidents took place in which crowds confronted merchants accused of holding scarce goods off the market. Often, they seized stocks of food and sold them at the traditional "just price," a form of protest common in eighteenth-century England. In one such incident, a crowd of 100 Massachusetts women accused an "eminent, wealthy, stingy merchant" of hoarding coffee, opened his warehouse, and carted off the goods. "A large concourse of men," wrote Abigail Adams, "stood amazed, silent spectators of the whole transaction."

The Debate over Free Trade

In 1779, with inflation totally out of control (in one month, prices in Philadelphia jumped 45 percent), Congress urged states to adopt measures to fix wages and prices. The policy embodied the belief that the task of republican government was to promote the public good, not individuals' self-interest. Bitter comments appeared in the Philadelphia press about the city's elite expending huge sums on "public dinners and other extravaganzas" while many in the city were "destitute of the necessities of life." But when a Committee of Safety tried to enforce price controls, it met spirited opposition from merchants and other advocates of a free market.

Against the traditional view that men should sacrifice for the public good, believers in **free trade** argued that economic development arose from economic self-interest. Just as Newton had revealed the inner workings of the natural

A cartoon from 1777 illustrates discontent with rising prices. One soldier identifies "extortioners" as "the worst enemies of the country." Another complains about serving "my country for sixteen pence per day."

universe, so the social world also followed unchanging natural laws, among them that supply and demand regulated the prices of goods. Adam Smith's great treatise on economics, ***The Wealth of Nations***, published in England in 1776, was beginning to become known in the United States. Smith's argument that the "invisible hand" of the free market directed economic life more effectively and fairly than governmental intervention offered intellectual justification for those who believed that the economy should be left to regulate itself.

Advocates of independence had envisioned America, released from the British Navigation Acts, trading freely with all the world. Opponents of price controls advocated free trade at home as well. "Let trade be as free as air," wrote one merchant. "Natural liberty" would regulate prices. Here were two competing conceptions of economic freedom—one based on the traditional view that the interests of the community took precedence over the property rights of individuals, the other insisting that unregulated economic freedom would produce social harmony and public gain. After 1779, the latter view gained ascendancy. State and federal efforts to regulate prices ceased. But the clash between these two visions of economic freedom would continue long after independence had been achieved.

"Yield to the mighty current of American freedom." So a member of the South Carolina legislature implored his colleagues in 1777. The current of freedom swept away not only British authority but also the principle of hereditary rule, the privileges of established churches, long-standing habits of deference and hierarchy, and old limits on the political nation. Yet in other areas, the tide of freedom encountered obstacles that did not yield as easily to its powerful flow.

THE LIMITS OF LIBERTY

Colonial Loyalists

Not all Americans shared in the democratization of freedom brought on by the American Revolution. **Loyalists**—those who retained their allegiance to the crown—experienced the conflict and its aftermath as a loss of liberty. Many leading Loyalists had supported American resistance in the 1760s but drew back at the prospect of independence and war. Loyalists included some of the most prominent Americans and some of the most humble. Altogether, an estimated 20 to 25 percent of free Americans remained loyal to the British, and nearly 20,000 fought on their side. At some points in the war, Loyalists serving with the British outnumbered Washington's army.

There were Loyalists in every colony, but they were most numerous in New York, Pennsylvania, and the backcountry of the Carolinas and Georgia. Some were wealthy men whose livelihoods depended on close working relationships with Britain—lawyers, merchants, Anglican ministers, and imperial officials. Many feared anarchy in the event of an American victory. "Liberty," one wrote, "can have no existence without obedience to the laws."

The struggle for independence heightened existing tensions between ethnic groups and social classes within the colonies. Some Loyalist ethnic minorities, like Highland Scots in North Carolina, feared that local majorities would infringe on their freedom to enjoy cultural autonomy. In the South, many backcountry farmers who had long resented the domination of public affairs by wealthy planters sided with the British. So did tenants on the New York estates of patriot landlords like the Livingston family. Robert Livingston had signed the Declaration of Independence. When the army of General Burgoyne approached Livingston's manor in 1777, tenants rose in revolt, hoping the British would confiscate his land and distribute it among themselves. Their hopes were dashed by Burgoyne's defeat at Saratoga. In the South, numerous slaves sided with the British, hoping an American defeat would bring them freedom.

A 1780 British cartoon commenting on the "cruel fate" of American Loyalists. Pro-independence colonists are likened to savage Indians.

The Loyalists' Plight

The War of Independence was in some respects a civil war among Americans. "This country," wrote a German colonel fighting with the British, "is the scene of the most cruel events. Neighbors are on opposite sides, children are against their fathers." Freedom of expression is often a casualty of war, and many Americans were deprived of basic rights in the name of liberty. After Dr. Abner Beebe, of East Haddam, Connecticut, spoke "very freely" in favor of the British, a mob attacked his house and destroyed his gristmill. Beebe himself was "assaulted, stripped naked, and hot pitch [tar] was poured upon him." The new state governments, or crowds of patriots, suppressed newspapers thought to be loyal to Britain.

Pennsylvania arrested and seized the property of Quakers, Mennonites, and Moravians—pacifist denominations who refused to bear arms because of their religious beliefs. With the approval of Congress, many states required residents to take oaths of allegiance to the new nation. Those who refused were denied the right to vote and in many cases forced into exile. "The flames of discord," wrote one British observer, "are sprouting from the seeds of liberty." Some wealthy Loyalists saw their land confiscated and sold at auction. Twenty-eight estates belonging to New Hampshire governor John Wentworth and his family were seized, as were the holdings of great New York Loyalist landlords like the De Lancey and Philipse families. Most of the buyers of this land were merchants, lawyers, and established landowners. Unable to afford the purchase price, tenants had no choice but to continue to labor for the new owners.

Loyalists after independence

The Revolution as a Borderlands Conflict

When the war ended, as many as 60,000 Loyalists were banished from the United States or emigrated voluntarily—mostly to Britain, Canada, or the West Indies—rather than live in an independent United States. So many Loyalists went to Nova Scotia, in Canada, that a new province, New Brunswick, was created to accommodate them. For those Loyalists who remained in the United States, hostility proved to be short-lived. In the Treaty of Paris of 1783, as noted in Chapter 5,

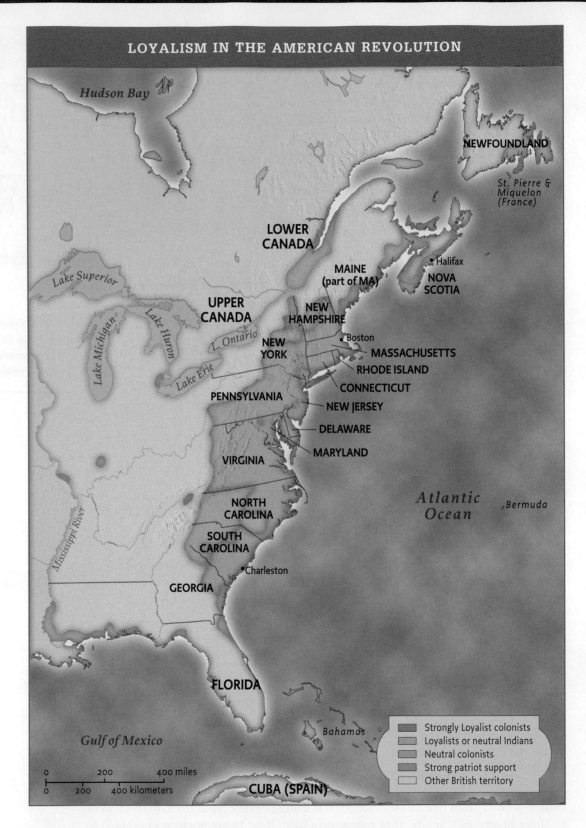

LOYALISM IN THE AMERICAN REVOLUTION

Hudson Bay

NEWFOUNDLAND

St. Pierre &
Miquelon
(France)

LOWER
CANADA

• Halifax

MAINE
(part of MA)

NOVA
SCOTIA

Lake Superior

UPPER
CANADA

NEW
HAMPSHIRE

Lake Michigan

Lake Huron

L. Ontario

NEW
YORK

• Boston

Lake Erie

MASSACHUSETTS

RHODE ISLAND

CONNECTICUT

PENNSYLVANIA

NEW JERSEY

DELAWARE

MARYLAND

VIRGINIA

*Atlantic
Ocean*

,Bermuda

Mississippi River

NORTH
CAROLINA

SOUTH
CAROLINA

• Charleston

GEORGIA

FLORIDA

Bahamas

Gulf of Mexico

	Strongly Loyalist colonists
	Loyalists or neutral Indians
	Neutral colonists
	Strong patriot support
	Other British territory

0   200   400 miles

0   200   400 kilometers

CUBA (SPAIN)

The Revolutionary War was, in some ways, a civil war within the colonies. There were Loyalists in every colony; they were most numerous in New York and North and South Carolina.

Americans pledged to end the persecution of Loyalists by state and local governments and to restore property seized during the war. American leaders believed the new nation needed to establish an international reputation for fairness and civility. States soon repealed their test oaths for voting and officeholding. Loyalists who did not leave the country were quickly reintegrated into American society, although despite the promise of the Treaty of Paris, confiscated Loyalist property was not returned.

Reintegration of Loyalists

The Loyalists' exile had a profound impact on the future development of North America. The War of Independence severed the British colonies of Nova Scotia and Quebec from the southern thirteen that formed the United States. Despite rejecting American independence, many Loyalists who settled in Canada brought with them not only a loyalty to the British crown but also a commitment to self-rule. They went on to agitate for responsible government in their new homeland. Their ideas would help to inspire rebellions in Canada in 1837 that helped close out the Age of Revolution the American revolt had launched. Although crushed by the British, the rebellions led eventually to the creation in 1867 of a single government for the Canadian provinces.

Thus, the American Revolution transformed the old boundary separating New England and New York from Quebec as provinces of the British empire into an international border. The consequences were profound. Without this development, Canada would not have been a refuge to slaves who left with the British when they evacuated the newly independent United States, or to those who escaped across the border later in the nineteenth century. Nor would Irish nationalists have been shielded from British law during and after the Civil War when they congregated in upstate New York and launched raids across the northern border as a way of striking a blow against British rule of their homeland. In Canada, the loyalist exiles would long be viewed as national founding fathers, and Canadians would often define their identity in opposition to their powerful neighbor to the south, even though goods and ideas always flowed easily across the border (today, each country is the other's largest trading partner).

Canada–United States border

The Indians' Revolution

Another region where the Revolution took on the character of a borderlands conflict as much as a struggle for independence was the trans-Appalachian West. Here, where British authority remained weak even after the expulsion of the French in the Seven Years' War and Indians enjoyed considerable authority, the patriots' victory marked a decisive shift of power away from native tribes and toward white settlers. The destruction of the "middle ground" would not be completed until after the War of 1812, but it received a major impetus from American independence.

Despite the Proclamation of 1763, discussed in Chapter 4, colonists had continued to move westward during the 1760s and early 1770s, leading Indian tribes to complain of intrusions on their land. Lord Dunmore, Virginia's royal governor, observed in 1772 that he had found it impossible "to restrain the Americans. . . . They do not conceive that government has any right to forbid their taking possession of a vast tract of country" or to force them to honor treaties with Indians.

Indian lands in the West

Kentucky, the principal hunting ground of southern Cherokees and numerous Ohio Valley Indians, became a flash point of conflict among settlers, land

Liberty Displaying the Arts and Sciences. This 1792 painting by Samuel Jennings is one of the few visual images of the early republic explicitly linking slavery with tyranny and liberty with abolition. The female figure offers books to newly freed slaves. Other forms of knowledge depicted include a globe and an artist's palette. Beneath her left foot lies a broken chain. In the background, free slaves enjoy some leisure time.

The Language of Slavery and Freedom

Slavery played a central part in the language of revolution. Apart from "liberty," it was the word most frequently invoked in the era's legal and political literature. Eighteenth-century writers frequently juxtaposed freedom and slavery as "the two extremes of happiness and misery in society." Yet in debates over British rule, slavery was primarily a political category, shorthand for the denial of one's personal and political rights by arbitrary government. Those who lacked a voice in public affairs, declared a 1769 petition demanding an expansion of the right to vote in Britain, were "enslaved." By the eve of independence, the contrast between Britain, "a kingdom of slaves," and America, a "country of free men," had become a standard part of the language of resistance. Such language was employed without irony even in areas where half the population in fact consisted of slaves. South Carolina, one writer declared in 1774, was a "sacred land" of freedom, where it was impossible to believe that "slavery shall soon be permitted to erect her throne."

Colonial writers of the 1760s occasionally made a direct connection between slavery as a reality and slavery as a metaphor. Few were as forthright as James Otis of Massachusetts, whose pamphlets did much to popularize the idea that Parliament lacked the authority to tax the colonies and regulate their commerce. Freedom, Otis insisted, must be universal: "What man is or ever was born free if every man is not?" Otis wrote of blacks not as examples of the loss of rights awaiting free Americans, but as flesh and blood British subjects "entitled to all the civil rights of such."

Otis was hardly typical of patriot leaders. But the presence of hundreds of thousands of slaves powerfully affected the meaning of freedom for the leaders of the American Revolution. In a famous speech to Parliament warning against attempts to intimidate the colonies, the British statesman Edmund Burke suggested that familiarity with slavery made colonial leaders unusually sensitive to threats to their own liberties. Where freedom was a privilege, not a common right, he observed, "those who are free are by far the most proud and jealous of their freedom." On the other hand, many British observers could not resist pointing out the colonists' apparent hypocrisy. "How is it," asked Dr. Samuel Johnson, "that we hear the loudest yelps for liberty from the drivers of negroes?"

Obstacles to Abolition

The contradiction between freedom and slavery seems so self-evident that it is difficult today to appreciate the power of the obstacles to **abolition**. At the time of the Revolution, slavery was already an old institution in America. It existed in every colony and formed the basis of the economy and social structure from Maryland southward. At least 40 percent of Virginia's population and even higher proportions in Georgia and South Carolina were slaves.

Virtually every founding father owned slaves at one point in his life, including not only southern planters but also northern merchants, lawyers, and farmers. (John Adams and Tom Paine were notable exceptions.) Thomas Jefferson owned more than 100 slaves when he wrote of mankind's unalienable right to liberty, and everything he cherished in his own manner of life, from lavish entertainments to the leisure that made possible the pursuit of arts and sciences, ultimately rested on slave labor.

Some patriots, in fact, argued that slavery for blacks made freedom possible for whites. Owning slaves offered a route to the economic autonomy widely deemed necessary for genuine freedom, a point driven home by a 1780 Virginia law that rewarded veterans of the War of Independence with 300 acres of land—and a slave. South Carolina and Georgia promised every white military volunteer a slave at the war's end.

So, too, the Lockean vision of the political community as a group of individuals contracting together to secure their natural rights could readily be invoked to defend bondage. Nothing was more essential to freedom, in this view, than the right of self-government and the protection of property against outside interference. These principles suggested that for the government to seize property—including slave property—against the owner's will would be an infringement on liberty. To require owners to give up their slave property would reduce *them* to slavery.

Slavery entrenched

The Cause of General Liberty

Nonetheless, by imparting so absolute a value to liberty and defining freedom as a universal entitlement rather than a set of rights specific to a particular place or people, the Revolution inevitably raised questions about the status of slavery in the new nation. Before independence, there had been little public discussion of the institution, even though enlightened opinion in the Atlantic world had come to view slavery as morally wrong and economically inefficient, a relic of a barbarous past.

As early as 1688, a group of German Quakers issued a "protest" regarding the rights of blacks, declaring it as unjust "to have them slaves, as it is to have other white ones." Samuel Sewall, a Boston merchant, published *The Selling of Joseph* in 1700, the first antislavery tract printed in America. All "the sons of Adam," Sewall insisted, were entitled to "have equal right unto liberty." During the course of the eighteenth century, antislavery sentiments had spread among Pennsylvania's Quakers, whose belief that all persons possessed the divine "inner light" made them particularly receptive. But it was during the revolutionary era that slavery for the first time became a focus of public debate. The Pennsylvania patriot Benjamin Rush in 1773 called upon "advocates for American liberty" to "espouse the cause of . . . general liberty" and warned that slavery was one of those "national crimes" that one day would bring "national punishment." Although a slaveholder himself, in private Jefferson condemned slavery as a system that every day imposed on its victims "more misery, than ages of that which [the colonists] rose in rebellion to oppose."

Freedom as universal

Early antislavery

Petitions for Freedom

The Revolution inspired widespread hopes that slavery could be removed from American life. Most dramatically, slaves themselves appreciated that by defining freedom as a universal right, the leaders of the Revolution had devised a weapon that could be used against their own bondage. The language of liberty

THE RATIFICATION DEBATE AND THE ORIGIN OF THE BILL OF RIGHTS

The Federalist

A national debate

Even though the Constitution provided that it would go into effect when nine states, not all thirteen as required by the Articles of Confederation, had given their approval, ratification was by no means certain. Each state held an election for delegates to a special ratifying convention. A fierce public battle ensued, producing hundreds of pamphlets and newspaper articles and spirited campaigns to elect delegates. To generate support, Hamilton, Madison, and Jay composed a series of eighty-five essays that appeared in newspapers under the pen name Publius and were gathered as a book, ***The Federalist***, in 1788. Hamilton wrote fifty, Madison thirty, and Jay the remainder. Today, the essays are regarded as among the most important American contributions to political thought. At the time, however, they represented only one part of a much larger national debate over ratification, reflected in innumerable pamphlets, newspaper articles, and public meetings.

Again and again, Hamilton and Madison repeated that rather than posing a danger to Americans' liberties, the Constitution in fact protected them. Hamilton's essays sought to disabuse Americans of their fear of political power. Government, he insisted, was an expression of freedom, not its enemy. Any government could become oppressive, but with its checks and balances and division of power, the Constitution made political tyranny almost impossible. Hamilton insisted that he was "as zealous an advocate for liberty as any man whatever." But "want of power" had been the fatal flaw of the Articles. At the New York ratifying con-

This satirical engraving by Amos Doolittle (who created the image of the Battle of Concord in Chapter 5) depicts some of the issues in the debate over the ratification of the Constitution. The wagon in the center is carrying Connecticut and sinking into the mud under the weight of debts and paper money as "Federals" and "Antifederals" try to pull it out. Federals call for the state to "comply with Congress" (that is, to pay money requisitioned by the national government); the Antifederals reply, "Tax luxury" and "Success to Shays," a reference to Shays's Rebellion. Underneath the three merchant ships is a phrase criticizing the tariffs that states were imposing on imports from one another (which the Constitution prohibited).

In this late-eighteenth-century engraving, Americans celebrate the signing of the Constitution beneath a temple of liberty.

vention, Hamilton assured the delegates that the Constitution had created "the perfect balance between liberty and power."

"Extend the Sphere"

Madison, too, emphasized how the Constitution was structured to prevent abuses of authority. But in several essays, especially *Federalist* nos. 10 and 51, he moved beyond such assurances to develop a strikingly new vision of the relationship between government and society in the United States. Madison identified the essential dilemma, as he saw it, of the new republic—government must be based on the will of the people, yet the people had shown themselves susceptible to dangerous enthusiasms. Most worrisome, they had threatened property rights, whose protection was the "first object of government." The problem of balancing democracy and respect for property would only grow in the years ahead because, he warned, economic development would inevitably increase the numbers of poor. What was to prevent them from using their political power to secure "a more equal distribution" of wealth by seizing the property of the rich?

The answer, Madison explained, lay not simply in the way power balanced power in the structure of government, but in the nation's size and diversity. Previous republics had existed only in small territories—the Dutch republic, or Italian city-states of the Renaissance. But, argued Madison, the very size of the United States was a source of stability, not, as many feared, weakness. "Extend the sphere," he wrote. In a nation as large as the United States, so many distinct interests—economic, regional, and political—would arise, that no single one would

Madison's Federalist *no. 10*

America's size and diversity

Order of Procession,

In honor of the Constitution of the United States.

THIS DAY.

AT 8 o'clock this morning, 23d of July, 10 guns will fire, when the Procession will parade, and proceed by the following rout, viz.
———Down Broad-way to Great Dock-Street, thence through Hanover-square, Queen, Chatham, Division and Arundel-Streets; and from thence through Bullock-street to Bayard's-house.

2 Horsemen with Trumpets.
1 piece of Artillery.
First Division.
Foresters in frocks, carrying axes.
Columbus in his ancient dress, on horseback.
6 Foresters, &c.
A Plough.
A Harrow.
Farmers.

Fourth Division.
Carpenters.
Farriers.
Hatters.
Peruke-makers and Hair-dressers.
Fifth Division.
White Smiths.
Cutlers.
Stone Masons.
Brick Layers.
Painters and Glaziers.
Cabinet Makers.
Windsor Chair Makers.
Upholsterers.
Fringe Makers,
Paper Stainers.
Civil Engineers.
Sixth Division.
Ship Wrights.
Black Smiths.
Ship Joiners.
Boat Builders.

In New York City's Grand Federal Procession of 1788, celebrating the ratification of the Constitution, members of each trade and occupation marched together. This document illustrates the variety of crafts in the pre-industrial city.

ever be able to take over the government and oppress the rest. Every majority would be a coalition of minorities, and thus "the rights of individuals" would be secure.

Madison's writings did much to shape the early nation's understanding of its new political institutions. In arguing that the size of the republic helped to secure Americans' rights, they reinforced the tradition that saw continuous westward expansion as essential to freedom. And in basing the preservation of freedom on the structure of government and size of the republic, not the character of the people, his essays represented a major shift away from the "republican" emphasis on a virtuous citizenry devoted to the common good as the foundation of proper government. Madison helped to popularize the "liberal" idea that men are generally motivated by self-interest, and that the good of society arises from the clash of these private interests.

The Anti-Federalists

Opponents of ratification, called **Anti-Federalists**, insisted that the Constitution shifted the balance between liberty and power too far in the direction of the latter. Anti-Federalists lacked the coherent leadership of the Constitution's defenders. They included state politicians fearful of seeing their influence diminish, among them such revolutionary heroes as Samuel Adams, John Hancock, and Patrick Henry. Small farmers, many of whom supported the state debtor-relief measures of the 1780s that the Constitution's supporters deplored, also saw no need for a stronger central government. Some opponents of the Constitution denounced the document's protections for slavery; others warned that the powers of Congress were so broad that it might enact a law for abolition.

Anti-Federalists repeatedly predicted that the new government would fall under the sway of merchants, creditors, and others hostile to the interests of ordinary Americans. Repudiating Madison's arguments in *Federalist* nos. 10 and 51, Anti-Federalists insisted that "a very extensive territory cannot be governed on the principles of freedom." Popular self-government, they claimed, flourished best in small communities, where rulers and ruled interacted daily. Only men of wealth, "ignorant of the sentiments of the middling and lower class of citizens," would have the resources to win election to a national government. The result of the Constitution, warned Melancton Smith of New York, a member of Congress under the Articles of Confederation, would be domination of the "common people" by the "well-born." "This," Smith predicted, "will be a government of oppression."

Liberty was the Anti-Federalists' watchword. America's happiness, they insisted, "arises from the freedom of our institutions and the limited nature of our government," both threatened by the new Constitution. Maryland Anti-Federalists had caps manufactured bearing the word "Liberty," to wear to the polls when members of the state's ratification convention were elected. To the vision of the United States as an energetic great power, Anti-Federalists counterposed a way of life grounded in local, democratic institutions. "What is Liberty?" asked James Lincoln of South Carolina. "The power of governing yourselves. If you adopt this constitution, have you this power? No."

Anti-Federalists also pointed to the Constitution's lack of a **Bill of Rights**, which left unprotected rights such as trial by jury and freedom of speech and the press.

Banner of the Society of Pewterers.
A banner carried by one of the many artisan groups that took part in New York City's Grand Federal Procession of 1788 celebrating the ratification of the Constitution. The banner depicts artisans at work in their shop and some of their products. The words "Solid and Pure," and the inscription at the upper right, link the quality of their pewter to their opinion of the new frame of government and hopes for the future. The inscription reads:

"The Federal Plan Most Solid and Secure Americans Their Freedom Will Endure All Arts Shall Flourish in Columbia's Land And All Her Sons Join as One Social Band"

The absence of a Bill of Rights, declared Patrick Henry, was "the most absurd thing to mankind that ever the world saw." State constitutions had bills of rights, yet the states, Henry claimed, were now being asked to surrender most of their powers to the federal government, with no requirement that it respect Americans' basic liberties.

In general, pro-Constitution sentiment flourished in the nation's cities and in rural areas closely tied to the commercial marketplace. The Constitution's most energetic supporters were men of substantial property. But what George Bryan of Pennsylvania, a supporter of ratification, called the "golden phantom" of prosperity also swung urban artisans, laborers, and sailors behind the movement for a government that would use its "energy and power" to revive the depressed economy. Anti-Federalism drew its support from small farmers in more isolated rural areas such as the Hudson Valley of New York, western Massachusetts, and the southern backcountry.

> Social bases of support and opposition

In the end, the supporters' energy and organization, coupled with their domination of the colonial press, carried the day. Ninety-two newspapers and magazines existed in the United States in 1787. Of these, only twelve published a significant number of Anti-Federalist pieces. Madison also won support for the new Constitution by promising that the first Congress would enact a Bill of Rights. By mid-1788, the required nine states had ratified. Although there was strong dissent in Massachusetts, New York, and Virginia, only Rhode Island and North Carolina voted against ratification, and they subsequently had little choice but to join the new government. Anti-Federalism died. But as with other movements in American history that did not immediately achieve their goals—for example, the Populists of the late nineteenth century—some of the Anti-Federalists' ideas eventually entered the political mainstream. To this day, their belief that a too-powerful central government is a threat to liberty continues to influence American political culture.

> Ratification

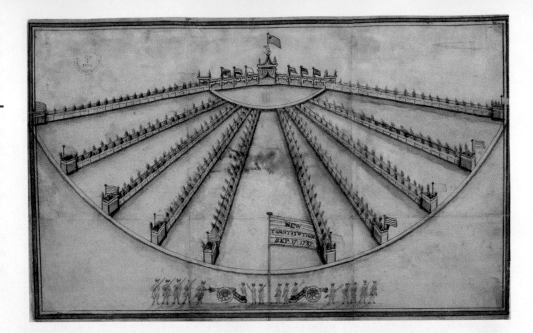

After the Grand Federal Procession, hundreds of marchers enjoyed a celebratory banquet. The ten tables represented the states that had ratified by July 1788 when the procession took place.

The Bill of Rights

Ironically, the parts of the Constitution Americans most value today—the freedoms of speech, the press, and religion; protection against unjust criminal procedures; equality before the law—were not in the original document. All of these but the last (which was enshrined in the Fourteenth Amendment after the Civil War) were contained in the first ten amendments, known as the Bill of Rights. Madison was so convinced that the balances of the Constitution would protect liberty that he believed a Bill of Rights "redundant or pointless." Amendments restraining federal power, he believed, would have no effect on the danger to liberty posed by unchecked majorities in the states, and no list of rights could ever anticipate the numerous ways that Congress might operate in the future. "Parchment barriers" to the abuse of authority, he observed, would prove least effective when most needed. Madison's prediction would be amply borne out at future times of popular hysteria, such as during the Red Scare following World War I and the McCarthy era of the 1950s, when all branches of government joined in trampling on freedom of expression, and during World War II, when hatred of a foreign enemy led to the internment of more than 100,000 Japanese-Americans, most of them citizens of the United States.

Nevertheless, every new state constitution contained some kind of declaration of citizens' rights, and large numbers of Americans—Federalist and Anti-Federalist alike—believed the new national Constitution should also have one. Indeed, many delegates at state conventions had refused to vote for ratification unless promised that a Bill of Rights would be added to the Constitution. In order to "conciliate the minds of the people," as Madison put it, he presented to Congress a series of amendments that became the basis of the Bill of Rights, which was ratified by the states in 1791. The First Amendment prohibited Congress from legislating with regard to religion or infringing on freedom of speech, freedom of the press, or the right of assembly. The Second upheld the people's right to "keep and bear arms" in conjunction with "a well-regulated militia." Others prohibited abuses such as arrests without warrants

Madison's objections

First Amendment rights

and forcing a person accused of a crime to testify against himself and reaffirmed the right to trial by jury.

In a sense, the Bill of Rights offered a definition of the "unalienable rights" Jefferson had mentioned in the Declaration of Independence—rights inherent in the human condition. Not having been granted by government in the first place, they could not be rescinded by government. In case any had been accidentally omitted, the Ninth Amendment declared that rights not specifically mentioned in the Constitution were "retained by the people." Its suggestion that the Constitution was not meant to be complete opened the door to future legal recognition of rights not grounded in the actual text (such as the right to privacy). The Tenth Amendment, meant to answer fears that the federal government would ride roughshod over the states, affirmed that powers not delegated to the national government or prohibited to the states continued to reside with the states.

> *Ninth Amendment rights*

The roots and even the specific language of some parts of the Bill of Rights lay far back in English history. The Eighth Amendment, prohibiting excessive bail and cruel and unusual punishments, incorporates language that originated in a declaration by the House of Lords in 1316 and was repeated centuries later in the English Bill of Rights and the constitutions of a number of American states.

Other provisions reflected the changes in American life brought about by the Revolution. The most remarkable of these was constitutional recognition of religious freedom. Unlike the Declaration of Independence, which invokes the blessing of divine providence, the Constitution is a purely secular document that contains no reference to God and bars religious tests for federal officeholders. The First Amendment prohibits the federal government from legislating on the subject of religion—a complete departure from British and colonial precedent. Under the Constitution it was and remains possible, as one critic complained, for "a papist, a Mohomatan, a deist, yea an atheist" to become president of the United States. Madison was so adamant about separating church and state that he even opposed the appointment of chaplains to serve Congress and the military.

> *Right to religious freedom*

An engraving and a poem, published in 1788 in an American newspaper, after New York became the eleventh state to ratify the new Constitution. North Carolina would ratify in 1789 and Rhode Island in 1790.

Today, when Americans are asked to define freedom, they instinctively turn to the Bill of Rights and especially the First Amendment, with its guarantees of freedom of speech, the press, and religion. Yet the Bill of Rights aroused little enthusiasm on ratification and for decades was all but ignored. Not until the twentieth century would it come to be revered as an indispensable expression of American freedom. Nonetheless, the Bill of Rights subtly affected the language of liberty. Applying only to the federal government, not the states, it reinforced the idea that concentrated national power posed the greatest threat to freedom. And it contributed to the long process whereby freedom came to be discussed in the vocabulary of rights.

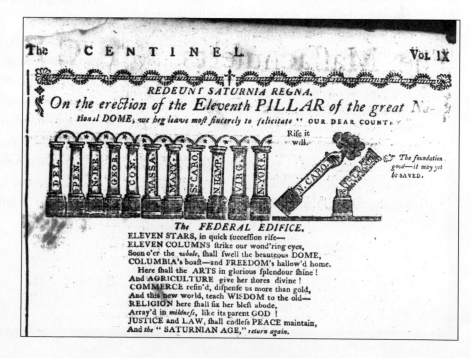

The CENTINEL. VOL IX

REDEUNT SATURNIA REGNA.

On the erection of the Eleventh PILLAR of the great National DOME, we beg leave most sincerely to felicitate "OUR DEAR COUNTRY"

Rise it will.

The foundation good—it may yet be SAVED.

The FEDERAL EDIFICE.

ELEVEN STARS, in quick succession rise—
ELEVEN COLUMNS strike our wond'ring eyes,
Soon o'er the whole, shall swell the beauteous DOME,
COLUMBIA's boast—and FREEDOM's hallow'd home.
  Here shall the ARTS in glorious splendour shine!
And AGRICULTURE give her stores divine!
COMMERCE refin'd, dispense us more than gold,
And this new world, teach WISDOM to the old—
RELIGION here shall fix her blest abode,
Array'd in mildness, like its parent GOD!
JUSTICE and LAW, shall endless PEACE maintain,
And the "SATURNIAN AGE," return again.

VOICES OF FREEDOM

From DAVID RAMSAY, *THE HISTORY OF THE AMERICAN REVOLUTION* (1789)

A member of the Continental Congress from South Carolina, David Ramsay published his history of the Revolution the year after the Constitution was ratified. In this excerpt, he lauds the principles of representative government and the right of future amendment, embodied in the state constitutions and adopted in the national one, as unique American political principles and the best ways of securing liberty.

The world has not hitherto exhibited so fair an opportunity for promoting social happiness. It is hoped for the honor of human nature, that the result will prove the fallacy of those theories that mankind are incapable of self government. The ancients, not knowing the doctrine of representation, were apt in their public meetings to run into confusion, but in America this mode of taking the sense of the people, is so well understood, and so completely reduced to system, that its most populous states are often peaceably convened in an assembly of deputies, not too large for orderly deliberation, and yet representing the whole in equal proportion. These popular

branches of legislature are miniature pictures of the community, and from their mode of election are likely to be influenced by the same interests and feelings with the people whom they represent. . . .

In no age before, and in no other country, did man ever possess an election of the kind of government, under which he would choose to live. The constituent parts of the ancient free governments were thrown together by accident. The freedom of modern European governments was, for the most part, obtained by concessions, or liberality of monarchs, or military leaders. In America alone, reason and liberty concurred in the formation of constitutions. . . . In one thing they were all perfect. They left the people in the power of altering and amending them, whenever they pleased. In this happy peculiarity they placed the science of politics on a footing with the other sciences, by opening it to improvements from experience, and the discoveries of future ages. By means of this power of amending American constitutions, the friends of mankind have fondly hoped that oppression will one day be no more.

From JAMES WINTHROP, ANTI-FEDERALIST ESSAY SIGNED "AGRIPPA" (1787)

A local official in Middlesex, Massachusetts, James Winthrop published sixteen public letters between November 1787 and February 1788 opposing ratification of the Constitution.

———————————

It is the opinion of the ablest writers on the subject, that no extensive empire can be governed upon republican principles, and that such a government will degenerate into a despotism, unless it be made up of a confederacy of smaller states, each having the full powers of internal regulation. This is precisely the principle which has hitherto preserved our freedom. No instance can be found of any free government of considerable extent which has been supported upon any other plan. Large and consolidated empires may indeed dazzle the eyes of a distant spectator with their splendor, but if examined more nearly are always found to be full of misery. . . . It is under such tyranny that the Spanish provinces languish, and such would be our misfortune and degradation, if we should submit to have the concerns of the whole empire managed by one empire. To promote the happiness of the people it is necessary that there should be local laws; and it is necessary that those laws should be made by the representatives of those who are immediately subject to [them]. . . .

It is impossible for one code of laws to suit Georgia and Massachusetts. They must, therefore, legislate for themselves. Yet there is, I believe, not one point of legislation that is not surrendered in the proposed plan. Questions of every kind respecting property are determinable in a continental court, and so are all kinds of criminal causes. The continental legislature has, therefore, a right to make rules in all cases. . . . No rights are reserved to the citizens. . . . This new system is, therefore, a consolidation of all the states into one large mass, however diverse the parts may be of which it is composed. . . .

A bill of rights . . . serves to secure the minority against the usurpation and tyranny of the majority. . . . The experience of all mankind has proved the prevalence of a disposition to use power wantonly. It is therefore as necessary to defend an individual against the majority in a republic as against the king in a monarchy.

QUESTIONS

1. *Why does Ramsay feel that the power to amend the Constitution is so important a political innovation?*

2. *Why does Winthrop believe that a Bill of Rights is essential in the Constitution?*

3. *How do Ramsay and Winthrop differ concerning how the principle of representation operates in the United States?*

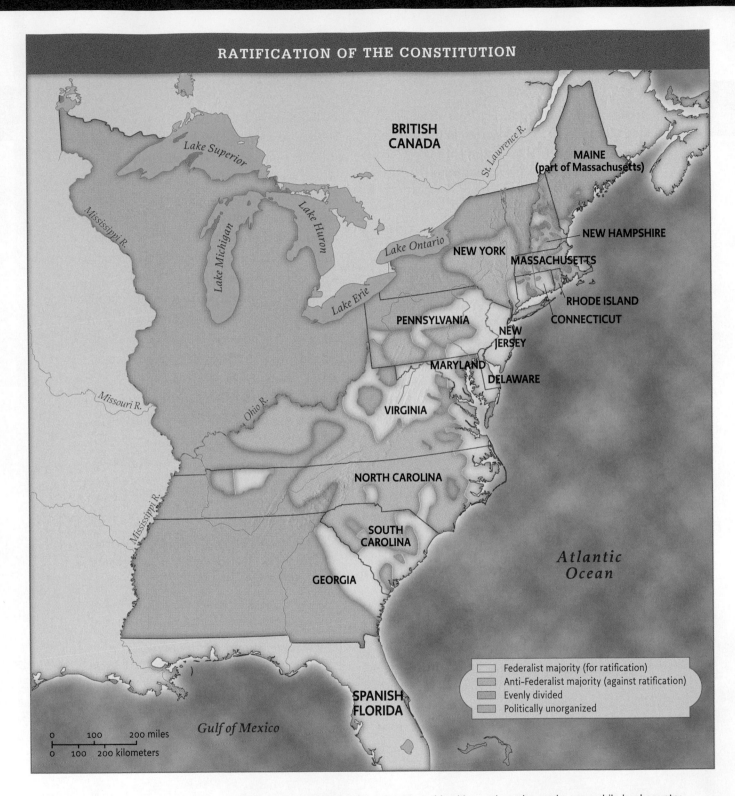

RATIFICATION OF THE CONSTITUTION

BRITISH CANADA

Lake Superior

Lake Michigan

Lake Huron

Lake Ontario

Lake Erie

Mississippi R.

Missouri R.

Ohio R.

St. Lawrence R.

MAINE (part of Massachusetts)

NEW HAMPSHIRE

NEW YORK

MASSACHUSETTS

RHODE ISLAND

CONNECTICUT

PENNSYLVANIA

NEW JERSEY

MARYLAND

DELAWARE

VIRGINIA

NORTH CAROLINA

SOUTH CAROLINA

GEORGIA

SPANISH FLORIDA

Atlantic Ocean

Gulf of Mexico

	Federalist majority (for ratification)
	Anti-Federalist majority (against ratification)
	Evenly divided
	Politically unorganized

0   100   200 miles
0   100   200 kilometers

Federalists—those who supported the new Constitution—tended to be concentrated in cities and nearby rural areas, while backcountry farmers were more likely to oppose the new frame of government.

Among the most important rights were freedom of speech and the press, vital building blocks of a democratic public sphere. Once an entitlement of members of Parliament and colonial assemblies, free speech came to be seen as a basic right of citizenship. Although the legal implementation remained to be worked out, and serious infringements would occur at many points in American history, the Bill of Rights did much to establish freedom of expression as a cornerstone of the popular understanding of American freedom.

"WE THE PEOPLE"

National Identity

The colonial population had been divided by ethnicity, religion, class, and status and united largely by virtue of their allegiance to Britain. The Revolution created not only a new nation but also a new collective body, the American people, whose members were to enjoy freedom as citizens in a new political community. Since government in the United States rested on the will of the people, it was all the more important to identify who the people were.

> *The American people*

The Constitution opens with the words "We the People," describing those who, among other things, are to possess "the Blessings of Liberty" as a birthright and pass them on to "Posterity." (Abraham Lincoln would later cite these words to argue that since the nation had been created by the people, not the states, the states could not dissolve it.) Although one might assume that the "people" of the United States included all those living within the nation's borders, the text made clear that this was not the case. The Constitution identifies three populations inhabiting the United States: Indians, treated as members of independent tribes and not part of the American body politic; "other persons"—that is, slaves; and the "people." Only the third were entitled to American freedom.

> *Exclusion of Indians and slaves*

Every nation confronts the task of defining its identity. Historians have traditionally distinguished between "civic nationalism," which envisions the nation as a community open to all those devoted to its political institutions and social values, and "ethnic nationalism," which defines the nation as a community of descent based on a shared ethnic heritage, language, and culture. At first glance, the United States appears to conform to the civic model. It lacked a clear ethnic identity or long-established national boundaries—the political principles of the Revolution held Americans together. To be an American, all one had to do was commit oneself to an ideology of liberty, equality, and democracy. From the outset, however, American nationality combined both civic and ethnic definitions. For most of our history, American citizenship has been defined by blood as well as by political allegiance.

Indians in the New Nation

The early republic's policies toward Indians and African-Americans illustrate the conflicting principles that shaped American nationality. American leaders agreed that the West should not be left in Indian hands, but they disagreed about the Indians' ultimate fate. The government hoped to encourage the westward expansion of white settlement, which implied one of three things: the removal of the Indian population to lands even

A medal issued to Red Jacket, a Seneca chief, during his visit to Philadelphia (then the national capital) in 1792. It depicts George Washington offering an Indian a peace pipe. The agricultural scene in the background was intended to suggest that Indians should take up farming.

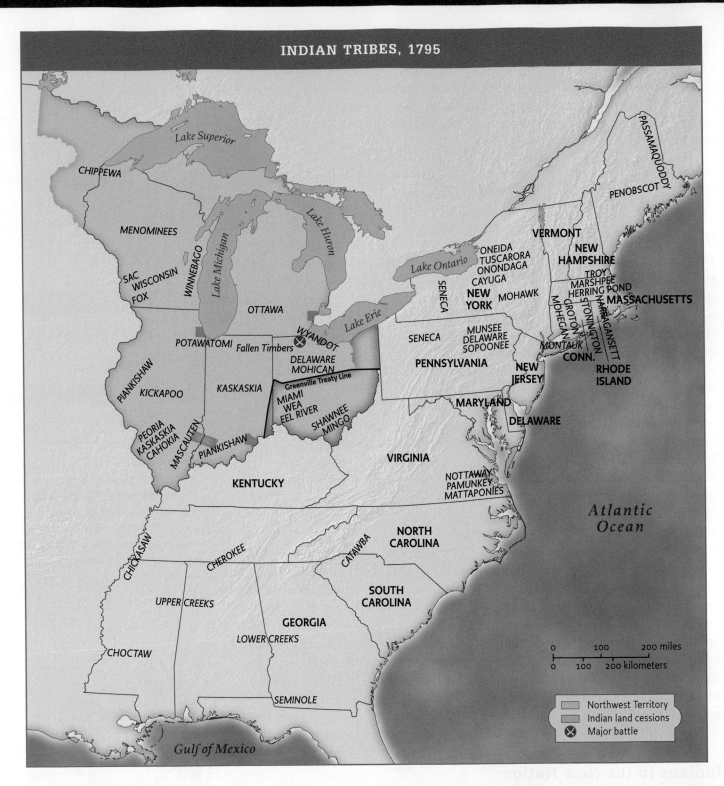

INDIAN TRIBES, 1795

CHIPPEWA

MENOMINEES

Lake Superior

Lake Huron

SAC
WISCONSIN
FOX

WINNEBAGO

Lake Michigan

OTTAWA

POTAWATOMI   Fallen Timbers
WYANDOT

Lake Erie

DELAWARE
MOHICAN

PIANKISHAW

KICKAPOO

KASKASKIA

Greenville Treaty Line

MIAMI
WEA
EEL RIVER

SHAWNEE
MINGO

PEORIA
KASKASKIA
CAHOKIA

MASCAUTEN

PIANKISHAW

Lake Ontario

SENECA

ONEIDA
TUSCARORA
ONONDAGA
CAYUGA

NEW
YORK   MOHAWK

SENECA

MUNSEE
DELAWARE
SOPOONEE

PENNSYLVANIA

NEW
JERSEY

MARYLAND

DELAWARE

PASSAMAQUODDY

PENOBSCOT

VERMONT

NEW
HAMPSHIRE

TROY
MARSHPEE
HERRING POND

MASSACHUSETTS

GROTON
MOHEGAN

STONINGTON

MONTAUK

CONN.

NARRAGANSETT

RHODE
ISLAND

KENTUCKY

VIRGINIA

NOTTAWAY
PAMUNKEY
MATTAPONIES

Atlantic
Ocean

CHICKASAW

CHEROKEE

CATAWBA

NORTH
CAROLINA

UPPER CREEKS

SOUTH
CAROLINA

CHOCTAW

GEORGIA

LOWER CREEKS

0   100   200 miles
0   100   200 kilometers

Northwest Territory
Indian land cessions
Major battle

SEMINOLE

Gulf of Mexico

By 1795, the Indian population had declined significantly from the early colonial era, but the area west of the Appalachian Mountains was still known as "Indian country."

farther west, their total disappearance, or their incorporation into white "civilization" with the expectation that they might one day become part of American society.

Many white Americans, probably most, deemed Indians savages unfit for citizenship. Indian tribes had no representation in the new government, and the Constitution excluded Indians "not taxed" from being counted in determining each state's number of congressmen. The treaty system gave them a unique status within the American political system. But despite this recognition of their sovereignty, treaties were essentially ways of transferring land from Indians to the federal government or the states. Often, a treaty was agreed to by only a small portion of a tribe, but the whole tribe was then forced to accept its legitimacy.

During Washington's administration, Secretary of War Henry Knox hoped to deal with Indians with a minimum of warfare and without undermining the new nation's honor. He recognized, he said in 1794, that American treatment of the continent's native inhabitants had been even "more destructive to the Indian" than Spain's conduct in Mexico and Peru. His conciliatory policy had mixed results. Congress forbade the transfer of Indian land without federal approval. But several states ignored this directive and continued to negotiate their own agreements.

Open warfare continued in the Ohio Valley. In 1791, Little Turtle, leader of the Miami Confederacy, inflicted a humiliating defeat on American forces led by Arthur St. Clair, the American governor of the Northwest Territory. With 630 dead, this was the costliest loss ever suffered by the United States Army at the hands of Indians. In 1794, 3,000 American troops under Anthony Wayne defeated Little Turtle's forces at the Battle of Fallen Timbers. This led directly to the **Treaty of Greenville** of 1795, in which twelve Indian tribes ceded most of Ohio and Indiana to the federal

The treaty system

War in the Ohio Valley

The signing of the Treaty of Greenville of 1795, painted by an unknown member of General Anthony Wayne's staff. In the treaty, a group of tribes ceded most of the area of the current states of Ohio and Indiana, along with the site that became the city of Chicago, to the United States.

The Plan of Civilization. Painted circa 1800 by an unidentified artist, this work depicts Hawkins explaining the advantages of settled agriculture as part of a plan to promote "civilization" among Native Americans. Having served in the Continental army during the War of Independence and as a senator from North Carolina, Hawkins was appointed in 1795 Superintendent of Indian Affairs for the southeastern United States. He supplied the Creeks, Cherokees, and Choctaws with agricultural training and farm implements and married a Creek woman.

Tribal identity

government. The treaty also established the **annuity system**—yearly grants of federal money to Indian tribes that institutionalized continuing government influence in tribal affairs and gave outsiders considerable control over Indian life.

Many prominent figures, however, rejected the idea that Indians were innately inferior to white Americans. Thomas Jefferson believed that Indians merely lived at a less advanced stage of civilization. Indians could become full-fledged members of the republic by abandoning communal landholding and hunting in favor of small-scale farming. Once they "possessed property," Jefferson told one Indian group, they could "join us in our government" and, indeed, "mix your blood with ours."

To pursue the goal of assimilation, Congress in the 1790s authorized President Washington to distribute agricultural tools and livestock to Indian men and spinning wheels and looms to Indian women. To whites, the adoption of American gender norms, with men working the land and women tending to their homes, would be a crucial sign that the Indians were becoming "civilized." But the American notion of civilization required so great a transformation of Indian life that most tribes rejected it. To Indians, freedom meant retaining tribal autonomy and identity, including the ability to travel widely in search of game. "Since our acquaintance with our brother white people," declared a Mohawk speaker at a 1796 treaty council, "that which we call freedom and liberty, becomes an entire stranger to us." There was no room for Indians who desired to retain their traditional way of life in the American empire of liberty.

Blacks and the Republic

By 1790, the number of African-Americans far exceeded the Indian population within the United States. The status of free blacks was somewhat indeterminate. Nowhere does the original Constitution define who in fact are citizens of the United

States. The individual states were left free to determine the boundaries of liberty. The North's **gradual emancipation** acts assumed that former slaves would remain in the country, not be colonized abroad. Northern statesmen like Hamilton, Jay, and Franklin worked for abolition, and some helped to establish schools for black children. During the era of the Revolution, free blacks enjoyed at least some of the legal rights accorded to whites, including, in most states, the right to vote. Some cast ballots in the election of delegates to conventions that ratified the Constitution. The large majority of blacks, of course, were slaves, and slavery rendered them all but invisible to those imagining the American community. Slaves, as Edmund Randolph, the nation's first attorney general, put it, were "not . . . constituent members of our society," and the language of liberty did not apply to them.

One of the era's most widely read books, **Letters from an American Farmer**, published in France in 1782 by Hector St. John de Crèvecoeur, strikingly illustrated this process of exclusion. Born in France, Crèvecoeur had taken part in the unsuccessful defense of Quebec during the Seven Years' War. Instead of returning home, he came to New York City in 1759. As a trader and explorer, he visited most of the British mainland colonies, as well as the Ohio and Mississippi Valleys. Crèvecoeur eventually married the daughter of a prominent New York landowner and lived with his own family on a farm in Orange County. Seeking to remain neutral during the War of Independence, he suffered persecution by both patriots and the British, and eventually returned to France.

In *Letters from an American Farmer*, Crèvecoeur popularized the idea, which would become so common in the twentieth century, of the United States as a melting pot. "Here," he wrote, "individuals of all nations are melted into a new one." The American left behind "all his ancient prejudices and manners [and received] new ones from the new mode of life he has embraced." Crèvecoeur was well aware of what he called "the horrors of slavery." But when he posed the famous question, "What then is the American, this new man?" he answered, "A mixture of English, Scotch, Irish, French, Dutch, Germans, and Swedes. . . . He is either a European, or the descendant of a European." This at a time when fully one-fifth of the population (the highest proportion in U.S. history) consisted of Africans and their descendants.

Like Crèvecoeur, many white Americans excluded blacks from their conception of the American people. The Constitution empowered Congress to create a uniform system by which immigrants became citizens, and the Naturalization Act of 1790 offered the first legislative definition of American nationality. With no debate, Congress restricted the process of becoming a citizen from abroad to "free white persons."

The law initiated a policy that some historians, with only partial accuracy, call **open immigration**. For Europeans, the process was indeed open. Only in the last quarter of the nineteenth century were groups of whites, beginning with prostitutes, convicted felons, lunatics, and persons likely to become a "public

TABLE 7.1 Total Population and Black Population of the United States, 1790

STATE	TOTAL POPULATION	SLAVES	FREE BLACKS
New England:			
New Hampshire	141,899	158	630
Vermont*	85,341	0	271
Massachusetts	378,556	0	5,369
Connecticut	237,655	2,764	2,771
Rhode Island	69,112	948	3,484
Maine**	96,643	0	536
Middle States:			
New York	340,241	21,324	4,682
New Jersey	184,139	11,423	2,762
Pennsylvania	433,611	3,737	6,531
South:			
Delaware	59,096	8,887	3,899
Maryland	319,728	103,036	8,043
Virginia	747,610	292,627	12,866
North Carolina	395,005	100,572	5,041
South Carolina	249,073	107,094	1,801
Georgia	82,548	29,264	398
Kentucky*	73,677	12,430	114
Tennessee*	35,691	3,417	361
Total	3,929,625	697,681	59,559

*Vermont, Kentucky, and Tennessee were territories that had not yet been admitted as states.
**Maine was part of Massachusetts in 1790.

Crèvecoeur

This painting by artist Gilbert Stuart, best known for his portraits of George Washington, is thought to depict Hercules, Washington's slave and the chief cook at his estate at Mount Vernon, Virginia. As president, Washington brought Hercules to Philadelphia, then the nation's capital, in violation of Pennsylvania's 1780 emancipation law, which freed any slave who resided in the state for six months. In 1797, as Washington and his family were preparing to return home at the end of his term in office, Hercules escaped. Washington died two years later; his will freed his slaves, including Hercules.

Benjamin Banneker

Jefferson's vision of American society

charge," barred from entering the country. For the first century of the republic, virtually the only white persons in the entire world ineligible to claim American citizenship were those unwilling to renounce hereditary titles of nobility, as required in an act of 1795. And yet, the word "white" in the Naturalization Act excluded a large majority of the world's population from emigrating to the "asylum for mankind" and partaking in the blessings of American freedom. For eighty years, no non-white immigrant could become a naturalized citizen. Africans were allowed to do so in 1870, but not until the 1940s did persons of Asian origin become eligible. (Native Americans were granted American citizenship in 1924.)

Jefferson, Slavery, and Race

Man's liberty, John Locke had written, flowed from "his having reason." To deny liberty to those who were not considered rational beings did not seem to be a contradiction. White Americans increasingly viewed blacks as permanently deficient in the qualities that made freedom possible—the capacity for self-control, reason, and devotion to the larger community. These were the characteristics that Jefferson, in a famous comparison of the races in his book ***Notes on the State of Virginia***, published in 1785, claimed blacks lacked, partly due to natural incapacity and partly because the bitter experience of slavery had (quite understandably, he felt) rendered them disloyal to the nation. Jefferson was reluctant to "degrade a whole race of men from the rank in the scale of beings which their Creator may perhaps have given them." He therefore voiced the idea "as a suspicion only" that blacks "are inferior to the whites in the endowments both of body and mind." Yet this "unfortunate" circumstance, he went on, "is a powerful obstacle to the emancipation of these people."

Jefferson was obsessed with the connection between heredity and environment, race and intelligence. His belief that individuals' abilities and achievements are shaped by social conditions inclined him to hope that no group was fixed permanently in a status of inferiority. He applied this principle, as has been noted, to Indians, whom he believed naturally the equal of whites in intelligence. In the case of blacks, however, he could not avoid the "suspicion" that nature had permanently deprived them of the qualities that made republican citizenship possible. Benjamin Banneker, a free African-American from Maryland who had taught himself the principles of mathematics, sent Jefferson a copy of an astronomical almanac he had published, along with a plea for the abolition of slavery. Jefferson replied, "Nobody wishes more than I do to see such proofs as you exhibit, that nature has given to our black brethren, talents equal to the other colors of men." To his friend Joel Barlow, however, Jefferson suggested that a white person must have helped Banneker with his calculations.

"Nothing is more certainly written in the book of fate," wrote Jefferson, "than that these people are to be free." Yet he felt that America should have a homogeneous citizenry with common experiences, values, and inborn abilities. Black Americans, Jefferson affirmed, should eventually enjoy the natural rights enumerated in the Declaration of Independence, but in Africa or the Caribbean, not in the United States. He foresaw Indians merging with whites into a single people, but he was horrified by the idea of miscegenation between blacks and whites. Unlike Indians, blacks, he believed, were unfit for economic independence and political

> RUN away from the subscriber in *Albemarle*, a Mulatto slave called *Sandy*, about 35 years of age, his stature is rather low, inclining to corpulence, and his complexion light; he is a shoemaker by trade, in which he uses his left hand principally, can do coarse carpenters work, and is something of a horse jockey; he is greatly addicted to drink, and when drunk is insolent and disorderly, in his conversation he swears much, and in his behaviour is artful and knavish. He took with him a white horse, much scarred with traces, of which it is expected he will endeavour to dispose; he also carried his shoemakers tools, and will probably endeavour to get employment that way. Whoever conveys the said slave to me, in *Albemarle*, shall have 40 s. reward, if taken up within the county, 4 l. if elsewhere within the colony, and 10 l. if in any other colony, from
>
> THOMAS JEFFERSON.

Thomas Jefferson, future author of the Declaration of Independence and in private a sharp critic of slavery, placed this advertisement in a Virginia newspaper in 1769, seeking the return of a runaway slave. Sandy was in fact recaptured, and Jefferson sold him in 1773.

self-government. Freeing the slaves without removing them from the country would endanger the nation's freedom.

Jefferson reflected the divided mind of his generation. Some prominent Virginians assumed that blacks could become part of the American nation. Edward Coles, an early governor of Illinois, brought his slaves from Virginia, freed them, and settled them on farms. Washington, who died in 1799, provided in his will that his 277 slaves would become free after the death of his wife, Martha. (Feeling uncomfortable living among men and women who looked forward to her death, she emancipated them the following year.) Jefferson thought of himself as a humane owner. Believing the slave trade immoral, Jefferson tried to avoid selling slaves to pay off his mounting debts. But his will provided for the freedom of only five, all relatives of his slave Sally Hemings, with whom he appears to have fathered one or more children. When he died in 1826, Jefferson owed so much money that his property, including the majority of his more than 200 slaves, was sold at auction, thus destroying the slave community he had tried to keep intact.

Jefferson as slaveholder

Principles of Freedom

Even as the decline of apprenticeship and indentured servitude narrowed the gradations of freedom among the white population, the Revolution widened the divide between free Americans and those who remained in slavery. Race, one among many kinds of legal and social inequality in colonial America, now emerged as a convenient justification for the existence of slavery in a land that claimed to be committed to freedom. Blacks' "natural faculties," Alexander Hamilton noted in 1779, were "probably as good as ours." But the existence of slavery, he added, "makes us fancy many things that are founded neither in reason nor experience."

Emergence of race

"We the people" increasingly meant only white Americans. "Principles of freedom, which embrace only half mankind, are only half systems," declared the anonymous author of a Fourth of July speech in Hartford, Connecticut, in 1800. "Declaration of Independence," he wondered, "where art thou now?" The answer came from a Richmond newspaper: "Tell us not of principles. Those principles have been annihilated by the existence of slavery among us."

SUGGESTED READING

BOOKS

- Amar, Akhil Reed. *Bill of Rights: Creation and Reconstruction* (1998). Presents the history of the Bill of Rights from its ratification through the Reconstruction era.

- Berkin, Carol. *A Brilliant Solution: Inventing the American Constitution* (2002). A lively account of the proceedings of the Constitutional Convention.

- Cornell, Saul. *The Other Founders: Anti-Federalism and the Dissenting Tradition in America, 1788–1828* (1999). A careful examination of the ideas of those who opposed ratification of the Constitution.

- Dowd, Gregory E. *A Spirited Resistance: The North American Indian Struggle for Unity, 1745–1815* (1992). Contains an important discussion of the place of Indians in the new American nation.

- Holton, Woody. *Unruly Americans and the Origins of the Constitution* (2007). Argues that the political activities of ordinary Americans helped to shape the Constitution.

- Kettner, James T. *The Development of American Citizenship, 1608–1870* (1978). Traces the development of the definition of American citizenship from early colonization to the aftermath of the Civil War.

- Levy, Leonard. *The Establishment Clause: Religion and the First Amendment* (1994). A historical account of one of the key components of the Bill of Rights.

- MacLeod, Duncan J. *Slavery, Race, and the American Revolution* (1974). A British scholar's interpretation of the role of race and slavery in the revolutionary era.

- Maier, Pauline. *Ratification: The People Debate the Constitution, 1787–1788* (2010). The most complete account of the state-by-state debates over ratification of the Constitution.

- McMillin, James A. *The Final Victims: Foreign Slave Trade to North America, 1783–1810* (2004). A study of the last phase of the American slave trade, as made possible by the new Constitution.

- Nash, Gary. *The Forgotten Fifth: African Americans in the Age of Revolution* (2006). A comprehensive survey of the Revolution's impact on blacks, slave and free.

- Nedelsky, Jennifer. *Private Property and the Limits of American Constitutionalism* (1990). Analyzes how the protection of private property shaped the writing of the Constitution.

- Rakove, Jack. *Original Meanings: Politics and Ideas in the Making of the Constitution* (1996). An influential interpretation of the ideas that went into the drafting of the Constitution.

- Richards, Leonard L. *Shays's Rebellion: The American Revolution's Final Battle* (2002). The most recent study of the uprising that helped to produce the Constitution.

- Wood, Gordon S. *The Creation of the American Republic, 1776–1789* (1969). Presents the evolution of American political ideas and institutions from the Declaration of Independence to the ratification of the Constitution.

WEBSITES

- Creating the United States: www.loc.gov/exhibits /creating-the-united-states

- Explore the Constitution: http://constitutioncenter.org

- The Presidency: http://americanhistory.si.edu/presidency /home.html

CHAPTER REVIEW AND ONLINE RESOURCES

REVIEW QUESTIONS

1. How did the limited central government created by the Articles of Confederation reflect the issues behind the Revolution and fears for individual liberties?

2. What were the ideas and motivations that pushed Americans to expand west?

3. What events and ideas led to the belief in 1786 and 1787 that the Articles of Confederation were not working well?

4. The Constitution has been described as a "bundle of compromises." Which compromises were the most significant in shaping the direction of the new nation and why?

5. What were the major arguments in support of the Constitution given by the Federalists?

6. What were the major arguments against the Constitution put forth by the Anti-Federalists?

7. How accurate was Hector St. John de Crèvecoeur's description of America as a melting pot?

KEY TERMS

Articles of Confederation (p. 240)
Ordinance of 1784 (p. 243)
Ordinance of 1785 (p. 243)
Northwest Ordinance of 1787 (p. 245)
empire of liberty (p. 245)
Shays's Rebellion (p. 246)
Constitutional Convention (pp. 247)
Virginia Plan (p. 248)
New Jersey Plan (p. 249)
federalism (p. 250)
division of powers (p. 250)
checks and balances (p. 250)
separation of powers (p. 250)
three-fifths clause (p. 251)
The Federalist (p. 254)
Anti-Federalists (p. 256)
Bill of Rights (p. 256)
Treaty of Greenville (p. 265)
annuity system (p. 266)
gradual emancipation (p. 267)
Letters from an American Farmer (p. 267)
open immigration (p. 267)
Notes on the State of Virginia (p. 268)

Go to 🐰 INQUIZITIVE

To see what you know—and learn what you've missed—with personalized feedback along the way.

Visit the *Give Me Liberty!* **Student Site** for primary source documents and images, interactive maps, author videos featuring Eric Foner, and more.

CHAPTER 8

SECURING THE REPUBLIC

★

1791–1815

UNDER ☆MY☆ ☆WINGS☆ ☆EVERY☆ ☆THING☆ PROSPERS

On April 30, 1789, in New York City, the nation's temporary capital, George Washington became the first president under the new Constitution. All sixty-nine electors had awarded him their votes. Dressed in a plain suit of "superfine American broad cloth" rather than European finery, Washington took the oath of office on the balcony of Federal Hall before a large crowd that reacted with "loud and repeated shouts" of approval. He then retreated inside to deliver his inaugural address before members of Congress and other dignitaries.

Washington's speech expressed the revolutionary generation's conviction that it had embarked on an experiment of enormous historical importance, whose outcome was by no means certain. "The preservation of the sacred fire of liberty and the destiny of the republican model of government," Washington proclaimed, depended on the success of the American experiment in self-government. Most Americans seemed to agree that freedom was the special genius of American institutions. In a resolution congratulating Washington on his inauguration, the House of Representatives observed that he had been chosen by "the freest people on the face of the earth." When the time came to issue the nation's first coins, Congress directed that they bear the image not of the head of state (as would be the case in a monarchy) but "an impression emblematic of liberty," with the word itself prominently displayed.

American leaders believed that the success of the new government depended, above all, on maintaining political harmony. They were especially anxious to avoid the emergence of organized political parties, which had already appeared in several states. Parties were considered divisive and disloyal. "They serve to organize faction," Washington would later declare, and to substitute the aims of "a small but artful" minority for the "will of the nation." The Constitution makes no mention of political parties, and the original method of electing the president assumes that candidates will run as individuals, not on a party ticket (otherwise, the second-place finisher would not have become vice president). Nonetheless, national political parties quickly arose. Originating in Congress, they soon spread to the general populace. Instead of harmony, the 1790s became, in the words of one historian, an "age of passion," with each party questioning the loyalty of the other and lambasting its opponent in the most extreme terms. Political rhetoric became inflamed because the stakes seemed so high—nothing less than the legacy of the Revolution, the new nation's future, and the survival of American freedom.

POLITICS IN AN AGE OF PASSION

President Washington provided a much-needed symbol of national unity. Having retired to private life after the War of Independence (despite some army officers' suggestion that he set himself up as a dictator), he was a model of self-sacrificing republican virtue. His vice president, John Adams, was widely respected as one of the main leaders in the drive for independence. Washington brought into his cabinet some of the new nation's most prominent political leaders, including Thomas

FOCUS QUESTIONS

What issues made the politics of the 1790s so divisive? *–p. 273*

How did competing views of freedom and global events promote the political divisions of the 1790s? *–p. 284*

What were the achievements and failures of Jefferson's presidency? *–p. 290*

What were the causes and significant results of the War of 1812? *–p. 297*

New Orleans in 1803, at the time of the Louisiana Purchase. The painting shows a view of the city from a nearby plantation. The town houses of merchants and plantation owners line the broad promenade along the waterfront. At the lower center, a slave goes about his work. An eagle holds aloft a banner that suggests the heady optimism of the young republic: Under My Wings Every Thing Prospers.

1789	Inauguration of George Washington
	French Revolution begins
1791	First Bank of the United States
	Hamilton's Report on Manufactures
1791–1804	Haitian Revolution
1791	Thomas Paine's *The Rights of Man*
1792	Mary Wollstonecraft's *A Vindication of the Rights of Woman*
1793	First federal fugitive slave law
1794	Whiskey Rebellion
	Jay's Treaty
1797	Inauguration of John Adams
1798	XYZ affair
	Alien and Sedition Acts
1800	Gabriel's Rebellion
1801	Inauguration of Thomas Jefferson
1801–1805	First Barbary War
1803	Louisiana Purchase
1804–1806	Lewis and Clark expedition
1809	Inauguration of James Madison
1812–1814	War of 1812
1814	Treaty of Ghent
	Hartford Convention

Jefferson as secretary of state and Alexander Hamilton to head the Treasury Department. He also appointed a Supreme Court of six members, headed by John Jay of New York. But harmonious government proved short-lived.

Hamilton's Program

Political divisions first surfaced over the financial plan developed by Secretary of the Treasury Hamilton in 1790 and 1791. Hamilton's immediate aims were to establish the nation's financial stability, bring to the government's support the country's most powerful financial interests, and encourage economic development. His long-term goal was to make the United States a major commercial and military power. Hamilton's model was Great Britain. The goal of national greatness, he believed, could never be realized if the government suffered from the same weaknesses as under the Articles of Confederation.

Hamilton's program had five parts. The first step was to establish the new nation's credit-worthiness—that is, to create conditions under which persons would loan money to the government by purchasing its bonds, confident that they would be repaid. Hamilton proposed that the federal government assume responsibility for paying off at its full face value the national debt inherited from the War of Independence, as well as outstanding debts of the states. Second, he called for the creation of a new national debt. The old debts would be replaced by new interest-bearing bonds issued to the government's creditors. This would give men of economic substance a stake in promoting the new nation's stability, since the stronger and more economically secure the federal government, the more likely it would be to pay its debts.

The third part of Hamilton's program called for the creation of a **Bank of the United States**, modeled on the Bank of England, to serve as the nation's main financial agent. A private corporation rather than a branch of the government, it would hold public funds, issue bank notes that would serve as currency, and make loans to the government when necessary, all the while returning a tidy profit to its stockholders. Fourth, to raise revenue, Hamilton proposed a tax on producers of whiskey. Finally, in a Report on Manufactures delivered to Congress in December 1791, Hamilton called for the imposition of a tariff (a tax on imported foreign goods) and government subsidies to encourage the development of factories that could manufacture products currently purchased from abroad. Privately, Hamilton promoted an unsuccessful effort to build an industrial city at present-day Paterson, New Jersey. He also proposed the creation of a national army to deal with uprisings like Shays's Rebellion.

The Emergence of Opposition

Hamilton's vision of a powerful commercial republic won strong support from American financiers, manufacturers, and merchants. But it alarmed those who believed the new nation's destiny lay in charting a different path of development. Hamilton's plans hinged on close ties with Britain, America's main trading partner. To James Madison and Thomas Jefferson, the future lay in westward expansion, not connections with Europe. They had little desire to promote manufacturing or urban growth or to see economic policy shaped in the interests of bankers and business leaders. Their goal was a republic of independent farmers marketing grain, tobacco, and other products freely to the entire world. Free trade, they believed, not a system of government favoritism through tariffs and subsidies, would promote American prosperity while fostering greater social equality. Jefferson and Madison quickly concluded that the greatest threat to American freedom lay in the alliance of a powerful central government with an emerging class of commercial capitalists, such as Hamilton appeared to envision.

To Jefferson, Hamilton's system "flowed from principles adverse to liberty, and was calculated to undermine and demolish the republic." Hamilton's plans for a standing army seemed to his critics a bold threat to freedom. The national bank and assumption of state debts, they feared, would introduce into American politics the same corruption that had undermined British liberty, and enrich those already wealthy at the expense of ordinary Americans. During the 1780s, speculators had bought up at great discounts (often only a few cents on the dollar) government bonds and paper notes that had been used to pay those who fought in the Revolution or supplied the army. Under Hamilton's plan, speculators would reap a windfall by being paid at face value while the original holders received nothing. Because transportation was so poor, moreover, many backcountry farmers were used to distilling their grain harvest into whiskey, which could then be carried more easily to market. Hamilton's whiskey tax seemed to single them out unfairly in order to enrich bondholders.

The Jefferson–Hamilton Bargain

At first, opposition to Hamilton's program arose almost entirely from the South, the region that had the least interest in manufacturing development and the least diversified economy. It also had fewer holders of federal bonds than the Middle States and New England. (Virginia had pretty much paid off its war debt; it did not see why it should be taxed to benefit states like Massachusetts that had failed to do so.) Hamilton insisted that all his plans were authorized by the Constitution's ambiguous clause empowering Congress to enact laws for the "general welfare." As a result, many southerners who had supported the new Constitution now became "strict constructionists," who insisted that the federal government could only exercise powers specifically listed in the document. Jefferson, for example, believed the new national bank unconstitutional, since the right of Congress to create a bank was not mentioned in the Constitution.

Opposition in Congress threatened the enactment of Hamilton's plans. Behind-the-scenes negotiations followed. They culminated at a famous dinner in 1790 at which Jefferson brokered an agreement whereby southerners accepted Hamilton's fiscal program (with the exception of subsidies to manufacturers) in exchange for the establishment of the permanent national capital on the Potomac River between Maryland and Virginia. Southerners hoped that the location would enhance their own power in the government while removing it from the influence of the northern financiers and merchants with whom Hamilton seemed to be allied. Major Pierre Charles L'Enfant, a French-born veteran of the War of Independence, designed a grandiose plan for the "federal city" modeled on the great urban centers of Europe, with wide boulevards, parks, and fountains. The job of surveying was done, in

An early American coin, bearing an image of liberty and the word itself, as directed by Congress in a 1792 law. The first U.S. coin to feature a real person rather than an idealized image of liberty was the Lincoln penny, issued in 1909 for the centennial of his birth.

Liberty and Washington, painted by an unknown artist around 1800, depicts a female figure of liberty placing a wreath on a bust of the first president. She carries an American flag and stands on a royal crown, which has been thrown to the ground. In the background is a liberty cap. Washington had died in 1799 and was now immortalized as a symbol of freedom, independence, and national pride.

The prominent Connecticut artist Amos Doolittle created this engraving, *A Display of the United States of America*, in 1794, during George Washington's second term as president. Washington is at the center with the motto "The protector of his country and the supporter of the rights of mankind." He is surrounded by the seals of the original thirteen states, plus the seal of Vermont in the lower right corner. The seals contain various images of commerce and liberty.

Edmond Genet

Jay's Treaty

part, by Benjamin Banneker, the free African-American scientist mentioned in the previous chapter. When it came to constructing public buildings in the nation's new capital, most of the labor was done by slaves.

The Impact of the French Revolution

Political divisions began over Hamilton's fiscal program, but they deepened in response to events in Europe. When the French Revolution began in 1789, nearly all Americans welcomed it, inspired in part by the example of their own rebellion. John Marshall later recalled, "I sincerely believed human liberty to depend in a great measure on the success of the French Revolution." But in 1793, the Revolution took a more radical turn with the execution of King Louis XVI along with numerous aristocrats and other foes of the new government, and war broke out between France and Great Britain.

Events in France became a source of bitter conflict in America. Jefferson and his followers believed that despite its excesses the Revolution marked a historic victory for the idea of popular self-government, which must be defended at all costs. Enthusiasm for France inspired a rebirth of symbols of liberty. Liberty poles and caps reappeared on the streets of American towns and cities. To Washington, Hamilton, and their supporters, however, the Revolution raised the specter of anarchy. America, they believed, had no choice but to draw closer to Britain.

American leaders feared being divided into parties "swayed by rival European powers," in the words of John Quincy Adams. But the rivalry between Britain and France did much to shape early American politics. The "permanent" alliance between France and the United States, which dated to 1778, complicated the situation. No one advocated that the United States should become involved in the European war, and Washington in April 1793 issued a proclamation of American neutrality. But that spring the French Revolution's American admirers organized tumultuous welcomes for Edmond Genet, a French envoy seeking to arouse support for his beleaguered government. When Genet began commissioning American ships to attack British vessels under the French flag, the Washington administration asked for his recall. (Deeming the situation in France too dangerous, he decided to remain in America and married the daughter of George Clinton, the governor of New York.)

Meanwhile, the British seized hundreds of American ships trading with the French West Indies and resumed the hated practice of **impressment**—kidnapping sailors, including American citizens of British origin, to serve in their navy. Sent to London to present objections, while still serving as chief justice, John Jay negotiated an agreement in 1794 that produced the greatest public controversy of Washington's presidency. **Jay's Treaty** contained no

British concessions on impressment or the rights of American shipping. Britain did agree to abandon outposts on the western frontier, which it was supposed to have done in 1783. In return, the United States guaranteed favored treatment to British imported goods. In effect, the treaty canceled the American-French alliance and recognized British economic and naval supremacy as unavoidable facts of life. Critics of the administration charged that it aligned the United States with monarchical Britain in its conflict with republican France. Ultimately, Jay's Treaty sharpened political divisions in the United States and led directly to the formation of an organized opposition party.

Political Parties

By the mid-1790s, two increasingly coherent parties had appeared in Congress, calling themselves **Federalists and Republicans**. (The latter had no connection with today's Republican Party, which was founded in the 1850s.) Both parties laid claim to the language of liberty, and each accused its opponent of engaging in a conspiracy to destroy it.

The Federalists, supporters of the Washington administration, favored Hamilton's economic program and close ties with Britain. Prosperous merchants, farmers, lawyers, and established political leaders (especially outside the South) tended to support the Federalists. Their outlook was generally elitist, reflecting the traditional eighteenth-century view of society as a fixed hierarchy and of public office as reserved for men of economic substance—the

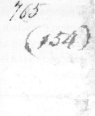

Philadelphia, August, 1793.

ALL able bodied seamen who are willing to engage in the cause of Liberty, and in the service of the French Republic, will please to apply to the French Consul, at No. 132, North Second-street.

Particular attention will be paid to the generous and intrepid natives of Ireland, who, it is presumed, will act like those warlike troops from that oppressed country, who took refuge in France about a century ago, and performed prodigies of valor under the old government of that country.

These, and volunteers from any other country, will be received into present pay, and comfortable accommodations.

N. B. The Republic has, at this present time, in her service, officers and soldiers from every civilized country in Europe, and natives of America, who, in imitation of the heroes from France in the American revolution, are a glory to themselves, and an honour to the country which gave them birth.

A recruiting poster seeking "able bodied seamen" willing to volunteer to fight for revolutionary France and "the cause of Liberty," issued in Philadelphia by Edmond Genet, a French envoy. Genet thought Irish immigrants in the United States would be especially willing to serve France in its war with Great Britain.

Infant Liberty Nursed by Mother Mob, a Federalist cartoon from 1807, illustrates the party's fear that the spirit of liberty was degenerating into anarchy. In the background, a mob assaults a building, while in the foreground a pile of books burns.

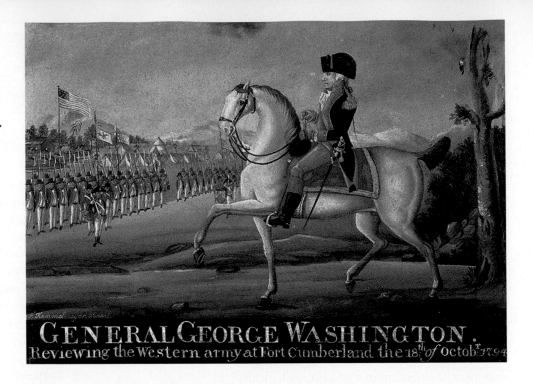

A 1794 painting by the Baltimore artist and sign painter Frederick Kemmelmeyer depicting President George Washington as commander-in-chief of the army dispatched to put down the Whiskey Rebellion.

GENERAL GEORGE WASHINGTON.
Reviewing the Western army at Fort Cumberland the 18.th of octob.r 1794

Venerate the Plough, a medal of the Philadelphia Society for the Promotion of Agriculture, 1786. Americans like Jefferson and Madison believed that farmers were the most virtuous citizens and therefore agriculture must remain the foundation of American life.

VENERATE THE PLOUGH.

"rich, the able, and the well-born," as Hamilton put it. Freedom, Federalists insisted, did not mean the right to stand up in opposition to the government. Federalists feared that the "spirit of liberty" unleashed by the American Revolution was degenerating into anarchy and "licentiousness." When the New York Federalist leader Rufus King wrote an essay on the "words . . . with wrong meaning" that had "done great harm" to American society, his first example was "Liberty."

The Whiskey Rebellion

The Federalists may have been the only major party in American history forthrightly to proclaim democracy and freedom dangerous in the hands of ordinary citizens. The **Whiskey Rebellion** of 1794, which broke out when backcountry Pennsylvania farmers sought to block collection of the new tax on distilled spirits, reinforced this conviction. The "rebels" invoked the symbols of 1776, displaying liberty poles and banners reading "Liberty or Death." "The citizens of the western country," one group wrote to the president, "consider [the tax] as repugnant to liberty, [and] an invasion of those privileges which the revolution bestowed upon them." But Washington dispatched 13,000 militiamen to western Pennsylvania (a larger force than he had commanded during the Revolution). He accompanied them part of the way to the scene of the disturbances, the only time in American history that the president has actually commanded an army in the field. The "rebels" offered no resistance. His vigorous response, Washington wrote, was motivated in part by concern for "the impression" the restoration of public order "will make on others"—the "others" being Europeans who did not believe the American experiment in self-government could survive.

The Republican Party

Republicans, led by Madison and Jefferson, were more sympathetic to France than the Federalists and had more faith in democratic self-government. They drew their support from an unusual alliance of wealthy southern planters and ordinary farmers throughout the country. Enthusiasm for the French Revolution increasingly drew urban artisans into Republican ranks as well. Republicans preferred what a New Hampshire editor called the "boisterous sea of liberty" to the "calm of despotism." They were far more critical than the Federalists of social and economic inequality, and more accepting of broad democratic participation as essential to freedom.

Each emerging party considered itself the representative of the nation and the other an illegitimate "faction." As early as 1792, Madison composed an imaginary dialogue between spokesmen for the two groups. The Federalist described ordinary people as "stupid, suspicious, licentious" and accused the Republican of being "an accomplice of atheism and anarchy." The latter called the Federalist an opponent of liberty and "an idolater of tyranny."

In real life, too, political language became more and more heated. Federalists denounced Republicans as French agents, anarchists, and traitors. Republicans called their opponents monarchists intent on transforming the new national government into a corrupt, British-style aristocracy. Each charged the other with betraying the principles of the War of Independence and of American freedom. Washington himself received mounting abuse. When he left office, a Republican newspaper declared that his name had become synonymous with "political iniquity" and "legalized corruption." One contemporary complained that the American press, "one of the great safeguards of free government," had become "the most scurrilous in the civilized world."

> The "boisterous sea of liberty"

An Expanding Public Sphere

The debates of the 1790s produced not only one of the most intense periods of partisan warfare in American history but also an enduring expansion of the public sphere, and with it the democratic content of American freedom. More and more citizens attended political meetings and became avid readers of pamphlets and newspapers. The establishment of nearly 1,000 post offices made possible the wider circulation of personal letters and printed materials. The era witnessed the rapid growth of the American press—the number of newspapers rose from around 100 to 260 during the 1790s, and reached nearly 400 by 1810.

Hundreds of "obscure men" wrote pamphlets and newspaper essays and formed political organizations. The decade's democratic ferment was reflected in writings like *The Key of Liberty* by William Manning, a self-educated Massachusetts

A print shop in the early republic. The increasing number of newspapers played a major role in the expansion of the public sphere.

An engraving from *The Lady's Magazine and Repository of Entertaining Knowledge*, published in Philadelphia in 1792. A woman identified as the "Genius of the Ladies Magazine" kneels before Liberty, presenting a petition for the "Rights of Women." In the foreground are symbols of the arts, science, and literature—knowledge that should be available to women as well as men.

Mary Wollstonecraft, author of the pioneering work *A Vindication of the Rights of Woman*, in a 1797 portrait.

farmer who had fought at the battle of Concord that began the War of Independence. Although not published until many years later, Manning's work, addressed to "friends to liberty and free government," reflected the era's popular political thought. The most important division in society, Manning declared, was between the "few" and the "many." He called for the latter to form a national political association to prevent the "few" from destroying "free government" and "tyrannizing over" the people.

The Democratic-Republican Societies

Inspired by the Jacobin clubs of Paris, supporters of the French Revolution and critics of the Washington administration in 1793 and 1794 formed nearly fifty **Democratic-Republican societies**. The Republican press publicized their meetings, replete with toasts to French and American liberty. The declaration of the Democratic Society of Addison County, Vermont, was typical: "That all men are naturally free, and possess equal rights. That all legitimate government originates in the voluntary social compact of the people."

Federalists saw the societies as another example of how liberty was getting out of hand. The government, not "self-created societies," declared the president, was the authentic voice of the American people. Forced to justify their existence, the societies developed a defense of the right of the people to debate political issues and organize to affect public policy. To the societies, "free inquiry" and "free communication" formed the first line of defense of "the unalienable rights of free men." Political liberty meant not simply voting at elections but constant involvement in public affairs. "We make no apology for thus associating ourselves," declared the Addison County society. "Political freedom" included the right to "exercise watchfulness and inspection, upon the conduct of public officers." Blamed by Federalists for helping to inspire the Whiskey Rebellion, the societies disappeared by the end of 1795. But much of their organization and outlook was absorbed into the emerging Republican Party. They helped to legitimize the right of "any portion of the people," regardless of station in life, to express political opinions and take an active role in public life.

The Republicans also gained support from immigrants from the British Isles, where war with France inspired a severe crackdown on dissent. Thomas Paine had returned to Britain in 1787. Five years later, after publishing *The Rights of Man*, a defense of the French Revolution and a stirring call for democratic change at home, he was forced to flee to France one step ahead of the law. But his writings inspired the emergence of a mass movement for political and social change, which authorities brutally suppressed.

The Rights of Women

The democratic ferment of the 1790s inspired renewed discussion about women's rights. In 1792, Mary Wollstonecraft published in England her extraordinary pamphlet, *A Vindication of the Rights of Woman*. Inspired by Paine's *Rights of Man*, she asserted that the "rights of humanity" should not be "confined to the male line." Wollstonecraft did not directly challenge traditional gender roles. Her call for greater access to education and to paid employment for women rested on the idea that this would enable single women to support themselves and married women to perform more capably as wives and mothers. But she did "drop a hint," as she put it, that women "ought to have representation" in government. Within two years, American editions of Wollstonecraft's work had appeared, along with pamphlets defending and attacking her arguments. A short-lived women's rights magazine was published in 1795 in New York City. For generations, Wollstonecraft's writings would remain an inspiration to women seeking greater rights. "She is alive and active," the British novelist Virginia Woolf wrote in the 1920s, "she argues and experiments, we hear her voice and trace her influence even now among the living."

The expansion of the public sphere offered new opportunities to women. Increasing numbers began expressing their thoughts in print. Hannah Adams of Massachusetts became the first American woman to support herself as an author, publishing works on religious history and the history of New England. Other women took part in political discussions, read newspapers, and listened to orations, even though outside of New Jersey none could vote.

Judith Sargent Murray, one of the era's most accomplished American women, wrote essays for the *Massachusetts Magazine* under the pen name "The Gleaner." Murray's father, a prosperous Massachusetts merchant, had taken an enlightened view of his daughter's education. Although Judith could not attend college because of her sex, she studied alongside her brother with a tutor preparing the young man for admission to Harvard. In her essay "On the Equality of the Sexes," written in 1779 and published in 1790, Murray insisted that women had as much right as men to exercise all their talents and should be allowed equal educational opportunities to enable them to do so. Women's apparent mental inferiority to men, she insisted, simply reflected the fact that they had been denied "the opportunity of acquiring knowledge." "The idea of the incapability of women," she maintained, was "totally inadmissable in this enlightened age."

Women and the Republic

Were women part of the new body politic? Until after the Civil War, the word "male" did not appear in the Constitution. Women were counted fully in determining representation in Congress, and there was nothing explicitly limiting the rights outlined in the Constitution to men. A few contributors to the pamphlet debate on women's rights admitted that, according to the logic of democracy, women ought to have a voice in government. The Constitution's use of the word "he" to describe officeholders, however, reflected an assumption so widespread that it scarcely required explicit defense: politics was a realm for men. The time had not yet arrived for a broad assault on gender inequality. But like the activities of

> *Wollstonecraft's* A Vindication of the Rights of Woman

An 1804 embroidery by sixteen-year-old Mary Green of Worcester, Massachusetts, based on *Liberty in the Form of the Goddess of Youth*, a widely reprinted engraving linking liberty and nationhood. Atop the American flag sits a liberty cap. At the goddess's feet lie symbols of Old World monarchy, including the key to the Bastille (the Paris prison stormed by a crowd at the outset of the French Revolution) and a broken royal scepter.

the Democratic-Republican societies, the discussion of women's status helped to popularize the language of rights in the new republic.

The men who wrote the Constitution did not envision the active and continuing involvement of ordinary citizens in affairs of state. But the rise of political parties seeking to mobilize voters in hotly contested elections, the emergence of the "self-created societies," the stirrings of women's political consciousness, and even armed uprisings like the Whiskey Rebellion broadened and deepened the democratization of public life set in motion by the American Revolution.

THE ADAMS PRESIDENCY

In 1792, Washington won unanimous reelection. Four years later, he decided to retire from public life, in part to establish the precedent that the presidency is not a life office. In his Farewell Address (mostly drafted by Hamilton and published in the newspapers rather than delivered orally; see the Appendix for excerpts from the speech), Washington defended his administration against criticism, warned against the party spirit, and advised his countrymen to steer clear of international power politics by avoiding "permanent alliances with any portion of the foreign world."

Washington's Farewell Address

The Election of 1796

George Washington's departure unleashed fierce party competition over the choice of his successor. In this, the first contested presidential election, two tickets presented themselves: John Adams, with Thomas Pinckney of South Carolina for vice president, representing the Federalists, and Thomas Jefferson, with Aaron Burr of New York, for the Republicans. In a majority of the sixteen states (Vermont, Kentucky, and Tennessee had been added to the original thirteen during Washington's presidency), the legislature chose presidential electors. But in the six states where the people voted for electors directly, intense campaigning took place. Adams received seventy-one electoral votes to Jefferson's sixty-eight. Because of factionalism among the Federalists, Pinckney received only fifty-nine votes, so Jefferson, the leader of the opposition party, became vice president. Voting fell almost entirely along sectional lines: Adams carried New England, New York, and New Jersey, while Jefferson swept the South, along with Pennsylvania.

The first contested presidential election

In 1797, John Adams assumed leadership of a divided nation. Brilliant but austere, stubborn, and self-important, he was disliked even by those who honored his long career of service to the cause of independence. His presidency was beset by crises.

On the international front, the country was nearly dragged into the ongoing European war. As a neutral nation, the United States claimed the right to trade nonmilitary goods with both Britain and France, but both countries seized American ships with impunity. In 1797, American diplomats were sent to Paris to negotiate a treaty to replace the old alliance of 1778. French officials presented them with a demand for bribes before negotiations could proceed. When Adams made public the envoys' dispatches, the French officials were designated by the last three letters of the alphabet. This **XYZ affair** poisoned America's relations with its former ally. By 1798, the United States and France were engaged in a "quasi-war" at sea, with French ships seizing American vessels in the Caribbean and a newly enlarged American navy harassing the French. In effect, the United States had become a military ally of Great Britain. But despite pressure from Hamilton, who desired a declaration of war, Adams in 1800 negotiated peace with France.

Adams was less cautious in domestic affairs. Unrest continued in many rural areas. In 1799, farmers in southeastern Pennsylvania obstructed the assessment of a tax on land and houses that Congress had imposed to help fund an expanded army and navy. A crowd led by John Fries, a local militia leader and auctioneer, released arrested men from prison. No shots were fired in what came to be called Fries's Rebellion, but Adams dispatched units of the federal army to the area. The army arrested Fries for treason and proceeded to terrorize his supporters, tear down liberty poles, and whip Republican newspaper editors. Adams pardoned Fries in 1800, but the area, which had supported his election in 1796, never again voted Federalist.

A New Display of the United States, an 1803 engraving by Amos Doolittle, depicts President John Adams surrounded by shields of sixteen states (the original thirteen plus Kentucky, Tennessee, and Vermont), with the population and number of senators and representatives of each. At the top, an eagle holds an arrow, an olive branch, and a banner reading "Millions for Our Defence Not a Cent for Tribute," a motto that originated during the XYZ affair of 1798 when French officials demanded bribes before entering into negotiations to avoid war with the United States.

The "Reign of Witches"

But the greatest crisis of the Adams administration arose over the **Alien and Sedition Acts** of 1798. Confronted with mounting opposition, some of it voiced by immigrant pamphleteers and editors, Federalists moved to silence their critics. A new Naturalization Act extended from five to fourteen years the residency requirement for immigrants seeking American citizenship. The Alien Act allowed the deportation of persons from abroad deemed "dangerous" by federal authorities. The Sedition Act (which was set to expire in 1801, by which time Adams hoped to have been reelected) authorized the prosecution of virtually any public assembly or publication critical of the government. While more lenient than many such measures in Europe (it did not authorize legal action before publication and allowed for trials by jury), the new law meant that opposition editors could be prosecuted for almost any political comment they printed. The main target was the Republican press, seen by Federalists as a group of upstart workingmen (most editors had started out as printers) whose persistent criticism of the administration fomented popular rebelliousness and endangered "genuine liberty."

The Alien and Sedition Acts

Congressional Pugilists, a 1798 cartoon depicting a fight on the floor of Congress between Connecticut Federalist Roger Griswold and Matthew Lyon, a Republican from Vermont. Lyon would soon be jailed under the Sedition Act for criticizing the Adams administration in his newspaper.

Opposition to the Sedition Act

The passage of these measures launched what Jefferson—recalling events in Salem, Massachusetts, a century earlier—termed a "reign of witches." Eighteen individuals, including several Republican newspaper editors, were charged under the Sedition Act. Ten were convicted for spreading "false, scandalous, and malicious" information about the government. Matthew Lyon, a member of Congress from Vermont and editor of a Republican newspaper, *The Scourge of Aristocracy*, received a sentence of four months in prison and a fine of $1,000. (Lyon had been the first former printer and most likely the first former indentured servant elected to Congress.) In Massachusetts, authorities indicted several men for erecting a liberty pole bearing the inscription "No Stamp Act, no Sedition, no Alien Bill, no Land Tax; Downfall to the Tyrants of America."

The Virginia and Kentucky Resolutions

The Alien and Sedition Acts failed to silence the Republican press. Some newspapers ceased publication, but new ones, with names like *Sun of Liberty* and *Tree of Liberty*, entered the field. The Sedition Act thrust freedom of expression to the center of discussions of American liberty. Madison and Jefferson mobilized opposition, drafting resolutions adopted by the Virginia and Kentucky legislatures. The **Virginia and Kentucky resolutions** attacked the Sedition Act as an unconstitutional violation of the First Amendment. Virginia's, written by Madison, called on the federal courts to protect free speech. The original version of Jefferson's Kentucky resolution went further, asserting that states could nullify laws of Congress that violated the Constitution—that is, states could unilaterally prevent the enforcement of such laws within their borders. The legislature prudently deleted this passage. The resolutions were directed against assaults on freedom of expression by the federal government, not the states. Jefferson took care to insist that the states "fully possessed" the authority to punish "seditious" speech, even if the national government did not. Indeed, state-level prosecutions of newspapers for seditious libel did not end when the Sedition Act expired in 1801.

No other state endorsed the Virginia and Kentucky resolutions. Many Americans, including many Republicans, were horrified by the idea of state action that might endanger the Union. But the "crisis of freedom" of the late 1790s strongly reinforced the idea that "freedom of discussion" was an indispensable attribute of American liberty and of democratic government. Free speech, as Massachusetts Federalist Harrison Gray Otis noted, had become the people's "darling privilege." The broad revulsion against the Alien and Sedition Acts contributed greatly to Jefferson's election as president in 1800.

The "Revolution of 1800"

"Jefferson and Liberty" became the watchword of the Republican campaign. By this time, Republicans had developed effective techniques for mobilizing voters, such as printing pamphlets, handbills, and newspapers and holding mass meetings to promote their cause. The Federalists, who viewed politics as an activity for a small group of elite men, found it difficult to match their opponents' mobilization. Nonetheless, they still dominated New England and enjoyed considerable support in the Middle Atlantic states. Jefferson triumphed, with seventy-three electoral votes to Adams's sixty-five.

Before assuming office, Jefferson was forced to weather an unusual constitutional crisis. Each party arranged to have an elector throw away one of his two votes for president, so that its presidential candidate would come out a vote ahead of the vice presidential. But the designated Republican elector failed to do so. As a result, both Jefferson and his running mate, Aaron Burr, received seventy-three electoral votes. With no candidate having a majority, the election was thrown into the House of Representatives that had been elected in 1798, where the Federalists enjoyed a slight majority. For thirty-five ballots, neither man received a majority of the votes. Finally, Hamilton intervened. He disliked Jefferson but believed him enough of a statesman to recognize that the Federalist financial system could not be dismantled. Burr, he warned, was obsessed with power, "an embryo Caesar."

Hamilton's support for Jefferson tipped the balance. To avoid a repetition of the crisis, Congress and the states soon adopted the Twelfth Amendment to the Constitution, requiring electors to cast separate votes for president and vice president. The election of 1800 also set in motion a chain of events that culminated four years later when Burr killed Hamilton in a duel. Burr appears to have subsequently engaged in a plot to form a new nation in the West from land detached from the United States and the Spanish empire. Acquitted of treason in 1807, he went into exile in Europe, eventually returning to New York, where he practiced law until his death in 1836.

The events of the 1790s demonstrated that a majority of Americans believed ordinary people had a right to play an active role in politics, express their opinions freely, and contest the policies of their government. His party, wrote Samuel Goodrich, a prominent Connecticut Federalist, was overthrown because democracy had become "the watchword of popular liberty." To their credit, Federalists never considered resistance to the election result. Adams's acceptance of defeat established the vital precedent of a peaceful transfer of power from a defeated party to its successor.

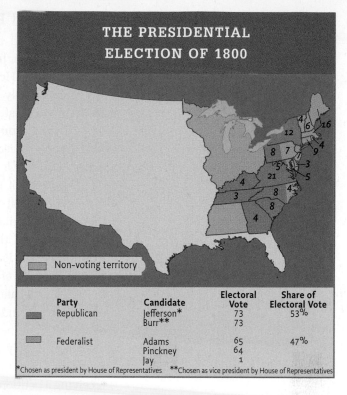

THE PRESIDENTIAL ELECTION OF 1800

Non-voting territory

Party	Candidate	Electoral Vote	Share of Electoral Vote
Republican	Jefferson*	73	53%
	Burr**	73	
Federalist	Adams	65	47%
	Pinckney	64	
	Jay	1	

*Chosen as president by House of Representatives   **Chosen as vice president by House of Representatives

An 1800 campaign banner, with a portrait of Thomas Jefferson and the words "John Adams is no more."

Slavery and Politics

Slavery's role in Jefferson's election

Lurking behind the political battles of the 1790s lay the potentially divisive issue of slavery. Jefferson, after all, received every one of the South's forty-one electoral votes. He always referred to his victory as the **Revolution of 1800** and saw it not simply as a party success but as a vindication of American freedom, securing for posterity the fruits of independence. Yet the triumph of "Jefferson and Liberty" would not have been possible without slavery. Had three-fifths of the slaves not been counted in apportionment, John Adams would have been reelected in 1800.

The issue of slavery would not disappear. The very first Congress under the new Constitution received petitions calling for emancipation. One bore the weighty signature of Benjamin Franklin, who in 1787 had agreed to serve as president of the Pennsylvania Abolition Society. The blessings of liberty, Franklin's petition insisted, should be available "without distinction of color to all descriptions of people."

Keeping slavery out of politics

A long debate followed, in which speakers from Georgia and South Carolina vigorously defended the institution and warned that behind northern criticism of slavery they heard "the trumpets of civil war." Madison found their forthright defense of slavery an embarrassment. But he concluded that the slavery question was so divisive that it must be kept out of national politics. He opposed Congress's even receiving a petition from North Carolina slaves on the grounds that they were not part of the American people and had "no claim" on the lawmakers' "attention." In 1793, to implement the Constitution's fugitive slave clause, Congress enacted a law providing for local officials to facilitate the return of escaped slaves.

The Haitian Revolution

Events during the 1790s underscored how powerfully slavery defined and distorted American freedom. The same Jeffersonians who hailed the French Revolution as a step in the universal progress of liberty reacted in horror against the slave revolution that began in 1791 in Saint Domingue, the jewel of the French overseas empire situated not far from the southern coast of the United States. Toussaint L'Ouverture, an educated slave on a sugar plantation, forged the rebellious slaves into an army able to defeat British forces seeking to seize the island and then an expedition hoping to reestablish French authority. The slave uprising led to the establishment of Haiti as an independent nation in 1804.

Reactions to the Haitian Revolution

Although much of the country was left in ruins by years of warfare, the **Haitian Revolution** affirmed the universality of the revolutionary era's creed of liberty. It inspired hopes for freedom among slaves in the United States. Throughout the nineteenth century, black Americans would look to Toussaint as a hero and celebrate the winning of Haitian independence. During the 1820s, several thousand free African-Americans emigrated to Haiti, whose government promised newcomers political rights and economic opportunity they did not enjoy in the United States.

Among white Americans, the response to the Haitian Revolution was different. Thousands of refugees from Haiti poured into the United States, fleeing the upheaval. Many spread tales of the massacres of slaveowners and the burning of their plantations, which reinforced white Americans' fears of slave insurrection at home. To most whites, the rebellious slaves seemed not men and women seeking liberty in the tradition of 1776, but a danger to American institutions. That the slaves had resorted to violence was widely taken to illustrate blacks' unfitness for republican freedom. Ironically, the Adams administration, which hoped that American merchants could replace their French counterparts in the island's lucrative sugar trade, encouraged the independence of black Haiti. When Jefferson became president, on the other hand, he sought to quarantine and destroy the hemisphere's second independent republic.

Toussaint L'Ouverture, leader of the slave revolution in Saint Domingue (modern-day Haiti). Painted in 1800 as part of a series of portraits of French military leaders, it depicts him as a courageous general.

Gabriel's Rebellion

The momentous year of 1800 witnessed not only the "revolution" of Jefferson's election but also an attempted real one, a plot by slaves in Virginia itself to gain their freedom. It was organized by a Richmond blacksmith, Gabriel, and his brothers Solomon, also a blacksmith, and Martin, a slave preacher. The conspirators planned to march on the city, which had recently become the state capital, from surrounding plantations. They would kill some white inhabitants and hold the rest, including Governor James Monroe, hostage until their demand for the abolition of slavery was met. Gabriel hoped that "poor white people" would join the insurrection, and he ordered that Quakers and Methodists (many of whom were critics of slavery) and "French people" (whose country was engaged in the "quasi-war" with the United States described earlier) be spared. On the night when the slaves were to gather, a storm washed out the roads to Richmond. The plot was soon discovered and the leaders arrested. Twenty-six slaves, including Gabriel, were hanged and dozens more transported out of the state.

Blacks in 1800 made up half of Richmond's population. One-fifth were free. A black community had emerged in the 1780s and 1790s, and the conspiracy was rooted in its institutions. Gabriel gathered recruits at black Baptist churches, funerals, barbecues, and other gatherings. In cities like Richmond, many skilled slave craftsmen, including Gabriel himself, could read and write and enjoyed the privilege of hiring themselves out to employers—that is, negotiating their own labor arrangements, with their owner receiving their "wages." Their relative autonomy helps account for slave artisans' prominent role in the conspiracy.

Gabriel's Rebellion was a product of its age. Gabriel himself had been born in 1776. Like other Virginians, the participants in the conspiracy spoke the language of liberty forged in the American Revolution and reinvigorated during the 1790s. The rebels even planned to carry a banner emblazoned with the slogan, reminiscent of Patrick Henry, "Death or Liberty." "We have as much right," one conspirator declared, "to fight for our liberty as any men." Another likened himself to George Washington, who had rebelled against established authority to "obtain the liberty of [his] countrymen."

If Gabriel's conspiracy demonstrated anything, commented the prominent Virginian George Tucker, it was that slaves possessed "the love of freedom" as fully as other men. Gabriel's words, he added, reflected "the advance of knowledge" among Virginia's slaves, including knowledge of the American language of liberty. When slaves escaped to join Lord Dunmore during the War of Independence, he wrote, "they sought freedom merely as a good; now they also claim it as a right."

The black community in Richmond

The slaves' "love of freedom"

1793 Eli Whitney's cotton gin

1790s–1830s Second Great Awakening

1806 Congress approves funds for the National Road

1807 Robert Fulton's steamboat

1814 Waltham textile factory

1819 *Dartmouth College v. Woodward*

Adams-Onís Treaty with Spain

1825 Erie Canal opens

1829 Lydia Maria Child's *The Frugal Housewife*

1831 Cyrus McCormick's reaper

1837 John Deere's steel plow

Depression begins

Ralph Waldo Emerson's "The American Scholar"

1844 Telegraph put into commercial operation

1845 John O'Sullivan coins phrase "manifest destiny"

1845–1851 Ireland's Great Famine

1854 Henry David Thoreau's *Walden*

alone. In several southern cities, public notices warned "persons of color" to stay away from the ceremonies honoring Lafayette. Half a century after the winning of independence, the coexistence of liberty and slavery, and their simultaneous expansion, remained the central contradiction of American life.

A NEW ECONOMY

In the first half of the nineteenth century, an economic transformation known to historians as the market revolution swept over the United States. Its catalyst was a series of innovations in transportation and communication. American technology had hardly changed during the colonial era. No important alterations were made in sailing ships, no major canals were built, and manufacturing continued to be done by hand, with skills passed on from artisan to journeyman and apprentice. At the dawn of the nineteenth century, most roads were little more than rutted paths through the woods. Transporting goods thirty miles inland by road cost as much as shipping the same cargo from England. In 1800, it took fifty days to move goods from Cincinnati to New York City, via a flatboat ride down the Mississippi River to New Orleans and then a journey by sail along the Gulf and Atlantic coasts.

To be sure, the market revolution represented an acceleration of developments already under way in the colonial era. As noted in previous chapters, southern planters were marketing the products of slave labor in the international market as early as the seventeenth century. By the eighteenth, many colonists had been drawn into Britain's commercial empire. Consumer goods like sugar and tea, and market-oriented tactics like the boycott of British goods, had been central to the political battles leading up to independence.

Nonetheless, as Americans moved across the Appalachian Mountains, and into interior regions of the states along the Atlantic coast, they found themselves more and more isolated from markets. In 1800, American farm families produced at home most of what they needed, from clothing to farm implements. What they could not make themselves, they obtained by bartering with their neighbors or purchasing from local stores and from rural craftsmen like blacksmiths and shoemakers. Those farmers not located near cities or navigable waterways found it almost impossible to market their produce.

The early life of Abraham Lincoln was typical of those who grew up in the pre-market world. Lincoln was born in Kentucky in 1809 and seven years later moved with his family to Indiana, where he lived until 1831. His father occasionally took pork down the Ohio and Mississippi Rivers to market in New Orleans, and Lincoln himself at age nineteen traveled by flatboat to that city to sell the goods of a local merchant. But essentially, the Lincoln family was self-sufficient. They hunted game for much of their food and sewed most of their clothing at home. They relied little on cash; Lincoln's father sometimes sent young Abraham to work for neighbors as a way of settling debts. As an adult, however, Lincoln embraced the market revolution. In the Illinois legislature in the 1830s, he eagerly promoted the improvement of rivers to facilitate access to markets. As a lawyer, he eventually came to represent the Illinois Central Railroad, which opened large areas of Illinois to commercial farming.

Roads and Steamboats

In the first half of the nineteenth century, in rapid succession, the **steamboat**, canal, railroad, and telegraph wrenched America out of its economic past. These innovations opened new land to settlement, lowered transportation costs, and made it far easier for economic enterprises to sell their products. They linked farmers to national and world markets and made them major consumers of manufactured goods. Americans, wrote Tocqueville, had "annihilated space and time."

The first advance in overland transportation came through the construction of toll roads, or "turnpikes," by localities, states, and private companies. Between 1800 and 1830, the New England and Middle Atlantic states alone chartered more than 900 companies to build new roads. In 1806, Congress authorized the construction of the paved National Road from Cumberland, Maryland, to the Old Northwest. It reached Wheeling, on the Ohio River, in 1818 and by 1838 extended to Illinois, where it ended.

Because maintenance costs were higher than expected and many towns built "shunpikes"—short detours that enabled residents to avoid tollgates—most private toll roads never turned a profit. Even on the new roads, horse-drawn wagons remained an inefficient mode of getting goods to market, except over short distances. It was improved water transportation that most dramatically increased the speed and lowered the expense of commerce.

Robert Fulton, a Pennsylvania-born artist and engineer, had experimented with steamboat designs while living in France during the 1790s. He even launched a steamboat on the Seine River in Paris in 1803. But not until 1807, when Fulton's ship the *Clermont* navigated the Hudson River from New York City to Albany, was the steamboat's technological and commercial feasibility demonstrated. The invention made possible upstream commerce (that is, travel against the current) on the country's major rivers as well as rapid transport across the Great Lakes and, eventually, the Atlantic Ocean. By 1811, the first steamboat had been introduced on the Mississippi River; twenty years later some 200 plied its waters.

A watercolor from 1829 by John William Hill depicts the Erie Canal five years after it opened. Boats carrying passengers and goods traverse the waterway, along whose banks farms and villages have sprung up.

Upstream commerce

The Erie Canal

The completion in 1825 of the 363-mile **Erie Canal** across upstate New York (a remarkable feat of engineering at a time when America's next-largest canal was only twenty-eight miles long) allowed goods to flow between the Great Lakes and New York City. Almost instantaneously, the canal attracted an influx of farmers migrating from New England, giving birth to cities like Buffalo, Rochester, and Syracuse along its path. Its water, wrote the novelist Nathaniel Hawthorne after a trip on the canal, served as a miraculous "fertilizer," for "it causes towns with their masses of brick and stone, their churches and theaters, their business . . . to spring up."

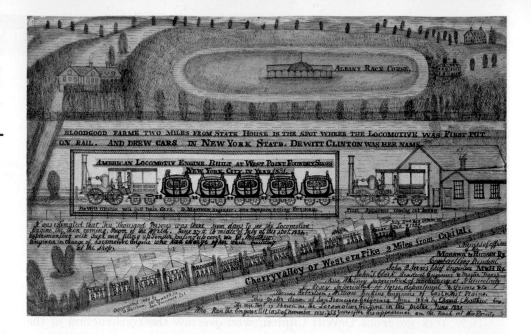

An 1884 watercolor, *Locomotive DeWitt Clinton*, recalls the early days of rail travel, and also depicts modes of transportation on canal and river. The train is driven by a steam-powered locomotive and the cars strongly resemble horse-drawn stagecoaches.

Samuel F. B. Morse

Morse, an artist and amateur scientist living in New York City, and was put into commercial operation in 1844. Using Morse code, messages could be sent over electric wires, with each letter and number represented by its own pattern of electrical pulses. Within sixteen years, some 50,000 miles of telegraph wire had been strung. Initially, the telegraph was a service for businesses, and especially newspapers, rather than individuals. It helped speed the flow of information and brought uniformity to prices throughout the country.

The Rise of the West

Improvements in transportation and communication made possible the rise of the West as a powerful, self-conscious region of the new nation. Between 1790 and 1840, some 4.5 million people crossed the Appalachian Mountains—more than the entire U.S. population at the time of Washington's first inauguration. Most of this migration took place after the War of 1812, which unleashed a flood of land-hungry settlers moving from eastern states. In the six years following the end of the war in 1815, six new states entered the Union (Indiana, Illinois, Missouri, Alabama, Mississippi, and Maine—the last an eastern frontier for New England).

Migration west

Few Americans moved west as lone pioneers. More frequently, people traveled in groups and, once they arrived in the West, cooperated with each other to clear land, build houses and barns, and establish communities. One stream of migration, including both small farmers and planters with their slaves, flowed out of the South to create the new Cotton Kingdom of Alabama, Mississippi, Louisiana, and Arkansas. Many farm families from the Upper South crossed into southern Ohio, Indiana, and Illinois. A third population stream moved from New England across New York to the Upper Northwest—northern Ohio, Indiana, and Illinois, and Michigan and Wisconsin.

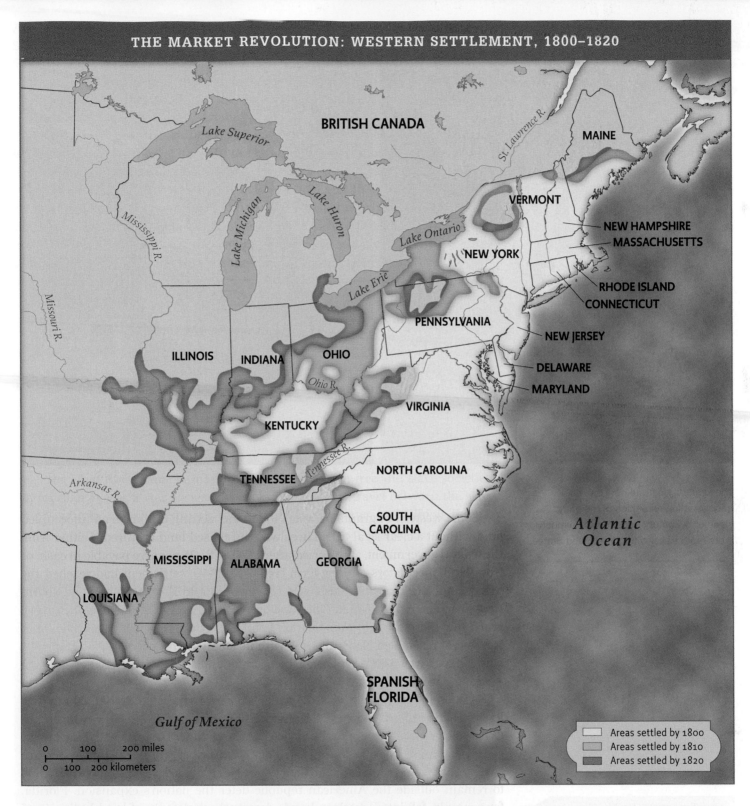

THE MARKET REVOLUTION: WESTERN SETTLEMENT, 1800–1820

BRITISH CANADA

Lake Superior

Lake Michigan

Lake Huron

Mississippi R.

Missouri R.

St. Lawrence R.

MAINE

VERMONT

NEW HAMPSHIRE

MASSACHUSETTS

Lake Ontario

NEW YORK

Lake Erie

RHODE ISLAND

CONNECTICUT

PENNSYLVANIA

NEW JERSEY

ILLINOIS

INDIANA

OHIO

DELAWARE

Ohio R.

MARYLAND

VIRGINIA

KENTUCKY

Tennessee R.

Arkansas R.

TENNESSEE

NORTH CAROLINA

SOUTH CAROLINA

Atlantic Ocean

MISSISSIPPI

ALABAMA

GEORGIA

LOUISIANA

SPANISH FLORIDA

Gulf of Mexico

0   100   200 miles
0   100   200 kilometers

Areas settled by 1800
Areas settled by 1810
Areas settled by 1820

In the first two decades of the nineteenth century, the westward movement of the population brought settlement to and across the Mississippi River. Before canals—and later, railroads—opened previously landlocked areas to commercial farming, settlement was concentrated near rivers.

within the United States, supplying the labor force required by the new Cotton Kingdom.

The Unfree Westward Movement

Historians estimate that around 1 million slaves were shifted from the older slave states to the Deep South between 1800 and 1860. Some traveled with their owners to newly established plantations, but the majority were transported by slave traders to be sold at auction for work in the cotton fields. Slave trading became a well-organized business, with firms gathering slaves in Maryland, Virginia, and South Carolina and shipping them to markets in Mobile, Natchez, and New Orleans. Slave coffles—groups chained to one another on forced marches to the Deep South—became a common sight. A British visitor to the United States in the 1840s encountered what he called a "disgusting and hideous spectacle," a file of "about two hundred slaves, manacled and chained together," being marched from Virginia to Louisiana. A source of greater freedom for many whites, the westward movement meant to African-Americans the destruction of family ties, the breakup of long-standing communities, and receding opportunities for liberty.

In 1793, when Whitney designed his invention, the United States produced 5 million pounds of cotton. By 1820, the crop had grown to nearly 170 million pounds. As the southern economy expanded westward, it was cotton produced on slave plantations that became the linchpin of southern development and by far the most important export of the empire of liberty.

Slave Trader, Sold to Tennessee, a watercolor sketch by the artist Lewis Miller from the mid-1850s. Miller depicts a group of slaves being marched from Virginia to Tennessee. Once Congress voted to prohibit the further importation of slaves into the country, slaveowners in newly opened areas of the country had to obtain slaves from other parts of the United States.

MARKET SOCIETY

Since cotton was produced solely for sale in national and international markets, the South was in some ways the most commercially oriented region of the United States. Yet rather than spurring economic change, the South's expansion westward simply reproduced the agrarian, slave-based social order of the older states. The region remained overwhelmingly rural. In 1860, roughly 80 percent of southerners worked the land—the same proportion as in 1800. The South's transportation and banking systems remained adjuncts of the plantation economy, geared largely to transporting cotton and other staple crops to market and financing the purchase of land and slaves.

> *Economic expansion with little change in the South*

Commercial Farmers

In the North, however, the market revolution and westward expansion set in motion changes that transformed the region into an integrated economy of commercial farms and manufacturing cities. As in the case of Lincoln's family, the slaughterhouses, where hundreds of thousands of pigs were butchered each year and the meat was shipped to eastern consumers. The greatest of all the western cities was Chicago. In the early 1830s, it was a tiny settlement on the shore of Lake Michigan. By 1860, thanks to the railroad, Chicago had become the nation's fourth-largest city, where farm products from throughout the Northwest were gathered to be sent east.

Like rural areas, urban centers witnessed dramatic changes due to the market revolution. The number of cities with populations exceeding 5,000 rose from 12 in 1820 to nearly 150 three decades later, by which time the urban population numbered more than 6 million. Urban merchants, bankers, and master craftsmen took advantage of the economic opportunities created by the expanding market among commercial farmers. The drive among these businessmen to increase production and reduce labor costs fundamentally altered the nature of work. Traditionally, skilled artisans had manufactured goods at home, where they controlled the pace and intensity of their own labor. Now, entrepreneurs gathered artisans into large workshops in order to oversee their work and subdivide their tasks. Craftsmen who traditionally produced an entire pair of shoes or piece of furniture saw the labor process broken down into numerous steps requiring far less skill and training. They found themselves subjected to constant supervision by their employers and relentless pressure for greater output and lower wages.

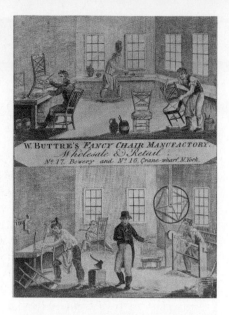

A trade card depicts the interior of a chair-manufacturing workshop in New York City. The owner stands at the center, dressed quite differently from his employees. The men are using traditional hand tools; furniture manufacturing had not yet been mechanized.

The Factory System

In some industries, most notably textiles, the factory superseded traditional craft production altogether. Factories gathered large groups of workers under central supervision and replaced hand tools with power-driven machinery. Samuel Slater, an immigrant from England, established America's first factory in 1790 at Pawtucket, Rhode Island. Since British law made it illegal to export the plans for industrial machinery, Slater, a skilled mechanic, built from memory a power-driven spinning jenny, one of the key inventions of the early industrial revolution.

Spinning factories such as Slater's produced yarn, which was then sent to traditional hand-loom weavers and farm families to be woven into cloth. This "outwork" system, in which rural men and women earned money by taking in jobs from factories, typified early industrialization. Before shoe production was fully mechanized, for example, various parts of the shoe were produced in factories, then stitched together in nearby homes, and then returned to the factories for finishing. Eventually, however, the entire manufacturing process in textiles, shoes, and many other products was brought under a single factory roof.

The cutoff of British imports because of the Embargo of 1807 and the War of 1812 stimulated the establishment of the first large-scale American factory utilizing power looms for weaving cotton cloth. This was constructed in 1814 at Waltham, Massachusetts, by a group of merchants who came to be called the Boston Associates. In the 1820s, they expanded their enterprise by creating an entirely new factory town (incorporated as the city of Lowell in 1836) on the Merrimack River, twenty-seven miles from Boston. Here they built a group of modern textile factories that brought together all phases of production from the spinning of thread to the weaving and finishing of cloth. By 1850, Lowell's fifty-two mills employed more than 10,000 workers. Across

The Lowell mills

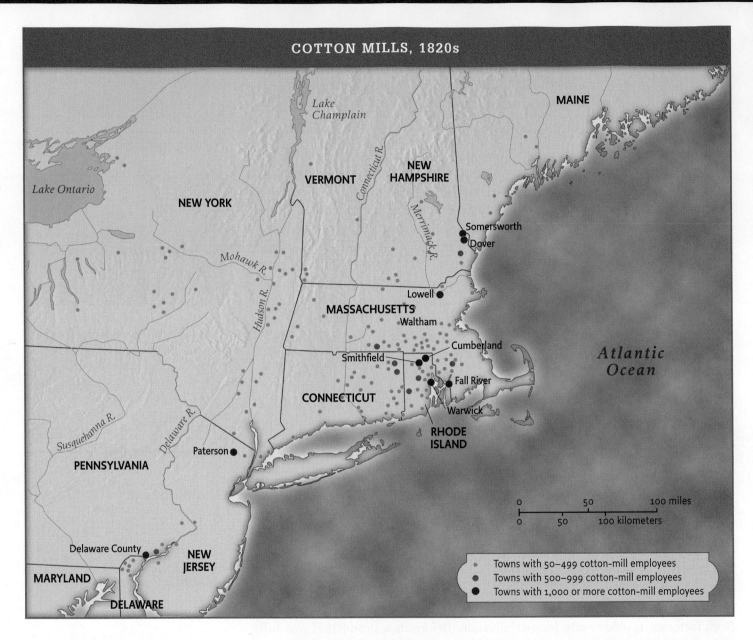

COTTON MILLS, 1820s

Towns with 50–499 cotton-mill employees
Towns with 500–999 cotton-mill employees
Towns with 1,000 or more cotton-mill employees

The early industrial revolution was concentrated in New England, where factories producing textiles from raw cotton sprang up along the region's many rivers, taking advantage of water power to drive their machinery.

Factory production

New England, small industrial cities sprang up patterned on Waltham and Lowell. Massachusetts soon became the second most industrialized region of the world, after Great Britain.

The earliest factories, including those at Pawtucket, Waltham, and Lowell, were located along the "fall line," where waterfalls and river rapids could be harnessed to provide power for spinning and weaving machinery. By the 1840s, steam power made it possible for factory owners to locate in towns like New Bedford nearer to the coast, and in large cities like Philadelphia and Chicago with their immense local markets. In 1850, manufacturers produced in factories not only textiles but also a wide variety of other goods, including tools, firearms, shoes, clocks, ironware, and agricultural machinery. What came to be called the **American system of manufactures** relied on the mass production of interchangeable parts that could be rapidly assembled into standardized finished products. This technique was first perfected in the manufacture

Mill on the Brandywine, an 1830 watercolor of a Pennsylvania paper mill. Because it relied on water power, much early manufacturing took place in the countryside.

of clocks by Eli Terry, a Connecticut craftsman, and in small-arms production by Eli Whitney, who had previously invented the cotton gin. More impressive, in a way, than factory production was the wide dispersion of mechanical skills throughout northern society. Every town, it seemed, had its sawmill, paper mill, iron works, shoemaker, hatmaker, tailor, and a host of other such small enterprises.

The early industrial revolution was largely confined to New England and a few cities outside it. Lacking a strong internal market, and with its slaveholding class generally opposed to industrial development, the South lagged in factory production. And outside New England, most northern manufacturing was still done in small-scale establishments employing a handful of workers, not in factories. In Cincinnati, for example, most workers in 1850 still labored in small unmechanized workshops.

A broadside from 1853 illustrates the long hours of work (from 5 AM to 6:30 PM with brief breaks for meals) in the textile mills of Holyoke, Massachusetts. Factory labor was strictly regulated by the clock.

The Industrial Worker

The market revolution helped to change Americans' conception of time itself. Farm life continued to be regulated by the rhythms of the seasons. But in cities, clocks became part of daily life, and work time and leisure time came to be clearly marked off from one another. In artisan workshops of the colonial and early national eras, bouts of intense work alternated with periods of leisure. Artisans would set down their tools to enjoy a drink at a tavern or attend a political discussion. As the market revolution accelerated, work in factories, workshops, and even for servants in Americans' homes took place for a specified number of hours per day. In colonial America, an artisan's pay was known as his "price," since it was linked to the goods he produced. In the nineteenth century, pay increasingly became a "wage," paid according to an hourly or daily rate. The increasing reliance on railroads, which operated

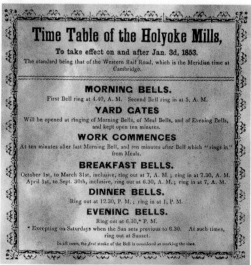

Women at work tending machines in the Lowell textile mills.

according to fixed schedules, also made Americans more conscious of arranging their lives according to "clock time."

Closely supervised work tending a machine for a period determined by a clock seemed to violate the independence Americans considered an essential element of freedom. Consequently, few native-born men could be attracted to work in the early factories. Employers turned instead to those who lacked other ways of earning a living.

The "Mill Girls"

Although some factories employed entire families, the early New England textile mills relied largely on female and child labor. At Lowell, the most famous center of early textile manufacturing, young unmarried women from Yankee farm families dominated the workforce that tended the spinning machines. To persuade parents to allow their daughters to leave home to work in the mills, Lowell owners set up boarding houses with strict rules regulating personal behavior. They also established lecture halls and churches to occupy the women's free time.

The constant supervision of the workers' private lives seems impossibly restrictive from a modern point of view. But this was the first time in history that large numbers of women left their homes to participate in the public world. Most valued the opportunity to earn money independently at a time when few other jobs were open to women. Home life, Lucy Larcom later recalled, was narrow and confining, while living and working at Lowell gave the **mill girls** a "larger, firmer idea of womanhood," teaching them "to go out of themselves and enter into the lives of others. . . . It was like a young man's pleasure in entering upon business for himself." But women like Larcom did not become a permanent class of factory workers. They typically remained in the factories for only a few years, after which they left to return home, marry, or move west. Larcom herself migrated to Illinois, where she became a teacher and writer. The shortage of industrial labor continued, easing only when large-scale immigration began in the 1840s and 1850s.

Young women workers from the Amoskeag textile mills in Manchester, New Hampshire, photographed in 1854.

The Growth of Immigration

Economic expansion fueled a demand for labor, which was met, in part, by increased immigration from abroad. Between 1790 and 1830, immigrants contributed only marginally to American population growth. But between 1840 and 1860, over 4 million people (more than the entire population of 1790) entered the United States, the majority from Ireland and Germany. About 90 percent headed for the northern states, where job opportunities were most abundant and the new arrivals would not have to compete with slave labor. Immigrants were virtually unknown in the slave states, except in cities on the periphery of the South, such as New Orleans, St. Louis, and Baltimore. In the North, however, they became a visible presence in both urban and rural areas. In 1860, the 814,000 residents of New York City, the major port of entry, included more than 384,000 immigrants, and one-third of the population of Wisconsin was foreign-born.

Numerous factors inspired this massive flow of population across the Atlantic. In Europe, the modernization of agriculture and the industrial revolution disrupted

Currency issued by a bank in Sanford, Maine, is embellished with images of women textile workers, illustrating their centrality to the state's economy. Before the Civil War, there was no national currency and banks issued their own paper money.

centuries-old patterns of life, pushing peasants off the land and eliminating the jobs of traditional craft workers. The introduction of the oceangoing steamship and the railroad made long-distance travel more practical. The Cunard Line began regular sailings with inexpensive fares from Britain to Boston and New York City in the 1840s. Beginning around 1840, emigration from Europe accelerated, not only to the United States but to Canada and Australia as well. Frequently, a male family member emigrated first; he would later send back money for the rest of the family to follow.

Irish and German Newcomers

To everyone discontented in Europe, commented the *New York Times*, "thoughts come of the New Free World." America's political and religious freedoms attracted Europeans who chafed under the continent's repressive governments and rigid social hierarchies, including political refugees from the failed revolutions of 1848. "In America," wrote a German newcomer, "there aren't any masters, here everyone is a free agent."

The largest number of immigrants, however, were refugees from disaster—Irish men and women fleeing the Great Famine of 1845–1851, when a blight destroyed the potato crop on which the island's diet rested. An estimated 1 million persons starved to death and another million emigrated in those years, most of them to the United States. Lacking industrial skills and capital, these impoverished agricultural laborers and small farmers ended up filling the low-wage unskilled jobs native-born Americans sought to avoid. Male Irish immigrants built America's railroads, dug canals, and worked as common laborers, servants, longshoremen, and factory operatives. Irish women frequently went to work as servants in the homes of native-born Americans, although some preferred factory work to domestic service. "It's the freedom that we want when the day's work is done," one Irish woman explained. "Our day is ten hours long, but when it's done it's done"; however, servants were on call at any time. By the end of the 1850s, the Lowell textile mills had largely replaced Yankee farm women with immigrant Irish families. Four-fifths of Irish immigrants remained in the Northeast. In Boston, New York, and smaller industrial cities, they congregated in overcrowded urban ghettos notorious for poverty, crime, and disease.

The second-largest group of immigrants, Germans, included a considerably larger number of skilled craftsmen than the Irish. Germans also settled in tightly knit neighborhoods in eastern cities, but many were able to move to the West, where they established themselves as craftsmen, shopkeepers, and farmers. The "German

The Great Famine of 1845–1851

TABLE 9.2 Total Number of Immigrants by Five-Year Period

YEARS	NUMBER OF IMMIGRANTS
1841–1845	430,000
1846–1850	1,283,000
1851–1855	1,748,000
1856–1860	850,000

Although our image of the West emphasizes the lone pioneer, many migrants settled in tightly knit communities and worked cooperatively. This painting by Olof Krans, who came to the United States from Sweden with his family in 1850 at the age of twelve, shows a group of women preparing to plant corn at the immigrant settlement of Bishop Hill, Illinois.

triangle," as the cities of Cincinnati, St. Louis, and Milwaukee were sometimes called, attracted large German populations. A vibrant German-language culture, with its own schools, newspapers, associations, and churches, developed wherever large numbers of Germans settled. "As one passes along the Bowery," one observer noted of a part of New York City known as Kleindeutschland (Little Germany), "almost everything is German."

Some 40,000 Scandinavians also emigrated to the United States in these years, most of whom settled on farms in the Old Northwest. The continuing expansion of industry and the failure of the Chartist movement of the 1840s, which sought to democratize the system of government in Britain, also inspired many English workers to emigrate to the United States.

The Rise of Nativism

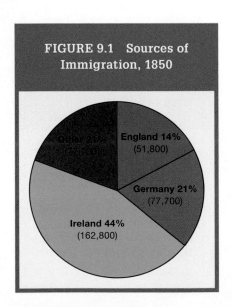

FIGURE 9.1 Sources of Immigration, 1850

Other 21% (74,100)
England 14% (51,800)
Germany 21% (77,700)
Ireland 44% (162,800)

Immigrants from England (whose ranks included the actor Junius Brutus Booth, father of John Wilkes Booth) were easily absorbed, but those from Ireland encountered intense hostility. As Roman Catholics, they faced discrimination in a largely Protestant society in which the tradition of "anti-popery" still ran deep. The Irish influx greatly enhanced the visibility and power of the Catholic Church, previously a minor presence in most parts of the country. During the 1840s and 1850s, Archbishop John Hughes of New York City made the church a more assertive institution. Hughes condemned the use of the Protestant King James Bible in New York City's public schools, pressed Catholic parents to send their children to an expanding network of parochial schools, and sought government funding to pay for them. He aggressively sought to win converts from Protestantism.

Many Protestants found such activities alarming. Catholicism, they feared, threatened American institutions and American freedom. In 1834, Lyman Beecher, a prominent Presbyterian minister (and father of the religious leader Henry Ward Beecher

Riot in Philadelphia, an 1844 lithograph, depicts street battles between nativists and Irish Catholics that left fifteen persons dead. The violence originated in a dispute over the use of the Protestant King James Bible in the city's public schools.

and the writers Harriet Beecher Stowe and Catharine Beecher), delivered a sermon in Boston, soon published as "A Plea for the West." Beecher warned that Catholics were seeking to dominate the American West, where the future of Christianity in the world would be worked out. His sermon inspired a mob to burn a Catholic convent in the city.

The idea of the United States as a refuge for those seeking economic opportunity or as an escape from oppression has always coexisted with suspicion of and hostility to foreign newcomers. American history has witnessed periods of intense anxiety over immigration. The Alien Act of 1798 reflected fear of immigrants with radical political views. During the early twentieth century, as will be discussed below, there was widespread hostility to the "new immigration" from southern and eastern Europe. In the early twenty-first century, the question of how many persons should be allowed to enter the United States, and under what circumstances, remains a volatile political issue.

Opposition to immigration

The Irish influx of the 1840s and 1850s thoroughly alarmed many native-born Americans. Those who feared the impact of immigration on American political and social life were called "nativists." They blamed immigrants for urban crime, political corruption, and a fondness for intoxicating liquor, and they accused them of undercutting native-born skilled laborers by working for starvation wages. The Irish were quickly brought into the urban political machines of the Democratic Party, whose local bosses provided jobs and poor relief to struggling newcomers. Nativists contended that the Irish, supposedly unfamiliar with American conceptions of liberty and subservient to the Catholic Church, posed a threat to democratic institutions, social reform, and public education. Stereotypes similar to those directed at blacks flourished regarding the Irish as well—childlike, lazy, and slaves of their passions, they were said to be unsuited for republican freedom.

Nativists

Nativism would not become a national political movement until the 1850s, as we will see in Chapter 13. But in the 1840s, New York City and Philadelphia witnessed violent anti-immigrant riots. Appealing mainly to skilled native-born workers who feared that immigrants were taking their jobs and undercutting their wages, a nativist candidate was elected New York City's mayor in 1844.

An engraving depicts the ruins of the Ursuline Convent in Charlestown, Massachusetts, burned by a mob in 1834 after a sermon by the Reverend Lyman Beecher, who warned that Catholics were conspiring to dominate the American West.

The Transformation of Law

American law increasingly supported the efforts of entrepreneurs to participate in the market revolution, while shielding them from interference by local governments and liability for some of the less desirable results of economic growth. The corporate form of business organization became central to the new market economy. A corporate firm enjoys special privileges and powers granted in a charter from the government, among them that investors and directors are not personally liable for the company's debts. Unlike companies owned by an individual, family, or limited partnership, in other words, a corporation can fail without ruining its directors and stockholders. Corporations were therefore able to raise far more capital than the traditional forms of enterprise. By the 1830s, many states had replaced the granting of charters through specific acts of legislation with "general incorporation laws," allowing any company to obtain a corporate charter if it paid a specified fee.

Corporations

Many Americans distrusted corporate charters as a form of government-granted special privilege. But the courts upheld their validity, while opposing efforts by established firms to limit competition from newcomers. In ***Dartmouth College v. Woodward*** (1819), John Marshall's Supreme Court defined corporate charters issued by state legislatures as contracts, which future lawmakers could not alter or rescind. Five years later, in ***Gibbons v. Ogden***, the Court struck down a monopoly the New York legislature had granted for steamboat navigation. And in 1837, with Roger B. Taney now the chief justice, the Court ruled that the Massachusetts legislature did not infringe the charter of an existing company that had constructed a bridge over the Charles River when it empowered a second company to build a competing bridge. The community, Taney declared, had a legitimate interest in promoting transportation and prosperity.

Court decisions on the economy

Local judges, meanwhile, held businessmen blameless for property damage done by factory construction (such as the flooding of upstream farmlands and the disruption of fishing when dams were built to harness water power). Numerous court decisions also affirmed employers' full authority over the workplace and invoked the old common law of conspiracy to punish workers who sought to strike for higher wages. Not until 1842, in **Commonwealth v. Hunt**, did Massachusetts chief justice Lemuel Shaw decree that there was nothing inherently illegal in workers organizing a union or a strike.

THE FREE INDIVIDUAL

By the 1830s, the market revolution and westward expansion had produced a society that amazed European visitors: energetic, materialistic, and seemingly in constant motion. Arriving in Chicago in 1835, the British writer Harriet Martineau found the streets "crowded with land speculators, hurrying from one sale to another. . . . As the gentlemen of our party walked the streets, store-keepers hailed them from their doors, with offers of farms, and all manner of land-lots, advising them to speculate before the price of land rose higher." Alexis de Tocqueville was struck by Americans' restless energy and apparent lack of attachment to place. "No sooner do you set foot on American soil," he observed, "than you find yourself in a sort of tumult. All around you, everything is on the move." Westward migration and urban development created a large mobile population no longer tied to local communities who sought to seize the opportunities offered by economic change. "In the United States," wrote Tocqueville, "a man builds a house in which to spend his old age, and sells it before the roof is on; he plants a garden and [rents] it just as the trees are coming into bearing; he brings a field into tillage and leaves other men to gather the crops."

> *An energetic society*

The West and Freedom

Westward expansion and the market revolution profoundly affected the lives of all Americans. They reinforced some older ideas of freedom and helped to create new ones. American freedom, for example, had long been linked with the availability of land in the West. A New York journalist, John L. O'Sullivan, first employed the phrase "**manifest destiny**," meaning that the United States had a divinely appointed mission, so obvious as to be beyond dispute, to occupy all of North America. Americans, he proclaimed, had a far better title to western lands than could be provided by any international treaty, right of discovery, or long-term settlement. Their right to the continent was provided by the nation's divinely inspired mission to extend the area of freedom. Other peoples' claims, O'Sullivan wrote, must give way to "our manifest destiny to overspread and to possess the whole of the continent which Providence has given us for the development of the great experiment in liberty." Those who stood in the way of expansion—European powers like Great Britain and Spain, Native Americans, Mexicans—were by definition obstacles to the progress of freedom.

O'Sullivan wrote these words in 1845, but the essential idea was familiar much earlier. As the population moved across the Appalachian Mountains, so did the linkage between westward expansion and freedom. "The Goddess

A song written in 1845 offers a satire of the widely held image of the West as "the land of the free," a place where the "humblest" American can achieve economic success. The pictures surrounding the text offer a somewhat different image of westerners, and the verses go on to complain about illness and hardship. But the opening words reflect the ways in which Americans have always viewed the West.

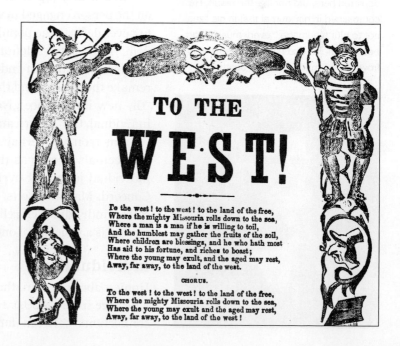

TO THE WEST!

To the west! to the west! to the land of the free,
Where the mighty Missouria rolls down to the sea,
Where a man is a man if he is willing to toil,
And the humblest may gather the fruits of the soil,
Where children are blessings, and he who hath most
Has aid to his fortune, and riches to boast;
Where the young may exult, and the aged may rest,
Away, far away, to the land of the west.

CHORUS.

To the west! to the west! to the land of the free,
Where the mighty Missouria rolls down to the sea,
Where the young may exult and the aged may rest,
Away, far away, to the land of the west!

of Liberty," declared Senator John Breckinridge of Kentucky, was not "governed by geographical limits." A sense of spatial openness, of the constant opportunity to pick up and move when the pursuit of happiness seemed to demand it, became more and more a central component of American freedom. Freedom in the United States, wrote the French historian Michel Chevalier, one of the many Europeans who visited the country in the 1830s, was a "practical idea" as much as a "mystical one"—it meant "a liberty of action and motion which the American uses to expand over the vast territory that Providence has given him and to subdue it to his uses."

In national myth and ideology, the West would long remain, as the writer Wallace Stegner would later put it, "the last home of the freeborn American." The settlement and economic exploitation of the West promised to prevent the United States from following down the path of Europe and becoming a society with fixed social classes and a large group of wage-earning poor. In the West, land was more readily available and oppressive factory labor far less common than in the East. With population and the price of land rising dramatically in the older states and young men's prospects for acquiring a farm or setting up an independent artisan shop declining, the West still held out the chance to achieve economic independence, the social condition of freedom.

The Transcendentalists

The restless, competitive world of the market revolution strongly encouraged the identification of American freedom with the absence of restraints on self-directed individuals seeking economic advancement and personal development. The "one important revolution" of the day, the philosopher Ralph Waldo Emerson wrote in the 1830s, was "the new value of the private man." The opportunity for personal growth offered a new definition of Jefferson's pursuit of happiness, one well suited to a world in which territorial expansion and the market revolution had shattered traditional spatial and social boundaries and made moving from place to place and status to status common features of American life.

In a widely reprinted 1837 address, "The American Scholar," Emerson called on the person engaged in writing and thinking to "feel all confidence in himself, . . . to never defer to the popular cry," and to find and trust his own "definition of freedom." In Emerson's definition, rather than a preexisting set of rights or privileges, freedom was an open-ended process of self-realization by which individuals could remake themselves and their own lives. The keynote of the times, he declared, was "the new importance given to the single person" and the "emancipation" of the individual, the "American idea."

Emerson was perhaps the most prominent member of a group of New England intellectuals known as the **transcendentalists**, who insisted on the primacy of individual judgment over existing social traditions and institutions. Emerson's Concord, Massachusetts, neighbor, the writer Henry David Thoreau, echoed his call for individual self-reliance. "Any man more right than his neighbors," Thoreau wrote, "is a majority of one."

Individualism

Ironies abounded in the era's "individualism" (a term that first entered the language in the 1820s). For even as the market revolution promoted commercial connections between far-flung people, the idea of the "sovereign individual"

The daguerreotype, an early form of photography, required the sitter to remain perfectly still for twenty seconds or longer. The philosopher Ralph Waldo Emerson, depicted here, did not like the result. He complained in his journal that in his "zeal not to blur the image," every muscle had become "rigid" and his face was fixed in a frown as "in madness, or in death."

proclaimed that Americans should depend on no one but themselves. Of course, personal independence had long been associated with American freedom. But eighteenth-century thinkers generally saw no contradiction between private happiness and self-sacrificing public virtue, defined as devotion to the common good. Now, Tocqueville observed, individualism led "each member of the community to sever himself from the mass of his fellows and to draw apart with his family and his friends . . . [leaving] society at large to itself." Americans increasingly understood the realm of the self—which came to be called "privacy"—as one with which neither other individuals nor government had a right to interfere. As will be discussed in the next chapter, individualism also helped to inspire the expansion of democracy. Ownership of one's self rather than ownership of property now made a person capable of exercising the right to vote.

Looking back from the 1880s, Emerson would recall the era before the Civil War as a time when "social existence" gave way to "the enlargement and independency of the individual, . . . driven to find all his resources, hopes, rewards, society, and deity within himself." In his own life, Thoreau illustrated Emerson's point about the primacy of individual conscience in matters political, social, and personal, and the need to find one's own way rather than following the crowd. Thoreau became persuaded that modern society stifled individual judgment by making men "tools of their tools," trapped in stultifying jobs by their obsession with acquiring wealth. Even in "this comparatively free country," he wrote, most persons were so preoccupied with material things that they had no time to contemplate the beauties of nature.

To escape this fate, Thoreau retreated for two years to a cabin on Walden Pond near Concord, where he could enjoy the freedom of isolation from the "economical and moral tyranny" he believed ruled American society. He subsequently published *Walden* (1854), an account of his experiences and a critique of how the market revolution was, in his opinion, degrading both Americans' values and the natural environment. An area that had been covered with dense forest in his youth, he observed,

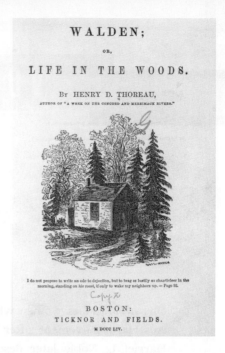

The sketch of Henry David Thoreau's cabin on Walden Pond illustrates his belief that Americans could enjoy what he called "absolute freedom" by rejecting market society and retreating into the wilderness. Only in this way, he insisted, could they preserve both individual independence and the natural environment.

Thomas Cole's 1846 painting *A Pic-Nic Party* exemplifies the work of the Hudson River School, a group of artists fascinated by the glory of nature. Cole portrays nature and civilization coexisting in harmony, although the prominence of the stump in the foreground, the remains of a tree felled by an axe, suggests that man poses a danger to the natural environment.

VOICES OF FREEDOM

From RECOLLECTIONS OF
HARRIET L. NOBLE
(1824)

One of countless women who took part in the westward movement after the War of 1812, Harriet L. Noble later described her family's migration from New York to Michigan, then a sparsely populated territory, and the burdens pioneer life placed on women.

My husband was seized with the mania, and accordingly made preparation to start and . . . we started about the 20th of September, 1824, for Michigan. . . . As we approached Detroit, the "Cantonment" with the American flag floating on its walls, was decidedly the most interesting of any part of the town; for a city it was certainly the most filthy, irregular place I had ever seen. . . . I said to myself, "if this be a Western city, give me a home in the woods." . . .

We passed two log houses between this and Ann Arbor. About the middle of the afternoon we found ourselves at our journey's end—but what a prospect? There were some six or seven log huts occupied by as many inmates as could be crowded into them. . . . We lived in this way until our husbands got a log house raised and the roof on. . . . We sold out and bought again ten miles west of Ann Arbor, a place which suited us better. . . . My husband and myself were four days

building it. I suppose most of my lady friends would think a woman quite out of "her legitimate sphere" in turning mason, but I was not at all particular what kind of labor I performed, so we were only comfortable and provided with the necessaries of life. . . .

I am not of a desponding disposition, nor often low-spirited, and having left New York to make Michigan my home, I had no idea of going back, or being very unhappy. Yet the want of society, of church privileges, and in fact almost every thing that makes life desirable, would often make me sad in spite of all effort to the contrary. . . .

When I look back upon my life, and see the ups and downs, the hardships and privations I have been called upon to endure, I feel no wish to be young again. I was in the prime of life when I came to Michigan—only twenty-one, and my husband was thirty-three. Neither of us knew the reality of hardship. Could we have known what it was to be pioneers in a new country, we should never have had the courage to come, but I am satisfied that with all the disadvantages of raising a family in a new country, there is a consolation in knowing that our children are prepared to brave the ills of life, I believe, far better than they would have been had we never left New York.

From "FACTORY LIFE AS IT IS, BY AN OPERATIVE" (1845)

Beginning in the 1830s, young women who worked in the cotton textile factories in Lowell, Massachusetts, organized to demand shorter hours of work and better labor conditions. In this pamphlet from 1845, a factory worker details her grievances as well as those of female domestic workers, the largest group of women workers.

———————————————

Philanthropists of the nineteenth century!—shall not the operatives of our country be permitted to speak for themselves?. . . Shall tyranny and cruel oppression be allowed to rivet the chains of physical and mental slavery on the millions of our country who are the real producers of all its improvements and wealth, and they fear to speak out in noble self-defense? Shall they fear to appeal to the sympathies of the people, or the justice of this far-famed republican nation? God forbid!

Much has been written and spoken in woman's behalf, especially in America; and yet a large class of females are, and have been, destined to a state of servitude as degrading as unceasing toil can make it. I refer to the female operatives of New England—the free states of our union—the states where no colored slave can breathe the balmy air, and exist as such—but yet there are those, a host of them, too, who are in fact nothing more nor less than slaves in every sense of the word! Slaves to a system of labor which requires them to toil from five until seven o'clock, with one hour only to attend to the wants of nature, allowed—slaves to the will and requirements of the "powers that be," however they may infringe on the rights or conflict with the feelings of the operative—slaves to ignorance—and how can it be otherwise? What time has the operative to bestow on moral, religious or intellectual culture? How can our country look for aught but ignorance and vice, under the existing state of things? When the whole system is exhausted by unremitting labor

during twelve and thirteen hours per day, can any reasonable being expect that the mind will retain its vigor and energy? Impossible! Common sense will teach every one the utter impossibility of improving the mind under these circumstances, however great the desire may be for knowledge.

Again, we hear much said on the subject of benevolence among the wealthy and so called, Christian part of community. Have we not cause to question the sincerity of those who, while they talk benevolence in the parlor, compel their help to labor for a mean, paltry pittance in the kitchen? And while they manifest great concern for the souls of the heathen in distant lands, care nothing for the bodies and intellects of those within their own precincts? . . .

In the strength of our united influence we will soon show these drivelling cotton lords, this mushroom aristocracy of New England, who so arrogantly aspire to lord it over God's heritage, that our rights cannot be trampled upon with impunity; that we WILL not longer submit to that arbitrary power which has for the last ten years been so abundantly exercised over us.

QUESTIONS

1. *In what ways did the experience of moving west alter traditional expectations of women's roles?*

2. *Why does the female factory worker compare her conditions with those of slaves?*

3. *What do these documents suggest about how different kinds of women were affected by economic change in the first part of the nineteenth century?*

was a "moral free agent"—that is, a person free to choose between a Christian life and sin. Sinners could experience a "change of heart" and embrace spiritual freedom, defined, in the words of evangelical minister Jonathan Blanchard, as "Christ ruling in and over rational creatures who are obeying him freely and from choice."

Revivalist ministers seized the opportunities offered by the market revolution to spread their message. They raised funds, embarked on lengthy preaching tours by canal, steamboat, and railroad, and flooded the country with mass-produced, inexpensive religious tracts. The revivals' opening of religion to mass participation and their message that ordinary Americans could shape their own spiritual destinies resonated with the spread of market values.

To be sure, evangelical preachers can hardly be described as cheerleaders for a market society. They regularly railed against greed and indifference to the welfare of others as sins. Finney called selfishness—an extreme form of individualism encouraged by the scramble for wealth produced by the market revolution—"the law of Satan's empire," not God's. Yet the revivals thrived in areas caught up in the rapid expansion of the market economy, such as the region of upstate New York along the path of the Erie Canal. Most of Finney's converts here came from the commercial and professional classes. Evangelical ministers promoted what might be called a controlled **individualism** as the essence of freedom. In stressing the importance of industry, sobriety, and self-discipline as examples of freely chosen moral behavior, evangelical preachers promoted the very qualities necessary for success in a market culture.

The Emergence of Mormonism

The Second Great Awakening illustrated how the end of governmental support for established churches promoted religious pluralism. Competition among religious groups kept religion vibrant and promoted the emergence of new denominations. Among the most successful of the religions that sprang up, hoping to create a Kingdom of God on earth, was the **Church of Jesus Christ of Latter-Day Saints**, or Mormons. The Mormons were founded in the 1820s by Joseph Smith, a farmer in upstate New York who as a youth began to experience religious visions. He claimed to have been led by an angel to a set of golden plates covered with strange writing. Smith translated and published them as *The Book of Mormon*, after a fourth-century prophet.

Depending on one's point of view, *The Book of Mormon* is either a divinely inspired holy book or an impressive work of American literature. It tells the story of three families who traveled from the ancient Middle East to the Americas, where they eventually evolved into Native American tribes. Jesus Christ plays a prominent role in the book, appearing to one of the family groups in the

Mass religion

The Awakening and market society

In this 1846 photograph the massive Mormon temple in Nauvoo, Illinois, towers over the ramshackle wooden buildings of this town along the Mississippi River.

Western Hemisphere after his death and resurrection. Thus, the word of God had been transmitted not only to people in the Biblical Middle East, but also directly to inhabitants of North America. The second coming of Christ would take place in the New World, where Smith was God's prophet. Smith mortgaged his farm to help pay for an edition of 5,000 copies, which appeared in 1830.

Mormonism emerged in a center of the Second Great Awakening, upstate New York. The church founded by Smith responded to the disruptions caused by the market revolution. It was self-consciously democratic, admitting anyone, regardless of wealth or occupation, who accepted Smith's message. (African-Americans could join, but could not enter the priesthood—a policy not overturned until 1978.) Like Jesus, Smith condemned the selfishness of the rich—in the ideal ancient society described in *The Book of Mormon* "there was no poor among them." At a time when paper money seemed to have little intrinsic worth, gold remained an unchallenged standard of value, which may help to explain the appeal of a religious text written on golden plates.

A democratic church

Gradually, however, Smith began to receive visions that led to more controversial doctrines, notably polygamy, which allows one man to have more than one wife. By the end of his life, Smith had married no fewer than thirty women. Along with the absolute authority Smith exercised over his followers, this doctrine outraged the Mormons' neighbors. Mobs drove Smith and his followers out of New York, Ohio, and Missouri before they settled in 1839 in Nauvoo, Illinois, where they hoped to await the Second Coming of Christ. There, five years later, Smith was arrested on the charge of inciting a riot that destroyed an anti-Mormon newspaper. While in jail awaiting trial, Smith was murdered by a group of intruders. In 1847, his successor as Mormon leader, Brigham Young, led more than 2,000 followers across the Great Plains and Rocky Mountains to the shores of the Great Salt Lake in present-day Utah, seeking a refuge where they could practice their faith undisturbed. (The area was then part of Mexico; the United States annexed it in 1848.) By 1852, the number of Mormons in various settlements in Utah had reached 16,000. The experience of expulsion helped to shape Mormon theology. Their distinctive practice of posthumous baptism, in which modern members of the church retrospectively baptize long-dead ancestors, seeks to unite across generations families separated not only by death but also by migration. The practice has also led the church to gather and make publicly available an enormous library of genealogical records from around the world—a goldmine for scholars of every religion.

Controversial doctrines

The Mormons' experience revealed the limits of religious toleration in nineteenth-century America but also the opportunities offered by religious pluralism. Today, Mormons constitute the fourth largest church in the United States and *The Book of Mormon* has been translated into over 100 languages.

THE LIMITS OF PROSPERITY

Liberty and Prosperity

As the market revolution progressed, the right to compete for economic advancement became a touchstone of American freedom. Official imagery linked the goddess of liberty ever more closely to emblems of material wealth. New Jersey, whose official seal, adopted in 1776, had paired liberty with Ceres, the Roman

Pat Lyon at the Forge, an 1826–1827 painting of a prosperous blacksmith. Proud of his accomplishments as a self-made man who had achieved success through hard work and skill rather than inheritance, Lyon asked the artist to paint him in his shop wearing his work clothes.

SUGGESTED READING

BOOKS

- Bergmann, William H. *The American National State and the Early West* (2014). Demonstrates how governmental action was crucial to early western development.

- Boydston, Jeanne. *Home and Work: Housework, Wages, and the Ideology of Work in the Early Republic* (1990). Examines how the market revolution affected ideas relating to women's work.

- Deyle, Steven. *Carry Me Back: The Domestic Slave Trade in American Life* (2005). The most comprehensive history of the internal slave trade, by which millions of slaves were transported to the Deep South.

- Dublin, Thomas. *Women at Work: The Transformation of Work in Lowell, Massachusetts, 1826–1860* (1975). A pioneering study of the working and nonworking lives of Lowell "factory girls."

- Faragher, John M. *Sugar Creek: Life on the Illinois Prairie* (1986). Traces the growth of a frontier community from early settlement to market society.

- Harris, Leslie. *In the Shadow of Slavery: African-Americans in New York City, 1626–1863* (2003). A study that emphasizes the exclusion of African-Americans from the economic opportunities offered by the market revolution.

- Haselby, Sam. *The Origins of American Religious Nationalism* (2015). Explores how the battle between frontier evangelists and more traditional New England ministers shaped religion and politics in the early republic.

- Howe, Daniel W. *What Hath God Wrought: The Transformation of America, 1815–1848* (2007). A comprehensive account of social and political changes in this era, emphasizing the significance of the communications revolution.

- Johnson, Paul E. *A Shopkeeper's Millennium: Society and Revivals in Rochester, New York, 1815–1837* (1978). Explores the impact of religious revivals on a key city of upstate New York.

- Larson, John L. *The Market Revolution in America: Liberty, Ambition, and the Eclipse of the Common Good* (2010). The most recent account of the market revolution and its impact on American society and values.

- Miller, Kerby A. *Exiles and Emigrants: Ireland and the Irish Exodus to North America* (1985). An examination of Irish immigration over the course of American history.

- Rockman, Seth. *Scraping By: Wage Labor, Slavery, and Survival in Early Baltimore* (2009). A pioneering study of the status of free laborers in a major city in a slave-based economy.

- Ryan, Mary P. *Cradle of the Middle Class: The Family in Oneida County, New York, 1790–1865* (1981). Examines how economic change helped to produce a new kind of middle-class family structure centered on women's dominance of the household.

- Stansell, Christine. *City of Women: Sex and Class in New York, 1789–1860* (1986). Considers how gender conventions and economic change shaped the lives of working-class women.

- Wilentz, Sean. *Chants Democratic: New York City and the Rise of the American Working Class, 1788–1850* (1984). A study of the early labor movement in one of its key centers in antebellum America.

WEBSITES

- American Transcendentalism: www.vcu.edu/engweb/transcendentalism/
- The First West: The Ohio Valley to 1820: http://loc.gov/ammem/award99/icuhtml/fawhome.html
- Women in America, 1820–1842: http://xroads.virginia.edu/~hyper/detoc/fem/home.htm

CHAPTER REVIEW AND ONLINE RESOURCES

REVIEW QUESTIONS

1. Identify the major transportation improvements in this period and explain how they influenced the market economy.

2. How did state and local governments promote the national economy in this period?

3. How did the market economy and westward expansion intensify the institution of slavery?

4. How did westward expansion and the market revolution drive each other?

5. What role did immigrants play in the new market society?

6. How did changes in the law promote development in the economic system?

7. As it democratized American Christianity, the Second Great Awakening both took advantage of the market revolution and criticized its excesses. Explain.

8. How did the market revolution change women's work and family roles?

9. Give some examples of the rise of individualism in these years.

KEY TERMS

steamboats (p. 309)

Erie Canal (p. 309)

Cotton Kingdom (p. 316)

cotton gin (p. 316)

Porkopolis (p. 319)

American system of manufactures (p. 322)

mill girls (p. 324)

nativism (p. 327)

Dartmouth College v. Woodward (p. 328)

Gibbons v. Ogden (p. 328)

Commonwealth v. Hunt (p. 329)

manifest destiny (p. 329)

transcendentalists (p. 330)

Second Great Awakening (p. 334)

individualism (p. 336)

Church of Jesus Christ of Latter-Day Saints (p. 336)

cult of domesticity (p. 339)

family wage (p. 341)

Go to **inQuizitive**

To see what you know—and learn what you've missed—with personalized feedback along the way.

Visit the *Give Me Liberty!* **Student Site** for primary source documents and images, interactive maps, author videos featuring Eric Foner, and more.

Jim Crow, a piece of sheet music from 1829. Minstrel shows were a form of nineteenth-century entertainment in which white actors impersonated blacks. One of the most popular characters was Jim Crow, the happy, childlike plantation slave created by the performer Thomas D. Rice. Years later, "Jim Crow" would come to mean the laws and customs of southern segregation.

Even today, controversy persists over the voting rights of immigrants, persons who have served prison terms, and the poor.

The political world of the nineteenth century, so crucial an arena for the exercise of American freedom, was in part defined in contrast to the feminine sphere of the home. The "most rabid Radical," Ralph Waldo Emerson remarked in his journal in 1841, was likely to be conservative "in relation to the theory of Marriage." Beyond the right to "decent treatment" by her husband and to whatever property the law allowed her to control, declared the *New York Herald*, a woman had "no rights . . . with which the public have any concern."

A Racial Democracy

If the exclusion of women from political freedom continued a long-standing practice, the increasing identification of democracy and whiteness marked something of a departure. Tocqueville noted that by the 1830s, "equality" had become an American obsession. In contrast to the highly stratified societies of Europe, white Americans of all social classes dressed the same, traveled in the same stagecoaches and railroad cars, and stayed in the same hotels. Yet at the same time, blacks were increasingly considered a group apart.

Racist imagery became the stock-in-trade of popular theatrical presentations like minstrel shows, in which white actors in blackface entertained the audience by portraying African-Americans as stupid, dishonest, and altogether ridiculous. With the exception of Herman Melville, who portrayed complex, sometimes heroic black characters in works like *Moby-Dick* and *Benito Cereno* (the latter a fictionalized account of a shipboard slave rebellion), American authors either ignored blacks entirely or presented them as stereotypes—happy slaves prone to superstition or long-suffering but devout Christians. Meanwhile, the somewhat tentative thinking of the revolutionary era about the status of non-whites flowered into an elaborate ideology of racial superiority and inferiority, complete with "scientific" underpinnings. These developments affected the boundaries of the political nation.

Race and the vote

In the revolutionary era, only Virginia, South Carolina, and Georgia explicitly confined the vote to whites, although elsewhere, custom often made it difficult for free blacks to exercise the **franchise**. As late as 1800, no northern state barred blacks from voting. But every state that entered the Union after that year, with the single exception of Maine, limited the right to vote to white males. And, beginning with Kentucky in 1799 and Maryland two years later, states that had allowed blacks to vote rescinded the privilege.

Race and Class

In 1821, the same New York constitutional convention that removed property qualifications for white voters raised the requirement for blacks to $250, a sum beyond the reach of nearly all of the state's black residents. North Carolina disenfranchised free blacks in 1835, and Pennsylvania, home of an articulate, economically successful black community in Philadelphia, did the same three years later. One delegate to the Pennsylvania constitutional convention refused to sign the completed document because of its provision limiting suffrage to whites. This was Thaddeus Stevens, who would later become a leader in the drive for equal rights

Disenfranchising free blacks

for African-Americans after the Civil War. By 1860, blacks could vote on the same basis as whites in only five New England states, which contained only 4 percent of the nation's free black population. A delegate to the Pennsylvania convention of 1837 described the United States as "a political community of white persons."

Despite racial inequalities, many whites of the revolutionary generation had thought of African-Americans as "citizens of color," potential members of the body politic. But in the nineteenth century, the definition of the political nation became more and more associated with race. The federal government barred free blacks from service in state militias and the army (although the navy did enroll some black sailors). No state accorded free blacks what today would be considered full equality before the law. In Illinois, for example, blacks could not vote, testify or sue in court, serve in the militia, or attend public schools. Blacks were aliens, not Americans, "intruders among us," declared a political leader in Minnesota.

In effect, race had replaced class as the boundary between those American men who were entitled to enjoy political freedom and those who were not. Even as this focus on race limited America's political community as a whole, it helped to solidify a sense of national identity among the diverse groups of European origin. In a country where the right to vote had become central to the meaning of freedom, it is difficult to overstate the importance of the fact that white male immigrants could vote in some states almost from the moment they landed in America, while nearly all free blacks (and, of course, slaves), whose ancestors had lived in the country for centuries, could not vote at all.

> *Race replaces class as a voting qualification*

NATIONALISM AND ITS DISCONTENTS

The American System

The War of 1812, which the United States and Great Britain—the world's foremost military power—fought to a draw, inspired an outburst of nationalist pride. But the war also revealed how far the United States still was from being a truly integrated nation. With the Bank of the United States having gone out of existence when its charter expired in 1811, the country lacked a uniform currency and found it almost impossible to raise funds for the war effort. Given the primitive state of transportation, it proved very difficult to move men and goods around the country. One shipment of supplies from New England had taken seventy-five days to reach New Orleans. With the coming of peace, the manufacturing enterprises that sprang up while trade with Britain had been suspended faced intense competition from low-cost imported goods. A younger generation of Republicans, including Henry Clay and John C. Calhoun, who had led the call for war in 1812, believed these "infant industries" deserved national protection. While retaining their Jeffersonian belief in an agrarian republic, they insisted that agriculture must be complemented by a manufacturing sector if the country were to become economically independent of Britain.

> *"Infant industries"*

In 1806, Congress, as noted in the previous chapter, had approved using public funds to build a paved National Road from Cumberland, Maryland, to the Ohio Valley. Two years later, Albert Gallatin, Jefferson's secretary of the treasury, outlined a plan for the federal government to tie the vast nation together by constructing

CHAPTER REVIEW AND ONLINE RESOURCES

REVIEW QUESTIONS

1. What global changes prompted the Monroe Doctrine? What were its key provisions? How does it show America's growing international presence?

2. How did Andrew Jackson represent the major developments of the era: westward movement, the market revolution, and the expansion of democracy for some alongside the limits on it for others?

3. How did the expansion of white male democracy run counter to the ideals of the founders, who believed government should be sheltered from excessive influence by ordinary people?

4. What were the components of the American System, and how were they designed to promote the national economy under the guidance of the federal government?

5. How did the Missouri Compromise and the nullification crisis demonstrate increasing sectional competition and disagreements over slavery?

6. According to Martin Van Buren, why were political parties a desirable element of public life? What did he do to build the party system?

7. What were the major economic, humanitarian, political, and social arguments for and against Indian removal?

8. What were the key issues that divided the Democratic and Whig parties? Where did each party stand on those issues?

9. Explain the causes and effects of the Panic of 1837.

KEY TERMS

the Dorr War (p. 348)

Democracy in America (p. 349)

franchise (p. 352)

American System (p. 354)

tariff of 1816 (p. 354)

Panic of 1819 (p. 355)

McCulloch v. Maryland (p. 356)

Era of Good Feelings (p. 356)

Missouri Compromise (p. 357)

Monroe Doctrine (p. 361)

spoils system (p. 368)

tariff of abominations (p. 371)

Exposition and Protest (p. 372)

Webster-Hayne debate (p. 372)

nullification crisis (p. 373)

Force Act (p. 373)

Indian Removal Act (p. 374)

Worcester v. Georgia (p. 375)

Trail of Tears (p. 376)

Bank War (p. 378)

soft money and hard money (p. 379)

pet banks (p. 379)

Panic of 1837 (p. 380)

Go to 🐰 INQUIZITIVE

To see what you know—and learn what you've missed—with personalized feedback along the way.

Visit the *Give Me Liberty!* **Student Site** for primary source documents and images, interactive maps, author videos featuring Eric Foner, and more.

SLAVERY, FREEDOM, AND THE CRISIS OF THE UNION, 1840-1877

During the middle part of the nineteenth century, the United States confronted its greatest crisis, as the division between slave and free societies tore the country apart. A new nation emerged from the Civil War, with slavery abolished and the meaning of freedom transformed for all Americans.

Despite the hope of some of the founders that slavery might die out, the institution grew in size and economic importance as the nineteenth century progressed. Slavery expanded westward with the young republic, and the slave population grew to nearly 4 million by 1860. After the northern states abolished slavery, it became the "peculiar institution" of the South, the basis of a society growing ever more different from the rest of the country in economic structure and social values. Planters who dominated southern life also exerted enormous influence in national affairs. They developed a defense of slavery that insisted the institution was the foundation of genuine freedom for white citizens. Slaves, meanwhile, created their own semiautonomous culture that nurtured from one generation to the next their hope for liberation from bondage. Nonetheless, slavery was in some ways a national institution. Slave-grown cotton, a source of wealth to slaveowners, also provided the raw material for the North's growing textile industry and became the country's most important export.

During the 1820s and 1830s, numerous social movements arose that worked to reform American society. Their inspiration lay primarily in the Second Great Awakening, the religious revivals that swept both North and South and offered salvation to sinners and improvement to society at large. While some reform movements were national in scope, others existed only in the North. Most notable among the latter was a new, militant movement demanding the immediate abolition of slavery and the incorporation of blacks as equal citizens of the republic. The abolitionists helped to focus discussions of freedom on the sharp contradiction between liberty and slavery. They promoted an understanding of freedom as control over one's self and participation as an equal member in social and political life. They not only helped to place the issue of slavery squarely on the national agenda but also inspired the stirrings of protest among a number of northern women, whose work in the antislavery movement led them to resent their own lack of legal rights and educational and economic opportunities.

In the 1840s, the conflict between free and slave societies moved to the center stage of American politics. It did so as a result of the nation's territorial expansion. The acquisition of a vast new area of land in the aftermath of the Mexican War raised the question of whether slavery would be able to expand farther westward. By the 1850s, this issue had destroyed the Whig Party, weakened the Democrats, and led to the creation of an entirely new party, the Republicans, dedicated to confining slavery to the states where it already existed. Exalting the superiority of northern society, based on "free labor," to southern society, based on slavery, Republicans elected Abraham Lincoln as president in 1860, even though he did not receive a single vote in most of the southern states. In response, seven slave states seceded from the Union and formed a new nation, the Confederate States of America. When southern forces fired on Fort Sumter, an enclave of Union control in Charleston harbor, they inaugurated the Civil War, by far the bloodiest conflict in American history.

Begun as a struggle to preserve the Union, the Civil War eventually became a crusade for emancipation, which brought the nation what President Lincoln called "a new birth of freedom." The North's failure to achieve military victory in the first two years of the war, coupled with the actions of slaves who by the thousands abandoned the plantations to flee to Union lines, propelled the Lincoln administration down the road to emancipation. Although it freed few slaves on the day it was issued, January 1, 1863, Lincoln's Emancipation Proclamation proved to be the turning point of the Civil War, for it announced that, henceforth, the Union army would serve as an agent of freedom. And by authorizing, for the first time, the enlistment of black men into the Union army, the Proclamation raised the question of black citizenship in the postwar world.

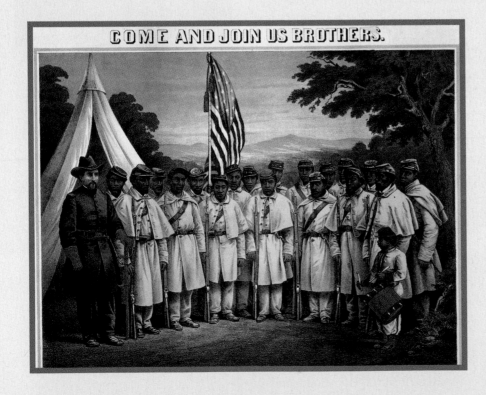

The era of Reconstruction that followed the Civil War was a time of intense political and social conflict, in which the definition of freedom and the question of who was entitled to enjoy it played a central role. Former slaves claimed that freedom meant full incorporation into American society, with the same rights and opportunities whites enjoyed. They also demanded that the government guarantee them access to land, to provide an economic foundation for their freedom. Most southern whites believed that blacks should go back to work on the plantations, enjoying very few political and civil rights. Andrew Johnson, who succeeded Lincoln as president, shared their view. But the majority of northern Republicans came to believe that the emancipated slaves should enjoy the same legal rights as whites. In 1867, they granted black men in the South the right to vote. During Reconstruction, northern Republicans rewrote the laws and Constitution to incorporate the ideal of equal citizenship for all Americans, regardless of race. This was a dramatic expansion of the meaning of freedom.

In the South, Reconstruction witnessed a short-lived period in which former slaves voted and held office alongside whites, a remarkable experiment in interracial democracy. On the other hand, the former slaves failed to achieve the economic freedom they desired, since the North proved unwilling to distribute land. As a result, most former slaves, and increasing numbers of whites in the war-devastated South, found themselves confined to working as sharecroppers on land owned by others. But the genuine advances achieved during Reconstruction, such as improved access to education, exercise of political rights, and the creation of new black institutions like independent churches, produced a violent reaction by upholders of white supremacy. During the 1870s, the North retreated from its commitment to equality. In 1877, Reconstruction came to an end. Many of the rights guaranteed to the former slaves were violated in the years that followed.

Although Reconstruction only lasted from 1865 to 1877, the issues debated then forecast many of the controversies that would envelop American society in the decades that followed. The definition of American citizenship, the power of the federal government and its relationship to the states, the future of political democracy in a society marked by increasing economic inequality—all these were Reconstruction issues, and all reverberated in the Gilded Age and Progressive era that followed.

The Civil War era resolved the contradiction of the existence of slavery in a land that celebrated freedom. But just as the American Revolution left to nineteenth-century Americans the problem of slavery, the Civil War and Reconstruction left to future generations the challenge of bringing genuine freedom to the descendants of slavery.

CHAPTER 11

THE PECULIAR INSTITUTION

In an age of "self-made" men, no American rose more dramatically from humble origins to national and international distinction than Frederick Douglass. Born into slavery in 1818, he became a major figure in the crusade for abolition, the drama of emancipation, and the effort during Reconstruction to give meaning to black freedom.

Douglass was the son of a slave mother and an unidentified white man, possibly his owner. As a youth in Maryland, he gazed out at the ships in Chesapeake Bay, seeing them as "freedom's swift-winged angels." In violation of Maryland law, Douglass learned to read and write, initially with the assistance of his owner's wife and then, after her husband forbade her to continue, with the help of local white children. "From that moment," he later wrote, he understood that knowledge was "the pathway from slavery to freedom." Douglass experienced slavery in all its variety, from work as a house servant and as a skilled craftsman in a Baltimore shipyard to labor as a plantation field hand. When he was fifteen, Douglass's owner sent him to a "slave breaker" to curb his independent spirit. After numerous whippings, Douglass defiantly refused to allow himself to be disciplined again. This confrontation, he recalled, was "the turning-point in my career as a slave." It rekindled his desire for freedom. In 1838, having borrowed the free papers of a black sailor, he escaped to the North.

Frederick Douglass went on to become the most influential African-American of the nineteenth century and the nation's preeminent advocate of racial equality. "He who has endured the cruel pangs of slavery," he wrote, "is the man to advocate liberty." Douglass lectured against slavery throughout the North and the British Isles, and he edited a succession of antislavery publications. He published a widely read autobiography that offered an eloquent condemnation of slavery and racism. Indeed, his own accomplishments testified to the incorrectness of prevailing ideas about blacks' inborn inferiority. Douglass was also active in other reform movements, including the campaign for women's rights. During the Civil War, he advised Abraham Lincoln on the employment of black soldiers and became an early advocate of giving the right to vote to the emancipated slaves. Douglass died in 1895, as a new system of white supremacy based on segregation and disenfranchisement was being fastened upon the South.

Throughout his career, Douglass insisted that slavery could only be overthrown by continuous resistance. "Those who profess to favor freedom, and yet deprecate agitation," he declared, "are men who want crops without plowing up the ground, they want rain without thunder and lightning, they want the ocean without the awful roar of its many waters." In effect, Douglass argued that in their desire for freedom, the slaves were truer to the nation's underlying principles than the white Americans who annually celebrated the Fourth of July while allowing the continued existence of slavery.

FOCUS QUESTIONS

How did slavery shape social and economic relations in the Old South? *–p. 390*

What were the legal and material constraints on slaves' lives and work? *–p. 400*

How did family, gender, religion, and values combine to create distinct slave cultures in the Old South? *–p. 410*

What were the major forms of resistance to slavery? *–p. 415*

The Slave Auction, by the British artist Eyre Crowe, depicts a scene in an auction house. A slave sale is in progress, while on the right, slaves wait apprehensively for their turn to be sold. A child clings to her mother, perhaps for the last time, while potential buyers examine the seated women. Crowe entered the auction house in March 1853 after seeing an advertisement for a slave sale, and began sketching. When the white crowd realized what he was doing, they "rushed on him savagely and obliged him to quit," Crowe's traveling companion wrote to a friend. The painting is based on his sketches.

389

THE OLD SOUTH

1791–1804	Haitian Revolution
1800	Gabriel's Rebellion
1811	Slave revolt in Louisiana
1822	Denmark Vesey's slave conspiracy
1830s	States legislate against teaching slaves to read or write
1831	William Lloyd Garrison's *The Liberator* debuts
	Nat Turner's Rebellion
1831–1832	Slave revolt in Jamaica
1832	Virginia laws tighten the slave system
1833	British Parliament mandates emancipation
1838	Great Britain abolishes slavery within its empire
	Frederick Douglass escapes slavery
1839	Slaves take control of the *Amistad*
1841	Slave uprising on the *Creole*
1849	Harriet Tubman escapes slavery
1855	Trial of Celia

When Frederick Douglass was born, slavery was already an old institution in America. Two centuries had passed since the first twenty Africans were landed in Virginia from a Dutch ship. After abolition in the North, slavery had become the "**peculiar institution**" of the South—that is, an institution unique to southern society. The Mason-Dixon Line, drawn by two surveyors in the eighteenth century to settle a boundary dispute between Maryland and Pennsylvania, eventually became the dividing line between slavery and freedom.

Despite the hope of some of the founders that slavery might die out, in fact the institution survived the crisis of the American Revolution and rapidly expanded westward. During the first forty years of Douglass's life, the number of slaves and the economic and political importance of slavery continued to grow. On the eve of the Civil War, the slave population had risen to nearly 4 million, its high rate of natural increase more than making up for the prohibition in 1808 of further slave imports from Africa. In the South as a whole, slaves made up one-third of the total population, and in the cotton-producing states of the Deep South, around half. By the 1850s, slavery had crossed the Mississippi River and was expanding rapidly in Arkansas, Louisiana, and eastern Texas. In 1860, one-third of the nation's cotton crop was grown west of the Mississippi.

Cotton Is King

In the nineteenth century, cotton replaced sugar as the world's major crop produced by slave labor. And although slavery survived in Brazil and the Spanish and French Caribbean, its abolition in the British empire in 1833 made the United States indisputably the center of New World slavery.

When measured by slavery's geographic extent, the numbers held in bondage, and the institution's economic importance both regionally and nationally, the Old South was the largest and most powerful slave society the modern world has known. Its strength rested on a virtual monopoly of cotton, the South's "white gold." Cotton had been grown for thousands of years in many parts of the globe. The conquistador Hernán Cortés was impressed by the high quality of woven cotton clothing worn by the Aztecs. But in the nineteenth century, cotton assumed an unprecedented role in the world economy.

Because the early industrial revolution centered on factories using cotton as the raw material to manufacture cloth, cotton became by far the most important commodity in international trade. And three-fourths of the world's cotton supply came from the southern United States. Throughout the world, hundreds of thousands of workers loaded, unloaded, spun, and wove cotton, and thousands of manufacturers and merchants owed their wealth to the cotton trade. Textile manufacturers in places as far-flung as Massachusetts, Lancashire in Great Britain, Normandy in France, and the suburbs of Moscow depended on a regular supply of American cotton.

Cotton sales earned the money from abroad that allowed the United States to pay for imported manufactured goods. On the eve of the Civil War, cotton represented well over half of the total value of American exports. In 1860, the economic investment represented by the slave population exceeded the value of the nation's factories, railroads, and banks combined.

The Second Middle Passage

As noted in Chapter 9, to replace the slave trade from Africa, which had been prohibited by Congress in 1808, a massive trade in slaves developed within the United States. More than 2 million slaves were sold between 1820 and 1860, a majority to local buyers but hundreds of thousands from older states to "importing" states of the Lower South, resulting in what came to be known as the **Second Middle Passage**. Slave trading was a visible, established business. The main commercial districts of southern cities contained the offices of slave traders, complete with signs reading "Negro Sales" or "Negroes Bought Here." Auctions of slaves took place at public slave markets, as in New Orleans, or at courthouses. Southern newspapers carried advertisements for slave sales, southern banks financed slave trading, southern ships and railroads carried slaves from buyers to sellers, and southern states and municipalities earned revenue by taxing the sale of slaves. The Cotton Kingdom could not have arisen without the internal slave trade, and the economies of older states like Virginia came increasingly to rely on the sale of slaves.

The internal slave trade

Slavery and the Nation

Slavery, Henry Clay proclaimed in 1816, "forms an exception . . . to the general liberty prevailing in the United States." But Clay, like many of his contemporaries, underestimated slavery's impact on the entire nation. The "free states" had ended slavery, but they were hardly unaffected by it. The Constitution, as we have seen, enhanced the power of the South in the House of Representatives and electoral college and required all states to return fugitives from bondage. Slavery shaped the lives of all Americans, white as well as black. It helped to determine where they

Slavery's influence

COTTON PRESSING IN LOUISIANA

"Cotton Processing in Louisiana," from *Ballou's Magazine* in 1856, illustrates how slaves were used to supply power for a partially mechanized work process.

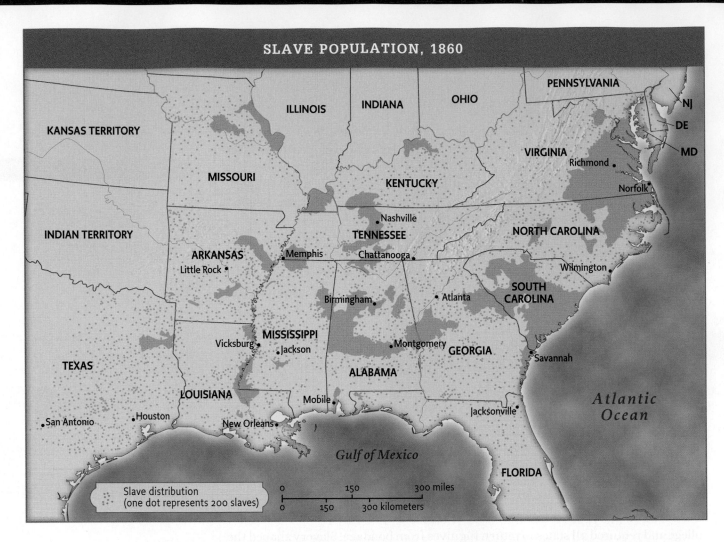

SLAVE POPULATION, 1860

Slave distribution
(one dot represents 200 slaves)

Rather than being evenly distributed throughout the South, the slave population was concentrated in areas with the most fertile soil and easiest access to national and international markets. By 1860, a significant percentage of the slave population had been transported from the Atlantic coast to the Deep South via the internal slave trade.

lived, how they worked, and under what conditions they could exercise their freedoms of speech, assembly, and the press.

Northern merchants and manufacturers participated in the slave economy and shared in its profits. Money earned in the cotton trade helped to finance industrial development and internal improvements in the North. Northern ships carried cotton to New York and Europe, northern bankers financed cotton plantations, northern companies insured slave property, and northern factories turned cotton into cloth. New York City's rise to commercial prominence depended as much on the establishment of shipping lines that gathered the South's cotton and transported it to Europe, as on the Erie Canal. The Lords of the Loom (New England's early factory owners) relied on cotton supplied by the Lords of the Lash (southern slaveowners). Northern manufacturers like Brooks

Slavery and the North

Brothers supplied cheap fabrics (called "Negro cloth") to clothe the South's slaves.

The Southern Economy

There was no single South before the Civil War. In the eight slave states of the Upper South, slaves and slaveowners made up a smaller percentage of the total population than in the seven Deep South states that stretched from South Carolina west to Texas. The Upper South had major centers of industry in Baltimore, Richmond, and St. Louis, and its economy was more diversified than that of the Deep South, which was heavily dependent on cotton. Not surprisingly, during the secession crisis of 1860–1861, the Deep South states were the first to leave the Union.

Nonetheless, slavery led the South down a very different path of economic development than the North's, limiting the growth of industry, discouraging immigrants from entering the region, and inhibiting technological progress. The South did not share in the urban growth experienced by the rest of the country. Most southern cities were located on the region's periphery and served mainly as centers for gathering and shipping cotton. Southern banks existed primarily to help finance the plantations. They loaned money for the purchase of land and slaves, not manufacturing development. Southern railroads mostly consisted of short lines that brought cotton from the interior to coastal ports.

In the Cotton Kingdom, the only city of significant size was New Orleans. With a population of 168,000 in 1860, New Orleans ranked as the nation's sixth-largest city. As the gathering point for cotton grown along the Mississippi River and sugar from the plantations of southeastern Louisiana, it was the world's leading exporter of slave-grown crops. Unlike other cities with slavery (apart from St. Louis and Baltimore, on the periphery of the South), New Orleans also attracted large numbers of European immigrants. In 1860, 40 percent of its population was foreign-born. And New Orleans's rich French heritage and close connections with the Caribbean produced a local culture quite different from that of the rest of the United States, reflected in the city's distinctive music, dance, religion, and cuisine.

In 1860, the South produced less than 10 percent of the nation's manufactured goods. Many northerners viewed slavery as an obstacle to American economic progress. But as New Orleans showed, slavery and economic growth could go hand in hand. In general, the southern economy was hardly stagnant, and slavery proved very profitable for most owners. The profits produced by slavery for the South and the nation as a whole formed a powerful obstacle to abolition. Speaking of cotton, Senator James Henry Hammond of South Carolina declared, "No power on earth dares to make war upon it. **Cotton is king.**"

A slave dealer's place of business in Alexandria, Virginia, then part of the District of Columbia, the nation's capital. The buying and selling of slaves was a regularized part of the southern economy, and such businesses were a common sight in every southern city. This building contained a "slave pen" that typically contained over 300 slaves being kept before their sale.

TABLE 11.1 Growth of the Slave Population	
YEARS	**SLAVE POPULATION**
1790	697,624
1800	893,602
1810	1,191,362
1820	1,538,022
1830	2,009,043
1840	2,487,355
1850	3,204,313
1860	3,953,760

This 1860 view of New Orleans captures the size and scale of the cotton trade in the South's largest city. More than 3,500 steamboats arrived in New Orleans in 1860.

Plain Folk of the Old South

The foundation of the Old South's economy, slavery powerfully shaped race relations, politics, religion, and the law. Its influence was pervasive: "Nothing escaped," writes one historian, "nothing and no one." This was true despite the fact that the majority of white southerners—three out of four white families—owned no slaves. Since planters monopolized the best land, most small white farmers lived outside the plantation belt in hilly areas unsuitable for cotton production. They worked the land using family labor rather than slaves or hired workers.

Many southern farmers lived lives of economic self-sufficiency remote from the market revolution. They raised livestock and grew food for their families, purchasing relatively few goods at local stores. Those residing on marginal land in isolated hill areas and the Appalachian Mountains were often desperately poor and, since nearly all the southern states lacked systems of free public education, were more often illiterate than their northern counterparts. Not until the arrival of railroads and coal mining later in the nineteenth century would such areas become integrated into the market economy. Most yeoman farmers enjoyed a comfortable standard of living, and many owned a slave or two. But even successful small farmers relied heavily on home production to supply their basic needs. Unlike northern farmers, therefore, they did not provide a market for manufactured goods. This was one of the main reasons why the South did not develop an industrial base.

Some poorer whites resented the power and privileges of the great planters. Politicians like Andrew Johnson of Tennessee and Joseph Brown of Georgia rose to power as self-proclaimed spokesmen of the common man against the "slavocracy." But most poor whites made their peace with the planters in whose hands economic and social power was concentrated. Racism, kinship ties, common participation in a democratic political culture, and regional loyalty in the face of outside criticism all served to cement bonds between planters and the South's "plain folk." In

TABLE 11.2 Slaveholding, 1850 (in Round Numbers)

NUMBER OF SLAVES OWNED	SLAVEHOLDERS
1	68,000
2–4	105,000
5–9	80,000
10–19	55,000
20–49	30,000
50–99	6,000
100–199	1,500
200 +	250

the plantation regions, moreover, small farmers manned the slave patrols that kept a lookout for runaway slaves and those on the roads without permission. Non-slaveholders regularly elected slaveowners to public offices in the South. Like other white southerners, most small farmers believed their economic and personal freedom rested on slavery.

The Planter Class

Even among slaveholders, the planter was far from typical. In 1850, a majority of slaveholding families owned five or fewer slaves. Fewer than 40,000 families possessed the twenty or more slaves that qualified them as planters. Fewer than 2,000 families owned a hundred slaves or more. Nonetheless, the planter's values and aspirations dominated southern life. The plantation, wrote Frederick Douglass, was "a little nation by itself, with its own language, its own rules, regulations, and customs." These rules and customs set the tone for southern society.

An upcountry family, dressed in home-spun, in Cedar Mountain, Virginia. Many white families in the pre–Civil War South were largely isolated from the market economy. This photograph was taken in 1862 but reflects the prewar way of life.

Ownership of slaves provided the route to wealth, status, and influence. Planters not only held the majority of slaves, but they controlled the most fertile land, enjoyed the highest incomes, and dominated state and local offices and the leadership of both political parties. Small slaveholders aspired to move up into the ranks of the planter class. Those who acquired wealth almost always invested it in land and slaves. But as the price of a "prime field hand" rose from $1,000 in 1840 to $1,800 in 1860 (the latter figure equivalent to around $40,000 today), it became more and more difficult for poorer white southerners to become slaveholders.

Slavery, of course, was a profit-making system, and slaveowners kept close watch on world prices for their products and invested in enterprises such as railroads and canals. They paid careful attention to every detail of their operations, adopted the most modern business and accounting practices, and carefully monitored market conditions and their own profits. Their wives—the "plantation mistresses" idealized in southern lore for femininity, beauty, and dependence on men—were hardly idle. They cared for sick slaves, directed the domestic servants, and supervised the entire plantation when their husbands were away. Of course, owners' sexual exploitation of slave women produced deep resentment among their wives, who sometimes took it out on the slaves themselves.

Alexis de Tocqueville observed that "the northerner loves to make money, the southerner to spend it." Many of the richest planters squandered their wealth in a lifestyle complete with lavish entertainments and summer vacations in Newport and Saratoga. House slaves were so numerous in Charleston, wrote one visitor to the city, that "the Charlestonians are obliged to exercise their wits to devise sufficient variety to keep them employed." On the cotton frontier, many planters lived in crude log homes. But in the older slave states, and as settled society developed in

Louisa, a slave woman, with her charge in an 1858 photograph. The slave had been purchased at age twenty-two at a slave auction in New Orleans to serve as a nursemaid. Because of a death in the white family, the child was her legal owner.

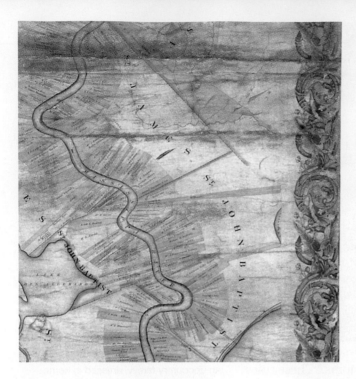

A detail from *Norman's Chart of the Lower Mississippi River* (1858) shows slave plantations laid out so that each fronted on the river and, therefore, had easy access to the market.

Significance of paternalism

Dueling

the Deep South, they constructed elegant mansions adorned with white columns in the Greek Revival style of architecture.

The Paternalist Ethos

The slave plantation was deeply embedded in the world market, and planters sought to accumulate land, slaves, and profits. But planters' values glorified not the competitive capitalist marketplace, but a hierarchical, agrarian society in which slaveholding gentlemen took personal responsibility for the physical and moral well-being of their dependents—women, children, and slaves. "The master," wrote one planter, "as the head of the system, has a right to the obedience and labor of the slave, but the slave has also his mutual rights in the master; the right of protection, the right of counsel and guidance, the right of subsistence, the right of care and attention in sickness and old age."

This outlook, known as **paternalism** (from the Latin word for "father"), had been a feature of American slavery even in the eighteenth century. But it became more ingrained after the closing of the African slave trade in 1808, which narrowed the cultural gap between master and slave. Unlike the absentee planters of the West Indies, many of whom resided in Great Britain, southern slaveholders lived on their plantations and thus had year-round contact with their slaves.

The paternalist outlook both masked and justified the brutal reality of slavery. It enabled slaveowners to think of themselves as kind, responsible masters even as they bought and sold their human property—a practice at odds with the claim that slaves formed part of the master's "family." Some slaveowners tried to reform the system to eliminate its most oppressive features. The Reverend Charles C. Jones, a wealthy planter of Liberty County, Georgia, organized his neighbors to promote the religious instruction of slaves, improve slave housing, diet, and medical care, and discourage severe punishments. But even Jones believed his slaves so "degraded" and lacking in moral self-discipline that he could not contemplate an end to slavery.

The Code of Honor

As time went on, the dominant southern conception of the good society diverged more and more sharply from that of the egalitarian, competitive, individualistic North. In the South, for example, both upper- and lower-class whites adhered to a code of personal honor, in which men were expected to defend, with violence if necessary, their own reputation and that of their families. Although dueling was illegal, many prominent southerners took part in duels to avenge supposed insults. In 1826, Henry Clay and John Randolph, two of the most important southern political leaders, fought a duel with pistols after Clay took exception to criticisms by Randolph on the floor of Congress. Fortunately, each missed the other. Twenty years later, however, John H. Pleasants, editor of the *Richmond Whig*, died in a duel with the son of a rival newspaperman.

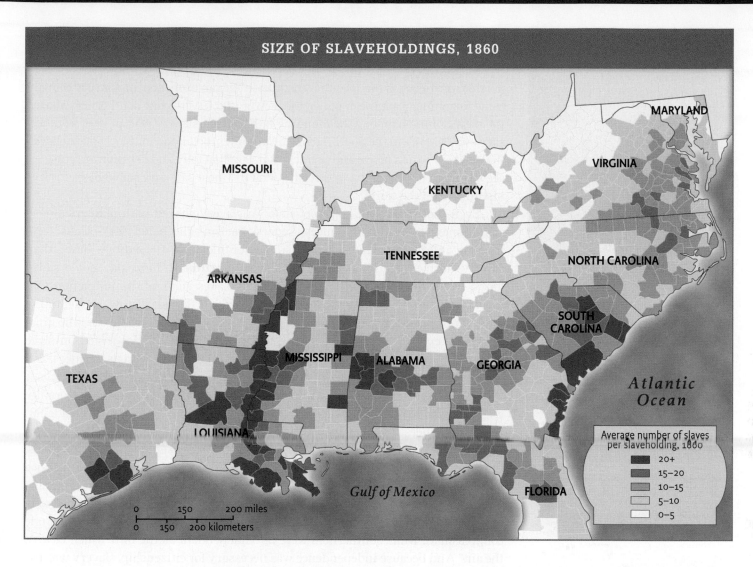

SIZE OF SLAVEHOLDINGS, 1860

Average number of slaves per slaveholding, 1860

- 20+
- 15–20
- 10–15
- 5–10
- 0–5

Just as southern men had a heightened sense of their own honor and masculinity, white southern women, even more than in the North, were confined within the "domestic circle." "A man loves his children," wrote George Fitzhugh, a Virginia lawyer and author of numerous books and articles on social issues, "because they are weak, helpless, and dependent. He loves his wife for similar reasons." As will be discussed in the next chapter, many northern women before the Civil War became part of a thriving female culture centered on voluntary religious and reform organizations. Few parallels existed in the South, and plantation mistresses often complained of loneliness and isolation.

Most southern slaveholders owned fewer than five slaves. The largest plantations were concentrated in coastal South Carolina and along the Mississippi River.

Women in southern ideology

The Proslavery Argument

Some southerners worried about their standing in the eyes of the world, especially how others viewed the intellectual life of their region. "We of the South," one wrote, "must, to Europe, continue to appear inferior to the North in intellectual cultivation." The free states outstripped the slave states in public education, in the number of colleges, and in newspapers, literary journals, and other publications.

A pre–Civil War engraving depicting the paternalist ideal. The old slave in the foreground says, "God Bless you massa! you feed and clothe us, . . . and when too old to work, you provide for us!" The master replies, "These poor creatures are a sacred legacy from my ancestors and while a dollar is left me, nothing shall be spared to increase their comfort and happiness."

Slavery and white equality

"Laws of the free womb"

Nonetheless, the life of the mind flourished in the Old South, and the region did not lack for novelists, political philosophers, scientists, and the like.

In the thirty years before the outbreak of the Civil War, however, even as northern criticism of the "peculiar institution" began to deepen, proslavery thought came to dominate southern public life. Fewer and fewer white southerners shared the view, common among the founding fathers, that slavery was, at best, a "necessary evil." "Many in the South," John C. Calhoun proclaimed in 1837, "once believed that [slavery] was a moral and political evil. . . . That folly and delusion are gone; we see it now in its true light, and regard it as the most safe and stable basis for free institutions in the world."

Even those who had no direct stake in slavery shared with planters a deep commitment to white supremacy. Indeed, racism—the belief that blacks were innately inferior to whites and unsuited for life in any condition other than slavery—formed one pillar of the **proslavery argument**. Most slaveholders also found legitimation for slavery in biblical passages such as the injunction that servants should obey their masters. Others argued that slavery was essential to human progress. Had not the ancient republics of Greece and Rome and the great European empires of the seventeenth and eighteenth centuries rested on slave labor? Without slavery, planters would be unable to cultivate the arts, sciences, and other civilized pursuits.

Still other defenders of slavery insisted that the institution guaranteed equality for whites by preventing the growth of a class doomed to a life of unskilled labor. Like northerners, they claimed to be committed to the ideal of freedom. Slavery for blacks, they declared, was the surest guarantee of "perfect equality" among whites, liberating them from the "low, menial" jobs like factory labor and domestic service performed by wage laborers in the North. Slavery made possible the considerable degree of economic autonomy (the social condition of freedom) enjoyed not only by planters but also by non-slaveholding whites. Because of slavery, claimed one congressman, white southerners were as "independent as the bird which cleaves the air." And because independence was necessary for citizenship, slavery was the "cornerstone of our republican edifice."

Abolition in the Americas

American slaveowners were well aware of developments in slave systems elsewhere in the Western Hemisphere. As noted in Chapter 8, the slave revolution in Haiti sent shock waves of fear throughout the American South. White southerners observed carefully the results of the wave of emancipations that swept the hemisphere in the first four decades of the century. In these years, slavery was abolished in most of Spanish America and in the British empire.

In most Latin American nations, the end of slavery followed the pattern established earlier in the northern United States—gradual emancipation accompanied by some kind of recognition of the owners' legal right to property in slaves. These "laws of the free womb" allowed slaveholders to retain ownership of existing slaves while freeing their slaves' children after they worked for the mother's owner for a specified number of years. Such laws, wrote one official, "respected the past and corrected only the future." Abolition was far swifter in the British empire, where

Parliament in 1833 mandated almost immediate emancipation, with a seven-year transitional period of "apprenticeship." This system produced so much conflict between former master and former slave that Britain decreed complete freedom in 1838. The law appropriated 20 million pounds to compensate the owners.

The experience of emancipation in other parts of the hemisphere strongly affected debates over slavery in the United States. Southern slaveowners judged the vitality of the Caribbean economy by how much sugar and other crops it produced for the world market. Since many former slaves preferred to grow food for their own families, defenders of slavery in the United States charged that British emancipation had been a failure. Abolitionists disagreed, pointing to the rising standard of living of freed slaves, the spread of education among them, and other improvements in their lives. In a hemispheric perspective, slavery was a declining institution. By 1840, slavery had been outlawed in Mexico, Central America, and Chile, and only small numbers of aging slaves remained in Venezuela, Colombia, and Peru. During the European revolutions of 1848, France and Denmark emancipated their colonial slaves. At mid-century, significant New World slave systems remained only in Cuba, Puerto Rico, Brazil—and the United States. Nonetheless, because of the rapid growth of the slave population in the Old South, there were more slaves in the hemisphere in 1860 than at any point prior to that.

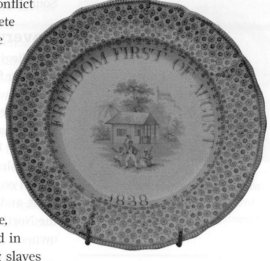

A plate manufactured in England to celebrate emancipation in the British empire. After a brief period of apprenticeship, all slaves were freed on August 1, 1838. At the center, a family of former slaves celebrates outside their cabin.

Slavery and Liberty

Many white southerners declared themselves the true heirs of the American Revolution. They claimed to be inspired by "the same spirit of freedom and independence" that motivated the founding generation. Like their ancestors of the 1760s and 1770s, their political language was filled with contrasts between liberty and slavery and complaints that outsiders proposed to reduce them to "slaves" by interfering with their local institutions. Southern state constitutions enshrined the idea of equal rights for free men, and the South participated fully in the movement toward political democracy for whites.

Beginning in the 1830s, however, proslavery writers began to question the ideals of liberty, equality, and democracy so widely shared elsewhere in the nation. South Carolina, the only southern state where a majority of white families owned slaves, became the home of an aggressive defense of slavery that repudiated the idea that freedom and equality were universal entitlements. The language of the Declaration of Independence—that all men were created equal and entitled to liberty—was "the most false and dangerous of all political errors," insisted John C. Calhoun. Proslavery spokesmen returned to the older definition of freedom as a privilege, a "reward to be earned, not a blessing to be gratuitously lavished on all alike."

Repudiating freedom and equality for all

As the sectional controversy intensified after 1830, a number of southern writers and politicians came to defend slavery less as the basis of equality for whites than as the foundation of an organic, hierarchical society. Inequality and hence the submission of inferior to superior—black to white, female to male, lower classes to upper classes—was a "fundamental law" of human existence. A hierarchy of "ranks

Embracing hierarchy

Slaves outside their cabin on a South Carolina plantation, probably photographed in the 1850s. They had brought their furniture outdoors to be included in the photo.

the South drew tighter and tighter the chains of bondage. If slaves in the United States enjoyed better health and diets than elsewhere in the Western Hemisphere, they had far less access to freedom. In Brazil, it was not uncommon for an owner to free slaves as a form of celebration—on the occasion of a wedding in the owner's family, for example—or to allow slaves to purchase their freedom. Although slavery in Brazil lasted until 1888, more than half the population of African descent was already free in 1850. (The comparable figure in the American South was well below 10 percent.) In the nineteenth-century South, more and more states set limits on voluntary manumission, requiring that such acts be approved by the legislature. "All the powers of earth," declared Abraham Lincoln in 1857, seemed to be "rapidly combining" to fasten bondage ever more securely upon American slaves. Few slave societies in history have so systematically closed off all avenues to freedom as the Old South did.

Free Blacks in the Old South

The existence of slavery helped to define the status of those blacks who did enjoy freedom. On the eve of the Civil War, nearly half a million free blacks lived in the United States, a majority in the South. Most were the descendants of slaves freed by southern owners in the aftermath of the Revolution or by the gradual emancipation laws of the northern states. Their numbers were supplemented by slaves who had been voluntarily liberated by their masters, who had been allowed to purchase their freedom, or who succeeded in running away.

When followed by "black" or "Negro," the word "free" took on an entirely new meaning. Whites defined their freedom, in part, by their distance from slavery. But among blacks, wrote Douglass, "the distinction between the slave and the free is not great." Northern free blacks, as noted in Chapter 10, generally could not vote and enjoyed few economic opportunities. Free blacks in the South could legally own property and marry and, of course, could not be bought and sold. But many regulations restricting the lives of slaves also applied to them. Free blacks had no voice in selecting public officials. Like slaves, they were prohibited from owning dogs, firearms, or liquor, and they could not strike a white person, even in self-defense. They were not allowed to testify in court against whites or serve on juries, and they had to carry at all times a certificate of freedom. Poor free blacks who required public assistance could be bound out to labor alongside slaves. "Free negroes," declared a South Carolina judge in 1848, "belong to a degraded caste of society" and should learn to conduct themselves "as inferiors."

As noted above, nineteenth-century Brazil had a large free black population. In the West Indies, many children of white owners and female slaves gained their

Restrictions on free blacks

DISTRIBUTION OF FREE BLACKS, 1860

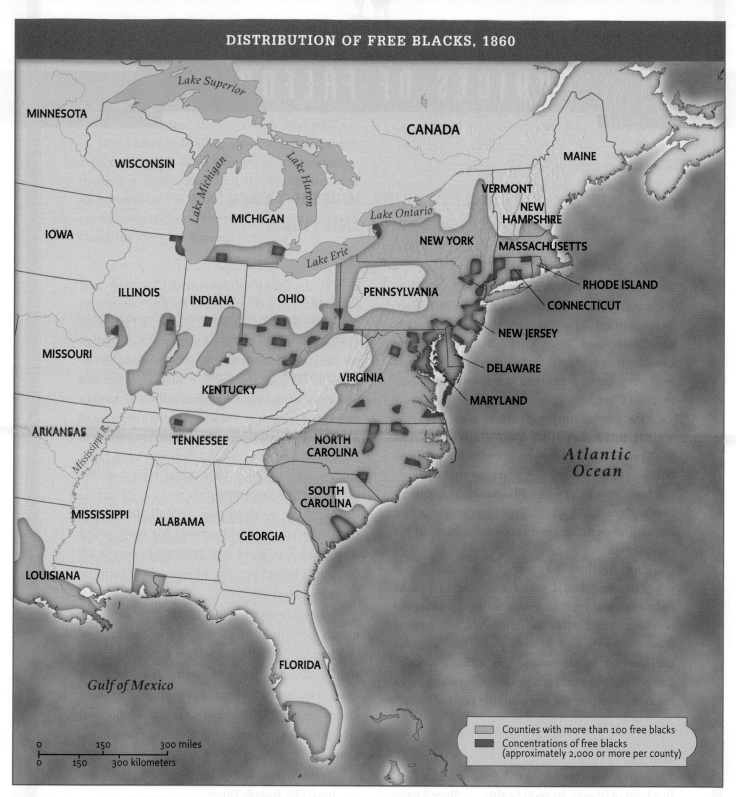

Counts with more than 100 free blacks

Concentrations of free blacks
(approximately 2,000 or more per county)

The nation's population in 1860 included nearly 500,000 free blacks. The majority lived in the slave states, especially Maryland and Virginia.

freedom, becoming part of a "free colored" population sharply distinguished from both whites above them and slaves below. In the absence of a white lower middle class, free blacks in Jamaica and other Caribbean islands operated shops and worked as clerks in government offices.

In the United States, a society that equated "black" and "slave" and left little room for a mulatto group between them, free blacks were increasingly considered an undesirable group, a potential danger to the slave system. By the 1850s, most southern states prohibited free blacks from entering their territory and a few states even moved to expel them altogether, offering the choice of enslavement or departure. Nonetheless, a few free blacks managed to prosper within slave society. William Johnson, a Natchez barber, acquired enough money to purchase a plantation with fifteen slaves; he hunted with upper-class whites and loaned them money. But he suffered from the legal disadvantages common to his race. He could not, for example, testify against his debtors in court when they failed to pay. In Virginia, the slaves freed and given land by the will of Richard Randolph (noted in Chapter 6) established a vibrant community they called Israel Hill. Despite the legal restrictions on free blacks in the state, they prospered as farmers and skilled craftsmen.

Prosperous free blacks

The Upper and Lower South

Very few free blacks (around 37,000 persons, or less than 2 percent of the area's black population) lived in the Lower South in 1860. Like William Johnson, a majority of them resided in cities. Mississippi, an overwhelmingly rural state with no real urban centers, had fewer than 800 free blacks on the eve of the Civil War. In New Orleans and Charleston, on the other hand, relatively prosperous free black communities developed, mostly composed of mixed-race descendants of unions between white men and slave women. Some became truly wealthy—Antoine Dubuclet of Louisiana, for example, owned 100 slaves. Many free blacks in these cities acquired an education and worked as skilled craftsmen such as tailors, carpenters, and mechanics. They established churches for their communities and schools for their children. Some New Orleans free blacks sent their children to France for an education. These elite free blacks did everything they could to maintain a separation from the slave population. The Brown Fellowship Society of Charleston, for example, would not even allow dark-skinned free men to join. Even in these cities, however, most free blacks were poor unskilled laborers.

In the Upper South, where the large majority of southern free blacks lived, they generally worked for wages as farm laborers. Here, where tobacco had exhausted the soil, many planters shifted to grain production, which required less year-round labor. They sold off many slaves to the Lower South and freed others. By 1860, half the African-American population of Maryland was free. Planters hired

REGION	FREE BLACK POPULATION	PERCENTAGE OF TOTAL BLACK POPULATION
North	226,152	100%
South	261,918	6.2
Upper South	224,963	12.8
Lower South	36,955	1.5
Delaware	19,829	91.7
Washington, D.C.	11,131	77.8
Kentucky	10,684	4.5
Maryland	83,942	49.1
Missouri	3,572	3.0
North Carolina	30,463	8.4
Tennessee	7,300	2.6
Virginia	58,042	10.6
Alabama	2,690	0.6
Arkansas	144	0.1
Florida	932	1.5
Georgia	3,500	0.8
Louisiana	18,647	5.3
Mississippi	773	0.2
South Carolina	9,914	2.4
Texas	355	0.2

TABLE 11.3 Free Black Population, 1860

local free blacks to work alongside their slaves at harvest time. Free blacks in Virginia and Maryland were closely tied to the slave community and often had relatives in bondage. Some owned slaves, but usually these were free men who had purchased their slave wives and children but could not liberate them because the law required any slave who became free to leave the state. Overall, in the words of Willis A. Hodges, a member of a free Virginia family that helped runaways to reach the North, free blacks and slaves were "one man of sorrow."

"One man of sorrow"

Slave Labor

First and foremost, slavery was a system of labor; "from sunup to first dark," with only brief interruptions for meals, work occupied most of the slaves' time. Large plantations were diversified communities, where slaves performed all kinds of work. The 125 slaves on one plantation, for instance, included a butler, two waitresses, a nurse, a dairymaid, a gardener, ten carpenters, and two shoemakers. Other plantations counted among their slaves engineers, blacksmiths, and weavers, as well as domestic workers from cooks to coachmen.

Slaves cut wood to provide fuel for steamboats, worked in iron and coal mines, manned the docks in southern seaports, and laid railroad track. They were set to work by local authorities to construct and repair bridges, roads, and other facilities and by the federal government to build forts and other public buildings in the South. Businessmen, merchants, lawyers, and civil servants owned slaves, and by 1860 some 200,000 worked in industry, especially in the ironworks and tobacco factories of the Upper South. Reliance on unfree labor, moreover, extended well beyond the ranks of slaveholders, for, as noted earlier, many small farmers and manufacturers rented slaves from plantation owners. A few owners gave trusted slaves extensive responsibilities. Simon Gray's owner made him the head of a riverboat crew on the Mississippi. Gray supervised both white and slave workers, sold his owner's lumber at urban markets, and handled large sums of money.

Slaves were an ever-present part of southern daily life. In this 1826 portrait of the five children of Commodore John Daniel Daniels, a wealthy Baltimore shipowner, a young slave lies on the floor at their side, holding the soap for a game of blowing bubbles, while another hovers in the background, almost depicted as part of the room's design.

Gang Labor and Task Labor

Gray's experience, of course, was hardly typical. The large majority of slaves—75 percent of women and nearly 90 percent of men, according to one study—worked in the fields. The precise organization of their labor varied according to the crop and the size of the holding. On small farms, the owner often toiled side-by-side with his slaves. The largest concentration of slaves, however, lived and worked on plantations in the Cotton Belt, where men, women, and children labored in gangs, often under the direction of an overseer and perhaps a slave "driver" who assisted him. Among slaves, overseers had a reputation for meting out harsh treatment. "The requisite qualifications for an overseer," wrote Solomon Northup, a free black who spent twelve years in slavery after being kidnapped

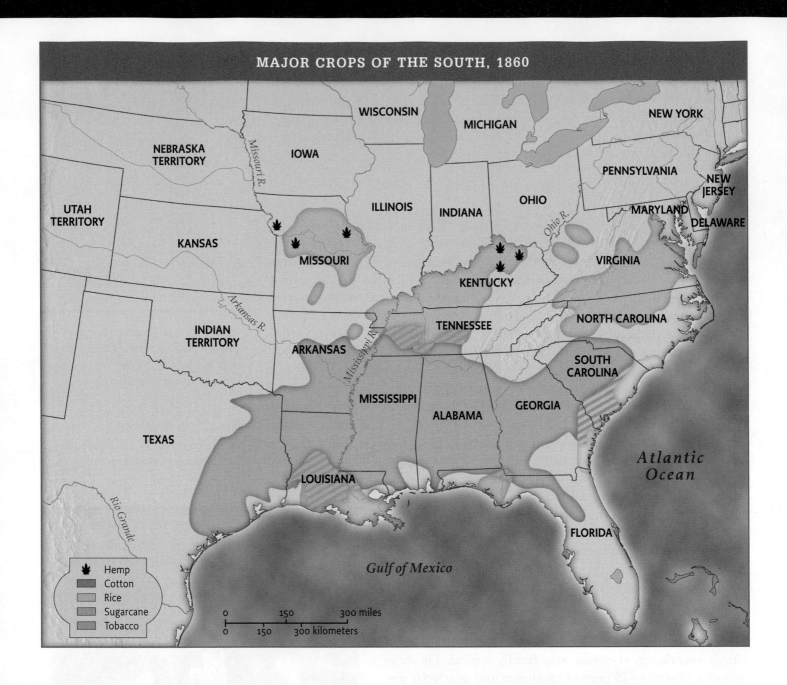

MAJOR CROPS OF THE SOUTH, 1860

Legend:
- Hemp
- Cotton
- Rice
- Sugarcane
- Tobacco

Cotton was the major agricultural crop of the South, and, indeed, the nation, but slaves also grew rice, sugarcane, tobacco, and hemp.

from the North, "are utter heartlessness, brutality, and cruelty. It is his business to produce large crops, no matter [what the] cost."

The 150,000 slaves who worked in the sugar fields of southern Louisiana also labored in large gangs. Conditions here were among the harshest in the South, for the late fall harvest season required round-the-clock labor to cut and process the sugarcane before it spoiled. On the rice plantations of South Carolina and Georgia, the system of task labor, which had originated in the colonial era, prevailed. With few whites willing to venture into the malaria-infested swamps, slaves were assigned daily tasks and allowed to set their own pace of work. Once a slave's task had been completed, he or she could spend the rest of the day hunting, fishing, or cultivating garden crops.

Slavery in the Cities

Skilled urban craftsmen also enjoyed considerable autonomy. Most city slaves were servants, cooks, and other domestic laborers. But owners sometimes allowed those with craft skills to "hire their own time." This meant that they could make work arrangements individually with employers, with most of the wages going to the slave's owner. Many urban slaves even lived on their own. But slaveholders increasingly became convinced that, as one wrote, the growing independence of skilled urban slaves "exerts a most injurious influence upon the relation of master and servant." For this reason, many owners in the 1850s sold city slaves to the countryside and sought replacements among skilled white labor.

During his time in Baltimore, Frederick Douglass "sought my own employment, made my own contracts, and collected my own earnings." Compared to conditions on the plantation, he concluded, "I was really well off." Douglass hastened to add, however, that his favored treatment in no way lessened his desire for freedom—"It was *slavery*, not its more incidents, that I hated."

In this undated photograph, men, women, and children pick cotton under the watchful eye of an overseer. Unlike sugarcane, cotton does not grow to a great height, allowing an overseer to supervise a large number of slaves.

Maintaining Order

Slaveowners employed a variety of means in their attempts to maintain order and discipline among their human property and persuade them to labor productively. At base, the system rested on force. Masters had almost complete discretion in inflicting punishment, and rare was the slave who went through his or her life without experiencing a whipping. Josiah Henson, who escaped to the North and published an autobiography, wrote that he could never erase from his memory the traumatic experience of seeing his father brutally whipped for striking a white man. Any infraction of plantation rules, no matter how minor, could be punished by the lash. One Georgia planter recorded in his journal that he had whipped a slave "for not bringing over milk for my coffee, being compelled to take it without."

Subtler means of control supplemented violence. Owners encouraged and exploited divisions among the slaves, especially between field hands and house servants. They created systems of incentives that rewarded good work with time off or even money payments. One Virginia slaveholder gave his slaves ten cents per day for good work and reported that this made them labor "with as much steadiness and cheerfulness as whites," thereby "saving all the expense of overseers." Probably the most powerful weapon wielded by slaveowners was the threat of sale, which separated slaves from their immediate families and from

Detail from *Rice Culture on the Ogeechee*. Published in January 1867 in *Harper's Weekly*, this engraving illustrates work on a rice plantation divided into a checkerboard pattern by irrigation ditches. Although a white person is present, most slaves in the rice fields worked under the task system, without daily oversight.

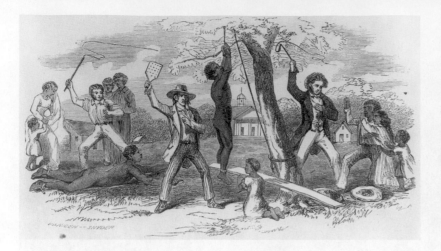

A Public Whipping of Slaves in Lexington, Missouri, in 1856, an illustration from the abolitionist publication *The Suppressed Book about Slavery*. Whipping was a common form of punishment for slaves.

the communities that, despite overwhelming odds, African-Americans created on plantations throughout the South.

SLAVE CULTURE

Slaves never abandoned their desire for freedom or their determination to resist total white control over their lives. In the face of grim realities, they succeeded in forging a semi-independent culture, centered on the family and church. This enabled them to survive the experience of bondage without surrendering their self-esteem and to pass from generation to generation a set of ideas and values fundamentally at odds with those of their masters.

Slave culture drew on the African heritage. African influences were evident in the slaves' music and dances, style of religious worship, and the use of herbs by slave healers to combat disease. (Given the primitive nature of professional medical treatment, some whites sought out slave healers instead of trained physicians.) Unlike the plantation regions of the Caribbean and Brazil, where the African slave trade continued into the nineteenth century and the black population far outnumbered the white, most slaves in the United States were American-born and lived amid a white majority. Slave culture was a new creation, shaped by African traditions and American values and experiences.

Kitchen Ball at White Sulphur Springs, Virginia, an 1838 painting by the German-born American artist Christian Mayr. Fashionably dressed domestic slaves celebrate the wedding of a couple, dressed in white at the center.

The Slave Family

At the center of the slave community stood the family. On the sugar plantations of the West Indies, the number of males far exceeded that of females, the workers lived in barracks-type buildings, and settled family life was nearly impossible. The United States, where the slave population grew from natural increase rather than continued importation from Africa, had an even male-female ratio, making the creation of families far more possible. To be sure, the law did not recognize the legality of slave marriages. The master had to consent before a man and woman could "jump over the broomstick" (the slaves' marriage ceremony), and families stood in constant danger of being broken up by sale.

Nonetheless, most adult slaves married, and their unions, when not disrupted by sale, typically lasted for a lifetime. To solidify a sense of family continuity, slaves frequently named children after cousins, uncles, grandparents, and other relatives. Nor did the slave family simply mirror kinship patterns among whites. Slaves, for example, did not marry first cousins, a practice common among white southerners. Because of constant sales, the slave community had a significantly higher number of female-headed households than among whites, as well as families in which grandparents, other relatives, or even non-kin assumed responsibility for raising children.

The Threat of Sale

As noted above, the threat of sale, which disrupted family ties, was perhaps the most powerful disciplinary weapon slaveholders possessed. As the domestic slave trade expanded with the rise of the Cotton Kingdom, about one slave marriage in three in slave-selling states like Virginia was broken by sale. Many children were separated from their parents by sale. According to one estimate, at least 10 percent of the teenage slaves in the Upper South were sold in the interstate slave trade. Fear of sale permeated slave life, especially in the Upper South. "Mother, is Massa going to sell us tomorrow?" ran a line in a popular slave song. As a reflection of their paternalist responsibilities, some owners encouraged slaves to marry. Others, however, remained unaware of their slaves' family connections, and their interest in slave children was generally limited to the children's ability to work in the fields. The federal census broke down the white population by five-year age categories, but it divided slaves only once, at age ten, the point at which they became old enough to enter the plantation labor force.

Slave traders gave little attention to preserving family ties. A public notice, "Sale of Slaves and Stock," announced the 1852 auction of property belonging to a recently deceased Georgia planter. It listed thirty-six individuals ranging from an infant to a sixty-nine-year-old woman and ended with the proviso "Slaves will be sold separate, or in lots, as best suits the purchaser." Sales like this were a human tragedy. "My dear wife," a Georgia slave wrote in 1858, "I take the pleasure of writing you these few [lines] with much regret to inform you that I am sold. . . . Give my love to my father and mother and tell them good bye for me, and if

> Slave marriages

A broadside advertising the public sale of slaves, along with horses, mules, and cattle, after the death of their owner. The advertisement notes that the slaves will be sold individually or in groups "as best suits the purchaser," an indication that families were likely to be broken up. The prices are based on each slave's sex, age, and skill.

Sale of Slaves and Stock.

The Negroes and Stock listed below, are a Prime Lot, and belong to the ESTATE OF THE LATE LUTHER McGOWAN, and will be sold on Monday, Sept. 22nd, 1852, at the Fair Grounds, in Savannah, Georgia, at 1:00 P. M. The Negroes will be taken to the grounds two days previous to the Sale, so that they may be inspected by prospective buyers.

On account of the low prices listed below, they will be sold for cash only, and must be taken into custody within two hours after sale.

No.	Name	Age	Remarks	Price
1	Lunesta	27	Prime Rice Planter,	$1,275.00
2	Violet	16	Housework and Nursemaid,	900.00
3	Lizzie	30	Rice, Unsound,	300.00
4	Minda	27	Cotton, Prime Woman,	1,200.00
5	Adam	28	Cotton, Prime Young Man,	1,100.00
6	Abel	41	Rice Hand, Eyesight Poor,	675.00
7	Tanney	22	Prime Cotton Hand,	950.00
8	Flementina	39	Good Cook, Stiff Knee,	400.00
9	Lanney	34	Prime Cottom Man,	1,000.00
10	Sally	10	Handy in Kitchen,	675.00
11	Maccabey	35	Prime Man, Fair Carpenter,	980.00
12	Dorcas Judy	25	Seamstress, Handy in House,	800.00
13	Happy	60	Blacksmith,	575.00
14	Mowden	15	Prime Cotton Boy,	700.00
15	Bills	21	Handy with Mules,	900.00
16	Theopolis	39	Rice Hand, Gets Fits,	575.00
17	Coolidge	29	Rice Hand and Blacksmith,	1,275.00
18	Bessie	69	Infirm, Sews,	250.00
19	Infant	1	Strong Likely Boy	400.00
20	Samson	41	Prime Man, Good with Stock,	975.00
21	Callie May	27	Prime Woman, Rice,	1,000.00
22	Honey	14	Prime Girl, Hearing Poor,	850.00
23	Angelina	16	Prime Girl, House or Field,	1,000.00
24	Virgil	21	Prime Field Hand,	1,100.00
25	Tom	40	Rice Hand, Lame Leg,	750.00
26	Noble	11	Handy Boy,	900.00
27	Judge Lesh	55	Prime Blacksmith,	800.00
28	Booster	43	Fair Mason, Unsound,	600.00
29	Big Kate	37	Housekeeper and Nurse,	950.00
30	Melie Ann	19	Housework, Smart Yellow Girl,	1,250.00
31	Deacon	26	Prime Rice Hand,	1,000.00
32	Coming	19	Prime Cotton Hand,	1,000.00
33	Mabel	47	Prime Cotton Hand,	800.00
34	Uncle Tim	60	Fair Hand with Mules,	600.00
35	Abe	27	Prime Cotton Hand,	1,000.00
36	Tennes	29	Prime Rice Hand and Coachman,	1,250.00

There will also be offered at this sale, twenty head of Horses and Mules with harness, along with thirty head of Prime Cattle. Slaves will be sold separate, or in lots, as best suits the purchaser. Sale will be held rain or shine.

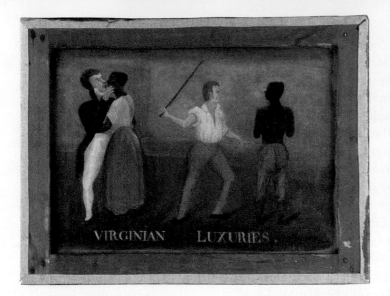

Virginian Luxuries. Originally painted on the back panel of a formal portrait, this image illustrates two "luxuries" of a Virginia slaveowner—the power to sexually abuse slave women and to whip slaves.

we shall not meet in this world I hope to meet in heaven. My dear wife for you and my children my pen cannot express the grief I feel to be parted from you all."

Gender Roles among Slaves

In some ways, gender roles under slavery differed markedly from those in the larger society. Slave men and women experienced, in a sense, the equality of powerlessness. The nineteenth century's "cult of domesticity," which defined the home as a woman's proper sphere, did not apply to slave women, who regularly worked in the fields. Slave men could not act as the economic providers for their families. Nor could they protect their wives from physical or sexual abuse by owners and overseers (a frequent occurrence on many plantations) or determine when and under what conditions their children worked.

When slaves worked "on their own time," however, more conventional gender roles prevailed. Slave men chopped wood, hunted, and fished, while women washed, sewed, and assumed primary responsibility for the care of children. Some planters allowed their slaves small plots of land on which to grow food to supplement the rations provided by the owner; women usually took charge of these "garden plots." But whatever its internal arrangements, the family was central to the slave community, allowing for the transmission of values, traditions, and survival strategies—in a word, of slave culture—from one generation to the next.

Slave Religion

A distinctive version of Christianity also offered solace to slaves in the face of hardship and hope for liberation from bondage. Some blacks, free and slave, had taken part in the Great Awakening of the colonial era, and even more were swept into the South's Baptist and Methodist churches during the religious revivals of the late eighteenth and early nineteenth centuries. As one preacher recalled of the great camp meeting that drew thousands of worshipers to Cane Ridge, Kentucky, in 1801, no distinctions were made "as to age, sex, color, or anything of a temporary nature; old and young, male and female, black and white, had equal privilege to minister the light which they received, in whatever way the Spirit directed."

The importance of religion

Even though the law prohibited slaves from gathering without a white person present, every plantation, it seemed, had its own black preacher. Usually the preacher was a "self-called" slave who possessed little or no formal education but whose rhetorical abilities and familiarity with the Bible made him one of the most respected members of the slave community. Especially in southern cities, slaves also worshiped in biracial congregations with white ministers, where they generally were required to sit in the back pews or in the balcony. Urban free blacks established their own churches, sometimes attended by slaves.

Religion and social control

To masters, Christianity offered another means of social control. Many required slaves to attend services conducted by white ministers, who preached that theft was immoral and that the Bible required servants to obey their masters. One slave later recalled being told in a white minister's sermon "how good God was in bringing us over to this country from dark and benighted Africa, and permitting us to listen to the sound of the gospel." Several slaves walked out of the service during a sermon by Charles C. Jones stressing that God had commanded servants to obey their masters and that they should not try to run away. One man came up to Jones at the end and said, "the doctrine is *one-sided*."

The Gospel of Freedom

The slaves transformed the Christianity they had embraced, turning it to their own purposes. A blend of African traditions and Christian belief, slave religion was practiced in secret nighttime gatherings on plantations and in "praise meetings" replete with shouts, dances, and frequent emotional interchanges between the preacher and the congregation. One former slave later recalled typical secret religious gatherings: "We used to slip off into the woods in the old slave days on Sunday evening way down in the swamps to sing and pray to our own liking. We prayed for this day of freedom."

The "Negro church" on Rockville Plantation near Charleston, South Carolina, in an 1863 photograph. Few plantations had such a building; most slaves worshiped secretly or in biracial churches with white ministers.

The biblical story of Exodus, in which God chose Moses to lead the enslaved Jews of Egypt into a promised land of freedom, played a central role in black Christianity. Slaves identified themselves as a chosen people, whom God in the fullness of time would deliver from bondage. At the same time, the figure of Jesus Christ represented to slaves a personal redeemer, one who truly cared for the oppressed. Slaves found other heroes and symbols in the Bible as well: Jonah, who overcame hard luck and escaped from the belly of a whale; David, who vanquished the more powerful Goliath; and Daniel, who escaped from the lion's den. And the Christian message of brotherhood and the equality of all souls before the Creator, in the slaves' eyes, offered an irrefutable indictment of the institution of slavery.

The Desire for Liberty

If their masters developed an elaborate ideology defending the South's "peculiar institution," slave culture rested on a conviction of the unjustness of bondage and the desire for freedom. "Nobody," the British political philosopher Edmund Burke had written during the American Revolution, "will be argued into slavery." Whatever proslavery writers asserted and ministers preached, blacks thought of themselves as a working people unjustly deprived of the fruits of their labor by idle planters who lived in luxury. "We bake the bread / they give us the crust," said a line from one slave song.

Most slaves fully understood the impossibility of directly confronting the system. Their folktales had no figures equivalent to Paul Bunyan, the powerful, larger-than-life backwoodsman popular in white folklore. Slaves' folklore, such as the Brer Rabbit stories, glorified the weak hare who outwitted stronger foes like

Slaves' adaptation of Christianity

Slave culture

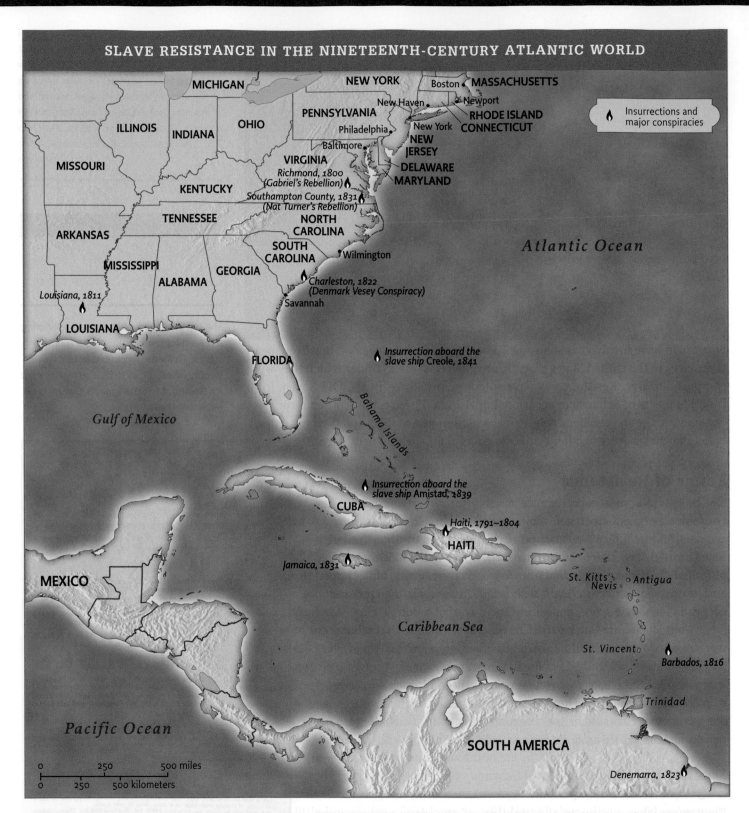

SLAVE RESISTANCE IN THE NINETEENTH-CENTURY ATLANTIC WORLD

Insurrections and major conspiracies

MICHIGAN

NEW YORK
Boston MASSACHUSETTS

PENNSYLVANIA
New Haven
Newport
RHODE ISLAND

ILLINOIS
INDIANA
OHIO
Philadelphia
New York
CONNECTICUT

NEW JERSEY

Baltimore
DELAWARE

MISSOURI
VIRGINIA
MARYLAND

Richmond, 1800
(Gabriel's Rebellion)

KENTUCKY

Southampton County, 1831
(Nat Turner's Rebellion)

TENNESSEE
NORTH CAROLINA

ARKANSAS

SOUTH CAROLINA
Wilmington

MISSISSIPPI
GEORGIA

ALABAMA
Charleston, 1822
(Denmark Vesey Conspiracy)

Louisiana, 1811
Savannah

LOUISIANA

Atlantic Ocean

FLORIDA
Insurrection aboard the
slave ship Creole, 1841

Gulf of Mexico

Bahama Islands

Insurrection aboard the
slave ship Amistad, 1839

CUBA

Haiti, 1791–1804

HAITI

Jamaica, 1831

St. Kitts
Nevis
Antigua

MEXICO

Caribbean Sea

St. Vincent
Barbados, 1816

Trinidad

Pacific Ocean

SOUTH AMERICA

Denemarra, 1823

0   250   500 miles
0   250   500 kilometers

Instances of slave resistance occurred throughout the Western Hemisphere, on land and at sea. This map shows the location of major events in the nineteenth century.

and War of 1812. Generally, however, formidable obstacles confronted the prospective **fugitive slave**. As Solomon Northup recalled, "Every white man's hand is raised against him, the patrollers are watching for him, the hounds are ready to follow in his track." Slaves had little or no knowledge of geography, apart from understanding that following the north star led to freedom. Not surprisingly, most of those who succeeded lived, like Frederick Douglass, in the Upper South, especially Maryland, Virginia, and Kentucky, which bordered on the free states. Douglass, who escaped at age twenty, was also typical in that the large majority of fugitives were young men. Most slave women were not willing to leave children behind, and to take them along on the arduous escape journey was nearly impossible.

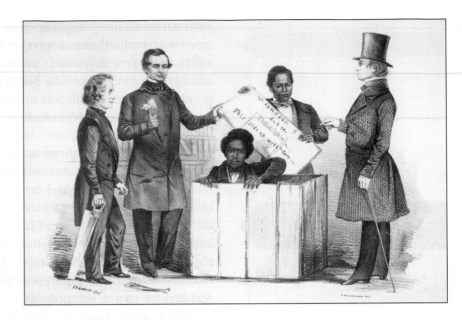

In the Deep South, fugitives tended to head for cities like New Orleans or Charleston, where they hoped to hide "in plain sight" among the growing communities of free blacks. Other escapees fled to remote areas like the Great Dismal Swamp of Virginia or the Florida Everglades, where the Seminole Indians offered refuge before they were forced to move west. Even in Tennessee, a study of newspaper advertisements for runaways finds that around 40 percent were thought to have remained in the local neighborhood and 30 percent to have headed to other locations in the South, while only 25 percent tried to reach the North.

In one of the most celebrated escapes of the antebellum years, Henry Brown, a slave in Richmond, had himself concealed in a crate and shipped to the antislavery office in Philadelphia. This lithograph from 1851 shows three white abolitionists, including J. Miller McKim, with a hatchet, as well as the African-American William Still, a leader of the underground railroad in the city, who holds the top of the crate as Brown emerges.

The Underground Railroad

The **Underground Railroad**, a loose organization of sympathetic abolitionists who hid fugitives in their homes and sent them on to the next "station," assisted some runaway slaves. A few courageous individuals made forays into the South to liberate slaves. The best known was **Harriet Tubman**. Born in Maryland in 1820, Tubman escaped to Philadelphia in 1849 and during the next decade risked her life by making numerous trips back to her state of birth to lead relatives and other slaves to freedom. Recent scholarship suggests that she rescued about seventy-five men, women, and children from slavery. But most who managed to reach the North did so on their own initiative, sometimes showing remarkable ingenuity. William and Ellen Craft impersonated a sickly owner traveling with her slave. Henry "Box" Brown packed himself inside a crate and literally had himself shipped from Richmond, Virginia, to freedom in the North. When his crate was opened, Brown emerged "with a face radiant with joy," and launched into a "hymn of praise." But because fugitives were always vulnerable to recapture, Brown soon departed for England, where he became a fixture on the antislavery lecture circuit.

Escapes to the North

Rather than a single, centralized system with tunnels, codes, and clearly defined routes and stations, the underground railroad was a series of interlocking

For many years, the American public sphere excluded discussion of slavery. Tocqueville had noted that in a democracy, individual dissenters found it difficult to stand up against the overwhelming power of majority opinion. Americans valued free speech, he wrote, but he did "not know any country where, in general, less independence of mind and genuine freedom of discussion reign than in America." The fight for the right to debate slavery openly and without reprisal led abolitionists to elevate "free opinion"—freedom of speech and of the press and the right of petition—to a central place in what Garrison called the "gospel of freedom." In defending free speech, abolitionists claimed to have become custodians of the "rights of every freeman."

"Free opinion"

THE ORIGINS OF FEMINISM

The Rise of the Public Woman

"When the true history of the antislavery cause shall be written," Frederick Douglass later recalled, "women will occupy a large space in its pages." Much of the movement's grassroots strength derived from northern women, who joined by the thousands. Most were evangelical Protestants, New England Congregationalists, or Quakers convinced, as Martha Higginson of Vermont wrote, that slavery was "a disgrace in this land of Christian light and liberty." A few became famous, but most antislavery women remain virtually unknown to history. One such activist was Lucy Colman, whose mother sang her antislavery songs when she was a child. Colman's career illustrated how the era's reform movements often overlapped. She became an abolitionist lecturer, a teacher at a school for blacks in upstate New York, an advocate of women's rights, and an opponent of capital punishment.

Women abolitionists

The public sphere was open to women in ways government and party politics were not. Women's letters and diaries reveal a keen interest in political issues, from slavery to presidential campaigns. Long before they could vote, women circulated petitions, attended mass meetings, marched in political parades, delivered public lectures, and raised money for political causes. Women organized a petition campaign against the policy of Indian removal. Although unsuccessful, the experience helped to produce a generation of women who then turned their attention to abolitionism, temperance, and other reforms. Harriet Beecher (later the author of *Uncle Tom's Cabin*) participated in the movement against Indian removal—of which her sister, Catharine, was a major organizer. **Dorothea Dix**, a Massachusetts schoolteacher, was the leading advocate of more humane treatment of the insane, who at the time generally were placed in jails alongside debtors and hardened criminals. Thanks to her efforts, twenty-eight states constructed mental hospitals before the Civil War. In 1834, middle-class women in New York City organized the Female Moral Reform Society, which sought to redeem prostitutes from lives of sin and to protect the morality of single women. They attacked the era's sexual double standard by publishing lists of men who frequented prostitutes

Petition against Indian removal

or abused women. By 1840, the society had been replicated in hundreds of American communities.

Women and Free Speech

All these activities enabled women to carve out a place in the public sphere. But it was participation in abolitionism that inspired the early movement for women's rights. In working for the rights of the slave, not a few women developed a new understanding of their own subordinate social and legal status. The daughters of a prominent South Carolina slaveholder, Angelina and Sarah Grimké had been converted first to Quakerism and then to abolitionism while visiting Philadelphia. During the 1830s, they began to deliver popular lectures that offered a scathing condemnation of slavery from the perspective of those who had witnessed its evils firsthand.

Abolitionism and women's rights

The Grimké sisters were neither the first women to lecture in public nor the first to be feverishly condemned by self-proclaimed guardians of female modesty. Frances Wright, a Scottish-born follower of reformer Robert Owen, spoke at New York's Hall of Science in the late 1820s and early 1830s, on subjects ranging from communitarianism to slavery, women's rights, and the plight of northern laborers. One New York newspaper called Wright a "female monster" for "shamefully obtruding herself upon the public." Maria Stewart, a black Bostonian, in 1832 became the first American woman to lecture to mixed male and female audiences. She, too, received intense criticism. "I have made myself contemptible in the eyes of many," Stewart wrote. "This is the land of freedom," she added, "and we claim our rights," including the right to speak in public.

Stewart left Boston in 1833 and rarely lectured again. The Grimké sisters, however, used the controversy over their speeches as a springboard for a vigorous argument against the idea that taking part in assemblies, demonstrations, and lectures was unfeminine. Outraged by the sight of females sacrificing all "modesty and delicacy" by appearing on the public lecture platform, a group of Massachusetts clergymen denounced the sisters. In reply, they forthrightly defended not only the right of women to take part in political debate but also their right to share the social and educational privileges enjoyed by men. "Since I engaged in the investigation of the rights of the slave," declared Angelina Grimké, "I have necessarily been led to a better understanding of my own." Her sister Sarah proceeded to publish *Letters on the Equality of the Sexes* (1838), a powerful call for equal rights for women and a critique of the notion of separate spheres. The book raised numerous issues familiar even today, including what later generations would call "equal pay for equal work." Why, Sarah Grimké wondered, did male teachers invariably receive higher wages than women, and a male tailor earn "two or three times as much" as a female counterpart "although the work done by each may be equally good?"

The Grimké sisters

Women's Rights

The Grimkés were the first to apply the abolitionist doctrine of universal freedom and equality to the status of women. When the prominent writer Catharine Beecher

The May Session of the Woman's Rights Convention, a cartoon published in *Harper's Weekly*, June 11, 1859. A female orator addresses the audience of men and women, while hecklers in the balcony disrupt the proceedings.

reprimanded the sisters for stepping outside "the domestic and social sphere," urging them to accept the fact that "heaven" had designated man "the superior" and woman "the subordinate," Angelina Grimké issued a stinging answer. "I know nothing," she wrote, "of men's rights and women's rights. My doctrine, then is, that whatever it is morally right for man to do, it is morally right for woman to do." Like their predecessors Frances Wright and Maria Stewart, the Grimké sisters soon retired from the fray, unwilling to endure the intense criticism to which they were subjected. But their writings helped to spark the movement for women's rights, which arose in the 1840s.

Elizabeth Cady Stanton and Lucretia Mott, the key organizers of the Seneca Falls Convention of 1848, were veterans of the antislavery crusade. In 1840, they had traveled to London as delegates to the World Anti-Slavery Convention, only to be barred from participating because of their sex. The Seneca Falls Convention, a gathering on behalf of women's rights held in the upstate New York town where Stanton lived, raised the issue of woman's suffrage for the first time. Stanton, the principal author, modeled the Seneca Falls Declaration of Sentiments on the Declaration of Independence (see the Appendix for the full text). But the document added "women" to Jefferson's axiom "all men are created equal," and in place of a list of injustices committed by George III, it condemned the "injuries and usurpations on the part of man toward woman." The first to be listed was denying her the right to vote. As Stanton told the convention, only the vote would make woman "free as man is free," since in a democratic society, freedom was impossible without access to the ballot. The argument was simple and irrefutable: in the words of Lydia Maria Child, "either the theory of our government [the democratic principle that government rests on the will of the people] is *false*, or women have a right to vote."

Seneca Falls marked the beginning of the seventy-year struggle for **woman suffrage**. The vote, however, was hardly the only issue raised at the convention.

The Seneca Falls Convention

The Declaration of Sentiments condemned the entire structure of inequality that denied women access to education and employment, gave husbands control over the property and wages of their wives and custody of children in the event of divorce, deprived women of independent legal status after they married, and restricted them to the home as their "sphere of action." Equal rights became the rallying cry of the early movement for women's rights, and equal rights meant claiming access to all the prevailing definitions of freedom.

The Declaration of Sentiments

Feminism and Freedom

Like abolitionism, temperance, and other reforms, **feminism** was an international movement. Lacking broad backing at home, early feminists found allies abroad. "Women alone will say what freedom they want," declared an article in *The Free Woman*, a journal established in Paris in 1832. With their household chores diminished because of the availability of manufactured goods and domestic servants, many middle-class women chafed at the restrictions that made it impossible for them to gain an education, enter the professions, and in other ways exercise their talents. Whether married or not, early feminists insisted, women deserved the range of individual choices—the possibility of self-realization—that constituted the essence of freedom.

Margaret Fuller

Women, wrote Margaret Fuller, had the same right as men to develop their talents, to "grow . . . to live freely and unimpeded." The daughter of a Jeffersonian congressman, Fuller was educated at home, at first under her father's supervision (she learned Latin before the age of six) and later on her own. She became part of New England's transcendentalist circle (discussed in Chapter 9) and from 1840 to 1842 edited *The Dial*, a magazine that reflected the group's views. In 1844, Fuller became literary editor of the *New York Tribune*, the first woman to achieve so important a position in American journalism.

An undated engraving of feminist writer Margaret Fuller (1810–1850).

In *Woman in the Nineteenth Century*, published in 1845, Fuller sought to apply to women the transcendentalist idea that freedom meant a quest for personal development. "Every path" to self-fulfillment, she insisted, should be "open to woman as freely as to man." Fuller singled out Abby Kelley as a "gentle hero" for continuing to speak in public despite being denounced by men for venturing "out of her sphere." Fearing that marriage to an American would inevitably mean subordination to male dictation, Fuller traveled to Europe as a correspondent for the *Tribune*. There she married an Italian patriot. Along with her husband and baby, she died in a shipwreck in 1850 while returning to the United States.

Women and Work

Women also demanded the right to participate in the market revolution. At an 1851 women's rights convention, the black abolitionist Sojourner Truth insisted that the movement devote attention to the plight of poor and working-class women and repudiate the idea that

VOICES OF FREEDOM

From ANGELINA GRIMKÉ, LETTER IN *THE LIBERATOR* (AUGUST 2, 1837)

The daughters of a prominent South Carolina slaveholder, Angelina and Sarah Grimké became abolitionists after being sent to Philadelphia for education. In this article, Angelina Grimké explains how participation in the movement against slavery led her to a greater recognition of women's lack of basic freedoms.

Since I engaged in the investigation of the rights of the slave, I have necessarily been led to a better understanding of my own; for I have found the Anti-Slavery cause to be . . . the school in which human rights are more fully investigated, and better understood and taught, than in any other [reform] enterprise. . . . Here we are led to examine why human beings have any rights. It is because they are moral beings. . . . Now it naturally occurred to me, that if rights were founded in moral being, then the circumstance of sex could not give to man higher rights and responsibilities, than to woman. . . .

When I look at human beings as moral beings, all distinction in sex sinks to insignificance and nothingness; for I believe it regulates rights and responsibilities no more than the color of the skin or the eyes. My doctrine, then is, that whatever it is morally right for man to do, it is morally right for woman to do. . . . This regulation of duty by the mere circumstance of sex . . . has led to all that [numerous] train of evils flowing out of the anti-christian doctrine of masculine and feminine virtues. By this doctrine, man has been converted into the warrior, and clothed in sternness . . . whilst woman has been taught to lean upon an arm of flesh, to . . . be admired for her personal charms, and caressed and humored like a spoiled child, or converted into a mere drudge to suit the convenience of her lord and master. . . . It has robbed woman of . . . the right to think and speak and act on all great moral questions, just as men think and speak and act. . . .

The discussion of the wrongs of slavery has opened the way for the discussion of other rights, and the ultimate result will most certainly be . . . the letting of the oppressed of every grade and description go free.

From CATHARINE BEECHER, *AN ESSAY ON SLAVERY AND ABOLITIONISM* (1837)

Most men, and many women, did not approve of women taking part in public debate. The writer Catharine Beecher responded to the activities of the Grimké sisters by urging them to accept that "heaven" had designated man "the superior" and woman "the subordinate."

———————

I have . . . been informed, that you contemplate a tour, during the ensuing year, for the purpose of exerting your influence to form Abolition Societies among ladies of the non-slave-holding States. . . . The object I have in view, is to present some reasons why it seems unwise and inexpedient for ladies of the non-slave-holding States to unite themselves in Abolition Societies; and thus, at the same time, to exhibit the inexpediency of the course you propose to adopt. . . .

Heaven has appointed to one sex the superior, and to the other the subordinate station, and this without any reference to the character or conduct of either. It is therefore as much for the dignity as it is for the interest of females, in all respects to conform to the duties of this relation. . . . But while woman holds a subordinate relation in society to the other sex, it is not because it was designed that her duties or her influence should be any the less important, or all-pervading. But it was designed that the mode of gaining influence and of exercising power should be altogether different and peculiar. . . . Woman is to win every thing by peace and love; by making herself so much respected, esteemed and loved, that to yield to her opinions and to gratify her wishes, will be the free-will offering of the heart. But this is to be all accomplished in the domestic and social circle. . . . The moment woman begins to feel the promptings of ambition, or the thirst for power, her ægis of defence is gone. All the sacred protection of religion, all the generous promptings of chivalry, all the poetry of romantic gallantry, depend upon woman's retaining her place as dependent and defenceless, and making no claims, and maintaining no right but what are the gifts of honour, rectitude and love.

A woman may seek the aid of cooperation and combination among her own sex, to assist her in her appropriate offices of piety, charity, maternal and domestic duty; but whatever, in any measure, throws a woman into the attitude of a combatant, either for herself or others—whatever binds her in a party conflict—whatever obliges her in any way to exert coercive influences, throws her out of her appropriate sphere. . . . In this country, petitions to congress, in reference to the official duties of legislators, seem, IN ALL CASES, to fall entirely without the sphere of female duty. Men are the proper persons to make appeals to the rulers whom they appoint, and if their female friends, by arguments and persuasions, can induce them to petition, all the good that can be done by such measures will be secured.

QUESTIONS

1. *What consequences does Grimké believe follow from the idea of rights being founded in the individual's "moral being"?*

2. *How does Beecher believe women should exert power within American society?*

3. *How do the two definitions of women's freedom differ from one another?*

women were too delicate to engage in work outside the home. Born a slave in New York State around 1799, Truth did not obtain her freedom until slavery finally ended in the state in 1827. A listener at her 1851 speech (which was not recorded at the time) later recalled that Truth had spoken of her years of hard physical labor, flexed her arm to show her strength, and exclaimed, "and aren't I a woman?"

Although those who convened at Seneca Falls were predominantly from the middle class—no representatives of the growing number of "factory girls" and domestic servants took part—the participants rejected the identification of the home as a woman's "sphere." Women, wrote Pauline Davis in 1853, "must go *to work*" to emancipate themselves from "bondage." During the 1850s, some feminists tried to popularize a new style of dress, devised by Amelia Bloomer, consisting of a loose-fitting tunic and trousers. In her autobiography, published in 1898, Elizabeth Cady Stanton recalled that women who adopted Bloomer's attire were ridiculed by the press and insulted by "crowds of boys in the streets." They found that "the physical freedom enjoyed did not compensate for the persistent persecution and petty annoyances suffered at every turn." The target of innumerable male jokes, the "bloomer" costume attempted to make a serious point—that the long dresses, tight corsets, and numerous petticoats considered to be appropriate female attire were so confining that they made it almost impossible for women to claim a place in the public sphere or to work outside the home.

In one sense, feminism demanded an expansion of the boundaries of freedom rather than a redefinition of the idea. Women, in the words of one reformer, should enjoy "the rights and liberties that every 'free white male citizen' takes to himself as God-given." But even as it sought to apply prevailing notions of freedom to women, the movement posed a fundamental challenge to some of society's central beliefs—that the capacity for independence and rationality were male traits, that the world was properly divided into public and private realms, and that issues of

Woman's Emancipation, a satirical engraving from *Harper's Monthly*, August 1851, illustrating the much-ridiculed "bloomer" costume.

justice and freedom did not apply to relations within the family. In every realm of life, including the inner workings of the family, declared Elizabeth Cady Stanton, there could be "no happiness without freedom."

The Slavery of Sex

The dichotomy between freedom and slavery powerfully shaped early feminists' political language. Just as the idea of "wage slavery" enabled northern workers to challenge the inequalities of the market revolution, the concept of the "slavery of sex" empowered the women's movement to develop an all-encompassing critique of male authority and their own subordination. Feminists of the 1840s and 1850s pointed out that the law of marriage made nonsense of the description of the family as a "private" institution independent of public authority. When the abolitionists and women's rights activitists Lucy Stone and Henry Blackwell married, they felt obliged to repudiate New York's laws that clothed the husband "with legal powers which . . . no man should possess."

Feminist abolitionists did not invent the analogy between marriage and slavery. The English writer Mary Wollstonecraft had invoked it as early as the 1790s in *A Vindication of the Rights of Woman* (discussed in Chapter 8). But the analogy between free women and slaves gained prominence as it was swept up in the accelerating debate over slavery. "Woman is a slave, from the cradle to the grave," asserted Ernestine Rose. "Father, guardian, husband—master still. One conveys her, like a piece of property, over to the other." For their part, southern defenders of slavery frequently linked slavery and marriage as natural and just forms of inequality. Eliminating the former institution, they charged, would threaten the latter.

Marriage was not, literally speaking, equivalent to slavery. The married woman, however, did not enjoy the fruits of her own labor—a central element of freedom. Beginning with Mississippi in 1839, numerous states enacted married women's property laws, shielding from a husband's creditors property brought into a marriage by his wife. Such laws initially aimed not to expand women's rights as much as to prevent families from losing their property during the depression that began in 1837. But in 1860, New York enacted a more far-reaching measure, allowing married women to sign contracts, buy and sell property, and keep their own wages. In most states, however, property accumulated after marriage, as well as wages earned by the wife, still belonged to the husband.

"Social Freedom"

Influenced by abolitionism, women's rights advocates turned another popular understanding of freedom—self-ownership, or control over one's own person—in an entirely new direction. The emphasis in abolitionist literature on the violation of the slave woman's body by her master helped to give the idea of self-ownership a concrete reality that encouraged application to free women as well. The law of domestic relations presupposed the husband's right of sexual access to his wife and to inflict corporal punishment on her. Courts proved reluctant to intervene in cases of physical abuse so long as it was not "extreme" or "intolerable." "Women's Rights," declared a Boston meeting in 1859, included "freedom and equal rights in

Am I Not a Woman and a Sister?, an illustration from *The Liberator*, 1849. Identifying with the plight of the female slave enabled free women to see more clearly the inequalities they themselves faced.

Marriage and slavery

Self-ownership

the family." The demand that women should enjoy the rights to regulate their own sexual activity and procreation and to be protected by the state against violence at the hands of their husbands challenged the notion that claims for justice, freedom, and individual rights should stop at the household's door.

The issue of women's private freedom revealed underlying differences within the movement for women's rights. Belief in equality between the sexes and in the sexes' natural differences coexisted in antebellum feminist thought. Even as they entered the public sphere and thereby challenged some aspects of the era's "cult of domesticity" (discussed in Chapter 9), many early feminists accepted other elements. Allowing women a greater role in the public sphere, many female reformers argued, would bring their "inborn" maternal instincts to bear on public life, to the benefit of the entire society.

Women's private freedom

Even feminists critical of the existing institution of marriage generally refrained from raising in public the explosive issue of women's "private" freedom. The question frequently arose, however, in the correspondence of feminist leaders. "Social Freedom," Susan B. Anthony observed to Lucy Stone, "lies at the bottom of all—and until woman gets that, she must continue the slave of men in all other things." Women like Anthony, who never married, and Stone, who with her husband created their own definition of marriage, reflected the same dissatisfactions with traditional family life as the women who joined communitarian experiments. Not until the twentieth century would the demand that freedom be extended to intimate aspects of life inspire a mass movement. But the dramatic fall in the birthrate over the course of the nineteenth century suggests that many women were quietly exercising "personal freedom" in their most intimate relationships.

The Abolitionist Schism

Even in reform circles, the demand for a greater public role for women remained extremely controversial. Massachusetts physician Samuel Gridley Howe pioneered humane treatment of the blind and educational reform, and he was an ardent abolitionist. But Howe did not support his wife's participation in the movement for female suffrage, which, he complained, caused her to "neglect domestic relations." When organized abolitionism split into two wings in 1840, the immediate cause was a dispute over the proper role of women in antislavery work. Abby Kelley's election to the business committee of the American Anti-Slavery Society sparked the formation of a rival abolitionist organization, the American and Foreign Anti-Slavery Society, which believed it wrong for a woman to occupy so prominent a position. The antislavery poet John Greenleaf Whittier compared Kelley to Eve, Delilah, and Helen of Troy, women who had sown the seeds of male destruction.

The role of women in abolitionism

Behind the split lay the fear among some abolitionists that Garrison's radicalism on issues like women's rights, as well as his refusal to support the idea of abolitionists voting or running for public office, impeded the movement's growth. Determined to make abolitionism a political movement, the seceders formed the **Liberty Party**, which nominated James G. Birney as its candidate for president.

He received only 7,000 votes (about one-third of 1 percent of the total). In 1840, antislavery northerners saw little wisdom in "throwing away" their ballots on a third-party candidate.

While the achievement of most of their demands lay far in the future, the women's rights movement succeeded in making "the woman question" a permanent part of the transatlantic discussion of social reform. As for abolitionism, although it remained a significant presence in northern public life until emancipation was achieved, by 1840 the movement had accomplished its most important work. More than 1,000 local antislavery societies were now scattered throughout the North, representing a broad constituency awakened to the moral issue of slavery. The "great duty of freedom," Ralph Waldo Emerson had declared in 1837, was "to open our halls to discussion of this question." The abolitionists' greatest achievement lay in shattering the conspiracy of silence that had sought to preserve national unity by suppressing public debate over slavery.

This image appeared on the cover of the sheet music for "Get Off the Track!," a song popularized by the Hutchinson singers, who performed antislavery songs. The trains *Immediate Emancipation* (with *The Liberator* as its front wheel) and *Liberty Party* pull into a railroad station. *The Herald of Freedom* and *American Standard* were antislavery newspapers. The song's lyrics praised William Lloyd Garrison and criticized various politicians, among them Henry Clay. The chorus went: "Roll it along! Through the nation / Freedom's car, Emancipation."

SUGGESTED READING

BOOKS

- Bestor, Arthur E. *Backwoods Utopias: The Sectarian and Owenite Phases of Communitarian Socialism in America* (1948). An account of some of the numerous communitarian experiments in pre–Civil War America.

- Boylan, Anne M. *The Origins of Women's Activism: New York and Boston, 1797–1840* (2002). Considers how middle-class urban women organized numerous associations for social improvement and thereby gained a place in the public sphere.

- Goodman, Paul. *Of One Blood: Abolitionists and the Origins of Racial Equality* (1998). Explores the origins of racial egalitarianism in the movement against slavery.

- Jeffrey, Julie R. *The Great Silent Army of Abolitionism: Ordinary Women in the Antislavery Movement* (1998). The role of women as the grassroots foot soldiers of the abolitionist movement.

- Jones, Martha S. *All Bound Up Together: The Woman Question in African American Public Culture, 1830–1900* (2007). How African-American leaders and organizations debated the proper social role of women.

- Kaestle, Carl F. *Pillars of the Republic: Common Schools and American Society, 1780–1860* (1983). Surveys the movement to introduce free public education in the United States.

- Kantrowitz, Stephen. *More than Freedom: Fighting for Black Citizenship in a White Republic, 1829–1889* (2012). A study of the black abolitionists of Boston and their struggle for an expansive understanding of freedom.

- Kraditor, Aileen S. *Means and Ends in American Abolitionism* (1969). An influential discussion of the political strategies of Garrisonian abolitionists.

- McGreevy, John T. *Catholicism and American Freedom* (2003). Contains an illuminating discussion of how Catholics responded to Protestant-based reform movements.

- Nye, Russell B. *Fettered Freedom: Civil Liberties and the Slavery Controversy, 1830–1860* (1949). Examines the impact of mob activities and other violations of civil liberties on the growth of abolitionism.

- Sinha, Manisha. *The Slave's Cause: A History of Abolition* (2016). A comprehensive history of the antislavery movement from the colonial era through the Civil War.

- Tyrrell, Ian. *Sobering Up: From Temperance to Prohibition in Antebellum America, 1800–1860* (1979). Traces the movement against the sale and use of liquor and how it changed in the first part of the nineteenth century.

- Zboray, Ronald J. and Mary. *Voices Without Votes: Women and Politics in Antebellum New England* (2010). Shows how women took part in Jacksonian-era politics in ways other than voting.

WEBSITES

- Samuel J. May Anti-Slavery Collection: http://dlxs.library.cornell.edu/m/mayantislavery/

- Women and Social Movements in the United States, 1600–2000: http://asp6new.alexanderstreet.com/wam2/wam2.index.map.aspx

CHAPTER REVIEW AND ONLINE RESOURCES

REVIEW QUESTIONS

1. How did the utopian communities challenge existing ideas about property and marriage?

2. How did the supporters and opponents of temperance understand the meaning of freedom differently?

3. What were the similarities and differences between the common school and institutions like asylums, orphanages, and prisons that were created by reformers?

4. Why did so many prominent white Americans, from both the North and South, support the colonization of freed slaves?

5. How was the abolition movement affected by other social and economic changes such as the rise in literacy, new print technology, and ideas associated with the market revolution?

6. How was racism evident even in the abolitionist movement, and what steps did some abolitionists take to fight racism in American society?

7. How could antebellum women participate in the public sphere even though they were excluded from government and politics?

8. How did white women's participation in the abolitionist movement push them to a new understanding of their own rights and oppression?

9. How did advocates for women's rights in these years both accept and challenge existing gender beliefs and social roles?

10. To what degree was antebellum reform international in scope?

KEY TERMS

utopian communities (p. 426)

Shakers (p. 426)

Oneida (p. 427)

Brook Farm (p. 429)

communitarianism (p. 429)

New Harmony (p. 429)

perfectionism (p. 431)

temperance movement (p. 431)

common school (p. 433)

American Colonization Society (p. 435)

American Anti-Slavery Society (p. 437)

moral suasion (p. 439)

Uncle Tom's Cabin (p. 442)

"gentlemen of property and standing" (p. 444)

gag rule (p. 445)

Dorothea Dix (p. 446)

woman suffrage (p. 448)

feminism (p. 449)

Liberty Party (p. 454)

Go to 🐾 INQUIZITIVE

To see what you know—and learn what you've missed—with personalized feedback along the way.

Visit the *Give Me Liberty!* **Student Site** for primary source documents and images, interactive maps, author videos featuring Eric Foner, and more.

CHAPTER 13

A HOUSE DIVIDED

★

1840–1861

In 1855, Thomas Crawford, one of the era's most prominent American sculptors, was asked to design a statue to adorn the Capitol's dome, still under construction in Washington, D.C. He proposed a statue of Freedom, a female figure wearing a liberty cap. Secretary of War Jefferson Davis of Mississippi, one of the country's largest slaveholders, objected to Crawford's plan. A familiar symbol in the colonial era, the liberty cap had fallen into disfavor among some Americans after becoming closely identified with the French Revolution. Davis's disapproval, however, rested on other grounds. Ancient Romans, he noted, regarded the cap as "the badge of the freed slave." Its use, he feared, might suggest that there was a connection between the slaves' longing for freedom and the liberty of freeborn Americans. Davis ordered the liberty cap replaced with a less controversial military symbol, a feathered helmet.

Crawford died in Italy, where he had spent most of his career, in 1857. Two years later, the colossal Statue of Freedom, which weighed 15,000 pounds, was transported to the United States in several pieces and assembled at a Maryland foundry under the direction of Philip Reed, a slave craftsman. In 1863, it was installed atop the Capitol, where it can still be seen today. By the time it was put in place, the country was immersed in the Civil War and Jefferson Davis had become president of the Confederate States of America. The dispute over the Statue of Freedom offers a small illustration of how, by the mid-1850s, nearly every public question was being swept up into the gathering storm over slavery.

FRUITS OF MANIFEST DESTINY

Continental Expansion

In the 1840s, slavery moved to the center stage of American politics. It did so not in the moral language or with the immediatist program of abolitionism, but as a result of the nation's territorial expansion. By 1840, with the completion of Indian removal, virtually all the land east of the Mississippi River was in white hands. The depression that began in 1837 sparked a large migration of settlers farther west. Some headed to Oregon, whose Willamette Valley was reputed to be one of the continent's most beautiful and fertile regions. Until the 1840s, the American presence in the area had been limited to a few fur traders and explorers. But between 1840 and 1845, some 5,000 emigrants made the difficult 2,000-mile journey by wagon train to Oregon from jumping-off places on the banks of the Missouri River. By 1860, nearly 300,000 men, women, and children braved disease, starvation, the natural barrier of the Rocky Mountains, and occasional Indian attacks to travel overland to Oregon and California.

During most of the 1840s, the United States and Great Britain jointly administered Oregon, and Utah was part of Mexico. This did not stop Americans from settling in either region. National boundaries meant little to those who moved west. The 1840s witnessed an intensification of the old belief that God intended the American nation to reach all the way to the Pacific Ocean. As noted in Chapter 9, the term that became a shorthand for this expansionist spirit was "manifest destiny."

FOCUS QUESTIONS

What were the major factors contributing to U.S. territorial expansion in the 1840s? *-p. 459*

Why did the expansion of slavery become the most divisive political issue in the 1840s and 1850s? *-p. 472*

What combination of issues and events fueled the creation of the Republican Party in the 1850s? *-p. 480*

What enabled Lincoln to emerge as president from the divisive party politics of the 1850s? *-p. 485*

What were the final steps on the road to secession? *-p. 495*

A lithograph from around 1860 depicts the town of Bridgewater, Massachusetts, home of a major ironworks. A railroad speeds along in the foreground, while factory smokestacks dot the horizon. The tidy buildings in the center suggest that industrialization has not upset social harmony. Industrial development in the north widened the gap between the sections.

1820	Moses Austin receives Mexican land grant
1836	Texas independence from Mexico
1845	Inauguration of James Polk
	United States annexes Texas
1846–1848	Mexican War
1846	Wilmot Proviso
1848	Treaty of Guadalupe Hidalgo
	Gold discovered in California
	Free Soil Party organized
1849	Inauguration of Zachary Taylor
1850	Compromise of 1850
	Fugitive Slave Act
1853	Inauguration of Franklin Pierce
1854	Kansas-Nebraska Act
	Know-Nothing Party established
	Ostend Manifesto
	Republican Party organized
1856	Bleeding Kansas
1857	Inauguration of James Buchanan
	Dred Scott decision
1858	Lincoln-Douglas debates
1859	John Brown's raid on Harpers Ferry
1860	South Carolina secedes
1861	Inauguration of Abraham Lincoln
	Fort Sumter fired upon

The original and final designs for Thomas Crawford's *Statue of Freedom* for the dome of the Capitol building. Secretary of War Jefferson Davis of Mississippi insisted that the liberty cap in the first design, a symbol of the emancipated slave in ancient Rome, be replaced.

The Mexican Frontier: New Mexico and California

Settlement of Oregon did not directly raise the issue of slavery. But the nation's acquisition of part of Mexico did. When Mexico achieved its independence from Spain in 1821, it was nearly as large as the United States and its population of 6.5 million was about two-thirds that of its northern neighbor. Mexico's northern provinces—California, New Mexico, and Texas—however, were isolated and sparsely settled outposts surrounded by Indian country. New Mexico's population at the time of Mexican independence consisted of around 30,000 persons of Spanish origin, 10,000 Pueblo Indians, and an indeterminate number of nomadic Indians—bands of Apaches, Comanches, Navajos, and Utes. With the opening in 1821 of the Santa Fe Trail linking that city with Independence, Missouri, the northern periphery of the new Mexican nation was quickly incorporated into the sphere of influence of the rapidly expanding western United States. New Mexico's commerce with the United States eclipsed trade with the rest of Mexico.

California's non-Indian population in 1821, some 3,200 missionaries, soldiers, and settlers, was vastly outnumbered by about 20,000 Indians living and working on land owned by religious missions and by 150,000 members of unsubdued tribes in the interior. In 1834, in the hope of reducing the power of the Catholic Church and attracting Mexican and foreign settlers to California, the Mexican government dissolved the great mission landholdings and emancipated Indians working for the friars. Most of the land ended up in the hands of a new class of Mexican cattle ranchers, the *Californios*, who defined their own identity in large measure against the surrounding Indian population. *Californios* referred to themselves as *gente de razón* (people capable of reason) as opposed to the *indios*, whom they called *gente sin razón* (people without reason). For the "common good," Indians were required to continue to work for the new landholders.

By 1840, California was already linked commercially with the United States. New England ships were trading with the region. California also attracted a small number of American newcomers. In 1846, Alfred Robinson, who had moved from Boston, published *Life in California*. "In this age of annexation," he wondered, "why not extend the 'area of freedom' by the annexation of California?"

> *Trade with California*

The Texas Revolt

The first part of Mexico to be settled by significant numbers of Americans was Texas, whose non-Indian population of Spanish origin (called **Tejanos**) numbered only about 2,000 when Mexico became independent. In order to develop the region, the Spanish government had accepted an offer by Moses Austin, a Connecticut-born farmer, to colonize it with Americans. In 1820, Austin received a large land grant. He died soon afterward and his son Stephen continued the plan, now in independent Mexico, reselling land in smaller plots to American settlers at twelve cents per acre. Although settlers were required to become Mexican citizens, by 1830, the population of American origin had reached around 7,000, considerably exceeding the number of *Tejanos*.

> *American settlers in Texas*

Alarmed that its grip on the area was weakening, the Mexican government in 1830 annulled existing land contracts and barred future emigration from the United States. Led by Stephen Austin, American settlers demanded greater autonomy within Mexico. Part of the area's tiny *Tejano* elite joined them. Mostly ranchers and large farmers, they had welcomed the economic boom that accompanied the settlers and had formed economic alliances with American traders. The issue of slavery further exacerbated matters. Mexico had abolished slavery, but local authorities allowed American settlers to bring slaves with them. When Mexico's ruler, General **Antonio López de Santa Anna**, sent an army in 1835 to

American Progress. This 1872 painting by John Gast, commissioned by the author of a travel guide to the Pacific coast, reflects the ebullient spirit of manifest destiny. A female figure descended from earlier representations of the goddess of liberty wears the star of empire and leads the movement westward while Indians retreat before her. Symbols of civilization abound: the eastern city in the upper right corner, railroads, fenced animals, stagecoaches, and telegraph wires and a "school book" held by the central figure.

FRUITS OF MANIFEST DESTINY | 461

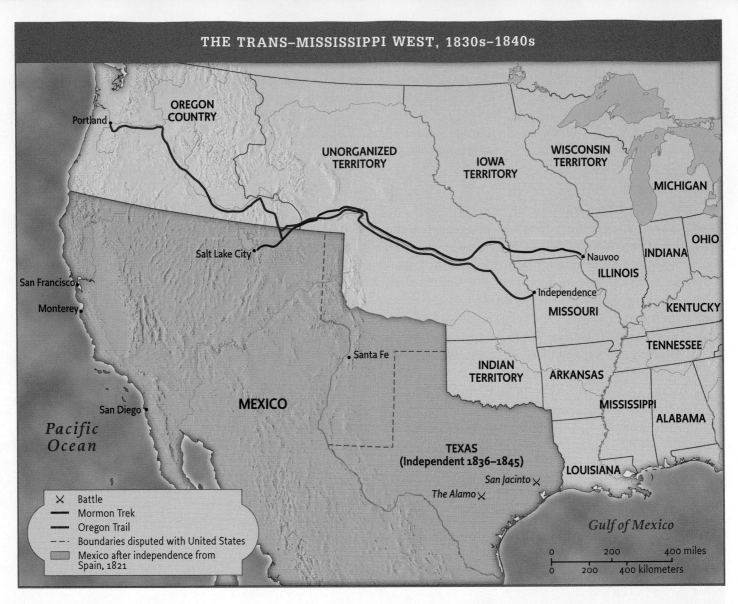

THE TRANS-MISSISSIPPI WEST, 1830s–1840s

OREGON COUNTRY

Portland

UNORGANIZED TERRITORY

IOWA TERRITORY

WISCONSIN TERRITORY

MICHIGAN

Salt Lake City

Nauvoo

ILLINOIS

OHIO

INDIANA

San Francisco

Monterey

Independence

MISSOURI

KENTUCKY

Santa Fe

TENNESSEE

INDIAN TERRITORY

ARKANSAS

San Diego

MEXICO

MISSISSIPPI

ALABAMA

Pacific Ocean

TEXAS
(Independent 1836–1845)

San Jacinto ✕

LOUISIANA

The Alamo ✕

✕   Battle
——   Mormon Trek
——   Oregon Trail
- - -   Boundaries disputed with United States
▨   Mexico after independence from Spain, 1821

Gulf of Mexico

| 0 | 200 | 400 miles |
| 0 | 200 | 400 kilometers |

Westward migration in the early and mid-1840s took American settlers across Indian country into the Oregon Territory, ownership of which was disputed with Great Britain. The Mormons migrated west to Salt Lake City, then part of Mexico.

The Republic of Texas ➤

impose central authority, a local committee charged that his purpose was "to give liberty to our slaves and make slaves of ourselves."

The appearance of Santa Anna's army sparked the chaotic **Texas revolt**. The rebels formed a provisional government that soon called for Texan independence. On March 6, 1836, Santa Anna's army stormed the Alamo, a mission compound in San Antonio, killing its 187 American and *Tejano* defenders. "Remember the Alamo" became the Texans' rallying cry. In April, forces under Sam Houston, a former governor of Tennessee, routed Santa Anna's army at the Battle of San Jacinto and forced him to recognize Texan independence. Houston was soon elected the first president of the Republic of Texas. In 1837, the Texas Congress called for union with the United States. But fearing the political disputes certain to result from an attempt to add another slave state to the Union, President Martin Van Buren shelved the question. Settlers from the United States nonetheless poured into the region, many of them slaveowners taking up fertile cotton land. By 1845, the population of Texas had reached nearly 150,000.

A flag carried at the Battle of San Jacinto during the Texas revolt of 1836 portrays a female figure displaying the rallying cry "Liberty or Death."

The Election of 1844

Texas annexation remained on the political back burner until President John Tyler revived it in the hope of rescuing his failed administration and securing southern support for renomination in 1844. In April 1844, a letter by John C. Calhoun, whom Tyler had appointed secretary of state, was leaked to the press. It linked the idea of absorbing Texas directly to the goal of strengthening slavery in the United States. Some southern leaders, indeed, hoped that Texas could be divided into several states, thus further enhancing the South's power in Congress. Late that month, Henry Clay and former president Van Buren, the prospective Whig and Democratic candidates for president and two of the party system's most venerable leaders, met at Clay's Kentucky plantation. They agreed to issue letters rejecting immediate annexation on the grounds that it might provoke war with Mexico. Clay and Van Buren were reacting to the slavery issue in the traditional manner—by trying to keep it out of national politics.

Texas annexation

Clay went on to receive the Whig nomination, but for Van Buren the letters proved to be a disaster. At the Democratic convention, southerners bent on annexation deserted Van Buren's cause, and he failed to receive the two-thirds majority necessary for nomination. The delegates then turned to the little-known James K. Polk, a former governor of Tennessee whose main assets were his support for annexation and his close association with Andrew Jackson, still the party's most popular figure. Like nearly all the presidents before him, Polk was a slaveholder. He owned substantial cotton plantations in Tennessee and Mississippi, where

James K. Polk

The plaza in San Antonio not long after the United States annexed Texas in 1845.

conditions were so brutal that only half of the slave children lived to the age of fifteen, and adults frequently ran away. To soothe injured feelings among northern Democrats over the rejection of Van Buren, the party platform called for not only the "reannexation" of Texas (implying that Texas had been part of the Louisiana Purchase and therefore once belonged to the United States) but also the "reoccupation" of all of Oregon. "Fifty-four forty or fight"—American control of Oregon all the way to its northern boundary at north latitude 54°40′—became a popular campaign slogan. But the bitterness of the northern Van Burenites over what they considered to be a betrayal on the part of the South would affect American politics for years to come.

Polk was the first "dark horse" candidate for president—that is, one whose nomination was completely unexpected. In the fall, he defeated Clay in an extremely close election. Polk's margin in the popular vote was less than 2 percent. Had not James G. Birney, running again as the Liberty Party candidate, received 16,000 votes in New York, mostly from antislavery Whigs, Clay would have been elected. In March 1845, only days before Polk's inauguration, Congress declared Texas part of the United States.

> *Polk's election*

The Road to War

James K. Polk may have been virtually unknown, but he assumed the presidency with a clearly defined set of goals: to reduce the tariff, reestablish the independent Treasury system, settle the dispute over ownership of Oregon, and bring California into the Union. Congress soon enacted the first two goals, and the third was accomplished in an agreement with Great Britain dividing Oregon at the forty-ninth parallel. Many northerners were bitterly disappointed by this compromise, considering it a betrayal of Polk's campaign promise not to give up any part of Oregon without a fight. But the president secured his main objectives, the Willamette Valley and the magnificent harbor of Puget Sound.

Acquiring California proved more difficult. Polk dispatched an emissary to Mexico offering to purchase the region, but the Mexican government refused to negotiate. By the spring of 1846, Polk was planning for military action. In April, American soldiers under Zachary Taylor moved into the region between the Nueces River and the Rio Grande, land claimed by both countries on the disputed border between Texas and Mexico. This action made conflict with Mexican forces inevitable. When fighting broke out, Polk claimed that the Mexicans had "shed blood upon American soil" and called for a declaration of war.

The War and Its Critics

The **Mexican War** was the first American conflict to be fought primarily on foreign soil and the first in which American troops occupied a foreign capital. Inspired by the expansionist fervor of manifest destiny, a majority of Americans supported the war. They were convinced, as Herman Melville put it in his novel *White-Jacket* (1850), that since Americans "bear the ark of Liberties" for all mankind, "national selfishness is unbounded philanthropy . . . to the world." But a significant minority in the North dissented, fearing that far from expanding the "great empire of liberty," the administration's real aim was to acquire new land for the expansion of slavery. Ulysses S. Grant, who served with distinction in Mexico, later called the war "one of the most unjust ever waged by a stronger nation against a weaker nation." Henry David Thoreau was jailed in Massachusetts in 1846 for refusing to pay taxes as a protest against the war. Defending his action, Thoreau wrote an important essay, "On Civil Disobedience," which inspired such later advocates of nonviolent resistance to unjust laws as Martin Luther King Jr. "Under a government which imprisons unjustly," wrote Thoreau, "the true place of a just man is also a prison."

> Support for the war

An image from a Mexican magazine depicts a Mexican soldier holding a flag emblazoned with the words "nation" and "liberty" and standing astride the American invader.

Among the war's critics was Abraham Lincoln, who had been elected to Congress in 1846 from Illinois. Like many Whigs, Lincoln questioned whether the Mexicans had actually inflicted casualties on American soil, as Polk claimed, and in 1847 he introduced a resolution asking the president to specify the precise "spot" where blood had first been shed. But Lincoln was also disturbed by Polk's claiming the right to initiate an invasion of Mexico. "Allow the president to invade a neighboring country whenever he shall deem it necessary to repel an invasion," he declared, "and you allow him to make war at pleasure." Lincoln's stance proved unpopular in Illinois. He had already agreed to serve only one term in Congress, but when Democrats captured his seat in 1848, many blamed the result on Lincoln's criticism of the war. But the concerns he raised regarding the president's power to "make war at pleasure" would continue to echo in the twentieth and twenty-first centuries.

Combat in Mexico

More than 60,000 volunteers enlisted and did most of the fighting. Combat took place on three fronts. In June 1846, a band of American insurrectionists proclaimed California freed from Mexican control and named Captain John C. Frémont, head of a small scientific expedition in the West, its ruler. Their aim was California's incorporation into the United States, but for the moment they adopted a flag depicting a large bear as the symbol of the area's independence. A month later, the U.S. Navy sailed into Monterey and San Francisco harbors, raised the American flag, and put an end to the "bear flag republic." At almost the same time, 1,600 American troops under General Stephen W. Kearny occupied Sante Fe without resistance and then set out for southern California, where they helped to put down a Mexican uprising against American rule.

War News from Mexico, an 1848 painting by Richard C. Woodville, shows how Americans received war news through the popular press.

The bulk of the fighting occurred in central Mexico. In February 1847, Taylor defeated Santa Anna's army at the Battle of Buena Vista. When the Mexican government still refused to negotiate, Polk ordered American forces under Winfield Scott to march inland from the port of Veracruz toward Mexico City. Scott's forces routed Mexican defenders and in September occupied the country's capital. In February 1848, the two governments agreed to the Treaty of Guadalupe Hidalgo, which confirmed the annexation of Texas and ceded California and present-day New Mexico, Arizona, Nevada, and Utah to the United States. In exchange, the United States paid Mexico $15 million. The Mexican Cession, as the land annexed from Mexico was called, established the present territorial boundaries on the North American continent except for the **Gadsden Purchase**, a parcel of additional land bought from Mexico in 1853, and Alaska, acquired from Russia in 1867.

The Mexican War is only a footnote in most Americans' historical memory. Unlike other wars, few public monuments celebrate the conflict. Mexicans, however, regard the war (or "the dismemberment," as it is called in that country) as a central event of their national history and a source of continued resentment over a century and a half after it was fought. As the Mexican negotiators of 1848 complained, it was unprecedented to launch a war because a country refused to sell part of its territory to a neighbor.

With the end of the Mexican War, the United States absorbed half a million square miles of Mexico's territory, one-third of that nation's total area. A region that for centuries had been united was suddenly split in two, dividing families and severing trade routes. An estimated 75,000 to 100,000 Spanish-speaking Mexicans and more than 150,000 Indians inhabited the Mexican Cession. The Treaty of

> *"The dismemberment"*

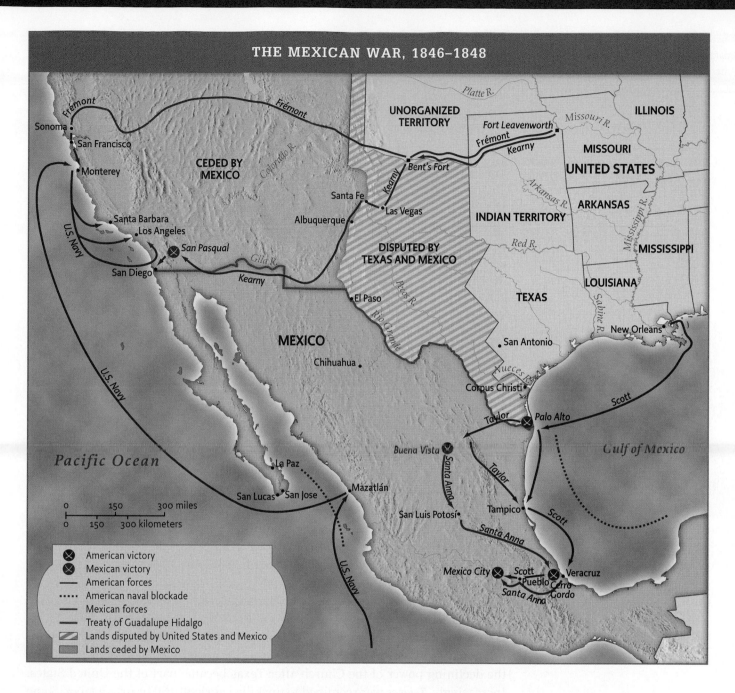

THE MEXICAN WAR, 1846–1848

⊗ American victory
⊗ Mexican victory
— American forces
···· American naval blockade
— Mexican forces
— Treaty of Guadalupe Hidalgo
▨ Lands disputed by United States and Mexico
▨ Lands ceded by Mexico

Guadalupe Hidalgo guaranteed to "male citizens" of the area "the free enjoyment of their liberty and property" and "all the rights" of Americans—a provision designed to protect the property of large Mexican landowners in California. Thus, in the first half of the nineteenth century, some residents of the area went from being Spaniards to Mexicans to Americans. Although not newcomers, they had to adjust to a new identity as if they were immigrants. As to Indians whose homelands and hunting grounds suddenly became part of the United States, the treaty referred to them only as "savage tribes" whom the United States must prevent from launching incursions into Mexico across the new border.

The Mexican War was the first in which an American army invaded another country and occupied its capital. As a result of the war, the United States acquired a vast new area in the modern-day Southwest.

A scene on a California ranch in 1849, with *Californios* (on horseback) and Native Americans at work.

The Texas Borderland

After achieving independence in 1836, Texas became a prime example of a western borderland. *Anglos* (white settlers from the East) and *Tejanos* had fought together to achieve independence, but soon relations between them soured. *Anglos* in search of land and resources expelled some Mexicans, including former allies, now suspected of loyalty to Mexico. Juan Seguín, a *Tejano*, had played an active role in the revolt and served for a time as mayor of San Antonio. In 1842, still mayor, he was driven from the town by vigilantes. He had become, he lamented, "a foreigner in my native land."

Tensions between Anglos and Tejanos

This was a problem inherent to borderlands—as boundaries shifted, longtime residents suddenly became aliens. Facing pressures to Americanize, some *Tejano* families sent their children to English-language schools established by Protestant missionaries from the East. But most refused to convert from Catholicism, despite the declining power of the Church after Texas became part of the United States. Increasingly, *Tejanos* were confined to unskilled agricultural or urban labor. Some *Tejanos* used their ambiguous identities to their own advantage. Women seeking divorces took advantage of new American laws, more liberal than those in Mexico. During the Civil War, some *Tejano* men avoided the Confederate draft by claiming to be citizens of Mexico.

Disputed territory

Meanwhile, in southern Texas, the disputed territory between the Nueces River and the Rio Grande, claimed by both Texas and Mexico but actually controlled by Comanche Indians, became a site of continual conflict. Authority in the area remained contested until Texas became part of the much more powerful United States and even then, Comanche power would not be broken until the 1860s and 1870s.

Race and Manifest Destiny

The spirit of manifest destiny gave a new stridency to ideas about racial superiority. During the 1840s, territorial expansion came to be seen as proof of the innate superiority of the "Anglo-Saxon race" (a mythical construct defined largely by its opposites: blacks, Indians, Hispanics, and Catholics). "*Race*," declared John L. O'Sullivan's *Democratic Review*, was the "key" to the "history of nations."

"Race" in the mid-nineteenth century was an amorphous notion involving color, culture, national origin, class, and religion. Newspapers, magazines, and scholarly works popularized the link between American freedom and the supposedly innate liberty-loving qualities of Anglo-Saxon Protestants. The annexation of Texas and conquest of much of Mexico became triumphs of civilization, progress, and liberty over the tyranny of the Catholic Church and the innate incapacity of "mongrel races." Indeed, calls by some expansionists for the United States to annex all of Mexico failed in part because of fear that the nation could not assimilate its large non-white Catholic population, supposedly unfit for citizenship in a republic.

The imposition of the American system of race relations proved detrimental to many inhabitants of the newly acquired territories. Texas had already demonstrated as much. Mexico had abolished slavery and declared persons of Spanish, Indian, and African origin equal before the law. The Texas Constitution adopted after independence not only included protections for slavery but also denied civil rights to Indians and persons of African origin. Only whites were permitted to purchase land, and the entrance of free blacks into the state was prohibited altogether. "Every privilege dear to a free man is taken away," one free black resident of Texas complained.

Local circumstances affected racial definitions in the former Mexican territories. Texas defined "Spanish" Mexicans, especially those who occupied important social positions, as white. Many New Mexicans, too, emphasized their "Spanish" heritage, hoping to acquire the freedoms that came with statehood. But the residents of New Mexico of both Mexican and Indian origin were long deemed "too Mexican" for democratic self-government. With white migration lagging, Congress did not allow New Mexico to become a state until 1912.

Gold-Rush California

California had a non-Indian population of fewer than 15,000 when the Mexican War ended. For most of the 1840s, five times as many Americans emigrated to Oregon as to California. But this changed dramatically after January 1848, when gold was discovered in the foothills of the Sierra Nevada Mountains at a sawmill owned by the Swiss immigrant Johann A. Sutter. A mania for gold spread throughout the world, fanned by newspaper accounts of instant wealth acquired by early migrants. By ship and land, newcomers poured into California, in what came to be called the **gold rush**. The non-Indian population rose to 200,000 by 1852 and more than 360,000 eight years later.

California's gold-rush population was incredibly diverse. Experienced miners flooded in from Mexico and South America. Tens of thousands of Americans who had never seen a mine arrived from the East, and from overseas came Irish, Germans, Italians, and Australians. Nearly 25,000 Chinese landed between 1849 and 1852,

A portrait from 1838 of Juan Seguín. Born in San Antonio, Seguín played an active role in the Texas Revolution, but later was forced by vigilantes to flee the city (where he was serving as mayor) for refuge in Mexico.

Emigration to California

Painted in 1850 by William S. Jewett, *The Promised Land—The Grayson Family* portrays a family that traveled overland from Missouri to California in 1846, two years before the gold rush. The husband, Andrew J. Grayson, commissioned the painting and gave the artist detailed instructions about the setting and the family's clothing (which is typical of domestic scenes of the period but seems inappropriate for the difficult overland journey). The painting suggests that the West was empty before the arrival of settlers from the East.

The gold rush brought thousands of fortune seekers, from nearly every corner of the globe, to California.

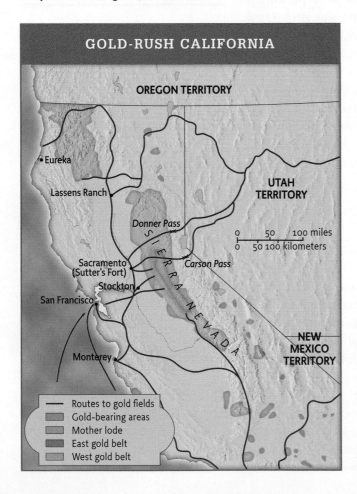

GOLD-RUSH CALIFORNIA

OREGON TERRITORY

Eureka

Lassens Ranch

UTAH TERRITORY

Donner Pass

SIERRA NEVADA

Sacramento (Sutter's Fort)

Carson Pass

Stockton

San Francisco

NEW MEXICO TERRITORY

Monterey

0   50   100 miles
0 50 100 kilometers

Routes to gold fields
Gold-bearing areas
Mother lode
East gold belt
West gold belt

almost all of them young men who had signed long-term labor contracts with Chinese merchants, who in turn leased them to mining and railroad companies and other employers. San Francisco, a town of 1,000 in 1848, became the gateway to the *El Dorado* of northern California. By 1850, it had 30,000 residents and had become perhaps the world's most racially and ethnically diverse city. Unlike farming frontiers settled by families, most of the gold-rush migrants were young men. Women played many roles in western mining communities, running restaurants and boardinghouses and working as laundresses, cooks, and prostitutes. But as late as 1860, California's male population outnumbered females by nearly three to one.

California and the Boundaries of Freedom

As early surface mines quickly became exhausted, they gave way to underground mining that required a large investment of capital. This economic development worsened conflicts among California's many racial and ethnic groups engaged in fierce competition for gold. The law was very fragile in gold-rush California. In 1851 and 1856, "committees of vigilance" took control of San Francisco, sweeping aside established courts to try and execute those accused of crimes. White miners organized extralegal groups that expelled "foreign miners"—Mexicans, Chileans, Chinese, French, and American Indians—from areas with gold. The state legislature imposed a tax of twenty dollars per month on foreign miners, driving many of them from the state.

California would long remain in the American imagination a place of infinite opportunity, where newcomers could start their lives anew. But the boundaries of freedom there were tightly drawn. The state constitution of 1850 limited voting and the right to testify in court to whites, excluding Indians, Asians, and the state's few blacks (who numbered only 962). California landowners who claimed Spanish descent or had intermarried with American settlers were deemed to be white. But with land titles derived from Mexican days challenged in court, many sold out to newcomers from the East.

Limits set by the state constitution

For California's Indians, the gold rush and absorption into the United States proved to be disastrous. Gold seekers overran Indian communities. Miners, ranchers, and vigilantes murdered thousands of Indians. Determined to reduce the native population, state officials paid millions in bounties to private militias that launched attacks on the state's Indians. Although California was a free state, thousands of Indian children, declared orphans or vagrants by local courts, were bought and sold as slaves. By 1860, California's Indian population, nearly 150,000 when the Mexican War ended, had been reduced to around 30,000.

The gold rush's toll on Indians

Opening Japan

The Mexican War ended with the United States in possession of the magnificent harbors of San Diego and San Francisco, long seen as jumping-off points for trade with the Far East. Between 1848 and 1860 American trade with China tripled. In 1850, New York businessman Asa Whitney submitted

A photograph from 1852 depicts miners at work in California. Chinese and white miners labor side by side searching for gold.

Transportation of Cargo by Westerners at the Port of Yokohama, 1861, by the Japanese artist Utagawa Sadahide, depicts ships in port, including an American one on the left, eight years after Commodore Perry's first voyage to Japan.

Slavery in the West

a plan to Congress for a transcontinental railroad that would speed eastern goods to Asian markets by eliminating the long and expensive sea route around South America. In a sense, he saw East Asia as a commercial extension of the American West. One congressman wrote in response to Whitney's proposal, "In the Bay of San Francisco will converge the commerce of Asia and the model republic."

In the 1850s, the United States took the lead in opening Japan, a country that had closed itself to nearly all foreign contact for more than two centuries. In 1853 and 1854, American warships under the command of **Commodore Matthew Perry** (the younger brother of Oliver Perry, a hero of the War of 1812) sailed into Tokyo Harbor. Perry, who had been sent by President Millard Fillmore to negotiate a trade treaty, demanded that the Japanese deal with him. Alarmed by European intrusions into China and impressed by Perry's armaments as well as a musical pageant he presented that included a blackface minstrel show, Japanese leaders agreed to do so. In 1854, they opened two ports to American shipping. Two years later, Townsend Harris, a merchant from New York City, arrived as the first American consul (and, according to some accounts, the inspiration for Puccini's great opera, *Madama Butterfly*, about an American who marries and then abandons a Japanese woman). Harris persuaded the Japanese to allow American ships into additional ports and to establish full diplomatic relations between the two countries. As a result, the United States acquired refueling places on the route to China. And Japan soon launched a process of modernization that transformed it into the region's major military power.

A DOSE OF ARSENIC

Victory over Mexico added more than 1 million square miles to the United States—an area larger than the Louisiana Purchase. But the acquisition of this vast territory raised the fatal issue that would disrupt the political system and plunge the nation into civil war—whether slavery should be allowed to expand into the West. Events soon confirmed Ralph Waldo Emerson's prediction that if the United States gobbled up part of Mexico, "it will be as the man who swallows arsenic. . . . Mexico will poison us."

Already, the bonds of union were fraying. In 1844 and 1845, the Methodists and Baptists, the two largest evangelical churches, divided into northern and southern branches. But it was the entrance of the slavery issue into the heart of American politics as the result of the Mexican War that eventually dissolved perhaps the strongest force for national unity—the two-party system.

The Wilmot Proviso

Before 1846, the status of slavery in all parts of the United States had been settled, either by state law or by the Missouri Compromise, which determined slavery's status in the Louisiana Purchase. The acquisition of new land reopened the question of slavery's expansion. The divisive potential of this issue became clear in 1846, when Congressman David Wilmot of Pennsylvania proposed a resolution prohibiting slavery from all territory acquired from Mexico. Party lines crumbled as every northerner, Democrat and Whig alike, supported what came to be known as the **Wilmot Proviso**, while nearly all southerners opposed it. The measure passed the House, where the more populous North possessed a majority, but failed in the Senate, with its even balance of free and slave states. The proviso, said one newspaper, "as if by magic, brought to a head the great question that is about to divide the American people."

> *Sectional division caused by the proviso*

In 1848, opponents of slavery's expansion organized the **Free Soil Party** and nominated Martin Van Buren for president and Charles Francis Adams, the son of John Quincy Adams, as his running mate. Democrats nominated Lewis Cass of Michigan, who proposed that the decision on whether to allow slavery should be left to settlers in the new territories (an idea later given the name "popular sovereignty"). Van Buren was motivated in part by revenge against the South for jettisoning him in 1844. But his campaign struck a chord among northerners opposed to the expansion of slavery, and he polled some 300,000 votes, 14 percent of the northern total. Victory in 1848 went to the Whig candidate, Zachary Taylor, a hero of the Mexican War and a Louisiana sugar planter. But the fact that a former president and the son of another abandoned their parties to run on a Free Soil platform showed that antislavery sentiment had spread far beyond abolitionist ranks. "Antislavery," commented Senator William H. Seward of New York, "is at length a respectable element in politics."

> *"Popular sovereignty"*

The Free Soil Appeal

The Free Soil position had a popular appeal in the North that far exceeded the abolitionists' demand for immediate emancipation and equal rights for blacks. While Congress possessed no constitutional power to abolish slavery within a state, well-known precedents existed for keeping territories (areas that had not yet entered the Union as states) free from slavery. Congress had done this in 1787 in the Northwest Ordinance and again in the Missouri Compromise of 1820–1821. Many northerners had long resented what they considered southern domination of the federal government. The idea of preventing the creation of new slave states appealed to those who favored policies, such as the protective tariff and government aid to internal improvements, that the majority of southern political leaders opposed.

For thousands of northerners, moreover, the ability to move to the new western territories held out the promise of economic betterment. The depression

> *Economic betterment in the West*

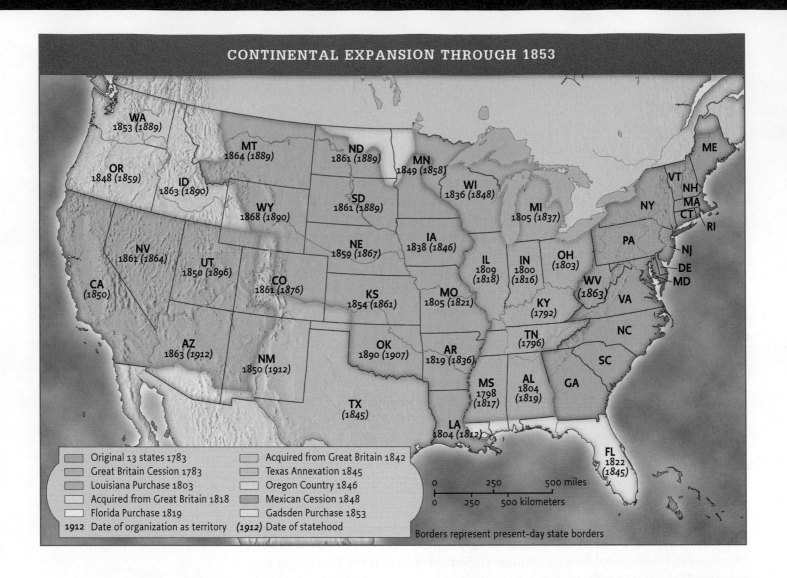

CONTINENTAL EXPANSION THROUGH 1853

WA 1853 (1889)
OR 1848 (1859)
ID 1863 (1890)
MT 1864 (1889)
ND 1861 (1889)
MN 1849 (1858)
WI 1836 (1848)
MI 1805 (1837)
ME
VT
NH
MA
CT
RI
NY
WY 1868 (1890)
SD 1861 (1889)
NV 1861 (1864)
UT 1850 (1896)
CO 1861 (1876)
NE 1859 (1867)
IA 1838 (1846)
IL 1809 (1818)
IN 1800 (1816)
OH (1803)
PA
NJ
DE
MD
CA (1850)
KS 1854 (1861)
MO 1805 (1821)
WV (1863)
VA
KY (1792)
AZ 1863 (1912)
NM 1850 (1912)
OK 1890 (1907)
AR 1819 (1836)
TN (1796)
NC
SC
MS 1798 (1817)
AL 1804 (1819)
GA
TX (1845)
LA 1804 (1812)
FL 1822 (1845)

Original 13 states 1783
Great Britain Cession 1783
Louisiana Purchase 1803
Acquired from Great Britain 1818
Florida Purchase 1819
Acquired from Great Britain 1842
Texas Annexation 1845
Oregon Country 1846
Mexican Cession 1848
Gadsden Purchase 1853
1912 Date of organization as territory   (1912) Date of statehood

0   250   500 miles
0   250   500 kilometers

Borders represent present-day state borders

By 1853, with the Gadsden Purchase, the present boundaries of the United States in North America, with the exception of Alaska, had been created.

Appeal of the "free soil" to northern racism

of the early 1840s had reinforced the traditional equation of landownership with economic freedom. The labor movement promoted access to western land as a way of combating unemployment and low wages in the East. "Freedom of the soil," declared George Henry Evans, the editor of a pro-labor newspaper, offered the only alternative to permanent economic dependence for American workers.

Such views merged easily with opposition to the expansion of slavery. If slave plantations were to occupy the fertile lands of the West, northern migration would be effectively blocked. The term "free soil" had a double meaning. The Free Soil platform of 1848 called both for barring slavery from western territories and for the federal government to provide free homesteads to settlers in the new territories. Unlike abolitionism, the "free soil" idea also appealed to the racism so widespread in northern society. Wilmot himself insisted that his controversial proviso was motivated not by "morbid sympathy for the slaves" but to advance "the cause and rights of the free white man," in part by preventing him from having to compete with "black labor."

To white southerners, the idea of barring slavery from territory acquired from Mexico seemed a violation of their equal rights as members of the Union.

Southerners had fought and died to win these territories; surely they had a right to share in the fruits of victory. A majority of slaves in 1848 lived in states that had not even existed when the Constitution was adopted. Many older plantation areas already suffered from soil exhaustion. Just as northerners believed westward expansion essential to their economic well-being, southern leaders became convinced that slavery must expand or die. Moreover, the admission of new free states would overturn the delicate political balance between the sections and make the South a permanent minority. Southern interests would not be secure in a Union dominated by non-slaveholding states.

The views of southern leaders

Crisis and Compromise

In world history, the year 1848 is remembered as the "springtime of nations," a time of democratic uprisings against the monarchies of Europe and demands by ethnic minorities for national independence. American principles of liberty and self-government appeared to be triumphing in the Old World. The Chartist movement in Great Britain organized massive demonstrations in support of democratic reforms. The French replaced their monarchy with a republic. Hungarians proclaimed their independence from Austrian rule. Patriots in Italy and Germany, both divided into numerous states, demanded national unification. But the revolutionary tide receded. Chartism faded away. In France, the Second Republic was soon succeeded by the reign of Emperor Napoleon III. Revolts in Budapest, Rome, and other cities were crushed. Would their own experiment in self-government, some Americans wondered, suffer the same fate as the failed revolutions of Europe?

Developments in Europe

With the slavery issue appearing more and more ominous, established party leaders moved to resolve differences between the sections. Some disputes were of long standing, but the immediate source of controversy arose from the acquisition of new lands after the Mexican War. In 1850, California asked to be admitted to the Union as a free state. Many southerners opposed the measure, fearing that it would upset the sectional balance in Congress. Senator Henry Clay offered a plan with four main provisions that came to be known as the Compromise of 1850. California would enter the Union as a free state. The slave trade, but not slavery itself, would be abolished in the nation's capital. A stringent new law would allow southerners to reclaim runaway slaves. And the status of slavery in the remaining territories acquired from Mexico would be left to the decision of the local white inhabitants. The United States would also agree to pay off the massive debt Texas had accumulated while independent.

The Compromise of 1850

The Great Debate

In the Senate debate on the Compromise, the divergent sectional positions received eloquent expression. Powerful leaders spoke for and against compromise. Daniel Webster of Massachusetts announced his willingness to abandon the Wilmot Proviso and accept a new fugitive slave law if this were the price of sectional peace. John C. Calhoun, again representing South Carolina, was too ill to speak. A colleague read his remarks rejecting the very idea of compromise. Slavery, Calhoun insisted, must be protected by the national government and extended into all the new territories. The North must yield or the Union could not survive. William

Arguments for and against the Compromise of 1850

Senator Daniel Webster of Massachusetts in a daguerreotype from 1850, the year his speech in support of the Compromise of 1850 contributed to its passage.

H. Seward of New York also opposed compromise. To southerners' talk of their constitutional rights, Seward responded that a "higher law" than the Constitution condemned slavery—the law of morality. Here was the voice of abolitionism, now represented in the U.S. Senate.

President Zachary Taylor, like Andrew Jackson a southerner but a strong nationalist, was alarmed by talk of disunion. He accused southern leaders in Congress of holding California hostage to their own legislative aims and insisted that all Congress needed to do was admit California to the Union. But Taylor died suddenly of an intestinal infection on July 9, 1850. His successor, Millard Fillmore of New York, threw his support to Clay's proposals. Fillmore helped to break the impasse in Congress and secure adoption of the **Compromise of 1850**.

The Fugitive Slave Issue

For one last time, political leaders had removed the dangerous slavery question from congressional debate. The new **Fugitive Slave Act**, however, made further controversy inevitable. The law allowed special federal commissioners to determine the fate of alleged fugitives without benefit of a jury trial or even testimony by the accused individual. It prohibited local authorities from interfering with the capture of fugitives and required individual citizens to assist in such capture when called upon by federal agents. Thus, southern leaders, usually strong defenders of states' rights and local autonomy, supported a measure that brought federal agents into communities throughout the North, armed with the power to override local law enforcement and judicial procedures to secure the return of runaway slaves. The security of slavery was more important to them than states'-rights consistency.

The fugitive slave issue affected all the free states, not just those that bordered on the South. Slave catchers, for example, entered California attempting to apprehend fugitives from Texas and New Mexico who hoped to reach freedom in British Columbia. The issue drew into politics individuals like Ralph Waldo Emerson, who, although antislavery, had previously remained aloof from the abolitionist crusade. Emerson and others influenced by transcendentalism viewed the Fugitive Slave Act as a dangerous example of how a government doing the bidding of the South could override an individual's ability to act according to his conscience—the foundation, for Emerson, of genuine freedom.

During the 1850s, federal tribunals heard more than 300 cases and ordered 157 fugitives returned to the South, many at the government's expense. But the law further widened sectional divisions and reinvigorated the underground railroad. In a series of dramatic confrontations, fugitives, aided by abolitionist allies, violently resisted recapture. A large crowd in 1851 rescued the escaped slave Jerry from jail in Syracuse, New York, and spirited him off to Canada. In the same year, an owner who attempted to recapture a fugitive was killed in Christiana, Pennsylvania. Later in the decade, Margaret Garner, a Kentucky slave who had escaped with her family to Ohio, killed her own young daughter rather than see her returned to slavery by federal marshals. (At the end of the twentieth century, this incident would become the basis for Toni Morrison's celebrated novel *Beloved*.)

Less dramatically, the men and women involved in the Underground Railroad redoubled their efforts to assist fugitives. Thanks to the consolidation of the railroad network in the North, it was now possible for escaping slaves who reached the free

Ralph Waldo Emerson

Resisting recapture

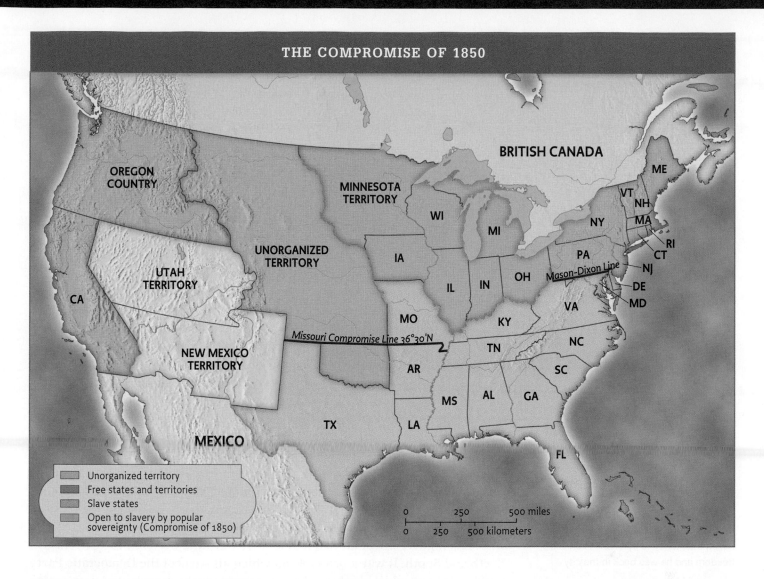

THE COMPROMISE OF 1850

Legend:
- Unorganized territory
- Free states and territories
- Slave states
- Open to slavery by popular sovereignty (Compromise of 1850)

states to be placed on trains that would take them to safety in Canada in a day or two. In 1855 and 1856, Sydney Howard Gay, an abolitionist editor in New York City and a key Underground Railroad operative, recorded in a notebook the arrival of over 200 fugitives—men, women, and children—a majority of whom had been sent by train from Philadelphia. Gay dispatched them to upstate New York and Canada.

Overall several thousand fugitives and freeborn blacks, worried that they might be swept up in the stringent provisions of the Fugitive Slave Act, fled to safety in Canada. The sight of so many refugees seeking liberty in a foreign land challenged the familiar image of the United States as an asylum for freedom. "Families are separating," reported a Toronto newspaper in October 1850, "leaving their homes, and flying in all directions to seek in Canada, under the British flag, the protection denied to them in the free republic."

The Compromise of 1850 attempted to settle issues arising from the acquisition of territory from Mexico by admitting California as a free state and providing that the status of slavery in Utah and New Mexico would be determined by the settlers.

Douglas and Popular Sovereignty

At least temporarily, the Compromise of 1850 seemed to restore sectional peace and party unity. In the 1852 presidential election, Democrat Franklin Pierce won

THE FUGITIVE SLAVE LAW.....HAMLET IN CHAINS.

An engraving from the *National Anti-Slavery Standard*, October 17, 1850, depicts James Hamlet, the first person returned to slavery under the Fugitive Slave Act of 1850, in front of City Hall in New York. Flags fly from the building, emblazoned with popular American maxims violated by Hamlet's rendition. By the time this appeared in print, New Yorkers had raised the money to purchase Hamlet's freedom and he was back in the city.

Appeal of the Independent Democrats

a sweeping victory over the Whig Winfield Scott on a platform that recognized the Compromise as a final settlement of the slavery controversy. Pierce received a broad popular mandate, winning 254 electoral votes to Scott's 42. Yet his administration turned out to be one of the most disastrous in American history. It witnessed the collapse of the party system inherited from the Age of Jackson.

In 1854, the old political order finally succumbed to the disruptive pressures of sectionalism. Early in that year, Illinois senator Stephen A. Douglas introduced a bill to provide territorial governments for Kansas and Nebraska, located within the Louisiana Purchase. With Calhoun, Clay, and Webster (the "great triumvirate") all having died between 1850 and 1852, Douglas, although only forty-one, saw himself as the new leader of the Senate. A strong believer in western development, he hoped that a transcontinental railroad could be constructed through Kansas or Nebraska. But he feared that this could not be accomplished unless formal governments had been established in these territories. Southerners in Congress, however, seemed adamant against allowing the organization of new free territories that might further upset the sectional balance. Douglas hoped to satisfy them by applying the principle of **popular sovereignty**, whereby the status of slavery would be determined by the votes of local settlers, not Congress. To Douglas, popular sovereignty embodied the idea of local self-government and offered a middle ground between the extremes of North and South. It was a principle on which all parts of the Democratic Party could unite, and which might enable him to capture the presidential nomination in 1856 to succeed the ineffectual Pierce.

The Kansas-Nebraska Act

Unlike the lands taken from Mexico, Kansas and Nebraska lay in the nation's heartland, directly in the path of westward migration. Slavery, moreover, was prohibited there under the terms of the Missouri Compromise, which Douglas's bill would repeal. In response, a group of antislavery congressmen issued the *Appeal of the Independent Democrats*. Written by two abolitionists from Ohio—Congressman Joshua Giddings and Senator Salmon P. Chase—the *Appeal* proved to be one of the most effective pieces of political persuasion in American history. It arraigned Douglas's bill as a "gross violation of a sacred pledge," part and parcel of "an atrocious plot" to convert free territory into a "dreary region of despotism, inhabited by masters and slaves." It helped to convince millions of northerners that southern leaders aimed at nothing less than extending their peculiar institution throughout the West.

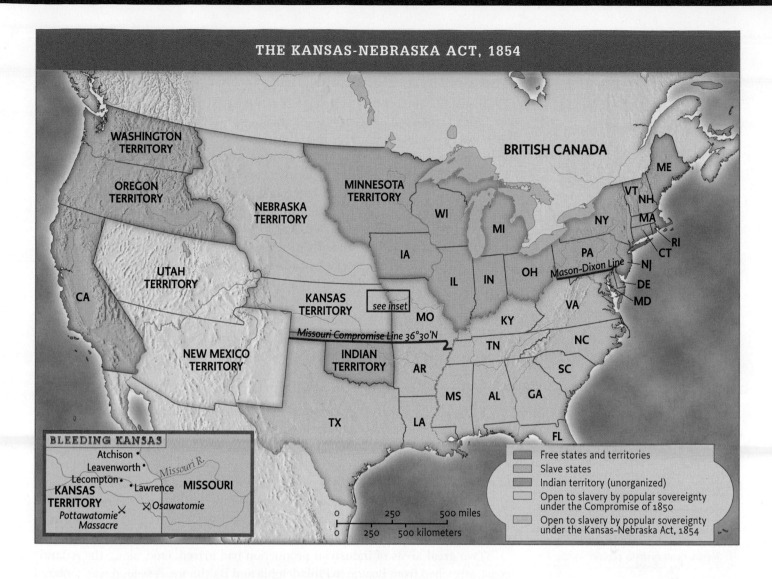

THE KANSAS-NEBRASKA ACT, 1854

WASHINGTON TERRITORY

OREGON TERRITORY

BRITISH CANADA

MINNESOTA TERRITORY

NEBRASKA TERRITORY

ME

VT
NH

UTAH TERRITORY

WI

MI

NY

MA

CA

IA

PA

RI
CT

IL   IN   OH

Mason-Dixon Line

NJ

KANSAS TERRITORY

see inset

MO

DE
MD

Missouri Compromise Line 36°30'N

KY

VA

NEW MEXICO TERRITORY

INDIAN TERRITORY

AR

TN

NC

SC

MS   AL   GA

TX

LA

FL

BLEEDING KANSAS

Atchison •
Leavenworth •
Lecompton •
• Lawrence   MISSOURI
KANSAS TERRITORY   × Osawatomie
× Pottawatomie Massacre

Missouri R.

Free states and territories
Slave states
Indian territory (unorganized)
Open to slavery by popular sovereignty under the Compromise of 1850
Open to slavery by popular sovereignty under the Kansas-Nebraska Act, 1854

0   250   500 miles
0   250   500 kilometers

Thanks to Douglas's energetic leadership, the **Kansas-Nebraska Act** became law. But it shattered the Democratic Party's unity. Even as Congress debated, protest meetings sprang up throughout the North. Fearing that the bill's unpopularity among their constituents would harm their chances for reelection, half the northern Democrats in the House cast negative votes. Loyalty to Pierce, Douglas, and their party led the other half to support the measure. It is difficult to think of a piece of legislation in American history that had a more profound impact on national life. In the wake of the bill's passage, American politics underwent a profound reorganization. During the next two years, the Whig Party, unable to develop a unified response to the political crisis, collapsed. From a region divided between the two parties, the South became solidly Democratic. Most northern Whigs, augmented by thousands of disgruntled Democrats, joined a new organization, the Republican Party, dedicated to preventing the further expansion of slavery.

The Kansas-Nebraska Act opened a vast area in the nation's heartland to the possible spread of slavery by repealing the Missouri Compromise and providing that settlers would determine the status of slavery in these territories.

ILLINIOS CENTRAL RAILROAD.

OPEN FROM LASALLE TO BLOOMINGTON.

Arrangements commencing May 23, 1853.

Passenger Trains leave as follows, daily, (Sundays excepted):

Bloomington,	8.00 A.M.	La Salle,		2.00 P.M.
Hudson,	8.35 "	Tonica,		2.35 "
Kappa,	8.54 "	Wenona,		3.15 "
Panola,	9.24 "	Minonk,		3.50 "
Minonk,	9.54 "	Panola,		4.30 "
Wenona,	10.40 "	Kappa,		5.00 "
Tonica,	11.25 "	Hudson,		5.20 "
La Salle, arr.	12.00 "	Bloomington, arr.		6.00 "

*Stopping at these places on signal to take or leave passengers.

A Freight Train, with Passenger Car attached, will leave La Salle on Mondays, Wednesdays and Fridays at 8.30, A. M. arriving at Bloomington 2.30, P. M. stopping at all stations.
Returning, leaves Bloomington on Tuesday, Thursday and Saturday at 5 A. M. arriving at La Salle at 11 A. M.
Stages, it is expected, will soon run in connection with the Cars between Bloomington, Springfield, Decatur and Urbana.

Chicago, May 23.   **R. B. MASON, Sup't.**

An 1853 broadside for one section of the Illinois Central Railroad. One of the most important new lines of the 1850s, the Illinois Central opened parts of the Old Northwest to settlement and commercial agriculture, and it helped to cement Chicago's place as the region's foremost city.

Northern industrial production

Hostility to immigrants

THE RISE OF THE REPUBLICAN PARTY

The Northern Economy

The disruptive impact of slavery on the traditional parties was the immediate cause of political transformation in the mid-1850s. But the rise of the Republican Party also reflected underlying economic and social changes, notably the completion of the market revolution and the beginning of mass immigration from Europe. The period from 1843, when prosperity returned, to 1857, when another economic downturn hit, witnessed explosive economic growth, especially in the North. The catalyst was the completion of the railroad network. From 5,000 miles in 1848, railroad track mileage grew to 30,000 by 1860, with most of the construction occurring in Ohio, Illinois, and other states of the Old Northwest. Four great trunk railroads now linked eastern cities with western farming and commercial centers. The railroads completed the reorientation of the Northwest's trade from the South to the East. As late as 1850, most western farmers still shipped their produce down the Mississippi River. Ten years later, however, railroads transported nearly all their crops to the East, at a fraction of the previous cost. By 1860, for example, 60 million bushels of wheat were passing through Buffalo on their way to market in eastern cities and abroad. The economic integration of the Northwest and Northeast created the groundwork for their political unification in the Republican Party.

By 1860, the North had become a complex, integrated economy, with eastern industrialists marketing manufactured goods to the commercial farmers of the West, while residents of the region's growing cities consumed the food westerners produced. Northern society stood poised between old and new ways. The majority of the population still lived not in large cities but in small towns and rural areas, where the ideal of economic independence—owning one's own farm or shop—still lay within reach. Yet the majority of the northern workforce no longer labored in agriculture, and the industrial revolution was spreading rapidly.

Two great areas of industrial production had arisen. One, along the Atlantic coast, stretched from Boston to Philadelphia and Baltimore. A second was centered on or near the Great Lakes, in inland cities like Buffalo, Cleveland, Pittsburgh, and Chicago. Driven by railroad expansion, coal mining and iron manufacturing were growing rapidly. Chicago, the Old Northwest's major rail center and the jumping-off place for settlers heading for the Great Plains, had become a complex manufacturing center, producing 5,000 reapers each year, along with barbed wire, windmills, and prefabricated "balloon frame" houses, all of which facilitated further western settlement. New York City by 1860 had become the nation's preeminent financial, commercial, and manufacturing center. Although the southern economy was also growing and the continuing expansion of cotton production brought wealth to slaveholders, the South did not share in these broad economic changes.

The Rise and Fall of the Know-Nothings

As noted in Chapter 9, nativism—hostility to immigrants, especially Catholics—emerged as a local political movement in the 1840s. But in 1854, with the party system in crisis, it burst on the national political scene with the sudden appearance of the American, or Know-Nothing, Party (so called because it began as a secret

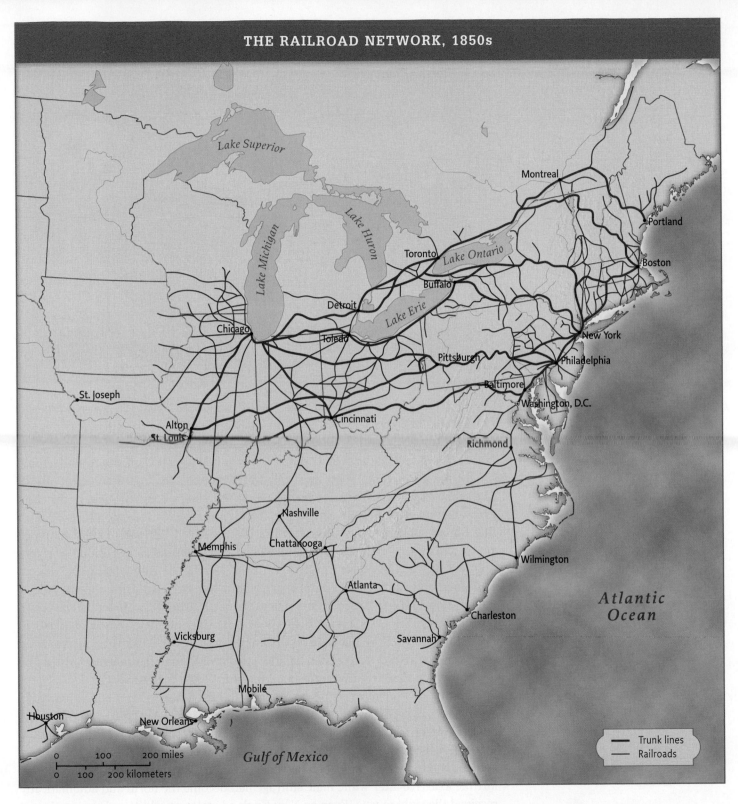

THE RAILROAD NETWORK, 1850s

The rapid expansion of the railroad network in the 1850s linked the Northeast and Old Northwest in a web of commerce. The South's rail network was considerably less developed, accounting for only 30 percent of the nation's track mileage.

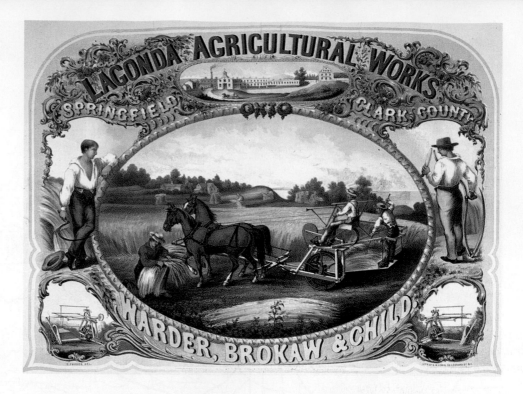

Lagonda Agricultural Works, a color lithograph from 1859 advertising an Ohio manufacturer of agricultural machinery, in this case a horse-drawn reaper.

organization whose members, when asked about its existence, were supposed to respond, "I know nothing"). The **Know-Nothing Party** trumpeted its dedication to reserving political office for native-born Americans and to resisting the "aggressions" of the Catholic Church, such as its supposed efforts to undermine public school systems. The Know-Nothings swept the 1854 state elections in Massachusetts, electing the governor, all of the state's congressmen, and nearly every member of the state legislature. They captured the mayor's office in cities like Philadelphia, Chicago, and San Francisco as well. In many states, nativists emerged as a major component of victorious "anti-Nebraska" coalitions of voters opposed to the Kansas-Nebraska Act. In the North, the Know-Nothings' appeal combined anti-Catholic and antislavery sentiment, with opposition to the sale of liquor often added to the equation. After all, most Catholics, as noted in the previous chapter, vigorously opposed the reform movements inspired by evangelical Protestantism, especially antislavery and temperance. The 1854 elections, said one observer, revealed "a deep seated feeling in favor of human freedom and also a fine determination that hereafter none but Americans shall rule America."

Despite severe anti-Irish discrimination in jobs, housing, and education, however, it is remarkable how little came of demands that immigrants be barred from the political nation. All European immigrants benefited from being white. During the 1850s, free blacks found immigrants pushing them out of even the jobs as servants and common laborers previously available to them. The newcomers had the good fortune to arrive after white male suffrage had become the norm and automatically received the right to vote. Even as New England states sought to reduce immigrant political power (Massachusetts and Connecticut made literacy a voting requirement, and Massachusetts mandated a two-year waiting period between becoming a naturalized citizen and voting), western states desperate for labor allowed

Nativism and anti-slavery

Immigrant suffrage

immigrants to vote well before they became citizens. In a country where the suffrage had become essential to understandings of freedom, it is significant that many white male immigrants could vote almost from the moment they landed in America, while non-whites, whose ancestors had lived in the country for centuries, could not.

The Free Labor Ideology

By 1856, it was clear that the Republican Party—a coalition of antislavery Democrats, northern Whigs, Free Soilers, and Know-Nothings opposed to the further expansion of slavery—would become the major alternative to the Democratic Party in the North. Republicans managed to convince most northerners that **the Slave Power**, as they called the South's proslavery political leadership, posed a more immediate threat to their liberties and aspirations than "popery" and immigration. The party's appeal rested on the idea of "free labor." In Republican hands, the antithesis between "free society" and "slave society" coalesced into a comprehensive worldview that glorified the North as the home of progress, opportunity, and freedom.

Free labor

The defining quality of northern society, Republicans declared, was the opportunity it offered each laborer to move up to the status of landowning farmer or independent craftsman, thus achieving the economic independence essential to freedom. Slavery, by contrast, spawned a social order consisting of degraded slaves, poor whites with no hope of advancement, and idle aristocrats. The struggle over the territories was a contest about which of two antagonistic labor systems would dominate the West and, by implication, the nation's future. If slavery were to spread into the West, northern free laborers would be barred, and their chances for social advancement severely diminished. Slavery, Republicans insisted, must be kept out of the territories so that free labor could flourish. The Republican platform of 1856 condemned slavery as one of the "twin relics of barbarism" in the United States (the other being Mormon polygamy).

The Propagation Society—More Free than Welcome, an anti-Catholic cartoon from the 1850s, illustrates the nativist fear that the Catholic Church poses a threat to American society. Pope Pius IX, cross in hand, steps ashore from a boat that also holds five bishops. Addressing "Young America," who holds a Bible, he says that he has come to "take charge of your spiritual welfare." A bishop adds, "I cannot bear to see that boy, with that horrible book."

SOUTHERN CHIVALRY — ARGUMENT versus CLUB'S.

A contemporary print denounces South Carolina congressman Preston S. Brooks's assault on Massachusetts senator Charles Sumner in May 1856. The attack on the floor of the Senate was in retaliation for Sumner's speech accusing Senator Andrew P. Butler (Brooks's distant cousin) of having taken "the harlot slavery" as his mistress.

To southern claims that slavery was the foundation of liberty, Republicans responded with the rallying cry "freedom national"—meaning not abolition, but ending the federal government's support of slavery. Under the banner of free labor, northerners of diverse backgrounds and interests rallied in defense of the superiority of their own society. Republicans acknowledged that some northern laborers, including most Irish immigrants, were locked into jobs as factory workers and unskilled laborers and found it extremely difficult to rise in the social scale. But Republicans concluded that it was their "dependent nature"—a lack of Protestant, middle-class virtues—that explained the plight of the immigrant poor.

Republicans were not abolitionists—they focused on preventing the spread of slavery, not attacking it where it existed. Nonetheless, many party leaders viewed the nation's division into free and slave societies as an "irrepressible conflict," as Senator William H. Seward of New York put it in 1858, that eventually would have to be resolved. These "two systems" of society, Seward insisted, were "incompatible" within a single nation. The market revolution, Seward argued, by drawing the entire nation closer together in a web of transportation and commerce, heightened the tension between freedom and slavery. The United States, he predicted, "must and will, sooner or later, become either entirely a slaveholding nation, or entirely a free-labor nation."

Bleeding Kansas and the Election of 1856

Their free labor outlook, which resonated so effectively with deeply held northern values, helps to explain the Republicans' rapid rise to prominence. But dramatic events in 1855 and 1856 also fueled the party's growth. When Kansas held elections in 1854 and 1855, hundreds of proslavery Missourians crossed the border to cast fraudulent ballots. President Franklin Pierce recognized the legitimacy of the resulting proslavery legislature and replaced the territorial governor, Andrew H. Reeder of Pennsylvania, when he dissented. Settlers from free states soon established a rival government, and a sporadic civil war broke out in Kansas in which some 200 persons eventually lost their lives. In one incident, in May 1856, a proslavery mob attacked the free-soil stronghold of Lawrence, burning public buildings and pillaging private homes.

Kansas elections

Brooks and Sumner

"**Bleeding Kansas**" seemed to discredit Douglas's policy of leaving the decision on slavery up to the local population, thus aiding the Republicans. The party also drew strength from an unprecedented incident in the halls of Congress. South Carolina representative Preston Brooks, wielding a gold-tipped cane, beat the antislavery senator Charles Sumner of Massachusetts unconscious after Sumner delivered a denunciation of "The Crime against Kansas." Many southerners applauded Brooks, sending him canes emblazoned with the words "Hit him again!"

In the election of 1856, the Republican Party chose as its candidate John C. Frémont and drafted a platform that strongly opposed the further expansion of slavery. Stung by the northern reaction to the Kansas-Nebraska Act, the Democrats nominated James Buchanan, who had been minister to Great Britain in 1854 and thus had no direct connection with that divisive measure. The Democratic platform endorsed the principle of popular sovereignty as the only viable solution to the slavery controversy. Meanwhile, the Know-Nothings presented ex-president Millard Fillmore as their candidate. Frémont outpolled Buchanan in the North, carrying eleven of sixteen free states—a remarkable achievement for an organization that had existed for only two years. But Buchanan won the entire South and the key northern states of Illinois, Indiana, and Pennsylvania, enough to ensure his victory. Fillmore carried only Maryland. But he ran well among former Whig voters in the Upper South and more conservative areas of the North, who were reluctant to join the Democrats but feared Republican victory might threaten the Union.

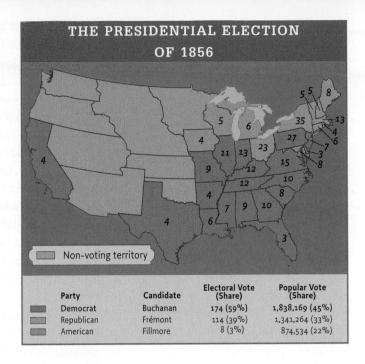

THE PRESIDENTIAL ELECTION OF 1856

Non-voting territory

Party	Candidate	Electoral Vote (Share)	Popular Vote (Share)
Democrat	Buchanan	174 (59%)	1,838,169 (45%)
Republican	Frémont	114 (39%)	1,341,264 (33%)
American	Fillmore	8 (3%)	874,534 (22%)

The 1856 election returns made starkly clear that parties had reoriented themselves along sectional lines. One major party had been destroyed, another had been seriously weakened, and a new one had arisen, devoted entirely to the interests of the North.

THE EMERGENCE OF LINCOLN

The final collapse of the party system took place during the administration of a president who epitomized the old political order. Born during George Washington's presidency, James Buchanan had served in Pennsylvania's legislature, in both houses of Congress, and as secretary of state under James K. Polk. A staunch believer in the Union, he committed himself to pacifying inflamed sectional emotions. Few presidents have failed more disastrously in what they set out to accomplish.

The Dred Scott Decision

Even before his inauguration, Buchanan became aware of an impending Supreme Court decision that held out the hope of settling the slavery controversy once and for all. This was the case of ***Dred Scott v. Sandford***. During the 1830s, Scott had accompanied his owner, Dr. John Emerson of Missouri, to Illinois, where slavery had been prohibited by the Northwest Ordinance of 1787 and by state law, and to Wisconsin Territory, where it was barred by the Missouri Compromise. After returning to Missouri, Scott sued for his freedom, claiming that residence on free soil had made him free.

The Dred Scott decision, one of the most famous—or infamous—rulings in the long history of the Supreme Court, was announced in March 1857, two days after Buchanan's inauguration. The justices addressed three questions. Could a black

Dred Scott as painted in 1857, the year the Supreme Court ruled that he and his family must remain in slavery.

person be a citizen and therefore sue in federal court? Did residence in a free state make Scott free? Did Congress possess the power to prohibit slavery in a territory? All nine justices issued individual opinions. But essentially, the Court divided 7-2 (with Justice Robert C. Grier of Pennsylvania, at Buchanan's behind-the-scenes urging, joining a southern majority). Speaking for the majority, Chief Justice Roger B. Taney declared that only white persons could be citizens of the United States. The nation's founders, Taney insisted, believed that blacks "had no rights which the white man was bound to respect." Descended from different ancestors and lacking a history of freedom, blacks, he continued, could never be part of the nation's "political family."

Congress's powerlessness to restrict slavery

The case could have ended there, since Scott had no right to sue, but inspired by the idea of resolving the slavery issue, Taney pressed on. Scott, he declared, remained a slave. Illinois law had no effect on him after his return to Missouri. As for his residence in Wisconsin, Congress possessed no power under the Constitution to bar slavery from a territory. The Missouri Compromise, recently repealed by the Kansas-Nebraska Act, had been unconstitutional, and so was any measure interfering with southerners' right to bring slaves into the western territories. The decision in effect declared unconstitutional the Republican platform of restricting slavery's expansion. It also seemed to undermine Douglas's doctrine of popular sovereignty. For if Congress lacked the power to prohibit slavery in a territory, how could a territorial legislature created by Congress do so? The Court, a Georgia newspaper exulted, "covers every question regarding slavery and settles it in favor of the South."

The Decision's Aftermath

The Scott family

Perhaps the person least directly affected by the Dred Scott decision was the plaintiff himself, for a new master immediately emancipated Scott and his family. Scott died in 1858, having enjoyed his freedom for less than two years. Harriet Scott lived until 1876, long enough to see Taney's ruling invalidated by the laws and constitutional amendments of Reconstruction. Their youngest daughter, Lizzie, survived to the age of 99. She died in 1954, having experienced the long era of segregation and the birth of the modern civil rights movement. The impact on the party system was more far-reaching. Among the decision's casualties was the reputation of the Court itself, which, in the North, sank to the lowest level in all of American history. Rather than abandoning their opposition to the expansion of slavery, Republicans now viewed the Court as controlled by the Slave Power.

The Lecompton battle

Slavery, announced President Buchanan, henceforth existed in all the territories, "by virtue of the Constitution." In 1858, his administration attempted to admit Kansas as a slave state under the Lecompton Constitution, which had been drafted by a pro-southern convention and never submitted to a popular vote. Outraged by this violation of popular sovereignty, Douglas formed an unlikely alliance with congressional Republicans to block the attempt. Kansas remained a territory; it would join the Union as a free state on the eve of the Civil War. The Lecompton battle convinced southern Democrats that they could not trust their party's most popular northern leader.

Lincoln and Slavery

The depth of Americans' divisions over slavery were brought into sharp focus in 1858 in one of the most storied election campaigns in the nation's history. Seeking reelection to the Senate as both a champion of popular sovereignty and the man who had prevented the administration from forcing slavery on the people of Kansas, Douglas faced an unexpectedly strong challenge from Abraham Lincoln, then little known outside of Illinois. Born into a modest farm family in Kentucky in 1809, Lincoln had moved as a youth to frontier Indiana and then Illinois. Although he began running for public office at the age of twenty-one, until the mid-1850s his career hardly seemed destined for greatness. He had served four terms as a Whig in the state legislature and one in Congress from 1847 to 1849.

Lincoln reentered politics in 1854 as a result of the Kansas-Nebraska Act. He once said that he "hated slavery as much as any abolitionist." Unlike abolitionists, however, Lincoln was willing to compromise with the South to preserve the Union. "I hate to see the poor creatures hunted down," he once wrote of fugitive slaves, "but I bite my lip and keep silent." But on one question he was inflexible—stopping the expansion of slavery.

Lincoln developed a critique of slavery and its expansion that gave voice to the central values of the emerging Republican Party and the millions of northerners whose loyalty it commanded. His speeches combined the moral fervor of the abolitionists with the respect for order and the Constitution of more conservative northerners. "I hate it," he said in 1854 of the prospect of slavery's expansion, "because of the monstrous injustice of slavery itself. I hate it because it deprives our republican example of its just influence in the world—enables the enemies of free institutions, with plausibility, to taunt us as hypocrites—causes the real friends of freedom to doubt our sincerity." If slavery were allowed to expand, he warned, the "love of liberty" would be extinguished and with it America's special mission to be a symbol of democracy for the entire world.

In a sense, Lincoln's own life personified the free labor ideology and the opportunities northern society offered to laboring men. During the 1850s, property-owning farmers, artisans, and shopkeepers far outnumbered wage earners in Illinois. Lincoln was fascinated and disturbed by the writings of proslavery ideologues like George Fitzhugh (discussed in Chapter 11), and he rose to the defense of northern society. "I want every man to have the chance," said Lincoln, "and I believe a black man is entitled to it, in which he *can* better his condition." Blacks might not be the equal of whites in all respects, but in their "natural right" to the fruits of their labor, they were "my equal and the equal of all others."

The Lincoln-Douglas Campaign

The campaign against Douglas, the North's preeminent political leader, created Lincoln's national reputation. Accepting his party's nomination for the Senate in June 1858, Lincoln etched sharply the differences between them. "A house divided against itself," he announced, "cannot stand. I believe this government cannot endure, permanently half *slave* and half

Abraham Lincoln

Abraham Lincoln's nickname "The Rail-splitter" recalled his humble origins. An unknown artist created this larger-than-life portrait. The White House is visible in the distance. The painting is said to have been displayed during campaign rallies in 1860.

free." Lincoln's point was not that civil war was imminent, but that Americans must choose between favoring and opposing slavery. There could be no middle ground. Douglas's policy of popular sovereignty, he insisted, reflected a moral indifference that could only result in the institution's spread throughout the entire country.

The **Lincoln-Douglas debates**, held in seven Illinois towns and attended by tens of thousands of listeners, remain classics of American political oratory. Clashing definitions of freedom lay at their heart. To Lincoln, freedom meant opposition to slavery. The nation needed to rekindle the spirit of the founding fathers, who, he claimed, had tried to place slavery on the path to "ultimate extinction." Douglas argued that the essence of freedom lay in local self-government and individual self-determination. A large and diverse nation could only survive by respecting the right of each locality to determine its own institutions. In response to a question posed by Lincoln during the Freeport debate, Douglas insisted that popular sovereignty was not incompatible with the Dred Scott decision. Although territorial legislatures could no longer exclude slavery directly, he argued, if the people wished to keep slaveholders out, all they needed to do was refrain from giving the institution legal protection.

In a critique not only of the antislavery movement but also of the entire reform impulse deriving from religious revivalism, Douglas insisted that politicians had no right to impose their own moral standards on society as a whole. "I deny the right of Congress," he declared, "to force a good thing upon a people who are unwilling to receive it." If a community wished to own slaves, it had a right to do so. Of course, when Douglas spoke of the "people," he meant whites alone. He spent much of his time in the debates attempting to portray Lincoln as a dangerous radical whose positions threatened to degrade white Americans by reducing them to equality with blacks. The United States government, Douglas proclaimed, had been created "by white men for the benefit of white men and their posterity for ever."

Lincoln shared many of the racial prejudices of his day. He opposed giving Illinois blacks the right to vote or serve on juries and spoke frequently of colonizing

Lincoln and Douglas's views of freedom

Douglas's critique of Lincoln

blacks overseas as the best solution to the problems of slavery and race. Yet, unlike Douglas, Lincoln did not use appeals to racism to garner votes. And he refused to exclude blacks from the human family. No less than whites, they were entitled to the inalienable rights of the Declaration of Independence, which applied to "all men, in all lands, everywhere," not merely to Europeans and their descendants.

The Illinois election returns revealed a state sharply divided, like the nation itself. Southern Illinois, settled from the South, voted strongly Democratic, while the rapidly growing northern part of the state was firmly in the Republican column. Until the adoption of the Seventeenth Amendment in the early twentieth century, each state's legislature chose its U.S. senators. In 1858, Republican candidates for the legislature won more votes statewide than Democrats. But because the apportionment of seats, based on the census of 1850, did not reflect the growth of northern Illinois since then, the Democrats emerged with a narrow margin in the legislature. Douglas was reelected. His victory was all the more remarkable because elsewhere in the North Republicans swept to victory in 1858. Resentment over the administration's Kansas policy split the Democratic Party, sometimes producing two Democratic candidates (pro-Douglas and pro-Buchanan) running against a single Republican. Coupled with the impact of the economic recession that began in 1857, this helped to produce Republican victories even in Indiana and Pennsylvania, which Democrats had carried two years earlier.

> *Illinois divided*

> *Douglas's win*

John Brown at Harpers Ferry

An armed assault by the abolitionist John Brown on the federal arsenal at **Harpers Ferry, Virginia**, further heightened sectional tensions. Brown had a long career of involvement in antislavery activities. In the 1830s and 1840s, he had befriended fugitive slaves and, although chronically in debt, helped to finance antislavery publications. Like other abolitionists, Brown was a deeply religious man. But his God was not the forgiving Jesus of the revivals, who encouraged men to save themselves through conversion, but the vengeful Father of the Old Testament. During the civil war in Kansas, Brown traveled to the territory. In May 1856, after the attack on Lawrence, he and a few followers murdered five proslavery settlers at Pottawatomie Creek. For the next two years, he traveled through the North and Canada, raising funds and enlisting followers for a war against slavery.

On October 16, 1859, with twenty-one men, five of them black, Brown seized Harpers Ferry. Militarily, the plan made little sense. Brown's band was soon surrounded and killed or captured by a detachment of federal soldiers headed by Colonel Robert E. Lee. Placed on trial for treason to the state of Virginia, Brown conducted himself with dignity and courage, winning admiration from millions of northerners who disapproved of his violent deeds. When Virginia's governor, Henry A. Wise, spurned pleas for clemency and ordered Brown executed, he turned Brown into a martyr to much of the North. Henry David Thoreau pronounced him "a crucified hero." Since Brown's death, radicals of both the left and right have revered Brown as a man willing to take action against an institution he considered immoral. Black leaders have long hailed him as a rare white person willing to sacrifice himself for the cause of racial justice.

To the South, the failure of Brown's assault seemed less significant than the adulation he seemed to arouse from much of the northern public. His raid and

John Brown, in an 1856 photograph.

VOICES OF FREEDOM

From THE LINCOLN-DOUGLAS DEBATES (1858)

The most famous political campaign in American history, the 1858 race for the U.S. Senate between Senator Stephen A. Douglas (a former Illinois judge) and Abraham Lincoln was highlighted by seven debates in which they discussed the politics of slavery and contrasting understandings of freedom.

DOUGLAS: Mr. Lincoln says that this government cannot endure permanently in the same condition in which it was made by its framers—divided into free and slave states. He says that it has existed for about seventy years thus divided, and yet he tells you that it cannot endure permanently on the same principles and in the same relative conditions in which our fathers made it. . . . One of the reserved rights of the states, was the right to regulate the relations between master and servant, on the slavery question.

Now, my friends, if we will only act conscientiously upon this great principle of popular sovereignty which guarantees to each state and territory the right to do as it pleases on all things local and domestic instead of Congress interfering, we will continue to be at peace one with another.

LINCOLN: Judge Douglas says, "Why can't this Union endure permanently, half slave and half free?" "Why can't we let it stand as our fathers placed it?" That is the exact difficulty between

us. . . . I say when this government was first established it was the policy of its founders to prohibit the spread of slavery into the new territories of the United States, where it had not existed. But Judge Douglas and his friends have broken up that policy and placed it upon a new basis by which it is to become national and perpetual. All I have asked or desired anywhere is that it should be placed back again upon the basis that the founders of our government originally placed it—restricting it from the new territories. . . .

Judge Douglas assumes that we have no interest in them—that we have no right to interfere. . . . Do we not wish for an outlet for our surplus population, if I may so express myself clear? Do we not feel an interest in getting to that outlet with such institutions as we would like to have prevail there? Now irrespective of the moral aspect of this question as to whether there is a right or wrong in enslaving a negro, I am still in favor of our new territories being in such a condition that white men may find a home. I am in favor of this not merely for our own people, but as an outlet for *free white people everywhere*, the world over—in which Hans and Baptiste and Patrick, and all other men from all the world, may find new homes and better their conditions in life.

DOUGLAS: For one, I am opposed to negro citizenship in any and every form. I believe this government was made on the white basis. I believe it was made by white men, for the benefit of white men and their posterity forever. . . . I do not believe that the Almighty made the negro capable of self-government. I say to you, my fellow-citizens, that in my opinion the signers of the Declaration of Independence had no reference to the negro whatever when they declared all men to be created equal. They desired to express by that phrase, white men, men of European birth and European descent . . . when they spoke of the equality of men.

LINCOLN: I have no purpose to introduce political and social equality between the white and the black races. There is a physical difference between the two, which in my judgment will probably forever forbid their living together upon the footing of perfect equality, and inasmuch as it becomes a necessity that there must be a difference, I, as well as Judge Douglas, am in favor of the race to which I belong, having the superior position. . . . But I hold that notwithstanding all this, there is no reason in the world why the negro is not entitled to all the natural rights enumerated in the Declaration of Independence, the right to life, liberty, and the pursuit of happiness. I hold that he is as much entitled to these as the white man. I agree with Judge Douglas he is not my equal in many respects—certainly not in color, perhaps not in moral or intellectual endowment. But in the right to eat the bread, without leave of anybody else, which his own hand earns, *he is my equal and the equal of Judge Douglas, and the equal of every living man.*

DOUGLAS: He tells you that I will not argue the question whether slavery is right or wrong. I tell you why I will not do it. . . . I hold that the people of the slaveholding states are civilized men as well as ourselves, that they bear consciences as well as we, and that they are accountable to God and their posterity and not to us. It is for them to decide therefore the moral and religious right of the slavery question for themselves within their own limits. . . . He says that he looks forward to a time when slavery shall be abolished everywhere. I look forward to a time when each state shall be allowed to do as it pleases.

LINCOLN: I suppose that the real difference between Judge Douglas and his friends, and the Republicans, is that the Judge is not in favor of making any difference between slavery and liberty . . . and consequently every sentiment he utters discards the idea that there is any wrong in slavery. . . . That is the real issue. That is the issue that will continue in this country when these poor tongues of Judge Douglas and myself shall be silent. It is the eternal struggle between these two principles—right and wrong—throughout the world.

QUESTIONS

1. *How do Lincoln and Douglas differ on what rights black Americans are entitled to enjoy?*

2. *Why does Lincoln believe the nation cannot exist forever half slave and half free, whereas Douglas believes it can?*

3. *How does each of the speakers balance the right of each state to manage its own affairs against the right of every person to be free?*

An 1835 painting of the federal arsenal at Harpers Ferry, Virginia (now West Virginia). John Brown's raid on Harpers Ferry in October 1859 helped to bring on the Civil War.

execution further widened the breach between the sections. Brown's last letter was a brief, prophetic statement: "I, John Brown, am quite certain that the crimes of this guilty land will never be purged away but with blood."

The Rise of Southern Nationalism

With the Republicans continuing to gain strength in the North, Democrats might have been expected to put a premium on party unity as the election of 1860 approached. By this time, however, a sizable group of southerners viewed their region's prospects as more favorable outside the Union than within it. Throughout the 1850s, influential writers and political leaders kept up a drumbeat of complaints about the South's problems. The sky-high price of slaves made it impossible for many planters' sons and upwardly mobile small farmers to become planters in their own right. Many white southerners felt that the opportunity was eroding for economic independence through ownership of land and slaves—liberty as they understood it. The North, secessionists charged, reaped the benefits of the cotton trade, while southerners fell deeper and deeper into debt. To remain in the Union meant to accept "bondage" to the North. But an independent South could become the foundation of a slave empire ringing the Caribbean and embracing Cuba, other West Indian islands, Mexico, and parts of Central America.

A slave empire

More and more southerners were speaking openly of southward expansion. In 1854, Pierre Soulé of Louisiana, the American ambassador to Spain, had persuaded the ministers to Britain and France to join him in signing the Ostend Manifesto, which called on the United States to purchase or seize Cuba, where slavery was still legal, from Spain. Meanwhile, the military adventurer William Walker led a series of "filibustering" expeditions (the term derived from the Spanish word for pirate, *filibustero*) in Central America.

Born in Tennessee, Walker had headed to California to join the gold rush. Failing to strike it rich, he somehow decided to try to become the leader of a Latin American country. Walker moved to establish himself as ruler of Nicaragua in Central America, and to open that country to slavery. Nicaragua at the time was engaged in a civil war, and one faction invited Walker to assist it by bringing 300 armed men. In 1855, Walker captured the city of Granada and in the following year proclaimed himself president. The administration of Franklin Pierce recognized Walker's government, but neighboring countries sent in troops, who forced Walker to flee. His activities represented clear violations of American neutrality laws. But Walker won acclaim in the South, and when federal authorities placed him on trial in New Orleans in 1858, the jury acquitted him.

William Walker

By the late 1850s, southern leaders were bending every effort to strengthen the bonds of slavery. "Slavery is our king," declared a South Carolina politician in 1860. "Slavery is our truth, slavery is our divine right." New state laws further restricted access to freedom. One in Louisiana stated simply: "After the passage of this act, no slave shall be emancipated in this state." Some southerners called for the reopening of the African slave trade, hoping that an influx of new slaves would lower the price, thereby increasing the number of whites with a vested interest in the peculiar institution. By early 1860, seven states of the Deep South had gone on record demanding that the Democratic platform pledge to protect slavery in all the territories that had not yet been admitted to the Union as states. Virtually no northern politician could accept this position. For southern leaders to insist on it would guarantee the destruction of the Democratic Party as a national institution. But southern nationalists, known as "fire-eaters," hoped to split the party and the country and form an independent southern Confederacy.

Strengthening slavery

The "fire-eaters"

The Democratic Split

When the Democratic convention met in April 1860, Douglas's supporters commanded a majority but not the two-thirds required for a presidential nomination. Because of his fight against Kansas's Lecompton Constitution and his refusal to support congressional laws imposing slavery on all the territories, Douglas had become unacceptable to political leaders of the Deep South. They were still determined to bring Kansas into the Union as a slave state. When the convention adopted a platform reaffirming the doctrine of popular sovereignty, delegates from the seven slave states of the Lower South walked out and the gathering recessed in confusion. Six weeks later, it reconvened, replaced the bolters with Douglas supporters, and nominated him for president. In response, southern Democrats placed their own ticket in the field, headed by John C. Breckinridge of Kentucky. Breckinridge insisted that slavery must be protected in the western territories.

The Democratic Party, the last great bond of national unity, had been shattered. National conventions had traditionally been places where party managers, mindful of the need for unity in the fall campaign, reconciled their differences. But in 1860, neither northern nor southern Democrats were interested in conciliation. Southern Democrats no longer trusted their northern counterparts. Douglas's backers, for

Democratic Party shattered

their part, would not accept a platform that doomed their party to certain defeat in the North.

The Nomination of Lincoln

Meanwhile, Republicans gathered in Chicago and chose Lincoln as their standard-bearer. Although he entered the convention with fewer delegates than William H. Seward, Lincoln did not suffer from Seward's political liabilities. Former Know-Nothings, a majority of whom had by now joined Republican ranks, bitterly resented Seward's efforts as governor of New York to channel state funds to Catholic schools. Seward had a not entirely deserved reputation for radicalism as a result of his "higher law" and "irrepressible conflict" speeches, discussed earlier.

Lincoln's appeal

Lincoln's devotion to the Union appealed to moderate Republicans, and his emphasis on the moral dimension of the sectional controversy made him acceptable to Republicans from abolitionist backgrounds. Having never associated with the Know-Nothings, he could appeal to immigrant voters, and nativists preferred him to the hated Seward. Most important, coming from Illinois, Lincoln was better positioned to carry the pivotal "doubtful states" essential for Republican victory. On the third ballot, he was nominated. The party platform denied the validity of the Dred Scott decision, reaffirmed Republicans' opposition to slavery's expansion, and added economic planks designed to appeal to a broad array of northern voters—free homesteads in the West, a protective tariff, and government aid in building a transcontinental railroad.

The Election of 1860

In effect, two presidential campaigns took place in 1860. In the North, Lincoln and Douglas were the combatants. In the South, the Republicans had no presence and three candidates contested the election—Douglas, Breckinridge, and John Bell of Tennessee, the candidate of the hastily organized Constitutional Union Party. A haven for Unionist former Whigs, this new party adopted a platform consisting of a single pledge—to preserve "the Constitution as it is [that is, with slavery] and the Union as it was [without sectional discord]."

The most striking thing about the election returns was their sectional character. Lincoln carried all of the North except New Jersey, receiving 1.8 million popular votes (54 percent of the regional total and 40 percent of the national) and 180 electoral votes (a clear majority). Breckinridge captured most of the slave states, although Bell carried three Upper South states and about 40 percent of the southern vote as a whole. Douglas placed first only in Missouri, but his 1.3 million popular votes were second in number only to Lincoln's. Douglas was the only candidate with significant support in all parts of the country, a vindication, in a sense, of his long effort to transcend sectional divisions. But his failure to carry either section suggested that a traditional political career based on devotion to the Union was no longer possible.

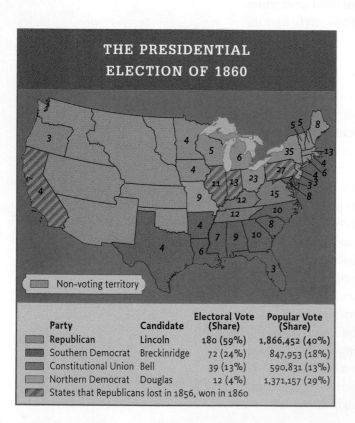

THE PRESIDENTIAL ELECTION OF 1860

Non-voting territory

Party	Candidate	Electoral Vote (Share)	Popular Vote (Share)
Republican	Lincoln	180 (59%)	1,866,452 (40%)
Southern Democrat	Breckinridge	72 (24%)	847,953 (18%)
Constitutional Union	Bell	39 (13%)	590,831 (13%)
Northern Democrat	Douglas	12 (4%)	1,371,157 (29%)
States that Republicans lost in 1856, won in 1860			

Without a single vote in ten southern states, Lincoln was elected the nation's sixteenth president. He failed to secure a majority of the national popular vote. But because of the North's superiority in population, Lincoln would still have carried the electoral college and thus been elected president even if the votes of his three opponents had all been cast for a single candidate.

THE IMPENDING CRISIS

The Secession Movement

In the eyes of many white southerners, Lincoln's victory placed their future at the mercy of a party avowedly hostile to their region's values and interests. Those advocating secession did not believe Lincoln's administration would take immediate steps against slavery in the states. But if, as seemed quite possible, the election of 1860 marked a fundamental shift in power, the beginning of a long period of Republican rule, who could say what the North's antislavery sentiment would demand in five years, or ten? Slaveowners, moreover, feared Republican efforts to extend their party into the South by appealing to non-slaveholders. Rather than accept permanent minority status in a nation governed by their opponents, Deep South political leaders boldly struck for their region's independence. At stake, they believed, was not a single election, but an entire way of life.

In the months that followed Lincoln's election, seven states stretching from South Carolina to Texas seceded from the Union. These were the states of the Cotton Kingdom, where slaves represented a larger part of the total population than in the Upper South. First to secede was South Carolina, the state with the highest percentage of slaves in its population and a long history of political radicalism. On December 20, 1860, the legislature unanimously voted to leave the Union. Its *Declaration of the Immediate Causes of Secession* placed the issue of slavery squarely at the center of the crisis. The first and longest complaint against the free states was interference with the return of fugitive slaves. The document indicated that not only northern actions but also northern public opinion regarding slavery compelled the state to leave the Union. The North had "assumed the right of deciding upon the propriety of our domestic institutions." Lincoln was a man "whose opinions and purposes are hostile to slavery." Experience had proved "that slaveholding states cannot be safe in subjection to nonslaveholding states." Secessionists equated their movement with the struggle for American independence. Proslavery ideologue George Fitzhugh, however, later claimed that southern secession was even more significant than the "commonplace affair" of 1776, since the South rebelled not merely against a particular government but against the erroneous modern idea of freedom based on "human equality" and "natural liberty."

A colorful Republican campaign banner from the 1860 campaign emphasizes the party's opposition to the expansion of slavery and promise of free homesteads for settlers in the West.

South Carolina

An Allegory of the North and the South, painted in 1858 by the Connecticut-born artist Luther Terry, offers a symbolic portrait of the United States on the eve of the Civil War. At the center is a female figure representing the nation and wearing a cap of liberty, with a horn of plenty at her feet. The figure of the South, on the left, is seated on a bale of cotton, with slaves visible in the fields behind her. The North, on the right, holds a book, *Useful Arts and Sciences*, and sits before a New England town with a church and textile mill. The sectional harmony portrayed here would soon be replaced by bloody warfare.

Lincoln's opposition to the Crittenden plan

The Secession Crisis

As the Union unraveled, President Buchanan seemed paralyzed. He denied that a state could secede, but he also insisted that the federal government had no right to use force against it. Other political leaders struggled to find a formula to resolve the crisis. Senator John J. Crittenden of Kentucky, a slave state on the border between North and South, offered the most widely supported compromise plan of the secession winter. Embodied in a series of unamendable constitutional amendments, Crittenden's proposal would have guaranteed the future of slavery in the states where it existed, and extended the Missouri Compromise line to the Pacific Ocean, dividing between slavery and free soil all territories "now held, or hereafter acquired." The seceding states rejected the compromise as too little, too late. But many in the Upper South and North saw it as a way to settle sectional differences and prevent civil war.

Crittenden's plan, however, foundered on the opposition of Abraham Lincoln. Willing to conciliate the South on issues like the return of fugitive slaves, Lincoln took an unyielding stand against the expansion of slavery. Here, he informed one Republican leader, he intended to "hold firm, as with a chain of steel." A fundamental principle of democracy, Lincoln believed, was at stake. "We have just carried an election," he wrote, "on principles fairly stated to the people. Now we are told in advance that the government shall be broken up unless we surrender to those we have beaten, before we take the offices. . . . If we surrender, it is the end of us and the end of the government." Lincoln, moreover, feared that Crittenden's reference to land "hereafter acquired" offered the South a thinly veiled invitation to demand the acquisition of Cuba, Mexico, and other territory suited to slavery.

Before Lincoln assumed office on March 4, 1861, the seven seceding states formed the Confederate States of America, adopted a constitution, and chose as their president Jefferson Davis of Mississippi. With a few alterations—the president served a single six-year term; cabinet members, as in Britain, could sit in Congress—the Confederate constitution was modeled closely on that of the United States. It departed from the federal Constitution, however, in explicitly guaranteeing slave property both in the states and in any territories the new nation acquired. The "cornerstone" of the Confederacy, announced Davis's vice president, Alexander H. Stephens of Georgia, was "the great truth that the negro is not equal to the white man, that slavery, subordination to the superior race, is his natural and normal condition."

The Confederate States of America

And the War Came

Even after rejecting the Crittenden Compromise, Lincoln did not believe war inevitable. When he became president, eight slave states of the Upper South remained in the Union. Here, slaves and slaveholders made up a considerably lower proportion of the population than in the Deep South, and large parts of the white population did not believe Lincoln's election justified dissolving the Union. Even within the Confederacy, whites had divided over secession, with considerable numbers of non-slaveholding farmers in opposition. In time, Lincoln believed, secession might collapse from within.

In his inaugural address, Lincoln tried to be conciliatory. He rejected the right of secession but denied any intention of interfering with slavery in the states. He said nothing of retaking the forts, arsenals, and customs houses the Confederacy

Lincoln's response to secession

An 1860 engraving of a mass meeting in Savannah, Georgia, shortly after Lincoln's elction as president, which called for the state to secede from the Union. The banner on the obelisk at the center reads, "Our Motto State's Rights, Equality of the States, Don't Tread on Me"—the last a slogan from the American Revolution.

A Richmond, Virginia, cartoonist in April 1861 depicts Lincoln as a cat seeking to catch the southern states as mice fleeing the Union, which lies dead on the left.

Fort Sumter

had seized, although he did promise to "hold" remaining federal property in the seceding states. But Lincoln also issued a veiled warning: "In your hands, my dissatisfied fellow countrymen, and not in mine, is the momentous issue of civil war."

In his first month as president, Lincoln walked a tightrope. He avoided any action that might drive more states from the Union, encouraged southern Unionists to assert themselves within the Confederacy, and sought to quiet a growing clamor in the North for forceful action against secession. Knowing that the risk of war existed, Lincoln strove to ensure that if hostilities did break out, the South, not the Union, would fire the first shot. And that is precisely what happened on April 12, 1861, at **Fort Sumter**, an enclave of Union control in the harbor of Charleston, South Carolina.

A few days earlier, Lincoln had notified South Carolina's governor that he intended to replenish the garrison's dwindling food supplies. Viewing Fort Sumter's presence as an affront to southern nationhood, and perhaps hoping to force the wavering Upper South to join the Confederacy, Jefferson Davis ordered batteries to fire on the fort. On April 14, its commander surrendered. The following day, Lincoln proclaimed that an insurrection existed in the South and called for 75,000 troops to suppress it. Civil war had begun. Within weeks, Virginia, North Carolina, Tennessee, and Arkansas joined the Confederacy. "Both sides deprecated war," Lincoln later said, "but one of them would *make* war rather than let the nation survive; and the other would *accept* war rather than let it perish. And the war came."

In 1842, Henry Wadsworth Longfellow published *Poems on Slavery*, a collection that included a work entitled simply "The Warning." In it, Longfellow compared the American slave to the mighty biblical figure of Samson, who after being blinded and chained, managed to destroy the temple of his tormentors:

> There is a poor, blind Samson in this land,
> Shorn of his strength, and bound in bonds of steel,
> Who may, in some grim revel, raise his hand,
> And shake the pillars of this Commonweal,
> Till the vast Temple of our liberties
> A shapeless mass of wreck and rubbish lies.

In 1861, Longfellow's warning came to pass. The Union created by the founders lay in ruins. The struggle to rebuild it would bring about a new birth of American freedom.

Inauguration of Mr. Lincoln, a photograph taken on March 4, 1861. The unfinished dome of the Capitol building symbolizes the precarious state of the Union at the time Lincoln assumed office.

SUGGESTED READING

BOOKS

- Anbinder, Tyler. *Nativism and Slavery: The Northern Know-Nothings and the Politics of the 1850s* (1992). A detailed study of the relationship between nativism and antislavery politics in the North.

- Cronon, William. *Nature's Metropolis: Chicago and the Great West* (1992). An influential account of the rise of Chicago and the city's relationship to its agricultural hinterland.

- Current, Richard N. *Lincoln and the First Shot* (1963). Examines the decisions and strategy of both Lincoln and Jefferson Davis that produced the firing on Fort Sumter that began the Civil War.

- Dean, Adam W. *An Agrarian Republic: Farming, Antislavery Politics, and Nature Parks in the Civil War Era* (2015). Challenges the idea of the coming of the Civil War as a clash between an agricultural South and an industrialized North by stressing the agrarian origins of political antislavery.

- DeLay, Brian. *War of a Thousand Deserts: Indian Raids and the U.S.-Mexican War* (2008). A history of the Mexican war that emphasizes its impact on Native Americans.

- Earle, Jonathan H. *Jacksonian Antislavery and the Politics of Free Soil, 1824–1854* (2004). Emphasizes the role of northern Jacksonians in antislavery politics.

- Foner, Eric. *Free Soil, Free Labor, Free Men: The Ideology of the Republican Party before the Civil War* (1970). A discussion of the basic ideas that united Republicans in the 1850s, especially their "free labor ideology."

- Haas, Lisbeth. *Conquests and Historical Identities in California, 1769–1936* (1995). Contains a detailed description of how California's acquisition by the United States affected the state's diverse population groups.

- Levine, Bruce. *Half Slave and Half Free: The Roots of the Civil War* (1992). A survey of the coming of the Civil War, stressing irreconcilable differences between North and South.

- Montejano, David. *Anglos and Mexicans in the Making of Texas* (1987). A history of cultural relations among the varied populations of Texas.

- Potter, David M. *The Impending Crisis, 1848–1861* (1976). Still the standard account of the nation's history in the years before the Civil War.

- Sinha, Manisha. *The Counterrevolution of Slavery: Politics and Ideology in Antebellum South Carolina* (2002). A detailed study of how a vigorous defense of slavery developed in South Carolina, which justified the decision for secession.

- Stampp, Kenneth. *And the War Came: The North and the Secession Crisis, 1860–61* (1950). An examination of northern actions and attitudes during the secession crisis.

- Stephanson, Anders. *Manifest Destiny: American Expansionism and the Empire of Right* (1995). Considers how the idea of an American mission to spread freedom and democracy has affected American foreign policy throughout the country's history.

WEBSITES

- Getting the Message Out! National Campaign Materials, 1840–1860: http://lincoln.lib.niu.edu/message/

- Gold Rush!: www.museumca.org/goldrush/

- The Mexican-American War and the Media, 1845–1858: www.history.vt.edu/MxAmWar/INDEX.HTM

- The Oregon Trail: http://oregontrail101.com

- Record of Fugitives: https://exhibitions.cul.columbia.edu/exhibits/show/fugitives/record_fugitives

- Uncle Tom's Cabin and American Culture: http://jefferson.village.virginia.edu/utc/

CHAPTER REVIEW AND ONLINE RESOURCES

REVIEW QUESTIONS

1. Explain the justifications for the doctrine of manifest destiny, including material and idealistic motivations.

2. Why did many Americans criticize the Mexican War? How did they see expansion as a threat to American liberties?

3. How did the concept of "race" develop by the mid-nineteenth century, and how did it enter into the manifest destiny debate?

4. How did western expansion affect the sectional tensions between the North and South?

5. How did the market revolution contribute to the rise of the Republican Party? How did those economic and political factors serve to unite groups in the Northeast and in the Northwest, and why was that unity significant?

6. What was the "Slave Power," and why did many northerners feel threatened by it?

7. Based on the Lincoln-Douglas debates, how did the two differ on the expansion of slavery, equal rights, and the role of the national government? Use examples of their words to illustrate your points.

8. Why did Stephen Douglas, among others, believe that "popular sovereignty" could resolve sectional divisions of the 1850s? Why did the idea not work out?

9. Explain how sectional voting patterns in the 1860 presidential election allowed southern "fire-eaters" to justify secession.

10. What do the California gold rush and the opening of Japan reveal about the United States' involvement in a global economic system?

KEY TERMS

Tejanos (p. 461)

Antonio López de Santa Anna (p. 461)

the Texas Revolt (p. 462)

Mexican War (p. 465)

Gadsden Purchase (p. 466)

gold rush (p. 469)

Commodore Matthew Perry (p. 472)

Wilmot Proviso (p. 473)

Free Soil Party (p. 473)

Compromise of 1850 (p. 476)

Fugitive Slave Act (p. 476)

popular sovereignty (p. 478)

Kansas-Nebraska Act (p. 479)

Know-Nothing Party (p. 482)

the Slave Power (p. 483)

"Bleeding Kansas" (p. 484)

Dred Scott v. Sandford (p. 485)

Lincoln-Douglas debates (p. 488)

Harpers Ferry, Virginia (p. 489)

Fort Sumter (p. 498)

Go to 🐰 INQUIZITIVE

To see what you know—and learn what you've missed—with personalized feedback along the way.

Visit the *Give Me Liberty!* **Student Site** for primary source documents and images, interactive maps, author videos featuring Eric Foner, and more.

1861   Civil War begins at Fort Sumter

        First Battle of Bull Run

1862   Forts Henry and Donelson captured

        Monitor v. *Merrimac* sea battle

        Battle of Shiloh

        Confederacy institutes the draft

        Homestead Act

        Seven Days' Campaign

        Second Battle of Bull Run

        Union Pacific and Central Pacific chartered

        Morrill Act of 1862

        Battle at Antietam

        Battle at Fredericksburg

1863   Emancipation Proclamation

        Siege of Vicksburg

        Battle at Gettysburg

        New York draft riots

        Lincoln introduces his Ten-Percent Plan

1864   General Grant begins a war of attrition

        Wade-Davis Bill

        General Sherman marches to the sea

1865   Thirteenth Amendment

        Union capture of Richmond

        General Lee surrenders to General Grant at Appomattox Courthouse

        Lincoln assassinated

1866   *Ex parte Milligan* ruling

leadership, the ability to mobilize economic resources, and a society's willingness to keep up the fight despite setbacks are as crucial to the outcome as success or failure on individual battlefields.

The Two Combatants

Almost any comparison between Union and Confederacy seemed to favor the Union. The population of the North and the loyal border slave states numbered 22 million in 1860, while only 9 million persons lived in the Confederacy, 3.5 million of them slaves. In manufacturing, railroad mileage, and financial resources, the Union far outstripped its opponent. On the other hand, the Union confronted by far the greater task. To restore the shattered nation, it had to invade and conquer an area larger than western Europe. Confederate soldiers were highly motivated fighters defending their homes and families. Like Washington's forces during the American Revolution, southern armies could lose most of the battles and still win the war if their opponent tired of the struggle. "No people," Confederate general P. G. T. Beauregard later claimed, "ever warred for independence with more relative advantages than the Confederacy."

On both sides, the outbreak of war stirred powerful feelings of patriotism. Recruits rushed to enlist, expecting a short, glorious war. Later, as enthusiasm waned, both sides resorted to a draft. The Confederacy in the spring of 1862 passed the first draft law in American history, and the North soon followed. By 1865, more than 2 million men had served in the Union army and 900,000 in the Confederate army. Each was a cross section of its society: the North's was composed largely of farm boys, shopkeepers, artisans, and urban workers, while the South's consisted mostly of non-slaveholding small farmers, with slaveowners dominating the officer corps.

Few recruits had any military experience. Ideas about war were highly romantic, based on novels, magazine articles, and lithographs of soldiers covering themselves with glory. One private wrote home in 1862 that his notion of combat had come from the pictures of battles he had seen: "they would all be in a line, all standing in a nice level field fighting, a number of ladies taking care of the wounded, etc. But it isn't so." Nor were the recruits ready for military regimentation. "It comes rather hard at first to be deprived of liberty," wrote an Illinois soldier. Initially, the constant round of drilling, ditch digging, and other chores was only occasionally interrupted by fierce bursts of fighting on the battlefield. According to one estimate, during the first two years of the war the main Union force, the Army of the Potomac, spent only thirty days in actual combat.

The Technology of War

Neither the soldiers nor their officers were prepared for the way technology had transformed warfare. The Civil War was the first major conflict in which the railroad transported troops and supplies and the first to see railroad junctions such as Atlanta and Petersburg become major military objectives. The famous sea battle between the Union vessel *Monitor* and the Confederate *Merrimac* in 1862 was the first demonstration of the superiority of ironclads over wooden ships, revolutionizing naval warfare. The war saw the use of the telegraph for military

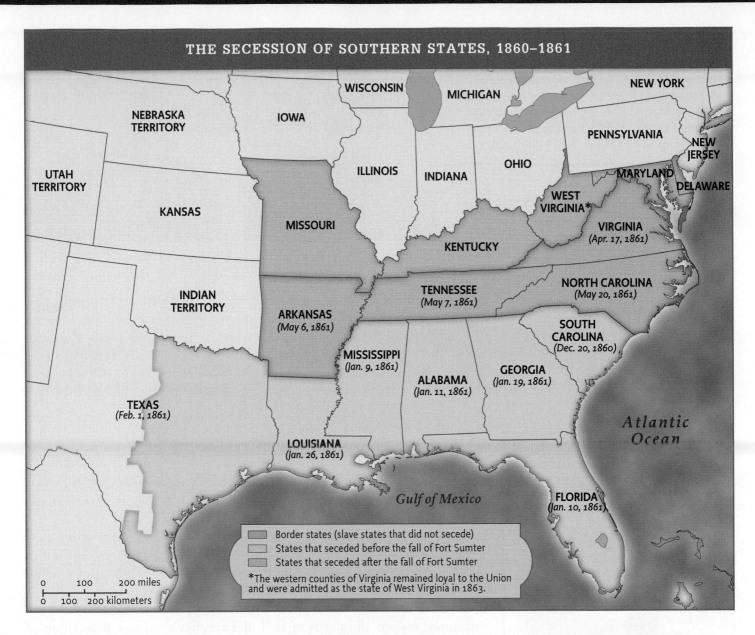

THE SECESSION OF SOUTHERN STATES, 1860–1861

WISCONSIN

MICHIGAN

NEW YORK

NEBRASKA TERRITORY

IOWA

PENNSYLVANIA

NEW JERSEY

UTAH TERRITORY

ILLINOIS

INDIANA

OHIO

MARYLAND

DELAWARE

KANSAS

MISSOURI

WEST VIRGINIA*

VIRGINIA
(Apr. 17, 1861)

KENTUCKY

INDIAN TERRITORY

TENNESSEE
(May 7, 1861)

NORTH CAROLINA
(May 20, 1861)

ARKANSAS
(May 6, 1861)

SOUTH CAROLINA
(Dec. 20, 1860)

MISSISSIPPI
(Jan. 9, 1861)

ALABAMA
(Jan. 11, 1861)

GEORGIA
(Jan. 19, 1861)

TEXAS
(Feb. 1, 1861)

Atlantic Ocean

LOUISIANA
(Jan. 26, 1861)

Gulf of Mexico

FLORIDA
(Jan. 10, 1861)

Border states (slave states that did not secede)
States that seceded before the fall of Fort Sumter
States that seceded after the fall of Fort Sumter

*The western counties of Virginia remained loyal to the Union and were admitted as the state of West Virginia in 1863.

0   100   200 miles
0   100   200 kilometers

communication, the introduction of observation balloons to view enemy lines, and even primitive hand grenades and submarines.

Perhaps most important, a revolution in arms manufacturing had replaced the traditional musket, accurate at only a short range, with the more modern rifle, deadly at 600 yards or more because of its grooved (or "rifled") barrel. This development changed the nature of combat, emphasizing the importance of heavy fortifications and elaborate trenches and giving those on the defensive—usually southern armies—a significant advantage over attacking forces. "My men," said Confederate general Thomas "Stonewall" Jackson, "sometimes fail to drive the enemy from his position, but to hold one, never." The war of rifle and trench produced the appalling casualty statistics of Civil War battles. The most recent estimate of those who perished in the war—around 750,000 men—represents the equivalent, in terms of today's population, of more than 7 million. These figures

By the time secession ran its course, eleven slave states had left the Union.

War of rifle and trench

Sergeant James W. Travis, Thirty-eighth Illinois Infantry, Union army, and Private Edwin Francis Jemison, Second Louisiana Regiment, Confederate army, two of the nearly 3 million Americans who fought in the Civil War. Before going off to war, many soldiers sat for photographs like these, reproduced on small cards called *cartes de visite*, which they distributed to friends and loved ones. Jemison was killed in the Battle of Malvern Hill in July 1862.

In nearly every resource for warfare, the Union enjoyed a distinct advantage. But this did not make Union victory inevitable; as during the War of Independence, the stronger side sometimes loses.

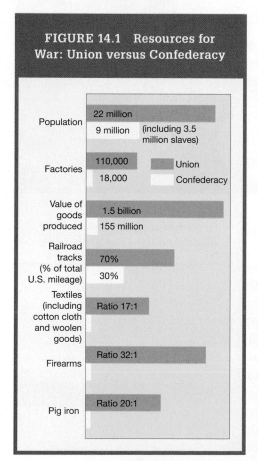

FIGURE 14.1   Resources for War: Union versus Confederacy

	Union	Confederacy
Population	22 million	9 million (including 3.5 million slaves)
Factories	110,000	18,000
Value of goods produced	1.5 billion	155 million
Railroad tracks (% of total U.S. mileage)	70%	30%
Textiles (including cotton cloth and woolen goods)	Ratio 17:1	
Firearms	Ratio 32:1	
Pig iron	Ratio 20:1	

do not include the thousands of civilians who became victims of battles or who perished in disease-ridden camps for runaway slaves or in conflicts between Unionist and Confederate families that raged in parts of the South. The death toll in the Civil War exceeds the total number of Americans who died in all the nation's other wars, from the Revolution to the wars in Iraq and Afghanistan.

Nor was either side ready for other aspects of modern warfare. Medical care remained primitive. "I believe the doctors kill more than they cure," wrote an Alabama private in 1862. Diseases like measles, dysentery, malaria, and typhus swept through army camps, killing more men than did combat. The Civil War was the first war in which large numbers of Americans were captured by the enemy and held in dire conditions in military prisons. Some 50,000 men died in these prisons, victims of starvation and disease, including 13,000 Union soldiers at Andersonville, Georgia.

Everywhere in the world, war was becoming more destructive. The scale of Civil War bloodshed was unique in American history, but not in the nineteenth-century world. The Taiping Rebellion in China (1850–1864) resulted in 23 million deaths. The War of the Triple Alliance in South America (1864–1870), which pitted Argentina, Brazil, and Uruguay against Paraguay, caused the death of half of Paraguay's prewar population of around 525,000.

The Public and the War

Another modern feature of the Civil War was that both sides were assisted by a vast propaganda effort to mobilize public opinion. In the Union, an outpouring of lithographs, souvenirs, sheet music, and pamphlets issued by patriotic organizations and the War Department reaffirmed northern values, tarred the Democratic Party with the brush of treason, and accused the South of numerous crimes against Union soldiers and loyal civilians. Comparable items appeared in the Confederacy.

At the same time, the war's brutal realities were brought home with unprecedented immediacy to the public at large. War correspondents accompanied the

War Spirit at Home, an 1866 painting by the New Jersey artist Lilly M. Spencer, depicts a family reading the news of the Union capture of Vicksburg in 1863. The household is now composed of women and children; the husband may be off in the army. While the children play as soldiers, the cross in the folds of the newspaper suggests a less celebratory reflection on the conflict. Newspapers brought news of the war into American homes.

armies, and newspapers reported the results of battles on the following day and quickly published long lists of casualties. The infant art of photography carried images of war into millions of American living rooms. Beginning in 1862, when photographers entered the battlefield to take shocking pictures of the dead at Antietam, the camera, in the words of one journalist, "brought the bodies and laid them in our door-yards." Mathew Brady, who organized a corps of photographers to cover the war, found the conflict a passport to fame and wealth. For photography itself, it was a turning point in its growth as an art and a business enterprise.

Reporting on the war

Mobilizing Resources

The outbreak of the war found both sides unprepared. In 1861, there was no national railroad gauge (the distance separating the two rails), so trains built for one line could not run on another. There were no national banking system, no tax system capable of raising the enormous funds needed to finance the war, and not even accurate maps of the southern states. Soon after the firing on Fort Sumter, Lincoln proclaimed a naval blockade of the South. But the navy, charged with patrolling the 3,500-mile coastline, consisted of only ninety vessels, fewer than half of them steam-powered. Not until late in the war did the blockade become effective.

Logistical problems

Then there was the problem of purchasing and distributing the food, weapons, and other supplies required by the soldiers. The Union army eventually became the best-fed and best-supplied military force in history. By the war's third year, on the other hand, southern armies were suffering from acute shortages of food, uniforms, and shoes. Yet the chief of the Confederacy's Ordnance Bureau, Josiah Gorgas

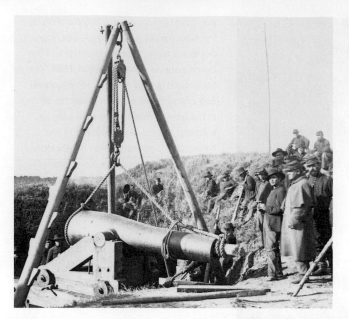

An eight-inch cannon, one of the weapons forged in the industrial revolution and deployed in the Civil War.

A surgeon's kit used in the Civil War, containing amputation instruments, knives, and tourniquets. With medical knowledge and practices primitive at best, far more men died from wounds, infections, and disease than in battle.

(a transplanted northerner), proved brilliantly resourceful in arming southern troops. Under his direction, the Confederate government imported weapons from abroad and established arsenals of its own to turn out rifles, artillery, and ammunition.

Military Strategies

Each side tried to find ways to maximize its advantages. Essentially, the Confederacy adopted a defensive strategy, with occasional thrusts into the North. General Robert E. Lee, the leading southern commander, was a brilliant battlefield tactician who felt confident of his ability to fend off attacks by larger Union forces. He hoped that a series of defeats would weaken the North's resolve and lead it eventually to abandon the conflict and recognize southern independence.

Lincoln's early generals found it impossible to bring the Union's advantages in manpower and technology to bear on the battlefield. In April 1861, the regular army numbered little more than 15,000 men, most of whom were stationed west of the Mississippi River. Its officers had been trained to lead small, professional forces into battle, not the crowds of untrained men who assembled in 1861. The North also suffered from narrowness of military vision. Its generals initially concentrated on occupying southern territory and attempting to capture Richmond, the Confederate capital. They attacked sporadically and withdrew after a battle, thus sacrificing the North's manpower superiority and allowing the South to concentrate its smaller forces when an engagement impended.

Well before his generals, Lincoln realized that simply capturing and occupying territory would not win the war, and that defeating the South's armies, not capturing its capital, had to be the North's battlefield objective. And when he came to adopt the policy of emancipation, Lincoln acknowledged that to win the war, the Union must make the institution that lay at the economic and social foundation of southern life a military target.

The War Begins

In the East, most of the war's fighting took place in a narrow corridor between Washington and Richmond—a distance of only 100 miles—as a succession of Union generals led the Army of the Potomac (as the main northern force in the East was called) toward the Confederate capital, only to be turned back by southern forces. The first significant engagement, the **first Battle of Bull Run**, took place in northern Virginia on July 21, 1861. It ended with the chaotic retreat of the Union soldiers, along with the sightseers and politicians who had come to watch the battle. Almost 800 men died at Bull Run, a toll eclipsed many times in the years to come, but more Americans than had been killed in any previous battle in the nation's history. The encounter disabused both sides of the idea that the war would be a brief lark.

In the wake of Bull Run, George B. McClellan, an army engineer who had recently won a minor engagement with Confederate troops in western Virginia, assumed command of the Union's Army of the Potomac. A brilliant organizer, McClellan succeeded in welding his men into a superb fighting force. He seemed reluctant, however, to commit them to battle, since he tended to overestimate the size of enemy forces. And as a Democrat, he hoped that compromise might end the war without large-scale loss of life or a weakening of slavery. Months of military inactivity followed.

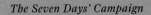

George B. McClellan

The War in the East, 1862

Not until the spring of 1862, after a growing clamor for action by Republican newspapers, members of Congress, and an increasingly impatient Lincoln, did McClellan lead his army of more than 100,000 men into Virginia. Here they confronted the smaller Army of Northern Virginia under the command of the Confederate general Joseph E. Johnston, and after he was wounded, Robert E. Lee. A brilliant battlefield tactician, Lee had been offered a command in the Union army but chose to fight for the Confederacy because of his devotion to Virginia. In the Seven Days' Campaign, a series of engagements in June 1862 on the peninsula south of Richmond, Lee blunted McClellan's attacks and forced him to withdraw to the vicinity of Washington, D.C. In August 1862, Lee again emerged victorious at the **second Battle of Bull Run** against Union forces under the command of General John Pope.

The Seven Days' Campaign

Successful on the defensive, Lee now launched an invasion of the North. He hoped to bring the border slave states into the Confederacy, persuade Britain and France to recognize southern independence, influence the North's fall elections, and perhaps capture Washington, D.C. At the **Battle of Antietam**, in Maryland, McClellan and the Army of the Potomac repelled Lee's advance. In a single day of fighting, nearly 4,000 men were killed and 18,000 wounded (2,000 of whom later died of their injuries). The dead, one survivor recalled, lay three deep in the field, mowed down "like grass before the scythe." More Americans died on September 17, 1862, when the Battle

Departure of the 7th Regiment, a lithograph from 1861 illustrating the departure of a unit of the New York State militia for service in the Civil War. A contemporary writer captured the exuberant spirit of the early days of the war: "New York was certainly raving mad with excitement. The ladies laughed, smiled, sighed, sobbed, and wept. The men cheered and shouted as never men cheered and shouted before."

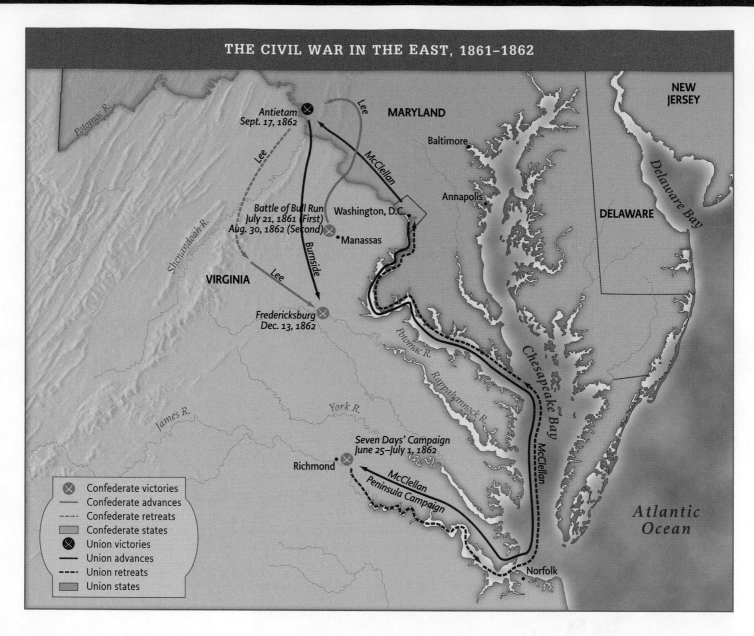

THE CIVIL WAR IN THE EAST, 1861–1862

Antietam
Sept. 17, 1862

MARYLAND

NEW JERSEY

Potomac R.

Lee

Lee

McClellan

Baltimore

Annapolis

DELAWARE

Delaware Bay

Battle of Bull Run
July 21, 1861 (First)
Aug. 30, 1862 (Second)

Washington, D.C.

Shenandoah R.

Manassas

Burnside

VIRGINIA

Lee

Fredericksburg
Dec. 13, 1862

Potomac R.

Rappahannock R.

Chesapeake Bay

McClellan

James R.

York R.

Seven Days' Campaign
June 25–July 1, 1862

Richmond

McClellan
Peninsula Campaign

McClellan

Atlantic Ocean

Norfolk

Confederate victories
Confederate advances
Confederate retreats
Confederate states
Union victories
Union advances
Union retreats
Union states

During the first two years of the war, most of the fighting took place in Virginia and Maryland.

Fredericksburg

of Antietam was fought, than on any other day in the nation's history, including Pearl Harbor and D-Day in World War II and the terrorist attacks of September 11, 2001.

Since Lee was forced to retreat, the North could claim Antietam as a victory. It was to be the Union's last success in the East for some time. In December 1862, the Union suffered one of its most disastrous defeats of the war when General Ambrose E. Burnside, who had replaced McClellan as the head of the Army of the Potomac, assaulted Lee's army, which was entrenched on heights near Fredericksburg, Virginia. "It was not a fight," wrote one Union soldier to his mother, "it was a massacre."

The War in the West

While the Union accomplished little in the East in the first two years of the war, events in the West followed a different course. Here, the architect of early success was Ulysses S. Grant. A West Point graduate who had resigned from the army in

1854 in part because of allegations of excessive drinking, Grant had been notably unsuccessful in civilian life. When the war broke out, he was working as a clerk in his brother's leather store in Galena, Illinois. But after being commissioned as a colonel in an Illinois regiment, Grant quickly displayed the daring, the logical mind, and the grasp of strategy he would demonstrate throughout the war.

In February 1862, Grant won the Union's first significant victory when he captured Forts Henry and Donelson in Tennessee. In April, naval forces under Admiral David G. Farragut steamed into New Orleans, giving the Union control of the South's largest city and the rich sugar plantation parishes to its south and west. At the same time, Grant withstood a surprise Confederate attack at Shiloh, Tennessee. But Union momentum in the West then stalled.

The Battle of Antietam, a painting of a Union advance by Captain James Hope of the Second Vermont Volunteers. More than 4,000 men died on September 17, 1862, when the Battle of Antietam was fought.

THE COMING OF EMANCIPATION

Slavery and the War

War, it has been said, is the midwife of revolution. And the Civil War produced far-reaching changes in American life. The most dramatic of these was the destruction of slavery, the central institution of southern society. Between 1831, when the British abolished slavery in their empire, and 1888, when emancipation came to Brazil, some 6 million slaves gained their freedom in the Western Hemisphere. Of these, nearly 4 million, two-thirds of the total, lived in the southern United States. In numbers, scale, and the economic power of the institution of slavery, American emancipation dwarfed that of any other country (although far

Emancipation in the Western Hemisphere

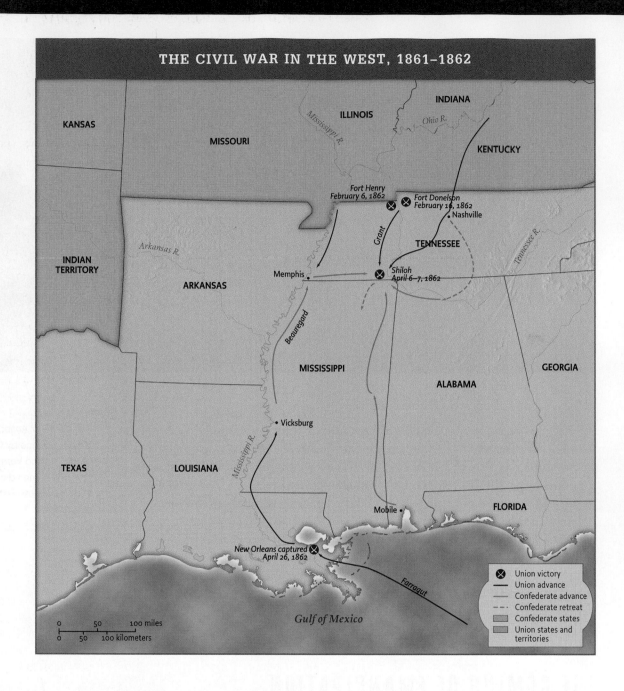

THE CIVIL WAR IN THE WEST, 1861–1862

Fort Henry
February 6, 1862

Fort Donelson
February 16, 1862

• Nashville

Grant

TENNESSEE

Memphis •

Shiloh
April 6–7, 1862

Beauregard

• Vicksburg

Mobile •

New Orleans captured
April 26, 1862

Farragut

Gulf of Mexico

KANSAS

MISSOURI

ILLINOIS

INDIANA

Mississippi R.

Ohio R.

KENTUCKY

Arkansas R.

Tennessee R.

INDIAN
TERRITORY

ARKANSAS

MISSISSIPPI

ALABAMA

GEORGIA

Mississippi R.

TEXAS

LOUISIANA

FLORIDA

	Union victory
	Union advance
	Confederate advance
	Confederate retreat
	Confederate states
	Union states and territories

0   50   100 miles
0   50   100 kilometers

Most of the Union's victories in the first two years of the war occurred in the West, especially at Shiloh and New Orleans.

more people were liberated in 1861 when Czar Alexander II abolished serfdom in the Russian empire).

At the outset of the war, Lincoln invoked time-honored northern values to mobilize public support. In a message to Congress, he identified the Union cause with the fate of democracy for the "whole family of man." He identified the differences between North and South in terms of the familiar free labor ideology: "This is essentially a people's struggle. On the side of the Union, it is a struggle for maintaining in the world, that form and substance of government, whose leading object is to elevate the condition of men . . . to afford all, an unfettered start, and a fair chance, in the race of life."

But while appealing to free labor values, Lincoln initially insisted that slavery was irrelevant to the conflict. In the war's first year, his paramount concerns were to keep the border slave states—Delaware, Maryland, Kentucky, and Missouri—in the Union and to build the broadest base of support in the North for the war effort. Action against slavery, he feared, would drive the border, with its white population of 2.6 million and nearly 500,000 slaves, into the Confederacy and alienate conservative northerners.

Early Union policy on slavery

The Unraveling of Slavery

Thus, in the early days of the war, a nearly unanimous Congress adopted a resolution proposed by Senator John J. Crittenden of Kentucky, which affirmed that the Union had no intention of interfering with slavery. Northern military commanders even returned fugitive slaves to their owners, a policy that raised an outcry in antislavery circles. Yet as the Confederacy set slaves to work as military laborers and blacks began to escape to Union lines, the policy of ignoring slavery unraveled. By the end of 1861, the military had adopted the plan, begun in Virginia by General Benjamin F. Butler, of treating escaped blacks as contraband of war—that is, property of military value subject to confiscation. Butler's order added a word to the war's vocabulary. Escaping slaves became known as "**the contrabands**." They were housed by the army in "contraband camps" and educated in new "contraband schools."

The Crittenden Resolution

Meanwhile, slaves took actions that helped propel a reluctant white America down the road to emancipation. Well before Lincoln made emancipation a war aim, blacks, in the North and the South, were calling the conflict the "freedom war." In 1861 and 1862, as the federal army occupied Confederate territory, slaves by the thousands headed for Union lines. Unlike fugitives before the war, these runaways included large numbers of women and children, as entire families abandoned the plantations. Not a few passed along military intelligence and detailed knowledge of the South's terrain. "The most valuable and reliable information of the enemy's movements in our vicinity that we have been able to get," noted the Union general Daniel E. Sickles, "derived from Negroes who came into our lines." In southern Louisiana, the arrival of the Union army in 1862 led slaves to sack plantation houses and refuse to work unless wages were paid. Slavery there, wrote a northern reporter, "is forever destroyed and worthless, no matter what Mr. Lincoln or anyone else may say on the subject."

A Civil War photograph depicts African-American men, women, and children who have escaped to Union lines in a mule-drawn covered wagon. The actions of fugitives like these helped propel the nation down the road to emancipation.

Steps toward Emancipation

At first, blacks' determination to seize the opportunity presented by the war proved a burden to the army and an embarrassment to the administration. But the failure of traditional strategies to produce victory strengthened the hand of antislavery northerners. Since slavery stood at the foundation of the southern economy, they insisted, emancipation was necessary to weaken the South's ability to sustain the war.

The most uncompromising opponents of slavery before the war, abolitionists and **Radical Republicans**, quickly concluded that the institution must become a target of the Union war effort. "It is plain," declared Thaddeus Stevens, a Radical Republican congressman from Pennsylvania, "that nothing approaching the present policy will subdue the rebels." Outside of Congress, few pressed the case for emancipation more eloquently than Frederick Douglass. From the outset, he insisted that it was futile to "separate the freedom of the slave from the victory of the government." "Fire must be met with water," Douglass declared, "darkness with light, and war for the destruction of liberty must be met with war for the destruction of slavery."

These appeals won increasing support in a Congress frustrated by lack of military success. In March 1862, Congress prohibited the army from returning fugitive slaves. Then came abolition in the District of Columbia (with monetary compensation for slaveholders) and the territories, followed in July by the Second Confiscation Act, which liberated slaves of disloyal owners in Union-occupied territory, as well as slaves who escaped to Union lines.

Throughout these months, Lincoln struggled to retain control of the emancipation issue. In August 1861, John C. Frémont, commanding Union forces in Missouri, a state racked by a bitter guerrilla war between pro-northern and pro-southern bands, decreed the freedom of its slaves. Fearful of the order's impact on the border states, Lincoln swiftly rescinded it. In November, the president proposed that the border states embark on a program of gradual emancipation with the federal government paying owners for their loss of property. He also revived the idea of colonization. In August 1862, Lincoln met at the White House with a delegation of black leaders and urged them to promote emigration from the United States. "You and we are different races," he declared. "It is better for us both to be separated." As late as December 1862, the president signed an agreement with a shady entrepreneur to settle former slaves on an island off the coast of Haiti.

Steps toward emancipation

The Second Confiscation Act

Abe Lincoln's Last Card, an engraving from the British magazine *Punch*, October 18, 1862, portrays the Preliminary Emancipation Proclamation as the last move of a desperate gambler

Lincoln's Decision

During the summer of 1862, Lincoln concluded that emancipation had become a political and military necessity. Many factors contributed to his decision—lack of military success, hope that emancipated slaves might help meet the army's growing manpower needs, changing northern public opinion, and the calculation that making slavery a target of the war effort would counteract sentiment in Britain for recognition of the Confederacy. But on the

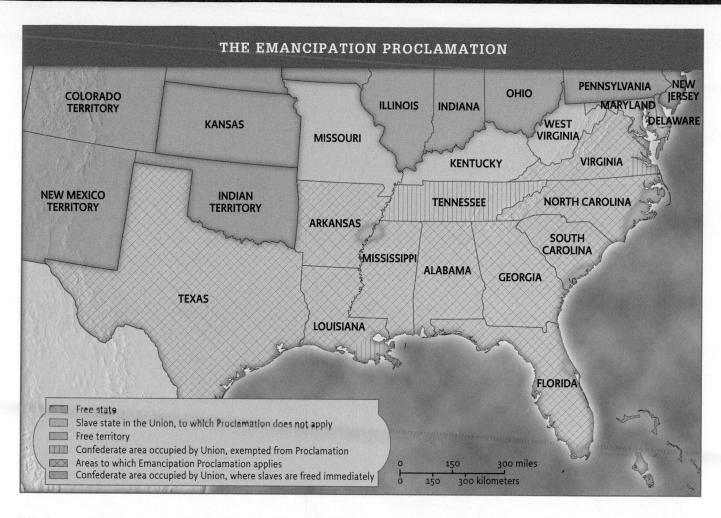

THE EMANCIPATION PROCLAMATION

Legend:
- Free state
- Slave state in the Union, to which Proclamation does not apply
- Free territory
- Confederate area occupied by Union, exempted from Proclamation
- Areas to which Emancipation Proclamation applies
- Confederate area occupied by Union, where slaves are freed immediately

0   150   300 miles
0   150   300 kilometers

With the exception of a few areas, the Emancipation Proclamation applied only to slaves in parts of the Confederacy not under Union control on January 1, 1863. Lincoln did not "free the slaves" with a stroke of his pen, but the Proclamation did change the nature of the Civil War.

advice of Secretary of State William H. Seward, Lincoln delayed his announcement until after a Union victory, lest it seem an act of desperation. On September 22, 1862, five days after McClellan's army forced Lee to retreat at Antietam, Lincoln issued the Preliminary Emancipation Proclamation. It warned that unless the South laid down its arms by the end of 1862, he would decree abolition.

The Preliminary Emancipation Proclamation

The initial northern reaction was not encouraging. In the fall elections of 1862, Democrats made opposition to emancipation the centerpiece of their campaign, warning that the North would be "Africanized"—inundated by freed slaves who would compete for jobs and seek to marry white women. The Republicans suffered sharp reverses. They lost control of the legislatures of Indiana and Illinois and the governorship of New York, and saw their majorities dangerously reduced in other states. In his annual message to Congress, early in December, Lincoln tried to calm northerners' racial fears, reviving the ideas of gradual emancipation and colonization. He concluded, however, on a higher note: "Fellow citizens, we cannot

Political backlash

"The fiery trial"

escape history. . . . The fiery trial through which we pass, will light us down, in honor or dishonor, to the latest generation. . . . In giving freedom to the slave, we assure freedom to the free—honorable alike in what we give, and what we preserve."

The Emancipation Proclamation

On January 1, 1863, after greeting visitors at the annual White House New Year's reception, Lincoln retired to his study to sign the **Emancipation Proclamation**. The document did not liberate all the slaves—indeed, on the day it was issued, it applied to very few. Because its legality derived from the president's authority as military commander-in-chief to combat the South's rebellion, the Proclamation exempted areas firmly under Union control (where the war, in effect, had already ended). Thus, it did not apply to the loyal border slave states that had never seceded or to areas of the Confederacy occupied by Union soldiers, such as Tennessee and parts of Virginia and Louisiana. But the vast majority of the South's slaves—more than 3 million men, women, and children—it declared "henceforward shall be free." Since most of these slaves were still behind Confederate lines, however, their liberation would have to await Union victories.

The reach of the Proclamation

Despite its limitations, the Proclamation set off scenes of jubilation among free blacks and abolitionists in the North and "contrabands" and slaves in the South. "Sound the loud timbrel o'er Egypt's dark sea," intoned a black preacher at a celebration in Boston. "Jehovah hath triumphed, his people are free." By making the Union army an agent of emancipation and wedding the goals of Union and abolition, the Proclamation sounded the eventual death knell of slavery.

Not only did the Emancipation Proclamation alter the nature of the Civil War and the course of American history, but it also represented a turning point in

Freed Negroes Celebrating President Lincoln's Decree of Emancipation, a fanciful engraving from the French periodical *Le Monde Illustré*, March 21, 1863.

Lincoln's own thinking. It contained no reference to compensation to slaveholders or to colonization of the freed people. For the first time, it committed the government to enlisting black soldiers in the Union army. Lincoln now became in his own mind the Great Emancipator—that is, he assumed the role that history had thrust upon him, and he tried to live up to it. He would later refuse suggestions that he rescind or modify the Proclamation in the interest of peace. Were he to do so, he told one visitor, "I should be damned in time and eternity."

The Civil War, begun to preserve the prewar Union, now portended a far-reaching transformation in southern life and a redefinition of American freedom. Decoupling emancipation from colonization meant that the freed slaves would become part of American life. A new system of labor, politics, and race relations would have to replace the shattered institution of slavery. "Up to now," wrote the socialist thinker Karl Marx, observing events from London, "we have witnessed only the first act of the Civil War—the constitutional waging of war. The second act, the revolutionary waging of war, is at hand." The evolution of Lincoln's emancipation policy displayed the hallmarks of his wartime leadership—his capacity for growth and his ability to develop broad public support for his administration.

The regimental banner and motto of a unit of African-American soldiers embodies the hope that service in the Union army will lead to citizenship in the postwar world.

Enlisting Black Troops

Of the Proclamation's provisions, few were more radical in their implications than the enrollment of blacks into military service. Since sailor had been one of the few occupations open to free blacks before the war, Secretary of the Navy Gideon Welles had already allowed African-Americans to serve on Union warships. But as during the American Revolution, when George Washington initially excluded blacks from the Continental army, blacks in the Civil War had to fight for the right to fight on land. Early in the war, Harry Jarvis, a Virginia slave, escaped to Fortress Monroe and offered to enlist in the Union army. General Benjamin F. Butler, Jarvis later recalled, "said *it wasn't a black man's war*. I told him it *would* be a black man's war before they got through."

At the outset, the Union army refused to accept northern black volunteers. The administration feared that whites would not be willing to fight alongside blacks, and that enlisting black soldiers would alienate the border slave states that remained in the Union. By the end of 1861, however, the army was employing escaped slaves as cooks, laundresses, and laborers. Preliminary steps to enlist combat troops were taken in a few parts of the South in 1862. White abolitionist Thomas Wentworth Higginson was sent to the South Carolina Sea Islands, which the Union navy had seized early in the war, to enroll slaves in the First South Carolina Volunteers. But only after the Emancipation Proclamation did the recruitment of black soldiers begin in earnest.

By the end of the war, more than 180,000 black men had served in the Union army, and 24,000 in the navy. One-third died in battle, or of wounds or disease. Fifteen black soldiers and eight sailors received the Medal of Honor, the highest

Concerns about volunteers

COME AND JOIN US BROTHERS.

PUBLISHED BY THE SUPERVISORY COMMITTEE FOR RECRUITING COLORED REGIMENTS
1210 CHESTNUT ST. PHILADELPHIA.

This widely reprinted recruiting poster urged African-American men to join the Union army after Congress and the president changed the policy of allowing only whites to serve.

A photograph of a black washerwoman for the Union army wearing a small American flag reflects how the war and emancipation led African-Americans to identify strongly with the nation.

award for military valor. Some black units won considerable notoriety, among them the Fifty-fourth Massachusetts Volunteers, a company of free blacks from throughout the North commanded by Robert Gould Shaw, a young reformer from a prominent Boston family. The bravery of the Fifty-fourth in the July 1863 attack on Fort Wagner, South Carolina, where nearly half the unit, including Shaw, perished, helped to dispel widespread doubts about blacks' ability to withstand the pressures of the Civil War battlefield. (The exploits of Shaw and the Fifty-fourth Massachusetts were popularized in the 1989 film *Glory*.)

Most black soldiers were emancipated slaves who joined the army in the South. After Union forces in 1863 seized control of the rich plantation lands of the Mississippi Valley, General Lorenzo Thomas raised fifty regiments of black soldiers—some 76,000 men in all. Another large group hailed from the border states exempted from the Emancipation Proclamation, where enlistment was, for most of the war, the only route to freedom. Here black military service undermined slavery, for Congress expanded the Emancipation Proclamation to liberate the families of black soldiers.

The Black Soldier

For black soldiers themselves, military service proved to be a liberating experience. "No negro who has ever been a soldier," wrote a northern official in 1865, "can again be imposed upon; they have learned what it is to be free and they will infuse their feelings into others." Service in the army established men as community leaders and opened a door to political advancement. Out of the army came many of the leaders of the Reconstruction era. At least 130 former soldiers served in political office after the Civil War. In time, the memory of black military service would fade from white America's collective memory. Of the hundreds of Civil War monuments that still dot the northern landscape, fewer than a dozen contain an image of a black soldier. But well into the twentieth century, it remained a point of pride in black families throughout the United States that their fathers and grandfathers had fought for freedom.

The Union navy treated black sailors pretty much the same as white sailors. Conditions on ships made racial segregation impossible. Black and white sailors lived and dined together in the same quarters. They received equal pay and had the same promotion opportunities. Within the army, however, black soldiers received treatment that was anything but equal to their white counterparts. Organized into segregated units under sometimes abusive white officers, they initially received lower pay (ten dollars per month, compared to sixteen dollars for white soldiers).

They were disproportionately assigned to labor rather than combat, and they could not rise to the rank of commissioned officer until the very end of the war. If captured by Confederate forces, they faced the prospect of sale into slavery or immediate execution. In a notorious incident in 1864, 200 of 262 black soldiers died when southern troops under the command of Nathan B. Forrest overran Fort Pillow in Tennessee. Some of those who perished had been killed after surrendering.

Nonetheless, black soldiers played a crucial role not only in winning the Civil War but also in defining the war's consequences. "Once let a black man get upon his person the brass letters U.S.," wrote Frederick Douglass in urging blacks to enlist, "and there is no power on earth which can deny that he has earned the right to citizenship in the United States." As Douglass predicted, thanks in part to black military service many Republicans in the last two years of the war came to believe that emancipation must bring with it equal protection of the laws regardless of race. One of the first acts of the federal government to recognize this principle was the granting of retroactive equal pay to black soldiers early in 1865. Racism was hardly eliminated from national life. But, declared George William Curtis, the editor of *Harper's Weekly*, the war and emancipation had transformed a government "for white men" into one "for mankind."

This is the only known photograph of a black Union soldier with his family.

The service of black soldiers affected Lincoln's own outlook. He insisted that they must be treated the same as whites when captured and suspended prisoner-of-war exchanges when the Confederacy refused to include black troops. In 1864, Lincoln, who before the war had never supported suffrage for African-Americans, urged the governor of Union-occupied Louisiana to work for the partial enfranchisement of blacks, singling out soldiers as especially deserving. At some future time, he observed, they might again be called upon to "keep the *jewel of Liberty* in the family of freedom."

A songbook compiled and illustrated by a Union soldier includes "John Brown's Body," sung to the melody of a Methodist hymn.

THE SECOND AMERICAN REVOLUTION

"Old things are passing away," wrote a black resident of California in 1862, "and eventually old prejudices must follow. The revolution has begun, and time alone must decide where it is to end." The changing status of black Americans was only one dramatic example of what some historians call the **Second American Revolution**—the transformation of American government and society brought about by the Civil War.

Liberty and Union

Never was freedom's contested nature more evident than during the Civil War. "We all declare for liberty," Lincoln observed in 1864, "but in using the same *word*

THE AMERICAN FLAG,
A NEW NATIONAL LYRIC.

The illustration accompanying "The American Flag," a piece of patriotic Civil War sheet music, exemplifies how the war united the ideals of liberty and nationhood.

Lincoln and the Female Slave, by the free black artist David B. Bowser. Working in Philadelphia, Bowser painted flags for a number of black Civil War regiments. Lincoln confers freedom on a kneeling slave, an image that downplays blacks' role in their own emancipation.

we do not all mean the same *thing*." To the North, he continued, freedom meant for "each man" to enjoy "the product of his labor." To southern whites, it conveyed mastership—the power to do "as they please with other men, and the product of other men's labor." The Union's triumph consolidated the northern understanding of freedom as the national norm.

The attack on Fort Sumter crystallized in northern minds the direct conflict between freedom and slavery that abolitionists had insisted upon for decades. The war, as Frederick Douglass recognized as early as 1862, merged "the cause of the slaves and the cause of the country." "Liberty and Union," he continued, "have become identical." As during the American Revolution, religious and secular understandings of freedom joined in a celebration of national destiny. "As He died to make men holy, let us die to make men free," proclaimed the popular song "Battle Hymn of the Republic," written by Julia Ward Howe and published in 1862.

Lincoln's Vision

But it was Lincoln himself who linked the conflict with the deepest beliefs of northern society. It is sometimes said that the American Civil War was part of a broader nineteenth-century process of nation building. Throughout the world, powerful, centralized nation-states developed in old countries, and new nations emerged where none had previously existed. The Civil War took place as modern states were consolidating their power and reducing local autonomy. The Meiji Restoration in Japan saw the emperor reclaim power from local lords, or shoguns. As in the United States, economic development quickly followed national unification. Japan soon emerged as a major economic power.

Lincoln has been called the American equivalent of Giuseppe Mazzini or Otto von Bismarck, who during this same era created nation-states in Italy and Germany from disunited collections of principalities. But Lincoln's nation was different from those being constructed in Europe. They were based on the idea of unifying a particular people with a common ethnic, cultural, and linguistic heritage. To Lincoln, the American nation embodied, instead, a set of universal ideas, centered on political democracy and human liberty. The United States represented to the world the principle that government should rest on popular consent and that all men should be free. These ideals, Lincoln declared, allowed immigrants from abroad, who could not "trace their connection by blood" to the nation's birth, nonetheless to become fully American.

Lincoln summarized his conception of the war's meaning in November 1863 in brief remarks at the dedication of a military cemetery at the site of the war's greatest battle. The Gettysburg Address is considered his finest speech (see the Appendix for the full text). In less than three minutes, he identified the nation's mission with the principle that "all men are created equal," spoke of the war as bringing about a "new birth of freedom," and defined the essence of democratic government. The sacrifices of Union soldiers, he declared, would ensure that "government of the people, by the people, for the people, shall not perish from the earth."

The mobilization of the Union's resources for modern war brought into being a new American nation-state with greatly expanded powers and responsibilities. The United States remained a federal republic with sovereignty divided between the state and national governments. But the war forged a new national

The Eagle's Nest, an 1861 antisecession cartoon promising "annihilation to traitors." The eggs representing seceding states have become rotten and are hatching monsters.

self-consciousness, reflected in the increasing use of the word "nation"—a unified political entity—in place of the older "Union" of separate states. In his inaugural address in 1861, Lincoln used the word "Union" twenty times, while making no mention of the "nation." By 1863, "Union" does not appear at all in the 269-word Gettysburg Address, while Lincoln referred five times to the "nation."

A new political identity

The War and American Religion

The upsurge of patriotism, and of national power, was reflected in many aspects of American life. Even as the war produced unprecedented casualties, the northern Protestant clergy strove to provide it with a religious justification and to reassure their congregations that the dead had not died in vain. The religious press now devoted more space to military and political developments than to spiritual matters. In numerous wartime sermons, Christianity and patriotism were joined in a civic religion that saw the war as God's mechanism for ridding the United States of slavery and enabling it to become what it had never really been—a land of freedom. Lincoln, one of the few American presidents who never joined a church, shrewdly marshaled religious symbolism to generate public support, declaring days of Thanksgiving after northern victories and encouraging northern clergymen to support Republican candidates for office. Of course, the southern clergy was equally convinced that the Confederate cause represented God's will. In 1863, Methodist bishop George Pierce, in an address to the Confederate Congress, declared that the struggle for southern independence enjoyed "the seal of the divine blessing."

Mass grief, religion, and patriotism

The Sisters of Charity, an order of nuns, photographed with doctors and soldiers at a hospital in Philadelphia in 1863. Many of the wounded from the Battle of Gettysburg were sent here for treatment. The Catholic contribution to the Union war effort mitigated the nativist bias so prominent in the 1850s.

Saterlee Hospital — West Phila.

Coping with mass death

A girl in mourning dress holds a framed photograph of her father, a cavalryman.

Religious beliefs enabled Americans to cope with the unprecedented mass death the war involved. Of course, equating death with eternal life is a central tenet of Christianity. But the war led to what one historian calls a "transformation of heaven," as Americans imagined future celestial family reunions that seemed more and more like gatherings in middle-class living rooms. Some Americans could not wait until their own deaths to see the departed. Spiritualism—belief in the ability to communicate with the dead—grew in popularity. Mary Todd Lincoln held seances in the White House to experience again the presence of her young son Willie, who succumbed to disease in 1862.

Coping with death also required unprecedented governmental action, from notifying next of kin to accounting for the dead and missing. Both the Union and Confederacy established elaborate systems for gathering statistics and maintaining records of dead and wounded soldiers, an effort supplemented by private philanthropic organizations. After the war ended, the federal government embarked on a program to locate and re-bury hundreds of thousands of Union soldiers in national military cemeteries. Between 1865 and 1871, the government reinterred more than 300,000 Union (but not Confederate) soldiers—including black soldiers, who were buried in segregated sections of military cemeteries.

Liberty in Wartime

This intense new nationalism made criticism of the war effort—or of the policies of the Lincoln administration—seem to Republicans equivalent to treason. Although there had been sporadic persecution of opponents of the Mexican War, the Civil War presented, for the first time since the Revolution, the issue of the limits of wartime dissent. During the conflict, declared the Republican *New York Times*, "the safety of the nation is the supreme law." Arbitrary arrests numbered in the thousands. They included opposition newspaper editors, Democratic politicians, individuals who discouraged enlistment in the army, and ordinary civilians like the Chicago man briefly imprisoned for calling the president a "damned fool." With the Constitution unclear as to who possessed the power to suspend the writ of habeas corpus (thus allowing prisoners to be held without charge), Lincoln claimed the right under the presidential war powers and twice suspended the writ throughout the entire Union for those accused of "disloyal activities."

Arbitrary arrests and the suspension of habeas corpus

The courts generally gave the administration a free hand. They refused to intervene when a military court convicted Clement L. Vallandigham, a leading Ohio Democrat known for his blistering antiwar speeches, of treason. On Lincoln's order, Vallandigham was banished to the Confederacy. In 1861, Chief Justice Roger B. Taney ordered the president to release John Merryman, a civilian who had been arrested by military authorities in Maryland, but the president ignored him. Not until 1866, after the fighting had ended, did the Supreme Court, in the case ***Ex parte Milligan***, declare it unconstitutional to bring accused persons before military tribunals where civil courts were operating. The Constitution, declared Justice David Davis, is not suspended in wartime—it remains "a law for rulers and people, equally in time of war and peace."

The Constitution in wartime

Lincoln was not a despot. Most of those arrested were quickly released, the Democratic press continued to flourish, and contested elections were held throughout the war. But the policies of the Lincoln administration offered proof—to be repeated during later wars—of the fragility of civil liberties in the face of assertive patriotism and wartime demands for national unity.

Fragility of civil liberties in wartime

The North's Transformation

Even as he invoked traditional values, Lincoln presided over far-reaching changes in northern life. The effort to mobilize the resources of the Union greatly enhanced the power not only of the federal government but also of a rising class of capitalist entrepreneurs. Unlike the South, which suffered economic devastation, the North experienced the war as a time of prosperity.

Northern prosperity

Nourished by wartime inflation and government contracts, the profits of industry boomed. New England mills worked day and night to supply the army with blankets and uniforms, and Pennsylvania coal mines and ironworks rapidly expanded their production. Mechanization proceeded apace in many industries, especially those like boot and shoe production and meatpacking that supplied the army's ever-increasing needs. Agriculture also flourished, for even as farm boys by the hundreds of thousands joined the army, the frontier of cultivation pushed westward, with machinery and immigrants replacing lost labor. Wisconsin furnished 90,000 men to the Union army, yet its population, grain production, and farm income continued to grow.

Government and the Economy

As in contemporary Germany and Japan, the new American nation-state that emerged during the Civil War was committed to rapid economic development.

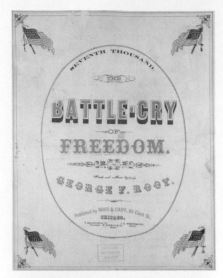

Sheet music for two of the best-known patriotic songs written during the Civil War.

Congress adopted policies that promoted economic growth and permanently altered the nation's financial system. With the South now unrepresented, the lawmakers adopted policies long advocated by many northerners. To spur agricultural development, the **Homestead Act** offered 160 acres of free public land to settlers in the West. It took effect on January 1, 1863, the same day as the Emancipation Proclamation, and like the Proclamation, tried to implement a vision of freedom. By the 1930s, more than 400,000 families had acquired farms under its provisions. In addition, the Morrill Land Grant College Act, named for Justin S. Morrill of Vermont, who introduced the measure, assisted the states in establishing "agricultural and mechanic colleges."

Congress also made huge grants of money and land for internal improvements, including up to 100 million acres to the Union Pacific and Central Pacific, two companies chartered in 1862 and charged with building a railroad from the Missouri River to the Pacific coast. (These were the first corporate charters issued by the federal government since the Second Bank of the United States in 1816.)

When first proposed by Asa Whitney in 1846, the idea of a **transcontinental railroad** had been considered by Congress "too gigantic" and "entirely impracticable." And, indeed, the project was monumental. The Central Pacific progressed only twenty miles a year for the first three years of construction because the Sierra Nevada range was almost impassable. It required some 20,000 men to lay the tracks across prairies and mountains, a substantial number of them immigrant Chinese contract laborers, called "coolies" by many Americans. Hundreds of Chinese workers died blasting tunnels and building bridges through this treacherous terrain. When it was completed in 1869, the transcontinental railroad, which ran from Omaha, Nebraska, to San Francisco, reduced the time of a cross-country journey from four or five months to six days. It expanded the national market, facilitated the spread of settlement and investment in the West, and heralded the doom of the Plains Indians.

The West and the War

Most accounts of the Civil War say little or nothing about the West. Yet the conflict engulfed Missouri, Kansas, and Indian Territory, and spread into the Southwest borderlands. The war divided western communities as residents flocked to both armies.

Since the beginning of the republic, the question of slavery had been tied up with the status of new western lands. Jefferson Davis had long been interested in the expansion of slavery into the Southwest. In pursuit of this goal, in October 1861, Confederate units from Texas launched an invasion of New Mexico (which Texans had long claimed as part of their state). They hoped to conquer the region as a gateway to acquisition of southern California and northern Mexico, a continuation of a southern version of manifest destiny, evidenced before the war in filibustering expeditions in the Caribbean. But the Confederates were defeated at Glorieta Pass in March 1862 by a small Union army contingent reinforced by volunteers from Colorado and California. With their retreat to Texas died the dream of a slave empire in the Far West.

The war had a profound impact on western Indians. One of Lincoln's first orders as president was to withdraw federal troops from the West so that they could protect Washington, D.C. Recognizing that this would make it impossible for the

The invasion of New Mexico

army to keep white interlopers from intruding on Indian land, as treaties required it to do, Indian leaders begged Lincoln to reverse this decision, but to no avail. Inevitably, conflict flared in the West between Native Americans and white settlers, with disastrous results. During the Civil War, the Sioux killed hundreds of white farmers in Minnesota before being subdued by the army at Fort Ridgely. After a military court sentenced more than 300 Indians to death, Lincoln commuted the sentences of all but 38. But their hanging in December 1862 remains the largest official execution in American history.

In November 1864, Colorado militiamen attacked a group of around 700 Cheyennes and Arapahos camped along Sand Creek in Colorado. Led by Colonel John Chivington, an abolitionist and a former Methodist minister, the soldiers were bent on punishing Indians responsible for raids on nearby settlements. They failed to locate the hostile Indians, but chose to assault the peaceful encampment with rifles and artillery, killing more than 150 men, women, and children. The incident sparked intensified warfare on the southern plains, as Cheyennes and Arapahos retaliated with attacks of their own. It also helped to inspire a movement for the reform of Indian policies to emphasize peaceful assimilation over military conquest. Congress investigated the massacre and condemned Chivington's actions. It even promised reparations to the survivors.

The Union army also launched a series of campaigns in the Southwest against tribes like the Kiowas and Comanches, whose violent raids on ranches and settlements had been an essential, although disruptive, part of the borderlands economy, organized around trading and exchanging captives (usually women), livestock, and horses. They had taken tens of thousands of horses and cattle each year, to use as a kind of currency in trade with other Indians and Anglos.

A lithograph depicts the hanging of thirty-eight Sioux Dakotas at Mankato, Minnesota, in December 1862, the largest mass execution in American history.

A Union soldier stands guard over a group of Indians during the Navajo's Long Walk, in which the army removed them from their New Mexico homeland to a reservation hundreds of miles away.

From FREDERICK DOUGLASS,
MEN OF COLOR TO ARMS (1863)

The Emancipation Proclamation opened the door to the large-scale recruitment of black men into the Union army. In March 1863, in a speech in Rochester, New York, Frederick Douglass called on northern blacks to volunteer for the Fifty-fourth Massachusetts Volunteers, a company of blacks from throughout the free states commanded by Robert Gould Shaw, a young reformer from a prominent Boston family.

_____

When first the rebel cannon shattered the walls of Sumter and drove away its starving garrison, I predicted that the war then and there inaugurated would not be fought out entirely by white men. Every month's experience during these dreary years has confirmed that opinion. A war undertaken and brazenly carried on for the perpetual enslavement of colored men, calls logically and loudly for colored men to help suppress it. . . . With every reverse to the national arms, with every exulting shout of victory raised by the slaveholding rebels, I have implored the imperiled nation to unchain against her foes, her powerful black hand. Slowly and reluctantly that appeal is beginning to be heeded. Stop not now to complain that it was not heeded sooner. . . . When the war is over, the country is saved, peace is established, and the black man's rights are secured, as they will

be, history with an impartial hand will dispose of that and sundry other questions. Action! Action! not criticism is the plain duty of this hour. . . . Liberty won by white men would lose half its luster. . . .

I have not thought lightly of the words I am now addressing you. The counsel I give comes of close observation of the great struggle now in progress, and of the deep conviction that this is your hour and mine. In good earnest then, and after the best deliberation, I now for the first time during this war feel at liberty to call and counsel you to arms. By every consideration which binds you to your enslaved fellow-countrymen, and the peace and welfare of your country; by every aspiration which you cherish for the freedom and equality of yourselves and your children; by all the ties of blood and identity which make us one with the brave black men now fighting our battles in Louisiana and in South Carolina, I urge you to fly to arms, and smite with death the power that would bury the government and your liberty in the same hopeless grave. . . . The chance is now given you to end in a day the bondage of centuries, and to rise in one bound from social degradation to the plane of common equality with all other varieties of men. . . . This is our golden opportunity.

From ABRAHAM LINCOLN,
ADDRESS AT SANITARY FAIR,
BALTIMORE (APRIL 18, 1864)

Abraham Lincoln's speech at a Sanitary Fair (a grand bazaar that raised money for the care of Union soldiers) offers a dramatic illustration of the contested meaning of freedom during the Civil War.

The world has never had a good definition of the word liberty, and the American people, just now, are much in want of one. We all declare for liberty; but in using the same *word* we do not all mean the same *thing*. With some the word liberty may mean for each man to do as he pleases with himself, and the product of his labor; while with others the same word may mean for some men to do as they please with other men, and the product of other men's labor. Here are two, not only different, but incompatible things, called by the same name— liberty. And it follows that each of the things is, by the respective parties, called by two different and incompatible names—liberty and tyranny.

The shepherd drives the wolf from the sheep's throat, for which the sheep thanks the shepherd as a *liberator*, while the wolf denounces him for the same act as the destroyer of liberty, especially as the sheep was a black one. Plainly the sheep and the wolf are not agreed upon a definition of the word liberty; and precisely the same difference prevails today among us human creatures, even in the North, and all professing to love liberty. Hence we behold the process by which thousands are daily passing from under the yoke of bondage, hailed by some as the advance of liberty, and bewailed by others as the destruction of all liberty. Recently, as it seems, the people of Maryland have been doing something to define liberty [abolishing slavery in the state]; and thanks to them that, in what they have done, the wolf's dictionary, has been repudiated.

QUESTIONS

1. *What benefits does Douglass think blacks will derive from service in the Union army?*

2. *What does Lincoln identify as the essential difference between northern and southern definitions of freedom?*

3. *While both men desire the end of slavery, are there subtle differences in how they seem to understand freedom?*

THE CIVIL WAR IN THE WESTERN TERRITORIES, 1862–1864

WASHINGTON TERRITORY

OREGON

MONTANA TERRITORY

Missouri River

IDAHO TERRITORY

Snake River

DAKOTA TERRITORY

MINNESOTA

Fort Ridgely, August 20–22, 1862

•Mankato

NEVADA

CHEYENNE

ARAPAHO

IOWA

UTAH TERRITORY

Colorado River

COLORADO TERRITORY

NEBRASKA TERRITORY

•San Francisco

CALIFORNIA

Sand Creek Massacre, November 29, 1864

KANSAS

MISSOURI

•St. Louis

NAVAJO

ARAPAHO

Fort Defiance•

Long Walk of the Navajo, 1864–66

Glorieta Pass, March 26–28, 1862

NEW MEXICO TERRITORY

■Fort Sumner

KIOWA

INDIAN TERRITORY

ARKANSAS

Rio Grande

COMANCHE

Mississippi River

Pacific Ocean

TEXAS

LOUISIANA

Houston•

Gulf of Mexico

— Long Walk of the Navajo
⊗ Major Indian conflict
⊗ Union victory
▨ Confederate states
☐ Union states
▨ Union territories

0   100   200 miles
0   100   200 kilometers

The army also made war on the Navajo, who were more victims than perpetrators of these raids. Indian raiding parties had stolen more than 50,000 sheep from their settlements in 1860 alone. Union forces destroyed their orchards and sheep and forced 8,000 people to move to a reservation set aside by the government. The **Navajo's Long Walk** became as central to their historical experience as the Trail of Tears to the Cherokee (see Chapter 10). Unlike the eastern Indians, however, the Navajo were eventually allowed to return to a portion of their lands. The wars against Native Americans, a small part of the violence that engulfed the nation during the Civil War, would continue for more than two decades after the sectional conflict ended.

> *War with the Navajo*

Ironically, the Confederacy, although defending slavery, treated Native Americans more fairly than the Union. The Confederate Constitution provided for Indian tribes to elect representatives to Congress, and the Davis administration removed state jurisdiction over Indian reservations, allowing them complete self-government. Some tribes that owned slaves, like the Cherokee, sided with the Confederacy. After 1865, they were forced to cede much of their land to the federal government and to accept former slaves into the Cherokee nation and give them land (the only slaveowners required to do so). Their status remains a point of controversy to this day. The Cherokee constitution was recently amended to exclude descendants of slaves from citizenship, leading to lawsuits that have yet to be resolved.

> *The Confederacy's treatment of Indians*

A New Financial System

The need to pay for the war produced dramatic changes in financial policy. To raise money, the government increased the tariff to unprecedented heights (thus promoting the further growth of northern industry), imposed new taxes on the production and consumption of goods, and enacted the nation's first income tax. It also borrowed more than $2 billion by selling interest-bearing bonds, thus creating an immense national debt. And it printed more than $400 million worth of paper money, called "greenbacks," declared to be legal tender—that is, money that must be accepted for nearly all public and private payments and debts. To rationalize banking, Congress established a system of nationally chartered banks, which were required to purchase government bonds and were given the right to issue bank notes as currency. A heavy tax drove money issued by state banks out of existence. Thus, the United States, whose money supply before the war was a chaotic mixture of paper notes issued by state and local banks, now had essentially two kinds of national paper currency—greenbacks printed directly by the federal government, and notes issued by the new national banks.

Along with profitable contracts to supply goods for the military effort, wartime economic policies greatly benefited northern manufacturers, railroad men, and financiers. Numerous Americans who would take the lead in reshaping the nation's postwar economy created or consolidated their fortunes during the Civil War, among them iron and steel entrepreneur Andrew Carnegie, oil magnate John D. Rockefeller, financiers Jay Gould and J. P. Morgan, and Philip D. Armour, who earned millions supplying beef to the Union army. These and other "captains of industry" managed to escape military service, sometimes by purchasing exemptions or hiring substitutes, as allowed by the draft law.

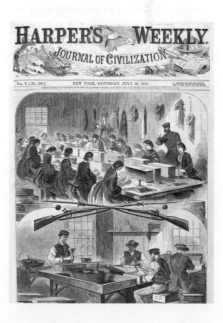

Filling Cartridges at the U.S. Arsenal of Watertown, Massachusetts, an engraving from *Harper's Weekly*, September 21, 1861. Both men and women were drawn to work in the booming war-related industries of the North.

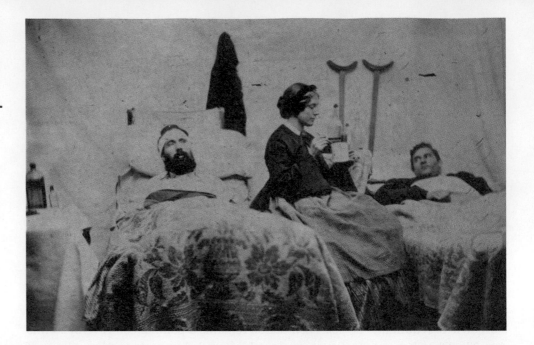

A female nurse photographed between two wounded Union soldiers in a Nashville military hospital in 1862. Many northern women served the army as nurses during the war.

Taken together, the Union's economic policies vastly increased the power and size of the federal government. The federal budget for 1865 exceeded $1 billion—nearly twenty times that of 1860. With its new army of clerks, tax collectors, and other officials, the government became the nation's largest employer. And while much of this expansion proved temporary, the government would never return to its weak and fragmented condition of the prewar period.

Women and the War

For many northern women, the conflict opened new doors of opportunity. Women took advantage of the wartime labor shortage to move into jobs in factories and into certain largely male professions, particularly nursing. The expansion of the activities of the national government opened new jobs for women as clerks in government offices. Many of these wartime gains were short-lived, but in white-collar government jobs, retail sales, and nursing, women found a permanent place in the workforce.

Some northern women took a direct part in military campaigns. Clara Barton, a clerk in the Patent Office in Washington, D.C., when the war began, traveled with the Army of Virginia, helping to organize supply lines and nursing wounded soldiers. Barton worked alone rather than as a part of the Department of Female Nurses, and she never received compensation from the government.

Hundreds of thousands of northern women took part in organizations that gathered money and medical supplies for soldiers and sent books, clothing, and food to freedmen. The United States Sanitary Commission emerged as a centralized national relief agency to coordinate donations on the northern home front. Although control at the national level remained in male hands, patriotic women did most of the grassroots work. Women played the leading role in organizing **Sanitary Fairs**—grand bazaars that displayed military banners, uniforms, and

Whimsical potholders expressing hope for a better life for emancipated slaves were sold at the Chicago Sanitary Fair of 1865, to raise money for soldiers' aid.

other relics of the war and sold goods to raise money for soldiers' aid. New York City's three-week fair of 1864 attracted a crowd of 30,000 and raised more than $1 million.

Many men understood women's war work as an extension of their "natural" capacity for self-sacrifice. But the very act of volunteering to work in local soldiers' aid societies brought many northern women into the public sphere and offered them a taste of independence. The suffrage movement suspended operations during the war to devote itself to the Union and emancipation. But women's continuing lack of the vote seemed all the more humiliating as their involvement in war work increased.

From the ranks of this wartime mobilization came many of the leaders of the postwar movement for women's rights. Mary Livermore, the wife of a Chicago minister, for example, toured military hospitals to assess their needs, cared for injured and dying soldiers, and organized two Sanitary Fairs. She emerged from the war with a deep resentment of women's legal and political subordination and organized her state's first woman suffrage convention. Women, she had concluded, must "think and act for themselves." After the war, Clara Barton not only became an advocate of woman suffrage but, as president of the American National Red Cross, lobbied for the United States to endorse the First Geneva Convention of 1864, which mandated the humane treatment of battlefield casualties. Largely as a result of Barton's efforts, the Senate ratified the convention in 1882. (Subsequent Geneva Conventions in the twentieth century would deal with the treatment of prisoners of war and civilians during wartime.)

Camp of Thirty-first Pennsylvania Infantry, Near Washington, D.C., an 1862 photograph by the Mathew Brady studio. Many women worked for the army as laundresses. Some accompanied their husbands and even brought their children.

The Divided North

Despite Lincoln's political skills, the war and his administration's policies divided northern society. Republicans labeled those opposed to the war Copperheads, after a poisonous snake that strikes without warning. Mounting casualties and rapid societal changes divided the North. Disaffection was strongest among the large southern-born population of states like Ohio, Indiana, and Illinois and working-class Catholic immigrants in eastern cities.

As the war progressed, it heightened existing social tensions and created new ones. The growing power of the federal government challenged traditional notions of local autonomy. The Union's draft law, which allowed individuals to provide a substitute or buy their way out of the army, caused widespread indignation. Workers resented manufacturers and financiers who reaped large profits while their own real incomes dwindled because of inflation. The war witnessed the rebirth of the northern labor movement, which organized numerous strikes for higher wages. The prospect of a sweeping change in the status of blacks called forth a racist reaction in many parts of the North. Throughout the war, the

Social tensions in the North

The Riots in New York: The Mob Lynching a Negro in Clarkson Street, an engraving from the British magazine Illustrated London News, August 8, 1863, reveals how the New York City draft riots escalated from an attempt to obstruct the draft into an assault on the city's black population.

Democratic Party subjected Lincoln's policies to withering criticism, although it remained divided between "War Democrats," who supported the military effort while criticizing emancipation and the draft, and those who favored immediate peace.

The New York City draft riots

On occasion, dissent degenerated into outright violence. In July 1863, the introduction of the draft provoked four days of rioting in New York City. The mob, composed largely of Irish immigrants, assaulted symbols of the new order being created by the war—draft offices, the mansions of wealthy Republicans, industrial establishments, and the city's black population, many of whom fled to New Jersey or took refuge in Central Park. Only the arrival of Union troops quelled the uprising, but not before more than 100 persons had died.

THE CONFEDERATE NATION

Leadership and Government

Jefferson Davis

The man charged with the task of rallying public support for the Confederacy proved unequal to the task. Born in 1808 in Kentucky, within eight months and 100 miles of Lincoln's birth, Jefferson Davis moved to Mississippi as a youth, attended West Point, and acquired a large plantation. Aloof, stubborn, and humorless, he lacked Lincoln's common touch and political flexibility. Although known before the war as the "Cicero of the Senate" for his eloquent speeches, Davis, unlike Lincoln, proved unable to communicate the war's meaning effectively to ordinary men and women. Moreover, the Confederacy's lack of a party system proved to be a political liability. Like the founders of the American republic, southern leaders saw parties as threats to national unity. As a result, Davis lacked a counterpart

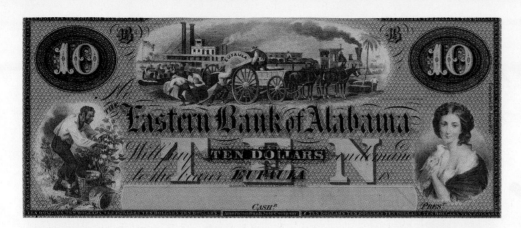

The centrality of slavery to the Confederacy is illustrated by the paper money issued by state governments and private banks, which frequently juxtaposed scenes of slaves at work with other revered images. The ten-dollar note of the Eastern Bank of Alabama depicts slaves working in the field and at a port, along with an idealized portrait of southern white womanhood. Alabama's five-dollar bill includes an overseer directing slaves in the field, and a symbol of liberty.

to the well-organized Republican Party, which helped to mobilize support for the Lincoln administration.

Under Davis, the Confederate nation became far more centralized than the Old South had been. The government raised armies from scratch, took control of southern railroads, and built manufacturing plants. But it failed to find an effective way of utilizing the South's major economic resource, cotton. In the early part of the war, the administration tried to suppress cotton production, urging planters to grow food instead and banning cotton exports. This, it was hoped, would promote economic self-sufficiency and force Great Britain, whose textile mills could not operate without southern cotton, to intervene on the side of the Confederacy.

Centralizing the South

"King Cotton diplomacy" turned out to be ineffective. Large crops in 1859 and 1860 had created a huge stockpile in English warehouses. By the time distress hit the manufacturing districts in 1862, the government of Prime Minister Palmerston had decided not to intervene, partly because Britain needed northern wheat almost as much as southern cotton. But the Confederate policy had far-reaching global consequences. Recognizing their overdependence on southern cotton, other nations moved to expand production. Britain promoted cultivation of the crop in Egypt and India, and Russia did the same in parts of Central Asia. As a result, the resumption of American cotton production after the war led directly to a world-wide crisis of overproduction that drove down the price of cotton, impoverishing farmers around the world.

The international dimension

A drawing by Langdon Cheves III, the teenage grandson of a prominent South Carolina political leader, depicts a Confederate killing a Yankee officer.

Commodity shortages

Nor did Davis deal effectively with obstructionist governors like Joseph E. Brown of Georgia, who denounced the Confederate draft as "a dangerous usurpation" of states' rights and individual liberty. All in all, Davis was so inferior to Lincoln as a wartime leader that one historian has suggested that had the North and South exchanged presidents, the South would have won the war.

The Inner Civil War

As the war progressed, social change and internal turmoil engulfed much of the Confederacy. At the outset, most white southerners rallied to the Confederate cause. No less fervently than northern troops, southern soldiers spoke of their cause in the language of freedom. "We are fighting for our liberty," wrote one volunteer, without any sense of contradiction, "against tyrants of the North . . . who are determined to destroy slavery." But public disaffection eventually became an even more serious problem for the Confederacy than for the Union.

One grievance was the draft. Like the Union, the Confederacy allowed individuals to provide a substitute. Because of the accelerating disintegration of slavery, it also exempted one white male for every twenty slaves on a plantation (thus releasing many overseers and planters' sons from service). The "twenty-negro" provision convinced many yeomen that the struggle for southern independence had become "a rich man's war and a poor man's fight."

Economic Problems

Economic deprivation also sparked disaffection. As the blockade tightened, areas of the Confederacy came under Union occupation, and production by slaves declined, shortages arose of essential commodities such as salt, corn, and meat. The war left countless farms, plantations, businesses, and railroads in ruins. The economic crisis, which stood in glaring contrast to the North's boom, was an unavoidable result of the war. But Confederate policies exaggerated its effects. War requires sacrifice, and civilian support for war depends, in part, on the belief that sacrifice is being fairly shared. Many non-slaveholders, however, became convinced that they were bearing an unfair share of the war's burdens.

Like the Union, the Confederacy borrowed heavily to finance the war. Unlike federal lawmakers, however, the planter-dominated Confederate Congress proved unwilling to levy heavy taxes that planters would have to pay. It relied on paper money, of which it issued $1.5 billion, far more than the North's greenbacks. Congress also authorized military officers to seize farm goods to supply the army, paying with increasingly worthless Confederate money. Small farmers deeply resented this practice, known as "impressment." "The Rebel army treated us a heap worse than [Union general William T.] Sherman did," a Georgia farmer later recalled. "I had hogs, and a mule, and a horse, and they took them all." Numerous yeoman families, many of whom had gone to war to preserve their economic independence, sank into poverty and debt. Food riots broke out in many places, including Richmond, Virginia, and Mobile, Alabama, where in 1863 large crowds of women plundered army food supplies.

Confederate financing of the war

In 1862, Joshua B. Moore, a slaveholder in northern Alabama, commented on how slavery threatened the Confederate war effort: "Men who have no interest in it," he wrote, "are not going to fight through a long war to save it—never. They will tire of it and quit." As the war progressed, desertion became what one officer called a "crying evil" for the southern armies. By the war's end, more than 100,000 men had deserted, almost entirely from among "the poorest class of nonslaveholders whose labor is indispensable to the daily support of their families." Men, another official noted, "cannot be expected to fight for the government that permits their wives and children to starve."

Desertion

Southern Unionists

Continued loyalty to the Union was a dangerous stance in the Confederate South. Georgia in 1861 passed a law making it punishable by death (hardly the action of a government committed to individual liberty and the rights of minorities). Nonetheless, by 1864, organized peace movements had appeared in several southern states, and secret societies such as the Heroes of America were actively promoting disaffection. Confederate military tribunals imprisoned hundreds of Unionists. Others were violently driven from their homes, and a few were executed by the

An engraving in the *New York Illustrated News* depicts the bread riot that took place in Mobile, Alabama, in the fall of 1863.

army or civilian authorities. But southerners loyal to the Union made a significant contribution to northern victory. By the end of the war, an estimated 50,000 white southerners had fought in the Union armies.

Elizabeth Van Lew

One of the most celebrated Union heroes of the war was Elizabeth Van Lew of Richmond, who had persuaded her mother to free the family's slaves when her father died in 1843. During the war she frequently visited Libby Prison in the Confederate capital, bringing supplies to Union prisoners of war and helping some of them to escape. With the aid of Mary Elizabeth Bowser, a former slave of the Van Lew family who worked as a servant in the southern White House, Van Lew passed information about Confederate plans to Union forces.

Women and the Confederacy

Experiences of white women in the South

Even more than in the North, the war placed unprecedented burdens on southern white women. Left alone on farms and plantations, they were often forced to manage business affairs and discipline slaves, previously the responsibility of men. As in the North, women mobilized to support soldiers in the field and stepped out of their traditional "sphere" to run commercial establishments and work in arms factories. In Richmond, "government girls" staffed many of the clerkships in the new Confederate bureaucracy. Rose Greenhow, the widow of a former American diplomat, headed an espionage ring in Washington, D.C., that passed valuable information about Union troop movements to the Confederacy early in the war. Even after her arrest and jailing, she managed to smuggle out intelligence until she was exiled to Richmond in 1862. Jefferson Davis rewarded Greenhow with $2,500 for her services.

Painted in 1864 by the Virginia artist William D. Washington, *The Burial of Latané* depicts a common wartime scene. The deceased is Confederate cavalry officer William Latané. The work illustrates how women, children, and slaves predominated on the southern homefront. Having finished digging the grave, the slave on the left has a faraway look in his eyes; perhaps he is listening for the sound of the approaching Union army. The painting was displayed in Richmond accompanied by a bucket into which viewers were urged to deposit contributions to the southern cause.

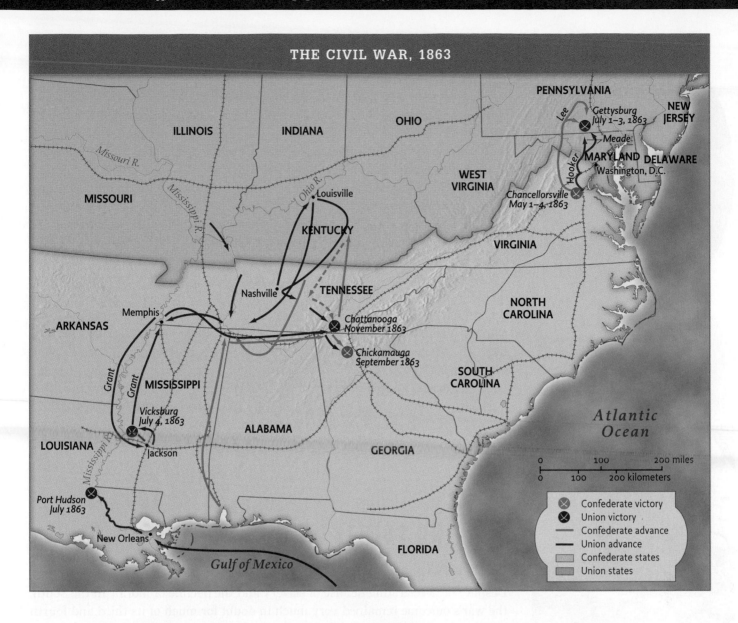

THE CIVIL WAR, 1863

In July 1863, the Union won major victories at Gettysburg and Vicksburg.

All Confederate women struggled to cope as their loved ones were drawn off into the army. The war led to the political mobilization, for the first time, of non-slaveholding white women. Lacking the aid of slave labor, they found that the absence of their husbands from their previously self-sufficient farms made it impossible to feed their families. They flooded Confederate authorities with petitions seeking assistance, not as charity but as a right. Politicians could not ignore the pleas of soldiers' wives, and state governments began to distribute supplies to needy families.

Southern women's self-sacrificing devotion to the cause became legendary. But as the war went on and the death toll mounted, increasing numbers of women came to believe that the goal of independence was not worth the cost. The growing disaffection of southern white women, conveyed in letters to loved ones at the front, contributed to the decline in civilian morale and encouraged desertion from the army.

Black Soldiers for the Confederacy

The growing shortage of white manpower eventually led Confederate authorities to a decision no one could have foreseen when the war began: they authorized the arming of slaves to fight for the South. As early as September 1863, a Mississippi newspaper had argued for freeing and enlisting able-bodied black men. "Let them," it wrote, "be declared free, placed in the ranks, and told to fight for their homes and country." But many slaveholders fiercely resisted this idea, and initially, the Confederate Senate rejected it. Not until March 1865, after Robert E. Lee had endorsed the plan, did the Confederate Congress authorize the arming of slaves. To be sure, enlisting blacks in the Confederate army did not necessarily mean the end of slavery. Both the British and Americans had used slave soldiers in the War of Independence, but slavery survived, as it undoubtedly would have had the Confederacy managed to win the Civil War.

The war ended before substantial recruitment of black Confederate soldiers— the only ones who reached the front were two companies impressed into service in Richmond a few days before the city's surrender. But the Confederate army did employ numerous blacks, nearly all of them slaves, as laborers. This later led to some confusion over whether blacks actually fought for the Confederacy—apart from a handful who "passed" for white, none in fact did. But the South's decision to raise black troops illustrates how the war undermined not only slavery but also the proslavery ideology. "The day you make soldiers of them is the beginning of the end of the revolution," declared Howell Cobb, a Georgia planter and politician. "If slaves make good soldiers, our whole theory of slavery is wrong."

Generals Robert E. Lee and Ulysses S. Grant, leaders of the opposing armies in the East, 1864–1865.

TURNING POINTS

Gettysburg and Vicksburg

Despite the accelerating demise of slavery and the decline of morale in the South, the war's outcome remained very much in doubt for much of its third and fourth years. In April 1863, "Fighting Joe" Hooker, who had succeeded Ambrose E. Burnside as the Union commander in the East, brought the Army of the Potomac into central Virginia to confront Lee. Outnumbered two to one, Lee repelled Hooker's attack at Chancellorsville, although he lost his ablest lieutenant, "Stonewall" Jackson, mistakenly killed by fire from his own soldiers.

Lee now gambled on another invasion of the North, although his strategic objective remains unclear. Perhaps he believed a defeat on its own territory would destroy the morale of the northern army and public. In any event, the two armies, with Union soldiers now under the command of General George G. Meade, met at Gettysburg, Pennsylvania, on the first three days of July 1863. With 165,000 troops involved, the **Battle of Gettysburg** remains the largest battle ever fought on the North American continent. Lee found himself in the unusual position of confronting entrenched Union forces. After two days of failing to dislodge them, he decided to attack the center of the Union line. On July 3, Confederate forces, led by Major General George E. Pickett's crack division, marched across an open field toward Union forces. Withering artillery and rifle fire met the charge, and most of Pickett's soldiers never reached Union lines. Of the 14,000 men who made the advance—the flower of Lee's army—fewer than half returned. Later remembered as "the high tide of the Confederacy," Pickett's Charge was also Lee's greatest blunder. His army retreated to Virginia, never again to set foot on northern soil.

Pickett's charge

On the same day that Lee began his retreat from Gettysburg, the Union achieved a significant victory in the West. Late in 1862, Grant had moved into Mississippi toward the city of Vicksburg. From its heights, defended by miles of trenches and earthworks, the Confederacy commanded the central Mississippi River. When direct attacks failed, as did an attempt to divert the river by digging a canal, Grant launched a siege. On July 4, 1863, Vicksburg surrendered, and with it John C. Pemberton's army of 30,000 men, a loss the Confederacy could ill afford. The entire Mississippi Valley now lay in Union hands. The simultaneous defeats at Gettysburg and the **Battle of Vicksburg** dealt a heavy blow to southern morale. "Today absolute ruin seems our portion," one official wrote in his diary. "The Confederacy totters to its destruction."

1864

Nearly two years, however, would pass before the war ended. Brought east to take command of Union forces, Grant in 1864 began a war of attrition against Lee's army in Virginia. That is, he was willing to accept high numbers of casualties, knowing that the North could replace its manpower losses while the South could not. Grant understood that to bring the North's manpower advantage into play, he must attack continuously "all along the line," thereby preventing the enemy from concentrating its forces or retreating to safety after an engagement.

A war of attrition

In May 1864, the 115,000-man Army of the Potomac crossed the Rapidan River to do battle with Lee's forces in Virginia. A month of the war's bloodiest fighting

Confederate dead at Spotsylvania, Virginia, the site of a bloody battle in 1864.

A sketch by William Waud, an artist who covered the war for *Harper's Weekly*, depicts Pennsylvania soldiers voting in their army camp in the 1864 election.

A political cartoon from 1864 suggests the difficulty faced by the Democratic candidate, George B. McClellan, in reconciling the party's war and peace wings.

YOU TRIED TO RIDE THEM TWO HOSSES ON THE PENINSULA FOR TWO YEARS MAC BUT IT WOULDN'T WORK

LITTLE MAC (confidentially)—Curse them faulty Horses—I can't manage the Act no how. One throws me in Virginia, and the other is bound the wrong way.

PEACE.

WAR

LITTLE MAC, IN HIS GREAT TWO HORSE ACT, IN THE PRESIDENTIAL CANVASS OF 1864.

followed. Grant and Lee first encountered each other in the Wilderness, a wild, shrub-covered region where, one participant recalled, "it was as though Christian men had turned to fiends, and hell itself had usurped the place of earth." Grant's army suffered 18,000 casualties, while Lee's far smaller forces incurred 7,500. Previous Union generals had broken off engagements after losses of this magnitude. But Grant continued to press forward, attacking again at Spotsylvania and then at Cold Harbor. At the end of six weeks of fighting, Grant's casualties stood at 60,000—almost the size of Lee's entire army—while Lee had lost 30,000 men. The sustained fighting in Virginia was a turning point in modern warfare. With daily combat and a fearsome casualty toll, it had far more in common with the trench warfare of World War I (discussed in Chapter 19) than the almost gentlemanly fighting with which the Civil War began.

Grant had become the only Union general to maintain the initiative against Lee, but at a cost that led critics to label him a "butcher of men." Victory still eluded him. Grant attempted to capture Petersburg, which controlled the railway link to Richmond, but Lee got to Petersburg first, and Grant settled in for a prolonged siege. Meanwhile, General William T. Sherman, who had moved his forces into Georgia from Tennessee, encountered dogged resistance from Confederate troops. Not until September 1864 did he finally enter Atlanta, seizing Georgia's main railroad center.

As casualty rolls mounted in the spring and summer of 1864, northern morale sank to its lowest point of the war. Lincoln for a time believed he would be unable to win reelection. In May, hoping to force Lincoln to step aside, Radical Republicans nominated John C. Frémont on a platform calling for a constitutional amendment to abolish slavery, federal protection of the freedmen's rights, and confiscation of the land of leading Confederates. The Democratic candidate for president, General George B. McClellan, was hampered from the outset of the campaign by a platform calling for an immediate cease-fire and peace conference—a plan that even war-weary northerners viewed as equivalent to surrender. In the end, Frémont withdrew, and buoyed by Sherman's capture of Atlanta, Lincoln won a sweeping victory. He captured every state but Kentucky, Delaware, and New Jersey. The result ensured that the war would continue until the Confederacy's defeat.

REHEARSALS FOR RECONSTRUCTION AND THE END OF THE WAR

As the war drew toward a close and more and more parts of the Confederacy came under Union control, federal authorities found themselves presiding over the transition from slavery to freedom. In South Carolina, Louisiana, and other parts of the South, debates took place over issues—access to land, control of labor, and the new structure of political power—that would reverberate in the postwar world.

The Sea Islands Experiment

The most famous "rehearsal for Reconstruction" took place on the Sea Islands just off the coast of South Carolina. The war was only a few months old when, in November 1861, the Union navy occupied the islands. Nearly the entire white population fled, leaving behind some 10,000 slaves. The navy was soon followed by other northerners—army officers, Treasury agents, prospective investors in cotton land, and a group known as Gideon's Band, which included black and white reformers and teachers committed to uplifting the freed slaves. Each of these groups, in addition to the islands' black population, had its own view of how the transition to freedom should be organized. And journalists reported every development on the islands to an eager reading public in the North.

> *Gideon's Band*

Convinced that education was the key to making self-reliant, productive citizens of the former slaves, northern-born teachers like Charlotte Forten, a member of one of Philadelphia's most prominent black families, and Laura M. Towne, a white native of Pittsburgh, devoted themselves to teaching the freed blacks. Towne, who in 1862 helped to establish Penn school on St. Helena Island,

> *Forten and Towne*

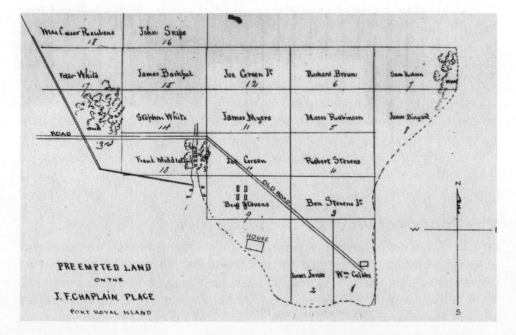

Diagram of plots selected by former slaves on Port Royal Island, South Carolina, January 25, 1864. Taking advantage of a sale of abandoned property, eighteen blacks (seventeen men and one woman) selected plots on a Sea Island plantation for purchase.

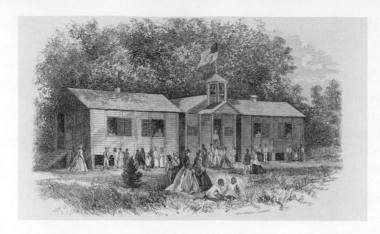

A school for freed people established in 1862 on St. Helena Island, South Carolina, by an aid association in Pennsylvania.

remained there as a teacher until her death in 1901. Like many of the Gideonites, Towne and Forten assumed that blacks needed outside guidance to appreciate freedom. But they sympathized with the former slaves' aspirations, central to which was the desire for land.

Other northerners, however, believed that the transition from slave to free labor meant not giving blacks land but enabling them to work for wages in more humane conditions than under slavery. When the federal government put land on the islands up for sale, most was acquired not by former slaves but by northern investors bent upon demonstrating the superiority of free wage labor and turning a tidy profit at the same time. By 1865, the **Sea Islands experiment** was widely held to be a success. Black families were working for wages, acquiring education, and enjoying better shelter and clothing and a more varied diet than under slavery. But the experiment also bequeathed to postwar Reconstruction the contentious issue of whether landownership should accompany black freedom.

Wartime Reconstruction in the West

Regulations for plantation labor

A very different rehearsal for Reconstruction, involving a far larger area and population than the Sea Islands, took place in Louisiana and the Mississippi Valley. After the capture of Vicksburg, the Union army established regulations for plantation labor. Military authorities insisted that the emancipated slaves must sign labor contracts with plantation owners who took an oath of loyalty. But, unlike before the war, the laborers would be paid wages and provided with education, physical punishment was prohibited, and their families were safe from disruption by sale.

Neither side was satisfied with the new labor system. Blacks resented having to resume working for whites and being forced to sign labor contracts. Planters complained that their workers were insubordinate. Without the whip, they insisted, discipline could not be enforced. But only occasionally did army officers seek to implement a different vision of freedom. At Davis Bend, Mississippi, site of the cotton plantations of Jefferson Davis and his brother Joseph, General Grant decided to establish a "negro paradise." Here, rather than being forced to labor for white owners, the emancipated slaves saw the land divided among themselves. In addition, a system of government was established that allowed the former slaves to elect their own judges and sheriffs.

The Politics of Wartime Reconstruction

Lincoln's Ten-Percent Plan

As the Civil War progressed, the future political status of African-Americans emerged as a key dividing line in public debates. Events in Union-occupied Louisiana brought the issue to national attention. Hoping to establish a functioning civilian government in the state, Lincoln in 1863 announced his **Ten-Percent Plan of Reconstruction**. He essentially offered an amnesty and full restoration of rights, including property except for slaves, to nearly all white southerners who took an oath affirming loyalty to the Union and support for emancipation. When 10 percent of the voters of 1860 had taken the oath, they could elect a new state government, which would be required to abolish slavery. Lincoln's plan offered no role to blacks in shaping the post-slavery order. His leniency toward southern whites seems to have been based on the assumption that many former slaveholders would come forward to accept his terms, thus weakening the Confederacy, shortening the war, and gaining white support for the ending of slavery.

Another group now stepped onto the stage of politics—the free blacks of New Orleans, who saw the Union occupation as a golden opportunity to press for equality before the law and a role in government for themselves. Their complaints at being excluded under Lincoln's Reconstruction plan won a sympathetic hearing from Radical Republicans in Congress. By the summer of 1864, dissatisfaction with events in Louisiana helped to inspire the **Wade-Davis Bill**, named for two leading Republican members of Congress. This bill required a majority (not one-tenth) of white male southerners to pledge support for the Union before Reconstruction could begin in any state, and it guaranteed blacks equality before the law, although not the right to vote. The bill passed Congress only to die when Lincoln refused to sign it and Congress adjourned. As the war drew to a close, it was clear that while slavery was dead, no agreement existed as to what social and political system should take its place.

> *Wade-Davis Bill*

Victory at Last

After Lincoln's reelection, the war hastened to its conclusion. In November 1864, Sherman and his army of 60,000 set out from Atlanta on their March to the Sea. Cutting a sixty-mile-wide swath through the heart of Georgia, they destroyed railroads, buildings, and all the food and supplies they could not use. His aim, Sherman wrote, was "to whip the rebels, to humble their pride, to follow them to their innermost recesses, and make them fear and dread us." Here was modern war in all its destructiveness, even though few civilians were physically harmed. In January 1865, after capturing Savannah, Sherman moved into South Carolina, bringing even greater destruction. Anarchy reigned on the plantations as slaves drove off remaining overseers, destroyed planters' homes, plundered smokehouses and storerooms, and claimed the land for themselves.

> *Sherman's March to the Sea*

General William T. Sherman photographed in 1864.

On January 31, 1865, Congress approved the **Thirteenth Amendment**, which abolished slavery throughout the entire Union—and in so doing, introduced the word "slavery" into the Constitution for the first time. In March, in his second inaugural address, Lincoln called for reconciliation: "with malice toward none, with charity for all, . . . let us . . . bind up the nation's wounds." Yet he also leveled a harsh judgment on the nation's past. Unlike the northern and southern clergy, who were sure of what God intended, Lincoln suggested that man does not know God's will—a remarkably modest statement on the eve of Union victory. Perhaps, Lincoln suggested, God had brought on the war to punish the entire nation, not just the South, for the sin of slavery. And if God willed that the war continue until all the wealth created by 250 years of slave labor had been destroyed, and "every drop

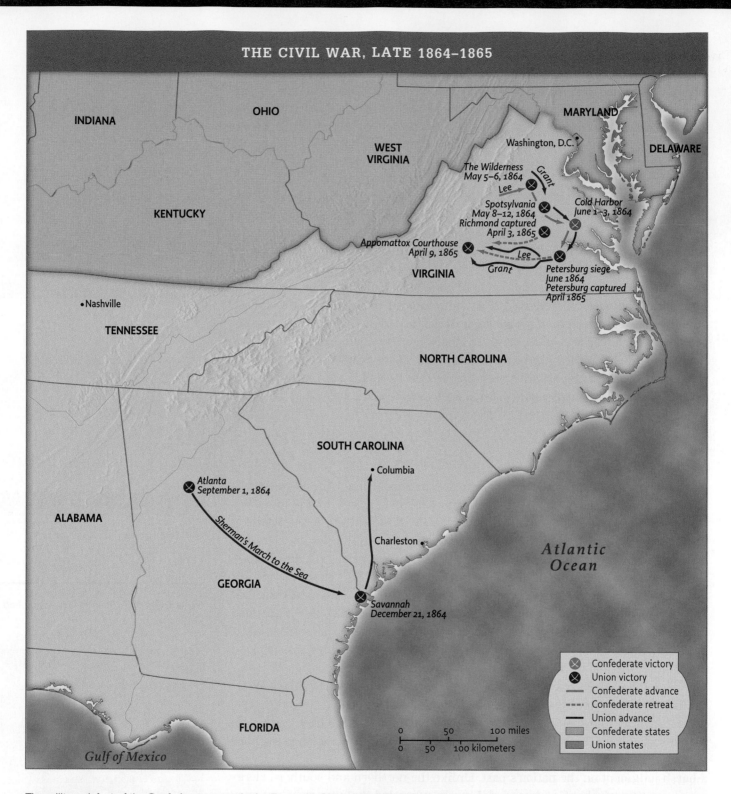

THE CIVIL WAR, LATE 1864–1865

INDIANA

OHIO

MARYLAND

DELAWARE

WEST VIRGINIA

Washington, D.C.

The Wilderness
May 5–6, 1864

Grant

Lee

KENTUCKY

Spotsylvania
May 8–12, 1864

Cold Harbor
June 1–3, 1864

Richmond captured
April 3, 1865

Appomattox Courthouse
April 9, 1865

Lee

VIRGINIA

Grant

Petersburg siege
June 1864
Petersburg captured
April 1865

Nashville

TENNESSEE

NORTH CAROLINA

SOUTH CAROLINA

Columbia

ALABAMA

Atlanta
September 1, 1864

Charleston

Atlantic
Ocean

Sherman's March to the Sea

GEORGIA

Savannah
December 21, 1864

FLORIDA

Gulf of Mexico

Legend:
- ⊗ Confederate victory
- ⊗ Union victory
- Confederate advance
- Confederate retreat
- Union advance
- Confederate states
- Union states

0   50   100 miles
0   50   100 kilometers

The military defeat of the Confederacy came in the East, with Sherman's March to the Sea, Grant's occupation of Richmond, and the surrender of Robert E. Lee's army.

of blood drawn with the lash shall be paid by another drawn with the sword," this too would be an act of justice (see the Appendix for the full text).

April 1865 brought some of the most momentous events in American history. On April 2, Grant finally broke through Lee's lines at Petersburg, forcing the Army of Northern Virginia to abandon the city and leaving Richmond defenseless. The following day, Union soldiers occupied the southern capital. At the head of one black army unit marched its chaplain, Garland H. White, a former fugitive from slavery. Called upon by a large crowd to make a speech, White, as he later recalled, proclaimed "for the first time in that city freedom to all mankind." Then the "doors of all the slave pens were thrown open and thousands came out shouting and praising God, and Father, or Master Abe."

Occupation at Richmond

On April 4, heedless of his own safety, Lincoln walked the streets of Richmond accompanied only by a dozen sailors. At every step he was besieged by former slaves, some of whom fell on their knees before the embarrassed president, who urged them to remain standing. Meanwhile, Lee and his army headed west, only to be encircled by Grant's forces. Realizing that further resistance was useless, Lee surrendered at **Appomattox Courthouse, Virginia**, on April 9. Although some Confederate units remained in the field, the Civil War was over.

Lincoln did not live to savor victory. On April 11, in what proved to be his last speech, he called publicly for the first time for limited black suffrage in the South. Three days later, while attending a performance at Ford's Theatre in Washington, D.C., the president was mortally wounded by John Wilkes Booth, one of the nation's most celebrated actors. Lincoln died the next morning. A train carried the

The ruins of a Charleston railroad depot, in an 1865 photograph by George N. Barnard.

president's body to its final resting place in Illinois on a winding 1,600-mile journey that illustrated how tightly the railroad now bound the northern states. Grieving crowds lined the train route, and solemn processions carried the president's body to lie in state in major cities so that mourners could pay their respects. It was estimated that 300,000 persons passed by the coffin in Philadelphia, 500,000 in New York, and 200,000 in Chicago. On May 4, 1865, Lincoln was laid to rest in Springfield.

The War and the World

In 1877, soon after retiring as president, Ulysses S. Grant embarked with his wife on a two-year tour of the world. At almost every location, he was greeted as a modern-day hero. What did America in the aftermath of the Civil War represent to the world? In England, the son of the duke of Wellington greeted Grant as a military genius, the primary architect of victory in one of the greatest wars in human history, and a fitting successor to Wellington's own father, the general who had vanquished Napoleon. In Newcastle, parading English workers hailed him as the man whose military prowess

A redesign of the American flag proposed in 1863 illustrates the linkage of nationalism and freedom that was solidified by the Civil War. The thirty-five stars forming the word "FREE" include the eleven Confederate states.

had saved the world's leading experiment in democratic government, and as a "Hero of Freedom," whose commander-in-chief, Abraham Lincoln, had vindicated the principles of free labor by emancipating America's slaves. In Berlin, Otto von Bismarck, the chancellor of Germany, welcomed Grant as a nation-builder, who had accomplished on the battlefield something—national unity—that Bismarck was attempting to create for his own people. "You had to save the Union," Bismarck commented, "just as we had to save Germany." Grant corrected him—"Not only to save the Union, but to destroy slavery."

The War in American History

The Civil War laid the foundation for modern America, guaranteeing the Union's permanence, destroying slavery, and shifting power in the nation from the South to the North (and, more specifically, from slaveowning planters to northern capitalists). It dramatically increased the power of the federal government and accelerated the modernization of the northern economy. And it placed on the postwar agenda the challenge of defining and protecting African-American freedom.

Paradoxically, both sides lost something they had gone to war to defend. Slavery was the cornerstone of the Confederacy, but the war led inexorably to slavery's destruction. In the North, the war hastened the transformation of Lincoln's America—the world of free labor, of the small shop and independent farmer—into an industrial giant. Americans, in the words of the abolitionist Wendell Phillips, would "never again . . . see the republic in which we were born."

Winslow Homer's painting *The Veteran in a New Field*, completed in the fall of 1865, offers a reflection on the Civil War and its legacy. The former Union soldier, whose army jacket lies in the right corner, is at work cutting wheat. The scythe brings to mind the grim reaper, a symbol of death, perhaps a reference not only to war casualties but also Lincoln's assassination. But the bountiful field suggests national regeneration.

Late in May 1865, a little over a month after Lincoln's death, some 200,000 veterans paraded through Washington, D.C., for the Grand Review of the Union armies, a final celebration of the nation's triumph. The scene inspired the poet Bret Harte to imagine a very different parade—a "phantom army" of the Union dead:

> The martyred heroes of Malvern Hill,
> Of Gettysburg and Chancellorsville,
> The men whose wasted figures fill
> The patriot graves of the nation . . .
> And marching beside the others,
> Came the dusky martyrs of Pillow's fight.

To Harte, the war's meaning ultimately lay in the sacrifices of individual soldiers. He included in his reverie the black troops, including those massacred at Fort Pillow. Blacks, Harte seemed to be saying, had achieved equality in death. Could the nation give it to them in life?

Here was the problem that confronted the United States as the postwar era known as Reconstruction began. "Verily," as Frederick Douglass declared, "the work does not *end* with the abolition of slavery, but only *begins*."

SUGGESTED READING

BOOKS

- Ayers, Edward L. *In the Presence of Mine Enemies: War in the Heart of America, 1859–1863* (2003). A study of the experiences of Americans in two counties—one in Pennsylvania, one in Virginia—in the early years of the Civil War.

- Foner, Eric. *The Fiery Trial: Abraham Lincoln and American Slavery* (2010). A study of the evolution of Lincoln's ideas and policies relating to slavery over the course of his life.

- Glatthaar, Joseph T. *Forged in Battle: The Civil War Alliance of Black Soldiers and White Officers* (1990). Relates the complex experience of black Civil War soldiers and their officers.

- Kelman, Ari. *A Misplaced Massacre: Struggling Over the Memory of Sand Creek* (2013). Examines the massacre at Sand Creek and the modern controversy over how to commemorate it.

- Lawson, Melinda. *Patriot Fires: Forging a New Nationalism in the Civil War North* (2002). Considers how both public and private groups, in order to mobilize support for the war effort, promoted a new idea of American nationalism.

- McCurry, Stephanie. *Confederate Reckoning: Power and Politics in the Civil War South* (2010). A pioneering study of the political mobilization of poorer white women and slaves in the Confederacy.

- McPherson, James M. *Battle Cry of Freedom: The Civil War Era* (1988). The standard account of the coming of the war, its conduct, and its consequences.

- Mitchell, Reid. *Civil War Soldiers* (1988). A look at the Civil War from the point of view of the experience of ordinary soldiers.

- Neely, Mark E. *The Fate of Liberty: Abraham Lincoln and Civil Liberties* (1991). Explores how the Lincoln administration did and did not meet the challenge of preserving civil liberties while fighting the war.

- Oakes, James. *Freedom National: The Destruction of Slavery in the United States* (2012). A careful account of the complex path to emancipation.

- Rable, George C. *God's Almost Chosen People: A Religious History of the Civil War* (2010). How on both sides religious conviction helped to sustain the war effort.

- Richardson, Heather C. *Greatest Nation of the Earth: Republican Economic Policies during the Civil War* (1997). Considers the far-reaching impact of the economic measures adopted by the Union during the war.

- Rose, Willie Lee. *Rehearsal for Reconstruction: The Port Royal Experiment* (1964). Traces the unfolding of the issues of Reconstruction in the Sea Islands of South Carolina in the midst of the war.

- Rubin, Anne S. *Shattered Nation: The Rise and Fall of the Confederacy, 1861–1868* (2005). An up-to-date account of the Confederate experience.

- Silber, Nina. *Daughters of the Union: Northern Women Fight the Civil War* (2005). Examines the participation of northern women in the war effort and how this did and did not alter their lives.

WEBSITES

- Civil War Photographs: http://memory.loc.gov/ammem /cwphtml/cwphome.html

- Civil War Women: http://library.duke.edu /specialcollections/collections/digitized/civil-war-women/

- A House Divided: America in the Age of Lincoln: www.digitalhistory.uh.edu/exhibits/ahd/index.html

- The Valley of the Shadow: Two Communities in the American Civil War: http://valley.vcdh.virginia.edu

CHAPTER REVIEW AND ONLINE RESOURCES

REVIEW QUESTIONS

1. What made the American Civil War the first modern war?

2. How was the North's victory over the South tied to the different ways the market revolution had developed in the two regions?

3. Describe how President Lincoln's war aims evolved between 1861 and 1863, changing from simply preserving the Union to also ending slavery.

4. How did the actions of slaves themselves, northern military strategy, and the Emancipation Proclamation combine to end slavery?

5. What role did blacks play in winning the Civil War and in defining the war's consequences?

6. How did federal policies undertaken during the Civil War transform the United States into a stronger nation-state—economically, politically, and ideologically?

7. What was the impact of the Civil War on civil liberties?

8. Compare and contrast women's efforts in the North and South to support the war effort and their families.

9. In what ways did the outcome of the Civil War change the United States' status in the world?

KEY TERMS

first Battle of Bull Run (p. 508)

second Battle of Bull Run (p. 509)

Battle of Antietam (p. 509)

"the contrabands" (p. 513)

Radical Republicans (p. 514)

Emancipation Proclamation (p. 516)

Second American Revolution (p. 519)

Ex parte Milligan (p. 523)

Homestead Act (p. 524)

transcontinental railroad (p. 524)

Navajo's Long Walk (p. 529)

Sanitary Fairs (p. 530)

"King Cotton diplomacy" (p. 533)

Battle of Gettysburg (p. 538)

Battle of Vicksburg (p. 539)

Sea Islands experiment (p. 542)

Ten-Percent Plan of Reconstruction (p. 542)

Wade-Davis Bill (p. 543)

Thirteenth Amendment (p. 543)

Appomattox Courthouse, Virginia (p. 545)

Go to 🐰 INQUIZITIVE

To see what you know—and learn what you've missed—with personalized feedback along the way.

Visit the *Give Me Liberty!* **Student Site** for primary source documents and images, interactive maps, author videos featuring Eric Foner, and more.

CHAPTER 15

"WHAT IS FREEDOM?": RECONSTRUCTION

★

1865-1877

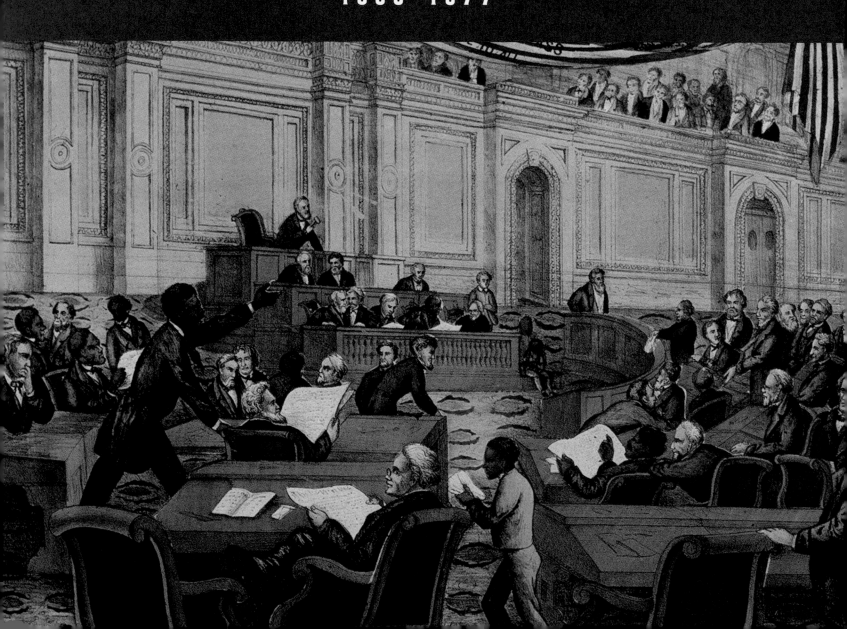

On the evening of January 12, 1865, less than a month after Union forces captured Savannah, Georgia, twenty leaders of the city's black community gathered for a discussion with General William T. Sherman and Secretary of War Edwin M. Stanton. Mostly Baptist and Methodist ministers, the group included several men who within a few years would assume prominent positions during the era of Reconstruction that followed the Civil War. Ulysses S. Houston, pastor of the city's Third African Baptist Church, and James Porter, an episcopal religious leader who had operated a secret school for black children before the war, in a few years would win election to the Georgia legislature. James D. Lynch, who had been born free in Baltimore and educated in New Hampshire, went on to serve as secretary of state of Mississippi.

The conversation revealed that the black leaders brought out of slavery a clear definition of freedom. Asked what he understood by slavery, Garrison Frazier, a Baptist minister chosen as the group's spokesman, responded that it meant one person's "receiving by irresistible power the work of another man, and not by his consent." Freedom he defined as "placing us where we could reap the fruit of our own labor, and take care of ourselves." The way to accomplish this was "to have land, and turn it and till it by our own labor." Frazier insisted that blacks possessed "sufficient intelligence" to maintain themselves in freedom and enjoy the equal protection of the laws.

Sherman's meeting with the black leaders foreshadowed some of the radical changes that would take place during the era known as Reconstruction (meaning, literally, the rebuilding of the shattered nation). In the years following the Civil War, former slaves and their white allies, North and South, would seek to redefine the meaning and boundaries of American freedom. Previously an entitlement of whites, freedom would be expanded to include black Americans. The laws and Constitution would be rewritten to guarantee African-Americans, for the first time in the nation's history, recognition as citizens and equality before the law. Black men would be granted the right to vote, ushering in a period of interracial democracy throughout the South. Black schools, churches, and other institutions would flourish, laying the foundation for the modern African-American community. Many of the advances of Reconstruction would prove temporary, swept away during a campaign of violence in the South and the North's retreat from the ideal of equality. But Reconstruction laid the foundation for future struggles to extend freedom to all Americans.

All this, however, lay in the future in January 1865. Four days after the meeting, Sherman responded to the black delegation by issuing Special Field Order 15. This set aside the Sea Islands and a large area along the South Carolina and Georgia coasts for the settlement of black families on forty-acre plots of land. He also offered them broken-down mules that the army could no longer use. In Sherman's order lay the origins of the phrase "forty acres and a mule," that would reverberate across the South in the next few years. By June, some 40,000 freed slaves had been settled on "Sherman land." Among the emancipated slaves, Sherman's order raised hopes that the end of slavery would be accompanied by the economic independence that they, like other Americans, believed essential to genuine freedom.

FOCUS QUESTIONS

What visions of freedom did the former slaves and slaveholders pursue in the postwar South? –*p. 552*

What were the sources, goals, and competing visions for Reconstruction? –*p. 564*

What were the social and political effects of Radical Reconstruction in the South? –*p. 574*

What were the main factors, in both the North and South, for the abandonment of Reconstruction? –*p. 579*

The Shackle Broken—by the Genius of Freedom. This 1874 lithograph depicts Robert B. Elliott, a black congressman from South Carolina, delivering a celebrated speech supporting the bill that became the Civil Rights Act of 1875.

THE MEANING OF FREEDOM

1865   Special Field Order 15

        Freedmen's Bureau
        established

        Lincoln assassinated;
        Andrew Johnson becomes
        president

1865–   Presidential Reconstruction
1867
        Black Codes

1866   Civil Rights Bill

        Ku Klux Klan established

1867   Reconstruction Act of 1867

        Tenure of Office Act

1867–   Radical Reconstruction
1877   of 1867

1868   Impeachment and trial of
        President Johnson

        Fourteenth Amendment
        ratified

1869   Inauguration of Ulysses S.
        Grant

        Women's rights
        organization splits into two
        groups

1870   Hiram Revels, first black
        U.S. senator

        Fifteenth Amendment
        ratified

1870–   Enforcement Acts
1871

1872   Liberal Republicans
        established

1873   Colfax Massacre

        Slaughterhouse Cases

        National economic
        depression begins

1876   United States v. Cruikshank

1877   Bargain of 1877

With the end of the Civil War, declared an Illinois congressman in 1865, the United States was a "new nation," for the first time "wholly free." The destruction of slavery, however, made the definition of freedom the central question on the nation's agenda. "What is freedom?" asked Congressman James A. Garfield in 1865. "Is it the bare privilege of not being chained? If this is all, then freedom is a bitter mockery, a cruel delusion." Did freedom mean simply the absence of slavery, or did it imply other rights for the former slaves, and if so, which ones: equal civil rights, the vote, ownership of property? During Reconstruction, freedom became a terrain of conflict, its substance open to different, often contradictory interpretations. Out of the conflict over the meaning of freedom arose new kinds of relations between black and white southerners, and a new definition of the rights of all Americans.

Blacks and the Meaning of Freedom

African-Americans' understanding of freedom was shaped by their experiences as slaves and their observation of the free society around them. To begin with, freedom meant escaping the numerous injustices of slavery—punishment by the lash, the separation of families, denial of access to education, the sexual exploitation of black women by their owners—and sharing in the rights and opportunities of American citizens. "If I cannot do like a white man," Henry Adams, an emancipated slave in Louisiana, told his former master in 1865, "I am not free."

Blacks relished the opportunity to demonstrate their liberation from the regulations, significant and trivial, associated with slavery. They openly held mass meetings and religious services free of white supervision, and they acquired dogs, guns, and liquor, all barred to them under slavery. No longer required to obtain a pass from their owners to travel, former slaves throughout the South left the plantations in search of better jobs, family members, or simply a taste of personal liberty. Many moved to southern towns and cities, where, it seemed, "freedom was free-er."

Families in Freedom

With slavery dead, institutions that had existed before the war, like the black family, free blacks' churches and schools, and the secret slave church, were strengthened, expanded, and freed from white supervision. The family was central to the postemancipation black community. Former slaves made remarkable efforts to locate loved ones from whom they had been separated under slavery. One northern reporter in 1865 encountered a freedman who had walked more than 600 miles from Georgia to North Carolina, searching for the wife and children from whom he had been sold away before the war. Meanwhile, widows of black soldiers successfully claimed survivors' pensions, forcing the federal government to acknowledge the validity of prewar relationships that slavery had attempted to deny.

But while Reconstruction witnessed the stabilization of family life, freedom subtly altered relationships within the family. Emancipation increased the power of black men and brought to many black families the nineteenth-century notion that men and women should inhabit separate "spheres." Immediately after the Civil War, planters complained that freedwomen had "withdrawn" from field labor and work as house servants. Many black women preferred to devote more time to their families than had been possible under slavery, and men considered it a badge of honor to see their wives remain at home. Eventually, the dire poverty of the black community would compel a far higher proportion of black women than white women to go to work for wages.

Church and School

At the same time, blacks abandoned white-controlled religious institutions to create churches of their own. On the eve of the Civil War, 42,000 black Methodists worshiped in biracial South Carolina churches; by the end of Reconstruction, only 600 remained. The rise of the independent black church, with Methodists and Baptists commanding the largest followings, redrew the religious map of the South. As the major institution independent of white control, the church played a central role in the black community. A place of worship, it also housed schools, social events, and political gatherings. Black ministers came to play a major role in politics. Some 250 held public office during Reconstruction.

Another striking example of the freedpeople's quest for individual and community improvement was their desire for education. Education, declared a Mississippi freedman, was "the next best thing to liberty." The thirst for learning sprang from many sources—a desire to read the Bible, the need to prepare for the economic marketplace, and the opportunity, which arose in 1867, to take part in politics. Blacks of all ages flocked to the schools established by northern missionary societies, the Freedmen's Bureau, and groups of ex-slaves themselves. Northern journalist Sidney Andrews, who toured the South in 1865, was impressed by how much education also took place outside of the classroom: "I had occasion very frequently to notice that porters in stores and laboring men in warehouses, and cart drivers on the streets, had spelling books with them, and were studying them during the time they were not occupied with their work." Reconstruction also witnessed the creation of the nation's first black colleges, including Fisk University in Tennessee, Hampton Institute in Virginia, and Howard University in the nation's capital.

Political Freedom

In a society that had made political participation a core element of freedom, the right to vote inevitably became central to the former slaves' desire for empowerment and equality. As Frederick Douglass put it soon after the South's surrender in 1865, "Slavery is not abolished until the black man has the ballot." In a "monarchial government," Douglass explained, no "special" disgrace applied to those denied the right to vote. But in a democracy, "where universal suffrage is the rule," excluding

Family Record, a lithograph marketed to former slaves after the Civil War, is an idealized portrait of a middle-class black family, with scenes of slavery and freedom.

Mother and Daughter Reading, Mt. Meigs, Alabama, an 1890 photograph by Rudolph Eickemeyer. During Reconstruction and for years thereafter, former slaves exhibited a deep desire for education, and learning took place outside of school as well as within.

Five Generations of a Black Family, an 1862 photograph that suggests the power of family ties among emancipated slaves

any group meant branding them with "the stigma of inferiority." As soon as the Civil War ended, and in some parts of the South even earlier, free blacks and emancipated slaves claimed a place in the public sphere. They came together in conventions, parades, and petition drives to demand the right to vote and, on occasion, to organize their own "freedom ballots."

Anything less than full citizenship, black spokesmen insisted, would betray the nation's democratic promise and the war's meaning. Speakers at black conventions reminded the nation of Crispus Attucks, who fell at the Boston Massacre, and of black soldiers' contribution to the War of 1812 and during "the bloody struggle through which we have just passed." To demonstrate their patriotism, blacks throughout the South organized Fourth of July celebrations. For years after the Civil War, white southerners would "shut themselves within doors" on Independence Day, as a white resident of Charleston recorded in her diary, while former slaves commemorated the holiday themselves.

Land, Labor, and Freedom

Former slaves' ideas of freedom, like those of rural people throughout the world, were directly related to landownership. Only land, wrote Merrimon Howard, a freedman from Mississippi, would enable "the poor class to enjoy the sweet boon of freedom." On the land they would develop independent communities free of white control. Many former slaves insisted that through their unpaid labor, they had acquired a right to the land. "The property which they hold," declared an Alabama black convention, "was nearly all earned by the sweat of *our* brows." In some parts of the South, blacks in 1865 seized property, insisting that it belonged

Landownership

The First African Church, Richmond, as depicted in *Harper's Weekly*, June 27, 1874. The establishment of independent black churches was an enduring accomplishment of Reconstruction.

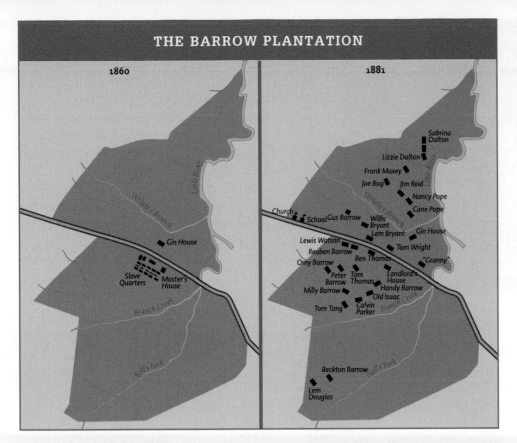

THE BARROW PLANTATION

Two maps of the Barrow plantation illustrate the effects of emancipation on rural life in the South. In 1860, slaves lived in communal quarters near the owner's house. Twenty-one years later, former slaves working as sharecroppers lived scattered across the plantation and had their own church and school.

to them. On one Tennessee plantation, former slaves claimed to be "joint heirs" to the estate and, the owner complained, took up residence "in the rooms of my house."

In its individual elements and much of its language, former slaves' definition of freedom resembled that of white Americans—self-ownership, family stability, religious liberty, political participation, and economic autonomy. But these elements combined to form a vision very much their own. For whites, freedom, no matter how defined, was a given, a birthright to be defended. For African-Americans, it was an open-ended process, a transformation of every aspect of their lives and of the society and culture that had sustained slavery in the first place. Although the freedpeople failed to achieve full freedom as they understood it, their definition did much to shape national debate during the turbulent era of Reconstruction.

Freedom's meaning to former slaves

Masters without Slaves

Most white southerners reacted to military defeat and emancipation with dismay, not only because of the widespread devastation but also because they must now submit to northern demands. "The demoralization is complete," wrote a Georgia girl. "We are whipped, there is no doubt about it." The appalling loss of life, a disaster without parallel in the American experience, affected all classes of southerners. Nearly 260,000 men died for the Confederacy—more than one-fifth of the

Confederate deaths

Winslow Homer's 1876 painting *A Visit from the Old Mistress* depicts an imaginary meeting between a southern white woman and her former slaves. Their stance and gaze suggest the tensions arising from the birth of a new social order. Homer places his subjects on an equal footing, yet maintains a space of separation between them. He exhibited the painting to acclaim at the Paris Universal Exposition in 1878.

Free labor and the good society

South's adult male white population. The wholesale destruction of work animals, farm buildings, and machinery ensured that economic revival would be slow and painful. In 1870, the value of property in the South, not counting that represented by slaves, was 30 percent lower than before the war.

Planter families faced profound changes in the war's aftermath. Many lost not only their slaves but also their life savings, which they had patriotically invested in now-worthless Confederate bonds. Some, whose slaves departed the plantation, for the first time found themselves compelled to do physical labor. General Braxton Bragg returned to his "once prosperous" Alabama home to find "*all, all* was lost, except my debts." Bragg and his wife, a woman "raised in affluence," lived for a time in a slave cabin.

Southern planters sought to implement an understanding of freedom quite different from that of the former slaves. As they struggled to accept the reality of emancipation, most planters defined black freedom in the narrowest manner. As journalist Sidney Andrews discovered late in 1865, "The whites seem wholly unable to comprehend that freedom for the negro means the same thing as freedom for them. They readily enough admit that the government has made him free, but appear to believe that they have the right to exercise the same old control." Southern leaders sought to revive the antebellum definition of freedom as if nothing had changed. Freedom still meant hierarchy and mastery; it was a privilege not a right, a carefully defined legal status rather than an open-ended entitlement. Certainly, it implied neither economic autonomy nor civil and political equality. "A man may be free and yet not independent," Mississippi planter Samuel Agnew observed in his diary in 1865. A Kentucky newspaper summed up the stance of much of the white South: the former slave was "*free*, but free only to labor."

The Free Labor Vision

Along with former slaves and former masters, the victorious Republican North tried to implement its own vision of freedom. Central to its definition was the antebellum principle of free labor, now further strengthened as a definition of the good society by the Union's triumph. In the free labor vision of a reconstructed South, emancipated blacks, enjoying the same opportunities for advancement as northern workers, would labor more productively than they had as slaves. At the same time, northern capital and migrants would energize the economy. The South would eventually come to resemble the "free society" of the North, complete with public schools, small towns, and independent farmers. Unified on the basis of free labor, proclaimed Carl Schurz, a refugee from the failed German revolution of 1848 who rose to become a leader of the Republican Party, America would become "a republic, greater, more populous, freer, more prosperous, and more powerful" than any in history.

With planters seeking to establish a labor system as close to slavery as possible, and former slaves demanding economic autonomy and access to land, a long period of conflict over the organization and control of labor followed on plantations throughout the South. It fell to **the Freedmen's Bureau**, an agency established by Congress in March 1865, to attempt to establish a working free labor system.

The Freedmen's Bureau

Under the direction of O. O. Howard, a graduate of Bowdoin College in Maine and a veteran of the Civil War, the Bureau took on responsibilities that can only be described as daunting. The Bureau was an experiment in government social policy that seems to belong more comfortably to the New Deal of the 1930s or the Great Society of the 1960s (see Chapters 21 and 25, respectively) than to nineteenth-century America. Bureau agents were supposed to establish schools, provide aid to the poor and aged, settle disputes between whites and blacks and among the freedpeople, and secure for former slaves and white Unionists equal treatment before the courts. "It is not . . . in your power to fulfill one-tenth of the expectations of those who framed the Bureau," General William T. Sherman wrote to Howard. "I fear you have Hercules' task."

The Bureau lasted from 1865 to 1870. Even at its peak, there were fewer than 1,000 agents in the entire South. Nonetheless, the Bureau's achievements in some areas, notably education and health care, were striking. While the Bureau did not establish schools itself, it coordinated and helped to finance the activities of

The Great Labor Question from a Southern Point of View, a cartoon by the artist Winslow Homer, published in *Harper's Weekly*, July 29, 1865. Homer satirizes the attitudes of many white southerners. While blacks labor in the fields, an idle planter warns a former slave, "My boy, we've toiled and taken care of you long enough—now you've got to work!"

The Freedmen's Bureau, an engraving from *Harper's Weekly*, July 25, 1868, depicts the Bureau agent as a promoter of racial peace in the violent postwar South.

Winslow Homer's 1876 painting *The Cotton Pickers*, one of a series of studies of rural life in Virginia, portrays two black women as dignified figures, without a trace of the stereotyping so common in the era's representations of former slaves. The expressions on their faces are ambiguous, perhaps conveying disappointment that eleven years after the end of slavery they are still at work in the fields.

A nursemaid and her charge, from a daguerreotype around 1865.

northern societies committed to black education. By 1869, nearly 3,000 schools, serving more than 150,000 pupils in the South, reported to the Bureau. Bureau agents also assumed control of hospitals established by the army during the war, and expanded the system into new communities. They provided medical care and drugs to both black and white southerners. In economic relations, however, the Bureau's activities proved far more problematic.

The Failure of Land Reform

The idea of free labor, wrote one Bureau agent, was "the noblest principle on earth." All that was required to harmonize race relations in the South was fair wages, good working conditions, and the opportunity to improve the laborer's situation in life. But blacks wanted land of their own, not jobs on plantations. One provision of the law establishing the Bureau gave it the authority to divide abandoned and confiscated land into forty-acre plots for rental and eventual sale to the former slaves.

In the summer of 1865, however, President Andrew Johnson, who had succeeded Lincoln, ordered nearly all land in federal hands returned to its former owners. A series of confrontations followed, notably in South Carolina and Georgia, where the army forcibly evicted blacks who had settled on "Sherman land." When O. O. Howard, head of the Freedmen's Bureau, traveled to the Sea Islands to inform blacks of the new policy, he was greeted with disbelief and protest. A committee of former slaves drew up petitions to Howard and President Johnson. "We want Homesteads," they declared, "we were promised Homesteads by the government." Land, the freedmen insisted, was essential to the meaning of freedom. Without it, they declared, "we have not bettered our condition" from the days of slavery—"you will see, this is not the condition of really free men."

Because no land distribution took place, the vast majority of rural freedpeople remained poor and without property during Reconstruction. They had no alternative but to work on white-owned plantations, often for their former owners. Far from

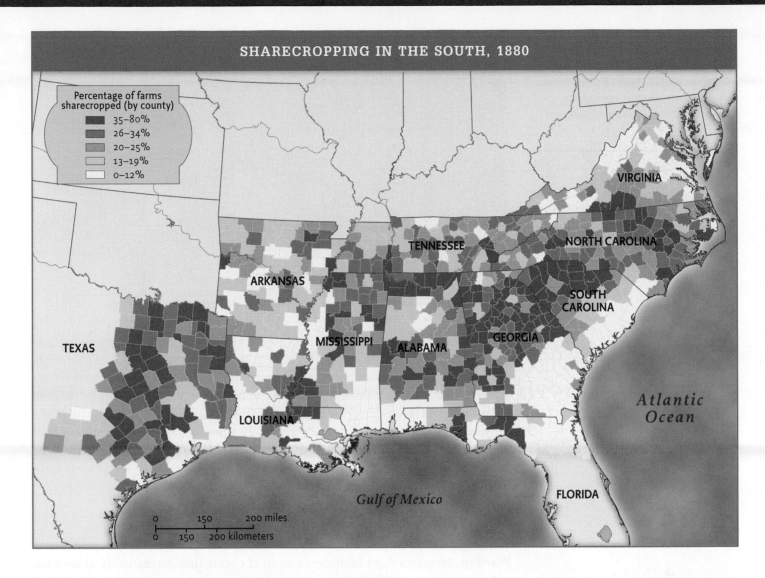

SHARECROPPING IN THE SOUTH, 1880

Percentage of farms
sharecropped (by county)

- 35–80%
- 26–34%
- 20–25%
- 13–19%
- 0–12%

being able to rise in the social scale through hard work, black men were largely confined to farm work, unskilled labor, and service jobs, and black women to positions in private homes as cooks and maids. Their wages remained too low to allow for any accumulation. By the turn of the century, a significant number of southern African-Americans had managed to acquire small parcels of land. But the failure of land reform produced a deep sense of betrayal that survived among the former slaves and their descendants long after the end of Reconstruction. "No sir," Mary Gaffney, an elderly ex-slave, recalled in the 1930s, "we were not given a thing but freedom."

By 1880, sharecropping had become the dominant form of agricultural labor in large parts of the South. The system involved both white and black farmers.

Toward a New South

Out of the conflict on the plantations, new systems of labor emerged in the different regions of the South. The task system, under which workers were assigned daily tasks, completion of which ended their responsibilities for that day, survived in the rice kingdom of South Carolina and Georgia. Closely supervised wage labor predominated on the sugar plantations of southern Louisiana. Sharecropping came to dominate the Cotton Belt and much of the Tobacco Belt of Virginia and North Carolina.

Labor systems

The cotton depot at Guthrie, Texas. Bales of cotton have been loaded onto trains for shipment. After the Civil War, more and more white farmers began growing cotton to support their families, permanently altering their formerly self-sufficient way of life.

Sharecropping initially arose as a compromise between blacks' desire for land and planters' demand for labor discipline. The system allowed each black family to rent a part of a plantation, with the crop divided between worker and owner at the end of the year. Sharecropping guaranteed the planters a stable resident labor force. Former slaves preferred it to gang labor because it offered them the prospect of working without day-to-day white supervision. But as the years went on, sharecropping became more and more oppressive. Sharecroppers' economic opportunities were severely limited by a world market in which the price of farm products suffered a prolonged decline.

The rise of sharecropping

The White Farmer

The plight of the small farmer was not confined to blacks in the postwar South. Wartime devastation set in motion a train of events that permanently altered the independent way of life of white yeomen, leading to what they considered a loss of freedom. Before the war, most small farmers had concentrated on raising food for their families and grew little cotton. With much of their property destroyed, many yeomen saw their economic condition worsened by successive crop failures after the war. To obtain supplies from merchants, farmers were forced to take up the growing of cotton and pledge a part of the crop as collateral (property the creditor can seize if a debt is not paid). This system became known as the **crop lien**. Since interest rates were extremely high and the price of cotton fell steadily, many farmers found themselves still in debt after marketing their portion of the crop at year's end. They had no choice but to continue to plant cotton to obtain new loans. By the mid-1870s, white farmers, who cultivated only 10 percent of the South's cotton crop in 1860, were growing 40 percent, and many who had owned their land had fallen into dependency as sharecroppers, who now rented land owned by others.

The crop-lien system

Both black and white farmers found themselves caught in the sharecropping and crop-lien systems. A far higher percentage of black than white farmers in the South rented land rather than owned it. But every census from 1880 to 1940 counted more white than black sharecroppers. The workings of sharecropping and the crop-lien system are illustrated by the case of Matt Brown, a Mississippi farmer who borrowed money each year from a local merchant. He began 1892 with a debt of $226 held over from the previous year. By 1893, although he produced cotton worth $171, Brown's debt had increased to $402, because he had borrowed $33 for food, $29 for clothing, $173 for supplies, and $112 for other items. Brown never succeeded in getting out of debt. He died in 1905; the last entry under his name in the merchant's account book is a coffin.

The burden of debt

The Urban South

Even as the rural South stagnated economically, southern cities experienced remarkable growth after the Civil War. As railroads penetrated the interior, they enabled merchants in market centers like Atlanta to trade directly with the North, bypassing coastal cities that had traditionally monopolized southern commerce. A new urban middle class of merchants, railroad promoters, and bankers reaped the benefits of the spread of cotton production in the postwar South.

Thus, Reconstruction brought about profound changes in the lives of southerners, black and white, rich and poor. In place of the prewar world of master, slave, and self-sufficient yeoman, the postwar South was peopled by new social classes—landowning employers, black and white sharecroppers, cotton-producing white farmers, wage-earning black laborers, and urban entrepreneurs. Each of these groups turned to Reconstruction politics in an attempt to shape to its own advantage the aftermath of emancipation.

Postwar southern society

Aftermath of Slavery

The United States, of course, was not the only society to confront the problem of the transition from slavery to freedom. Indeed, many parallels exist between the debates during Reconstruction and struggles that followed slavery in other parts of the Western Hemisphere over the same issues of land, control of labor, and political power. In every case, former planters (or, in Haiti, where the planter class had been destroyed, the government itself) tried to encourage or require former slaves to go back to work on plantations to grow the same crops as under slavery. Planters elsewhere held the same stereotypical views of black laborers as were voiced by their counterparts in the United States—former slaves were supposedly lazy, were lacking in ambition, and thought that freedom meant an absence of labor.

Emancipation in the Western Hemisphere

For their part, former slaves throughout the hemisphere tried to carve out as much independence as possible, both in their daily lives and in their labor. They attempted to reconstruct family life by withdrawing women and children from field labor (in the West Indies, women turned to marketing their families' crops to earn income). Wherever possible, former slaves acquired land of their own and devoted more time to growing food for their families than to growing crops for the international market. In many places, the plantations either fell to pieces, as in Haiti, or continued operating with a new labor force composed of indentured servants from India and China, as in Jamaica, Trinidad, and British Guiana. Southern planters in the United States brought in a few Chinese laborers in an attempt to replace freedmen, but since the federal government opposed such efforts, the Chinese remained only a tiny proportion of the southern workforce.

VOICES OF FREEDOM

From PETITION OF COMMITTEE IN BEHALF OF THE FREEDMEN TO ANDREW JOHNSON (1865)

In the summer of 1865, President Andrew Johnson ordered land that had been distributed to freed slaves in South Carolina and Georgia returned to its former owners. A committee of freedmen drafted a petition asking for the right to obtain land. Johnson did not, however, change his policy.

———————————

We the freedmen of Edisto Island, South Carolina, have learned from you through Major General O. O. Howard . . . with deep sorrow and painful hearts of the possibility of [the] government restoring these lands to the former owners. We are well aware of the many perplexing and trying questions that burden your mind, and therefore pray to god (the preserver of all, and who has through our late and beloved President [Lincoln's] proclamation and the war made us a free people) that he may guide you in making your decisions and give you that wisdom that cometh from above to settle these great and important questions for the best interests of the country and the colored race.

Here is where secession was born and nurtured. Here is where we have toiled nearly all our lives as slaves and treated like dumb driven cattle.

This is our home, we have made these lands what they were, we are the only true and loyal people that were found in possession of these lands. We have been always ready to strike for liberty and humanity, yea to fight if need be to preserve this glorious Union. Shall not we who are freedmen and have always been true to this Union have the same rights as are enjoyed by others? . . . Are not our rights as a free people and good citizens of these United States to be considered before those who were found in rebellion against this good and just government? . . .

[Are] we who have been abused and oppressed for many long years not to be allowed the privilege of purchasing land but be subject to the will of these large land owners? God forbid. Land monopoly is injurious to the advancement of the course of freedom, and if government does not make some provision by which we as freedmen can obtain a homestead, we have not bettered our condition. . . .

We look to you . . . for protection and equal rights with the privilege of purchasing a homestead—a homestead right here in the heart of South Carolina.

From A SHARECROPPING CONTRACT (1866)

Few former slaves were able to acquire land in the post–Civil War South. Most ended up as sharecroppers, working on white-owned land for a share of the crop at the end of the growing season. This contract, typical of thousands of others, originated in Tennessee. The laborers signed with an X, as they were illiterate.

Thomas J. Ross agrees to employ the Freedmen to plant and raise a crop on his Rosstown Plantation. . . . On the following Rules, Regulations and Remunerations.

The said Ross agrees to furnish the land to cultivate, and a sufficient number of mules & horses and feed them to make and house said crop and all necessary farming utensils to carry on the same and to give unto said Freedmen whose names appear below one half of all the cotton, corn and wheat that is raised on said place for the year 1866 after all the necessary expenses are deducted out that accrues on said crop. Outside of the Freedmen's labor in harvesting, carrying to market and selling the same the said Freedmen . . . covenant and agrees to and with said Thomas J. Ross that for and in consideration of one half of the crop before mentioned that they will plant, cultivate, and raise under the management control and Superintendence of said Ross, in good faith, a cotton, corn and oat crop under his management for the year 1866. And we the said Freedmen agrees to furnish ourselves & families in provisions, clothing, medicine and medical bills and all, and every kind of other expenses that we may incur on said plantation for the year 1866 free of charge to said Ross. Should the said Ross furnish us any of the above supplies or any other kind of expenses, during said year, [we] are to settle and pay him out of the net proceeds of our part of the crop the retail price of the county at time of sale or any price we may agree upon—The said Ross shall keep a regular book account, against each and every one or the head of every family to be adjusted and settled at the end of the year.

We furthermore bind ourselves to and with said Ross that we will do good work and labor ten hours a day on an average, winter and summer. . . . We further agree that we will lose all lost time, or pay at the rate of one dollar per day, rainy days excepted. In sickness and women lying in childbed are to lose the time and account for it to the other hands out of his or her part of the crop. . . .

We furthermore bind ourselves that we will obey the orders of said Ross in all things in carrying out and managing said crop for said year and be docked for disobedience. All is responsible for all farming utensils that is on hand or may be placed in care of said Freedmen for the year 1866 to said Ross and are also responsible to said Ross if we carelessly, maliciously maltreat any of his stock for said year to said Ross for damages to be assessed out of our wages.

Samuel (X) Johnson, Thomas (X) Richard, Tinny (X) Fitch, Jessie (X) Simmons, Sophe (X) Pruden, Henry (X) Pruden, Frances (X) Pruden, Elijah (X) Smith

---

QUESTIONS

1. *Why do the black petitioners believe that owning land is essential to the enjoyment of freedom?*

2. *In what ways does the contract limit the freedom of the laborers?*

3. *What do these documents suggest about competing definitions of black freedom in the aftermath of slavery?*

Chinese laborers at work on a Louisiana plantation during Reconstruction.

Emancipation and the right to vote

But if struggles over land and labor united its postemancipation experience with that of other societies, in one respect the United States was unique. Only in the United States were former slaves, within two years of the end of slavery, granted the right to vote and, thus, given a major share of political power. Few anticipated this development when the Civil War ended. It came about as the result of one of the greatest political crises of American history—the battle between President Andrew Johnson and Congress over Reconstruction. The struggle resulted in profound changes in the nature of citizenship, the structure of constitutional authority, and the meaning of American freedom.

THE MAKING OF RADICAL RECONSTRUCTION

Andrew Johnson

To Lincoln's successor, Andrew Johnson, fell the task of overseeing the restoration of the Union. Born in poverty in North Carolina, as a youth Johnson worked as a tailor's apprentice. After moving to Tennessee, he achieved success through politics. Beginning as an alderman (a town official), he rose to serve in the state legislature, the U.S. Congress, and for two terms as governor of Tennessee. Johnson identified himself as the champion of his state's "honest yeomen" and a foe of large planters, whom he described as a "bloated, corrupted aristocracy." A strong defender of the Union, he became the only senator from a seceding state to remain at his post in Washington, D.C., when the Civil War began in 1861. When northern forces occupied Tennessee, Abraham Lincoln named him military governor. In 1864, Republicans nominated him to run for vice president as a symbol of the party's hope of extending its organization into the South.

Background and outlook

In personality and outlook, Johnson proved unsuited for the responsibilities he shouldered after Lincoln's death. A lonely, stubborn man, he was intolerant of criticism and unable to compromise. He lacked Lincoln's political skills and keen sense of public opinion. A fervent believer in states' rights, Johnson insisted that since secession was illegal, the southern states had never actually left the Union or surrendered the right to govern their own affairs. Moreover, while Johnson had supported emancipation once Lincoln made it a goal of the war effort, he held deeply racist views. African-Americans, Johnson believed, had no role to play in Reconstruction.

The Failure of Presidential Reconstruction

A little over a month after Lee's surrender at Appomattox, and with Congress out of session until December, Johnson in May 1865 outlined his plan for reuniting the nation. He issued a series of proclamations that began the period of Presidential Reconstruction (1865–1867). Johnson offered a pardon (which restored political and property rights, except for slaves) to nearly all white southerners who took an oath of allegiance to the Union. He excluded Confederate leaders and wealthy planters whose prewar property had been valued at more than $20,000. This exemption suggested at first that Johnson planned a more punitive Reconstruction than Lincoln had intended. Most of those exempted, however, soon received individual pardons from the president. Johnson also appointed provisional governors and ordered them to call state conventions, elected by whites alone, that would establish loyal governments in the South. Apart from the requirement that they abolish slavery, repudiate secession, and refuse to pay the Confederate debt—all unavoidable consequences of southern defeat—he granted the new governments a free hand in managing local affairs.

Johnson's program

At first, most northerners believed Johnson's policy deserved a chance to succeed. The conduct of the southern governments elected under his program, however, turned most of the Republican North against the president. By and large, white voters returned prominent Confederates and members of the old elite to power. Reports of violence directed against former slaves and northern visitors in the South further alarmed Republicans.

The Black Codes

But what aroused the most opposition to Johnson's Reconstruction policy were the **Black Codes**, laws passed by the new southern governments that attempted to regulate the lives of the former slaves. These laws granted blacks certain rights, such as legalized marriage, ownership of property, and limited access to the courts. But they denied them the rights to testify against whites, to serve on juries or in state militias, or to vote. And in response to planters' demands that the freedpeople be required to work on the plantations, the Black Codes declared that those who failed to sign yearly labor contracts could be arrested and hired out to white landowners. Some states limited the occupations open to blacks and barred them from acquiring land, and others provided that judges could assign black children to work for their former owners without the consent of the parents. "We are not permitted to own the land whereon to build a schoolhouse or a church," complained a black convention in Mississippi. "Where is justice? Where is freedom?"

Regulating the former slaves

Thaddeus Stevens, leader of the Radical Republicans in the House of Representatives during Reconstruction.

Clearly, the death of slavery did not automatically mean the birth of freedom. But the Black Codes so completely violated free labor principles that they called forth a vigorous response from the Republican North. Wars—especially civil wars—often generate hostility and bitterness. But few groups of rebels in history have been treated more leniently than the defeated Confederates. A handful of southern leaders were arrested but most were quickly released. Only one was executed—Henry Wirz, the commander of Andersonville prison, where thousands of Union prisoners of war had died. Most of the Union army was swiftly demobilized. What motivated the North's turn against Johnson's policies was not a desire to "punish" the white South, but the inability of the South's political leaders to accept the reality of emancipation. "We must see to it," announced Republican senator William Stewart of Nevada, "that the man made free by the Constitution of the United States is a freeman indeed."

The Radical Republicans

When Congress assembled in December 1865, Johnson announced that with loyal governments functioning in all the southern states, the nation had been reunited. In response, Radical Republicans, who had grown increasingly disenchanted with Johnson during the summer and fall, called for the dissolution of these governments and the establishment of new ones with "rebels" excluded from power and black men guaranteed the right to vote. Radicals tended to represent constituencies in New England and the "burned-over" districts of the rural North that had been home to religious revivalism, abolitionism, and other reform movements. Although they differed on many issues, Radicals shared the conviction that Union victory created a golden opportunity to institutionalize the principle of equal rights for all, regardless of race.

The Radicals fully embraced the expanded powers of the federal government born during the Civil War. Traditions of federalism and states' rights, they insisted, must not obstruct a sweeping national effort to protect the rights of all Americans.

The most prominent Radicals in Congress were Charles Sumner, a senator from Massachusetts, and Thaddeus Stevens, a lawyer and iron manufacturer who represented Pennsylvania in the House of Representatives. Before the Civil War, both had been outspoken foes of slavery and defenders of black rights. Early in the Civil War, both had urged Lincoln to free and arm the slaves, and both in 1865 favored black suffrage in the South. "The same national authority," declared Sumner, "that destroyed slavery must see that this other pretension [racial inequality] is not permitted to survive."

Thaddeus Stevens's most cherished aim was to confiscate the land of disloyal planters and divide it among former slaves and northern migrants to the South. "The whole fabric of southern society," he declared, "*must* be changed. Without this, this Government can never be, as it has never been, a true republic." But his plan to make "small independent landholders" of the former slaves proved too radical even for many of his Radical colleagues. Congress, to be sure, had already offered free land to settlers in the West in the Homestead Act of 1862. But this land had been in the possession of the federal government, not private individuals (although originally, of course, it had belonged to Indians). Most congressmen believed too deeply in the sanctity of property rights to be willing to take land from one group of owners and distribute it to others. Stevens's proposal failed to pass.

> *Thaddeus Stevens*

The Origins of Civil Rights

With the South unrepresented, Republicans enjoyed an overwhelming majority in Congress. But the party was internally divided. Most Republicans were moderates, not Radicals. Moderates believed that Johnson's plan was flawed, but they desired to work with the president to modify it. They feared that neither northern nor southern whites would accept black suffrage. Moderates and Radicals joined in refusing to seat the southerners recently elected to Congress, but moderates broke with the Radicals by leaving the Johnson governments in place.

Early in 1866, Senator Lyman Trumbull of Illinois proposed two bills, reflecting the moderates' belief that Johnson's policy required modification. The first extended the life of the Freedmen's Bureau, which had originally been established for only one year. The second, the **Civil Rights Bill of 1866**, was described by one congressman as "one of the most important bills ever presented to the House for its action." It defined all persons born in the United States as citizens and spelled out rights they were to enjoy without regard to race. Equality before the law was central to the measure—no longer could states enact laws like the Black Codes discriminating between white and black citizens. So were free labor values. According to the law, no state could deprive any citizen of the right to make contracts, bring lawsuits, or enjoy equal protection of one's person and property. These, said Trumbull, were the "fundamental rights belonging to every man as a free man." The bill made no mention of the right to vote for blacks. In constitutional terms, the Civil Rights Bill represented the first attempt to give concrete meaning to the Thirteenth Amendment, which had abolished slavery, to define in law the essence of freedom.

To the surprise of Congress, Johnson vetoed both bills. Both, he said, would centralize power in the national government and deprive the states of the authority to regulate their own affairs. Moreover, he argued, blacks did not deserve the rights of citizenship. By acting to secure their rights, Congress was discriminating

President Andrew Johnson, in an 1868 lithograph by Ourrler and Ives. Because of Johnson's stubborn opposition to the congressional Reconstruction policy, one disgruntled citizen drew a crown on his head with the words, "I am King."

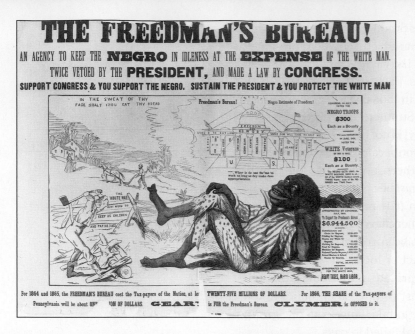

THE FREEDMAN'S BUREAU!
AN AGENCY TO KEEP THE NEGRO IN IDLENESS AT THE EXPENSE OF THE WHITE MAN.
TWICE VETOED BY THE PRESIDENT, AND MADE A LAW BY CONGRESS.
SUPPORT CONGRESS & YOU SUPPORT THE NEGRO. SUSTAIN THE PRESIDENT & YOU PROTECT THE WHITE MAN

A Democratic Party broadside from the election of 1866 in Pennsylvania uses racist imagery to argue that government assistance aids lazy former slaves at the expense of hardworking whites.

Black suffrage

Significance of the Fourteenth Amendment

"against the white race." The vetoes made a breach between the president and nearly the entire Republican Party inevitable. Congress failed by a single vote to muster the two-thirds majority necessary to override the veto of the Freedmen's Bureau Bill (although later in 1866, it did extend the Bureau's life to 1870). But in April 1866, the Civil Rights Bill became the first major law in American history to be passed over a presidential veto.

The Fourteenth Amendment

Congress now proceeded to adopt its own plan of Reconstruction. In June, it approved and sent to the states for ratification the **Fourteenth Amendment**, which placed in the Constitution the principle of citizenship for all persons born in the United States, and which empowered the federal government to protect the rights of all Americans. The amendment prohibited the states from abridging the "privileges or immunities" of citizens or denying any person of the "equal protection of the laws." This broad language opened the door for future Congresses and the federal courts to breathe meaning into the guarantee of legal equality.

In a compromise between the radical and moderate positions on black suffrage, the amendment did not grant blacks the right to vote. But it did provide that if a state denied the vote to any group of men, that state's representation in Congress would be reduced. (This provision did not apply when states barred women from voting.) The abolition of slavery threatened to increase southern political power, since now all blacks, not merely three-fifths as in the case of slaves, would be counted in determining a state's representation in Congress. The Fourteenth Amendment offered the leaders of the white South a choice—allow black men to vote and keep their state's full representation in the House of Representatives, or limit the vote to whites and sacrifice part of their political power.

The Fourteenth Amendment produced an intense division between the parties. Not a single Democrat in Congress voted in its favor, and only 4 of 175 Republicans were opposed. Radicals, to be sure, expressed their disappointment that the amendment did not guarantee black suffrage. (It was far from perfect, Stevens told the House, but he intended to vote for it, "because I live among men and not among angels.") Nonetheless, by writing into the Constitution the principle that equality before the law regardless of race is a fundamental right of all American citizens, the amendment made the most important change in that document since the adoption of the Bill of Rights.

The Reconstruction Act

The Fourteenth Amendment became the central issue of the political campaign of 1866. Johnson embarked on a speaking tour of the North, called by journalists the "swing around the circle," to urge voters to elect members of Congress committed to his own Reconstruction program. Denouncing his critics, the president made wild accusations that the Radicals were plotting to assassinate him. His behavior further undermined public support for his policies, as did riots that broke out in Memphis and New Orleans, in which white policemen and citizens killed dozens of blacks.

In the northern congressional elections that fall, Republicans opposed to Johnson's policies won a sweeping victory. Nonetheless, at the president's urging, every southern state but Tennessee refused to ratify the Fourteenth Amendment. The intransigence of Johnson and the bulk of the white South pushed moderate Republicans toward the Radicals. In March 1867, over Johnson's veto, Congress adopted the **Reconstruction Act**, which temporarily divided the South into five military districts and called for the creation of new state governments, with black men given the right to vote. Thus began the period of Radical Reconstruction, which lasted until 1877.

A variety of motives combined to produce Radical Reconstruction—demands by former slaves for the right to vote, the Radicals' commitment to the idea of equality, widespread disgust with Johnson's policies, the desire to fortify the Republican Party in the South, and the determination to keep ex-Confederates from office. But the conflict between President Johnson and Congress did not end with the passage of the Reconstruction Act.

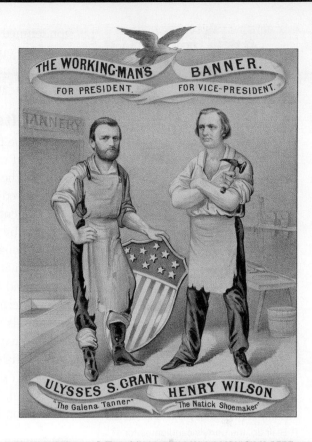

A Republican campaign poster from 1868 depicts Ulysses S. Grant and his running mate Henry Wilson not as a celebrated general and U.S. senator but as ordinary workingmen, embodiments of the dignity of free labor.

Impeachment and the Election of Grant

In March 1867, Congress adopted the **Tenure of Office Act**, barring the president from removing certain officeholders, including cabinet members, without the consent of the Senate. Johnson considered this an unconstitutional restriction on his authority. In February 1868, he removed Secretary of War Edwin M. Stanton, an ally of the Radicals. The House of Representatives responded by approving articles of **impeachment**—that is, it presented charges against Johnson to the Senate, which had to decide whether to remove him from office.

That spring, for the first time in American history, a president was placed on trial before the Senate for "high crimes and misdemeanors." By this point, virtually all Republicans considered Johnson a failure as president. But some moderates disliked Benjamin F. Wade, a Radical who, as temporary president of the Senate, would become president if Johnson were removed. Others feared that conviction would damage the constitutional separation of powers between Congress and the executive. Johnson's lawyers assured moderate Republicans that, if acquitted, he would stop interfering with Reconstruction policy. The final tally was 35–19 to convict Johnson, one vote short of the two-thirds necessary to remove him. Seven Republicans had joined the Democrats in voting to acquit the president.

Johnson's acquittal

A few days after the vote, Republicans nominated Ulysses S. Grant, the Union's most prominent military hero, as their candidate for president. Grant's Democratic opponent was Horatio Seymour, the former governor of New York. Reconstruction became the central issue of the bitterly fought 1868 campaign. Republicans identified their opponents with secession and treason, a tactic known as "waving the bloody shirt." Democrats denounced Reconstruction as unconstitutional and

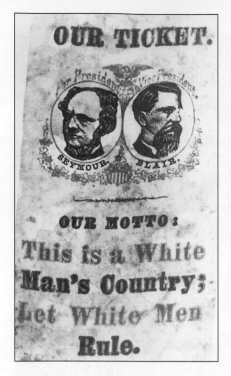

A Democratic ribbon from the election of 1868, with Horatio Seymour and Francis P. Blair Jr., the party's candidates for president and vice president. The ribbon illustrates the explicit appeals to racism that marked the campaign.

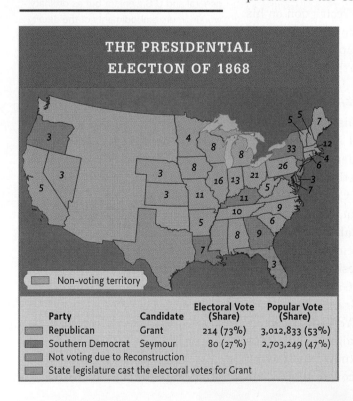

Party	Candidate	Electoral Vote (Share)	Popular Vote (Share)
Republican	Grant	214 (73%)	3,012,833 (53%)
Southern Democrat	Seymour	80 (27%)	2,703,249 (47%)
Not voting due to Reconstruction			
State legislature cast the electoral votes for Grant			

condemned black suffrage as a violation of America's political traditions. They appealed openly to racism. Seymour's running mate, Francis P. Blair Jr., charged Republicans with placing the South under the rule of "a semi-barbarous race" who longed to "subject the white women to their unbridled lust."

The Fifteenth Amendment

Grant won the election of 1868, although by a margin—300,000 of 6 million votes cast—that many Republicans found uncomfortably slim. The result led Congress to adopt the era's third and final amendment to the Constitution. In February 1869, it approved the **Fifteenth Amendment**, which prohibited the federal and state governments from denying any citizen the right to vote because of race. Bitterly opposed by the Democratic Party, it was ratified in 1870.

Although the Fifteenth Amendment opened the door to suffrage restrictions not explicitly based on race—literacy tests, property qualifications, and poll taxes—and did not extend the right to vote to women, it marked the culmination of four decades of abolitionist agitation. As late as 1868, even after Congress had enfranchised black men in the South, only eight northern states allowed African-American men to vote. With the Fifteenth Amendment, the American Anti-Slavery Society disbanded, its work, its members believed, now complete. "Nothing in all history," exclaimed veteran abolitionist William Lloyd Garrison, equaled "this wonderful, quiet, sudden transformation of four millions of human beings from . . . the auction-block to the ballot-box."

The "Great Constitutional Revolution"

The laws and amendments of Reconstruction reflected the intersection of two products of the Civil War era—a newly empowered national state and the idea of a national citizenry enjoying equality before the law. What Republican leader Carl Schurz called the "great Constitutional revolution" of Reconstruction transformed the federal system and with it, the language of freedom so central to American political culture.

Before the Civil War, American citizenship had been closely linked to race. The first Congress, in 1790, had limited to whites the right to become a naturalized citizen when immigrating from abroad. No black person, free or slave, the Supreme Court had declared in the *Dred Scott* decision of 1857, could be a citizen of the United States. The laws and amendments of Reconstruction repudiated the idea that citizenship was an entitlement of whites alone. The principle of equality before the law, moreover, did not apply only to the South. The Reconstruction amendments voided many northern laws discriminating on the basis of race. And, as one congressman noted, the amendments expanded the liberty of whites as well as blacks, including "the millions of people of foreign birth who will flock to our shores."

The new amendments also transformed the relationship between the federal government and the states. The Bill of Rights had linked civil liberties to the autonomy of the states.

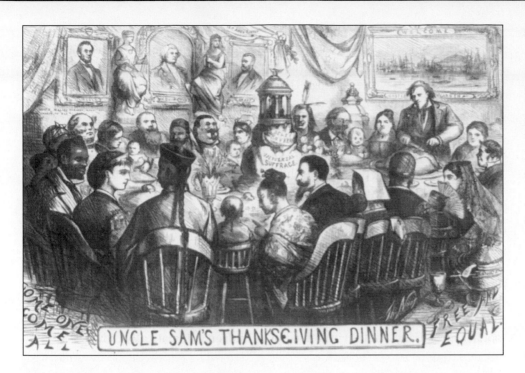

UNCLE SAM'S THANKSGIVING DINNER.

Uncle Sam's Thanksgiving Dinner, an engraving by Thomas Nast from *Harper's Weekly*, November 20, 1868, shortly after the election of Ulysses S. Grant, graphically illustrates how the boundaries of freedom had expanded during Reconstruction. The guests include, among others, African-Americans, Asian-Americans, and Native Americans, men and women, all enjoying a harmonious feast. The table's centerpiece contains the slogan, "universal suffrage."

Its language—"Congress shall make no law"—reflected the belief that concentrated national power posed the greatest threat to freedom. The authors of the Reconstruction amendments assumed that rights required national power to enforce them. Rather than a threat to liberty, the federal government, in Charles Sumner's words, had become "the custodian of freedom."

The Reconstruction amendments transformed the Constitution from a document primarily concerned with federal-state relations and the rights of property into a vehicle through which members of vulnerable minorities could stake a claim to freedom and seek protection against misconduct by all levels of government. In the twentieth century, many of the Supreme Court's most important decisions expanding the rights of American citizens were based on the Fourteenth Amendment, perhaps most notably the 1954 *Brown* ruling that outlawed school segregation (see Chapter 24).

Boundaries of Freedom

Reconstruction redrew the boundaries of American freedom. Lines of exclusion that limited the privileges of citizenship to white men had long been central to the practice of American democracy. Only in an unparalleled crisis could they have been replaced, even temporarily, by the vision of a republic of equals embracing black Americans as well as white. That the United States was a "white man's government" had been a widespread belief before the Civil War. It is not difficult to understand why Andrew Johnson, in one of his veto messages, claimed that federal protection of blacks' civil rights violated "all our experience as a people."

Race and rights

Another illustration of the new spirit of racial inclusiveness was the Burlingame Treaty, negotiated by Anson Burlingame, an antislavery congressman from Massachusetts before being named American envoy to China. Other treaties with China had been one-sided, securing trading and political advantages for European

The Burlingame Treaty

powers. The Burlingame Treaty reaffirmed China's national sovereignty, and provided reciprocal protection for religious freedom and against discrimination for citizens of each country emigrating or visiting the other. When Burlingame died, Mark Twain wrote a eulogy that praised him for "outgrow[ing] the narrow citizenship of a state [to] become a citizen of the world."

Reconstruction Republicans' belief in universal rights had its limits. In his remarkable "Composite Nation" speech of 1869, Frederick Douglass condemned prejudice against immigrants from China. America's destiny, he declared, was to transcend race by serving as an asylum for people "gathered here from all corners of the globe by a common aspiration for national liberty." A year later, Charles Sumner moved to strike the word "white" from naturalization requirements. Senators from the western states objected. At their insistence, the naturalization law was amended to make Africans eligible to obtain citizenship when migrating from abroad. But Asians remained ineligible. The racial boundaries of nationality had been redrawn, but not eliminated. The juxtaposition of the amended naturalization law and the Fourteenth Amendment created a significant division in the Asian-American community. Well into the twentieth century, Asian immigrants could not become citizens, but their native-born children automatically did.

Amendment of naturalization law

The Rights of Women

"The contest with the South that destroyed slavery," wrote the Philadelphia lawyer Sidney George Fisher in his diary, "has caused an immense increase in the popular passion for liberty and equality." But advocates of women's rights encountered the limits of the Reconstruction commitment to equality. Women activists saw Reconstruction as the moment to claim their own emancipation. No less than blacks, proclaimed Elizabeth Cady Stanton, women had arrived at a "transition period, from slavery to freedom." The rewriting of the Constitution, declared suffrage leader Olympia Brown, offered the opportunity to sever the blessings of freedom from sex as well as race and to "bury the black man and the woman in the citizen."

Women activists

The destruction of slavery led feminists to search for ways to make the promise of free labor real for women. Every issue of the new women's rights journal, *The Agitator*, edited by Mary Livermore, who had led fund-raising efforts for aid to Union soldiers during the war, carried stories complaining of the limited job opportunities and unequal pay for females who entered the labor market. Other feminists debated how to achieve "liberty for married women." Demands for liberalizing divorce laws (which generally required evidence of adultery, desertion, or extreme abuse to terminate a marriage) and for recognizing "woman's control over her own body" (including protection against domestic violence and access to what later generations would call birth control) moved to the center of many feminists' concerns. "Our rotten marriage institution," one Ohio woman wrote, "is the main obstacle in the way of woman's freedom."

Feminists and Radicals

In one place, women's political rights did expand during Reconstruction—not, however, in a bastion of radicalism such as Massachusetts, but in the Wyoming territory. This had less to do with the era's egalitarian impulse than with the desire to attract female emigrants to an area where men outnumbered women five to one. In 1869, Wyoming's diminutive legislature (it consisted of fewer than twenty men) extended the right to vote to women, and the bill was then signed by the governor, a federal appointee. Wyoming entered the Union in 1890, becoming the first state since New Jersey in the late eighteenth century to allow women to vote.

In general, however, talk of woman suffrage and redesigning marriage found few sympathetic male listeners. Even Radical Republicans insisted that Reconstruction was the "Negro's hour" (the hour, that is, of the black male). The Fourteenth Amendment for the

A Delegation of Advocates of Woman Suffrage Addressing the House Judiciary Committee, an engraving from *Frank Leslie's Illustrated Newspaper*, February 4, 1871. The group includes Elizabeth Cady Stanton, seated just to the right of the speaker, and Susan B. Anthony, at the table on the extreme right.

first time introduced the word "male" into the Constitution, in its clause penalizing a state for denying any group of men the right to vote. The Fifteenth Amendment outlawed discrimination in voting based on race but not gender. These measures produced a bitter split both between feminists and Radical Republicans, and within feminist circles.

Some leaders, like Stanton and Susan B. Anthony, opposed the Fifteenth Amendment because it did nothing to enfranchise women. They denounced their former abolitionist allies and moved to sever the women's rights movement from its earlier moorings in the antislavery tradition. On occasion, they appealed to racial and ethnic prejudices, arguing that native-born white women deserved the vote more than non-whites and immigrants. "Patrick and Sambo and Hans and Yung Tung, who do not know the difference between a monarchy and a republic," declared Stanton, had no right to be "making laws for [feminist leader] Lucretia Mott." But other abolitionist-feminists, like Abby Kelley and Lucy Stone, insisted that despite their limitations, the Reconstruction amendments represented steps in the direction of truly universal suffrage and should be supported. The result was a split in the movement and the creation in 1869 of two hostile women's rights organizations—the National Woman Suffrage Association, led by Stanton, and the American Woman Suffrage Association, with Lucy Stone as president. They would not reunite until 1890.

Thus, even as it rejected the racial definition of freedom that had emerged in the first half of the nineteenth century, Reconstruction left the gender boundary largely intact. When women tried to use the rewritten legal code and Constitution to claim equal rights, they found the courts unreceptive. Myra Bradwell invoked the idea of free labor in challenging an Illinois statute limiting the practice of law to men, but the Supreme Court in 1873 rebuffed her claim. Free labor principles, the justices declared, did not apply to women, since "the law of the Creator" had assigned them to "the domestic sphere."

Despite their limitations, the Fourteenth and Fifteenth Amendments and the Reconstruction Act of 1867 marked a radical departure in American history.

The gender boundary intact

"We have cut loose from the whole dead past," wrote Timothy Howe, a Republican senator from Wisconsin, "and have cast our anchor out a hundred years" into the future. The Reconstruction Act of 1867 inaugurated America's first real experiment in interracial democracy.

RADICAL RECONSTRUCTION IN THE SOUTH

"The Tocsin of Freedom"

Among the former slaves, the passage of the Reconstruction Act inspired an outburst of political organization. At mass political meetings—community gatherings attended by men, women, and children—African-Americans staked their claim to equal citizenship. Blacks, declared an Alabama meeting, deserved "exactly the same rights, privileges and immunities as are enjoyed by white men. We ask for nothing more and will be content with nothing less."

These gatherings inspired direct action to remedy long-standing grievances. Hundreds took part in sit-ins that integrated horse-drawn public streetcars in cities across the South. Plantation workers organized strikes for higher wages. Speakers, male and female, fanned out across the South. Frances Ellen Watkins Harper, a black veteran of the abolitionist movement, embarked on a two-year tour, lecturing on "Literacy, Land, and Liberation." James D. Lynch, a member of the group that met with General Sherman in 1865, organized Republican meetings. He became known, in the words of a white contemporary, as "a great orator, fluid and graceful," who "stirred the emotions" of his listeners "as no other man could do."

Determined to exercise their new rights as citizens, thousands joined the Union League, an organization closely linked to the Republican Party, and the vast majority of eligible African-Americans registered to vote. James K. Green,

Electioneering at the South, an engraving from *Harper's Weekly*, July 25, 1868, depicts a speaker at a political meeting in the rural South. Women as well as men took part in these grassroots gatherings.

a former slave in Hale County, Alabama, and a League organizer, went on to serve eight years in the Alabama legislature. In the 1880s, Green looked back on his political career. Before the war, he declared, "I was entirely ignorant; I knew nothing more than to obey my master; and there were thousands of us in the same attitude. . . . But the tocsin [warning bell] of freedom sounded and knocked at the door and we walked out like free men and shouldered the responsibilities."

By 1870, all the former Confederate states had been readmitted to the Union, and in a region where the Republican Party had not existed before the war, nearly all were under Republican control. Their new state constitutions, drafted in 1868 and 1869 by the first public bodies in American history with substantial black representation, marked a considerable improvement over those they replaced. The constitutions greatly expanded public responsibilities. They established the region's first state-funded systems of free public education, and they created new penitentiaries, orphan asylums, and homes for the insane. The constitutions guaranteed equality of civil and political rights and abolished practices of the antebellum era such as whipping as a punishment for crime, property qualifications for officeholding, and imprisonment for debt. A few states initially barred former Confederates from voting, but this policy was quickly abandoned by the new state governments.

From the Plantation to the Senate, an 1883 lithograph celebrating African-American progress during Reconstruction. Among the black leaders pictured at the top are Reconstruction congressmen Benjamin S. Turner, Josiah T. Walls, and Joseph H. Rainey; Hiram Revels of Mississippi, the first African-American senator; religious leader Richard Allen; and abolitionists Frederick Douglass and William Wells Brown. At the center emancipated slaves work in the cotton fields, and below children attend school and a black family stands outside its home.

The Black Officeholder

Throughout Reconstruction, black voters provided the bulk of the Republican Party's support. But African-Americans did not control Reconstruction politics, as their opponents frequently charged. The highest offices remained almost entirely in white hands, and only in South Carolina, where blacks made up 60 percent of the population, did they form a majority of the legislature. Nonetheless, the fact that some 2,000 African-Americans occupied public offices during Reconstruction represented a fundamental shift of power in the South and a radical departure in American government.

African-Americans were represented at every level of government. Fourteen were elected to the national House of Representatives. Two blacks served in the U.S. Senate during Reconstruction, both representing Mississippi. Hiram Revels, who had been born free in North Carolina, was educated in Illinois, and served as a chaplain in the wartime Union army, in 1870 became the first black senator in American history. The second, Blanche K. Bruce, a former slave, was elected in 1875. The next African-American elected to the Senate was Edward W. Brooke of Massachusetts, who served 1967–1978.

Pinckney B. S. Pinchback of Louisiana, the Georgia-born son of a white planter and a free black woman, served briefly during the winter of 1872–1873 as America's first black governor. More than a century would pass before L. Douglas Wilder of Virginia, elected in 1989, became the second. Some 700 blacks sat in state legislatures during Reconstruction, and scores held local offices ranging

The First Vote, an engraving from *Harper's Weekly*, November 16, 1867, depicts the first biracial elections in southern history. The voters represent key sources of the black political leadership that emerged during Reconstruction—the artisan carrying his tools, the well-dressed city person (probably free before the war), and the soldier.

from justice of the peace to sheriff, tax assessor, and policeman. The presence of black officeholders and their white allies made a real difference in southern life, ensuring that blacks accused of crimes would be tried before juries of their peers and enforcing fairness in such aspects of local government as road repair, tax assessment, and poor relief.

In South Carolina and Louisiana, homes of the South's wealthiest and best-educated free black communities, most prominent Reconstruction officeholders had never experienced slavery. In addition, a number of black Reconstruction officials, like Pennsylvania-born Jonathan J. Wright, who served on the South Carolina Supreme Court, had come from the North after the Civil War. The majority, however, were former slaves who had established their leadership in the black community by serving in the Union army, working as ministers, teachers, or skilled craftsmen, or engaging in Union League organizing. Among the most celebrated black officeholders was Robert Smalls, who had worked as a slave on the Charleston docks before the Civil War and who won national fame in 1862 by secretly guiding the *Planter*, a Confederate vessel, out of the harbor and delivering it to Union forces. Smalls became a powerful political leader on the South Carolina Sea Islands and was elected to five terms in Congress.

Carpetbaggers and Scalawags

The new southern governments also brought to power new groups of whites. Many Reconstruction officials were northerners who for one reason or another had made their homes in the South after the war. Their opponents dubbed them **carpetbaggers**, implying that they had packed all their belongings in a suitcase and left their homes in order to reap the spoils of office in the South. Some carpetbaggers were undoubtedly corrupt adventurers. The large majority, however, were former Union soldiers who decided to remain in the South when the war ended, before there was

Black and white members of the Mississippi senate, 1874–1875, shortly before the end of Reconstruction in the state. The woman in the bottom row is a postmistress.

any prospect of going into politics. Others were investors in land and railroads who saw in the postwar South an opportunity to combine personal economic advancement with a role in helping to substitute, as one wrote, "the civilization of freedom for that of slavery." Teachers, Freedmen's Bureau officers, and others who came to the region genuinely hoping to assist the former slaves represented another large group of carpetbaggers.

Most white Republicans had been born in the South. Former Confederates reserved their greatest scorn for these **scalawags**, whom they considered traitors to their race and region. Some southern-born Republicans were men of stature and wealth, like James L. Alcorn, the owner of one of Mississippi's largest plantations and the state's first Republican governor.

Most scalawags, however, were non-slaveholding white farmers from the southern upcountry. Many had been wartime Unionists, and they now cooperated with the Republicans in order to prevent "rebels" from returning to power. Others hoped Reconstruction governments would help them recover from wartime economic losses by suspending the collection of debts and enacting laws protecting small property holders from losing their homes to creditors. In states like North Carolina, Tennessee, and Arkansas, Republicans initially commanded a significant minority of the white vote. Even in the Deep South, the small white Republican vote was important, because the population remained almost evenly divided between blacks (almost all of whom voted for the party of Lincoln) and whites (overwhelmingly Democratic).

A portrait of Hiram Revels, the first black U.S. senator, by Theodore Kaufmann, a German-born artist who emigrated to the United States in 1855. Lithograph copies sold widely in the North during Reconstruction. Frederick Douglass, commenting on the dignified image, noted that African-Americans "so often see ourselves described and painted as monkeys, that we think it a great piece of fortune to find an exception to this general rule."

Southern Republicans in Power

In view of the daunting challenges they faced, the remarkable thing is not that Reconstruction governments in many respects failed, but how much they did accomplish. Perhaps their greatest achievement lay in establishing the South's first state-supported public schools. The new educational systems served both black and white children, although generally in schools segregated by race. Only in New Orleans were the public schools integrated during Reconstruction, and only in South Carolina did the state university admit black students (elsewhere, separate colleges were established). By the 1870s, in a region whose prewar leaders had made it illegal for slaves to learn and had done little to provide education for poorer whites, more than half the children, black and white, were attending public schools. The new governments also pioneered civil rights legislation. Their laws made it illegal for railroads, hotels, and other institutions to discriminate on the basis of race. Enforcement varied considerably from locality to locality, but Reconstruction established for the first time at the state level a standard of equal citizenship and a recognition of blacks' right to a share of public services.

> *State-supported public schools*

Republican governments also took steps to strengthen the position of rural laborers and promote the South's economic recovery. They passed laws to ensure that agricultural laborers and sharecroppers had the first claim on harvested crops, rather than merchants to whom the landowner owed money. South Carolina created a state Land Commission, which by 1876 had settled 14,000 black families and a few poor whites on their own farms.

> *Plans for economic recovery*

Emancipation, an 1865 lithograph, is unusual because along with the familiar images of Lincoln and emancipated slaves, it also portrays a poor white family, suggesting that all Americans will benefit from the end of slavery and Reconstruction.

The Quest for Prosperity

Rather than land distribution, however, the Reconstruction governments pinned their hopes for southern economic growth and opportunity for African-Americans and poor whites alike on regional economic development. Railroad construction, they believed, was the key to transforming the South into a society of booming factories, bustling towns, and diversified agriculture. "A free and living republic," declared a Tennessee Republican, would "spring up in the track of the railroad." Every state during Reconstruction helped to finance railroad construction, and through tax reductions and other incentives tried to attract northern manufacturers to invest in the region. The program had mixed results. Economic development in general remained weak. With abundant opportunities existing in the West, few northern investors ventured to the Reconstruction South.

To their supporters, the governments of Radical Reconstruction presented a complex pattern of disappointment and accomplishment. A revitalized southern economy failed to materialize, and most African-Americans remained locked in poverty. On the other hand, biracial democratic government, a thing unknown in American history, for the first time functioned effectively in many parts of the South. Public facilities were rebuilt and expanded, school systems established, and legal codes purged of racism. The conservative elite that had dominated southern government from colonial times to 1867 found itself excluded from political power, while poor whites, newcomers from the North, and former slaves cast ballots, sat on juries, and enacted and administered laws. "We have gone through one of the most remarkable changes in our relations to each other," declared a white South Carolina lawyer in 1871, "that has been known, perhaps, in the history of the world." It is a measure of how far change had progressed that the reaction against Reconstruction proved so extreme.

A group of black students and their teacher in a picture taken by an amateur photographer, probably a Union army veteran, while touring Civil War battlefields.

THE OVERTHROW OF RECONSTRUCTION

Reconstruction's Opponents

The South's traditional leaders—planters, merchants, and Democratic politicians—bitterly opposed the new governments. They denounced them as corrupt, inefficient, and examples of "black supremacy." "Intelligence, virtue, and patriotism" in public life, declared a protest by prominent southern Democrats, had given way to "ignorance, stupidity, and vice." Corruption did exist during Reconstruction, but it was confined to no race, region, or party. The rapid growth of state budgets and the benefits to be gained from public aid led in some states to a scramble for influence that produced bribery, insider dealing, and a get-rich-quick atmosphere. Southern frauds, however, were dwarfed by those practiced in these years by the Whiskey Ring, which involved high officials of the Grant administration, and by New York's Tweed Ring, controlled by the Democrats, whose thefts ran into the tens of millions of dollars. (These are discussed in the next chapter.) The rising taxes needed to pay for schools and other new public facilities and to assist railroad development were another cause of opposition to Reconstruction. Many poor whites who had initially supported the Republican Party turned against it when it became clear that their economic situation was not improving.

The most basic reason for opposition to Reconstruction, however, was that most white southerners could not accept the idea of former slaves voting, holding office, and enjoying equality before the law. In order to restore white supremacy in southern public life and to ensure planters a disciplined, reliable labor force, they believed, Reconstruction must be overthrown. Opponents launched a campaign of violence in an effort to end Republican rule. Their actions posed a fundamental challenge both for Reconstruction governments in the South and for policymakers in Washington, D.C.

Sources of opposition

Campaign of violence

"A Reign of Terror"

The Civil War ended in 1865, but violence remained widespread in large parts of the postwar South. In the early years of Reconstruction, violence was mostly

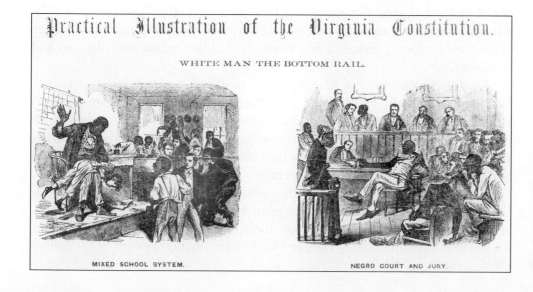

A cartoon from around 1870 illustrates a key theme of the racist opposition to Reconstruction—that blacks had forced themselves upon whites and gained domination over them. A black schoolteacher inflicts punishment on a white student in an integrated classroom, and a racially mixed jury judges a white defendant.

A Prospective Scene in the City of Oaks, a cartoon in the September 1, 1868, issue of the *Independent Monitor*, a Democratic newspaper published in Tuscaloosa, Alabama. The cartoon sent a warning to the Reverend A. S. Lakin, who had moved from Ohio to become president of the University of Alabama, and Dr. N. B. Cloud, a southern-born Republican serving as Alabama's superintendent of public education. The Ku Klux Klan forced both men from their positions. While most of the Klan's victims were black, the two men pictured here are white.

Colfax

The Enforcement Acts

local and unorganized. Blacks were assaulted and murdered for refusing to give way to whites on city sidewalks, using "insolent" language, challenging end-of-year contract settlements, and attempting to buy land. The violence that greeted the advent of Republican governments after 1867, however, was far more pervasive and more directly motivated by politics. In wide areas of the South, secret societies sprang up with the aim of preventing blacks from voting and destroying the organization of the Republican Party by assassinating local leaders and public officials.

The most notorious such organization was the **Ku Klux Klan**, which in effect served as a military arm of the Democratic Party in the South. From its founding in 1866 in Tennessee, the Klan was a terrorist organization. It quickly spread into nearly every southern state. Led by planters, merchants, and Democratic politicians, men who liked to style themselves the South's "respectable citizens," the Klan committed some of the most brutal criminal acts in American history. In many counties, it launched what one victim called a "reign of terror" against Republican leaders, black and white.

The Klan's victims included white Republicans, among them wartime Unionists and local officeholders, teachers, and party organizers. William Luke, an Irish-born teacher in a black school, was lynched in 1870. But African-Americans—local political leaders, those who managed to acquire land, and others who in one way or another defied the norms of white supremacy—bore the brunt of the violence. In York County, South Carolina, where nearly the entire white male population joined the Klan (and women participated by sewing the robes and hoods Klansmen wore as disguises), the organization committed eleven murders and hundreds of whippings.

On occasion, violence escalated from assaults on individuals to mass terrorism and even local insurrections. In Meridian, Mississippi, in 1871, some thirty blacks were murdered in cold blood, along with a white Republican judge. The bloodiest act of violence during Reconstruction took place in Colfax, Louisiana, in 1873, where armed whites assaulted the town with a small cannon. Hundreds of former slaves were murdered, including fifty members of a black militia unit after they had surrendered.

Unable to suppress the Klan, the new southern governments appealed to Washington for help. In 1870 and 1871, Congress adopted three **Enforcement Acts**, outlawing terrorist societies and allowing the president to use the army against them. These laws continued the expansion of national authority during Reconstruction. They defined crimes that aimed to deprive citizens of their civil and political rights as federal offenses rather than violations of state law. In 1871, President Grant dispatched federal marshals, backed up by troops in some areas, to arrest hundreds of accused Klansmen. Many Klan leaders fled the South. After a series of well-publicized trials, the Klan went out of existence. In 1872, for the first time since before the Civil War, peace reigned in most of the former Confederacy.

The Liberal Republicans

Despite the Grant administration's effective response to Klan terrorism, the North's commitment to Reconstruction waned during the 1870s. Many Radicals, including Thaddeus Stevens, who died in 1868, had passed from the scene. Within the Republican Party, their place was taken by politicians less committed to the ideal of equal rights for blacks. Northerners increasingly felt that the South should be able to solve its own problems without constant interference from Washington. The federal government had freed the slaves, made them citizens, and given them the right to vote. Now, blacks should rely on their own resources, not demand further assistance.

In 1872, an influential group of Republicans, alienated by corruption within the Grant administration and believing that the growth of federal power during and after the war needed to be curtailed, formed their own party. They included Republican founders like Lyman Trumbull and prominent editors and journalists such as E. L. Godkin of *The Nation*. Calling themselves Liberal Republicans, they nominated Horace Greeley, editor of the *New York Tribune*, for president.

The Liberals' alienation from the Grant administration initially had little to do with Reconstruction. They claimed that corrupt politicians had come to power in the North by manipulating the votes of immigrants and workingmen, while men of talent and education like themselves had been pushed aside. Democratic criticisms of Reconstruction, however, found a receptive audience among the Liberals. As in the North, they became convinced, the "best men" of the South had been excluded from power while "ignorant" voters controlled politics, producing corruption and misgovernment. Power in the South should be returned to the region's "natural leaders." During the campaign of 1872, Greeley repeatedly called on Americans to "clasp hands across the bloody chasm" by putting the Civil War and Reconstruction behind them.

A Tennessee member of the Ku Klux Klan, photographed in his hooded disguise around 1870.

The Old Plantation Home, a lithograph from 1872 produced by the prominent firm of Currier and Ives in New York City, illustrates how a nostalgic image of slavery as a time of carefree happiness for African-Americans was being promoted even as Reconstruction took place.

Changes in graphic artist Thomas Nast's depiction of blacks in *Harper's Weekly* mirrored the evolution of Republican sentiment in the North. *And Not This Man?*, August 5, 1865, shows the black soldier as an upstanding citizen deserving of the vote. *Colored Rule in a Reconstructed (?) State*, March 14, 1874, suggests that Reconstruction legislatures had become travesties of democratic government.

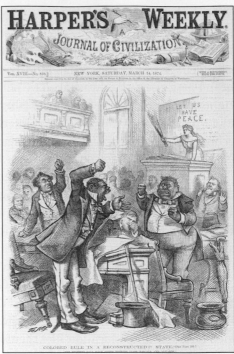

A bankbook issued by the Freedman's Savings and Trust Company, a private corporation established by Congress to promote thrift among the former slaves. Black individuals, families, church groups, and civic organizations deposited nearly $2 million in branches scattered across the South. The bank failed in 1874 because of mismanagement, and thousands of depositors lost their savings.

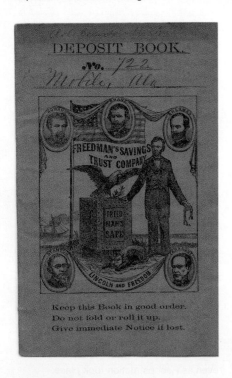

Greeley had spent most of his career, first as a Whig and then as a Republican, denouncing the Democratic Party. But with the Republican split presenting an opportunity to repair their political fortunes, Democratic leaders endorsed Greeley as their candidate. Many rank-and-file Democrats, unable to bring themselves to vote for Greeley, stayed at home on election day. As a result, Greeley suffered a devastating defeat by Grant, whose margin of more than 700,000 popular votes was the largest in a nineteenth-century presidential contest. But Greeley's campaign placed on the northern agenda the one issue on which the Liberal reformers and the Democrats could agree—a new policy toward the South.

The North's Retreat

The Liberal attack on Reconstruction, which continued after 1872, contributed to a resurgence of racism in the North. Journalist James S. Pike, a leading Greeley supporter, in 1874 published *The Prostrate State*, an influential account of a visit to South Carolina. The book depicted a state engulfed by political corruption, drained by governmental extravagance, and under the control of "a mass of black barbarism." The South's problems, Pike insisted, arose from "Negro government." The solution was to restore leading whites to political power. Newspapers that had long supported Reconstruction now began to condemn black participation in southern government. They expressed their views visually as well. Engravings depicting the former slaves as heroic Civil War veterans, upstanding citizens, or victims of violence were increasingly replaced by caricatures presenting them as little more than unbridled animals. Resurgent racism offered a convenient explanation for the alleged "failure" of Reconstruction.

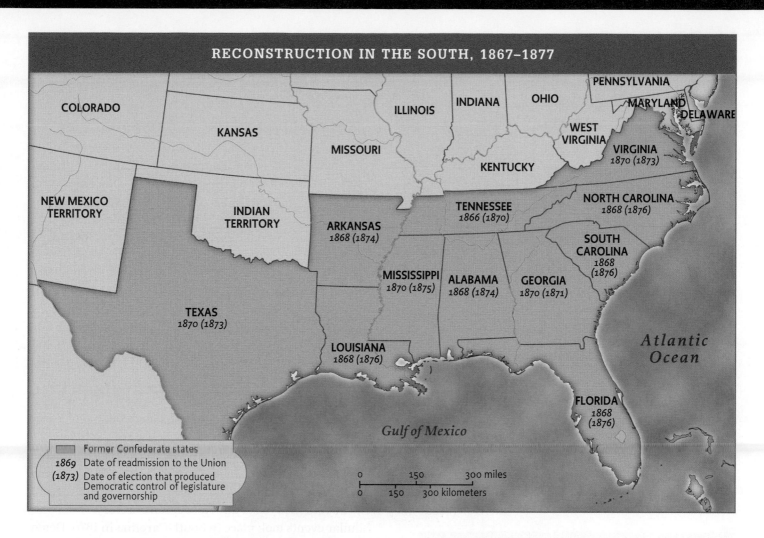

RECONSTRUCTION IN THE SOUTH, 1867–1877

COLORADO

KANSAS

NEW MEXICO
TERRITORY

INDIAN
TERRITORY

TEXAS
1870 (1873)

ILLINOIS

MISSOURI

INDIANA

OHIO

PENNSYLVANIA

MARYLAND

DELAWARE

WEST
VIRGINIA

VIRGINIA
1870 (1873)

KENTUCKY

ARKANSAS
1868 (1874)

TENNESSEE
1866 (1870)

NORTH CAROLINA
1868 (1876)

SOUTH
CAROLINA
*1868
(1876)*

MISSISSIPPI
1870 (1875)

ALABAMA
1868 (1874)

GEORGIA
1870 (1871)

LOUISIANA
1868 (1876)

FLORIDA
*1868
(1876)*

*Atlantic
Ocean*

Gulf of Mexico

Former Confederate states

1869 Date of readmission to the Union

(1873) Date of election that produced
Democratic control of legislature
and governorship

0   150   300 miles

0   150   300 kilometers

Other factors also weakened northern support for Reconstruction. In 1873, the country plunged into a severe economic depression. Distracted by economic problems, Republicans were in no mood to devote further attention to the South. The depression dealt the South a severe blow and further weakened the prospect that Republicans could revitalize the region's economy. Democrats made substantial gains throughout the nation in the elections of 1874. For the first time since the Civil War, their party took control of the House of Representatives. Before the new Congress met, the old one enacted a final piece of Reconstruction legislation, the **Civil Rights Act of 1875**. This outlawed racial discrimination in places of public accommodation like hotels and theaters. But it was clear that the northern public was retreating from Reconstruction.

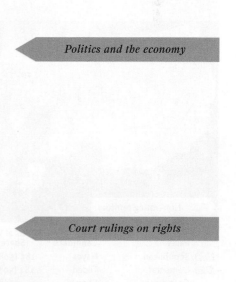

Politics and the economy

The Supreme Court whittled away at the guarantees of black rights Congress had adopted. In the *Slaughterhouse Cases* (1873), white butchers excluded from a state-sponsored monopoly in Louisiana went to court, claiming that their right to equality before the law guaranteed by the Fourteenth Amendment had been violated. The justices rejected their claim, ruling that the amendment had not altered traditional federalism. Most of the rights of citizens, it declared, remained under state

Court rulings on rights

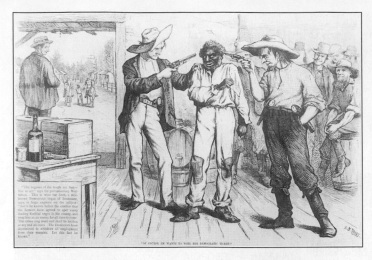

Of Course He Wants to Vote the Democratic Ticket, a cartoon from Harper's Weekly, October 21, 1876, comments on the campaign of terror launched by South Carolina Democrats in an attempt to carry the election of 1876.

control. Three years later, in *United States v. Cruikshank*, the Court gutted the Enforcement Acts by throwing out the convictions of some of those responsible for the Colfax Massacre of 1873.

The Triumph of the Redeemers

By the mid-1870s, Reconstruction was clearly on the defensive. Democrats had already regained control of states with substantial white voting majorities such as Tennessee, North Carolina, and Texas. The victorious Democrats called themselves **Redeemers**, since they claimed to have "redeemed" the white South from corruption, misgovernment, and northern and black control.

In those states where Reconstruction governments survived, violence again erupted. This time, the Grant administration showed no desire to intervene. In contrast to the Klan's activities—conducted at night by disguised men—the violence of 1875 and 1876 took place in broad daylight, as if to underscore Democrats' conviction that they had nothing to fear from Washington. In Mississippi, in 1875, white rifle clubs drilled in public and openly assaulted and murdered Republicans. When Governor Adelbert Ames, a Maine-born Union general, frantically appealed to the federal government for assistance, President Grant responded that the northern public was "tired out" by southern problems. On election day, armed Democrats destroyed ballot boxes and drove former slaves from the polls. The result was a Democratic landslide and the end of Reconstruction in Mississippi. "A revolution has taken place," wrote Ames, "and a race are disfranchised—they are to be returned to . . . an era of second slavery."

Similar events took place in South Carolina in 1876. Democrats nominated for governor former Confederate general Wade Hampton. Hampton promised to respect the rights of all citizens of the state, but his supporters, inspired by Democratic tactics in Mississippi, launched a wave of intimidation. Democrats intended to carry the election, one planter told a black official, "if we have to wade in blood knee-deep."

The Disputed Election and Bargain of 1877

Events in South Carolina directly affected the outcome of the presidential campaign of 1876. To succeed Grant, the Republicans nominated Governor Rutherford B. Hayes of Ohio. Democrats chose as his opponent New York's governor, Samuel J. Tilden. By this time, only South Carolina, Florida, and Louisiana remained under Republican control. The election turned out to be so close that whoever captured these states—which both parties claimed to have carried—would become the next president.

Unable to resolve the impasse on its own, Congress in January 1877 appointed a fifteen-member Electoral Commission, composed of senators, representatives, and Supreme Court

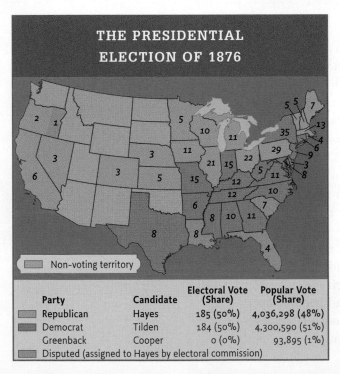

THE PRESIDENTIAL ELECTION OF 1876

Non-voting territory

Party	Candidate	Electoral Vote (Share)	Popular Vote (Share)
Republican	Hayes	185 (50%)	4,036,298 (48%)
Democrat	Tilden	184 (50%)	4,300,590 (51%)
Greenback	Cooper	0 (0%)	93,895 (1%)
Disputed (assigned to Hayes by electoral commission)			

justices. Republicans enjoyed an 8–7 majority on the commission, and to no one's surprise, the members decided by that margin that Hayes had carried the disputed southern states and had been elected president. Even as the commission deliberated, however, behind-the-scenes negotiations took place between leaders of the two parties. Hayes's representatives agreed to recognize Democratic control of the entire South and to avoid further intervention in local affairs. They also pledged that Hayes would place a southerner in the cabinet position of postmaster general and that he would work for federal aid to the Texas and Pacific railroad, a transcontinental line projected to follow a southern route. For their part, Democrats promised not to dispute Hayes's right to office and to respect the civil and political rights of blacks.

Thus was concluded the **Bargain of 1877**. Not all of its parts were fulfilled. But Hayes became president, and he did appoint David M. Key of Tennessee as postmaster general. Hayes quickly ordered federal troops to stop guarding the state houses in Louisiana and South Carolina, allowing Democratic claimants to become governor. (Contrary to legend, Hayes did not remove the last soldiers from the South—he simply ordered them to return to their barracks.) But the Texas and Pacific never did get its land grant. Of far more significance, the triumphant southern Democrats failed to live up to their pledge to recognize blacks as equal citizens.

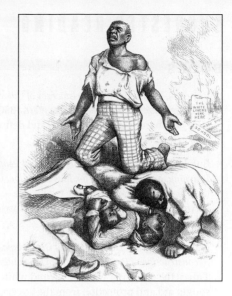

Is This a Republican Form of Government?, a cartoon by Thomas Nast in *Harper's Weekly*, September 2, 1876, illustrates his conviction that the overthrow of Reconstruction meant that the United States was not prepared to live up to its democratic ideals or protect the rights of black citizens threatened by violence.

The End of Reconstruction

As a historical process—the nation's adjustment to the destruction of slavery—Reconstruction continued well after 1877. Blacks continued to vote and, in some states, hold office into the 1890s. But as a distinct era of national history—when Republicans controlled much of the South, blacks exercised significant political power, and the federal government accepted the responsibility for protecting the fundamental rights of all American citizens—Reconstruction had come to an end. Despite its limitations, Reconstruction was a remarkable chapter in the story of American freedom. Nearly a century would pass before the nation again tried to bring equal rights to the descendants of slaves. The civil rights era of the 1950s and 1960s would sometimes be called the Second Reconstruction.

Even while it lasted, however, Reconstruction revealed some of the tensions inherent in nineteenth-century discussions of freedom. The policy of granting black men the vote while denying them the benefits of land ownership strengthened the idea that the free citizen could be a poor, dependent laborer. Reconstruction placed on the national agenda a problem that would dominate political discussion for the next half-century—how, in a modern society, to define the economic essence of freedom.

SUGGESTED READING

BOOKS

- Bottoms, D. Michael. *An Aristocracy of Color: Race and Reconstruction in California and the West*, 1850–1890 (2013). A study of changing race relations, and definitions of race, in the western states.

- Butchart, Ronald E. *Schooling the Freed People: Teaching, Learning, and the Struggle for Black Freedom* (2010). Relates the efforts of black and white teachers to educate the former slaves and some of the conflicts that arose over the purposes of such education.

- Downs, Gregory. *Declarations of Dependence: The Long Reconstruction of Popular Politics in the South, 1861–1908* (2011). Traces the changing ways black and white southerners sought aid and protection from the government during and after the Civil War and Reconstruction.

- Downs, James. *Sick from Freedom: The Deadly Consequences of Emancipation* (2012). How disease shaped the experience of freedom and how the Freedmen's Bureau and other agencies sought to cope with widespread illness among former slaves.

- DuBois, Ellen C. *Feminism and Suffrage: The Emergence of an Independent Women's Movement in America, 1848–1869* (1978). Explores how the split over the exclusion of women from the Fourteenth and Fifteenth Amendments gave rise to a movement for woman suffrage no longer tied to the abolitionist tradition.

- Edwards, Laura. *Gendered Strife and Confusion: The Political Culture of Reconstruction* (1997). Considers how issues relating to gender relations affected the course of southern Reconstruction.

- Fields, Barbara J. *Slavery and Freedom on the Middle Ground: Maryland during the Nineteenth Century* (1985). A study of slavery and emancipation in a key border state.

- Foner, Eric. *Nothing but Freedom: Emancipation and Its Legacy* (1983). Includes a comparison of the emancipation experience in different parts of the Western Hemisphere.

- Foner, Eric. *Reconstruction: America's Unfinished Revolution, 1863–1877* (1988). A comprehensive account of the Reconstruction era.

- Hahn, Steven. *A Nation under Our Feet: Black Political Struggles in the Rural South from Slavery to the Great Migration* (2003). A detailed study of black political activism, stressing nationalist consciousness and emigration movements.

- Hyman, Harold M. *A More Perfect Union: The Impact of the Civil War and Reconstruction on the Constitution* (1973). Analyzes how the laws and constitutional amendments of Reconstruction changed the Constitution and the rights of all Americans.

- Jung, Moon-Ho. *Coolies and Cane: Race, Labor, and Sugar in the Age of Emancipation* (2006). Tells the story of Chinese laborers brought to work in the sugar fields after the end of slavery.

- Litwack, Leon F. *Been in the Storm So Long: The Aftermath of Slavery* (1979). A detailed look at the immediate aftermath of the end of slavery and the variety of black and white responses to emancipation.

- Rable, George C. *But There Was No Peace: The Role of Violence in the Politics of Reconstruction* (1984). The only full-scale study of violence in the Reconstruction South.

- Richardson, Heather C. *West from Appomattox* (2007). An account that fully integrates the West into the history of the Reconstruction era.

- Rodrigue, John C. *Reconstruction in the Cane Fields: From Slavery to Free Labor in Louisiana's Sugar Parishes, 1862–1880* (2001). A study of how an often-neglected part of the South experienced the aftermath of slavery.

- Summers, Mark W. *Railroads, Reconstruction, and the Gospel of Prosperity: Aid under the Radical Republicans, 1865–1877* (1984). A detailed look at southern governments' efforts to promote economic development, and the political corruption that sometimes accompanied it.

WEBSITES

- After Slavery: Race, Labor, and Politics in the Post-Emancipation Carolinas: www.afterslavery.com

- America's Reconstruction: People and Politics after the Civil War: www.digitalhistory.uh.edu/exhibits/reconstruction/index.html

- The Andrew Johnson Impeachment Trial: www.law.umkc.edu/faculty/projects/ftrials/impeach/impeachmt.htm

- Freedmen and Southern Society Project: www.history.umd.edu/Freedmen/

- Freedmen's Bureau Online: http://www.freedmensbureau.com/

CHAPTER REVIEW AND ONLINE RESOURCES

REVIEW QUESTIONS

1. In 1865, former Confederate general Robert Richardson remarked that "the emancipated slaves own nothing, because nothing but freedom has been given to them." Explain whether this would be an accurate assessment of Reconstruction twelve years later.

2. The women's movement split into two separate national organizations in part because the Fifteenth Amendment did not give women the vote. Explain why the two groups split.

3. How did black families, churches, schools, and other institutions contribute to the development of African-American culture and political activism in this period?

4. Why did ownership of land and control of labor become major points of contention between former slaves and whites in the South?

5. By what methods did southern whites seek to limit African-American civil rights and liberties? How did the federal government respond?

6. How did the failure of land reform and continued poverty lead to new forms of servitude for both blacks and whites?

7. What caused the confrontation between President Johnson and Congress over Reconstruction policies?

8. What national issues and attitudes combined to bring an end to Reconstruction by 1877?

9. By 1877, how did the condition of former slaves in the United States compare with that of freedpeople around the globe?

KEY TERMS

the Freedmen's Bureau (p. 557)

sharecropping (p. 560)

crop lien (p. 560)

Black Codes (p. 565)

Civil Rights Bill of 1866 (p. 567)

Fourteenth Amendment (p. 568)

Reconstruction Act (p. 569)

Tenure of Office Act (p. 569)

impeachment (p. 569)

Fifteenth Amendment (p. 570)

carpetbaggers (p. 576)

scalawags (p. 577)

Ku Klux Klan (p. 580)

Enforcement Acts (p. 580)

Civil Rights Act of 1875 (p. 583)

Redeemers (p. 584)

Bargain of 1877 (p. 585)

Go to 🐰 INQUIZITIVE

To see what you know—and learn what you've missed—with personalized feedback along the way.

Visit the *Give Me Liberty!* **Student Site** for primary source documents and images, interactive maps, author videos featuring Eric Foner, and more.

APPENDIX

DOCUMENTS

The Declaration of Independence (1776)   A-2

The Constitution of the United States (1787)   A-5

From George Washington's Farewell Address (1796)   A-16

The Seneca Falls Declaration of Sentiments and Resolutions
  (1848)   A-21

From Frederick Douglass's "What, to the Slave, Is the Fourth of
  July?" Speech (1852)   A-24

The Gettysburg Address (1863)   A-27

Abraham Lincoln's Second Inaugural Address (1865)   A-28

The Populist Platform of 1892   A-29

Franklin D. Roosevelt's First Inaugural Address (1933)   A-32

From The Program for the March on Washington for
  Jobs and Freedom (1963)   A-35

Ronald Reagan's First Inaugural Address (1981)   A-36

Barack Obama's First Inaugural Address (2009)   A-39

TABLES AND FIGURES

Presidential Elections   A-42

Admission of States   A-50

Population of the United States   A-51

Historical Statistics of the United States:
  Labor Force—Selected Characteristics Expressed as a
    Percentage of the Labor Force, 1800–2010   A-52
  Immigration, by Origin   A-52
  Unemployment Rate, 1890–2015   A-53
  Union Membership as a Percentage of Nonagricultural
    Employment, 1880–2015   A-53
  Voter Participation in Presidential Elections, 1824–2012   A-53
  Birthrate, 1820–2015   A-53

THE DECLARATION OF INDEPENDENCE (1776)

When in the course of human events, it becomes necessary for one people to dissolve the political bands which have connected them with another, and to assume among the Powers of the earth, the separate and equal station to which the Laws of Nature and of Nature's God entitle them, a decent respect to the opinions of mankind requires that they should declare the causes which impel them to the separation.

We hold these truths to be self-evident, that all men are created equal, that they are endowed by their Creator with certain unalienable rights, that among these are Life, Liberty, and the pursuit of Happiness. That to secure these rights, Governments are instituted among Men, deriving their just powers from the consent of the governed. That whenever any Form of Government becomes destructive of these ends, it is the Right of the People to alter or to abolish it, and to institute new Government, laying its foundation on such principles and organizing its powers in such form, as to them shall seem most likely to effect their Safety and Happiness. Prudence, indeed, will dictate that Governments long established should not be changed for light and transient causes; and accordingly all experience hath shown, that mankind are more disposed to suffer, while evils are sufferable, than to right themselves by abolishing the forms to which they are accustomed. But when a long train of abuses and usurpations, pursuing invariably the same Object evinces a design to reduce them under absolute Despotism, it is their right, it is their duty, to throw off such Government, and to provide new Guards for their future security.—Such has been the patient sufferance of these Colonies; and such is now the necessity which constrains them to alter their former Systems of Government. The history of the present King of Great Britain is a history of repeated injuries and usurpations, all having in direct object the establishment of an absolute Tyranny over these States. To prove this, let Facts be submitted to a candid world.

He has refused his Assent to Laws, the most wholesome and necessary for the public good.

He has forbidden his Governors to pass Laws of immediate and pressing importance, unless suspended in their operation till his Assent should be obtained; and when so suspended, he has utterly neglected to attend to them.

He has refused to pass other Laws for the accommodation of large districts of people, unless those people would relinquish the right of Representation in the Legislature, a right inestimable to them and formidable to tyrants only.

He has called together legislative bodies at places unusual, uncomfortable, and distant from the depository of their public Records, for the sole purpose of fatiguing them into compliance with his measures.

He has dissolved Representative Houses repeatedly, for opposing with manly firmness his invasions on the rights of the people.

He has refused for a long time, after such dissolutions, to cause others to be elected; whereby the Legislative powers, incapable of Annihilation, have returned to the People at large for their exercise; the State remaining in the mean time exposed to all dangers of invasion from without, and convulsions within.

He has endeavoured to prevent the population of these States; for that purpose obstructing the Laws of Naturalization of Foreigners; refusing to pass others to encourage their migrations hither, and raising the conditions of new Appropriations of Lands.

He has obstructed the Administration of Justice, by refusing his Assent to Laws for establishing Judiciary powers.

He has made Judges dependent on his Will alone, for the tenure of their offices, and the amount and payment of their salaries.

He has erected a multitude of New Offices, and sent hither swarms of Officers to harass our People, and eat out their substance.

He has kept among us, in times of peace, Standing Armies without the Consent of our legislatures.

He has affected to render the Military independent of and superior to the Civil Power.

He has combined with others to subject us to a jurisdiction foreign to our constitution, and unacknowledged by our laws; giving his Assent to their Acts of pretended Legislation:

For quartering large bodies of armed troops among us:

For protecting them, by a mock Trial, from Punishment for any Murders which they should commit on the Inhabitants of these States:

For cutting off our Trade with all parts of the world:

For imposing taxes on us without our Consent:

For depriving us of many cases, of the benefits of Trial by jury:

For transporting us beyond Seas to be tried for pretended offences:

For abolishing the free System of English Laws in a neighbouring Province, establishing therein an Arbitrary government, and enlarging its Boundaries so as to render it at once an example and fit instrument for introducing the same absolute rule into these Colonies:

For taking away our Charters, abolishing our most valuable Laws, and altering fundamentally the Forms of our Governments:

For suspending our own Legislatures, and declaring themselves invested with Power to legislate for us in all cases whatsoever.

He has abdicated Government here, by declaring us out of his Protection and waging War against us.

He has plundered our seas, ravaged our Coasts, burnt our towns, and destroyed the lives of our people.

He is at this time transporting large armies of foreign mercenaries to compleat the works of death, desolation, and tyranny, already begun with circumstances of Cruelty & perfidy scarcely paralleled in the most barbarous ages, and totally unworthy the Head of a civilized nation.

He has constrained our fellow Citizens taken Captive on the high Seas to bear Arms against their Country, to become the executioners of their friends and Brethren, or to fall themselves by their Hands.

He has excited domestic insurrections amongst us, and has endeavoured to bring on the inhabitants of our frontiers, the merciless Indian Savages, whose known rule of warfare, is an undistinguished destruction of all ages, sexes, and conditions.

In every stage of these Oppressions We have Petitioned for Redress in the most humble terms: Our repeated Petitions have been answered only by repeated injury. A Prince, whose character is thus marked by every act which may define a Tyrant, is unfit to be the ruler of a free people.

Nor have We been wanting in attention to our British brethren. We have warned them from time to time of attempts by their legislature to extend an unwarrantable jurisdiction over us. We have reminded them of the circumstances of our emigration and settlement here. We have appealed to their native justice and magnanimity, and we have conjured them by the ties of our common kindred to disavow these usurpations, which, would inevitably interrupt our connections and correspondence. They too must have been deaf to the voice of justice and of consanguinity. We must, therefore, acquiesce in the necessity, which denounces our Separation, and hold them, as we hold the rest of mankind, Enemies in War, in Peace Friends.

WE, THEREFORE, the Representatives of the UNITED STATES OF AMERICA, in General Congress, Assembled, appealing to the Supreme Judge of the world for the rectitude of our intentions, do, in the Name, and by Authority of the good People of these Colonies, solemnly publish and declare, That these United Colonies are, and of Right ought to be FREE AND INDEPENDENT STATES; that they are Absolved from all Allegiance to the British Crown, and that all political connection between them and the State of Great Britain, is and ought to be totally dissolved; and that as Free and Independent States, they have full Power to levy War, conclude Peace, contract Alliances, establish Commerce, and to do all other Acts and Things which Independent States may of right do. And for the support of this Declaration, with a firm reliance on the Protection of Divine Providence, we mutually pledge to each other our Lives, our Fortunes, and our sacred Honor.

The foregoing Declaration was, by order of Congress, engrossed, and signed by the following members:

John Hancock

NEW HAMPSHIRE
Josiah Bartlett
William Whipple
Matthew Thornton

MASSACHUSETTS BAY
Samuel Adams
John Adams
Robert Treat Paine
Elbridge Gerry

RHODE ISLAND
Stephen Hopkins
William Ellery

CONNECTICUT
Roger Sherman
Samuel Huntington
William Williams
Oliver Wolcott

NEW YORK
William Floyd
Philip Livingston
Francis Lewis
Lewis Morris

NEW JERSEY
Richard Stockton
John Witherspoon
Francis Hopkinson
John Hart
Abraham Clark

PENNSYLVANIA
Robert Morris
Benjamin Rush
Benjamin Franklin
John Morton
George Clymer
James Smith
George Taylor
James Wilson
George Ross

DELAWARE
Caesar Rodney
George Read
Thomas M'Kean

MARYLAND
Samuel Chase
William Paca
Thomas Stone
Charles Carroll, of Carrollton

VIRGINIA
George Wythe
Richard Henry Lee
Thomas Jefferson
Benjamin Harrison
Thomas Nelson, Jr.
Francis Lightfoot Lee
Carter Braxton

NORTH CAROLINA
William Hooper
Joseph Hewes
John Penn

SOUTH CAROLINA
Edward Rutledge
Thomas Heyward, Jr.
Thomas Lynch, Jr.
Arthur Middleton

GEORGIA
Button Gwinnett
Lyman Hall
George Walton

Resolved, That copies of the Declaration be sent to the several assemblies, conventions, and committees, or councils of safety, and to the several commanding officers of the continental troops; that it be proclaimed in each of the United States, at the head of the army.

THE CONSTITUTION OF THE UNITED STATES (1787)

We the People of the United States, in order to form a more perfect Union, establish Justice, insure domestic Tranquility, provide for the common defence, promote the general Welfare, and secure the Blessings of Liberty to ourselves and our Posterity, do ordain and establish this Constitution for the United States of America.

ARTICLE. I.

Section. 1. All legislative Powers herein granted shall be vested in a Congress of the United States, which shall consist of a Senate and House of Representatives.

Section. 2. The House of Representatives shall be composed of Members chosen every second Year by the People of the several States, and the Electors in each State shall have the Qualifications requisite for Electors of the most numerous Branch of the State Legislature.

No Person shall be a Representative who shall not have attained to the Age of twenty five Years, and been seven Years a Citizen of the United States, and who shall not, when elected, be an Inhabitant of that State in which he shall be chosen.

Representatives and direct Taxes shall be apportioned among the several States which may be included within this Union, according to their respective Numbers, which shall be determined by adding to the whole Number of free Persons, including those bound to Service for a Term of Years, and excluding Indians not taxed, three fifths of all other Persons. The actual Enumeration shall be made within three Years after the first Meeting of the Congress of the United States, and within every subsequent Term of ten Years, in such Manner as they shall by Law direct. The Number of Representatives shall not exceed one for every thirty Thousand, but each State shall have at Least one Representative; and until such enumeration shall be made, the State of New Hampshire shall be entitled to chuse three, Massachusetts eight, Rhode-Island and Providence Plantations one, Connecticut five, New York six, New Jersey four, Pennsylvania eight, Delaware one, Maryland six, Virginia ten, North Carolina five, South Carolina five, and Georgia three.

When vacancies happen in the Representation from any state, the Executive Authority thereof shall issue Writs of Election to fill such Vacancies.

The House of Representatives shall chuse their Speaker and other Officers; and shall have the sole Power of Impeachment.

Section. 3. The Senate of the United States shall be composed of two Senators from each State, chosen by the legislature thereof, for six Years; and each Senator shall have one Vote.

Immediately after they shall be assembled in Consequence of the first Election, they shall be divided as equally as may be into three Classes. The Seats of the Senators of the first Class shall be vacated at the Expiration of the second Year, of the second Class at the Expiration of the fourth Year, and of the third Class at the Expiration of the sixth Year, so that one third may be chosen every second Year; and if Vacancies happen by Resignation, or otherwise, during the Recess of the Legislature of any State, the Executive thereof may make temporary Appointments until the next Meeting of the Legislature, which shall then fill such Vacancies.

No Person shall be a Senator who shall not have attained to the Age of thirty Years, and been nine Years a Citizen of the United States, and who shall not, when elected, be an Inhabitant of that State for which he shall be chosen.

The Vice President of the United States shall be President of the Senate, but shall have no Vote, unless they be equally divided.

The Senate shall chuse their other Officers, and also a President pro tempore, in the Absence of the Vice President, or when he shall exercise the Office of President of the United States.

The Senate shall have the sole Power to try all Impeachments. When sitting for that Purpose, they shall be on Oath or Affirmation. When the President of the United States is tried, the Chief Justice shall preside: And no Person shall be convicted without the Concurrence of two thirds of the Members present.

Judgment in Cases of Impeachment shall not extend further than to removal from Office, and disqualification to hold and enjoy any Office of honor, Trust or Profit under the United States: but the Party convicted shall nevertheless be liable and subject to Indictment, Trial, Judgment and Punishment, according to Law.

Section. 4. The Times, Places and Manner of holding Elections for Senators and Representatives, shall be prescribed in each State by the Legislature thereof; but the Congress may at any time by Law make or alter such Regulations, except as to the Places of chusing Senators.

The Congress shall assemble at least once in every Year, and such Meeting shall be on the first Monday in December, unless they shall by Law appoint a different Day.

Section. 5. Each House shall be the Judge of the Elections, Returns and Qualifications of its own Members, and a Majority of each shall constitute a Quorum to do Business; but a smaller Number may adjourn from day to day, and may be authorized to compel the Attendance of absent Members, in such Manner, and under such Penalties as each House may provide.

Each House may determine the Rules of its Proceedings, punish its Members for disorderly Behaviour, and, with the Concurrence of two thirds, expel a Member.

Each House shall keep a Journal of its Proceedings, and from time to time publish the same, excepting such Parts as may in their Judgment require Secrecy; and the Yeas and Nays of the Members of either House on any question shall, at the Desire of one fifth of those Present, be entered on the Journal.

Neither House, during the Session of Congress, shall, without the Consent of the other, adjourn for more than three days, not to any other Place than that in which the two Houses shall be sitting.

Section. 6. The Senators and Representatives shall receive a Compensation for their Services, to be ascertained by Law, and paid out of the Treasury of the United States. They shall in all Cases, except Treason, Felony and Breach of the Peace, be privileged from Arrest during their Attendance at the Session of their respective Houses, and in going to and returning from the same; and for any Speech or Debate in either House, they shall not be questioned in any other Place.

No Senator or Representative shall, during the Time for which he was elected, be appointed to any civil Office under the Authority of the United States, which shall have been created, or the Emoluments whereof shall have been encreased during such time; and no Person holding any Office under the United States, shall be a Member of either House during his Continuance in Office.

Section. 7. All Bills for raising Revenue shall originate in the House of Representatives; but the Senate may propose or concur with Amendments as on other Bills.

Every Bill which shall have passed the House of Representatives and the Senate shall, before it become a Law, be presented to the President of the United States; If he approve he shall sign it, but if not he shall return it, with his Objections to that House in which it shall have originated, who shall enter the Objections at large on their Journal, and proceed to reconsider it. If after such Reconsideration two thirds of that House shall agree to pass the Bill, it shall be sent, together with the Objections, to the other House, by which it shall likewise be reconsidered, and if approved by two thirds of that House, it shall become a Law. But in all such Cases the Votes of both Houses shall be determined by Yeas and Nays, and the Names of the Persons voting for and against the Bill shall be entered on the Journal of each House respectively. If any Bill shall not be returned by the President within ten Days (Sundays excepted) after it shall have been presented to him, the Same shall be a Law, in like Manner as if he had signed it, unless the Congress by their Adjournment prevent its Return, in which Case it shall not be a Law.

Every Order, Resolution, or Vote to which the Concurrence of the Senate and House of Representatives may be necessary (except on a question of Adjournment) shall be presented to the President of the United States; and before the Same shall take Effect, shall be approved by him, or being disapproved by him, shall be repassed by two thirds of the Senate and House of Representatives, according to the Rules and Limitations prescribed in the Case of a Bill.

Section. 8. The Congress shall have Power To lay and collect Taxes, Duties, Imposts and Excises, to pay the Debts and provide for the common Defence and general Welfare of the United States; but all Duties, Imposts and Excises shall be uniform throughout the United States;

To borrow Money on the credit of the United States;

To regulate Commerce with foreign Nations, and among the several States, and with the Indian Tribes;

To establish an uniform Rule of Naturalization, and uniform Laws on the subject of Bankruptcies throughout the United States;

To coin Money, regulate the Value thereof, and of foreign Coin, and fix the Standard of Weights and Measures;

To provide for the Punishment of counterfeiting the Securities and current Coin of the United States;

To establish Post Offices and Post Roads;

To promote the Progress of Science and useful Arts, by securing for limited Times to Authors and Inventors the exclusive Right to their respective Writings and Discoveries;

To constitute Tribunals inferior to the supreme Court;

To define and punish Piracies and Felonies committed on the high Seas, and Offences against the Law of Nations;

To declare War, grant Letters of Marque and Reprisal, and make Rules concerning Captures on Land and Water;

To raise and support Armies, but no Appropriation of Money to that Use shall be for a longer Term than two Years;

To provide and maintain a Navy;

To make Rules for the Government and Regulation of the land and naval Forces;

To provide for calling forth the Militia to execute the Laws of the Union, suppress Insurrections and repel Invasions;

To provide for organizing, arming, and disciplining, the Militia, and for governing such Part of them as may be employed in the Service of the United States, reserving to the States respectively, the Appointment of the Officers, and the Authority of training the Militia according to the discipline prescribed by Congress;

To exercise exclusive Legislation in all Cases whatsoever, over such District (not exceeding ten Miles square) as may, by Cession of Particular States, and the Acceptance of Congress, become the Seat of the Government of the United States, and to exercise like Authority over all Places purchased by the Consent of the Legislature of the State in which the Same shall be, for the Erection of Forts, Magazines, Arsenals, dock-Yards, and other needful Buildings;—And

To make all Laws which shall be necessary and proper for carrying into Execution the foregoing Powers, and all other Powers vested by this Constitution in the Government of the United States, or in any Department or Officer thereof.

Section. 9. The Migration or Importation of such Persons as any of the States now existing shall think proper to admit, shall not be prohibited by the Congress prior to the Year one thousand eight hundred and eight, but a Tax or duty may be imposed on such Importation, not exceeding ten dollars for each Person.

The Privilege of the Writ of Habeas Corpus shall not be suspended, unless when in Cases of Rebellion or Invasion the public Safety may require it.

No Bill of Attainder or ex post facto Law shall be passed.

No Capitation, or other direct, Tax shall be laid, unless in Proportion to the Census or Enumeration herein before directed to be taken.

No Tax or Duty shall be laid on Articles exported from any State.

No Preference shall be given by any Regulation of Commerce or Revenue to the Ports of one State over those of another: nor shall Vessels bound to, or from, one State, be obliged to enter, clear, or pay Duties in another.

No Money shall be drawn from the Treasury, but in Consequence of Appropriations made by Law; and a regular Statement and Account of the Receipts and Expenditures of all public Money shall be published from time to time.

No Title of Nobility shall be granted by the United States: And no Person holding any Office of Profit or Trust under them, shall, without the Consent of the Congress, accept of any present, Emolument, Office, or Title, of any kind whatever, from any King, Prince, or foreign State.

Section. 10. No State shall enter into any Treaty, Alliance, or Confederation; grant Letters of Marque and Reprisal; coin Money; emit Bills of Credit; make any Thing but gold and silver Coin a Tender in Payment of Debts; pass any Bill of Attainder, ex post facto Law, or Law impairing the Obligation of Contracts, or grant any Title of Nobility.

No State shall, without the Consent of the Congress, lay any Imposts or Duties on Imports or Exports, except what may be absolutely necessary for executing its inspection Laws: and the net Produce of all Duties and Imposts, laid by any State on Imports or Exports, shall be for the Use of the Treasury of the United States; and all such Laws shall be subject to the Revision and Controul of the Congress.

No State shall, without the Consent of Congress, lay any Duty of Tonnage, keep Troops, or Ships of War in time of Peace, enter into any Agreement or Compact with another State, or with a foreign Power, or engage in War, unless actually invaded, or in such imminent Danger as will not admit of delay.

ARTICLE. II.

Section. 1. The executive Power shall be vested in a President of the United States of America. He shall hold his Office during the term of four Years, and, together with the Vice President, chosen for the same Term, be elected, as follows:

Each State shall appoint, in such Manner as the Legislature thereof may direct, a Number of Electors, equal to the whole Number of Senators and Representatives to which the State may be entitled in the Congress: but no Senator or Representative, or Person holding an Office of Trust or Profit under the United States, shall be appointed an Elector.

The Electors shall meet in their respective States, and vote by Ballot for two Persons, of whom one at least shall not be an Inhabitant of the same State with themselves. And they shall make a List of all the Persons voted for, and of the Number of Votes for each; which List they shall sign and certify, and transmit sealed to the Seat of the Government of the United States, directed to the President of the Senate. The President of the Senate shall, in the Presence of the Senate and House of Representatives, open all the Certificates, and the Votes shall then be counted. The Person having the greatest Number of Votes shall be the President, if such Number be a Majority of the whole Number of Electors appointed; and if there be more than one who have such Majority, and have an equal Number of Votes, then the House of Representatives shall immediately chuse by Ballot one of them for President; and if no Person have a Majority, then from the five highest on the List the said House shall in like Manner chuse the President. But in chusing the President, the Votes shall be taken by States, the Representation from each State having one Vote; A quorum for this Purpose shall consist of a Member or Members from two thirds of the States, and a Majority of all the States shall be necessary to a Choice. In every Case, after the Choice of the President, the Person having the greatest Number of Votes of the Electors shall be the Vice President. But if there should remain two or more who have equal Votes, the Senate shall chuse from them by Ballot the Vice President.

The Congress may determine the Time of chusing the Electors, and the Day on which they shall give their Votes; which Day shall be the same throughout the United States.

No Person except a natural born Citizen, or a Citizen of the United States, at the time of the Adoption of this Constitution, shall be eligible to the Office of President; neither shall any Person be eligible to that Office who shall not have attained to the Age of thirty five Years, and been fourteen Years a Resident within the United States.

In Case of the Removal of the President from Office, or of his Death, Resignation, or Inability to discharge the Powers and Duties of the said Office, the Same shall devolve on the Vice President, and the Congress may by Law provide for the Case of Removal, Death, Resignation or Inability, both of the President and Vice President, declaring what Officer shall then act as President, and such Officer shall act accordingly, until the Disability be removed, or a President shall be elected.

The President shall, at stated Times, receive for his Services, a Compensation, which shall neither be encreased or diminished during the Period for which he shall have been elected, and he shall not receive within that Period any other Emolument from the United States, or any of them.

Before he enters on the Execution of his Office, he shall take the following Oath or Affirmation:—"I do solemnly swear (or affirm) that I will faithfully execute the Office of President of the United States, and will to the best of my Ability, preserve, protect and defend the Constitution of the United States."

Section. 2. The President shall be Commander in Chief of the Army and Navy of the United States, and of the Militia of the several States, when called into the actual Service of the United States; he may require the Opinion, in writing, of the principal Officer in each of the executive Departments, upon any Subject relating to the Duties of their respective Offices, and he shall have Power to grant Reprieves and Pardons for Offences against the United States, except in Cases of Impeachment.

He shall have Power, by and with the Advice and Consent of the Senate, to make Treaties, provided two thirds of the Senators present concur; and he shall nominate, and by and with the Advice and Consent of the Senate, shall appoint Ambassadors, other public Ministers and Consuls, Judges of the supreme Court, and all other Officers of the United States, whose Appointments are not herein otherwise provided for, and which shall be established by Law; but the Congress may by Law vest the Appointment of such inferior Officers, as they think proper, in the President alone, in the Courts of Law, or in the Heads of Departments.

The President shall have Power to fill up all Vacancies that may happen during the Recess of the Senate, by granting Commissions which shall expire at the End of their next Session.

Section. 3. He shall from time to time give to the Congress Information of the State of the Union, and recommend to their Consideration such Measures as he shall judge necessary and expedient; he may, on extraordinary Occasions, convene both Houses, or either of them, and in Case of Disagreement between them, with Respect to the Time of Adjournment, he may adjourn them to such Time as he shall think proper; he shall receive Ambassadors and other public Ministers; he shall take Care that the Laws be faithfully executed, and shall Commission all the Officers of the United States.

Section. 4. The President, Vice President and all civil Officers of the United States, shall be removed from Office on Impeachment for, and Conviction of, Treason, Bribery, or other high Crimes and Misdemeanors.

ARTICLE. III.

Section. 1. The judicial Power of the United States, shall be vested in one supreme Court, and in such inferior Courts as the Congress may from time to time ordain and establish. The Judges, both of the supreme and inferior Courts, shall hold their Offices during good Behavior, and shall, at stated Times, receive for their Services, a Compensation, which shall not be diminished during their Continuance in Office.

Section. 2. The judicial Power shall extend to all Cases, in Law and Equity, arising under this Constitution, the Laws of the United States, and Treaties made, or which shall be made, under their Authority;—to all Cases affecting Ambassadors, other public Ministers and Consuls;—to all Cases of admiralty and maritime Jurisdiction;—the Controversies to which the United States shall be a Party;—to Controversies between two or more States;—between a State and Citizens of another State;—between Citizens of different States;—between Citizens of the same State claiming Lands under Grants of different States, and between a State, or the Citizens thereof, and foreign States, Citizens or Subjects.

In all cases affecting Ambassadors, other public Ministers and Consuls, and those in which a State shall be Party, the supreme Court shall have original Jurisdiction. In all the other Cases before mentioned, the supreme Court shall have appellate Jurisdiction, both as to Law and Fact, with such Exceptions, and under such Regulations as the Congress shall make.

The Trial of all Crimes, except in Cases of Impeachment, shall be by Jury; and such Trial shall be held in the State where the said Crimes shall have been committed; but when not committed within any State, the Trial shall be at such Place or Places as the Congress may by Law have directed.

Section. 3. Treason against the United States, shall consist only in levying War against them, or in adhering to their Enemies, giving them Aid and Comfort. No Person shall be convicted of Treason unless on the Testimony of two Witnesses to the same overt Act, or on Confession in open Court.

The Congress shall have Power to declare the Punishment of Treason, but no Attainder of Treason shall work Corruption of Blood, or Forfeiture except during the Life of the Person attainted.

ARTICLE. IV.

Section. 1. Full Faith and Credit shall be given in each State to the public Acts, Records, and judicial Proceedings of every other State. And the Congress may by general Laws prescribe the Manner in which such Acts, Records and Proceedings shall be proved, and the Effect thereof.

Section. 2. The Citizens of each State shall be entitled to all Privileges and Immunities of Citizens in the several States.

A Person charged in any State with Treason, Felony, or other Crime, who shall flee from Justice, and be found in another State, shall on Demand of the executive Authority of the State from which he fled, be delivered up, to be removed to the State having Jurisdiction of the Crime.

No Person held to Service or Labour in one State, under the Laws thereof, escaping into another, shall, in Consequence of any Law or Regulation therein, be discharged from such Service or Labour, but shall be delivered up on Claim of the Party to whom such Service or Labour may be due.

Section. 3. New States may be admitted by the Congress into this Union; but no new State shall be formed or erected within the Jurisdiction of any other State; nor any State be formed by the Junction of two or more States, or Parts of States, without the consent of the Legislatures of the States concerned as well as of the Congress.

The Congress shall have Power to dispose of and make all needful Rules and Regulations respecting the Territory or other Property belonging to the United States; and nothing in this Constitution shall be so construed as to Prejudice any Claims of the United States, or of any particular States.

Section. 4. The United States shall guarantee to every State in this Union a Republican Form of Government, and shall protect each of them against Invasion; and on Application of the Legislature, or of the Executive (when the Legislature cannot be convened) against domestic Violence.

ARTICLE. V.

The Congress, whenever two thirds of both Houses shall deem it necessary, shall propose Amendments to this Constitution, or, on the Application of the Legislatures of two thirds of the several States, shall call a Convention for proposing Amendments, which, in either Case, shall be valid to all Intents and Purposes, as Part of this Constitution, when ratified by the Legislatures of three fourths of the several States, or by Conventions in three fourths thereof, as the one or the other Mode of Ratification may be proposed by the Congress; Provided that no Amendment which may be made prior to the Year One thousand eight hundred and eight shall in any Manner affect the first and fourth Clauses in the Ninth Section of the first Article; and that no State, without its Consent, shall be deprived of its equal Suffrage in the Senate.

ARTICLE. VI.

All Debts contracted and Engagements entered into, before the Adoption of this Constitution, shall be as valid against the United States under this Constitution, as under the Confederation.

This Constitution, and the Laws of the United States which shall be made in Pursuance thereof; and all Treaties made, or which shall be made, under the Authority of the United States, shall be the supreme Law of the Land; and the Judges in every State shall be bound thereby, any Thing in the Constitution or Laws of any State to the Contrary notwithstanding.

The Senators and Representatives before mentioned, and the Members of the several State Legislatures, and all executive and judicial Officers, both of the United States and of the several States, shall be bound by Oath or Affirmation, to support this Constitution; but no religious Test shall ever be required as a Qualification to any Office or public Trust under the United States.

ARTICLE. VII.

The Ratification of the Conventions of nine States, shall be sufficient for the Establishment of this Constitution between the States so ratifying the Same.

Done in Convention by the Unanimous Consent of the States present the Seventeenth Day of September in the Year of our Lord one thousand seven hundred and Eighty seven and of the Independence of the United States of America the Twelfth. In witness thereof We have hereunto subscribed our Names,

G⁰. WASHINGTON—Presdᵗ.
and deputy from Virginia

NEW HAMPSHIRE
John Langdon
Nicholas Gilman

MASSACHUSETTS
Nathaniel Gorham
Rufus King

CONNECTICUT
Wᵐ Samˡ Johnson
Roger Sherman

NEW YORK
Alexander Hamilton

NEW JERSEY
Wil: Livingston
David A. Brearley
Wᵐ Paterson
Jona: Dayton

PENNSYLVANIA
B Franklin
Thomas Mifflin
Robᵗ Morris
Geo. Clymer
Thoˢ FitzSimons
Jared Ingersoll
James Wilson
Gouv Morris

DELAWARE
Geo: Read
Gunning Bedford jun
John Dickinson
Richard Bassett
Jaco: Broom

MARYLAND
James McHenry
Dan of Sᵗ Thoˢ Jenifer
Danˡ Carroll

VIRGINIA
John Blair—
James Madison Jr.

NORTH CAROLINA
Wᵐ Blount
Richᵈ Dobbs Spaight
Hu Williamson

SOUTH CAROLINA
J. Rutledge
Charles Cotesworth
   Pinckney
Charles Pinckney
Pierce Butler

GEORGIA
William Few
Abr Baldwin

AMENDMENTS TO THE CONSTITUTION

Articles in addition to, and Amendment of the Constitution of the United States of America, proposed by Congress, and ratified by the Legislatures of the several States, pursuant to the fifth Article of the original Constitution.

AMENDMENT I.*
Congress shall make no law respecting an establishment of religion, or prohibiting the free exercise thereof; or abridging the freedom of speech, or of the press; or the right of the people peaceably to assemble, and to petition the Government for a redress of grievances.

AMENDMENT II.
A well regulated Militia, being necessary to the security of a free State, the right of the people to keep and bear Arms, shall not be infringed.

AMENDMENT III.
No Soldier shall, in time of peace be quartered in any house, without the consent of the Owner, nor in time of war, but in a manner to be prescribed by law.

AMENDMENT IV.
The right of the people to be secure in their persons, houses, papers, and effects, against unreasonable searches and seizures, shall not be violated, and no Warrants shall issue, but upon probable cause, supported by Oath or affirmation, and particularly describing the place to be searched, and the persons or things to be seized.

AMENDMENT V.
No person shall be held to answer for a capital, or otherwise infamous crime, unless on a presentment or indictment of a Grand Jury, except in cases arising in the land or naval forces, or in the Militia, when in actual service in time of War or public danger; nor shall any person be subject for the same offence to be twice put in jeopardy of life or limb; nor shall be compelled in any criminal case to be a witness against himself, nor be deprived of life, liberty, or property, without due process of law; nor shall private property be taken for public use, without just compensation.

*The first ten Amendments (the Bill of Rights) were ratified in 1791.

AMENDMENT VI.
In all criminal prosecutions, the accused shall enjoy the right to a speedy and public trial, by an impartial jury of the State and district wherein the crime shall have been committed, which district shall have been previously ascertained by law, and to be informed of the nature and cause of the accusation; to be confronted with the witnesses against him; to have compulsory process for obtaining witnesses in his favor, and to have the Assistance of Counsel for his defence.

AMENDMENT VII.
In Suits at common law, where the value in controversy shall exceed twenty dollars, the right of trial by jury shall be preserved, and no fact tried by a jury, shall be otherwise re-examined in any Court of the United States, than according to the rules of the common law.

AMENDMENT VIII.
Excessive bail shall not be required, nor excessive fines imposed, nor cruel and unusual punishments inflicted.

AMENDMENT IX.
The enumeration in the Constitution, of certain rights, shall not be construed to deny or disparage others retained by the people.

AMENDMENT X.
The powers not delegated to the United States by the Constitution, nor prohibited by it to the States, are reserved to the States respectively, or to the people.

AMENDMENT XI.
The Judicial power of the United States shall not be construed to extend to any suit in law or equity, commenced or prosecuted against one of the United States by Citizens of another State, or by Citizens or Subjects of any Foreign State. [January 8, 1798]

AMENDMENT XII.
The Electors shall meet in their respective states, and vote by ballot for President and Vice-President, one of whom, at least, shall not be an inhabitant of the same state with themselves; they shall name in their ballots the person voted for as President, and in distinct ballots the person voted for as Vice-President, and they shall

make distinct lists of all persons voted for as President, and of all persons voted for as Vice President, and of the number of votes for each, which lists they shall sign and certify, and transmit sealed to the seat of the government of the United States, directed to the President of the Senate;—The President of the Senate shall, in the presence of the Senate and House of Representatives, open all the certificates and the votes shall then be counted;—The person having the greatest number of votes for President, shall be the President, if such number be a majority of the whole number of Electors appointed; and if no person have such majority, then from the persons having the highest numbers not exceeding three on the list of those voted for as President, the House of Representatives shall choose immediately, by ballot, the President. But in choosing the President, the votes shall be taken by states, the representation from each state having one vote; a quorum for this purpose shall consist of a member or members from two-thirds of the states, and a majority of all the states shall be necessary to a choice. And if the House of Representatives shall not choose a President whenever the right of choice shall devolve upon them, before the fourth day of March next following, then the Vice-President shall act as President, as in the case of the death or other constitutional disability of the President.— The person having the greatest number of votes as Vice-President, shall be the Vice-President, if such number be a majority of the whole number of Electors appointed, and if no person have a majority, then from the two highest numbers on the list, the Senate shall choose the Vice-President; a quorum for the purpose shall consist of two-thirds of the whole number of Senators, and a majority of the whole number shall be necessary to a choice. But no person constitutionally ineligible to the office of President shall be eligible to that of Vice-President of the United States. [September 25, 1804]

AMENDMENT XIII.
Section 1. Neither slavery nor involuntary servitude, except as a punishment for crime whereof the party shall have been duly convicted, shall exist within the United States, or any place subject to their jurisdiction.

Section 2. Congress shall have power to enforce this article by appropriate legislation. [December 18, 1865]

AMENDMENT XIV.
Section 1. All persons born or naturalized in the United States, and subject to the jurisdiction thereof, are citizens of the United States and of the State wherein they reside. No State shall make or enforce any law which shall abridge the privileges or immunities of citizens of the United States; nor shall any State deprive any person of life, liberty, or property, without due process of law; nor deny to any person within its jurisdiction the equal protection of the laws.

Section 2. Representatives shall be apportioned among the several States according to their respective numbers, counting the whole number of persons in each State, excluding Indians not taxed. But when the right to vote at any election for the choice of electors for President and Vice President of the United States, Representatives in Congress, the Executive and Judicial officers of a State, or the members of the Legislature thereof, is denied to any of the male inhabitants of such State, being twenty-one years of age, and citizens of the United States, or in any way abridged, except for participation in rebellion, or other crime, the basis of representation therein shall be reduced in the proportion which the number of such male citizens shall bear to the whole number of male citizens twenty-one years of age in such State.

Section 3. No person shall be a Senator or Representative in Congress, or elector of President and Vice President, or hold any office, civil or military, under the United States, or under any State, who, having previously taken an oath, as a member of Congress, or as an officer of the United States, or as a member of any State legislature, or as an executive or judicial officer of any State, to support the Constitution of the United States, shall have engaged in insurrection or rebellion against the same, or given aid or comfort to the enemies thereof. But Congress may by a vote of two-thirds of each House, remove such disability.

Section 4. The validity of the public debt of the United States, authorized by law, including debts incurred for payment of pensions and bounties for services in suppressing insurrection or rebellion, shall not be questioned. But neither the United States nor any State shall assume or pay any debt or obligation incurred in aid of insurrection or rebellion against the United States, or any claim for the loss or emancipation of any slave; but all such debts, obligations and claims shall be held illegal and void.

Section 5. The Congress shall have power to enforce, by appropriate legislation, the provisions of this article. [July 28, 1868]

AMENDMENT XV.

Section 1. The right of citizens of the United States to vote shall not be denied or abridged by the United States or by any State on account of race, color, or previous condition of servitude—

Section 2. The Congress shall have power to enforce this article by appropriate legislation. [March 30, 1870]

AMENDMENT XVI.

The Congress shall have power to lay and collect taxes on incomes, from whatever source derived, without apportionment among the several States, and without regard to any census or enumeration. [February 25, 1913]

AMENDMENT XVII.

The Senate of the United States shall be composed of two senators from each State, elected by the people thereof, for six years; and each Senator shall have one vote. The electors in each State shall have the qualifications requisite for electors of the most numerous branch of the State legislatures.

When vacancies happen in the representation of any State in the Senate, the executive authority of such State shall issue writs of election to fill such vacancies: *Provided,* That the legislature of any State may empower the executive thereof to make temporary appointments until the people fill the vacancies by election as the legislature may direct.

This amendment shall not be so construed as to affect the election or term of any senator chosen before it becomes valid as part of the Constitution. [May 31, 1913]

AMENDMENT XVIII.

After one year from the ratification of this article, the manufacture, sale, or transportation of intoxicating liquors within, the importation thereof into, or the exportation thereof from the United States and all territory subject to the jurisdiction thereof for beverage purposes is hereby prohibited.

The Congress and the several States shall have concurrent power to enforce this article by appropriate legislation.

This article shall be inoperative unless it shall have been ratified as an amendment to the Constitution by the legislatures of the several States, as provided in the Constitution, within seven years from the date of the submission thereof to the States by Congress. [January 29, 1919]

AMENDMENT XIX.

The right of citizens of the United States to vote shall not be denied or abridged by the United States or by any State on account of sex.

The Congress shall have power by appropriate legislation to enforce the provisions of this article. [August 26, 1920]

AMENDMENT XX.

Section 1. The terms of the President and Vice-President shall end at noon on the twentieth day of January, and the terms of Senators and Representatives at noon on the third day of January, of the years in which such terms would have ended if this article had not been ratified; and the terms of their successors shall then begin.

Section 2. The Congress shall assemble at least once in every year, and such meeting shall begin at noon on the third day of January, unless they shall by law appoint a different day.

Section 3. If, at the time fixed for the beginning of the term of the President, the President-elect shall have died, the Vice-President-elect shall become President. If a President shall not have been chosen before the time fixed for the beginning of his term, or if the President-elect shall have failed to qualify, then the Vice-President-elect shall act as President until a President shall have qualified; and the Congress may by law provide for the case wherein neither a President-elect nor a Vice-President-elect shall have qualified, declaring who shall then act as President, or the manner in which one who is to act shall be selected, and such person shall act accordingly until a President or Vice-President shall have qualified.

Section 4. The Congress may by law provide for the case of the death of any of the persons from whom the House of Representatives may choose a President whenever the right of choice shall have devolved upon them, and for the case of the death of any of the persons from whom the Senate may choose a Vice-President whenever the right of choice shall have devolved upon them.

Section 5. Sections 1 and 2 shall take effect on the 15th day of October following the ratification of this article.

Section 6. This article shall be inoperative unless it shall have been ratified as an amendment to the Constitution by the legislatures of three-fourths of the several States within seven years from the date of its submission. [February 6, 1933]

AMENDMENT XXI.

Section 1. The eighteenth article of amendment to the Constitution of the United States is hereby repealed.

Section 2. The transportation or importation into any State, Territory or possession of the United States for delivery or use therein of intoxicating liquors, in violation of the laws thereof, is hereby prohibited.

Section 3. This article shall be inoperative unless it shall have been ratified as an amendment to the Constitution by convention in the several States, as provided in the Constitution, within seven years from the date of the submission thereof to the States by the Congress. [December 5, 1933]

AMENDMENT XXII.

Section 1. No person shall be elected to the office of the President more than twice, and no person who has held the office of President, or acted as President, for more than two years of a term to which some other person was elected President shall be elected to the office of the President more than once. But this Article shall not apply to any person holding the office of President when this Article was proposed by the Congress, and shall not prevent any person who may be holding the office of President, or acting as President, during the term within which this Article becomes operative from holding the office of President or acting as President during the remainder of such term.

Section 2. This article shall be inoperative unless it shall have been ratified as an amendment to the Constitution by the legislatures of three-fourths of the several States within seven years from the date of its submission to the States by the Congress. [February 27, 1951]

AMENDMENT XXIII.

Section 1. The District constituting the seat of government of the United States shall appoint in such manner as the Congress may direct:

A number of electors of President and Vice-President equal to the whole number of Senators and Representatives in Congress to which the District would be entitled if it were a State, but in no event more than the least populous State; they shall be in addition to those appointed by the States, but they shall be considered, for the purposes of

the election of President and Vice-President, to be electors appointed by a State; and they shall meet in the District and perform such duties as provided by the twelfth article of amendment.

Section 2. The Congress shall have the power to enforce this article by appropriate legislation. [March 29, 1961]

AMENDMENT XXIV.

Section 1. The right of citizens of the United States to vote in any primary or other election for President or Vice President, for electors for President or Vice President, or for Senator or Representative in Congress, shall not be denied or abridged by the United States or any State by reason of failure to pay any poll tax or other tax.

Section 2. The Congress shall have power to enforce this article by appropriate legislation. [January 23, 1964]

AMENDMENT XXV.

Section 1. In case of the removal of the President from office or of his death or resignation, the Vice President shall become President.

Section 2. Whenever there is a vacancy in the office of Vice President, the President shall nominate a Vice President who shall take office upon confirmation by a majority vote of both Houses of Congress.

Section 3. Whenever the President transmits to the President pro tempore of the Senate and the Speaker of the House of Representatives his written declaration that he is unable to discharge the powers and duties of his office, and until he transmits to them a written declaration to the contrary, such powers and duties shall be discharged by the Vice President as Acting President.

Section 4. Whenever the Vice President and a majority of either the principal officers of the executive departments or of such other body as Congress may by law provide, transmit to the President pro tempore of the Senate and the Speaker of the House of Representatives their written declaration that the President is unable to discharge the powers and duties of his office, the Vice President shall immediately assume the powers and duties of the office as Acting President.

Thereafter, when the President transmits to the President pro tempore of the Senate and the Speaker of the House of Representatives his written declaration that no inability exists, he shall resume the powers and duties of his office unless the Vice President and a majority of either the principal officers of the executive departments or of such other body as Congress may by law provide, transmit within four days to the President pro tempore of the Senate and the Speaker of the House of Representatives their written declaration that the President is unable to discharge the powers and duties of his office. Thereupon Congress shall decide the issue, assembling within forty-eight hours for that purpose if not in session. If the Congress, within twenty-one days after receipt of the latter written declaration, or, if Congress is not in session, within twenty-one days after Congress is required to assemble, determines by two-thirds vote of both Houses that the President is unable to discharge the powers and duties of his office, the Vice-President shall continue to discharge the same as Acting President; otherwise, the President shall resume the powers and duties of his office. [February 10, 1967]

AMENDMENT XXVI.

Section 1. The right of citizens of the United States, who are eighteen years of age or older, to vote shall not be denied or abridged by the United States or by any State on account of age.

Section 2. The Congress shall have power to enforce this article by appropriate legislation. [June 30, 1971]

AMENDMENT XXVII.

No law, varying the compensation for the services of the Senators and Representatives shall take effect, until an election of Representatives shall have intervened. [May 8, 1992]

FROM GEORGE WASHINGTON'S FAREWELL ADDRESS (1796)

Friends and Citizens:

The period for a new election of a citizen to administer the executive government of the United States being not far distant, and the time actually arrived when your thoughts must be employed in designating the person who is to be clothed with that important trust, it appears to me proper, especially as it may conduce to a more distinct expression of the public voice, that I should now apprise you of the resolution I have formed, to decline being considered among the number of those out of whom a choice is to be made.

In looking forward to the moment which is intended to terminate the career of my public life, my feelings do not permit me to suspend the deep acknowledgment of that debt of gratitude which I owe to my beloved country for the many honors it has conferred upon me; still more for the steadfast confidence with which it has supported me; and for the opportunities I have thence enjoyed of manifesting my inviolable attachment, by services faithful and persevering, though in usefulness unequal to my zeal. If benefits have resulted to our country from these services, let it always be remembered to your praise, and as an instructive example in our annals, that under circumstances in which the passions, agitated in every direction, were liable to mislead, amidst appearances sometimes dubious, vicissitudes of fortune often discouraging, in situations in which not unfrequently want of success has countenanced the spirit of criticism, the constancy of your support was the essential prop of the efforts, and a guarantee of the plans by which they were effected. Profoundly penetrated with this idea, I shall carry it with me to my grave, as a strong incitement to unceasing vows that heaven may continue to you the choicest tokens of its beneficence; that your union and brotherly affection may be perpetual; that the free Constitution, which is the work of your hands, may be sacredly maintained; that its administration in every department may be stamped with wisdom and virtue; that, in fine, the happiness of the people of these States, under the auspices of liberty, may be made complete by so careful a preservation and so prudent a use of this blessing as will acquire to them the glory of recommending it to the applause, the affection, and adoption of every nation which is yet a stranger to it.

Here, perhaps, I ought to stop. But a solicitude for your welfare, which cannot end but with my life, and the apprehension of danger, natural to that solicitude, urge me, on an occasion like the present, to offer to your solemn contemplation, and to recommend to your frequent review, some sentiments which are the result of much reflection, of no inconsiderable observation, and which appear to me all-important to the permanency of your felicity as a people. These will be offered to you with the more freedom, as you can only see in them the disinterested warnings of a parting friend, who can possibly have no personal motive to bias his counsel. Nor can I forget, as an encouragement to it, your indulgent reception of my sentiments on a former and not dissimilar occasion.

Interwoven as is the love of liberty with every ligament of your hearts, no recommendation of mine is necessary to fortify or confirm the attachment.

The unity of government which constitutes you one people is also now dear to you. It is justly so, for it is a main pillar in the edifice of your real independence, the support of your tranquility at home, your peace abroad; of your safety; of your prosperity; of that very liberty which you so highly prize. But as it is easy to foresee that, from different causes and from different quarters, much pains will be taken, many artifices employed to weaken in your minds the conviction of this truth; as this is the point in your political fortress against which the batteries of internal and external enemies will be most constantly and actively (though often covertly and insidiously) directed, it is of infinite moment that you should properly estimate the immense value of your national union to your collective and individual happiness; that you should cherish a cordial, habitual, and immovable attachment to it; accustoming yourselves to think and speak of it as of the palladium of your political safety and prosperity; watching for its preservation with jealous anxiety; discountenancing whatever may suggest even a suspicion that it can in any event be abandoned; and indignantly frowning upon the first dawning of every attempt to alienate any portion of our country from the rest, or to enfeeble the sacred ties which now link together the various parts.

For this you have every inducement of sympathy and interest. Citizens, by birth or choice, of a common country, that country has a right to concentrate your affections. The name of American, which belongs to you in your national capacity, must always exalt the just pride of patriotism more than any appellation derived from local discriminations. With slight shades of difference, you have the same religion, manners, habits, and political principles. You have in a common cause fought and triumphed together; the independence and liberty you possess are the work of joint counsels, and joint efforts of common dangers, sufferings, and successes.

But these considerations, however powerfully they address themselves to your sensibility, are greatly outweighed by those which apply more immediately to your interest. Here every portion of our country finds the most commanding motives for carefully guarding and preserving the union of the whole.

The North, in an unrestrained intercourse with the South, protected by the equal laws of a common government, finds in the productions of the latter great additional resources of maritime and commercial enterprise and precious materials of manufacturing industry. The South, in the same intercourse, benefiting by the agency of the North, sees its agriculture grow and its commerce expand. Turning partly into its own channels the seamen of the North, it finds its particular navigation invigorated; and, while it contributes, in different ways, to nourish and increase the general mass of the national navigation, it looks forward to the protection of a maritime strength, to which itself is unequally adapted. The East, in a like intercourse with the West, already finds, and in the progressive improvement of interior communications by land and water, will more and more find a valuable vent for the commodities which it brings from abroad, or manufactures at home. The West derives from the East supplies requisite to its growth and comfort, and, what is perhaps of still greater consequence, it must of necessity owe the secure enjoyment of indispensable outlets for its own productions to the weight, influence, and the future maritime strength of the Atlantic side of the Union, directed by an indissoluble community of interest as one nation. Any other tenure by which the West can hold this essential advantage, whether derived from its own separate strength, or from an apostate and unnatural connection with any foreign power, must be intrinsically precarious.

While, then, every part of our country thus feels an immediate and particular interest in union, all the parts combined cannot fail to find in the united mass of means and efforts greater strength, greater resource, proportionably greater security from external danger, a less frequent interruption of their peace by foreign nations; and, what is of inestimable value, they must derive from union an

exemption from those broils and wars between themselves, which so frequently afflict neighboring countries not tied together by the same governments, which their own rival ships alone would be sufficient to produce, but which opposite foreign alliances, attachments, and intrigues would stimulate and embitter. Hence, likewise, they will avoid the necessity of those overgrown military establishments which, under any form of government, are inauspicious to liberty, and which are to be regarded as particularly hostile to republican liberty. In this sense it is that your union ought to be considered as a main prop of your liberty, and that the love of the one ought to endear to you the preservation of the other.

These considerations speak a persuasive language to every reflecting and virtuous mind, and exhibit the continuance of the Union as a primary object of patriotic desire. Is there a doubt whether a common government can embrace so large a sphere? Let experience solve it. To listen to mere speculation in such a case were criminal. We are authorized to hope that a proper organization of the whole with the auxiliary agency of governments for the respective subdivisions, will afford a happy issue to the experiment. It is well worth a fair and full experiment. With such powerful and obvious motives to union, affecting all parts of our country, while experience shall not have demonstrated its impracticability, there will always be reason to distrust the patriotism of those who in any quarter may endeavor to weaken its bands.

★ ★ ★

To the efficacy and permanency of your Union, a government for the whole is indispensable. No alliance, however strict, between the parts can be an adequate substitute; they must inevitably experience the infractions and interruptions which all alliances in all times have experienced. Sensible of this momentous truth, you have improved upon your first essay, by the adoption of a constitution of government better calculated than your former for an intimate union, and for the efficacious management of your common concerns. This government, the offspring of our own choice, uninfluenced and unawed, adopted upon full investigation and mature deliberation, completely free in its principles, in the distribution of its powers, uniting security with energy, and containing within itself a provision for its own amendment, has a just claim to your confidence and your support. Respect for its authority, compliance with its laws, acquiescence in its measures, are duties enjoined by the fundamental maxims of true liberty. The basis of our political systems is the

his progenitors for several generations, I anticipate with pleasing expectation that retreat in which I promise myself to realize, without alloy, the sweet enjoyment of partaking, in the midst of my fellow-citizens, the benign influence of good laws under a free government, the ever-favorite object of my heart, and the happy reward, as I trust, of our mutual cares, labors, and dangers.

Geo. Washington

THE SENECA FALLS DECLARATION OF SENTIMENTS AND RESOLUTIONS (1848)

1. DECLARATION OF SENTIMENTS

When, in the course of human events, it becomes necessary for one portion of the family of man to assume among the people of the earth a position different from that which they have hitherto occupied, but one to which the laws of nature and of nature's God entitle them, a decent respect to the opinions of mankind requires that they should declare the causes that impel them to such a course.

We hold these truths to be self-evident: that all men and women are created equal; that they are endowed by their Creator with certain inalienable rights; that among these are life, liberty, and the pursuit of happiness; that to secure these rights governments are instituted, deriving their just powers from the consent of the governed. Whenever any form of government becomes destructive of these ends, it is the right of those who suffer from it to refuse allegiance to it, and to insist upon the institution of a new government, laying its foundation on such principles, and organizing its powers in such form, as to them shall seem most likely to effect their safety and happiness. Prudence, indeed, will dictate that governments long established should not be changed for light and transient causes; and accordingly all experience hath shown that mankind are more disposed to suffer, while evils are sufferable, than to right themselves by abolishing the forms to which they are accustomed. But when a long train of abuses and usurpations, pursuing invariably the same object, evinces a design to reduce them under absolute despotism, it is their duty to throw off such government, and to provide new guards for their future security. Such has been the patient sufferance of the women under this government, and such is now the necessity which constrains them to demand the equal station to which they are entitled. The history of mankind is a history of repeated injuries and usurpations on the part of man toward woman, having in direct object the establishment of an absolute tyranny over her. To prove this, let facts be submitted to a candid world.

He has never permitted her to exercise her inalienable right to the elective franchise.

He has compelled her to submit to laws, in the formation of which she had no voice.

He has withheld from her rights which are given to the most ignorant and degraded men—both natives and foreigners.

Having deprived her of this first right of a citizen, the elective franchise, thereby leaving her without representation in the halls of legislation, he has oppressed her on all sides.

He has made her, if married, in the eye of the law, civilly dead. He has taken from her all right in property, even to the wages she earns.

He has made her, morally, an irresponsible being, as she can commit many crimes with impunity, provided they be done in the presence of her husband.

In the covenant of marriage, she is compelled to promise obedience to her husband, he becoming, to all intents and purposes, her master—the law giving him power to deprive her of her liberty, and to administer chastisement.

He has so framed the laws of divorce, as to what shall be the proper causes, and in case of separation, to whom the guardianship of the children shall be given, as to be wholly regardless of the happiness of women—the law, in all cases, going upon a false supposition of the supremacy of man, and giving all power into his hands.

After depriving her of all rights as a married woman, if single, and the owner of property, he has taxed her to support a government which recognizes her only when her property can be made profitable to it.

He has monopolized nearly all the profitable employments, and from those she is permitted to follow, she receives but a scanty remuneration. He closes against her all the avenues to wealth and distinction which he considers most honorable to himself. As a teacher of theology, medicine, or law, she is not known.

He has denied her the facilities for obtaining a thorough education, all colleges being closed against her.

He allows her in Church, as well as State, but a subordinate position, claiming Apostolic authority for her exclusion from the ministry, and, with some exceptions, from any public participation in the affairs of the Church.

He has created a false public sentiment by giving to the world a different code of morals for men and women, by which moral delinquencies which exclude women from society, are not only tolerated, but deemed of little account in man.

He has usurped the prerogative of Jehovah himself, claiming it as his right to assign for her a sphere of action, when that belongs to her conscience and to her God.

He has endeavored, in every way that he could, to destroy her confidence in her own powers, to lessen her self-respect and to make her willing to lead a dependent and abject life.

Now, in view of this entire disfranchisement of one-half the people of this country, their social and religious degradation—in view of the unjust laws above mentioned, and because women do feel themselves aggrieved, oppressed, and fraudulently deprived of their most sacred rights, we insist that they have immediate admission to all the rights and privileges which belong to them as citizens of the United States.

In entering upon the great work before us, we anticipate no small amount of misconception, misrepresentation, and ridicule; but we shall use every instrumentality within our power to effect our object. We shall employ agents, circulate tracts, petition the State and National legislatures, and endeavor to enlist the pulpit and the press in our behalf. We hope this Convention will be followed by a series of Conventions embracing every part of the country.

2. RESOLUTIONS

WHEREAS, The great precept of nature is conceded to be, that "man shall pursue his own true and substantial happiness." Blackstone in his Commentaries remarks, that this law of Nature being coeval with mankind, and dictated by God himself, is of course superior in obligation to any other. It is binding over all the globe, in all countries and at all times; no human laws are of any validity if contrary to this, and such of them as are valid, derive all their force, and all their validity, and all their authority, mediately and immediately, from this original; therefore,

Resolved, That such laws as conflict, in any way, with the true and substantial happiness of woman, are contrary to the great precept of nature and of no validity, for this is "superior in obligation to any other."

Resolved, That all laws which prevent woman from occupying such a station in society as her conscience shall dictate, or which place her in a position inferior to that of man, are contrary to the great precept of nature, and therefore of no force or authority.

Resolved, That woman is man's equal—was intended to be so by the Creator, and the highest good of the race demands that she should be recognized as such.

Resolved, That the women of this country ought to be enlightened in regard to the laws under which they live, that they may no longer publish their degradation by declaring themselves satisfied with their present position, nor their ignorance, by asserting that they have all the rights they want.

Resolved, That inasmuch as man, while claiming for himself intellectual superiority, does accord to woman moral superiority, it is pre-eminently his duty to encourage her to speak and teach, as she has an opportunity, in all religious assemblies.

Resolved, That the same amount of virtue, delicacy, and refinement of behavior that is required of woman in the social state, should also be required of man, and the same transgressions should be visited with equal severity on both man and woman.

Resolved, That the objection of indelicacy and impropriety, which is so often brought against woman when she addresses a public audience, comes with a very ill-grace from those who encourage, by their attendance, her appearance on the stage, in the concert. Or in feats of the circus.

Resolved, That woman has too long rested satisfied in the circumscribed limits which corrupt customs and a perverted application of the Scriptures have marked out for her, and that it is time she should move in the enlarged sphere which her great Creator has assigned her.

Resolved, That it is the duty of the women of this country to secure to themselves their sacred right to the elective franchise.

Resolved, That the equality of human rights results necessarily from the fact of the identity of the race in capabilities and responsibilities.

Resolved, therefore, That, being invested by the Creator with the same capabilities, and the same consciousness of responsibility for their exercise, it is demonstrably the right and duty of woman, equally with man, to promote every righteous cause by every righteous means; and especially in regard to the great subjects of morals and religion, it is self-evidently her right to participate with her brother in teaching them, both in private and in public, by writing and by speaking, by any instrumentalities proper to be used, and in any assemblies proper to be held; and this being a self-evident truth growing out of the divinely implanted principles of human nature, any custom or authority adverse to it, whether modern or wearing the hoary sanction of antiquity, is to be regarded as a self-evident falsehood, and at war with mankind.

Resolved, That the speedy success of our cause depends upon the zealous and untiring efforts of both men and women, for the overthrow of the monopoly of the pulpit, and for the securing to women an equal participation with men in the various trades, professions, and commerce.

FROM FREDERICK DOUGLASS'S "WHAT, TO THE SLAVE, IS THE FOURTH OF JULY?" SPEECH (1852)

★ ★ ★

This, for the purpose of this celebration, is the Fourth of July. It is the birthday of your National Independence, and of your political freedom. This, to you, is what the Passover was to the emancipated people of God. It carries your minds back to the day, and to the act of your great deliverance; and to the signs and to the wonders associated with that act and that day. This celebration also marks the beginning of another year of your national life; and reminds you that the Republic of America is now seventy-six years old. I am glad, fellow citizens, that your nation is so young. Seventy-six years, though a good old age for a man, is but a mere speck in the life of a nation. Three score years and ten is the allotted time for individual men; but nations number their years by thousands. According to this fact, you are, even now, only in the beginning of your national career, still lingering in the period of childhood. I repeat, I am glad this is so. There is hope in the thought, and hope is much needed, under the dark clouds which lower above the horizon. The eye of the reformer is met with angry flashes, portending disastrous times; but his heart may well beat lighter at the thought that America is young, and that she is still in the impressible stage of her existence. May he not hope that high lessons of wisdom, of justice and of truth, will yet give direction to her destiny? Were the nation older, the patriot's heart might be sadder and the reformer's brow heavier. Its future might be shrouded in gloom and the hope of its prophets go out in sorrow. There is consolation in the thought that America is young. Great streams are not easily turned from channels worn deep in the course of ages. They may sometimes rise in quiet and stately majesty, and inundate the land, refreshing and fertilizing the earth with their mysterious properties. They may also rise in wrath and fury, and bear away on their angry waves the accumulated wealth of years of toil and hardship. They, however, gradually flow back to the same old channel and flow on as serenely as ever. But, while the river may not be turned aside, it may dry up and leave nothing behind but the withered branch and the unsightly rock, to howl in the abyss-sweeping wind, the sad tale of departed glory. As with rivers, so with nations.

Fellow citizens, I shall not presume to dwell at length on the associations that cluster about this day. The simple story of it is, that seventy-six years ago the people of this country were British subjects. The style and title of your "sovereign people" (in which you now glory) was not then born. You were under the British Crown. Your fathers esteemed the English government as the home government, and England as the fatherland. This home government, you know, although a considerable distance from your home, did, in the exercise of its parental prerogatives, impose upon its colonial children such restraints, burdens and limitations as, in its mature judgment, it deemed wise, right and proper.

★ ★ ★

Feeling themselves harshly and unjustly treated by the home government, your fathers, like men of honesty and men of spirit, earnestly sought redress. They petitioned and remonstrated; they did so in a decorous, respectful and loyal manner. Their conduct was wholly unexceptionable. This, however, did not answer the purpose. They saw themselves treated with sovereign indifference, coldness and scorn. Yet they persevered. They were not the men to look back.

★ ★ ★

Citizens, your fathers . . . succeeded; and today you reap the fruits of their success. The freedom gained is yours; and you, therefore, may properly celebrate this anniversary. The Fourth of July is the first great fact in your nation's history—the very ringbolt in the chain of your yet undeveloped destiny.

Pride and patriotism, not less than gratitude, prompt you to celebrate and to hold it in perpetual remembrance. I have said that the Declaration of Independence is the ringbolt to the chain of your nation's destiny; so, indeed, I regard it. The principles contained in that instrument are saving principles. Stand by those principles, be true to them on all occasions, in all places, against all foes, and at whatever cost.

★ ★ ★

[The fathers of this republic] were peace men, but they preferred revolution to peaceful submission to bondage. They were quiet men; but they did not shrink from agitating against oppression. They showed forbearance, but that they knew its limits. They believed in order, but not in the order of tyranny. With them, nothing was "settled" that was not right. With them, justice, liberty and humanity were "final," not slavery and oppression. You may well cherish the memory of such men. They were great in their day and generation. Their solid manhood stands out the more as we contrast it with these degenerate times.

★ ★ ★

Fellow citizens, pardon me, allow me to ask, why am I called upon to speak here today? What have I, or those I represent, to do with your national independence? Are the great principles of political freedom and of natural justice, embodied in that Declaration of Independence, extended to us? and am I, therefore, called upon to bring our humble offering to the national altar and to confess the benefits and express devout gratitude for the blessings resulting from your independence to us?

★ ★ ★

But such is not the state of the case. I say it with a sad sense of the disparity between us. I am not included within the pale of this glorious anniversary! Your high independence only reveals the immeasurable distance between us. The blessings in which you, this day, rejoice, are not enjoyed in common. The rich inheritance of justice, liberty, prosperity and independence, bequeathed by your fathers, is shared by you, not by me. The sunlight that brought light and healing to you, has brought stripes and death to me. This Fourth of July is *yours*, not *mine*. *You* may rejoice, *I* must mourn.

★ ★ ★

Fellow citizens, above your national, tumultuous joy I hear the mournful wail of millions! whose chains, heavy and grievous yesterday, are today rendered more intolerable by the jubilee shouts that reach them. If I do forget, if I do not faithfully remember those bleeding children of sorrow this day, "may my right hand forget her cunning, and may my tongue cleave to the roof of my mouth!" To forget them, to pass lightly over their wrongs and to chime in with the popular theme would be treason most scandalous and shocking and would make me a reproach before God and the world. My subject, then, fellow citizens, is American slavery. I shall see this day and its popular characteristics from the slave's point of view. Standing there identified with the American bondman, making his wrongs mine, I do not hesitate to declare, with all my soul, that the character and conduct of this nation never looked blacker to me than on this Fourth of July. Whether we turn to the declarations of the past or to the professions of the present, the conduct of the nation seems equally hideous and revolting. America is false to the past, false to the present, and solemnly binds herself to be false to the future.

★ ★ ★

For the present, it is enough to affirm the equal manhood of the Negro race. It is not astonishing that, while we are plowing, planting and reaping, using all kinds of mechanical tools, erecting houses, constructing bridges, building ships, working in metals of brass, iron, copper, silver and gold; that, while we are reading, writing and ciphering, acting as clerks, merchants and secretaries, having among us lawyers, doctors, ministers, poets, authors, editors, orators and teachers; that, while we are engaged in all manner of enterprises common to other men, digging gold in California, capturing the whale in the Pacific, feeding sheep and cattle on the hillside, living, moving, acting, thinking, planning, living in families as husbands, wives and children, and, above all, confessing and worshiping the Christian's God and looking hopefully for life and immortality beyond the grave, we are called upon to prove that we are men!

Would you have me argue that man is entitled to liberty? that he is the rightful owner of his own body? You have already declared it. Must I argue the wrongfulness of slavery? Is that a question for republicans? Is it to be settled by the rules of logic and argumentation, as a matter beset with great difficulty, involving a doubtful application of the principle of justice, hard to be understood? How should I look today, in the presence of Americans, dividing and subdividing a discourse, to show that men have a natural right to freedom, speaking of it relatively and positively, negatively and affirmatively? To do so would be to make myself ridiculous and to offer an insult to your understanding. There is not a man beneath the canopy of heaven that does not know that slavery is wrong *for him*.

★ ★ ★

What, to the American slave, is your Fourth of July? I answer: a day that reveals to him, more than all other days in the year, the gross injustice and cruelty to which he is the constant victim. To him, your celebration is a sham; your boasted liberty an unholy license; your national greatness swelling vanity; your sounds of rejoicing are empty and heartless; your denunciation of tyrants brass-fronted impudence; your shouts of liberty and equality hollow mockery; your prayers and hymns, your sermons and thanksgivings, with all your religious parade and solemnity, are to Him mere bombast, fraud, deception, impiety and hypocrisy—a thin veil to cover up crimes which would disgrace a nation of savages. There is not a nation on the earth guilty of practices more shocking and bloody than are the people of the United States at this very hour.

Go where you may, search where you will, roam through all the monarchies and despotisms of the Old World, travel through South America, search out every abuse, and when you have found the last, lay your facts by the side of the everyday practices of this nation, and you will say with me, that, for revolting barbarity and shameless hypocrisy, America reigns without a rival.

Americans! your republican politics, not less than your republican religion, are flagrantly inconsistent. You boast of your love of liberty, your superior civilization and your pure Christianity, while the whole political power of the nation (as embodied in the two great political parties) is solemnly pledged to support and perpetuate the enslavement of three millions of your countrymen. You hurl your anathemas at the crowned-headed tyrants of Russia and Austria and pride yourselves on your democratic institutions, while you yourselves consent to be the mere *tools* and *bodyguards* of the tyrants of Virginia and Carolina. You invite to your shores fugitives of oppression from abroad, honor them with banquets, greet them with ovations, cheer them, toast them, salute them, protect them, and pour out your money to them like water; but the fugitives from your own land you advertise, hunt, arrest, shoot and kill. You glory in your refinement and your universal education; yet you maintain a system as barbarous and dreadful as ever stained the character of a nation—a system begun in avarice, supported in pride, and perpetuated in cruelty. You shed tears over fallen Hungary, and make the sad story of her wrongs the theme of your poets, statesmen and orators, till your gallant sons are ready to fly to arms to vindicate her cause against the oppressor;* but, in regard to the ten thousand wrongs of the American slave, you would enforce the strictest silence and would hail him as an enemy of the nation who dares to make those wrongs the subject of public discourse! You are all on fire at the mention of liberty for France or for Ireland, but are as cold as an iceberg at the thought of liberty for the enslaved of America. You discourse eloquently on the dignity of labor; yet, you sustain a system which, in its very essence, casts a stigma upon labor. You can bare your bosom to the storm of British artillery to throw off a three-penny tax on tea, and yet wring the last hard-earned farthing from the grasp of the black laborers of your country. You profess to believe "that of one blood God made all nations of men to dwell on the face of all the earth"† and hath commanded all men, everywhere, to love one another; yet you notoriously hate (and glory in your hatred) all men whose skins are not colored like your own. You declare before the world, and are understood by the world to declare, that you "*hold these truths to be self-evident, that all men are created equal; and are endowed by their Creator with certain unalienable rights; and that among these are, life, liberty and the pursuit of happiness*"; and yet, you hold securely, in a bondage which, according to your own Thomas Jefferson, "*is worse than ages of that which your fathers rose in rebellion to oppose,*" a seventh part of the inhabitants of your country.

Fellow citizens, I will not enlarge further on your national inconsistencies. The existence of slavery in this country brands your republicanism as a sham, your humanity as a base pretense, and your Christianity as a lie. It destroys your moral power abroad; it corrupts your politicians at home. It saps the foundation of religion; it makes your name a hissing and a byword to a mocking earth. It is the antagonistic force in your government, the only thing that seriously disturbs and endangers your union. It fetters your progress; it is the enemy of improvement; the deadly foe of education; it fosters pride; it breeds insolence; it promotes vice; it shelters crime; it is a curse to the earth that supports it; and yet you cling to it as if it were the sheet anchor of all your hopes.

★ ★ ★

Allow me to say, in conclusion, notwithstanding the dark picture I have this day presented, of the state of the nation, I do not despair of this country. There are forces in operation which must inevitably work the downfall of slavery.

★ ★ ★

---

*The fledgling Hungarian republic was invaded by Austria and Russia in 1849.
†Acts 17:26.

THE GETTYSBURG ADDRESS (1863)

Four score and seven years ago our fathers brought forth on this continent, a new nation, conceived in Liberty, and dedicated to the proposition that all men are created equal.

Now we are engaged in a great civil war, testing whether that nation, or any nation so conceived and so dedicated, can long endure. We are met on a great battle field of that war. We have come to dedicate a portion of that field, as a final resting place for those who here gave their lives that that nation might live. It is altogether fitting and proper that we should do this.

But, in a larger sense, we can not dedicate—we can not consecrate—we can not hallow—this ground. The brave men, living and dead, who struggled here, have consecrated it, far above our poor power to add or detract. The world will little note, nor long remember what we say here, but it can never forget what they did here. It is for us the living, rather, to be dedicated here to the unfinished work which they who fought here have thus far so nobly advanced. It is rather for us to be here dedicated to the great task remaining before us—that from these honored dead we take increased devotion to that cause for which they gave the last full measure of devotion—that we here highly resolve that these dead shall not have died in vain—that this nation, under God, shall have a new birth of freedom—and that government of the people, by the people, for the people, shall not perish from the earth.

Abraham Lincoln
November 19, 1863

ABRAHAM LINCOLN'S SECOND INAUGURAL ADDRESS (1865)

Fellow Countrymen:

At this second appearing to take the oath of the presidential office, there is less occasion for an extended address than there was at the first. Then a statement, somewhat in detail, of a course to be pursued, seemed fitting and proper. Now, at the expiration of four years, during which public declarations have been constantly called forth on every point and phase of the great contest which still absorbs the attention, and engrosses the energies of the nation, little that is new could be presented. The progress of our arms, upon which all else chiefly depends, is as well known to the public as to myself; and it is, I trust, reasonably satisfactory and encouraging to all. With high hope for the future, no prediction in regard to it is ventured.

On the occasion corresponding to this four years ago, all thoughts were anxiously directed to an impending civil war. All dreaded it—all sought to avert it. While the inaugural address was being delivered from this place, devoted altogether to *saving* the Union without war, insurgent agents were in the city seeking to *destroy* it without war—seeking to dissolve the Union, and divide effects, by negotiation. Both parties deprecated war; but one of them would *make* war rather than let the nation survive; and the other would *accept* war rather than let it perish. And the war came.

One eighth of the whole population were colored slaves, not distributed generally over the Union, but localized in the southern part of it. These slaves constituted a peculiar and powerful interest. All knew that this interest was, somehow, the cause of the war. To strengthen, perpetuate, and extend this interest was the object for which the insurgents would rend the Union, even by war; while the government claimed no right to do more than to restrict the territorial enlargement of it. Neither party expected for the war, the magnitude, or the duration, which it has already attained. Neither anticipated that the *cause* of the conflict might cease with, or even before, the conflict itself should cease. Each looked for an easier triumph, and a result less fundamental and astounding. Both read the same Bible, and pray to the same God; and each invokes His aid against the other. It may seem strange that any men should dare to ask a just God's assistance in wringing their bread from the sweat of other men's faces; but let us judge not that we be not judged. The prayers of both could not be answered; that of neither has been answered fully. The Almighty has His own purposes. "Woe unto the world because of offences! for it must needs be that offences come; but woe to that man by whom the offence cometh." If we shall suppose that American slavery is one of those offences which, in the providence of God, must needs come, but which, having continued through His appointed time, He now wills to remove, and that He gives to both North and South, this terrible war, as the woe due to those by whom the offence came, shall we discern therein any departure from those divine attributes which the believers in a living God always ascribe to Him? Fondly do we hope, fervently do we pray—that this mighty scourge of war may speedily pass away. Yet, if God wills that it continue until all the wealth piled by the bondsman's two hundred and fifty years of unrequited toil shall be sunk, and until every drop of blood drawn with the lash shall be paid by another drawn with the sword, as was said three thousand years ago, so still it must be said "the judgments of the Lord are true and righteous altogether."

With malice toward none; with charity for all; with firmness in the right as God gives us to see the right, let us strive on to finish the work we are in; to bind up the nation's wounds; to care for him who shall have borne the battle and for his widow and his orphan, to do all which may achieve and cherish a just and a lasting peace, among ourselves and with all nations.

THE POPULIST PLATFORM OF 1892

Assembled upon the 116th anniversary of the Declaration of Independence, the People's Party of America, in their first national convention, invoking upon their action the blessing of Almighty God, puts forth in the name and on behalf of the people of this country, the following preamble and declaration of principles:

PREAMBLE

The conditions which surround us best justify our co-operation; we meet in the midst of a nation brought to the verge of moral, political, and material ruin. Corruption dominates the ballot-box, the Legislatures, the Congress, and touches even the ermine of the bench. The people are demoralized; most of the States have been compelled to isolate the voters at the polling places to prevent universal intimidation and bribery. The newspapers are largely subsidized or muzzled, public opinion silenced, business prostrated, homes covered with mortgages, labor impoverished, and the land concentrating in the hands of the capitalists. The urban workmen are denied the right to organize for self-protection, imported pauperized labor beats down their wages, a hireling standing army, unrecognized by our laws, is established to shoot them down, and they are rapidly degenerating into European conditions. The fruits of the toil of millions are boldly stolen to build up the fortunes for a few, unprecedented in the history of mankind; and the possessors of these, in turn, despise the Republic and endanger liberty. From the same prolific womb of governmental injustice we breed the two great classes—tramps and millionaires.

The national power to create money is appropriated to enrich bondholders; a vast public debt, payable in legal tender currency, has been funded into gold-bearing bonds, thereby adding millions to the burdens of the people. Silver, which has been accepted as coin since the dawn of history, has been demonetized to add to the purchasing power of gold by decreasing the value of all forms of property as well as human labor, and the supply of currency is purposely abridged to fatten usurers, bankrupt enterprise, and enslave industry. A vast conspiracy against mankind has been organized on two continents, and it is rapidly taking possession of the world. If not met and overthrown at once it forebodes terrible social convulsions, the destruction of civilization, or the establishment of an absolute despotism.

We have witnessed for more than a quarter of a century the struggles of the two great political parties for power and plunder, while grievous wrongs have been inflicted upon the suffering people. We charge that the controlling influences dominating both these parties have permitted the existing dreadful conditions to develop without serious effort to prevent or restrain them. Neither do they now promise us any substantial reform. They have agreed together to ignore in the coming campaign every issue but one. They propose to drown the outcries of a plundered people with the uproar of a sham battle over the tariff, so that capitalists, corporations, national banks, rings, trusts, watered stock, the demonetization of silver, and the oppressions of the usurers may all be lost sight of. They propose to sacrifice our homes, lives, and children on the altar of mammon; to destroy the multitude in order to secure corruption funds from the millionaires.

Assembled on the anniversary of the birthday of the nation, and filled with the spirit of the grand general and chief who established our independence, we seek to restore the government of the Republic to the hands of "the plain people," with which class it originated. We assert our purpose to be identical with the purposes of the National Constitution, "to form a more perfect union and establish justice, insure domestic tranquility, provide for the common defense, promote the general welfare, and secure the blessings of liberty for ourselves and our posterity." We declare that this Republic can only endure as a free government while built upon the love of the whole people for each other and for the nation; that it cannot be pinned together by bayonets; that the civil war is over, and that every passion and resentment which grew out of it must die with it; and that we must be in fact, as we are in name, one united brotherhood of free men.

Our country finds itself confronted by conditions for which there is no precedent in the history of the world; our annual agricultural productions amount to billions of dollars in value, which must, within a few weeks or months, be exchanged for billions of dollars of commodities consumed in their production; the existing currency supply is wholly inadequate to make this exchange; the results are falling prices, the formation of combines and rings, the impoverishment of the producing class. We pledge ourselves, if given power, we will labor to correct these evils by wise and reasonable legislation, in accordance with the terms of our platform. We believe that the power of government—in other words, of the people—should be expanded (as in the case of the postal service) as rapidly and as far as the good sense of an intelligent people and the teaching of experience shall justify, to the end that oppression, injustice, and poverty shall eventually cease in the land.

While our sympathies as a party of reform are naturally upon the side of every proposition which will tend to make men intelligent, virtuous, and temperate, we nevertheless regard these questions—important as they are—as secondary to the great issues now pressing for solution, and upon which not only our individual prosperity but the very existence of free institutions depend; and we ask all men to first help us to determine whether we are to have a republic to administer before we differ as to the conditions upon which it is to be administered, believing that the forces of reform this day organized will never cease to move forward until every wrong is remedied, and equal rights and equal privileges securely established for all the men and women of this country.

PLATFORM

We declare, therefore—

First.—That the union of the labor forces of the United States this day consummated shall be permanent and perpetual; may its spirit enter into all hearts for the salvation of the Republic and the uplifting of mankind!

Second.—Wealth belongs to him who creates it, and every dollar taken from industry without an equivalent is robbery. "If any will not work, neither shall he eat." The interests of rural and civic labor are the same; their enemies are identical.

Third.—We believe that the time has come when the railroad corporations will either own the people or the people must own the railroads; and, should the government enter upon the work of owning and managing all railroads, we should favor an amendment to the Constitution by which all persons engaged in the government service shall be placed under a civil-service regulation of the most rigid character, so as to prevent the increase of the power of the national administration by the use of such additional government employees.

FINANCE.—We demand a national currency, safe, sound, and flexible, issued by the general government only, a full legal tender for all debts, public and private, and that without the use of banking corporations, a just, equitable, and efficient means of distribution direct to the people, at a tax not to exceed two per cent per annum, to be provided as set forth in the sub-treasury plan of the Farmers' Alliance, or a better system; also by payments in discharge of its obligations for public improvements.

1. We demand free and unlimited coinage of silver and gold at the present legal ratio of 16 to 1.

2. We demand that the amount of circulating medium be speedily increased to not less than $50 per capita.

3. We demand a graduated income tax.

4. We believe that the money of the country should be kept as much as possible in the hands of the people, and hence we demand that all State and national revenues shall be limited to the necessary expenses of the government, economically and honestly administered.

5. We demand that postal savings banks be established by the government for the safe deposit of the earnings of the people and to facilitate exchange.

TRANSPORTATION.—Transportation being a means of exchange and a public necessity, the government should own and operate the railroads in the interest of the people. The telegraph and telephone, like the post-office system, being a necessity for the transmission of news, should be owned and operated by the government in the interest of the people.

LAND.—The land, including all the natural sources of wealth, is the heritage of the people, and should not be monopolized for speculative purposes, and alien ownership of land should be prohibited. All land now held by railroads and other corporations in excess of their actual needs, and all lands now owned by aliens should be reclaimed by the government and held for actual settlers only.

EXPRESSION OF SENTIMENTS

Your committee on Platform and Resolutions beg leave unanimously to report the following:

Whereas, Other questions have been presented for our consideration, we hereby submit the following, not as a part of the Platform of the People's Party, but as resolutions expressive of the sentiment of this Convention:

1. *Resolved*, That we demand a free ballot and a fair count in all elections, and pledge ourselves to secure it to every legal voter without federal intervention, through the adoption by the States of the unperverted Australian or secret ballot system.

2. *Resolved*, That the revenue derived from a graduated income tax should be applied to the reduction of the burden of taxation now levied upon the domestic industries of this country.

3. *Resolved,* That we pledge our support to fair and liberal pensions to ex-Union soldiers and sailors.

4. *Resolved,* That we condemn the fallacy of protecting American labor under the present system, which opens our ports to the pauper and criminal classes of the world, and crowds out our wage-earners; and we denounce the present ineffective laws against contract labor, and demand the further restriction of undesirable emigration.

5. *Resolved,* that we cordially sympathize with the efforts of organized workingmen to shorten the hours of labor, and demand a rigid enforcement of the existing eight-hour law on Government work, and ask that a penalty clause be added to the said law.

6. *Resolved,* That we regard the maintenance of a large standing army of mercenaries, known as the Pinkerton system, as a menace to our liberties, and we demand its abolition; and we condemn the recent invasion of the Territory of Wyoming by the hired assassins of plutocracy, assisted by federal officers.

7. *Resolved,* That we commend to the favorable consideration of the people and the reform press the legislative system known as the initiative and referendum.

8. *Resolved,* That we favor a constitutional provision limiting the office of President and Vice-President to one term, and providing for the election of Senators of the United States by a direct vote of the people.

9. *Resolved,* That we oppose any subsidy or national aid to any private corporation for any purpose.

10. *Resolved,* That this convention sympathizes with the Knights of Labor and their righteous contest with the tyrannical combine of clothing manufacturers of Rochester, and declare it to be the duty of all who hate tyranny and oppression to refuse to purchase the goods made by the said manufacturers, or to patronize any merchants who sell such goods.

FRANKLIN D. ROOSEVELT'S FIRST INAUGURAL ADDRESS (1933)

I am certain that my fellow Americans expect that on my induction into the Presidency I will address them with a candor and a decision which the present situation of our Nation impels. This is preeminently the time to speak the truth, the whole truth, frankly and boldly. Nor need we shrink from honestly facing conditions in our country today. This great Nation will endure as it has endured, will revive and will prosper. So, first of all, let me assert my firm belief that the only thing we have to fear is fear itself—nameless, unreasoning, unjustified terror which paralyzes needed efforts to convert retreat into advance. In every dark hour of our national life a leadership of frankness and vigor has met with that understanding and support of the people themselves which is essential to victory. I am convinced that you will again give that support to leadership in these critical days.

In such a spirit on my part and on yours we face our common difficulties. They concern, thank God, only material things. Values have shrunken to fantastic levels; taxes have risen; our ability to pay has fallen; government of all kinds is faced by serious curtailment of income; the means of exchange are frozen in the currents of trade; the withered leaves of industrial enterprise lie on every side; farmers find no markets for their produce; the savings of many years in thousands of families are gone.

More important, a host of unemployed citizens face the grim problem of existence, and an equally great number toil with little return. Only a foolish optimist can deny the dark realities of the moment.

Yet our distress comes from no failure of substance. We are stricken by no plague of locusts. Compared with the perils which our forefathers conquered because they believed and were not afraid, we have still much to be thankful for. Nature still offers her bounty and human efforts have multiplied it. Plenty is at our doorstep, but a generous use of it languishes in the very sight of the supply. Primarily this is because the rulers of the exchange of mankind's goods have failed, through their own stubbornness and their own incompetence, have admitted their failure, and abdicated. Practices of the unscrupulous money changers stand indicted in the court of public opinion, rejected by the hearts and minds of men.

True they have tried, but their efforts have been cast in the pattern of an outworn tradition. Faced by failure of credit they have proposed only the lending of more money. Stripped of the lure of profit by which to induce our people to follow their false leadership, they have resorted to exhortations, pleading tearfully for restored confidence. They know only the rules of a generation of self-seekers. They have no vision, and when there is no vision the people perish.

The money changers have fled from their high seats in the temple of our civilization. We may now restore that temple to the ancient truths. The measure of the restoration lies in the extent to which we apply social values more noble than mere monetary profit.

Happiness lies not in the mere possession of money; it lies in the joy of achievement, in the thrill of creative effort. The joy and moral stimulation of work no longer must be forgotten in the mad chase of evanescent profits. These dark days will be worth all they cost us if they teach us that our true destiny is not to be ministered unto but to minister to ourselves and to our fellow men.

Recognition of the falsity of material wealth as the standard of success goes hand in hand with the abandonment of the false belief that public office and high political position are to be valued only by the standards of pride of place and personal profit; and there must be an end to a conduct in banking and in business which too often has given to a sacred trust the likeness of callous and selfish wrongdoing. Small wonder that confidence languishes, for it thrives only on honesty, on honor, on the sacredness of obligations, on faithful protection, on unselfish performance; without them it cannot live.

Restoration calls, however, not for changes in ethics alone. This Nation asks for action, and action now.

Our greatest primary task is to put people to work. This is no unsolvable problem if we face it wisely and courageously. It can be accomplished in part by direct recruiting by the Government itself, treating the task as we would treat the emergency of a war, but at the same time, through this employment, accomplishing greatly needed projects to stimulate and reorganize the use of our natural resources.

Hand in hand with this we must frankly recognize the overbalance of population in our industrial centers and, by engaging on a national scale in a redistribution, endeavor to provide a better use of the land for those best fitted for the land. The task can be helped by definite efforts to raise the values of agricultural products and with this the power to purchase the output of our cities. It can be helped by preventing realistically the tragedy of the growing loss through foreclosure of our small homes and our farms. It can be helped by insistence that the Federal, State, and local governments act forthwith on the demand that their cost be drastically reduced. It can be helped by the unifying of relief activities which today are often scattered, uneconomical, and unequal. It can be helped by national planning for and supervision of all forms of transportation and of communications and other utilities which have a definitely public character. There are many ways in which it can be helped, but it can never be helped merely by talking about it. We must act and act quickly.

Finally, in our progress toward a resumption of work we require two safeguards against a return of the evils of the old order; there must be a strict supervision of all banking and credits and investments; there must be an end to speculation with other people's money, and there must be provision for an adequate but sound currency.

There are the lines of attack. I shall presently urge upon a new Congress, in special session, detailed measures for their fulfillment, and I shall seek the immediate assistance of the several States.

Through this program of action we address ourselves to putting our own national house in order and making income balance outgo. Our international trade relations, though vastly important, are in point of time and necessity secondary to the establishment of a sound national economy. I favor as a practical policy the putting of first things first. I shall spare no effort to restore world trade by international economic readjustment, but the emergency at home cannot wait on that accomplishment.

The basic thought that guides these specific means of national recovery is not narrowly nationalistic. It is the insistence, as a first consideration, upon the interdependence of the various elements in all parts of the United States—a recognition of the old and permanently important manifestation of the American spirit of the pioneer. It is the way to recovery. It is the immediate way. It is the strongest assurance that the recovery will endure.

In the field of world policy I would dedicate this Nation to the policy of the good neighbor—the neighbor who resolutely respects himself and, because he does so, respects the rights of others—the neighbor who respects his obligations and respects the sanctity of his agreements in and with a world of neighbors.

If I read the temper of our people correctly, we now realize as we have never realized before our interdependence on each other; that we cannot merely take but we must give as well; that if we are to go forward, we must move as a trained and loyal army willing to sacrifice for the good of a common discipline, because without such discipline no progress is made, no leadership becomes effective. We are, I know, ready and willing to submit our lives and property to such discipline, because it makes possible a leadership which aims at a larger good. This I propose to offer, pledging that the larger purposes will bind upon us all as a sacred obligation with a unity of duty hitherto evoked only in time of armed strife.

With this pledge taken, I assume unhesitatingly the leadership of this great army of our people dedicated to a disciplined attack upon our common problems.

Action in this image and to this end is feasible under the form of government which we have inherited from our ancestors. Our Constitution is so simple and practical that it is possible always to meet extraordinary needs by changes in emphasis and arrangement without loss of essential form. That is why our constitutional system has proved itself the most superbly enduring political mechanism the modern world has produced. It has met every stress of vast expansion of territory, of foreign wars, of bitter internal strife, of world relations.

It is to be hoped that the normal balance of executive and legislative authority may be wholly adequate to meet the unprecedented task before us. But it may be that an unprecedented demand and need for undelayed action may call for temporary departure from that normal balance of public procedure.

I am prepared under my constitutional duty to recommend the measures that a stricken nation in the midst of a stricken world may require. These measures, or such other measures as the Congress may build out of its experience and wisdom, I shall seek, within my constitutional authority, to bring to speedy adoption.

But in the event that the Congress shall fail to take one of these two courses, and in the event that the national emergency is still critical, I shall not evade the clear course of duty that will then confront me. I shall ask the Congress for the one remaining instrument to meet the crisis—broad Executive power to wage a war against the emergency, as great as the power that would be given to me if we were in fact invaded by a foreign foe.

For the trust reposed in me I will return the courage and the devotion that befit the time. I can do no less.

We face the arduous days that lie before us in the warm courage of national unity; with the clear consciousness of seeking old and precious moral values; with the clean satisfaction that comes from the stern performance of duty by old and young alike. We aim at the assurance of a rounded and permanent national life.

We do not distrust the future of essential democracy. The people of the United States have not failed. In their need they have registered a mandate that they want direct, vigorous action. They have asked for discipline and direction under leadership. They have made me the present instrument of their wishes. In the spirit of the gift I take it.

In this dedication of a Nation we humbly ask the blessing of God. May He protect each and every one of us. May He guide me in the days to come.

FROM THE PROGRAM FOR THE MARCH ON WASHINGTON FOR JOBS AND FREEDOM (1963)

WHAT WE DEMAND*

1. Comprehensive and effective *civil rights legislation* from the present Congress—without compromise or filibuster—to guarantee all Americans

    access to all public accommodations
    decent housing
    adequate and integrated education
    the right to vote

2. Withholding of Federal funds from all programs in which discrimination exists.

3. *Desegregation of all school districts in 1963.*

4. Enforcement of the *Fourteenth Amendment*—reducing Congressional representation of states where citizens are disfranchised.

5. A new *Executive Order* banning discrimination in all housing supported by federal funds.

6. Authority for the Attorney General to institute *injunctive suits* when any constitutional right is violated.

7. A massive federal program to train and place all unemployed workers—Negro and white—on meaningful and dignified jobs at decent wages.

8. A national *minimum wage* act that will give all Americans a decent standard of living. (Government surveys show that anything less than $2.00 an hour fails to do this.)

9. A broadened *Fair Labor Standards Act* to include all areas of employment which are presently excluded.

10. A federal *Fair Employment Practices Act* barring discrimination by federal, state, and municipal governments, and by employers, contractors, employment agencies, and trade unions.

*Support of the March does not necessarily indicate endorsement of every demand listed. Some organizations have not had an opportunity to take an official position on all of the demands advocated here.

RONALD REAGAN'S FIRST INAUGURAL ADDRESS (1981)

WEST FRONT OF THE U.S. CAPITOL, JANUARY 20, 1981

Senator Hatfield, Mr. Chief Justice, Mr. President, Vice President Bush, Vice President Mondale, Senator Baker, Speaker O'Neill, Reverend Moomaw, and my fellow citizens:

To a few of us here today this is a solemn and most momentous occasion, and yet in the history of our nation it is a commonplace occurrence. The orderly transfer of authority as called for in the Constitution routinely takes place, as it has for almost two centuries, and few of us stop to think how unique we really are. In the eyes of many in the world, this every-four-year ceremony we accept as normal is nothing less than a miracle.

Mr. President, I want our fellow citizens to know how much you did to carry on this tradition. By your gracious cooperation in the transition process, you have shown a watching world that we are a united people pledged to maintaining a political system which guarantees individual liberty to a greater degree than any other, and I thank you and your people for all your help in maintaining the continuity which is the bulwark of our republic. The business of our nation goes forward. These United States are confronted with an economic affliction of great proportions. We suffer from the longest and one of the worst sustained inflations in our national history. It distorts our economic decisions, penalizes thrift, and crushes the struggling young and the fixed-income elderly alike. It threatens to shatter the lives of millions of our people.

Idle industries have cast workers into unemployment, human misery, and personal indignity. Those who do work are denied a fair return for their labor by a tax system which penalizes successful achievement and keeps us from maintaining full productivity. But great as our tax burden is, it has not kept pace with public spending. For decades we have piled deficit upon deficit, mortgaging our future and our children's future for the temporary convenience of the present. To continue this long trend is to guarantee tremendous social, cultural, political, and economic upheavals.

You and I, as individuals, can, by borrowing, live beyond our means, but for only a limited period of time. Why, then, should we think that collectively, as a nation, we're not bound by that same limitation? We must act today in order to preserve tomorrow. And let there be no misunderstanding: We are going to begin to act, beginning today. The economic ills we suffer have come upon us over several decades. They will not go away in days, weeks, or months, but they will go away. They will go away because we as Americans have the capacity now, as we've had in the past, to do whatever needs to be done to preserve this last and greatest bastion of freedom.

In this present crisis, government is not the solution to our problem; government is the problem. From time to time we've been tempted to believe that society has become too complex to be managed by self-rule, that government by an elite group is superior to government for, by, and of the people. Well, if no one among us is capable of governing himself, then who among us has the capacity to govern someone else? All of us together, in and out of government, must bear the burden. The solutions we seek must be equitable, with no one group singled out to pay a higher price.

We hear much of special interest groups. Well, our concern must be for a special interest group that has been too long neglected. It knows no sectional boundaries or ethnic and racial divisions, and it crosses political party lines. It is made up of men and women who raise our food, patrol our streets, man our mines and factories, teach our children, keep our homes, and heal us when we're sick—professionals, industrialists, shopkeepers, clerks, cabbies, and truck drivers. They are, in short, "we the people," this breed called Americans.

Well, this administration's objective will be a healthy, vigorous, growing economy that provides equal opportunities for all Americans, with no barriers born of bigotry or discrimination. Putting America back to work means putting all Americans back to work. Ending inflation means freeing all Americans from the terror of runaway living costs. All must share in the productive work of this "new beginning," and all must share in the bounty of a revived economy. With the idealism and fair play which are the core of our system and our strength, we can have a strong and prosperous America, at peace with itself and the world.

So, as we begin, let us take inventory. We are a nation that has a government—not the other way around. And this makes us special among the nations of the Earth. Our government has no power except that granted it by the people. It is time to check and reverse the growth of government, which shows signs of having grown beyond the consent of the governed.

It is my intention to curb the size and influence of the federal establishment and to demand recognition of the distinction between the powers granted to the federal government and those reserved to the states or to the people. All of us need to be reminded that the federal government did not create the states; the states created the federal government.

Now, so there will be no misunderstanding, it's not my intention to do away with government. It is rather to make it work—work with us, not over us; to stand by our side, not ride on our back. Government can and must provide opportunity, not smother it; foster productivity, not stifle it.

If we look to the answer as to why for so many years we achieved so much, prospered as no other people on earth, it was because here in this land we unleashed the energy and individual genius of man to a greater extent than has ever been done before. Freedom and the dignity of the individual have been more available and assured here than in any other place on earth. The price for this freedom at times has been high, but we have never been unwilling to pay the price.

It is no coincidence that our present troubles parallel and are proportionate to the intervention and intrusion in our lives that result from unnecessary and excessive growth of government. It is time for us to realize that we're too great a nation to limit ourselves to small dreams. We're not, as some would have us believe, doomed to an inevitable decline. I do not believe in a fate that will fall on us no matter what we do. I do believe in a fate that will fall on us if we do nothing. So, with all the creative energy at our command, let us begin an era of national renewal. Let us renew our determination, our courage, and our strength. And let us renew our faith and our hope.

We have every right to dream heroic dreams. Those who say that we're in a time when there are no heroes, they just don't know where to look. You can see heroes every day going in and out of factory gates. Others, a handful in number, produce enough food to feed all of us and then the world beyond. You meet heroes across a counter, and they're on both sides of that counter. There are entrepreneurs with faith in themselves and faith in an idea who create new jobs, new wealth and opportunity. They're individuals and families whose taxes support the government and whose voluntary gifts support church, charity, culture, art, and education. Their patriotism is quiet, but deep. Their values sustain our national life.

Now, I have used the words "they" and "their" in speaking of these heroes. I could say "you" and "your," because I'm addressing the heroes of whom I speak—you, the citizens of this blessed land. Your dreams, your hopes, your goals are going to be the dreams, the hopes, and the goals of this administration, so help me God.

We shall reflect the compassion that is so much a part of your makeup. How can we love our country and not love our countrymen; and loving them, reach out a hand when they fall, heal them when they're sick, and provide opportunity to make them self-sufficient so they will be equal in fact and not just in theory?

Can we solve the problems confronting us? Well, the answer is an unequivocal and emphatic "yes." To paraphrase Winston Churchill, I did not take the oath I've just taken with the intention of presiding over the dissolution of the world's strongest economy.

In the days ahead I will propose removing the roadblocks that have slowed our economy and reduced productivity. Steps will be taken aimed at restoring the balance between the various levels of government. Progress may be slow, measured in inches and feet, not miles, but we will progress. It is time to reawaken this industrial giant, to get government back within its means, and to lighten our punitive tax burden. And these will be our first priorities, and on these principles there will be no compromise.

On the eve of our struggle for independence a man who might have been one of the greatest among the Founding Fathers, Dr. Joseph Warren, president of the Massachusetts Congress, said to his fellow Americans, "Our country is in danger, but not to be despaired of . . . . On you depend the fortunes of America. You are to decide the important questions upon which rests the happiness and the liberty of millions yet unborn. Act worthy of yourselves." Well, I believe we, the Americans of today, are ready to act worthy of ourselves, ready to do what must be done to ensure happiness and liberty for ourselves, our children, and our children's children. And as we renew ourselves here in our own land, we will be seen as having greater strength throughout the world. We will again be the exemplar of freedom and a beacon of hope for those who do not now have freedom.

To those neighbors and allies who share our freedom, we will strengthen our historic ties and assure them of our support and firm commitment. We will match loyalty with loyalty. We will strive for mutually beneficial relations. We will not use our friendship to impose on their sovereignty, for our own sovereignty is not for sale. As for the enemies of freedom, those who are potential adversaries, they will be reminded that peace is the highest aspiration of the American people. We will negotiate for it, sacrifice for it; we will not surrender for it, now or ever.

Our forbearance should never be misunderstood. Our reluctance for conflict should not be misjudged as a failure of will. When action is required to preserve our national security, we will act. We will maintain sufficient strength to prevail if need be, knowing that if we do so we have the best chance of never having to use that strength. Above all, we must realize that no arsenal or no weapon in the arsenals of the world is so formidable as the will and moral courage of free men and women. It is a weapon our adversaries in today's world do not have. It is a weapon that we as Americans do have. Let that be understood by those who practice terrorism and prey upon their neighbors. I'm told that tens of thousands of prayer meetings are being held on this day, and for that I'm deeply grateful. We are a nation under God, and I believe God intended for us to be free. It would be fitting and good, I think, if on each Inaugural Day in future years it should be declared a day of prayer.

This is the first time in our history that this ceremony has been held, as you've been told, on the West Front of the Capitol. Standing here, one faces a magnificent vista, opening up on the city's special beauty and history. At the end of this open mall are those shrines to the giants on whose shoulders we stand.

Directly in front of me, the monument to a monumental man, George Washington, father of our country. A man of humility who came to greatness reluctantly. He led Americans out of revolutionary victory into infant nationhood. Off to one side, the stately memorial to Thomas Jefferson. The Declaration of Independence flames with his eloquence. And then, beyond the Reflecting Pool, the dignified columns of the Lincoln Memorial. Whoever would understand in his heart the meaning of America will find it in the life of Abraham Lincoln.

Beyond those monuments to heroism is the Potomac River, and on the far shore the sloping hills of Arlington National Cemetery, with its row upon row of simple white markers bearing crosses and Stars of David. They add up to only a tiny fraction of the price that has been paid for our freedom. Each one of those markers is a monument to the kind of hero I spoke of earlier. Their lives ended in places called Belleau Wood, the Argonne, Omaha Beach, Salerno, and halfway around the world on Guadalcanal, Tarawa, Pork Chop Hill, the Chosin Reservoir, and in a hundred rice paddies and jungles of a place called Vietnam.

Under one such marker lies a young man, Martin Treptow, who left his job in a small town barbershop in 1917 to go to France with the famed Rainbow Division. There, on the western front, he was killed trying to carry a message between battalions under heavy artillery fire.

We're told that on his body was found a diary. On the flyleaf under the heading "My Pledge," he had written these words: "America must win this war. Therefore I will work, I will save, I will sacrifice, I will endure, I will fight cheerfully and do my utmost, as if the issue of the whole struggle depended on me alone."

The crisis we are facing today does not require of us the kind of sacrifice that Martin Treptow and so many thousands of others were called upon to make. It does require, however, our best effort and our willingness to believe in ourselves and to believe in our capacity to perform great deeds, to believe that together with God's help we can and will resolve the problems which now confront us.

And after all, why shouldn't we believe that? We are Americans.

God bless you, and thank you.

BARACK OBAMA'S FIRST INAUGURAL ADDRESS (2009)

My fellow citizens: I stand here today humbled by the task before us, grateful for the trust you've bestowed, mindful of the sacrifices borne by our ancestors.

I thank President Bush for his service to our nation—(*applause*)—as well as the generosity and cooperation he has shown throughout this transition.

Forty-four Americans have now taken the presidential oath. The words have been spoken during rising tides of prosperity and the still waters of peace. Yet, every so often, the oath is taken amidst gathering clouds and raging storms. At these moments, America has carried on not simply because of the skill or vision of those in high office, but because we, the people, have remained faithful to the ideals of our forebears and true to our founding documents.

So it has been: so it must be with this generation of Americans.

That we are in the midst of crisis is now well understood. Our nation is at war against a far-reaching network of violence and hatred. Our economy is badly weakened, a consequence of greed and irresponsibility on the part of some, but also our collective failure to make hard choices and prepare the nation for a new age. Homes have been lost, jobs shed, businesses shuttered. Our health care is too costly, our schools fail too many—and each day brings further evidence that the ways we use energy strengthen our adversaries and threaten our planet.

These are the indicators of crisis, subject to data and statistics. Less measurable, but no less profound, is a sapping of confidence across our land; a nagging fear that America's decline is inevitable, that the next generation must lower its sights.

Today I say to you that the challenges we face are real. They are serious and they are many. They will not be met easily or in a short span of time. But know this America: They will be met. (*Applause*)

On this day, we gather because we have chosen hope over fear, unity of purpose over conflict and discord. On this day, we come to proclaim an end to the petty grievances and false promises, the recriminations and worn-out dogmas that for far too long have strangled our politics. We remain a young nation. But in the words of Scripture, the time has come to set aside childish things. The time has come to reaffirm our enduring spirit; to choose our better history; to carry forward that precious gift, that noble idea passed on from generation to generation; the God-given promise that all are equal, all are free, and all deserve a chance to pursue their full measure of happiness. (*Applause*)

In reaffirming the greatness of our nation we understand that greatness is never a given. It must be earned. Our journey has never been one of short-cuts or settling for less. It has not been the path for the faint-hearted, for those that prefer leisure over work, or seek only the pleasures of riches and fame. Rather, it has been the risk-takers, the doers, the makers of things—some celebrated, but more often men and women obscure in their labor—who have carried us up the long rugged path towards prosperity and freedom.

For us, they packed up their few worldly possessions and traveled across oceans in search of a new life. For us, they toiled in sweatshops, and settled the West, endured the lash of the whip, and plowed the hard earth. For us, they fought and died in places like Concord and Gettysburg, Normandy and Khe Sahn.

Time and again these men and women struggled and sacrificed and worked till their hands were raw so that we might live a better life. They saw America as bigger than the sum of our individual ambitions, greater than all the differences of birth or wealth or faction.

This is the journey we continue today. We remain the most prosperous, powerful nation on Earth. Our workers are no less productive than when this crisis began. Our minds are no less inventive, our goods and services no less needed than they were last week, or last month, or last year. Our capacity remains undiminished. But our time of standing pat, of protecting narrow interests and putting off unpleasant decisions—that time has surely passed. Starting today, we must pick ourselves up, dust ourselves off, and begin again the work of remaking America. (*Applause*)

For everywhere we look, there is work to be done. The state of our economy calls for action, bold and swift. And we will act, not only to create new jobs, but to lay a new foundation for growth. We will build the roads and bridges, the electric grids and digital lines that feed our commerce and bind us together. We'll restore science to its rightful place, and wield technology's wonders to raise health care's quality and lower its cost. We will harness the sun and the winds and the soil to fuel our cars and run our factories. And we will transform our schools and colleges and universities to meet the demands of a new age. All this we can do. All this we will do.

Now, there are some who question the scale of our ambitions, who suggest that our system cannot tolerate too many big plans. Their memories are short, for they have forgotten what this country has already done, what free men and women can achieve when imagination is joined to common purpose, and necessity to courage. What the cynics fail to understand is that the ground has shifted beneath them, that the stale political arguments that have consumed us for so long no longer apply.

The question we ask today is not whether our government is too big or too small, but whether it works—whether it helps families find jobs at a decent wage, care they can afford, a retirement that is dignified. Where the answer is yes, we intend to move forward. Where the answer is no, programs will end. And those of us who manage the public's dollars will be held to account, to spend wisely, reform bad habits, and do our business in the light of day, because only then can we restore the vital trust between a people and their government.

Nor is the question before us whether the market is a force for good or ill. Its power to generate wealth and expand freedom is unmatched. But this crisis has reminded us that without a watchful eye, the market can spin out of control. The nation cannot prosper long when it favors only the prosperous. The success of our economy has always depended not just on the size of our gross domestic product, but on the reach of our prosperity, on the ability to extend opportunity to every willing heart—not out of charity, but because it is the surest route to our common good. (*Applause*)

As for our common defense, we reject as false the choice between our safety and our ideals. Our Founding Fathers—(*applause*)—our Founding Fathers, faced with perils that we can scarcely imagine, drafted a charter to assure the rule of law and the rights of man—a charter expanded by the blood of generations. Those ideals still light the world, and we will not give them up for expedience sake. (*Applause*)

And so, to all the other peoples and governments who are watching today, from the grandest capitals to the small village where my father was born, know that America is a friend of each nation, and every man, woman and child who seeks a future of peace and dignity. And we are ready to lead once more. (*Applause*)

Recall that earlier generations faced down fascism and communism not just with missiles and tanks, but with the sturdy alliances and enduring convictions. They understood that our power alone cannot protect us, nor does it entitle us to do as we please. Instead they knew that our power grows through its prudent use; our security emanates from the justness of our cause, the force of our example, the tempering qualities of humility and restraint.

We are the keepers of this legacy. Guided by these principles once more we can meet those new threats that demand even greater effort, even greater cooperation and understanding between nations. We will begin to responsibly leave Iraq to its people and forge a hard-earned peace in Afghanistan. With old friends and former foes, we'll work tirelessly to lessen the nuclear threat, and roll back the specter of a warming planet.

We will not apologize for our way of life, nor will we waver in its defense. And for those who seek to advance their aims by inducing terror and slaughtering innocents, we say to you now that our spirit is stronger and cannot be broken—you cannot outlast us, and we will defeat you. (*Applause*)

For we know that our patchwork heritage is a strength, not a weakness. We are a nation of Christians and Muslims, Jews and Hindus, and non-believers. We are shaped by every language and culture, drawn from every end of this Earth: and because we have tasted the bitter swill of civil war and segregation, and emerged from that dark chapter stronger and more united, we cannot help but believe that the old hatreds shall someday pass; that the lines of tribe shall soon dissolve; that as the world grows smaller, our common humanity shall reveal itself; and that America must play its role in ushering in a new era of peace.

To the Muslim world, we seek a new way forward, based on mutual interest and mutual respect. To those leaders around the globe who seek to sow conflict, or blame their society's ills on the West, know that your people will judge you on what you can build, not what you destroy. (*Applause*)

To those who cling to power through corruption and deceit and the silencing of dissent, know that you are on the wrong side of history, but that we will extend a hand if you are willing to unclench your fist. (*Applause*)

To the people of poor nations, we pledge to work alongside you to make your farms flourish and let clean waters flow; to nourish starved bodies and feed hungry minds. And to those nations like ours that enjoy relative plenty, we say we can no longer afford indifference to the suffering outside our borders, nor can we consume the world's resources without regard to effect. For the world has changed, and we must change with it.

As we consider the role that unfolds before us, we remember with humble gratitude those brave Americans who at this very hour patrol far-off deserts and distant mountains. They have something to tell us, just as the fallen heroes who lie in Arlington whisper through the ages.

We honor them not only because they are the guardians of our liberty, but because they embody the spirit of service—a willingness to find meaning in something greater than themselves.

And yet at this moment, a moment that will define a generation, it is precisely this spirit that must inhabit us all. For as much as government can do, and must do, it is ultimately the faith and determination of the American people upon which this nation relies. It is the kindness to take in a stranger when the levees break, the selflessness of workers who would rather cut their hours than see a friend lose their job which sees us through our darkest hours. It is the firefighter's courage to storm a stairway filled with smoke, but also a parent's willingness to nurture a child that finally decides our fate.

Our challenges may be new. The instruments with which we meet them may be new. But those values upon which our success depends—honesty and hard work, courage and fair play, tolerance and curiosity, loyalty and patriotism—these things are old. These things are true. They have been the quiet force of progress throughout our history.

What is demanded, then, is a return to these truths. What is required of us now is a new era of responsibility—a recognition on the part of every American that we have duties to ourselves, our nation and the world; duties that we do not grudgingly accept, but rather seize gladly, firm in the knowledge that there is nothing so satisfying to the spirit, so defining of our character than giving our all to a difficult task.

This is the price and the promise of citizenship. This is the source of our confidence—the knowledge that God calls on us to shape an uncertain destiny. This is the meaning of our liberty and our creed, why men and women and children of every race and every faith can join in celebration across this magnificent mall; and why a man whose father less than 60 years ago might not have been served in a local restaurant can now stand before you to take a most sacred oath. (*Applause*)

So let us mark this day with remembrance of who we are and how far we have traveled. In the year of America's birth, in the coldest of months, a small band of patriots huddled by dying campfires on the shores of an icy river. The capital was abandoned. The enemy was advancing. The snow was stained with blood. At the moment when the outcome of our revolution was most in doubt, the father of our nation ordered these words to be read to the people:

"Let it be told to the future world...that in the depth of winter, when nothing but hope and virtue could survive... that the city and the country, alarmed at one common danger, came forth to meet [it]."

America: In the face of our common dangers, in this winter of our hardship, let us remember these timeless words. With hope and virtue, let us brave once more the icy currents, and endure what storms may come. Let it be said by our children's children that when we were tested we refused to let this journey end, that we did not turn back nor did we falter; and with eyes fixed on the horizon and God's grace upon us, we carried forth that great gift of freedom and delivered it safely to future generations.

Thank you. God bless you. And God bless the United States of America. (*Applause*)

PRESIDENTIAL ELECTIONS

Year	Number of States	Candidates	Parties	Popular Vote	% of Popular Vote	Electoral Vote	% Voter Participation
1789	11	**GEORGE WASHINGTON**	NO PARTY			69	
		John Adams	DESIGNATIONS			34	
		Other candidates				35	
1792	15	**GEORGE WASHINGTON**	NO PARTY			132	
		John Adams	DESIGNATIONS			77	
		George Clinton				50	
		Other candidates				5	
1796	16	**JOHN ADAMS**	FEDERALIST			71	
		Thomas Jefferson	Republican			68	
		Thomas Pinckney	Federalist			59	
		Aaron Burr	Republican			30	
		Other candidates				48	
1800	16	**THOMAS JEFFERSON**	REPUBLICAN			73	
		Aaron Burr	Republican			73	
		John Adams	Federalist			65	
		Charles C. Pinckney	Federalist			64	
		John Jay	Federalist			1	
1804	17	**THOMAS JEFFERSON**	REPUBLICAN			162	
		Charles C. Pinckney	Federalist			14	
1808	17	**JAMES MADISON**	REPUBLICAN			122	
		Charles C. Pinckney	Federalist			47	
		George Clinton	Republican			6	
1812	18	**JAMES MADISON**	REPUBLICAN			128	
		DeWitt Clinton	Federalist			89	

Year	Number of States	Candidates	Parties	Popular Vote	% of Popular Vote	Electoral Vote	% Voter Participation
1816	19	**JAMES MONROE**	REPUBLICAN			183	
		Rufus King	Federalist			34	
1820	24	**JAMES MONROE**	REPUBLICAN			231	
		John Quincy Adams	Independent			1	
1824	24	**JOHN QUINCY ADAMS**	NO PARTY	108,740	31.0	84	26.9
		Andrew Jackson	DESIGNATIONS	153,544	43.0	99	
		William H. Crawford		46,618	13.0	41	
		Henry Clay		47,136	13.0	37	
1828	24	**ANDREW JACKSON**	DEMOCRAT	647,286	56.0	178	57.6
		John Quincy Adams	National Republican	508,064	44.0	83	
1832	24	**ANDREW JACKSON**	DEMOCRAT	687,502	54.5	219	55.4
		Henry Clay	National Republican	530,189	37.5	49	
		William Wirt	Anti-Masonic	101,051	8.0	7	
		John Floyd	Democrat			11	
1836	26	**MARTIN VAN BUREN**	DEMOCRAT	765,483	51.0	170	57.8
		William H. Harrison	Whig			73	
		Hugh L. White	Whig	739,795	49.0	26	
		Daniel Webster	Whig			14	
		William P. Mangum	Whig			11	
1840	26	**WILLIAM H. HARRISON**	WHIG	1,274,624	53.0	234	80.2
		Martin Van Buren	Democrat	1,127,781	47.0	60	

Year	Number of States	Candidates	Parties	Popular Vote	% of Popular Vote	Electoral Vote	% Voter Participation
1844	26	**JAMES K. POLK**	DEMOCRAT	1,338,464	50.0	170	78.9
		Henry Clay	Whig	1,300,097	48.0	105	
		James G. Birney	Liberty	62,300	2.0		
1848	30	**ZACHARY TAYLOR**	WHIG	1,360,967	47.5	163	72.7
		Lewis Cass	Democrat	1,222,342	42.5	127	
		Martin Van Buren	Free Soil	291,263	10.0		
1852	31	**FRANKLIN PIERCE**	DEMOCRAT	1,601,117	51.0	254	69.6
		Winfield Scott	Whig	1,385,453	44.0	42	
		John P. Hale	Free Soil	155,825	5.0		
1856	31	**JAMES BUCHANAN**	DEMOCRAT	1,832,955	45.0	174	78.9
		John C. Frémont	Republican	1,339,932	33.0	114	
		Millard Fillmore	American	871,731	22.0	8	
1860	33	**ABRAHAM LINCOLN**	REPUBLICAN	1,865,593	40.0	180	81.2
		Stephen A. Douglas	Northern Democrat	1,382,713	29.0	12	
		John C. Breckinridge	Southern Democrat	848,356	18.0	72	
		John Bell	Constitutional Union	592,906	13.0	39	
1864	36	**ABRAHAM LINCOLN**	REPUBLICAN	2,206,938	55.0	212	73.8
		George B. McClellan	Democrat	1,803,787	45.0	21	
1868	37	**ULYSSES S. GRANT**	REPUBLICAN	3,013,421	53.0	214	78.1
		Horatio Seymour	Democrat	2,706,829	47.0	80	

Year	Number of States	Candidates	Parties	Popular Vote	% of Popular Vote	Electoral Vote	% Voter Participation
1872	37	**ULYSSES S. GRANT**	REPUBLICAN	3,596,745	55.6	286	71.3
		Horace Greeley	Democrat	2,843,446	43.9	66	
1876	38	**RUTHERFORD B. HAYES**	REPUBLICAN	4,036,572	48.0	185	81.8
		Samuel J. Tilden	Democrat	4,284,020	51.0	184	
1880	38	**JAMES A. GARFIELD**	REPUBLICAN	4,453,295	48.4	214	79.4
		Winfield S. Hancock	Democrat	4,414,082	48.3	155	
		James B. Weaver	Greenback-Labor	308,578	3.5		
1884	38	**GROVER CLEVELAND**	DEMOCRAT	4,879,507	48.5	219	77.5
		James G. Blaine	Republican	4,850,293	48.2	182	
		Benjamin F. Butler	Greenback-Labor	175,370	1.8		
		John P. St. John	Prohibition	150,369	1.5		
1888	38	**BENJAMIN HARRISON**	REPUBLICAN	5,447,129	47.9	233	79.3
		Grover Cleveland	Democrat	5,537,857	48.6	168	
		Clinton B. Fisk	Prohibition	249,506	2.2		
		Anson J. Streeter	Union Labor	146,935	1.3		
1892	44	**GROVER CLEVELAND**	DEMOCRAT	5,555,426	46.1	277	74.7
		Benjamin Harrison	Republican	5,182,690	43.0	145	
		James B. Weaver	People's	1,029,846	8.5	22	
		John Bidwell	Prohibition	264,133	2.2		
1896	45	**WILLIAM McKINLEY**	REPUBLICAN	7,102,246	51.0	271	79.3
		William J. Bryan	Democrat	6,492,559	47.0	176	

LABOR FORCE—SELECTED CHARACTERISTICS EXPRESSED AS A PERCENTAGE OF THE LABOR FORCE, 1800–2010

Year	Agriculture	Manufacturing	Domestic service	Clerical, sales, and service	Professions	Slave	Nonwhite	Foreign-born	Female
1800	74.4	—	2.4	—	—	30.2	32.6	—	21.4
1860	55.8	13.8	5.4	4.8[1]	3.0[1]	21.7	23.6	24.5[1]	19.6
1910	30.7	20.8	5.5	14.1	4.7	—	13.4	22.0	20.8
1950	12.0	26.4	2.5	27.3	8.9	—	10.0	8.7	27.9
2000	2.4	14.7	0.6	38.0[2]	15.6	—	16.5	10.3[2]	46.6
2010	1.6	10.1	1.6	40.2	22.2	—	18.7	15.8	46.7

[1]Values for 1870 are presented here because the available data for 1860 exclude slaves.
[2]1990.
Note: "Clerical, sales, and service" excludes domestic service.

IMMIGRATION, BY ORIGIN (in thousands)

Period	Europe	Americas	Asia
1820–30	106	12	—
1831–40	496	33	—
1841–50	1,597	62	—
1851–60	2,453	75	42
1861–70	2,065	167	65
1871–80	2,272	404	70
1881–90	4,735	427	70
1891–1900	3,555	39	75
1901–10	8,065	362	324
1911–20	4,322	1,144	247
1921–30	2,463	1,517	112
1931–40	348	160	16
1941–50	621	355	32
1951–60	1,326	997	150
1961–70	1,123	1,716	590
1971–80	800	1,983	1,588
1981–90	762	3,616	2,738
1991–2000	1,360	4,487	2,796
2001–10	1,318	4,478	3,621

UNEMPLOYMENT RATE, 1890–2015

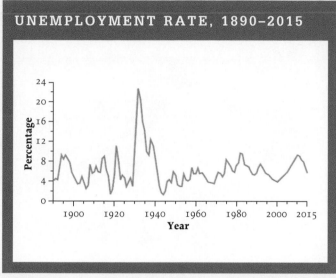

UNION MEMBERSHIP AS A PERCENTAGE OF NONAGRICULTURAL EMPLOYMENT, 1880–2015

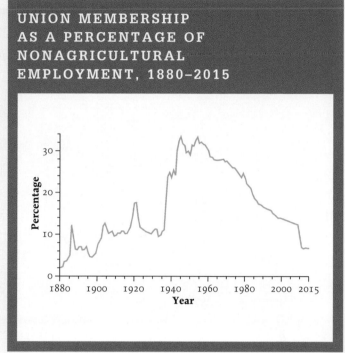

VOTER PARTICIPATION IN PRESIDENTIAL ELECTIONS, 1824–2016

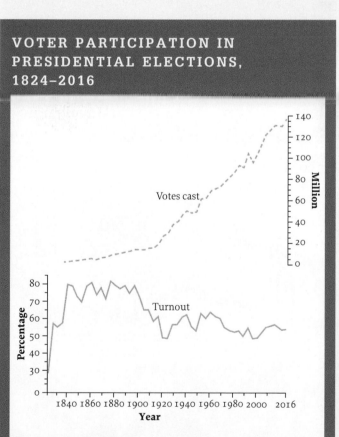

BIRTHRATE, 1820–2015

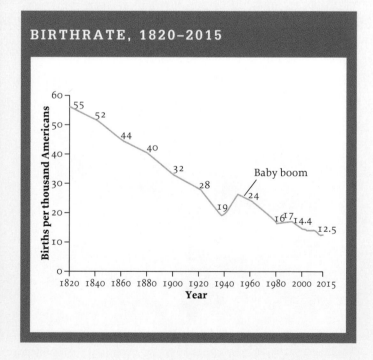

GLOSSARY

abolition Social movement of the pre–Civil War era that advocated the immediate emancipation of the slaves and their incorporation into American society as equal citizens.

Act Concerning Religion (or Maryland Toleration Act) 1649 law that granted free exercise of religion to all Christian denominations in colonial Maryland.

Adkins v. Children's Hospital 1923 Supreme Court case that reversed *Muller v. Oregon,* the 1908 case that permitted states to set maximum hours to protect working women. Justices ruled in *Adkins* that women no longer deserved special treatment because they could vote.

affirmative action Policy efforts to promote greater employment opportunities for minorities.

Agricultural Adjustment Act New Deal legislation passed in 1933 that established the Agricultural Adjustment Administration (AAA) to improve agricultural prices by limiting market supplies; declared unconstitutional in *United States v. Butler* (1936).

Albany Plan of Union A failed 1754 proposal by the seven northern colonies in anticipation of the French and Indian War, urging the unification of the colonies under one crown-appointed president.

Alien and Sedition Acts Four measures passed in 1798 during the undeclared war with France that limited the freedoms of speech and press and restricted the liberty of noncitizens.

American Anti-Slavery Society Founded in 1833, the organization that sought an immediate end to slavery and the establishment of equality for black Americans. It split in 1840 after disputes about the role of women within the organization and other issues.

American Civil Liberties Union Organization founded during World War I to protest the suppression of freedom of expression in wartime; played a major role in court cases that achieved judicial recognition of Americans' civil liberties.

American Colonization Society Organized in 1816 to encourage colonization of free blacks to Africa; West African nation of Liberia founded in 1822 to serve as a homeland for them.

American exceptionalism The belief that the United States has a special mission to serve as a refuge from tyranny, a symbol of freedom, and a model for the rest of the world.

American Federation of Labor A federation of trade unions founded in 1881, composed mostly of skilled, white, native-born workers; its long-term president was Samuel Gompers.

American Indian Movement (AIM) Movement founded in 1963 by Native Americans who were fed up with the poor conditions on Indian reservations and the federal government's unwillingness to help. In 1973, AIM led 200 Sioux in the occupation of Wounded Knee. After a ten-week standoff with the federal authorities, the government agreed to reexamine Indian treaty rights and the occupation ended.

"American standard of living" The Progressive-era idea that American workers were entitled to a wage high enough to allow them full participation in the nation's mass consumption economy.

American System Program of internal improvements and protective tariffs promoted by Speaker of the House Henry Clay in his presidential campaign of 1824; his proposals formed the core of Whig ideology in the 1830s and 1840s.

American system of manufactures A system of production that relied on the mass production of interchangeable parts that could be rapidly assembled into standardized finished products. First perfected in Connecticut by clockmaker Eli Terry and by small-arms producer Eli Whitney in the 1840s and 50s.

Americans with Disabilities Act 1990 law that prohibited the discrimination against persons with disabilities in both hiring and promotion. It also mandated accessible entrances for public buildings.

the *Amistad* Ship that transported slaves from one port in Cuba to another, seized by the slaves in 1839. They made their way northward to the United States, where the status of the slaves became the subject of a celebrated court case; eventually most were able to return to Africa.

Anglican Church The established state church of England, formed by Henry VII after the pope refused to annul his marriage to Catherine of Aragon.

annuity system System of yearly payments to Native American tribes by which the federal government justified and institutionalized its interference in Indian tribal affairs.

Antietam, Battle of One of the bloodiest battles of the Civil War, fought to a standoff on September 17, 1862, in western Maryland.

Anti-Federalists Opponents of the Constitution who saw it as a limitation on individual and states' rights; their demands led to the addition of a Bill of Rights to the document.

Anti-Imperialist League Coalition of anti-imperialist groups united in 1899 to protest American territorial expansion, especially in the Philippine Islands; its membership included prominent politicians, industrialists, labor leaders, and social reformers.

Appomattox Courthouse, Virginia Site of the surrender of Confederate general Robert E. Lee to Union general Ulysses S. Grant on April 9, 1865, marking the end of the Civil War.

Army-McCarthy hearings Televised U.S. Senate hearings in 1954 on Senator Joseph McCarthy's charges of disloyalty in the army; his tactics contributed to his censure by the Senate.

Arnold, Benedict A traitorous American commander who planned to sell out the American garrison at West Point to the British. His plot was discovered before it could be executed and he joined the British army.

Articles of Confederation First frame of government for the United States; in effect from 1781 to 1788, it provided for a weak central authority and was soon replaced by the Constitution.

Atlanta Compromise Speech to the Cotton States and International Exposition in 1895 by educator Booker T. Washington, the leading black spokesman of the day; black

scholar W. E. B. Du Bois gave the speech its derisive name and criticized Washington for encouraging blacks to accommodate segregation and disenfranchisement.

Atlantic Charter Agreement issued August 12, 1941, following meetings in Newfoundland between President Franklin D. Roosevelt and British Prime Minister Winston Churchill, that signaled the Allies' cooperation and stated their war aims.

Atlantic slave trade The systematic importation of African slaves from their native continent across the Atlantic Ocean to the New World, largely fueled by rising demand for sugar, rice, coffee, and tobacco.

Attucks, Crispus During the Boston Massacre, the individual who was supposedly at the head of the crowd of hecklers and who baited the British troops. He was killed when the British troops fired on the crowd.

Axis powers In World War II, the nations of Germany, Italy, and Japan.

Aztec Mesoamerican people who were conquered by the Spanish under Hernan Cortes, 1519–1528.

baby boom Markedly higher birthrate in the years following World War II; led to the biggest demographic "bubble" in American history.

backcountry In colonial America, the area stretching from central Pennsylvania southward through the Shenandoah Valley of Virginia and into upland North and South Carolina.

Bacon's Rebellion Unsuccessful 1676 revolt led by planter Nathaniel Bacon against Virginia governor William Berkeley's administration because of governmental corruption and because Berkeley had failed to protect settlers from Indian raids and did not allow them to occupy Indian lands.

Balkan crisis A series of ethnic and political crises that arose following the dissolution of Yugoslavia in the 1990s. Many atrocities were committed during the conflict, and NATO, the United Nations, and the United States intervened several times.

Bank of the United States Proposed by the first secretary of the treasury, Alexander Hamilton, the bank that opened in 1791 and operated until 1811 to issue a uniform currency, make business loans, and collect tax monies. The Second Bank of the United States was chartered in 1816 but President Andrew Jackson vetoed the recharter bill in 1832.

Bank War Political struggle in the early 1830s between President Jackson and financier Nicholas Biddle over the renewing of the Second Bank's charter.

Barbary Wars The first wars fought by the United States, and the nation's first encounter with the Islamic world. The wars were fought from 1801 to 1805 against plundering pirates off the Mediterranean coast of Africa after President Thomas Jefferson's refusal to pay them tribute to protect American ships.

Bargain of 1877 Deal made by a Republican and Democratic special congressional commission to resolve the disputed presidential election of 1876; Republican Rutherford B. Hayes, who had lost the popular vote, was declared the winner in exchange for the withdrawal of federal troops from involvement in politics in the South, marking the end of Reconstruction.

Bay of Pigs invasion U.S. mission in which the CIA, hoping to inspire a revolt against Fidel Castro, sent 1,500 Cuban exiles to invade their homeland on April 17, 1961; the mission was a spectacular failure.

the Beats A term coined by Jack Kerouac for a small group of poets and writers who railed against 1950s mainstream culture.

Bill for Establishing Religious Freedom A Virginia law, drafted by Thomas Jefferson in 1777 and enacted in 1786, that guarantees freedom of, and from, religion.

Bill of Rights First ten amendments to the U.S. Constitution, adopted in 1791 to guarantee individual rights against infringement by the federal government.

birth control movement An offshoot of the early twentieth-century feminist movement that saw access to birth control and "voluntary motherhood" as essential to women's freedom. The birth-control movement was led by Margaret Sanger.

Black Codes Laws passed from 1865 to 1866 in southern states to restrict the rights of former slaves; to nullify the codes, Congress passed the Civil Rights Act of 1866 and the Fourteenth Amendment.

Black Legend Idea that the Spanish New World empire was more oppressive toward the Indians than other European empires; was used as a justification for English imperial expansion.

Black Lives Matter Civil rights movement sparked by a series of incidents of police brutality and lethal force against people of color.

Black Power Post-1966 rallying cry of a more militant civil rights movement.

"Bleeding Kansas" Violence between pro- and antislavery settlers in the Kansas Territory, 1856.

bonanza farms Large farms that covered thousands of acres and employed hundreds of wage laborers in the West in the late nineteenth century.

borderland A place between or near recognized borders where no group of people has complete political control or cultural dominance.

Boston Massacre Clash between British soldiers and a Boston mob, March 5, 1770, in which five colonists were killed.

Boston Tea Party The incident on December 16, 1773, in which the Sons of Liberty, dressed as Indians, dumped hundreds of chests of tea into Boston Harbor to protest the Tea Act of 1773. Under the Tea Act, the British exported to the colonies millions of pounds of cheap—but still taxed—tea, thereby undercutting the price of smuggled tea and forcing payment of the tea duty.

***bracero* program** System agreed to by Mexican and American governments in 1942 under which tens of thousands of Mexicans entered the United States to work temporarily in agricultural jobs in the Southwest; lasted until 1964 and inhibited labor organization among farm workers since *braceros* could be deported at any time.

Brant, Joseph The Mohawk leader who led the Iroquois against the Americans in the Revolutionary War.

Bretton Woods conference International meeting held in the town of Bretton Woods, New Hampshire, in 1944 in which participants agreed that the American dollar would replace the British pound as the most important international currency. The conference also created the World Bank and International Monetary Fund to promote rebuilding after

World War II and to ensure that countries did not devalue their currencies.

Brook Farm Transcendentalist commune in West Roxbury, Massachusetts, populated from 1841 to 1847 principally by writers (Nathaniel Hawthorne, for one) and other intellectuals.

Brown v. Board of Education 1954 U.S. Supreme Court decision that struck down racial segregation in public education and declared "separate but equal" unconstitutional.

Bull Run, first Battle of The first land engagement of the Civil War which took place on July 21, 1861, at Manassas Junction, Virginia, and at which Union troops quickly retreated.

Bull Run, second Battle of Civil War engagement that took place one year after the first Battle of Bull Run, on August 29–30, during which Confederates captured the federal supply depot at Manassas Junction, Virginia, and forced Union troops back to Washington.

Bunker Hill, Battle of First major battle of the Revolutionary War; it actually took place at nearby Breed's Hill, Massachusetts, on June 17, 1775.

the Bush Doctrine President George W. Bush's foreign policy principle wherein the United States would launch a war on terrorism.

Bush v. Gore U.S. Supreme Court case that determined the winner of the disputed 2000 presidential election.

busing The means of transporting students via buses to achieve school integration in the 1970s.

Camp David Accords Peace agreement between the leaders of Israel and Egypt, brokered by President Jimmy Carter in 1978.

captivity narratives Accounts written by colonists after their time in Indian captivity, often stressing the captive's religious convictions.

caravel A fifteenth-century European ship capable of long-distance travel.

carpetbaggers Derisive term for northern emigrants who participated in the Republican governments of the Reconstruction South.

checks and balances A systematic balance to prevent any one branch of the national government from dominating the other two.

Chinese Exclusion Act 1882 law that halted Chinese immigration to the United States.

Church of Jesus Christ of Latter-Day Saints Religious sect founded in 1830 by Joseph Smith; it was a product of the intense revivalism of the "burned-over district" of New York. Smith's successor Brigham Young led 15,000 followers to Utah in 1847 to escape persecution.

Civil Rights Act (1964) Law that outlawed discrimination in public accommodations and employment.

Civil Rights Act of 1875 The last piece of Reconstruction legislation, which outlawed racial discrimination in places of public accommodation such as hotels and theaters. Many parts of it were ruled unconstitutional by the Supreme Court in 1883.

Civil Rights Bill of 1866 Along with the Fourteenth Amendment, legislation that guaranteed the rights of citizenship to former slaves.

Civil Service Act of 1883 Law that established the Civil Service Commission and marked the end of the spoils system.

Civilian Conservation Corps (CCC) 1933 New Deal public work relief program that provided outdoor manual work for unemployed men, rebuilding infrastructure and implementing conservation programs. The program cut the unemployment rate, particularly among young men.

Cold War Term for tensions, 1945–1989, between the Soviet Union and the United States, the two major world powers after World War II.

collective bargaining The process of negotiations between an employer and a group of employees to regulate working conditions.

Columbian Exchange The transatlantic flow of goods and people that began with Columbus's voyages in 1492.

Committee of Correspondence Group organized by Samuel Adams in retaliation for the *Gaspée* incident to address American grievances, assert American rights, and form a network of rebellion.

common school Tax-supported state schools of the early nineteenth century open to all children.

Common Sense A pamphlet anonymously written by Thomas Paine in January 1776 that attacked the English principles of hereditary rule and monarchical government.

Commonwealth v. Hunt Landmark 1842 ruling of the Massachusetts Supreme Court establishing the legality of labor unions.

communitarianism Social reform movement of the nineteenth century driven by the belief that by establishing small communities based on common ownership of property, a less competitive and individualistic society could be developed.

Compromise of 1850 Complex compromise devised by Senator Henry Clay that admitted California as a free state, included a stronger fugitive slave law, and delayed determination of the slave status of the New Mexico and Utah territories.

Congress of Industrial Organizations Umbrella organization of semiskilled industrial unions, formed in 1935 as the Committee for Industrial Organization and renamed in 1938.

conquistadores Spanish term for "conquerors," applied to Spanish and Portuguese soldiers who conquered lands held by indigenous peoples in central and southern America as well as the current states of Texas, New Mexico, Arizona, and California.

conservation movement A progressive reform movement focused on the preservation and sustainable management of the nation's natural resources.

Constitutional Convention Meeting in Philadelphia, May 25–September 17, 1787, of representatives from twelve colonies—excepting Rhode Island—to revise the existing Articles of Confederation; the convention soon resolved to produce an entirely new constitution.

containment General U.S. strategy in the Cold War that called for containing Soviet expansion; originally devised by U.S. diplomat George F. Kennan.

Continental army Army authorized by the Continental Congress in 1775 to fight the British; commanded by General George Washington.

Continental Congress First meeting of representatives of the colonies, held in Philadelphia in 1774 to formulate actions against British policies; in the Second Continental Congress (1775–1789), the colonial representatives conducted the war and adopted the Declaration of Independence and the Articles of Confederation.

"the contrabands" Slaves who sought refuge in Union military camps or who lived in areas of the Confederacy under Union control.

Contract with America A list of conservatives' promises in response to the supposed liberalism of the Clinton administration, that was drafted by Speaker of the House Newt Gingrich and other congressional Republicans as the GOP platform for the 1994 midterm elections. It was more a campaign tactic than a practical program; few of its proposed items ever became law.

cotton gin Invented by Eli Whitney in 1793, the machine that separated cotton seed from cotton fiber, speeding cotton processing and making profitable the cultivation of the more hardy, but difficult to clean, short-staple cotton; led directly to the dramatic nineteenth-century expansion of slavery in the South.

"Cotton Is King" Phrase from Senator James Henry Hammond's speech extolling the virtues of cotton, and, implicitly, the slave system of production that led to its bounty for the South. "King Cotton" became a shorthand for Southern political and economic power.

Cotton Kingdom Cotton-producing region, relying predominantly on slave labor, that spanned from North Carolina west to Louisiana and reached as far north as southern Illinois.

counterculture "Hippie" youth culture of the 1960s, which rejected the values of the dominant culture in favor of illicit drugs, communes, free sex, and rock music.

Court packing President Franklin D. Roosevelt's failed 1937 attempt to increase the number of U.S. Supreme Court justices from nine to fifteen in order to save his Second New Deal programs from constitutional challenges.

Covenant Chain Alliance formed in the 1670s between the English and the Iroquois nations.

coverture Principle in English and American law that a married woman lost her legal identity, which became "covered" by that of her husband, who therefore controlled her person and the family's economic resources.

Coxey's Army A march on Washington organized by Jacob Coxey, an Ohio member of the People's Party. Coxey believed in abandoning the gold standard and printing enough legal tender to reinvigorate the economy. The marchers demanded that Congress create jobs and pay workers in paper currency not backed by gold.

creoles Persons born in the New World of European ancestry.

crop lien Credit extended by merchants to tenants based on their future crops; under this system, high interest rates and the uncertainties of farming often led to inescapable debts.

Cuban missile crisis Tense confrontation caused when the United States discovered Soviet offensive missile sites in Cuba in October 1962; the U.S.-Soviet confrontation was the Cold War's closest brush with nuclear war.

cult of domesticity The nineteenth-century ideology of "virtue" and "modesty" as the qualities that were essential to proper womanhood.

Culture Wars Battles over moral values that occurred throughout the 1990s. The Culture Wars touched many areas of American life—from popular culture to academia. Flashpoints included the future of the nuclear family and the teaching of evolution.

Dartmouth College v. Woodward 1819 U.S. Supreme Court case in which the Court upheld the original charter of the college against New Hampshire's attempt to alter the board of trustees; set the precedent of support of contracts against state interference.

Dawes Act Law passed in 1887 meant to encourage adoption of white norms among Indians; broke up tribal holdings into small farms for Indian families, with the remainder sold to white purchasers.

D-Day June 6, 1944, when an Allied amphibious assault landed on the Normandy coast and established a foothold in Europe, leading to the liberation of France from German occupation.

Declaration of Independence Document adopted on July 4, 1776, that made the break with Britain official; drafted by a committee of the Second Continental Congress, including principal writer Thomas Jefferson.

decolonization The process by which African and Asian colonies of European empires became independent in the years following World War II.

Defense of Marriage Act 1996 law that barred gay couples from receiving federal benefits. Ruled unconstitutional in 2013.

deindustrialization Term describing decline of manufacturing in old industrial areas in the late twentieth century as companies shifted production to low-wage centers in the South and West or in other countries.

Deism Enlightenment thought applied to religion; emphasized reason, morality, and natural law.

Democracy in America Two works, published in 1835 and 1840, by the French thinker Alexis de Tocqueville on the subject of American democracy. Tocqueville stressed the cultural nature of American democracy, and the importance and prevalence of equality in American life.

Democratic-Republican societies Organizations created in the mid-1790s by opponents of the policies of the Washington administration and supporters of the French Revolution.

Denmark Vesey's conspiracy An 1822 failed slave uprising in Charleston, South Carolina, purported to have been led by Denmark Vesey, a free black man.

deregulation Reagan-Clinton era legislation that removed regulations on many industries, including finance and air travel.

détente Period of improving relations between the United States and Communist nations, particularly China and the Soviet Union, during the Nixon administration.

disenfranchisement To deprive of the right to vote; in the United States, exclusionary policies were used to deny groups, especially African-Americans and women, their voting rights.

Dissenters Protestants who belonged to denominations outside of the established Anglican Church.

division of powers The division of political power between the state and federal governments under the U.S. Constitution (also known as federalism).

Dix, Dorothea An important figure in increasing the public's awareness of the plight of the mentally ill. After a two-year investigation of the treatment of the mentally ill in Massachusetts, she presented her findings and won the support of leading reformers. She eventually convinced twenty states to reform their treatment of the mentally ill.

Dixiecrats Deep South delegates who walked out of the 1948 Democratic National Convention in protest of the party's support for civil rights legislation and later formed the States' Rights Democratic (Dixiecrat) Party, which nominated Strom Thurmond of South Carolina for president.

Dollar Diplomacy A foreign policy initiative under President William Howard Taft that promoted the spread of American influence through loans and economic investments from American banks.

Dominion of New England Consolidation into a single colony of the New England colonies—and later New York and New Jersey—by royal governor Edmund Andros in 1686; dominion reverted to individual colonial governments three years later.

"Don't ask, don't tell" President Clinton's compromise measure that allowed gay people to serve in the military incognito, as officers could no longer seek them out for dismissal but they could not openly express their identity. "Don't ask, don't tell" was ended under the Obama administration, when gay military service was allowed.

the Dorr War A movement in Rhode Island against property qualifications for voting. The movement formed an extralegal constitutional convention for the state and elected Thomas Dorr as a governor, but was quashed by federal troops dispatched by President John Tyler.

double-V Led by *The Pittsburgh Courier*, the movement that pressed for victory over fascism abroad and over racism at home. It argued that since African-Americans were risking their lives abroad, they should receive full civil rights at home.

dower rights In colonial America, the right of a widowed woman to inherit one-third of her deceased husband's property.

Dred Scott v. Sandford 1857 U.S. Supreme Court decision in which Chief Justice Roger B. Taney ruled that Congress could not prohibit slavery in the territories, on the grounds that such a prohibition would violate the Fifth Amendment rights of slaveholders, and that no black person could be a citizen of the United States.

Dust Bowl Great Plains counties where millions of tons of topsoil were blown away from parched farmland in the 1930s; massive migration of farm families followed.

Eighteenth Amendment Prohibition amendment passed in 1919 that made illegal the manufacture, sale, or transportation of alcoholic beverages; repealed in 1933.

Ellis Island Reception center in New York Harbor through which most European immigrants to America were processed from 1892 to 1954.

Emancipation Proclamation Declaration issued by President Abraham Lincoln; the preliminary proclamation on September 22, 1862, freed the slaves in areas under Confederate control as of January 1, 1863, the date of the final proclamation, which also authorized the enrollment of black soldiers into the Union army.

Embargo Act Attempt in 1807 to exert economic pressure by prohibiting all exports from the United States, instead of waging war in reaction to continued British impressment of American sailors; smugglers easily circumvented the embargo, and it was repealed two years later.

Emergency Banking Act Passed in 1933, the First New Deal measure that provided for reopening the banks under strict conditions and took the United States off the gold standard.

empire of liberty The idea, expressed by Jefferson, that the United States would not rule its new territories as colonies, but rather would eventually admit them as full member states.

enclosure movement A legal process that divided large farm fields in England that were previously collectively owned by groups of peasants into smaller, individually owned plots. The enclosure movement took place over several centuries, and resulted in eviction for many peasants.

Enforcement Acts Three laws passed in 1870 and 1871 that tried to eliminate the Ku Klux Klan by outlawing it and other such terrorist societies; the laws allowed the president to deploy the army for that purpose.

English Bill of Rights A series of laws enacted in 1689 that inscribed the rights of Englishmen into law and enumerated parliamentary powers such as taxation.

English liberty The idea that English people were entitled to certain liberties, including trial by jury, habeas corpus, and the right to face one's accuser in court. These rights meant that even the English king was subject to the rule of law.

English Toleration Act A 1690 act of Parliament that allowed all English Protestants to worship freely.

Enlightenment Revolution in thought in the eighteenth century that emphasized reason and science over the authority of traditional religion.

Equal Rights Amendment Amendment to guarantee equal rights for women, introduced in 1923 but not passed by Congress until 1972; it failed to be ratified by the states.

Era of Good Feelings Contemporary characterization of the administration of popular Republican president James Monroe, 1817–1825.

Erie Canal Most important and profitable of the canals of the 1820s and 1830s; stretched from Buffalo to Albany, New York, connecting the Great Lakes to the East Coast and making New York City the nation's largest port.

Espionage Act 1917 law that prohibited spying and interfering with the draft as well as making "false statements" that hurt the war effort.

ethnic cleansing The systematic removal of an ethnic group from a territory through violence or intimidation in order to create a homogeneous society; the term was popularized by the Yugoslav policy brutally targeting Albanian Muslims in Kosovo.

Ex parte Milligan 1866 Supreme Court case that declared it unconstitutional to bring accused persons before military tribunals where civil courts were operating.

Exposition and Protest Document written in 1828 by Vice President John C. Calhoun of South Carolina to protest the so-called Tariff of Abominations, which seemed to favor northern industry; introduced the concept of state interposition and became the basis for South Carolina's Nullification Doctrine of 1833.

Fair Deal Domestic reform proposals of the Truman administration; included civil rights legislation, national health insurance, and repeal of the Taft-Hartley Act, but only extensions of some New Deal programs were enacted.

family values Set of beliefs usually associated with conservatism that stressed the superiority of nuclear family, heterosexual marriage, and traditional gender roles.

family wage Idea that male workers should earn a wage sufficient to enable them to support their entire family without their wives' having to work outside the home.

Federal Housing Administration (FHA) A government agency created during the New Deal to guarantee mortgages, allowing lenders to offer long-term (usually thirty-year) loans with low down payments (usually 10 percent of the asking price). The FHA seldom underwrote loans in racially mixed or minority neighborhoods.

Federal Trade Commission (FTC) Independent agency created by the Wilson administration that replaced the Bureau of Corporations as an even more powerful tool to combat unfair trade practices and monopolies.

federalism A system of government in which power is divided between the central government and the states.

The Federalist Collection of eighty-five essays that appeared in the New York press in 1787–1788 in support of the Constitution; written by Alexander Hamilton, James Madison, and John Jay and published under the pseudonym "Publius."

Federalists and Republicans The two increasingly coherent political parties that appeared in Congress by the mid-1790s. The Federalists, led by George Washington, John Adams, and Alexander Hamilton, favored a strong central government. The Republicans, first identified during the early nineteenth century, supported a strict interpretation of the Constitution, which they believed would safeguard individual freedoms and states' rights from the threats posed by a strong central government.

The Feminine Mystique The book widely credited with sparking second-wave feminism in the United States. Author Betty Friedan focused on college-educated women, arguing that they would find fulfillment by engaging in paid labor outside the home.

feminism Term that entered the lexicon in the early twentieth century to describe the movement for full equality for women, in political, social, and personal life.

Fifteenth Amendment Constitutional amendment ratified in 1870, which prohibited states from discriminating in voting privileges on the basis of race.

flappers Young women of the 1920s whose rebellion against prewar standards of femininity included wearing shorter dresses, bobbing their hair, dancing to jazz music, driving cars, smoking cigarettes, and indulging in illegal drinking and gambling.

Force Act 1833 legislation, sparked by the nullification crisis in South Carolina, that authorized the president's use of the army to compel states to comply with federal law.

Fordism Early twentieth-century term describing the economic system pioneered by Ford Motor Company based on high wages and mass consumption.

Fort McHenry Fort in Baltimore Harbor unsuccessfully bombarded by the British in September 1814; Francis Scott Key, a witness to the battle, was moved to write the words to "The Star-Spangled Banner."

Fort Sumter First battle of the Civil War, in which the federal fort in Charleston (South Carolina) Harbor was captured by the Confederates on April 14, 1861, after two days of shelling.

Four Freedoms Freedom of speech, freedom of worship, freedom from want, and freedom from fear, as described by President Franklin D. Roosevelt during his January 6, 1941, State of the Union Address.

Fourteen Points President Woodrow Wilson's 1918 plan for peace after World War I; at the Versailles peace conference, however, he failed to incorporate all of the points into the treaty.

Fourteenth Amendment 1868 constitutional amendment that guaranteed rights of citizenship to former slaves, in words similar to those of the Civil Rights Act of 1866.

franchise The right to vote.

free blacks African-American persons not held in slavery; immediately before the Civil War, there were nearly a half

million in the United States, split almost evenly between North and South.

Free Soil Party Political organization formed in 1848 to oppose slavery in the territory acquired in the Mexican War; nominated Martin Van Buren for president in 1848. By 1854 most of the party's members had joined the Republican Party.

free trade The belief that economic development arises from the exchange of goods between different countries without governmental interference.

the Freedmen's Bureau Reconstruction agency established in 1865 to protect the legal rights of former slaves and to assist with their education, jobs, health care, and landowning.

freedom petitions Arguments for liberty presented to New England's courts and legislatures in the early 1770s by enslaved African-Americans.

Freedom Rides Bus journeys challenging racial segregation in the South in 1961.

French and Indian War The last—and most important—of four colonial wars fought between England and France for control of North America east of the Mississippi River.

Fugitive Slave Act 1850 law that gave the federal government authority in cases involving runaway slaves; aroused considerable opposition in the North.

fugitive slaves Slaves who escaped from their owners.

fundamentalism Anti-modernist Protestant movement started in the early twentieth century that proclaimed the literal truth of the Bible; the name came from *The Fundamentals*, published by conservative leaders.

Gabriel's Rebellion An 1800 uprising planned by Virginian slaves to gain their freedom. The plot was led by a blacksmith named Gabriel, but was discovered and quashed.

Gadsden Purchase Thirty thousand square miles in present-day Arizona and New Mexico bought by Congress from Mexico in 1853 primarily for the Southern Pacific Railroad's transcontinental route.

gag rule Rule adopted by House of Representatives in 1836 prohibiting consideration of abolitionist petitions;

opposition, led by former president John Quincy Adams, succeeded in having it repealed in 1844.

Garvey, Marcus The leading spokesman for Negro Nationalism, which exalted blackness, black cultural expression, and black exclusiveness. He called upon African-Americans to liberate themselves from the surrounding white culture and create their own businesses, cultural centers, and newspapers. He was also the founder of the Universal Negro Improvement Association.

Geneva Accords A 1954 document that had promised elections to unify Vietnam and established the Seventeenth Parallel demarcation line which divided North and South Vietnam.

"gentlemen of property and standing" Well-to-do merchants who often had commercial ties to the South and resisted abolitionism, occasionally inciting violence against its adherents.

Gettysburg, Battle of Battle fought in southern Pennsylvania, July 1–3, 1863; the Confederate defeat and the simultaneous loss at Vicksburg marked the military turning point of the Civil War.

Ghost Dance A spiritual and political movement among Native Americans whose followers performed a ceremonial "ghost dance" intended to connect the living with the dead and make the Indians bulletproof in battles intended to restore their homelands.

GI Bill of Rights The 1944 legislation that provided money for education and other benefits to military personnel returning from World War II.

Gibbons v. Ogden 1824 U.S. Supreme Court decision reinforcing the "commerce clause" (the federal government's right to regulate interstate commerce) of the Constitution; Chief Justice John Marshall ruled against the State of New York's granting of steamboat monopolies.

the Gilded Age The popular but derogatory name for the period from the end of the Civil War to the turn of the century, after the title of the 1873 novel by Mark Twain and Charles Dudley Warner.

globalization Term that became prominent in the 1990s to describe the rapid acceleration of international flows of commerce, financial resources, labor, and cultural products.

Glorious Revolution A coup in 1688 engineered by a small group of aristocrats that led to William of Orange taking the British throne in place of James II.

gold rush The massive migration of Americans into California territory in the late 1840s and 1850s in pursuit of gold, which was discovered there in 1848.

gold standard Policy at various points in American history by which the value of a dollar is set at a fixed price in terms of gold (in the post–World War II era, for example, $35 per ounce of gold).

Good Neighbor Policy Policy proclaimed by President Franklin D. Roosevelt in his first inaugural address in 1933 that sought improved diplomatic relations between the United States and its Latin American neighbors.

gradual emancipation A series of acts passed in state legislatures throughout the North in the years following the Revolution that freed slaves after they reached a certain age, following lengthy "apprenticeships."

grandfather clause Loophole created by southern disenfranchising legislatures of the 1890s for illiterate white males whose grandfathers had been eligible to vote before the Civil War.

Great Awakening Fervent religious revival movement in the 1720s through the 1740s that was spread throughout the colonies by ministers like New England Congregationalist Jonathan Edwards and English revivalist George Whitefield.

Great Depression Worst economic depression in American history; it was spurred by the stock market crash of 1929 and lasted until World War II.

Great League of Peace An alliance of the Iroquois tribes, originally formed sometime between 1450 and 1600, that used their combined strength to pressure Europeans to work with them in the fur trade and to wage war across what is today eastern North America.

Great Migration Large-scale migration of southern blacks during and after World War I to the North, where jobs had become available during the labor shortage of the war years.

Great Migration (1630s) The migration of approximately 21,000 English Puritans to the Massachusetts Bay Colony.

Great Railroad Strike A series of demonstrations, some violent, held nationwide in support of striking railroad workers in Martinsburg, West Virginia, who refused to work due to wage cuts.

Great Recession A period of major economic stagnation across the United States and western Europe, characterized by rising unemployment and inflation and a 37 percent decline in the stock market between March and December 1974.

Great Society Term coined by President Lyndon B. Johnson in his 1965 State of the Union address, in which he proposed legislation to address problems of voting rights, poverty, diseases, education, immigration, and the environment.

Griswold v. Connecticut Supreme Court decision that, in overturning Connecticut law prohibiting the use of contraceptives, established a constitutional right to privacy.

Guantánamo Bay A detention center at the American naval base at Guantánamo Bay, Cuba, where beginning in 2002 suspected terrorists and war prisoners were held indefinitely and tried by extrajudicial military tribunals. During his 2008 presidential campaign, Senator Barack Obama pledged to close the prison, but as of 2015 it remained open.

Gulf of Tonkin resolution Legislation passed by Congress in 1964 in reaction to supposedly unprovoked attacks on American warships off the coast of North Vietnam; it gave the president unlimited authority to defend U.S. forces and members of SEATO.

Gulf oil spill Environmental disaster that occurred in 2010 after an explosion on the *Deepwater Horizon* oil rig. Hundreds of millions of gallons of oil were spilled into the Gulf of Mexico, resulting in one of the largest environmental calamities in human history.

Gulf War Military action in 1991 in which an international coalition led by the United States drove Iraq from Kuwait, which it had occupied the previous year.

hacienda Large-scale farm in the Spanish New World empire worked by Indian laborers.

Haitian Revolution A slave uprising that led to the establishment of Haiti as an independent country in 1804.

Half-Way Covenant A 1662 religious compromise that allowed baptism and partial church membership to colonial New Englanders whose parents were not among the Puritan elect.

Harlem Renaissance African-American literary and artistic movement of the 1920s centered in New York City's Harlem neighborhood; writers Langston Hughes, Jean Toomer, Zora Neale Hurston, and Countee Cullen were among those active in the movement.

Harpers Ferry, Virginia Site of abolitionist John Brown's failed raid on the federal arsenal, October 16–17, 1859; Brown became a martyr to his cause after his capture and execution.

Hart-Celler Act 1965 law that eliminated the national origins quota system for immigration established by laws in 1921 and 1924; led to radical change in the origins of immigrants to the United States, with Asians and Latin Americans outnumbering Europeans.

Hartford Convention Meeting of New England Federalists on December 15, 1814, to protest the War of 1812; proposed seven constitutional amendments (limiting embargoes and changing requirements for officeholding, declaration of war, and admission of new states), but the war ended before Congress could respond.

Haymarket Affair Violence during an anarchist protest at Haymarket Square in Chicago on May 4, 1886; the deaths of eight, including seven policemen, led to the trial of eight anarchist leaders for conspiracy to commit murder.

Haynes, Lemuel A black member of the Massachusetts militia and celebrated minister who urged that Americans extend their conception of freedom to enslaved Africans during the Revolutionary Era.

headright system A land-grant policy that promised fifty acres to any colonist who could afford passage to Virginia, as well as fifty more for any accompanying servants. The headright policy was eventually expanded to include any colonists—and was also adopted in other colonies.

Helsinki Accords 1975 agreement between the USSR and the United States that recognized the post–World War II boundaries of Europe and guaranteed the basic liberties of each nation's citizens.

Hessians German soldiers, most from Hesse-Cassel principality (hence, the name), paid to fight for the British in the Revolutionary War.

Hollywood Ten A group called before the House Un-American Activities Committee who refused to speak about their political leanings or "name names"—that is, identify communists in Hollywood. Some were imprisoned as a result.

Holocaust Systematic racist attempt by the Nazis to exterminate the Jews of Europe, resulting in the murder of over 6 million Jews and more than a million other "undesirables."

Homestead Act 1862 law that authorized Congress to grant 160 acres of public land to a western settler, who had to live on the land for five years to establish title.

horizontal expansion The process by which a corporation acquires or merges with its competitors.

House of Burgesses The first elected assembly in colonial America, established in 1619 in Virginia. Only wealthy landowners could vote in its elections.

House Un-American Activities Committee (HUAC) Committee formed in 1938 to investigate subversives in the government and holders of radical ideas more generally; best-known investigations were of Hollywood notables and of former State Department official Alger Hiss, who was accused in 1948 of espionage and Communist Party membership. Abolished in 1975.

Hundred Days Extraordinarily productive first three months of President Franklin D. Roosevelt's administration in which a special session of Congress enacted fifteen of his New Deal proposals.

Hurricane Katrina 2005 hurricane that devastated much of the Gulf Coast, especially New Orleans. The Bush administration's response was widely criticized as inadequate.

illegal alien A new category established by the Immigration Act of 1924 that referred to immigrants crossing U.S. borders in excess of the new immigration quotas.

Immigration Restriction League A political organization founded in 1894 that called for reducing immigration to the United States by requiring a literacy test for immigrants.

impeachment Bringing charges against a public official; for example, the House of Representatives can impeach a president for "treason, bribery, or other high crimes and misdemeanors" by majority vote, and after the trial the Senate can remove the president by a vote of two-thirds. Two presidents, Andrew Johnson and Bill Clinton, have been impeached and tried before the Senate; neither was convicted.

impressment The British navy's practice of using press-gangs to kidnap men in British and colonial ports who were then forced to serve in the British navy.

"In God We Trust" Phrase placed on all new U.S. currency as of 1954.

indentured servants Settlers who signed on for a temporary period of servitude to a master in exchange for passage to the New World; Virginia and Pennsylvania were largely peopled in the seventeenth and eighteenth centuries by English and German indentured servants.

Indian New Deal Phrase that refers to the reforms implemented for Native Americans during the New Deal era. John Collier, the commissioner of the Bureau of Indian Affairs (BIA), increased the access Native Americans had to relief programs and employed more Native Americans at the BIA. He worked to pass the Indian Reorganization Act. However, the version of the act passed by Congress was a much diluted version of Collier's original proposal and did not greatly improve the lives of Native Americans.

Indian Removal Act 1830 law signed by President Andrew Jackson that permitted the negotiation of treaties to obtain the Indians' lands in exchange for their relocation to what would become Oklahoma.

individualism Term that entered the language in the 1820s to describe the increasing emphasis on the pursuit of personal advancement and private fulfillment free of outside interference.

Industrial Workers of the World Radical union organized in Chicago in 1905 and nicknamed the Wobblies; its opposition to World War I led to its destruction by the federal government under the Espionage Act.

inflation An economic condition in which prices rise continuously.

Insular Cases Series of cases between 1901 and 1904 in which the Supreme Court ruled that constitutional protection of individual rights did not fully apply to residents of "insular" territories acquired by the United States in the Spanish-American War, such as Puerto Rico and the Philippines.

Interstate Commerce Commission Organization established by Congress, in reaction to the U.S. Supreme Court's ruling in *Wabash Railroad v. Illinois* (1886), in order to curb abuses in the railroad industry by regulating rates.

interstate highway system National network of interstate superhighways; its construction began in the late 1950s for the purpose of commerce and defense. The interstate highways would enable the rapid movement of military convoys and the evacuation of cities after a nuclear attack.

Intolerable Acts Four parliamentary measures in reaction to the Boston Tea Party that forced payment for the tea, disallowed colonial trials of British soldiers, forced their quartering in private homes, and reduced the number of elected officials in Massachusetts.

Iran-Contra Affair Scandal of the second Reagan administration involving sales of arms to Iran in partial exchange for release of hostages in Lebanon and use of the arms money to aid the Contras in Nicaragua, which had been expressly forbidden by Congress.

Iraq War Military campaign in 2003 in which the United States, unable to gain approval by the United Nations, unilaterally occupied Iraq and removed dictator Saddam Hussein from power.

iron curtain Term coined by Winston Churchill to describe the Cold War divide between western Europe and the Soviet Union's eastern European satellites.

ISIS An insurgency that emerged from the sectarian civil wars that destabilized Syria and post–Saddam Hussein Iraq. Beginning in 2014, ISIS forces attacked towns and cities in Iraq, Syria, and Lybia, systematically murdering members of ethnic and religious minorities.

isolationism The desire to avoid foreign entanglements that dominated the U.S. Congress in the 1930s; beginning in 1935, lawmakers passed a series of Neutrality Acts that banned travel on belligerents' ships and the sale of arms to countries at war.

Japanese-American internment Policy adopted by the Roosevelt administration in 1942 under which 110,000 persons of Japanese descent, most of them American citizens, were removed from the West Coast and forced to spend most of World War II in internment camps; it was the largest violation of American civil liberties in the twentieth century.

Jay's Treaty Treaty with Britain negotiated in 1794 by Chief Justice John Jay; Britain agreed to vacate forts in the Northwest Territories, and festering disagreements (border with Canada, prewar debts, shipping claims) would be settled by commission.

Kansas Exodus A migration in 1879 and 1880 by some 40,000–60,000 blacks to Kansas to escape the oppressive environment of the New South.

Kansas-Nebraska Act 1854 law sponsored by Illinois senator Stephen A. Douglas to allow settlers in newly organized territories north of the Missouri border to decide the slavery issue for themselves; fury over the resulting repeal of the Missouri Compromise of 1820 led to violence in Kansas and to the formation of the Republican Party.

"King Cotton diplomacy" An attempt during the Civil War by the South to encourage British intervention by banning cotton exports.

King Philip's War A multiyear conflict that began in 1675 with an Indian uprising against white colonists. Its end result was broadened freedoms for white New Englanders and the dispossession of the region's Indians.

Knights of Labor Founded in 1869, the first national union; lasted, under the leadership of Terence V. Powderly, only into the 1890s; supplanted by the American Federation of Labor.

Know-Nothing Party Nativist, anti-Catholic third party organized in 1854 in reaction to large-scale German and Irish immigration; the party's only presidential candidate was Millard Fillmore in 1856.

Korean War Conflict touched off in 1950 when Communist North Korea invaded South Korea; fighting, largely by U.S. forces, continued until 1953.

Korematsu v. United States 1944 Supreme Court case that found Executive Order 9066 to be constitutional. Fred Korematsu, an American-born citizen of Japanese descent, defied the military order that banned all persons of Japanese ancestry from designated western coastal areas. The Court upheld Korematsu's arrest and internment.

Ku Klux Klan Group organized in Pulaski, Tennessee, in 1866 to terrorize former slaves who voted and held political offices during Reconstruction; a revived organization in the 1910s and 1920s that stressed white, Anglo-Saxon, fundamentalist Protestant supremacy; revived a third time to fight the civil rights movement of the 1950s and 1960s in the South.

Kyoto Protocol A 1997 international agreement that sought to combat global warming. To great controversy, the Bush administration announced in 2001 that it would not abide by the Kyoto Protocol.

Las Casas, Bartolomé de A Catholic missionary who renounced the Spanish practice of coercively converting Indians and advocated their better treatment. In 1552, he wrote *A Brief Relation of the Destruction of the Indies*, which described the Spanish's cruel treatment of the Indians.

League of Nations Organization of nations to mediate disputes and avoid war established after World War I as part of the Treaty of Versailles; President Woodrow Wilson's "Fourteen Points" speech to Congress in 1918 proposed the formation of the league, which the United States never joined.

League of United Latin American Citizens Often called LULAC, an organization that challenged restrictive housing, employment discrimination, and other inequalities faced by Latino Americans.

Lend-Lease Act 1941 law that permitted the United States to lend or lease arms and other supplies to the Allies, signifying increasing likelihood of American involvement in World War II.

Letters from an American Farmer 1782 book by Hector St. John de Crèvecoeur that popularized the notion that the United States was a "melting pot" while excluding people of color from the process of assimilation.

Levittown Low-cost, mass-produced developments of suburban tract housing built by William Levitt after World War II on Long Island and elsewhere.

Lewis and Clark expedition Led by Meriwether Lewis and William Clark, a mission to the Pacific coast commissioned for the purposes of scientific and geographical exploration.

Lexington and Concord, Battles of The first shots fired in the Revolutionary War, on April 19, 1775, near Boston; approximately 100 minutemen and 250 British soldiers were killed.

liberal internationalism Woodrow Wilson's foreign policy theory, which rested on the idea that economic and political freedom went hand in hand, and encouraged American intervention abroad in order to secure these freedoms globally.

liberalism Originally, political philosophy that emphasized the protection of liberty by limiting the power of government to interfere with the natural rights of citizens; in the twentieth century, belief in an activist government promoting greater social and economic equality.

liberty of contract A judicial concept of the late nineteenth and early twentieth centuries whereby the courts overturned laws regulating labor conditions as violations of the economic freedom of both employers and employees.

Liberty Party Abolitionist political party that nominated James G. Birney for president in 1840 and 1844; merged with the Free Soil Party in 1848.

Lincoln-Douglas debates Series of senatorial campaign debates in 1858 focusing on the issue of slavery in the territories; held in Illinois between Republican Abraham Lincoln, who made a national reputation for himself, and incumbent Democratic senator Stephen A. Douglas, who managed to hold on to his seat.

the Little Bighorn, Battle of Most famous battle of the Great Sioux War; took place in 1876 in the Montana Territory; combined Sioux and Cheyenne warriors massacred a vastly outnumbered U.S. Cavalry commanded by Lieutenant Colonel George Armstrong Custer.

Long Telegram A telegram by American diplomat George Kennan in 1946 outlining his views of the Soviet Union that eventually inspired the policy of containment.

Lord Dunmore's proclamation A proclamation issued in 1775 by the earl of Dunmore, the British governor of Virginia, that offered freedom to any slave who fought for the king against the rebelling colonists.

Lords of Trade An English regulatory board established to oversee colonial affairs in 1675.

the Lost Cause A romanticized view of slavery, the Old South, and the Confederacy that arose in the decades following the Civil War.

Louisiana Purchase President Thomas Jefferson's 1803 purchase from France of the important port of New Orleans and 828,000 square miles west of the Mississippi River to the Rocky Mountains; it more than doubled the territory of the United States at a cost of only $15 million.

Loyalists Colonists who remained loyal to Great Britain during the War of Independence.

Lusitania British passenger liner sunk by a German U-boat, May 7, 1915, creating a diplomatic crisis and public outrage at the loss of 128 Americans (roughly 10 percent of the total aboard); Germany agreed to pay reparations, and the United States waited two more years to enter World War I.

lynching Practice, particularly widespread in the South between 1890 and 1940, in which persons (usually black) accused of a crime were murdered by mobs before standing trial. Lynchings often took place before large crowds, with law enforcement authorities not intervening.

Manhattan Project Secret American program during World War II to develop an atomic bomb; J. Robert Oppenheimer led the team of physicists at Los Alamos, New Mexico.

manifest destiny Phrase first used in 1845 to urge annexation of Texas; used thereafter to encourage American settlement of European colonial and Indian lands in the Great Plains and the West and, more generally, as a justification for American empire.

Marbury v. Madison First U.S. Supreme Court decision to declare a federal law—the Judiciary Act of 1801—unconstitutional.

March on Washington Civil rights demonstration on August 28, 1963, where the Reverend Martin Luther King Jr. gave his "I Have a Dream" speech on the steps of the Lincoln Memorial.

Marshall Plan U.S. program for the reconstruction of post–World War II Europe through massive aid to former enemy nations as well as allies; proposed by General George C. Marshall in 1947.

massive retaliation Strategy that used the threat of nuclear warfare as a means of combating the global spread of communism.

maternalist reforms Progressive-era reforms that sought to encourage women's child-bearing and -rearing abilities and to promote their economic independence.

Mayflower Compact Document signed in 1620 aboard the *Mayflower* before the Pilgrims landed at Plymouth; the document committed the group to majority-rule government.

McCarran-Walter Act Immigration legislation passed in 1952 that allowed the government to deport immigrants who had been identified as communists, regardless of whether or not they were citizens.

McCarthyism Post–World War II Red Scare focused on the fear of Communists in U.S. government positions; peaked during the Korean War; most closely associated with Joseph McCarthy, a major instigator of the hysteria.

McCulloch v. Maryland 1819 U.S. Supreme Court decision in which Chief Justice John Marshall, holding that Maryland could not tax the Second Bank of the United States, supported the authority of the federal government versus the states.

McNary-Haugen bill Vetoed by President Calvin Coolidge in 1927 and 1928, the bill to aid farmers that would have artificially raised agricultural prices by selling surpluses overseas for low prices and selling the reduced supply in the United States for higher prices.

mercantilism Policy of Great Britain and other imperial powers of regulating the economies of colonies to benefit the mother country.

mestizos Spanish word for persons of mixed Native American and European ancestry.

Metacom The chief of the Wampanoags, whom the colonists called King Philip. He resented English efforts to convert Indians to Christianity and waged a war against the English colonists, one in which he was killed.

métis Children of marriages between Indian women and French traders and officials.

Mexican War Controversial war with Mexico for control of California and New Mexico, 1846–1848; the Treaty of Guadalupe

Hidalgo fixed the border at the Rio Grande and extended the United States to the Pacific coast, annexing more than a half-million square miles of Mexican territory.

middle ground A borderland between European empires and Indian sovereignty where various native peoples and Europeans lived side by side in relative harmony.

Middle Passage The hellish and often deadly middle leg of the transatlantic "Triangular Trade" in which European ships carried manufactured goods to Africa, then transported enslaved Africans to the Americas and the Caribbean, and finally conveyed American agricultural products back to Europe; from the late sixteenth to the early nineteenth centuries, some 12 million Africans were transported via the Middle Passage, unknown millions more dying en route.

military-industrial complex The concept of "an immense military establishment" combined with a "permanent arms industry," which President Eisenhower warned against in his 1961 Farewell Address.

mill girls Women who worked at textile mills during the Industrial Revolution who enjoyed new freedoms and independence not seen before.

missile gap The claim, raised by John F. Kennedy during his campaign for president in 1960, that the Soviet Union had developed a technological and military advantage during Eisenhower's presidency.

Missouri Compromise Deal proposed by Kentucky senator Henry Clay in 1820 to resolve the slave/free imbalance in Congress that would result from Missouri's admission as a slave state; Maine's admission as a free state offset Missouri, and slavery was prohibited in the remainder of the Louisiana Territory north of the southern border of Missouri.

Monroe Doctrine President James Monroe's declaration to Congress on December 2, 1823, that the American continents would be thenceforth closed to European colonization, and that the United States would not interfere in European affairs.

Montgomery bus boycott Sparked by Rosa Parks's arrest on December 1, 1955, for refusing to surrender her seat to a white passenger, a successful year-long boycott protesting segregation on city buses; led by the Reverend Martin Luther King Jr.

moral imperialism The Wilsonian belief that U.S. foreign policy should be guided by morality, and should teach other peoples about democracy. Wilson used this belief to both repudiate Dollar Diplomacy and justify frequent military interventions in Latin America.

moral suasion The abolitionist strategy that sought to end slavery by persuading both slaveowners and complicit northerners that the institution was evil.

muckraking Writing that exposed corruption and abuses in politics, business, meatpacking, child labor, and more, primarily in the first decade of the twentieth century; included popular books and magazine articles that spurred public interest in reform.

Muller v. Oregon 1908 Supreme Court decision that held that state interest in protecting women could override liberty of contract. Louis D. Brandeis, with help from his sister-in-law Josephine Goldmark of the National Consumers League, filed a brief in *Muller* that used statistics about women's health to argue for their protection.

multiculturalism Term that became prominent in the 1990s to describe a growing emphasis on group racial and ethnic identity and demands that jobs, education, and politics reflect the increasingly diverse nature of American society.

Murray, Judith Sargent A writer and early feminist thinker prominent in the years following the American Revolution.

My Lai massacre Massacre of 347 Vietnamese civilians in the village of My Lai by Lieutenant William Calley and troops under his command. U.S. army officers covered up the massacre for a year until an investigation uncovered the events. Eventually twenty-five army officers were charged with complicity in the massacre and its cover-up, but only Calley was convicted. He served little time for his crimes.

Nat Turner's Rebellion Most important slave uprising in nineteenth-century America, led by a slave preacher who, with his followers, killed about sixty white persons in Southampton County, Virginia, in 1831.

National Association for the Advancement of Colored People Founded in 1910, the civil rights organization that brought lawsuits against discriminatory practices and published *The Crisis*, a journal edited by African-American scholar W. E. B. Du Bois.

National Defense Education Act 1958 law passed in reaction to America's perceived inferiority in the space race; encouraged education in science and modern languages through student loans, university research grants, and aid to public schools.

National Industrial Recovery Act 1933 law passed on the last of the Hundred Days; it created public-works jobs through the Federal Emergency Relief Administration and established a system of self-regulation for industry through the National Recovery Administration, which was ruled unconstitutional in 1935.

National Organization for Women Organization founded in 1966 by writer Betty Friedan and other feminists; it pushed for abortion rights, nondiscrimination in the workplace, and other forms of equality for women.

National Recovery Administration (NRA) Controversial federal agency created in 1933 that brought together business and labor leaders to create "codes of fair competition" and "fair labor" policies, including a national minimum wage.

nativism Anti-immigrant and anti-Catholic feeling especially prominent in the 1830s through the 1850s; the largest group of its proponents was New York's Order of the Star-Spangled Banner, which expanded into the American (Know-Nothing) Party in 1854.

Navajo's Long Walk The forced removal of 8,000 Navajos from their lands by Union forces to a reservation in the 1860s.

Navigation Act Law passed by the English Parliament to control colonial trade and bolster the mercantile system, 1650–1775; enforcement of the act led to growing resentment by colonists.

neoconservatives The leaders of the conservative insurgency of the early 1980s. Their brand of conservatism was personified in Ronald Reagan, who believed in less government, supply-side economics, and "family values."

Neolin A Native American religious prophet who, by preaching pan-Indian unity and rejection of European technology and commerce, helped inspire Pontiac's Rebellion.

Neutrality Acts Series of laws passed between 1935 and 1939 to keep the United States from becoming involved in war by prohibiting American trade and travel to warring nations.

New Deal Franklin D. Roosevelt's campaign promise, in his speech to the Democratic National Convention of 1932, to combat the Great Depression with a "new deal for the American people"; the phrase became a catchword for his ambitious plan of economic programs.

new feminism A new aspect of the women's rights movement that arose in the early part of the twentieth century. New feminism added a focus on individual and sexual freedom to the movement, and introduced the word "feminism" into American life.

New Freedom Democrat Woodrow Wilson's political slogan in the presidential campaign of 1912; Wilson wanted to improve the banking system, lower tariffs, and, by breaking up monopolies, give small businesses freedom to compete.

New Harmony Community founded in Indiana by British industrialist Robert Owen in 1825; the short-lived New Harmony Community of Equality was one of the few nineteenth-century communal experiments not based on religious ideology.

new immigrants Wave of newcomers from southern and eastern Europe, including many Jews, who became a majority among immigrants to America after 1890.

New Jersey Plan New Jersey's delegation to the Constitutional Convention's plan for one legislative body with equal representation for each state.

New Left Radical youth protest movement of the 1960s, named by leader Tom Hayden to distinguish it from the Old (Marxist-Leninist) Left of the 1930s.

New Nationalism Platform of the Progressive Party and slogan of former president Theodore Roosevelt in the presidential campaign of 1912; stressed government activism, including regulation of trusts, conservation, and recall of state court decisions that had nullified progressive programs.

New Negro Term used in the 1920s, in reference to a slow and steady growth of black political influence that occurred in northern cities, where African-Americans were freer to speak and act. This political activity created a spirit of protest that expressed itself culturally in the Harlem Renaissance and politically in "new Negro" nationalism.

New Orleans, Battle of Last battle of the War of 1812, fought on January 8, 1815, weeks after the peace treaty was signed but prior to the news' reaching America; General Andrew Jackson led the victorious American troops.

New South *Atlanta Constitution* editor Henry W. Grady's 1886 term for the prosperous post–Civil War South he envisioned: democratic, industrial, urban, and free of nostalgia for the defeated plantation South.

new world order President George H. W. Bush's term for the post–Cold War world.

Ninety-Five Theses The list of moral grievances against the Catholic Church by Martin Luther, a German priest, in 1517.

"no taxation without representation" The rallying cry of opponents to the 1765 Stamp Act. The slogan decried the colonists' lack of representation in Parliament.

North American Free Trade Agreement (NAFTA) Approved in 1993, the agreement with Canada and Mexico that allowed goods to travel across their borders free of tariffs. Critics of the agreement argued that American workers would lose their jobs to cheaper Mexican labor.

North Atlantic Treaty Organization (NATO) Alliance founded in 1949 by ten western European nations, the United States, and Canada to deter Soviet expansion in Europe.

Northwest Ordinance of 1787 Law that created the Northwest Territory (area north of the Ohio River and west of Pennsylvania), established conditions for self-government and statehood, included a Bill of Rights, and permanently prohibited slavery.

Notes on the State of Virginia Thomas Jefferson's 1785 book that claimed, among other things, that black people were incapable of becoming citizens and living in harmony alongside white people due to the legacy of slavery and what Jefferson believed were the "real distinctions that nature has made" between races.

NSC-68 Top-secret policy paper approved by President Truman in 1950 that outlined a militaristic approach to combating the spread of global communism.

nullification crisis The 1832 attempt by the State of South Carolina to nullify, or invalidate within its borders, the 1832 federal tariff law. President Jackson responded with the Force Act of 1833.

Obergefell v. Hodges 2015 Supreme Court decision that allowed same-sex couples to marry throughout the United States.

Occupy Wall Street A grassroots movement in 2011 against growing economic inequality, declining opportunity, and the depredations of Wall Street banks.

oil embargo Prohibition on trade in oil declared by the Organization of Petroleum Exporting Countries, dominated by Middle Eastern producers, in October 1973 in response to U.S. and western European support for Israel in the 1973 Yom Kippur War. The rise in gas prices and fuel shortages resulted in a global economic recession and profoundly affected the American economy.

Oneida Utopian community founded in 1848; the Perfectionist religious group practiced "complex marriage" under leader John Humphrey Noyes.

Open Door Policy Demand in 1899 by Secretary of State John Hay, in hopes of protecting the Chinese market for U.S. exports, that Chinese trade be open to all nations.

open immigration American immigration laws under which nearly all white people could immigrate to the United States and become naturalized citizens.

Operation Dixie CIO's largely ineffective post–World War II campaign to unionize southern workers.

Ordinance of 1784 A law drafted by Thomas Jefferson that regulated land ownership and defined the terms by which western land would be marketed and settled; it established stages of self-government for the West. First Congress would govern a territory; then the territory would be admitted to the Union as a full state.

Ordinance of 1785 A law that regulated land sales in the Old Northwest. The land surveyed was divided into 640-acre plots and sold at $1 per acre.

Oslo Accords 1993 roadmap for peace between Israel and the newly created Palestinian Authority, negotiated under the Clinton administration.

Panama Canal Zone The small strip of land on either side of the Panama Canal. The Canal Zone was under U.S. control from 1903 to 1979 as a result of Theodore Roosevelt's assistance in engineering a coup in Colombia that established Panama's independence.

Panic of 1819 Financial collapse brought on by sharply falling cotton prices, declining demand for American exports, and reckless western land speculation.

Panic of 1837 Beginning of major economic depression lasting about six years; touched off by a British financial crisis and made worse by falling cotton prices, credit and currency problems, and speculation in land, canals, and railroads.

paternalism A moral position developed during the first half of the nineteenth century which claimed that slaves were deprived of liberty for their own "good." Such a rationalization was adopted by some slaveowners to justify slavery.

the "peculiar institution" A phrase used by whites in the antebellum South to refer to slavery without using the word "slavery."

Pentagon Papers Informal name for the Defense Department's secret history of the Vietnam conflict; leaked to the press by former official Daniel Ellsberg and published in the *New York Times* in 1971.

Pequot War An armed conflict in 1637 that led to the destruction of one of New England's most powerful Indian groups.

perfectionism The idea that social ills once considered incurable could in fact be eliminated, popularized by the religious revivalism of the nineteenth century.

Perry, Commodore Matthew U.S. naval officer who negotiated the Treaty of Kanagawa in 1854. That treaty was the first step in starting a political and commercial relationship between the United States and Japan.

pet banks Local banks that received deposits while the charter of the Bank of the United States was about to expire in 1836. The choice of these banks was influenced by political and personal connections.

Philippine War American military campaign that suppressed the movement for Philippine independence after the Spanish-American War; America's death toll was over 4,000 and the Philippines' was far higher.

Pilgrims Puritan separatists who broke completely with the Church of England and sailed to the New World aboard the *Mayflower*, founding Plymouth Colony on Cape Cod in 1620.

plantation An early word for a colony, a settlement "planted" from abroad among an alien population in Ireland or the New World. Later, a large agricultural enterprise that used unfree labor to produce a crop for the world market.

Platt Amendment 1901 amendment to the Cuban constitution that reserved the United States' right to intervene in Cuban affairs and forced newly independent Cuba to host American naval bases on the island.

Plessy v. Ferguson U.S. Supreme Court decision supporting the legality of Jim Crow laws that permitted or required "separate but equal" facilities for blacks and whites.

Pontiac's Rebellion An Indian attack on British forts and settlements after France ceded to the British its territory east of the Mississippi River, as part of the Treaty of Paris in 1763, without consulting France's Indian allies.

Popular Front A period during the mid-1930s when the Communist Party sought to ally itself with socialists and New Dealers in movements for social change, urging reform of the capitalist system rather than revolution.

popular sovereignty Program that allowed settlers in a disputed territory to decide the slavery issue for themselves; most closely associated with Senator Stephen A. Douglas of Illinois.

Populists Founded in 1892, a group that advocated a variety of reform issues, including free coinage of silver, income tax, postal savings, regulation of railroads, and direct election of U.S. senators.

Porkopolis Nickname of Cincinnati, coined in the mid-nineteenth century, after its numerous slaughter houses.

Port Huron Statement A manifesto by Students for a Democratic Society that criticized institutions ranging from political parties to corporations, unions, and the military-industrial complex, while offering a new vision of social change.

Potsdam conference Last meeting of the major Allied powers; the conference that took place outside Berlin from July 17 to August 2, 1945, at which U.S. president Harry Truman, Soviet dictator Joseph Stalin, and British prime minister Clement Attlee finalized plans begun at Yalta.

Proclamation of 1763 Royal directive issued after the French and Indian War prohibiting settlement, surveys, and land grants west of the Appalachian Mountains; caused considerable resentment among colonists hoping to move west.

Progressive Party Political party created when former president Theodore Roosevelt broke away from the Republican Party to run for president again in 1912; the party supported progressive reforms similar to those of the Democrats but stopped short of seeking to eliminate trusts. Also the name of the party backing Robert La Follette for president in 1924.

Progressivism Broad-based reform movement, 1900–1917, that sought governmental action in solving problems in many areas of American life, including education, public health, the economy, the environment, labor, transportation, and politics.

proslavery argument The series of arguments defending the institution of slavery in the South as a positive good, not a necessary evil. The arguments included the racist belief that black people were inherently inferior to white people, as well as the belief that slavery, in creating a permanent underclass of laborers, made freedom possible for whites. Other elements of the argument included biblical citations.

Public Works Administration A New Deal agency that contracted with private construction companies to build roads, bridges, schools, hospitals, and other public facilities.

Pueblo Revolt Uprising in 1680 in which Pueblo Indians temporarily drove Spanish colonists out of modern-day New Mexico.

Pure Food and Drug Act Passed in 1906, the first law to regulate manufacturing of food and medicines; prohibited dangerous additives and inaccurate labeling.

Puritans English religious group that sought to purify the Church of England; founded the Massachusetts Bay Colony under John Winthrop in 1630.

Radical Republicans Group within the Republican Party in the 1850s and 1860s that advocated strong resistance to the expansion of slavery, opposition to compromise with the South in the secession crisis of 1860–1861, emancipation and

arming of black soldiers during the Civil War, and equal civil and political rights for blacks during Reconstruction.

Reagan Revolution The rightward turn of American politics following the 1980 election of Ronald Reagan. The Reagan Revolution made individual "freedom" a rallying cry for the right.

Reaganomics Popular name for President Ronald Reagan's philosophy of "supply side" economics, which combined tax cuts with an unregulated marketplace.

reconquista The "reconquest" of Spain from the Moors completed by King Ferdinand and Queen Isabella in 1492.

Reconstruction Act 1867 law that established temporary military governments in ten Confederate states—excepting Tennessee—and required that the states ratify the Fourteenth Amendment and permit freedmen to vote.

Reconstruction Finance Corporation Federal program established in 1932 under President Herbert Hoover to loan money to banks and other institutions to help them avert bankruptcy.

Red Scare of 1919–1920 Fear among many Americans after World War I of Communists in particular and noncitizens in general, a reaction to the Russian Revolution, mail bombs, strikes, and riots.

Redeemers Post–Civil War Democratic leaders who supposedly saved the South from Yankee domination and preserved the primarily rural economy.

redemptioners Indentured families or persons who received passage to the New World in exchange for a promise to work off their debt in America.

Regulators Groups of backcountry Carolina settlers who protested colonial policies.

repartimiento **system** Spanish labor system under which Indians were legally free and able to earn wages but were also required to perform a fixed amount of labor yearly. Replaced the *encomienda* system.

republic Representative political system in which citizens govern themselves by electing representatives, or legislators, to make key decisions on the citizens' behalf.

republican motherhood The ideology that emerged as a result of American independence where women played an indispensable role by training future citizens.

republicanism Political theory in eighteenth-century England and America that celebrated active participation in public life by economically independent citizens as central to freedom.

reverse discrimination Belief that affirmative action programs discriminate against white people.

Revolution of 1800 First time that an American political party surrendered power to the opposition party; Jefferson, a Republican, had defeated incumbent Adams, a Federalist, for president.

Roanoke colony English expedition of 117 settlers, including Virginia Dare, the first English child born in the New World; the colony disappeared from Roanoke Island in the Outer Banks sometime between 1587 and 1590.

robber barons Also known as "captains of industry"; Gilded-Age industrial figures who inspired both admiration, for their economic leadership and innovation, and hostility and fear, due to their unscrupulous business methods, repressive labor practices, and unprecedented economic control over entire industries.

Roe v. Wade 1973 U.S. Supreme Court decision requiring states to permit first-trimester abortions.

Roosevelt Corollary 1904 Announcement by President Theodore Roosevelt, essentially a corollary to the Monroe Doctrine, that the United States could intervene militarily to prevent interference from European powers in the Western Hemisphere.

Rwandan genocide 1994 Genocide conducted by the Hutu ethnic group upon the Tutsi minority in Rwanda.

Sacco-Vanzetti case A case held during the 1920s in which two Italian-American anarchists were found guilty and executed for a crime in which there was very little evidence linking them to the particular crime.

Salem witch trials A crisis of trials and executions in Salem, Massachusetts, in 1692 that resulted from anxiety over witchcraft.

salutary neglect Informal British policy during the first half of the eighteenth century that allowed the American colonies considerable freedom to pursue their economic and political interests in exchange for colonial obedience.

Sanitary Fairs Fund-raising bazaars led by women on behalf of Civil War soldiers. The fairs offered items such as uniforms and banners, as well as other emblems of war.

Santa Anna, Antonio López de The military leader who, in 1834, seized political power in Mexico and became a dictator. In 1835, Texans rebelled against him, and he led his army to Texas to crush their rebellion. He captured the missionary called the Alamo and killed all of its defenders, which inspired Texans to continue their resistance and Americans to volunteer to fight for Texas. The Texans captured Santa Anna during a surprise attack, and he bought his freedom by signing a treaty recognizing Texas's independence.

Saratoga, Battle of Major defeat of British general John Burgoyne and more than 5,000 British troops at Saratoga, New York, on October 17, 1777.

scalawags Southern white Republicans—some former Unionists—who supported Reconstruction governments.

Schenck v. United States 1919 U.S. Supreme Court decision upholding the wartime Espionage and Sedition Acts; in the opinion he wrote for the case, Justice Oliver Wendell Holmes set the now-familiar "clear and present danger" standard.

scientific management Management campaign to improve worker efficiency using measurements like "time and motion" studies to achieve greater productivity; introduced by Frederick Winslow Taylor in 1911.

Scopes trial 1925 trial of John Scopes, Tennessee teacher accused of violating state law prohibiting teaching of the theory of evolution; it became a nationally celebrated confrontation between religious fundamentalism and civil liberties.

Scottsboro case Case in which nine black youths were convicted of raping two white women; in overturning the verdicts of this case, the Court established precedents in *Powell v. Alabama* (1932) that adequate counsel must be appointed in capital cases, and in *Norris v. Alabama* (1935) that African-Americans cannot be excluded from juries.

Sea Islands experiment The 1861 pre-Reconstruction social experiment that involved converting slave plantations into places where former slaves could work for wages or own land. Former slaves also received education and access to improved shelter and food.

Second American Revolution The transformation of American government and society brought about by the Civil War.

Second Great Awakening Religious revival movement of the early decades of the nineteenth century, in reaction to the growth of secularism and rationalist religion; began the predominance of the Baptist and Methodist Churches.

second Great Migration The movement of black migrants from the rural South to the cities of the North and West, which occurred from 1941 through World War II, that dwarfed the Great Migration of World War I.

Second Middle Passage The massive trade of slaves from the upper South (Virginia and the Chesapeake) to the lower South (the Gulf states) that took place between 1820 and 1860.

Sedition Act 1918 law that made it a crime to make spoken or printed statements that criticized the U.S. government or encouraged interference with the war effort.

Selective Service Act Law passed in 1917 to quickly increase enlistment in the army for the United States' entry into World War I; required men to register with the draft.

"separate but equal" Principle underlying legal racial segregation, upheld in *Plessy v. Ferguson* (1896) and struck down in *Brown v. Board of Education* (1954).

separation of powers Feature of the U.S. Constitution, sometimes called "checks and balances," in which power is divided between executive, legislative, and judicial branches of the national government so that no one can dominate the other two and endanger citizens' liberties.

Serra, Father Junípero Missionary who began and directed the California mission system in the 1770s and 1780s. Serra presided over the conversion of many Indians to Christianity, but also engaged them in forced labor.

settlement house Late-nineteenth-century movement to offer a broad array of social services in urban immigrant neighbor-

hoods; Chicago's Hull House was one of hundreds of settlement houses that operated by the early twentieth century.

Seven Years' War The last—and most important—of four colonial wars fought between England and France for control of North America east of the Mississippi River.

Seventeenth Amendment Progressive reform passed in 1913 that required U.S. senators to be elected directly by voters; previously, senators were chosen by state legislatures.

Shakers Religious sect founded by Mother Ann Lee in England. The United Society of Believers in Christ's Second Appearing settled in Watervliet, New York, in 1774, and subsequently established eighteen additional communes in the Northeast, Indiana, and Kentucky.

Share Our Wealth movement Program offered by Huey Long as an alternative to the New Deal. The program proposed to confiscate large personal fortunes, which would be used to guarantee every poor family a cash grant of $5,000 and every worker an annual income of $2,500. It also promised to provide pensions, reduce working hours, and pay veterans' bonuses and ensured a college education to every qualified student.

sharecropping Type of farm tenancy that developed after the Civil War in which landless workers—often former slaves—farmed land in exchange for farm supplies and a share of the crop.

Shays's Rebellion Attempt by Massachusetts farmer Daniel Shays and 1,200 compatriots, seeking debt relief through issuance of paper currency and lower taxes, to prevent courts from seizing property from indebted farmers.

Sherman Antitrust Act Passed in 1890, first law to restrict monopolistic trusts and business combinations; extended by the Clayton Antitrust Act of 1914.

Silent Spring A 1962 book by biologist Rachel Carson about the destructive impact of the widely used insecticide DDT that launched the modern environmentalist movement.

single tax Concept of taxing only landowners as a remedy for poverty, promulgated by Henry George in *Progress and Poverty* (1879).

sit-down strike Tactic adopted by labor unions in the mid- and late 1930s, whereby striking workers refused to leave factories, making production impossible; proved highly effective in the organizing drive of the Congress of Industrial Organizations.

sit-ins Tactic adopted by young civil rights activists, beginning in 1960, of demanding service at lunch counters or public accommodations and refusing to leave if denied access; marked the beginning of the most militant phase of the civil rights struggle.

Sixteenth Amendment Constitutional amendment passed in 1913 that legalized the federal income tax.

the Slave Power The Republican and abolitionist term for pro-slavery dominance of southern and national governments.

Smith, John A swashbuckling soldier of fortune with rare powers of leadership and self-promotion who was appointed to the resident council to manage Jamestown.

Smoot-Hawley Tariff 1930 act that raised tariffs to an unprecedented level and worsened the Great Depression by raising prices and discouraging foreign trade.

Snowden, Edward An NSA contractor turned whistleblower, who released classified information relating to the United States' intelligence gathering both at home and abroad.

social contract Agreement hammered out between labor and management in leading industries; called a new "social contract." Unions signed long-term agreements that left decisions regarding capital investment, plant location, and output in management's hands, and they agreed to try to prevent unauthorized "wildcat" strikes.

Social Darwinism Application of Charles Darwin's theory of natural selection to society; used the concept of the "survival of the fittest" to justify class distinctions and to explain poverty.

Social Gospel Ideals preached by liberal Protestant clergymen in the late nineteenth and early twentieth centuries; advocated the application of Christian principles to social problems generated by industrialization.

Social Security Act 1935 law that created the Social Security system with provisions for a retirement pension, unemployment insurance, disability insurance, and public assistance (welfare).

Socialist Party Political party demanding public ownership of major economic enterprises in the United States as well as reforms like recognition of labor unions and women's suffrage; reached peak of influence in 1912 when presidential candidate Eugene V. Debs received over 900,000 votes.

Society of American Indians Organization founded in 1911 that brought together Native American intellectuals of many tribal backgrounds to promote discussion of the plight of Indian peoples.

Society of Friends (Quakers) Religious group in England and America whose members believed all persons possessed the "inner light" or spirit of God; they were early proponents of abolition of slavery and equal rights for women.

soft money and hard money In the 1830s, "soft money" referred to paper currency issued by banks. "Hard money" referred to gold and silver currency—also called specie.

Sons of Liberty Organizations formed by Samuel Adams, John Hancock, and other radicals in response to the Stamp Act.

Sotomayor, Sonia First Supreme Court Justice of Hispanic descent. Justice Sotomayor was appointed by President Barack Obama in 2009.

Southern Christian Leadership Conference (SCLC) Civil rights organization founded in 1957 by the Reverend Martin Luther King Jr. and other civil rights leaders.

Southern Manifesto A document written in 1956 that repudiated the Supreme Court decision in *Brown v. Board of Education* and supported the campaign against racial integration in public places.

spoils system The term meaning the filling of federal government jobs with persons loyal to the party of the president; originated in Andrew Jackson's first term.

Sputnik First artificial satellite to orbit the earth; launched October 4, 1957, by the Soviet Union.

stagflation A combination of stagnant economic growth and high inflation present during the 1970s.

Stamp Act Parliament's 1765 requirement that revenue stamps be affixed to all colonial printed matter, documents, and playing cards; the Stamp Act Congress met to formulate a response, and the act was repealed the following year.

staple crops Important cash crops; for example, cotton or tobacco.

steamboats Paddlewheelers that could travel both up- and down-river in deep or shallow waters; they became commercially viable early in the nineteenth century and soon developed into America's first inland freight and passenger service network.

stock market crash Also known as Black Tuesday, a stock market panic in 1929 that resulted in the loss of more than $10 billion in market value (worth approximately ten times more today). One among many causes of the Great Depression.

Stonewall Inn A gathering place for New York's gay community, the site of the 1969 police raids and resulting riots that launched the modern gay rights movement.

Stono Rebellion A slave uprising in 1739 in South Carolina that led to a severe tightening of the slave code and the temporary imposition of a prohibitive tax on imported slaves.

Strategic Arms Limitation Talks 1972 talks between President Nixon and Secretary Brezhnev that resulted in the Strategic Arms Limitation Treaty (or SALT), which limited the quantity of nuclear warheads each nation could possess, and prohibited the development of missile defense systems.

Student Nonviolent Coordinating Committee (SNCC) Organization founded in 1960 to coordinate civil rights sit-ins and other forms of grassroots protest.

Students for a Democratic Society (SDS) Major organization of the New Left, founded at the University of Michigan in 1960 by Tom Hayden and Al Haber.

suffrage The right to vote.

Sugar Act 1764 decision by Parliament to tax refined sugar and many other colonial products.

Sunbelt The label for an arc that stretched from the Carolinas to California. During the postwar era, much of the urban population growth occurred in this area.

Taft-Hartley Act 1947 law passed over President Harry Truman's veto; the law contained a number of provisions to weaken labor unions, including the banning of closed shops.

tariff of abominations Tariff passed in 1828 by Parliament that taxed imported goods at a very high rate; aroused strong opposition in the South.

tariff of 1816 First true protective tariff, intended to protect certain American goods against foreign competition.

Tea Party A grassroots Republican movement that emerged in 2009 named for the Boston Tea Party of the 1770s. The Tea Party opposed the Obama administration's sweeping legislative enactments and advocated for a more stringent immigration policy.

Teapot Dome Harding administration scandal in which Secretary of the Interior Albert B. Fall profited from secret leasing to private oil companies of government oil reserves at Teapot Dome, Wyoming, and Elk Hills, California.

Tecumseh and Tenskwatawa Tecumseh—a leader of the Shawnee tribe who tried to unite all Indians into a confederation to resist white encroachment on their lands. His beliefs and leadership made him seem dangerous to the American government. He was killed at the Battle of the Thames. His brother, Tenskwatawa—a religious prophet who called for complete separation from whites, the revival of traditional Indian culture, and resistance to federal policies.

Tejanos Texas settlers of Spanish or Mexican descent.

temperance movement A widespread reform movement, led by militant Christians, focused on reducing the use of alcoholic beverages.

Tennessee Valley Authority Administrative body created in 1933 to control flooding in the Tennessee River valley, provide work for the region's unemployed, and produce inexpensive electric power for the region.

Tenochtitlán The capital city of the Aztec Empire. The city was built on marshy islands on the western side of Lake Tetzcoco, which is the site of present-day Mexico City.

Ten-Percent Plan of Reconstruction President Lincoln's proposal for reconstruction, issued in 1863, in which southern states would rejoin the Union if 10 percent of the 1860 electorate signed loyalty pledges, accepted emancipation, and had received presidential pardons.

Tenure of Office Act 1867 law that required the president to obtain Senate approval to remove any official whose appointment had also required Senate approval; President Andrew Johnson's violation of the law by firing Secretary of War Edwin Stanton led to Johnson's impeachment.

Tet offensive Surprise attack by the Viet Cong and North Vietnamese during the Vietnamese New Year of 1968; turned American public opinion strongly against the war in Vietnam.

the Texas Revolt The 1830s rebellion of residents of the territory of Texas—many of them Americans emigrants—against Mexican control of the region.

Thirteenth Amendment Constitutional amendment adopted in 1865 that irrevocably abolished slavery throughout the United States.

Three Mile Island Nuclear power plant near Harrisburg, Pennsylvania, site of 1979 accident that released radioactive steam into the air; public reaction ended the nuclear power industry's expansion.

three-fifths clause A provision signed into the Constitution in 1787 that three-fifths of the slave population would be counted in determining each state's representation in the House of Representatives and its electoral votes for president.

Title IX Part of the Educational Amendments Act of 1972 that banned gender discrimination in higher education.

totalitarianism The term that describes aggressive, ideologically driven states that seek to subdue all of civil society to their control, thus leaving no room for individual rights or alternative values.

Townshend Acts 1767 parliamentary measures (named for the chancellor of the Exchequer) that taxed tea and other commodities, and established a Board of Customs Commissioners and colonial vice-admiralty courts.

Trail of Tears Cherokees' own term for their forced removal, 1838–1839, from the Southeast to Indian lands (later Oklahoma); of 15,000 forced to march, 4,000 died on the way.

transcendentalists Philosophy of a small group of mid-nineteenth-century New England writers and thinkers, including Ralph Waldo Emerson, Henry David Thoreau, and Margaret Fuller; they stressed personal and intellectual self-reliance.

transcontinental railroad First line across the continent from Omaha, Nebraska, to Sacramento, California, established in 1869 with the linkage of the Union Pacific and Central Pacific railroads at Promontory, Utah.

Treaty of Greenville 1795 treaty under which twelve Indian tribes ceded most of Ohio and Indiana to the federal government, and which also established the "annuity" system.

Treaty of Paris Signed on September 3, 1783, the treaty that ended the Revolutionary War, recognized American independence from Britain, established the border between Canada and the United States, fixed the western border at the Mississippi River, and ceded Florida to Spain.

Truman Doctrine President Harry S. Truman's program announced in 1947 of aid to European countries—particularly Greece and Turkey—threatened by communism.

trusts Companies combined to limit competition.

Tubman, Harriet Abolitionist who was born a slave, escaped to the North, and then returned to the South nineteen times and guided 300 slaves to freedom.

Tulsa riot A race riot in 1921—the worst in American history—that occurred in Tulsa, Oklahoma, after a group of black veterans tried to prevent a lynching. Over 300 African-Americans were killed, and 10,000 lost their homes in fires set by white mobs.

Uncle Tom's Cabin Harriet Beecher Stowe's 1852 antislavery novel that popularized the abolitionist position.

Underground Railroad Operating in the decades before the Civil War, a clandestine system of routes and safehouses through which slaves were led to freedom in the North.

United Nations Organization of nations to maintain world peace, established in 1945 and headquartered in New York.

Uprising of 1622 Unsuccessful uprising of Virginia Native Americans that wiped out one-quarter of the settler population, but ultimately led to the settlers gaining supremacy.

urban renewal A series of policies supported by all levels of government that allowed local governments and housing authorities to demolish so-called blighted areas in urban centers to replace them with more valuable real estate usually reserved for white people.

USA Patriot Act A 2001 mammoth bill that conferred unprecedented powers on law-enforcement agencies charged with preventing domestic terrorism, including the power to wiretap, read private messages, and spy on citizens.

U.S.S. *Maine* Battleship that exploded in Havana Harbor on February 15, 1898, resulting in 266 deaths; the American public, assuming that the Spanish had mined the ship, clamored for war, and the Spanish-American War was declared two months later.

utopian communities Ideal communities that offered innovative social and economic relationships to those who were interested in achieving salvation.

V-E Day May 8, 1945, the day World War II officially ended in Europe.

Versailles Treaty The treaty signed at the Versailles peace conference after World War I which established President Woodrow Wilson's vision of an international regulating body, redrew parts of Europe and the Middle East, and assigned economically crippling war reparations to Germany, but failed to incorporate all of Wilson's Fourteen Points.

vertical integration Company's avoidance of middlemen by producing its own supplies and providing for distribution of its product.

Vicksburg, Battle of The fall of Vicksburg, Mississippi, to General Ulysses S. Grant's army on July 4, 1863, after two months of siege; a turning point in the war because it gave the Union control of the Mississippi River.

Vietnam Syndrome The belief that the United States should be extremely cautious in deploying its military forces overseas that emerged after the end of the Vietnam War.

Virginia and Kentucky resolutions Legislation passed in 1798 and 1799 by the Virginia and the Kentucky legislatures; written by James Madison and Thomas Jefferson in response to the Alien and Sedition Acts, the resolutions advanced the state-compact theory of the Constitution. Virginia's resolution called on the federal courts to protect free speech. Jefferson's draft for Kentucky stated that a state could nullify federal law, but this was deleted.

Virginia Company A joint-stock enterprise that King James I chartered in 1606. The company was to spread Christianity in the New World as well as find ways to make a profit in it.

Virginia Plan Virginia's delegation to the Constitutional Convention's plan for a strong central government and a two-house legislature apportioned by population.

virtual representation The idea that the American colonies, although they had no actual representative in Parliament, were "virtually" represented by all members of Parliament.

Voting Rights Act Law passed in the wake of Martin Luther King Jr.'s Selma-to-Montgomery March in 1965; it authorized federal protection of the right to vote and permitted federal enforcement of minority voting rights in individual counties, mostly in the South.

Wade-Davis Bill Radical Republicans' 1864 plan for reconstruction that required loyalty oaths, abolition of slavery, repudiation of war debts, and denial of political rights to high-ranking Confederate officials; President Lincoln refused to sign the bill.

Wagner Act (National Labor Relations Act of 1935) Law that established the National Labor Relations Board and facilitated unionization by regulating employment and bargaining practices.

Walking Purchase An infamous 1737 purchase of Indian land in which Pennsylvanian colonists tricked the Lenni Lanape Indians. The Lanape agreed to cede land equivalent to the distance a man could walk in thirty-six hours, but the colonists marked out an area using a team of runners.

war in Afghanistan War fought against the Taliban and Al-Qaeda in Afghanistan following the attacks of September 11, 2001. It remains the longest war in American history.

War Industries Board Board run by financier Bernard Baruch that planned production and allocation of war materiel, supervised purchasing, and fixed prices, 1917–1919.

War of 1812 War fought with Britain, 1812–1814, over issues that included impressment of American sailors, interference with shipping, and collusion with Northwest Territory Indians; settled by the Treaty of Ghent in 1814.

War on Poverty Plan announced by President Lyndon B. Johnson in his 1964 State of the Union address; under the Economic Opportunity Bill signed later that year, Head Start, VISTA, and the Jobs Corps were created, and programs were created for students, farmers, and businesses in efforts to eliminate poverty.

war on terrorism Global crusade to root out anti-American, anti-Western Islamist terrorist cells; launched by President George W. Bush as a response to the 9/11 attacks.

War Powers Act Law passed in 1973, reflecting growing opposition to American involvement in the Vietnam War; required congressional approval before the president sent troops abroad.

Watergate Washington office and apartment complex that lent its name to the 1972–1974 scandal of the Nixon administration; when his knowledge of the break-in at the Watergate and subsequent cover-up were revealed, Nixon resigned the presidency under threat of impeachment.

The Wealth of Nations The 1776 work by economist Adam Smith that argued that the "invisible hand" of the free market directed economic life more effectively and fairly than governmental intervention.

Webster-Hayne debate U.S. Senate debate of January 1830 between Daniel Webster of Massachusetts and Robert Hayne of South Carolina over nullification and states' rights.

welfare state A term that originated in Britain during World War II to refer to a system of income assistance, health coverage, and social services for all citizens.

Whiskey Rebellion Violent protest by western Pennsylvania farmers against the federal excise tax on whiskey, 1794.

Wilmot Proviso Proposal to prohibit slavery in any land acquired in the Mexican War; defeated by southern senators, led by John C. Calhoun of South Carolina, in 1846 and 1847.

Winthrop, John Puritan leader and governor of the Massachusetts Bay Colony who resolved to use the colony as a refuge for persecuted Puritans and as an instrument of building a "wilderness Zion" in America.

woman suffrage Movement to give women the right to vote through a constitutional amendment, spearheaded by Susan B. Anthony and Elizabeth Cady Stanton's National Woman Suffrage Association.

Worcester v. Georgia 1832 Supreme Court case that held that the Indian nations were distinct peoples who could not be dealt with by the states—instead, only the federal government could negotiate with them. President Jackson refused to enforce the ruling.

Works Progress Administration (WPA) Part of the Second New Deal; it provided jobs for millions of the unemployed on construction and arts projects.

Wounded Knee massacre Last incident of the Indian Wars; it took place in 1890 in the Dakota Territory, where the U.S. Cavalry killed over 200 Sioux men, women, and children.

writs of assistance One of the colonies' main complaints against Britain; the writs allowed unlimited search warrants without cause to look for evidence of smuggling.

XYZ affair Affair in which French foreign minister Talleyrand's three anonymous agents demanded payments to stop French plundering of American ships in 1797; refusal to pay the bribe was followed by two years of undeclared sea war with France (1798–1800).

Yalta conference Meeting of Franklin D. Roosevelt, Winston Churchill, and Joseph Stalin at a Crimean resort to discuss the postwar world on February 4–11, 1945; Joseph Stalin claimed large areas in eastern Europe for Soviet domination.

Yamasee uprising Revolt of Yamasee and Creek Indians, aggravated by rising debts and slave traders' raids, against

Carolina settlers. Resulted in the expulsion of many Indians to Florida.

yellow press Sensationalism in newspaper publishing that reached a peak in the circulation war between Joseph Pulitzer's *New York World* and William Randolph Hearst's *New York Journal* in the 1890s; the papers' accounts of events in Havana Harbor in 1898 led directly to the Spanish-American War.

yeoman farmers Small landowners (the majority of white families in the Old South) who farmed their own land and usually did not own slaves.

Yorktown, Battle of Last battle of the Revolutionary War; General Lord Charles Cornwallis along with over 7,000 British troops surrendered at Yorktown, Virginia, on October 17, 1781.

Zimmermann Telegram Telegram from the German foreign secretary to the German minister in Mexico, February 1917, instructing the minister to offer to recover Texas, New Mexico, and Arizona for Mexico if it would fight the United States to divert attention from Germany in the event that the United States joined the war.

zoot suit riots 1943 riots in which sailors on leave attacked Mexican-American youths.

CREDITS

PHOTOS

Title page: Library of Congress; Frontispiece: Granger Collection; **Author photo:** Flynn Larsen; **p. viii:** Nuestra Senora de Copacabana, Lima, Peru / Bridgeman Images; **p. ix:** Museum of Art, Rhode Island School of Design. Gift of Robert Winthrop. Photography by Erik Gould; **p. x:** *Free Women of Color with Their Children and Servants in a Landscape*, 1770–1796 (oil on canvas), Brunias, Agostino (1728–96) / Brooklyn Museum of Art, New York, USA / Gift of Mrs. Carl H. de Silver in memory of her husband, by exchange and gift of George S. Hellman, by exchange / Bridgeman Images; **p. xi:** Image copyright © The Metropolitan Museum of Art. Image source: Art Resource, NY; **p. xii:** Collection of the New-York Historical Society; **p. xiii:** Shelburne Museum, Vermont / Museum purchase, 1957, acquired from Harry Shaw Newman, The Old Print Shop / Bridgeman Images; **p. xiv:** MPI / Getty Images; **p. xv:** National Portrait Gallery, Smithsonian Institution / Art Resource, NY; **p. xvi:** Art Resource; **p. xvii:** Artist / maker unknown, American Fourth Pennsylvania Cavalry American After 1861 Oil on canvas The Collection of Edgar William and Bernice Chrysler Garbisch, 1968, 1968–222–3 Philadelphia Museum of Art; **p. xviii:** Digital Image © 2016 Museum Associates / LACMA. Licensed by Art Resource, NY; **p. xxi:** Granger Collection; **p. xxii:** Jewett, William S. (1812–1873) *The Promised Land - the Grayson family*, 1850, Oil on canvas, 50 3/4 x 64 in. Daniel J. Terra Collection, 1999.79. Terra Foundation for American Art. Photo Credit: Terra Foundation for American Art, Chicago / Art Resource, NY; **p. xxiv:** Library of Congress; **p. xxvi:** National Archives; **p. 1:** Library of Congress. **Chapter 1: p. 2 (top):** Bridgeman Images; **(bottom):** Self-Portrait, by Thomas Smith, 1948.19, Worcester Art Museum, Worcester, Massachusetts; **p. 3 (top):** Unidentified artist, British, 18th century or first quarter 19th century; Quaker Meeting; Oil on canvas; 64.1 × 76.2cm (25 1/4 × 30in.); Museum of Fine Arts, Boston; Bequest of Maxim Karolik; 64.456. Photograph © 2013 Museum of Fine Arts, Boston; **(bottom):** Granger Collection; **p. 4:** Nuestra Senora de Copacabana, Lima, Peru / Bridgeman Images; **p. 8:** Library of Congress; **p. 9:** Bridgeman Images; **p. 10 (top):** Georg Gerster/Science Source; **(bottom):** Library of Congress; **p. 12:** Bridgeman Images; **p. 13:** Library of Congress; **p. 14:** Bridgeman Images; **p. 15:** Courtesy Lilly Library, Indiana University, Bloomington, IN; **p. 16:** Library of Congress; **p. 17:** Wikimedia Commons, public domain; **p. 20 (top):** Ellen Mack / Getty Images; **(bottom):** Granger Collection; **p. 21:** Granger Collection; **p. 23:** Granger Collection; **p. 24:** akg-images; **p. 25:** Gianni Dagli Orti / The Art Archive at Art Resource, NY; **p. 26 (top):** Denver Art Museum, Collection of Frederick and Jan Mayer; **(bottom):** Bridgeman Images; **p. 27:** Library of Congress; **p. 28 (top):** Museo de la Basilica de Guadalupe, Mexico City; **(bottom):** Rare Books Division, The New York Public Library, Astor, Lenox, and Tilden Foundations. Art Resource, NY;

p. 29: Library of Congress; **p. 30:** Granger Collection; **p. 33:** Library of Congress, Prints & Photographs Division, Edward S. Curtis Collection; **p. 34:** National Museum of American History, Smithsonian Institution, Behring Center; **p. 38:** Bettmann / Corbis; **p. 42:** GLC03582 Novi Belgi Novaeque Angliae (New Netherland and New England) by Nicholas Visscher, 1682 / Courtesy of The Gilder Lehrman Institute of American History; **p. 43:** Museum of the City of New York; **p. 44:** The Colonial Williamsburg Foundation. **Chapter 2: p. 48:** Granger Collection; **p. 51 (top):** GL Archive / Alamy Stock Photo; **(bottom):** Woburn Abbey, Bedfordshire, UK / Bridgeman Images; **p. 52:** The John Carter Brown Library at Brown University; **p. 53:** Wikimedia, public domain; **p. 54:** Granger Collection; **p. 55:** GLC 4110. Document signed: contracts relating to the indenture of James Mahony, 31 March 1773. (The Gilder Lehrman Collection, courtesy of the Gilder Lehrman Institute of American History, New York.); **p. 56:** © The Trustees of the British Museum / Art Resource, NY; **p. 57:** Museum of Art, Rhode Island School of Design. Gift of Robert Winthrop. Photography by Erik Gould; **p. 59 (top):** Corbis; **(bottom):** National Portrait Gallery, Smithsonian Institution / Art Resource, NY; **p. 60:** Granger Collection; **p. 61 (top):** Library of Congress; **(bottom):** George Arents Collection, New York Public Library, Art Resource, NY; **p. 62:** Mary Evans Picture Library / Alamy; **p. 63:** MPI / Getty Images; **p. 64:** Library of Congress; **p. 65:** American Antiquarian Society; **p. 66:** Granger Collection; **p. 67:** Courtesy of the Massachusetts Archives; **p. 68:** Worcester Art Museum, Worcester, Massachusetts, Gift of William A. Savage; **p. 69:** Massachusetts Historical Society; **p. 70:** The New York Public Library / Art Resource, NY; **p. 73:** Annenberg Rare Book and Manuscript Library, Van Pelt-Dietrich Library Center, U Penn; **p. 76:** Library of Congress; **p. 77:** Self-Portrait, by Thomas Smith, 1948.19, Worcester Art Museum, Worcester, Massachusetts; **p. 78:** Mrs. Elizabeth Freake and Baby Mary, unknown artist, 1963.134, Worcester Art Museum, Worcester, Massachusetts; **p. 79:** Historical Picture Archive / Corbis; **p. 81:** Granger Collection; **p. 82 (top):** Private Collection / Bridgeman Images; **(bottom):** British Library Board / Robana / Art Resource, NY; **p. 83:** The Cromwell Museum, Huntingdon. **Chapter 3: p. 86:** Emmet Collection, Miriam and Ira D. Wallach Division of Art, Prints and Photographs, The New York Public Library, Astor, Lenox and Tilden Foundations; **p. 91:** Library of Congress; **p. 92:** Historical Society of Pennsylvania; **p. 93:** Germantown Historical Society, Philadelphia, PA; **p. 94:** Unidentified artist, British, 18th century or first quarter 19th century; Quaker Meeting; Oil on canvas; 64.1 × 76.2cm (25 1/4 × 30in.); Museum of Fine Arts, Boston; Bequest of Maxim Karolik; 64.456. Photograph © 2013 Museum of Fine Arts, Boston; **p. 95:** *Free Women of Color with Their Children and Servants in a Landscape*, 1770-1796 (oil on can-

vas), Brunias, Agostino (1728-96) / Brooklyn Museum of Art, New York, USA / Gift of Mrs. Carll H. de Silver in memory of her husband, by exchange and gift of George S. Hellman, by exchange / Bridgeman Images; **p. 96:** © British Library Board. All Rights Reserved / The Bridgeman Art Library; **p. 97:** Private Collection / Bridgeman Art Library; **p. 98:** Colonial Williamsburg Foundation; **p. 100:** National Maritime Museum, London; **p. 102:** The John Carter Brown Library at Brown University; **p. 103:** Springhill, County Londonderry, Northern Ireland, National Trust Photographic Library / Derrick E. Witty / Bridgeman Art Library; **p. 105:** Rare Books Division, The New York Public Library, Astor, Lenox and Tilden Foundations. Art Resource, NY; **p. 110 (top):** Houghton Library, Harvard University, Typ 632.96.202; **(bottom):** The Historical Society of Pennsylvania; **p. 114:** Eileen Tweedy / The Art Archive at Art Resource, NY; **p. 115:** The Library Company of Philadelphia; **p. 116:** Winterthur Museum; **p. 117:** The Colonial Williamsburg Foundation; **p. 118:** Photograph © 2015 Museum of Fine Arts, Boston; **p. 119:** Geoffrey Clements / Corbis; **p. 120:** Carter's Grove. Aug 1995. Photo by Melissa Wilkins. http://creativecommons.org/licenses/by-sa/2.0/deed.en; **p. 121:** Art Resource; **p. 122:** Gift of Edgar William and Bernice Chrysler Garbisch, Image © 2006 Board of Trustees, National Gallery of Art, Washington, D.C. **Chapter 4: p. 126:** Granger Collection; **p. 130 (top):** The John Carter Library at Brown University; **(bottom):** Library of Congress; **p. 132:** © Musée d'histoire de Nantes – Château des ducs de Bretagne / Alain Guillard; **p. 133:** Granger Collection; **p. 134:** Granger Collection; **p. 136:** Jamestown-Yorktown Foundation; **p. 137:** Abby Aldrich Rockefeller Folk Art Museum, Colonial Williamsburg Foundation, Williamsburg, VA; **p. 138:** Image copyright © The Metropolitan Museum of Art. Image source: Art Resource, NY; **p. 139:** Schomburg Center for Research in Black Culture, Photographs and Prints Division, The New York Public Library; **p. 141:** Chicago Historical Museum; **p. 142:** Eileen Tweedy / The Art Archive at Art Resource, NY; **p. 143 (top):** Library of Congress; **(bottom):** © National Portrait Gallery, London; **p. 144:** The Library Company of Philadelphia; **p. 146:** This item is reproduced by permission of The Huntington Library, San Marino, California; **p. 148:** Library of Congress; **p. 149:** Portrait of Benjamin Franklin, Mason Chamberlin, Oil on canvas, 1762, Philadelphia Museum of Art: Gift of Mr. and Mrs Wharton Sinkler, 1956; **p. 150 (top):** Wikimedia, public domain; **(bottom):** National Portrait Gallery, London; **p. 151:** The John Carter Brown Library at Brown University; **p. 152:** Zisterzienserstift Zwettl, Bibliothek; Cod. 420, Appendix: Rolle 2; **p. 154:** Library of Congress; **p. 155:** Czech National Library; **p. 157:** Granger Collection; **p. 158:** Library of Congress; **p. 164:** Library of Congress. **Chapter 5: p. 167 (both):** Library of Congress; **p. 168 (top):** Granger Collection;

(bottom): Chicago Historical Society; **p. 169 (top):** © New Bedford Whaling Museum; **(bottom):** Private Collection / Bridgeman Images; **p. 170:** Library of Congress; **p. 173:** By permission of the Houghton Library, Harvard University; **p. 174:** Library of Congress; **p. 175 (top):** Corbis; **(bottom):** The Colonial Williamsburg Foundation; **p. 176:** Library of Congress; **p. 180 (top):** Library of Congress; **(bottom):** Michael Nicholson / Corbis; **p. 181:** Library of Congress; **p. 182:** Library of Congress; **p. 183:** Special Collections Research Center, University of Chicago Library; **p. 184:** Miriam and Ira D. Wallach Division of Art, Prints and Photographs, New York Public Library. Art Resource, NY; **p. 185:** Chicago Historical Society; **p. 186 (top):** National Portrait Gallery, London; **(bottom):** American Philosophical Society; **p. 190:** Library of Congress; **p. 191:** American Antiquarian Society; **p. 192:** Sid Lapidus Collection. Rare Books Division. Department of Rare Books and Special Collections. Princeton University Library; **p. 193:** © The Trustees of the British Museum / Art Resource, NY; **p. 194:** Anne S. K. Brown Military Collection, Brown University; **p. 195:** Morristown National Historic Park, Morristown, New Jersey, USA; **p. 199 (both):** Library of Congress; **p. 200:** Harvard University Portrait Collection, Bequest of Ward Nicholas Boylston to Harvard College, 1828. **Chapter 6: p. 204:** Collection of the New-York Historical Society; **p. 206:** National Gallery of Art, Washington, Gift of Mrs. Robert Homans; **p. 207:** Winterthur Museum; **p. 208:** Gianni Dagli Orti / The Art Archive at Art Resource, NY; **p. 209:** Historical Society of Pennsylvania; **p. 210:** Courtesy of the Beinecke Rare Book and Manuscript Library, Yale University; **p. 211:** Courtesy of the New-York Historical Society; **p. 212:** North Eastern view, Watertown, Ct. 1836 John Warner Barber / The Connecticut Historical Society, Hartford CT; **p. 213:** York County Historical Society, USA / The Bridgeman Art Library; **p. 215:** American Antiquarian Society; **p. 216:** Library of Congress; **p. 217:** Reproduced by permission of the Huntington Library, San Marino, California; **p. 219:** Library of Congress; **p. 223:** Corbis; **p. 224:** Library Company of Philadelphia. Gift of the artist, 1792; **p. 226 (top):** American Antiquarian Society; **(bottom):** Library of Congress; **p. 227:** Library and Archives Canada, Acc. No. 1938-220-1; **p. 228 (top):** National Archives, London; **(bottom):** Collection of The New-York Historical Society; **p. 229:** Bequest of Miss Lucy T. Aldrich, 39.002; Museum of Art, Rhode Island School of Design, Providence; **p. 232 (top):** Library of Congress; **(bottom):** Southern Historical Collection, Wilson Library, The University of North Carolina at Chapel Hill; **p. 233:** The Philadelphia Museum of Art / Art Resource, NY; **p. 235:** Library of Congress. **Chapter 7: p. 238:** Granger Collection; **p. 242:** National Archives; **p. 243:** American Antiquarian Society; **p. 245:** Print Collection, Miriam and Ira D. Wallach Division of Art, Prints, and Photographs, The New York Public Library; Astor, Lenox, and Tilden Foundations. Art Resource, NY; **p. 247 (top):** Library of Congress; **(bottom):** Image copyright © The Metropolitan Museum of Art. Image source: Art Resource, NY; **p. 248:** Wikimedia, public domain; **p. 249:** Library of Congress; **p. 251:** The Library of Virginia; **p. 252:** From the collection of the National Constitution Center, Philadelphia, gift of Robert L.

McNeil, Jr.; **p. 253:** MPI / Getty Images; **p. 254:** Library of Congress; **p. 255:** Granger Collection; **p. 256:** Courtesy of the New-York Historical Society; **p. 257:** Collection of the New-York Historical Society / Bridgeman Art Library; **p. 258:** Collection of The New-York Historical Society; **p. 259:** Library of Congress; **p. 263:** Old Paper Studios / Alamy Stock Photo; **p. 265:** Chicago Historical Society; **p. 266:** Greenville County Museum of Art, Museum purchase with funds from The Museum Association's 1990 and 1991 Collectors Groups and the 1989, 1990 and 1991 Museum Antiques Shows, sponsored by Elliott, Davis & Company, CPAs; artist: unknown (circle of E. Savage) title: *The Plan of Civilization*; date: circa 1800; medium: oil on canvas.; **p. 269:** Virginia Historical Society, Richmond / Bridgeman Art Library. **Chapter 8: p. 272:** Chicago Historical Society; **p. 275 (top):** Chicago Historical Society; **(bottom):** Fenimore Art Museum, Cooperstown, New York. Photo by Richard Walker; **p. 276:** Library of Congress; **p. 277 (top):** Rare Book and Special Collections Division, Library of Congress; **(bottom):** Library of Congress; **p. 278 (top):** Courtesy, Winterthur Museum, Bequest of Hery F. DuPont; **(bottom):** Library of Congress; **p. 279:** The New York Public Library / Art Resource, NY; **p. 280 (top):** Chicago Historical Society; **(bottom):** © National Portrait Gallery, London; **p. 281:** Liberty in the Form of the Goddess of Youth, by Mary Green, 1963.86, Worcester Art Museum, Worcester, Massachusetts; **p. 285:** Library of Congress; **p. 286:** Library of Congress; **p. 287:** Division of Political History, National Museum of American History, Smithsonian Institution; **p. 289:** Photos 12 / Alamy; **p. 290:** I.N. Stokes Collection, Miriam and Ira D. Wallach Division of Art, Prints, and Photographs, The New York Public Library; Astor, Lenox, and Tilden Foundations. Art Resource, NY; **p. 292:** Private Collection; **p. 294:** Missouri Historical Society, St. Louis; **p. 295:** GLC07730 *The attack made on Tripoli on the 3d. August 1804 by John Guerrazzi, August 23rd.* 1852 / Courtesy of The Gilder Lehrman Institute of American History; **p. 296:** Courtesy of the New-York Historical Society; **p. 298 (top):** Royal Ontario Museum; **(bottom):** National Portrait Gallery, Smithsonian Institution / Art Resource, NY; **p. 299 (top):** Photo by Mark Sexton. © Peabody Essex Museum, 2003, all rights reserved; **(bottom):** Library Company of Philadelphia; **p. 300:** Collection of the New-York Historical Society / Bridgeman Images; **p. 302:** American Antiquarian Society, Massachusetts / Bridgeman Art Library; **p. 303:** Photography by Erik Arneson © Nicholas S. West. **Chapter 9: p. 306:** Shelburne Museum, Vermont / Museum purchase, 1957, acquired from Harry Shaw Newman, The Old Print Shop / Bridgeman Images; **p. 309:** I.N. Phelps Stokes Collection, Miriam and Ira D. Wallach Division of Art, Prints and Photographs, The New York Public Library, Astor, Lenox and Tilden Foundations. Art Resource, NY; **p. 311 (top):** Chicago Historical Society; **(bottom):** www.Archive.org, public domain; **p. 312:** Collection of the New-York Historical Society / Bridgeman Images; **p. 315:** Edwin Whitefield, Minnesota Historical Society; **p. 318:** Abby Aldrich Rockefeller Folk Art Museum, Colonial Williamsburg Foundation, Williamsburg, VA; **p. 319:** Cincinnati Museum Center / Getty Images; **p. 321:** Courtesy, The Winterthur Library: Joseph Downs Collection of

Manuscripts and Printed Ephemera; **p. 323 (top):** Library of Congress; **(bottom):** Granger Collection; **p. 324 (top):** Barfoot, American, Progress of Cotton, Reeding or Drawing In, No. 9, Mabel Brady Garvan Collection, Yale University Art Gallery; **(bottom):** Courtesy of the Manchester (N.H.) Historic Association; **p. 325:** Granger Collection; **p. 326:** Bishop Hill State Historic Site/Illinois Historic Preservation Agency; **p. 327:** Historical Society of Pennsylvania, medium graphics collection, H. Bucholzer; **p. 328:** Granger Collection; **p. 329:** Library of Congress; **p. 330:** George Eastman Museum; **p. 331 (top):** Corbis; **(bottom):** Brooklyn Museum, HIP / Art Resource, NY; **p. 334:** Library of Congress; **p. 335:** Library of Congress; **p. 336:** Church Archives of The Church of Jesus-Christ of Latter-day Saints; **p. 337:** John Neagle, American, 1796-1865; *Pat Lyon at the Forge, 1826-27*; Oil on canvas; 238.12 × 172.72 cm (93 3/4 × 68 in.); Museum of Fine Arts, Boston; Henry H. and Zoe Oliver Sherman Fund; 1975.806. Photograph © 2013 Museum of Fine Arts, Boston; **p. 338:** Library of Congress; **p. 339:** American Antiquarian Society; **p. 340 (both):** Library of Congress, **p. 341:** Library of Congress; **p. 342:** Granger Collection; **p. 343:** Library of Congress. **Chapter 10: p. 346:** Gift of Stephen C. Clark, Fenimore Art Museum, Cooperstown, New York. Photo by Milo Stewart; **p. 349 (top):** Library of Congress; **(bottom):** Courtesy the Rhode Island Historical Society, Dorr Liberation Society, Rhode Island, 1844, engraving, Rhi X3 6692; **p. 350:** Historical Society of Pennsylvania, large graphics collection, John Lewis Krimmel; **p. 351:** Library of Congress; **p. 352:** Granger Collection; **p. 354:** Library of Congress; **p. 358:** Granger Collection; **p. 361:** Huntington Library, San Marino, California; **p. 365:** Bettmann / Corbis; **p. 366:** Library of Congress; **p. 367:** Private Collection / The Bridgeman Art Library; **p. 368:** The Art Archive at Art Resource, NY; **p. 370:** Saint Louis Art Museum, Missouri / Gift of Bank of America / The Bridgeman Art Library; **p. 371:** Library of Congress; **p. 372:** Library of Congress; **p. 373:** Library of Congress; **p. 374:** Library of Congress; **p. 376 (top):** MPI / Getty Images; **(bottom):** Charles Deas, The Trapper and his Family, Photograph © 2013 Museum of Fine Arts, Boston; **p. 377:** Smithsonian American Art Museum, Washington, DC / Art Resource, NY; **p. 378:** Library of Congress; **p. 380:** Library of Congress; **p. 381:** Library of Congress. **Chapter 11: p. 385:** Bettmann / Corbis; **p. 386 (top):** Hulton Archive / Getty Images; **(bottom):** Chicago History Museum; **p. 387 (top):** Collection of Dr. and Mrs. John Livingston and Mrs. Elizabeth Livingston Jaeger, Photo: Hearts and Hands Media Arts. Photography courtesy of Hearts & Hands Media Arts, from the book and film "Hearts and Hands: A Social History of 19th Century Women and their Quilts" (New Day Films); **(bottom):** Fine Arts Museums of San Francisco, Gift of Joseph Martin, Jr., 1994.120.4; **p. 388:** Hirshhorn Museum & Sculpture Garden, Washington D.C. / Bridgeman Art Library; **p. 391:** MPI / Getty Images; **p. 393:** Library of Congress; **p. 394:** Hulton Archive / Getty Images; **p. 395 (top):** Library of Congress; **(bottom):** Missouri History Museum, St. Louis; **p. 396:** Library of Congress; **p. 398:** Library of Congress; **p. 399:** Merseyside Maritime Museum, Liverpool; **p. 400:** Granger Collection; **p. 401 (top):** Chicago Historical Society; **(bottom):** New

Hampshire Historical Society; **p. 402:** Courtesy of South Caroliniana Library, University of South Carolina, Columbia; **p. 407:** Courtesy of the Maryland Historical Society; **p. 409 (top):** Library of Congress; **(bottom):** Library of Congress; **p. 410 (top):** Library of Congress; **(bottom):** North Carolina Museum of Art, Raleigh, Purchased with funds from the State of North Carolina; **p. 411:** Chicago History Museum; **p. 412:** Abby Aldrich Rockefeller Folk Art Museum, Colonial Williamsburg Foundation, Williamsburg, VA; **p. 413:** Library of Congress; **p. 414:** Historic New Orleans Collection 1960.46; **p. 415:** GLCO7238 *$2,500 Reward*! Mississippi Co., Missouri broadside advertising runaway slaves, August 23, 1852 / Courtesy of The Gilder Lehrman Institute of American History; **p. 417:** Library Company of Philadelphia; **p. 420:** Library of Congress. **Chapter 12: p. 424:** Collection of Dr. and Mrs. John Livingston and Mrs. Elizabeth Livingston Jaeger, Photo: Hearts and Hands Media Arts. Photography courtesy of Hearts & Hands Media Arts, from the book and film "Hearts and Hands: A Social History of 19th Century Women and their Quilts" (New Day Films); **p. 427:** Library of Congress; **p. 429:** Bibliotheque Nationale, Paris, France / Archives Charmet / The Bridgeman Art Library; **p. 430:** Library of Congress; **p. 431:** Library of Congress; **p. 432:** NYPL Digital; **p. 433:** Collection of New-York Historical Society; **p. 434:** Granger Collection; **p. 435:** Library of Congress; **p. 436 (top):** Library of Congress; **(bottom):** Courtesy of the Massachusetts Historical Society. Banner, William Lloyd Garrison (1805-1879) "Proclaim Liberty Throughout all the Land unto all the inhabitants thereof." MHS image #332; **p. 437:** Bettmann / Corbis; **p. 438:** The Boston Athenaeum, TBMR VEP. An 847. The Anti-Slavery Alphabet, a children's book (1847); **p. 439:** Library of Congress; **p. 440 (top)** Granger Collection; **(bottom):** Susan Torrey Merritt American, 1826-1879 Anti-Slavery Picnic at Weymouth Landing, Massachusetts, c. 1845 Watercolor, gouache, and collage on paper 660 × 914 mm Gift of Elizabeth R. Vaughan, 1950.1846 The Art Institute of Chicago; **p. 441:** Chicago Historical Society; **p. 442:** Library of Congress; **p. 443 (top):** Samuel J. Miller, Frederick Douglass, 1847-52, cased half-plate daguerreotype, plate: 14x10.6 cm, Major Acquisitions Centennial Endowment, The Art Institute of Chicago; **(bottom):** Library of Congress; **p. 444 (top):** Library of Congress; **(bottom):** American Antiquarian Society, Massachusetts / Bridgeman Art Library; **p. 445:** Destruction by Fire of Pennsylvania Hall, on the Night of the 17th May, 1838 by J.C. Wild, printed by J.T. Bowen. The Library Company of Philadelphia; **p. 448:** Library of Congress; **p. 449:** National Portrait Gallery, Smithsonian Institution / Art Resource, NY; **p. 452:** Bettmann / Corbis; **p. 453:** Bettmann / Corbis; **p. 455:** Library of Congress. **Chapter 13: p. 458:** John Perry Newell, Lazell, Perkins & Co. Bridgewater, Mass., ca. 1860. Yale University Art Gallery, Mabel Brady Garvan Collection; **p. 460 (left):** Library of Congress; **(right):** Architect of the Capitol; **p. 461:** Library of Congress; **p. 463:** Courtesy of the State Preservation Board, Austin, Texas, photographer F. Thomson, Post 1990, CHA 1989.68, post conservation; **p. 464:** Bettmann / Corbis; **p. 465:** Anonymous cartoon published in *El Calavera*, May 7, 1847; **p. 466:** Granger Collection; **p. 468:** Alfred Sully

Monterey, California Rancho Scene drawing work on paper c. 1849, Watercolor, Oakland Museum of California Kahn Collection A65.43; **p. 469:** Seguin, Juan Nepomuceno; Accession ID: CHA 1989.096; Courtesy State Preservation Board; Original Artist: Wright, Thomas Jefferson / 1798-1846; Photographer: Perry Huston, 7/28/95 post conservation; **p. 470:** Jewett, William S. (1812-1873) *The Promised Land - The Grayson family*, 1850. Oil on canvas, 50 3/4 × 64 in. Daniel J. Terra Collection, 1999.79. Terra Foundation for American Art Photo Credit: Terra Foundation for American Art, Chicago / Art Resource, NY; **p. 471:** Art Resource; **p. 472:** Image copyright © The Metropolitan Museum of Art/ Art Resource, NY; **p. 476** © The Metropolitan Museum of Art / Art Resource, NY; **p. 478:** Fugitive slave law. *Hamlet in chains*. National anti-slavery standard. Vol. 21 (Oct. 17, 1850), page 82, Rare Book & Manuscript Library, Columbia University in the City of New York; **p. 480:** Chicago Historical Society; **p. 482:** Library of Congress; **p. 483:** Library of Congress; **p. 484:** Bettmann / Corbis; **p. 485:** Collection of New-York Historical Society; **p. 487:** Bettmann / Corbis; **p. 488 (left):** Chicago Historical Society; **(right):** George Eastman House / Getty Images; **p. 489:** Collection of The New-York Historical Society; **p. 492:** Courtesy of the Maryland Historical Society; **p. 495:** Abraham Lincoln Presidential Library and Museum; **p. 496:** Greenville County Museum of Art, Greenville, SC; **p. 497:** Library of Congress; **p. 498:** Fotosearch / Getty Images; **p. 499:** Library of Congress. **Chapter 14: p. 502:** Artist/maker unknown, American; Fourth Pennsylvania Cavalry American, After 1861 Oil on canvas, The Collection of Edgar William and Bernice Chrysler Garbisch, 1968; 1968-222-3, Philadelphia Museum of Art; **p. 506 (both):** Library of Congress; **p. 507:** Newark Museum / Art Resource, NY; **p. 508 (top):** Library of Congress; **(bottom):** Chicago Historical Society; **p. 509:** Museum of Fine Arts, Boston / M. and M. Karolik Collection of American Watercolors and / Drawings, 1800-75 / The Bridgeman Art Library; **p. 511:** Edward Owen / Art Resource, NY; **p. 513:** Library of Congress; **p. 514:** Chicago Historical Society; **p. 516:** Chicago History Museum; **p. 517:** Library of Congress; **p. 518 (top):** Chicago History Museum; **(bottom):** Smithsonian Institution, Photographic History Collection, Division of Information Technology; **p. 519 (top):** Library of Congress; **(bottom):** GLC00968 Unknown (Civil War Songbook). November 24, 1862, p.4 / Courtesy of The Gilder Lehrman Institute of American History; **p. 520 (top):** Library of Congress; **(bottom):** David Bustill Bowser (American, 1820-1900) Untitled (Lincoln and the Female Slave) 1863 Oil on canvas, 19 × 14 1987.1.83 Simpson Collection, The Amistad Center for Art & Culture. Photo by John Groo/The Amistad Center for Art & Culture; **p. 521:** Library of Congress; **p. 522 (top):** Courtesy, Daughters of Charity, Province of St. Louise, St. Louis, MO.; **(bottom):** Library of Congress; **p. 524 (both):** Chicago Historical Society; **p. 525 (top):** Granger Collection; **(bottom):** National Archives; **p. 529:** Chicago Historical Society; **p. 530 (top):** U.S. Army Military History Institute; **(bottom):** Chicago Historical Society; **p. 531:** Library of Congress; **p. 532:** Granger Collection; **p. 533:** Louisiana State University Special Collections From the U.S. Civil War Center exhibit Beyond Face Value,

courtesy of Jules d'Hemecourt; **p. 533:** Louisiana State University Special Collections From the U.S. Civil War Center exhibit Beyond Face Value, courtesy of Jules d'Hemecourt; **p. 534:** From the Collections of the South Carolina Historical Society; **p. 539:** Library of Congress; **p. 535:** provided courtesy © HarpWeek., LLC; **p. 536:** The Johnson Collection; **p. 538 (both):** Library of Congress; **p. 540 (both):** Library of Congress; **p. 541:** National Archives; **p. 542:** Library of Congress; **p. 543:** National Archives; **p. 545:** Library of Congress; **p. 546 (top):** provided courtesy © HarpWeek LLC; **(bottom):** © The Metropolitan Museum of Art / Art Resource, NY. **Chapter 15: p. 550:** Chicago Historical Society; **p. 553 (top):** Library of Congress; **(bottom):** Photographic History Collection, Division of Information Technology and Communications, National Museum of American History, Smithsonian Institution; **p. 554 (top):** Library of Congress; **(bottom):** Granger Collection; **p. 556:** Smithsonian American Art Museum, Washington, DC / Art Resource, NY; **p. 557 (both):** Library of Congress; **p. 558 (top):** Digital Image © [year] Museum Associates / LACMA. Licensed by Art Resource, NY; **(bottom):** Cook Collection, Valentine Richmond History Center; **p. 560:** Library of Congress; **p. 564:** Kemper Leila Williams Foundation / The Historic New Orleans Collection; **p. 566 (both):** Library of Congress; **p. 567:** Ed Sullivan Collection, Special Collections, University of Hartford; **p. 568:** Library of Congress; **p. 569:** Library of Congress; **p. 570:** Manuscripts, Archives & Rare Books Division, Schomburg Center for Research in Black Culture, The New York Public Library, Astor, Lenox and Tilden Foundations / Art Resource, NY; **p. 571:** Library of Congress; **p. 573:** Library of Congress; **p. 574:** Library of Congress; **p. 575:** Library of Congress; **p. 567 (both):** Library of Congress; **p. 577:** Granger Collection; **p. 578 (top):** Library of Congress; **(bottom):** Clements Library Collection, University of Michigan; **p. 579:** Granger Collection; **p. 580:** Wikimedia, public domain; **p. 581 (top):** Niday Picture Library / Alamy; **(bottom):** © Fine Arts Museums of San Francisco, Gift of Joseph Martin, Jr., 1994.120.4; **p. 582 (both top):** Library of Congress; **(bottom):** National Archives; **p. 584:** Granger Collection; **p. 585:** Library of Congress.

TEXT

Abigail Adams: "Abigail Adams to John Adams, 31 March 1776." Reprinted by permission of the publisher from *The Adams Papers: Adams Family Correspondence, Volume I and II: December 1761-March 1778*, edited by L. H. Butterfield, Cambridge, Mass.: The Belknap Press of Harvard University Press, Copyright © 1963 by the Massachusetts Historical Society. **Bartolomé de las Casas:** "History of the Indies [1528]", excerpt from *History of the Indies*, translated and edited by Andrée Collard (New York: Harper & Row, 1971), pp. 82, 112-115. Copyright © 1971 by Andrée M. Collard, renewed © 1999 by Joyce J. Contrucci. Reprinted by permission of Joyce J. Contrucci. **Democratic-Republican Society of Pennsylvania:** Excerpt from minutes of The Democratic Society of Pennsylvania, December 18, 1794. The Historical Society of Pennsylvania (HSP), Collection # Am. 315/315O. Reprinted with

INDEX

Page numbers in *italics* refer to illustrations.

AAA, *see* Agricultural Adjustment Act
Abe Lincoln's Last Card, 514
abolition, in western hemisphere,
   398–99
abolitionist movement, moral suasion
   and, 439
abolition movement, 129, 135, 207,
   224–26, *224, 226*, 339, 385, 390,
   436–46, *436, 437, 438, 439, 440,*
   443, 444, 445, 451, 454–55, 476,
   516
   Abby Kelley and, 425
   Abraham Lincoln and, 487–88
   African-Americans and, 389, 415–
     21, 435, 436, 441–43
   British, 227
   in Civil War, 514, 543
   colonization and, 435–36
   in early U.S., 167, 226–29, 288, 358
   Frederick Douglass and, 389
   John Brown and, 489–92
   The Liberator newspaper for, 351, *455*
   moral suasion and, 442
   obstacles to, in early U.S., 224–25
   pacifism and, 439
   rise in militant form of, 436
   after Turner's rebellion, 420–21
   U.S. Constitution and, 256
   in Virginia, 420
   women's rights linked to, 446, 447,
     453–54
Acadians, 158
Acoma pueblo, 33, *33*
Act Concerning Religion (1649), 82
Act of Union (1707), 127
Adams, Abigail (1744–1818), 205, *206*,
   217, 232
   letters to John Adams by, 205, 230,
     234
Adams, Charles Francis (1807–1886),
   473
Adams, Hannah, 281
Adams, Henry (b. 1843), 552
Adams, John (1735–1826), 173, 216, 225,
   239, *287*, 291, 358, 361
   Abigail Adams's letters to, 205,
     230, 234
   Boston Massacre and, 179
   Constitutional Convention and, 247
   education and, 215
   in election of 1796, 284
   in election of 1800, 287
   expansion of navy by, 295
   in First Continental Congress, 182
   Fries's Rebellion and, 285
   Haiti and, 289
   and Native Americans, 377
   presidency of, 284–90, *285*
   religion and, 212
   on the right to vote, 208, 209

in Second Continental Congress, 185
   selected vice president, 273
   on the Stamp Act, 176
   Thomas Paine and, 186
   Treaty of Paris and, 200, *200*
   on women's rights, 232, 233
   XYZ affair and, 285, *285*
Adams, John Quincy (1767–1848),
   276, 315, 347, 356, 358, 360, *361*,
   445, 473
   in *Amistad* case, 418
   in election of 1824, 361–65, *365*
   in election of 1828, 366
   views on federal power, 365
Adams, Samuel (1722–1803), 182, 215,
   256
Adams-Onís Treaty (1819), 315
Addison County society, 280
Address at Sanitary Fair, Baltimore
   (Lincoln), 527
Address to the Slaves, 436
Africa, 2, 3, 5, 6, 18, 19–20, *19, 20*, 24,
   88, 127
African-Americans, 352–53
   in abolition movement, 389, 415–21,
     435, 441–43
   in American Revolution, 193, 194,
     194
   barred from Missouri, 357
   barred from public land, 339
   and Black Codes, 565–66, 567
   citizenship and, 440, 573, 574
   in Civil War, 517–19, *517, 518, 519,*
     526, 541–42, *541*, 546
   Constitution and, 266–68
   decline in economic status of, 339
   early emancipation struggles of,
     226, 234–35
   as Ethiopian Regiment, 194
   as First Rhode Island Regiment, *194*
   free blacks, 98, 133–34, 228–32,
     402–7, *406*, 435
   Freedom's Journal newspaper for,
     351, 443
   in gold rush, 471
   immigrants vs., 482
   Jefferson on, 268–69
   and jobs in New York City, 339
   in Korean War, 194
   and Ku Klux Klan, *see* Ku Klux Klan
   labor and, 339
   in Louisiana, 294
   market revolution and, 338–39, 343
   in Maryland colony, 97–98
   as part of society, 437, 440
   Pennsylvania disenfranchisement
     of, 363
   in politics, 575–76, *576*
   population of, *267*
   in Quaker society, 93

in Reconstruction, 386–87, 561,
     567–68, *568*, 570–72, *571*, 574–76
   religion of, 412–13, *413*
   and segregation, *see* segregation
   in Seminole War, 376
   as soldiers for Confederacy, 538
   as viewed by Jackson, 367
   voting rights of, 143–44, 347,
     348–49, 351
   wages and, 339, 542
   westward expansion and, 318
   see also Great Migration; slavery;
     slaves
African Chief, The, 281
African Methodist Episcopal Church,
   338, *338*, 419
African religion, in American colonies, 137
Age of Jackson, 210, 349, 366, 367–77,
   382, 435, 439, 478
Age of Revolution, 167
Agitator, 572
Agnew, Samuel (1833–1902), 556
Agreement of the People, 80, 147
agriculture, 5, 10, 20, 25, 121, 155–56,
   168, 266, 275, 277, *278*, 307, 380,
   395–96
   American Revolution and, 217
   in Civil War, 523
   Democratic Party and, 369
   and immigration, 109
   Indian, 57
   industrial revolution and, 480
   invention of, 6
   Jamestown and, 58
   Jefferson's views on, 292, 353
   market revolution and, 307, 318–19
   in Panic of 1837, 380
   promotion by J. Q. Adams of, 365
   Pueblo Indians and, 10, 14
   tobacco and, 60–61, 114
   women and, 14, 15, 122–23
"Agrippa," 261
Alabama, 156, 312, 315, 374
Alamance, Battle of, 177
Alamo, 462
*Alarm To the Legislature of the Province in
   New-York* (Seabury), 188
Alaska:
   acquisition from Russia of, 466
   Russian fur traders in, 154
Albany, N.Y., 39, 309
Albany Plan of Union (1754), 164
Albuquerque, N.Mex., 152
Alcorn, James L. (1816–1894), 577
Alexander I, czar of Russia (1777–
   1825), 512
Alexander VI, Pope (1431?–1503), 27
Alexandria, Va., slave trade in, *393*
Alger, John B., 400

Algonquian Indians, 44
Alien Act (1798), 285–86, 327
Allegory of the North and the South, An
   (Terry), *496*
Allen, Ethan (1738–1789), 178, 185
Allen, Joseph, 183
Allen, Richard (1760–1831), 338, *575*
America, democracy in, 346–84
American and Foreign Anti-Slavery
   Society, 454
American Anti-Slavery Society, 437,
   439, 442, 454, 570
American Bible Society, 432
American colonies, 3, 49, 53–54
   African religion in, 137
   Anglicization of, 118–19
   artisans of, 115
   assemblies in, 145–46
   cities of, 115–16
   diversity of, 6, 107, 123
   election campaigns in, 207
   elite class in, 117–18
   and English Civil War, 81–82
   expansion of, 3, 127
   expansion of England's, 88–94
   Glorious Revolution in, 103–4
   government in, 145
   hierarchical structure in, 119–22
   Islam in, 137
   liberties in, 55
   literacy in, 146
   maps of, *108, 153*
   middle class in, 121–22
   politics in, 143–49
   population of, 3, 61, 106–7, 132
   poverty in, 120–21
   Protestantism in, 42, 64, 82, 91, 101,
     103–4, 109, 110
   reduced death rate in, 122
   as refuge, 52
   relationship with Indians in, 91–92
   salutary neglect and, 145
   society of, 114, 117–23
   voting rights in, 143–44, 207–8
   western frontier of, 156–57
   women's role in, 122–23
   see also American Revolution
American Colonization Society, 435,
   435, 436, 441
American Crisis, The (Paine), 195
American Dictionary (Webster), 343, 349
American Flag, The, 520
*American Foot Soldiers, Yorktown
   Campaign*, 194
American Husbandry (Anon.), 121
American Magazine, The, 158
American National Red Cross, 531
American Party, *see* Know-Nothing
   Party
American Philosophical Society, 146

American Progress (Gast), *461*
American Railway Union, 644
American Revolution, 170–203, *192*, 224, *232*, 279, 289, 307, 387, 390, 437, 517
  American advantages in, 193
  American mutinies in, 199
  Andrew Jackson in, 347
  Articles of Confederation and, 240
  background of, 171–82
  battles of, 194–200
  black soldiers in, 194, *194*
  as borderlands conflict, 219–21
  British advantages in, 193
  casualties in, 193, 506
  creation of national identity and, 263
  debt created by, 274
  democracy and, 168, 206–10, 284
  early battles of, 184–85, 194–99
  economic effect of, 216–18, 245–46
  equality and, 205
  family life and, 233–34
  force strength in, 193, *193*
  French assistance in, 193, *199*
  indentured servitude and, 193, 205, 215, 234
  Indians and, 205, 221–23, 234
  low point of, 195
  Loyalists in, 218–21, *220*
  map of battles in, *196*
  Paine's view of, 186–87, 189
  religious freedom and, 210–15
  slavery and, 167, 205, 223–29, 231, 234–35, 413, 435
  in South, 197–99, *198*
  Spanish help in, 197
  views of elite on, 207–8
  voting rights and, 209–10
  women and, 179, 229–32, *232*
"American Scholar, The" (Emerson), 330
American Standard, 455
American Sunday School Union, *339*
American System, 353–55, *354*, 364, 369, 382
American system of manufactures, 322–23
American Temperance Society, 431
American Tract Society, 432–33
American Woman's Home, The (Beecher and Beecher Stowe), *351*
American Woman Suffrage Association, 573
America Triumphant and Britannia in Distress, 235
Ames, Adelbert (1835–1933), 584
Am I Not a Man and a Brother?, 442, *443*
Am I Not a Woman and a Sister? (Bourne), *453*
Amistad, 418
Amity and Commerce, Treaty of (1778), 197
Amsterdam, 41
Anabaptists, 110, *334*
Andersonville, Ga., Confederate prison at, 506, 566
Andes Mountains, 8, 24–25
And Not This Man (Nast), *582*
Andrews, Sidney (1837–1880), 553, 556

Andros, Edmund (1637–1714), 90–91, 103–4
Anglican Church, 41, 70, 80, 82, 102–3, 104, 110, 118, 180
  American Revolution and, 211–12, 214, 218
  creation of, 50
  Dissenters and, 82, 102, 210
  Puritans and, 64–66
Anglo-Dutch war, 88
Anglos, 468
Angola, as source of slaves, 98
"annuity" system (for Native Americans), 265
Anthony, Saint, *34*
Anthony, Susan B. (1820–1906), 454, 573, *573*
Antietam, Battle of, 507, 509–10, *511*, 515
Anti-Federalists, 256, 257, 258, 261
Antigua, *96*
Antinomianism, 72
Antislavery Picnic at Weymouth Landing, Massachusetts (Merritt), *440*
Antrobus, John (1837–1907), *414*
Antwerp, *44*
Apaches, 34, 152, 153, *154*, 460
Apess, William (1798–1839), 222, 377
Appalachian Mountains, 242, 243, *264*, 308
  crossing of, 312
  population west of, 315
Appeal in Favor of That Class of Americans Called Africans, An (Child), 440
Appeal of the Independent Democrats, 478
Appeal to the Coloured Citizens of the World, An (Walker), 436, *436*, 442
Appomattox Courthouse, 545, 565
Arabella, 68
Aragon, 21
Arapahos, 525
Aristotle (384–322 B.C.E.), 17, 207
  on democracy, 349
Arizona, 10, *10*, 466
Arkansas, 312
  enters Union, 338
Armada Portrait (Gower), *51*
Arminianism, 149
Armour, Philip D. (1832–1901), 529
Army, U.S.:
  African-Americans in, 353, 517–19, *517*, 526
  fear of standing, 275
Army of Northern Virginia, Confederate, 509
Army of the Potomac, Union, 508–9, 538, 539–40
Arnold, Benedict (1741–1801), 185, 199, 211, *235*
Articles of Confederation (1781), 240–47, *241*, 249, 250, 254, 274
  weaknesses of, 245–46
artisans, 321, 323, 339
  African-Americans as, 339
  see also craftsmen
Ashanti people, 130, 136
Asia, 2, 18, *19*
  and Native Americans, 6
  sea route to, 2

asiento, 128
assemblies, colonial, 145–46
  governor vs., 145
  Parliament vs., 173
  rise of, 145–46
Astor, John Jacob (1763–1848), 338
Astor House, 338
asylum of liberty, U.S. as, 167, 187, 191, 214, 268
asylums, 433
Atlanta, Ga., Sherman's capture of, 540
Atlantic trade, of New England colonies, 128–30, *129*
Attack Made on Tripoli, 295
Attucks, Crispus (ca. 1723–1770), 179, 554
Augusta County, Va., 120
Austin, Moses (1761–1821), 461
Austin, Stephen (1793–1836), 461
Autobiography (Franklin), 146, *146*
Avilés, Pedro Menéndez de, *see* Menéndez de Avilés, Pedro
Azores, 20
Aztecs, 8, *9*, 23, *23*, 25, *25*, 27, 390
  smallpox epidemic and, 23

Bache, Sarah Franklin (1743–1808), 232
backcountry, in Colonial America, 114
Backus, Isaac (1724–1806), 151, 212
Bacon, Nathaniel (1647–1676), 100
Bacon's Rebellion, 99–101, *100*, 161
Bahamas, 21
Baja California, Mexico, *155*
Balboa, Vasco Núñez de (1475–1519), *8*, 22, 23
balloons, hot air, 504
Ballous's Magazine, 391
Baltimore and Ohio (B&O), 311
Bank of England, 140, 380
Bank of the United States, 274, 299, 353, 370
  battle with Jackson of, 378–80
  Congress and, 378–79
  Second, 355, 356, *378*
bankruptcy, 342, 355
Bankruptcy Scene, A, 245
banks, 369, 560
  national, 169, 275, 354–56, 529; *see also* Bank of the United States
  Southern, 393
Banneker, Benjamin (1731–1806), 268, 276
Banner of the Society of Pewterers, 239, 257
Baptists, 110, 150, 151
  African-American, 412, 553
  in American colonies, 143
  Free-Will, 214
  in Gabriel's Rebellion, 289
  in Great Awakening, 150, 151
  in Massachusetts colony, 82, 210–11
  in Second Great Awakening, 335, 412
  Seventh Day, 110
  slavery and, 472
Barbados, 97, 127, 134, 721
  as founder of Carolina colony, 92
  population of, 97
Barbary Coast, 95, 295
Barbary Wars, 294–95, *295*

Bargain of 1877, 584–85
Barlow, Joel (1754–1812), 268
Barnard, George N., *545*
Barrow plantation, maps of, *555*
Barton, Clara (1821–1912), 530, 531
Bastille, *281*
Baton Rouge, La., 156, 314
"Battle Hymn of the Republic" (Howe), 520
Battle of Antietam, The (Hope), *511*
Battle of Concord, The (Doolittle), *184*
Beaufort, South Carolina, *137*
Beauregard, P. G. T. (1818–1893), 504
Bedford Basin near Halifax (Petley), *227*
Beebe, Abner, 219
Beecher, Catharine (1800–1878), 327, 351, *351*, 446, 447–48, 451
Beecher, Henry Ward, 326
Beecher, Lyman (1775–1863), 326–27, *328*
Belgium, *44*
Bell, John (1797–1869), 494
Beloved (Morrison), 476
Benin, 19
Benito Cereno (Melville), 352
Benjamin Hawkins Trading with the Creek Indians, 266
Bennett, Thomas, Jr. (1781–1865), 419
Bentham, Jeremy, 234
Benton, Thomas Hart (1782–1858), 374
Bering Strait, 6
Berkeley, John (1602–1678), 93
Berkeley, William (1606–1677), 99–100, *100*, 103
Bernard, Francis (1712–1779), 174–75
Bible, 2, 28, 64, *67*, 68–70, 73, *74*, *130*, *142*, 149, 151, *151*, 412, 419, 432
  Jefferson's version of, 212
  King James, 327, *327*
  slavery in, 398, 405
  see also New Testament
Bible Commonwealth, 69, 70, 77, 104
Biddle, Nicholas (1786–1844), 378–79, *378*
Bill of Rights (American), 256, 258–63, 373, 568, 570–71
Bill of Rights (English), 103, 259, 263
Bingham, George Caleb (1811–1879), *367, 370*
Birney, James G. (1825–1864), 444, 454–55, 464
birthrate, decline in U.S., 340
Bishop Hill, Ill., *326*
Bismarck, Otto von (1815–1898), 520
black Americans, *see* African-Americans
Black Codes, 565–66, *566*, 567
Black Hawk (1767–1838), 13, *373*, 374
Black Hawk and His Son, Whirling Thunder (Jarvis), *373*
Black Hawk War, 373
Black Hills, 191–92
Black Legend, *29*, 30, 35, 36, 43, 152
Black Pioneers, 227
Blackstone, William (1723–1780), 178
"black supremacy," 579
Blackwell, Henry (1825?–1909), 453
Blair, Francis P., Jr. (1821–1875), 570, *570*

Blanchard, Jonathan (1811–1892), 335

"Bleeding Kansas," 484–85

Blithedale Romance, The (Hawthorne), 429

Bloomer, Amelia (1818–1894), 452

Blue Ridge Mountains, 212

Boardman, Elijah (1760–1823), *119*

Board of Trade (English), 172

Body of Liberties (1641), 69–70, 77

Book of Mormon, The, 336–37

Book of Negroes, *228*

Booth, John Wilkes (1838–1865), 326, 545

Booth, Junius Brutus, 326

borderlands and boundaries in North America, shifting, 44–45

border states:
    in Civil War, 513, 514
    Emancipation Proclamation and, 516

Boston, Mass., 115, *138*, 146, 147, 173
    population of, 115
    poverty in, 120
    Puritans in, 77–78
    religious tolerance in, 211
    Townshend boycott in, 178
    Washington's army abandons, 194

Boston Almanack, *175*

Boston Associates, 321

Boston Gazette, 141

Bostonians Paying the Excise-Man, The, 181

Boston Massacre, 179–80, *180*, 554

Boston Massacre, The (Revere), *180*

Boston News-Letter, 147

Boston Tea Party, 181, *181*

Bowdoin, James (1726–1790), 246

Bowser, David B., *520*

Bowser, Mary Elizabeth (b. 1840s), *536*

Braddock, Edward (1695–1755), 158

Bradford, William (1590–1657), 76

Bradwell, Myra (1831–1894), 573

Brady, Mathew (1823?–1896), 507, *531*

Bragg, Braxton (1817–1876), 556

Brant, Joseph (c. 1742–1807), 223

Brazil, 23, 27, 42, 96, *97*, 128, *131*, 132, 506
    abolition of slavery in, 511
    Dutch control of, 41
    slavery in, 137, 401–2, 410, 415

Breckinridge, John C. (1821–1875), 330, 493

Breed's Hill, Battle of, 185

Brent, Margaret (1601–1670?), 62

Brer Rabbit stories, 413–14

Bridgewater, Mass., *459*

Bristol, England, 129

British Empire, 81, 96–98, 186
    abolition in, 398–99, *399*
    abolition of slavery in, 511
    American vs. British view of, 174–75
    expansion of, 88–94

British Isles, abolitionsits in, 438

British liberty, *see* English liberty

British navy, 296

bronze, 19

Brooke, Edward W. (1919–), 575

Brook Farm, 429

Brooks, Preston (1819–1857), 484, *484*

Brown, Henry "Box" (b. 1816), 417, *417*

Brown, John (1800–1859), 442, 489–92, *489*, *492*

Brown, Joseph E. (1821–1894), 394, 534

Brown, Matt, 561

Brown, Olympia, 572

Brown, William Wells, *575*

Brown Fellowship Society, 406

Brownson, Orestes (1803–1876), 343

Brown v. Board of Education, 571

Bruce, Blanche K. (1841–1898), 575

Brunias, Agostino, *95*

Bryan, George (1731–1791), 257, 260

Buchanan, James (1791–1868), 485, 496

Buena Vista, Battle of, 466

buffalo, 10, 32

Bulger, Andrew (1789–1858), *298*

Bull Dance (Catlin), *377*

Bull Run, First Battle of, 508

Bull Run, Second Battle of, 509

Bunker Hill, Battle of, 185, 364

Burgoyne, John (1722–1792), 195, 219

Burial of Latané, The (Washington), *536*

Burk, John D. (1776?–1808), 281

Burke, Edmund (1729–1797), 164, 224, 413

Burlingame, Anson, 571

Burlingame Treaty, 571–72

Burnside, Ambrose E. (1824–1881), 510, 538

Burr, Aaron (1756–1836), 284, 287

Burwell, Carter (1716–1756), 120

Bute, Lord, *182*

Butler, Andrew P. (1796–1857), *484*

Butler, Benjamin F. (1818–1893), 513, 517

Byllesby, Langdon (1803–1890), 343

Byrd, William, III (1728–1777), 119

Cabeza de Vaca, Alvar Núñez (ca. 1490–1557?), 32

Cabot, John (ca. 1450–ca. 1499), 22, 23, 50

Cabral, Pedro (1467–1520), 22, 23

Cabrillo, Juan Rodriguez (d. 1543), 32

Cadwalader family, *233*

Caesar (former slave), *228*

Cahokia, 9

Caitlin, George, *377*

Cajuns, 158

Calhoun, Floride (1792–1866), 372

Calhoun, John C. (1782–1850), 475
    American System and, 353, 354
    annexation of Texas and, 463
    compact theory of, 371–73
    concurrent majority theory of, 373
    death of, 478
    Declaration of Independence as viewed by, 399
    Democratic Party and, 382
    Missouri Controversy and, 356
    nationalism and, 371–72
    nullification crisis and, 371–73, *371*, *372*
    sectionalism and, 372
    slavery as viewed by, 398, 399
    states' rights and, 371–73
    as vice president, 372
    as War Hawk, 297

California, *30*, 464, 466, *468*
    constitution of, 471
    enters Union, 475
    gold rush in, 469–70, *470*, *471*, 493
    population of, 154–55, 460, 469, 470, 471
    Russian fur traders in, 154
    Spanish settlements in, 154–55, *155*

Californios, 155, 460–61, *468*

Calvert, Cecilius, Lord Baltimore (1605–1675), 63, 82–83

Calvert, Charles, *133*

Calvert, Charles, Lord Baltimore (1637–1715), 101, 104

Calvin, John (1509–1564), 65

Calvinists, 41, 104

Cambridge, Mass., 68
    first American printing press in, *64*, 68

Camp of Thirty-first Pennsylvania Infantry, Near Washington, D.C., 531

Canada, 9, 10, 87, 155, 164, 174, 299, 365
    border with United States, 365
    ceded to Great Britain, 158
    French, 38–39
    Loyalists exiled in, 219–21
    Native Americans in, 87
    as slave refuge, 414, 418, 476–77
    U.S. invasion of, 299, 377
    War Hawks' plan for annexation of, 297
    see also French Canada

canals, 168, *307*, 309–11, *310*, 354, 379
    plan of Gallatin for, 354

Canary Islands, 20, 21

Cantino, Alberto, *20*

Cantino World Map, 20

Canyon de Chelly, *10*

Cape Breton Island, 158

Cape Cod, 66, *66*

Cape Henry, 49

Cape of Good Hope, 20

Cape Verde Islands, 20

capitalism:
    development of, 40–41
    as threat to freedom, 275
    women and, 341

"captains of industry," 529

captivity narratives, 73

caravels, 18

Caribbean, 25, 30, 127, 128–29, 155, 285
    abolition in, 399
    free blacks in, 406
    French, 158
    influence on New Orleans of, 393
    as part of slave empire, 492
    see also West Indies

Carleton, Guy, 227

Carlos II, king of Spain, 152

Carlos III, king of Spain, 152

Carnegie, Andrew (1835–1919), 529

Carolina colony, 102, 103
    founding of, 92
    hierarchical society of, 92
    Indians in, 92
    slave trade in, 134

Caroline, Fort, 32

carpetbaggers, 576–77

Carroll, John, 211

Carson, Ann Baker, 234

Carter, Landon (1710–1778), 133

Carter, Robert, III (1728–1804), 151, 228

Carter, Robert "King" (1663–1732), 118, 151

Carter family, 157

Carter's Grove, *120*

Cartwright, John (1740–1824), *192*

Cass, Lewis (1782–1866), 473

Castile, 21

castizo, 26

Catawba Indians, *13*, 111

Catherine of Aragon (1485–1536), 50

Catholics, Catholicism, 21, 23, 39, 51–52, 64, 73, 102–4, 140, 141, 154, 164, 181–82, *182*, 210–11, 326, *327*, 460, *468*, 469, 480–82, *483*, 494
    in American colonies, 110, 143, 210–11, 213
    banned in Ireland, 83
    Church of England and, 64, 80, 102
    Civil War and, *522*
    as Democrats, 370
    and freeing of slaves, 98
    French and, 164
    Germans as, 109
    Know-Nothing Party vs., 480–82
    liberties of, 213
    in Maryland colony, 63–64, 82, 104
    Native Americans and, 3, 28–29, *28*, 33–35, 39
    in New Netherland, 42–43
    in Pennsylvania colony, 110
    slavery and, 137
    Spanish colonies and, 25, 28–29, *28*, 33–35, 43
    temperance movement and, 432

Cato's Letters (Trenchard and Gordon), 141–42, 148

Cayugas, 12

Celia (slave; d. 1855), 401

census, federal, 411

Central America, *7*, *8*, *31*
    Spain in, 155

Central Pacific, 524

Chaco Canyon, 10, *10*

Chain of Friendship, 93, 111

Chamberlain, Mason, *149*

Champlain, Samuel de (1567–1635), 35–39, *38*

Chancellorsville, Battle of, 538

Chapman, Maria Weston, 438

Chariot of Liberty, A, 183

Charles I, king of England (1600–1649), 63, 65, 80, *81*, 82, *82*, *83*, 141

Charles II, king of England (1630–1685), 80, 82, 88, 90, 91, 102, 103

Charleston, S.C., 115, 119, *134*, 138, 226, 228, *413*, 545
    black community in, 406, 417
    demands return of slaves, 227
    slave trade in, 92

Charleston Harbor, 386

Charles Town Harbor (Roberts), *117*

Charter of Liberties and Privileges (1683), 91

Charter of Liberty (1682), 93

Chartist movement, 326, 475

Chase, Salmon P. (1808–1873), 478
checks and balances, 250, 254
Cherokee Nation v. Georgia, 374
Cherokee Phoenix, 351
Cherokees, 12, 111, 156, 221, 222–23, 242, 266, 298, 300, 374–76, 374, 529
Constitution of, 374, 375
Chesapeake, 296
Chesapeake Bay, 49, 200
Chesapeake region, 41, 54, 57, 58, 60–61, 67–68, 77, 99–101, 107, 109, 128
boycott in, 179
Great Awakening in, 151
indentured servants in, 133
as runaway slave refuge, 138
settlement of, 58–64
slavery in, 132–33, 134, 138
society in, 133
tenant farmers in, 133
tobacco in, 58, 60–61, 61, 62, 94, 98, 99, 107, 109, 116, 123, 133
Chevalier, Michel (1806–1879), 330
Cheves, Langdon, III, 534
Cheyennes, 525
Chicago, Ill., 321, 322
as manufacturing center, 480
Chicago Sanitary Fair, 530
Chickasaws, 12, 156, 242, 374
Child, Lydia Maria (1802–1880), 341, 351, 440, 448
China, 18, 20, 24, 471, 506
Burlingame Treat and, 571–72
early trade with, 245–46
china (Chinese porcelain), 245
Chinese, Chinese immigrants, 469–70, 524, 561, 564, 572
California gold rush and, 471
Chinese porcelain (china), 245
chinos, 26
Chivington, John (1821–1894), 525
Choctaws, 12, 222, 223, 242, 266, 374
Christianity, 12, 15, 16–17, 21, 26–27, 27, 28–29, 59, 59, 71, 73–74, 214–15, 295
Civil War and, 521–22
and free exercise of religion, 82, 93
Great Awakening and, 149–51
growth of, in U.S., 335
liberty and, 432
Native Americans and, 12, 32, 36, 37, 52, 87, 154–55
in New World, 45
Second Great Awakening, 334–36
sects of, 110
slavery and, 99, 137, 151, 412–13, 446
see also specific denominations
"Christian liberty," 16–17
Christian Republicanism, 214–15
"Christian Sparta", America as, 215
church and state, separation of, 212–15
churches, tax support of, 110, 151, 211, 213, 214
Church of England, *see* Anglican Church
Church of Jesus Christ of Latter-day Saints, *see* Mormons
Church of Latter-Day Saints, *see* Mormons

Cibola, seven golden cities of, 32
Cincinnati, Ohio, 319–21, 319, 323
race riots in, 338
Circle of the Social and Benevolent Affections, 215
cities, growth of, 319–21, 320
citizenship, 567, 568, 570, 574
of African-Americans, 440, 574
of Asian-Americans, 572
Fourteenth Amendment and, 440, 572, 573
Native Americans and, 263, 265, 615
second-class, *see* segregation
civic nationalism, 263
Civil Rights Act (1875), 551, 583
abuses of, 258
Alien and Sedition Acts and, 285–86, 327
in American colonies, 49–50, 55, 143–44, 206, 207–8
American Revolution and, 209–15
Civil War and, 522–23
in England, 80–81
legislation on, 577
violations as federal offenses, 580
see also Bill of Rights (American); constitutional amendments, U.S.; freedom; McCarthy era; women's rights
Civil Rights Bill (1866), 567, 568
Civil War, U.S., 385, 386–87, 395, 459, 496, 502–48, 509, 551, 553
agriculture in, 523
beginning of, 498–99
black soldiers in, 517–19, 517, 519
blockade in, 507, 534
campaigns of, 510, 512, 537
casualties in, 503, 505–6, 507, 509–10, 511, 517, 522, 539, 539, 555
civil liberties and, 522–23
Confederate advantages in, 504
draft in, 504, 529, 531–32, 534
emancipation and, 385, 386, 503, 511–19, 515, 518, 520, 543, 546, 552–60
end of, 543–45
financing of, 529
as first modern war, 503–11
food riots in, 535
industry in, 523
message to Congress, 512
photography in, 507
propaganda in, 506–7
religion and, 521–22, 522
resources for, 506
as Second American Revolution, 519–32
Sherman's March to the Sea in, 544
songs of, 524
technology of, 504–6, 508
transportation in, 507
Union advantages in, 504
in West, 528
West in, 510–11, 512, 539
and westward expansion, 524–29
women in, 530–31, 530
Clark, William (1770–1838), 293–94, 294

class:
in American Society, 338, 341–42, 351, 352–53, 371
development of, 341–42
education and, 434
race and, 352–53, 352
see also middle class
Clay, Henry (1777–1852), 315, 378, 382, 414
American Colonization Society and, 435
American System and, 354
annexation of Texas and, 463
Compromise of 1850 and, 475
death of, 478
in duel with Randolph, 396
election of 1824 and, 361–64
election of 1828 and, 366
in election of 1832, 379
Missouri Controversy and, 356, 357
nickname of, 367
nullification crisis and, 373
on slavery, 391
as War Hawk, 297
Clermont, 309
cliff dwellings, 10
Clinton, De Witt (1769–1828), 302–3, 311
Clinton, George (1739–1812), 164, 276
Clinton, Henry (1738–1795), 197, 227
Cloud, N. B. (1809–1875), 580
Coats, William, 115
Cobb, Howell (1815–1868), 538
Coercive Acts, *see* Intolerable Acts
coffee, 115, 128
coinage, 145, 273, 275
Cold Harbor, Battle of, 539
Cole, Thomas (1801–1848), 331
Coles, Edward (1786–1868), 269
Colfax, La., massacre in, 580, 584
Colman, Lucy (1817–1906), 446
colonialization, of slaves, 435–36, 514, 517
Colored Rule in a Reconstructed (?) State (Nast), 582
Columbian Exchange, 24, 24
Columbian Magazine, 215, 216
Columbia River, 10
Columbus, Christopher (1451–1506), 5, 18, 20–23
voyages of, 20–23, 21, 22, 24
Columbus's Landfall, 21
Comanches, 152, 153, 154, 460, 468, 525
Come and Join Us Brothers, 518
"comity," 357
Committee of Correspondence, 175, 226, 232
Committee of Safety, 104, 183, 217
common law, development of English, 79–80
Common Sense (Paine), 186–87, 186, 189, 191, 207, 234
"Commonwealth and Free State", England as, 80
Commonwealth v. Hunt, 329
communication, 168, 239, 308
communism, 426
communitarians, 430
Company of New France, 35
compass, 18

"Composite Nation" (Douglass), 572
Compromise of 1850, 475–76, 476, 477, 477
Concord, Battle of, 184, 184, 185, 196, 216, 280
"Concord Hymn" (Emerson), 184
concurrent majority theory, 373
Conestoga Indians, massacre of, 161
Confederate Constitution, 529
Confederate States of America, 386, 497–98, 532–38, 544, 546
black soldiers and, 538
currency of, 533
division among, 534
economic problems of, 534–35
government of, 532–33
Senate of, 538
states' rights and, 534
Union sympathizers in, 535–36
women and, 536–37
Confidence Man, The (Melville), 355
Congregationalists, 64, 68, 110, 150, 210–11, 212, 446
American Revolution and, 214
Half-Way Covenant and, 79
in Massachusetts, 212–13
Congress, U.S., 242, 374, 582
under Articles of Confederation, 240–42
authority of, 356, 372
Bank of the United States and, 378–79
and coinage, 273, 275
under Constitution, 249–50
and currency, 217, 529
Deborah Sampson pensioned by, 232
Independent Treasury policy and, 381
Missouri Compromise and, 357
National Road authorized by, 309, 353
oaths of allegiance and, 219
petitioned for emancipation, 288
political parties in, 273
presidential veto and, 379, 567–68
Reconstruction policies of, 565
slavery and, 288, 473
and wage and price controls, 217
see also House of Representatives, U.S.; Senate, U.S.
Congressional Medal of Honor, 517–18
"Congressional Pugilists," 286
Connecticut, 240, 254
slavery in, 228
Connecticut colony, 71, 116, 150
government in, 144
militia of, 185
in Pequot War, 76
women in, 122
Connecticut River valley, settlement of, 76
conquistadores, 9, 23–24, 25, 29
constitution:
of California, 471
Cherokee, 374, 375
English, 140–41, 186
of Texas, 469

Constitution, U.S., 168, 247–63, *259*, 283, 364, 391
  African-Americans and, 551, 571, 572
  American System and, 354
  Andrew Jackson and, *349*
  Calhoun's view of, 372
  celebration pageants for, 239
  checks and balances in, 250, 254
  compact theory of, 371–73
  Confederate constitution and, 497
  free blacks and, 266–67
  Garrison's suggested abrogation of, 437
  J. Q. Adams and, 365
  Louisiana Purchase and, 292
  map of ratification of, *262*
  Marbury v. Madison in, 291
  Missouri Compromise and, 357
  national bank and, 356
  Native Americans and, 263, 265
  political parties and, 273
  powers granted under, 250
  preamble to, *252*, 253
  ratification of, 239, *239*, 254–63, *254, 256, 257*
  signing of, *255*
  slavery and, 251–52, *251*, 263, 440–41, 474, 486
  state vs. federal powers in, 259
  strict constructionism and, 275, 354, 356, 365
  tariffs in, 253
  three-fifths clause of, 251, 252, 288, 303
  trade in, 253
  Webster's view of, 372
  women's rights and, 281, 573
  see also Constitutional Convention
Constitution, USS, 299, *299*
constitutional amendments, U.S.:
  First, 258, 263, 286
  Second, 258
  Eighth, 259
  Ninth, 259
  Tenth, 259
  Twelfth, 287
  Thirteenth, 543, 567
  Fourteenth, 440, 568, 571, 572, 573, 583
  Fifteenth, 570, 573
  Seventeenth, 489
Constitutional Convention (1787), 247–53, *247, 249, 253*
Constitutional Union Party, 494
constitutions, state, 208–9
Continental Army, *171*, 185, 187, 193, *194*, 216
  demoralization of, 195
  strength of, 193
Continental Association, 182–83
Continental Congress, *see* First Continental Congress; Second Continental Congress
"coolies," 524
Cooper, Mary, 123
Coote, Richard (1636–1701), 114
Copley, John Singleton, *200*
Copperheads, 531

Cornish, Samuel (ca. 1795–1858), 443
Cornwallis, Lord Charles (1738–1805), *199*, 200
Coronado, Francisco Vásquez de (1510–1554), 32
Coronation of Louis XVI, 208
corporations, 328
  see also specific corporations
Cortés, Hernán (1485–1547), *9, 22, 23, 23, 27*, 390
Cortland family, 177
Cosby, William (1690–1736), 148
cotton, *317*, 321, 355, 380, 385, 390–91, *408*, 533, 559, 560–61, *560, 575*
  compressing of, *391*
  exporting of, 392
  market revolution and, 312, *317*
  in New Orleans, *394*
  and North, 392, 492
  and Northern textile industry, 385
  plantations, *see* planters, plantations, cotton
  and wealth in South, 480
  see also Cotton Kingdom
Cotton, John (1584–1652), 71–72
Cotton Belt, 407, 559
cotton gin, 316, 318
Cotton Kingdom, 312, 316–18, *317*, 347, 355, 391, 393, 411, 495, 533
Cotton Pickers, The (Homer), *558*
Cotton Pressing in Lousiana, 391
Council of the Indies, 25
Country Party, 141
County Election (Bingham), *370*
Court of Common Pleas, The, *79*
"cousinocracy," 118
Covenant Chain, 90–91
coverture, 17, 233
Cowpens, S.C., American victory at, 199–200
coyotes, 26
Craft, Ellen (1826?–1891), 417
Craft, William (1824–1900), 417
craftsmen, 321, 323, 325, 342
  African-Americans as, 339, 389, 406, 459
  see also artisans
Crawford, Thomas (1813?–1857), 459, *460*
Crawford, William H. (1732–1782), 361–64
Creek Confederacy, 111
Creek Indians, 92, 111, 134, 222, 223, *266*, 297, 300, 361, 374, 376
Creole, 418
Creoles, 136
Crèvecoeur, Hector St. John de (1735–1813), 267
cricket, 140
criollos, 25
Crisis, The, 429
Crittenden, John J. (1786–1863), 496–97, 513
"Croaton," 51
Cromwell, Oliver (1599–1658), 80, 82, 83, *83*, 88
De Lancey family, 118, 144, 176, 207
Delany, Martin R. (1812–1885), 442
Delaware colony, 92
Delaware Indians, 156, 158, 161
Crowe, Eyre (1824–1910), *389*

Cruikshank, U.S. v., 584
crypto-Jews, 135
Cuba, 21, 29, 33, 36, 158, 359, 361, 365, 492, 497
  slavery in, 137
"cult of domesticity," 339–40, 454
currency, 145, 172, *183*, 217, 246, *248*, 250, 274, 275, *325*, 355, 369, 378, 379, 381, 529
  Confederate, *533*, 534
  lack of uniform, 353
Currency Act (1764), 173, 175
Currier, Nathaniel (1813–1888), *311, 567, 581*
Curtis, George William (1824–1892), 519
Cutting Sugar Cane, 96
Cuzco, 29

Dahl, Michael (1659–1743), *143*
Dahomey people, 130
"Dandy Jim," 352
Daniels, John Daniel, *407*
Dartmouth College v. Woodward, 328
Daughters of Liberty, 179
David (Indian), *57*
Davis, David (1815–1886), 523
Davis, Jefferson (1808–1889), 459, *460*, 497, 498, 524, 532–34, 536, 542
  Abraham Lincoln compared to, 532, 534
Davis, Joseph (1784–1870), 542
Davis, Pauline (1813–1876), 452
D-Day, 510
de Anza, Juan Bautista, 154
Deas, Charles, *376*
De Bow's Review, 405
de Bry, Theodor (1528–1598), *16, 29, 52, 61, 66*
debt, imprisonment for, 342
Declaration of Independence (1776), 187–92, *190*, 213, 234, 239, *249*, 259, 399
  ideas of equality in, 206
  Lincoln's views on, 489
  Native Americans and, 222
  Robert Livingston and, 219
  slavery and, 187, 225, 268, 270, 419, 436, 441
"Declaration of Josephe" (Josephe), 37
Declaration of Sentiments, 448, 449
Declaration of the Immediate Causes of Secession, 495
Declaratory Act (1766), 177
Deep South, 316, 347, 390, 395–96, 417, 492, 493, 495, 497, 577
Deere, John (1804–1886), 319
Deer Island, 87
deference, tradition of, 144
deficit, federal, *see* national debt
de Islas, Andrés, *26*
deism, 149
  in Second Great Awakening, 335
  separation of church and state and, 212, 215
crop-lien system, 560–61
crop rotation, 52

Delegation of Advocates of Women's Suffrage Addressing the House Judiciary Committee, A, 573
democracy, in America, 346–84
Democracy in America (Tocqueville), 307, 349
Democratic Party, 169, 368–69, *370*, 373, 381–82, *381*, 386, 463–64, 465, 473, 478–79, 483, 485, 489, 492, 503, 515, 523
  and Bank of the United States, 378, *378*
  in the Civil War, 532, 540
  creation of, 364
  1860 convention of, 493–94
  Fifteenth amendment and, 570
  Irish and, 327
  John C. Calhoun and, 382
  nomination of Buchanan and, 485
  press of, 369, 382, 523
  in Reconstruction, 568, *568*, 577, 579, 580, 581–84, *584*
  see also specific elections and campaigns
Democratic-Republican societies, 280, 281, 283, 284
  Federalist Party views on, 280
Democratic Review, 469
Denmark, 139
  in the West Indies, 96
Department of Female Nurses, 530
Departure of the 7th Regiment, 509
depression, economic:
  of early 1840s, 473–74
  of 1819, 341, 356
  of 1837, 311, 341, 380, *380*, 453, 459
  of 1857, 480
  of 1873, 581, 583
de Soto, Hernando (1496–1542), 32
Destruction by Fire of Pennsylvannia Hall, 445
Detroit, Mich., 159
Dew, Thomas R. (1802–1846), 420
Dial, 449
Diallo, Ayuba, *136*
Dias, Bartholomeu (1450–1500), 20
Dickinson, John (1731–1808), 178, 187, *208, 209*
Diego, Juan, 27
Diggers, 81
Dinwiddie, Robert (1693–1770), 157
Discourse Concerning Western Planting, A (Hakluyt), *52*
diseases:
  Africans and, 94, 131
  in Civil War, 506
  Indians and, 2, 3, 5, 23, 26, 30, 32, 39, 54, 57, 73, 76, 87, 97, 106, 155
  in Jamestown, 58
  Pilgrims and, 66
Display of the United States of America, A (Doolittle), *276*
Dissenters, 71, 82, 102–3, 110, 143, 150, 180, 210–11
diversity, *211*
division of powers, in U.S. Constitution, 250, 254
Dix, Dorothea (1802–1887), 446
Dominican Republic, 21
Dominion of New England, 104

Donelson, Fort, 511
Doolittle, Amos (1754–1832), *184, 254, 276, 285*
Dorr, Thomas (1805–1854), 348–49, *349*
Dorr Liberation Stock, 349
Dorr War, 348–49, *349*
Douglas, Stephen A. (1813–1861), 477–79, 485, 486–89, *488,* 490–91, 493–94
Douglass, Frederick (1817–1895), 390, 402, 418, *440, 443,* 446, 514, 526
    on abolition, 547, 553
    autobiography of, 442
    biography of, 389
    on black soldiers, 519
    "Composite Nation" speech of, 572
    on the Constitution, 441
    Independence Day speech of, 443
    on plantations, 395
    on slavery, 402, 409, 417, 446, 520
"dower rights," 62
Downfall of Mother Bank, The, 378
draft, in Civil War, 504, 529, 531–32, 534
Drayton, William Henry (1742–1779), 222
Dred Scott case, 485–86, *485,* 488, 494, 570
Drunkard's Progress, The, 430
Dubuclet, Antoine (1810–1887), 406
dueling, 396
Duguid, William, *138*
Dunkers, 109, 110
Dunmore, John Murray, earl of (1732–1809), 185, 194, 221, 227, 289
Duquesne, Fort, 158
Dutch East India Company, 39
Dutch East Indies, *see* Indonesia
Dutch Empire, 39–41, 90, 128
    see also Netherlands
Dutch Reformed Church, 41, 42
Dutch South Africa, *110*
Dutch West India Company, 39, 43, *43*
Dyer, Mary (d. 1660), 81

Eagle's Nest, The, 521
East, 319–21
East Anglia, England, 76–77
Eastern Bank of Alabama, *533*
East India Company, 181
East Indies, 18, 23
Eaton, Peggy (1799?–1879), 372
economic freedom:
    American Revolution and, 215–18
    hoarding and, 217
    monopolies and, 217
    price controls and, 217, *217*
economy:
    of Confederate States of America, 534–35
    early U.S., 215–18, 239, 242, 245–46
    government and, 168–69
    of New England colonies, 76–78
    1819 downturn of, 341, 355
    Northern vs. Southern, 216
    slavery and, 224–25
    of West Indies, 96–98
    see also depression, economic; market revolution

Ecuador, 359
Eden, Richard (1521?–1576), 16
Edict of Nantes (1598), 38, *110*
Edisto Island, S.C., 562
education:
    of freed slaves, 541–42, *542,* 553, *553, 555,* 557–58
    individualism and, 434
    in New World, 25
    public, 208, 215, 342, 433–35, *434, 575, 577, 579*
    reform, 425
    slaves barred from, 401
    social classes and, 434
    women and, 281, 282
Edwards, Jonathan (1703–1758), 150, *150*
Edward VI, king of England (1537–1853), 50
Eickemeyer, Rudolph (1831–1895), *553*
Eighth Amendment, 259
Electioneering at the South, 574
elections and campaigns:
    of 1789, 273
    of 1792, 284
    of 1796, 284–85
    of 1800, 287, *287*
    of 1804, 296
    of 1808, 296
    of 1816, 356
    of 1820, 356
    of 1824, 361–64, *364,* 366
    of 1828, 365, 366, *366*
    of 1836, 381
    of 1840, 381–82, *381, 382*
    of 1844, 463–64
    of 1848, 473
    of 1852, 477–78
    of 1856, 483–85, *485*
    of 1858, 486–89
    of 1860, *485,* 494–95, *494, 495*
    of 1862, 515
    of 1864, 540
    of 1868, 569, *569, 570, 571*
    of 1872, 582, 583
    of 1876, 584–85, *584*
    in Middle Colonies, 144
    in New England colonies, 144
Electoral College, 249–50, 251, 252, 284, 288, 296, 366, *366*
    Twelfth Amendment and voting by, 287
    as undemocratic, 349
Electoral Commission (1877), 584–85
Eliot, John (1604–1690), 73
Elizabeth I, queen of England (1533–1603), 49–50, *51,* 52, 53
Elliott, Robert B. (1842–1884), *551*
Emancipation, 578
Emancipation Proclamation, Preliminary (1862), *514,* 515
Emancipation Proclamation (1862), 386, 503, *515,* 516–19, 524, 526, 562
Embargo (1807), 295–96, *296,* 302, 321
Emerson, John (d. 1843), 485
Emerson, Ralph Waldo (1803–1882), 184, *184,* 330, *330,* 331, 343, 352, 369–70, 425, 455, 472, 476

Empress of China, 245
enclosure movement, 52
encomienda system, 29
Enforcement Acts (1870–71), 580, 584
England, 49, 127
    Civil War of, 80–82, *81,* 102, 140, 143, 147
    and colonization of America, 48–85
    as "Commonwealth and Free State," 80
    debate over freedom in, 80–81
    emigration from, 3, 54
    empire expansion by, 88–94
    Glorious Revolution of, 102–3, 140
    as haven for former slaves, 227
    Ireland conquered by, 50–51
    justification for colonization by, 3, 15, 52–54, 81
    political upheavals of, 80–81
    poor economic conditions in, 53–54
    population of, 52, 54
    prejudice in, 94–95
    Protestantism in, 50, 51, 80, 82, 140
    Reformation in, 50
    War of Jenkins' Ear and, 139
    in West Indies, 96
    see also British Empire; Great Britain
England, Church of, *see* Anglican Church
England's Grievance Discovered (Gardiner), *105*
English colonies, *see* American Colonies
English common law, development of, 79–80
English Country Party, 145
English liberty, 3, 79–80, *79,* 80–81, 91, 100, 135, 141, 171, 172, 173, 175, 183
English Toleration Act (1690), 104
Enlightenment, 148, 178, 212
    American, 148–49
    religion and, 149–50
entail, 217
Episcopalians, 188, *212*
Equiano, Olaudah (1745–1797), 127, *130,* 131
"Era of Good Feelings," 356
Erie, Lake, 299
Erie Canal, 307, *309,* 309–11, *309,* 392
Escape of the Reformed Refugees from France, 110
Essay on Slavery and Abolitionism, An (Beecher), 451
Essex County, Mass., 121
Ethiopian Regiment, of Lord Dunmore, 194
ethnic nationalism, 259
eugenics, 428
Europe, European powers, 2, 5, *19,* 278, 290
    Enlightenment in, 148
    expansion of, 6–9, 18–21
    hierarchical society of, 17
    negative views of Indians in, 15
    New World rivalry of, 127–28, 151–56
    social status in, 17
    speed of American exploration by, 23–24

    Western, 5
    see also specific countries
Evans, George Henry (1805–1856), 474
executive branch, U.S. government, 291
Ex parte Milligan, 523
Exposition and Protest, 372
extraterritoriality, 252

factories, system, 321–23
Fallen Timbers, Battle of, 265
Falmouth, Maine, 187
Family Record, 553
family wage, 341
Farmer's and Mechanics Almanac, 243
Farmington, Conn., 182
farms, *see* agriculture
Farragut, David G. (1801–1870), 511
Federal Hall, 273
federalism, 250, *254*
Federalist, The (Hamilton, Madison, and Jay), 254–55, 292
Federalist Party, 277, 279, 284, 299, 356, 371
    in election of 1800, 287
    in election of 1804, 296
    in election of 1824, 364
    elimination of, 303
    in Missouri Compromise, 358
    and national bank, 169
    platform of, 277–78
    views on Democratic-Republican societies of, 280
    views on press of, 285
Federal Reserve Bank, 355
Female Anti-Slavery Society, 425
Female Moral Reform Society, 446–47
feminism, 446–55
    see also gender relations; women; women's rights
femme sole (unmarried woman), 62
Ferdinand, king of Spain (1452–1516), 21, *21*
feudalism, 92, 123
field labor, 61
Fifteenth Amendment, 570, 573
54th Massachusetts Volunteers, 518, 526
Filling Cartridges at the U.S. Arsenal of Watertown, Massachusetts, 529
Fillmore, Millard (1800–1874), 472, 476, 485
Finney, Charles Grandison (1792–1875), 334, 335–36, 437
"fire-eaters," 493
First African Church, 554
First Amendment, 258, 263, 286
First Continental Congress (1775), 182–84, 211
First Rhode Island Regiment, *194*
First Seminole War, 376
First South Carolina Volunteers, 515
First Vote, The, 576
fish, 129
Fisher, Sidney George, 572
Fisk University, 553
Fitzhugh, George (1806–1881), 397, 400, 487, 495
Five Civilized Tribes, 374, 375
Five Generations of a Black Family, 554

Five Iroquois Nations, 90–91, *91*
flag, U.S., *546*
Flanders, 192
flappers, 764, 771
Fletcher v. Peck, 291
Florentine Codex, 23
Florida, *16*, 25, 31–32, 91–92, 139, 146, 197, 314–15, 374, 376
  ceded to Great Britain, 158
  colonization of, 32–33
  as haven for fleeing slaves, 138
  population of, 152, 154
  Seminoles in, 376–77
  U.S. acquisition of, 316, 365
  War Hawks' plan for conquest of, 297
Flushing Remonstrance, 42
Force Bill, 373
Foreign Trade, 88
Forrest, Nathan B. (1821–1877), 519
Fort Caroline, 32
Fort Donelson, 511
Fort Duquesne, 158
Forten, Charlotte (1837–1914), 541–42
Forten, James (1766–1842), 441
Fort Henry, 511
Fort Knox, 355
Fort Louisbourg, 158
Fort McHenry, 299
Fort McIntosh, 242
Fort Necessity, 158
Fort Orange, 39
Fort Pillow, 519, 547
Fort Ridgely, 525
Fort Ross, 154
Fort Stanwix, 242
Fort Sumter, 386, 498, 507, 520
Fort Ticonderoga, 158, 185
Fort Wagner, 518
Fort Washington, 195
Foster, Stephen S. (1809–1881), 425
Founding Fathers:
  as slaveholders, 225, 227, 228, 251, *268*, 269
  western land speculation of, 222
Fourier, Charles (1772–1837), 429
Four Racial Groups (de Islas), *26*
Fourteenth Amendment, 440, 568, 571, 572, 573, 583
Fox, Ebenezer (1763–1843), 216
Fragment on Government (Bentham), 234
Frame of Government, 93
France, 23, 35–39, 52, 104, *110*, 111, 139, 140, 157–58, 186, 239, 492
  American Revolution and, 193, 197, *199*, *208*, 211
  Catholicism and, 164
  change of government in, 475
  designs on Cuba by, 361
  justification for colonization by, 3, 15
  Louisiana Purchase and, 291–92
  New World exploration of, 35–39
  population compared to England, 54
  seizure of American ships by, 284–85
  trade with, 284
  U.S. Civil War and, 509
  in wars with American colonists, 127

in wars with Great Britain, 276, *277*, 280, 295–96
  in West Indies, 96
  see also French Empire
Franciscans, 33, *34*, 154
Frank Leslie's Illustrated Newspaper, *343*, *566*, *573*
Franklin, Benjamin (1706–1790), 146, *146*, 147, 148–49, *149*, 164, *164*, *183*, 232, 243, 267
  at Constitutional Convention, 248, 253
  as deist, 149
  as head of Pennsylvania Abolition Society, 288
  Treaty of Amity and Commerce and, 197
  Treaty of Paris and, 200
  writings of, 116, 141, 146, 148
Franklin, James (1697–1735), 147
Frazier, Garrison (b. 1797), 551
Freake, Elizabeth (1642–1713), *78*
Freake, John (1635–1675), *78*
Fredericksburg, Va., *127*
Fredricksburg, Battle of, 510
free blacks:
  in Caribbean, 406
  as laborers, 406–7
  in New Orleans, 406
  population of, *403*, 406, *406*
  see also African-Americans; slaves, emancipated
"freeborn Englishman," 80, 127
Freedman's Savings and Trust Company, *582*
Freedmen's Bureau, 553, 557–58, 567–68, *568*, 577
Freedmen's Bureau, The, *557*
Freedmen's Bureau Bill (1866), 568
freedom, 126–66, *331*
  in Age of Jackson, 369–70
  American Revolution and, 168, 171, 206, 207–8, 234–35
  Civil War and, 385, 520, 522–23
  Democratic vs. Whig view of, 369
  desire of slaves for, 101, 138–39, 226, 231, 413–15
  economic, 53–54
  European idea of, 15–18
  expansion of, 127
  of expression, 147–48, 208, 219, 258, 263, 283, 286, 392, 445, 446
  feminism and, 449
  Indians and, 15–16, 221–23, 266
  individualism and, 331, 336
  as inducement to English colonization, 53–54
  industrialization and, 323–24
  land possession and, 177–78
  Lincoln's views of, 520, 527
  Locke on, 268
  market revolution and, 336
  in New Netherland, 41–45
  political power vs., 145–46
  of the press, 147–48, 258, 263, 290, 392, 445, 446
  in Reconstruction, 552–53
  reform and, 432–33
  of religion, 258, 290

religious, *see* religious freedom
  slaveholders' views of, 385
  of speech, *see* freedom, of expression
  Stamp Act and, 171, 174
  in utopian societies, 430
  after War of 1812, 307
  Webster's definition of, 343
  Whig views of, 370–71
  white vs. Indian, 221–23
  see also religious freedom
freedom dues, 55
freedom of religion, *see* religious freedom
freedom petitions, of New England slaves, 226
"Freedoms and Exemptions," 43
Freedom's Journal, 350–51, 443
Freed Slaves Celebrating President Lincoln's Decree of Emancipation, *516*
freeholders, 362
freemen, in Pennsylvania, 94
Free Soil Party, 473–75, 483
free trade, 217–18
Free Woman, 449
Free Women of Color with their Children and Servants in a Landscape (Brunias), *95*
Frelinghuysen, Theodore (1817–1885), 150
Frémont, John C. (1813–1890), 466, 485, 514, 540
French and Indian War, *see* Seven Years' War
French Canada, 35–39
French Empire, 3, 25, 26, 35–39, *44*, 49, 97, 152, *153*, 155–56
  end of, *160*
French Revolution, 159, 235, 276–77, *277*, 279, 280, *281*
Fries, John (1750–1818), 285
Fries's Rebellion, 285
From Factory Life as It Is., 333
From the Plantation to the Senate, *575*
Frugal Housewife, The (Child), 341
Fugitive Slave Act (1850), 476–77, *478*
fugitive slaves, 288, 376, 475, 476–77, 513, *513*
  Abraham Lincoln and, 487, 495
  as contraband in Civil War, 513, 516
  in U.S. Constitution, 288
Fuller, Margaret (1810–1850), 449, *449*
Fulton, Robert (1765–1815), 309
Fundamental Constitutions of Carolina (1669), 92
Fundamental Orders (1639), 71
fur trade, 35, 39, 43, 56–57, 116, 123, 154, 156
  animal populations and, 57
  Five Iroquois Nations and, 91
  in New France, 38
  of Pequots, 76
  Russian, 154
  Treaty of Paris and, 159

Gabriel (slave; 1776–1800), 289–90, 418, 420
Gabriel's Rebellion, 289–90
Gadsden Purchase, 466, *474*
Gaffney, Mary (b. 1846), 559

Gage, Thomas (1721–1787), 193
gag rule, regarding abolition, 445
Gales, Joseph (1786–1860), 281
Gallatin, Albert (1761–1849), 353–54
Galloway, Joseph (1731–1803), 186
Gama, Vasco da (1460–1524), 20
Gardiner, Ralph, *105*
Garfield, James A. (1831–1881), 552
Garner, Margaret, 476
Garnet, Henry Highland (1815–1882), *436*, 442
Garrison, William Lloyd (1805–1879), 421, 437, *437*, 439, 441–42, 444, 446, 454, *455*, 570
Gast, John, *461*
Gay, Sydney Howard, 477
gender relations:
  European, 15
  Native American, 14
  see also women; women's rights
General Court (Conn.), 73
General Court (Mass.), 68, 69, 75, 77, 78, 103, 104
General History of Virginia (Smith), *60*
Genet, Edmond (1763–1834), 276, *277*
Geneva Conventions, First, 531
Genoa, 20, 23
"gentlemen of property and standing," abolition movement and, 444
George III, king of England (1738–1820), 171, *171*, 186, 187, 191, *199*
Georgia, 288, 314–15, 374–76, 562
  government in, 209
  population of slaves in, 135
  slavery in, 132, 252
  Trail of Tears in, 376
  voting rights in, 352
Georgia colony, 32, 143
  in American Revolution, 194, 199
  creation of, 135
  Declaration of Independence and, 187
  French in, 156
  Loyalists in, 218
  rice plantations in, 134
  slavery in, 134, 138, 227
German-Americans, 110, 157, 324–26, 370
German Beer Garden on Sunday Evening, A, *432*
Germans, German immigrants, 109, 110, 111, 112, 157, 324–26, 432, *432*
  as Democrats, 370
  English liberty and, 183
"German triangle," 325–26
Gettysburg, Battle of, *522*, *537*, 538–39
Gettysburg Address, The, 520, 521
Ghent, Treaty of (1814), 300
Gibbons v. Ogden, 328
Giddings, Joshua (1795–1864), 478
Gideon's Band, 541, 542
Gifford, Abigail, 70
Gilbert, Humphrey (1539–1583), 51
Gilded Age, 387
Gin Lane (Hogarth), *53*
"Gleaner, The," 281
Gliddon, George R. (1809–1857), 442
Glorieta Pass, Battle of, 524
Glorious Revolution, 102–3, *103*

Glory, 518
Goddess of Liberty, 307, 329–30
Godkin, E. L. (1831–1902), 581
"God Save the King," 140
gold, 18, 24, 29, 32, 35, 49, 53–54, 58, 88,
    97, 106, 380
    in California gold rush, 381, 469–70,
      470, 471, 493
    coinage, 145
    currency and, 355, 378, 379
    as inducement to exploration, 2,
      18–19, 31, 32, 35
    tobacco as substitute for, 61
Goodell, William (1792–1878), 439
Goodrich, Samuel (1793–1860), 287
Gordon, Thomas (d. 1750), 141–42,
    148
Gorgas, Josiah (1818–1883), 508
Gould, Jay (1836–1892), 529
government, U.S.:
    Constitutional debate over, 168,
      248, 261
    debt of, *see* national debt
    economy and, 168–69
    society and, 256
    structure of, 248–49
    see also specific branches
grain, 129, 275
Grand Council of the Five Iroquois
    Nations, *91*
"grandees," 100, 119
Grand Federal Procession, 239, *239,
    256, 257, 258*
Grand Review of the Union armies,
    547
Grant, Ulysses S. (1822–1885),
    510–11, *538,* 539, 542, *544,* 545,
    580, 581
    background of, 510–11
    in election of 1868, 569, *569, 571*
    Ku Klux Klan and, 580
    Lee's surrender to, 545
    on Mexican War, 465
    at Petersburg, 545
    scandals under, 579
    Southern violence and, 584
Gray, Simon, 407
Grayson, Andrew J., *470*
Great Awakening, 110, 138, 149–51,
    150, 151
    impact of, 151
Great Awakening, Second, 334–36, *335,*
    385, 431, 437
    individualism and, 335
Great Awakening, slavery and, 151,
    412
Great Britain, 2–3, *22,* 23, 115, 222, 239,
    364, 365, 492
    American boycott of, 182–83
    Chartist movement in, 475
    creation of, 127
    empire of, 25, 26, 157–58
    as obstacle to westward expansion,
      329
    Oregon Territory and, 459, *462,*
      464–65
    patriotism of, 140
    regulation of American trade with,
      117

    seizure of American ships by, 284
    trade with, 284
    U.S. Civil War and, 509
    war debt of, 172–73
    in war with France, 276, *277,* 280,
      295–96
    see also British Empire; England
Great Council, 12
Great Famine, as cause of Irish immi-
    gration, 325
*Great Labor Question from a Southern
    Point of View, The* (Homer), 557
Great Lakes, 39, 44, 307, 354
Great Lakes region, 91, 155, 159
Great League of Peace, 12
Great Migration, 67, 78
Great Plains, 10, 32, 152
Great Seal of the United States, *242*
Great Society, 557
"Great Sun," 13
Great Triumvirate, 478
*Great Voyage to the Country of the Hurons,
    The* (Sagard), *17*
Greece, ancient, slavery in, 398
Greeley, Horace (1811–1872), 581–82
Green, James K. (1823–1891), 574–75
Green, Mary, *281*
Greene, Nathanael (1742–1786),
    199–200
Greenglass, David (1922–), 914–15
Greenhow, Rose, 536
Green Mountain Boys, 177–78, 185
Greenville, Treaty of (1795), 265, *265,*
    298
Grenville, George (1712–1770), 173, *176*
Grier, Robert C. (1794–1870), 486
Grimké, Angelina (1805–1879), 441,
    447–48, 450
Grimké, Sarah (1792–1873), 447–48
Griswold, Roger (1762–1812), *286*
Grotius, Hugo (1583–1645), 27
Guadalupe Hidalgo, Treaty of (1848),
    466–67
Guadeloupe, 106, 158
    slave uprising in, 139
Guale Indians, 32
Guerriere, 299
Guilford Courthouse, N.C., American
    victory at, 199–200
Gulf Coast, 32, 156
Gulf of Mexico, *9,* 10, 35
Gullah Jack, 419
Gullah language, 138
guns, 130
Gutenberg, Johannes (1390–1468), 23
Guthrie, Tex., *560*

haciendas, 25
Hagerty, John, *151*
Haiti, 21, 97, 288–89, *289,* 415, 419, 514
    creation of, 288
Haitian Revolution, 288–89, *444*
Hakluyt, Richard (1552?–1616), 52, 53
Half-Way Covenant (1662), 78
Hamilton, Alexander (1757?–1804),
    247, 247, 248, 254, 267, 269, 287
    centralized state sought by, 291
    French Revolution as viewed by, 276
    proposes standing army, 274

    religion and, 212
    selected as head of Treasury
      Department, 274
    social hierarchy as viewed by,
      277–78
    Treasury program of, 274, *276,* 277
    war with France desired by, 285
Hamilton, Andrew (ca. 1676–1741), 148
Hamlet, James, *478*
Hammond, James Henry (1807–1864),
    372, 393, 414
Hampton, Wade (1818–1902), 584
Hampton University, 553
Hancock, John (1737–1793), 179, 191,
    226, 256
Handsome Lake, 298
Hänner, Johannes, 112
Hansford, Charles (1735?–1815), 136
Hardenbroeck, Margaret (d. ca. 1690),
    41
Harmony community, 429
Harper, Frances Ellen Watkins (1825–
    1911), 574
Harpers Ferry, 489–92, *492*
Harper's Magazine, 427
Harper's Monthly, 452
Harper's Weekly, 409, 432, 448, 519, 529,
    *540, 554, 557, 571, 574, 576, 582,
    584, 585*
Harris, Townsend (1804–1878), 472
Harrison, William Henry (1773–1841),
    298, 299–300, *381,* 382
Harte, Bret (1839–1902), 547
Hartford, Conn., 71
Hartford Convention, 303–4
Harvard College, 68, *69,* 281
Hat Act (1732), 172
Havana, Cuba, 32
Hawkins, Benjamin (1754–1818), *266,*
    297
Hawley, Joseph (1723–1788), 187
Hawthorne, Nathaniel (1804–1864),
    309, 429
Hayes, Rutherford B. (1822–1893),
    584–85
Hayne, Robert Y. (1791–1839), *372,
    372,* 419
Haynes, Lemuel (1753–1833), 226, *229*
headright system, 59, 61, 64
Hemings, Sally (1773–1835), 269
Henry, Fort, 511
Henry, Patrick (1736–1799), 175, 182,
    252, 256–57, 289
    as slaveholder, 227
    western land speculation of, 222
Henry VII, king of England (1457–
    1509), 50
Henry VIII, king of England (1491–
    1547), 50, 53
Henson, Josiah (1789–1883), 409, 442
Herald Of Freedom, 455
Hercules, 175
Hercules (Washington's slave), *268*
Heroes of America, 535
Hesselius, John, *133*
Hessians, 193, 195
Hicks, Edward, *121*
Hiding in a Mangrove Swamp, 376
Higginson, Martha, 446

Higginson, Thomas Wentworth
    (1823–1911), 517
Highland Scots, 218–19
Hill, John William, *309*
Hispaniola, 21, 24, 36
History of the American Revolution, The
    (Ramsay), 260
History of the Indies (Las Casas), 36
hoarding, to fix prices, 217
Hoare, William, *136*
Hobbes, Thomas, *81*
Hodges, Willis A. (1815–1890), 407
Hogarth, William (1697–1764), *53,
    142, 180*
Holland, *see* Netherlands
Holy Experiment, Pennsylvania
    colony's, 161
Holyoke, Mass., 323
Holy Trinity, 83
Homer, Winslow (1836–1910), *546, 556,
    557, 558*
Homestead Act (1862), 245, 524, 567
homesteads, free, *495*
Hone, Philip (1780–1851), 347
Hooker, "Fighting Joe" (1814–1879), 538
Hooker, Thomas (1586–1647), 71
Hope, James, *511*
Hopis, 10
*Horse America Throwing His Master,
    The, 199*
horses, 8, 10
Horseshoe Bend, Battle of, 300
House of Burgesses, Va., 59, 99, 101,
    118, 144, 175, 213
House of Commons, British, 18, 80, 82,
    140, 145, *174,* 175
House of Lords, British, 80, 140
House of Representatives, U.S., 249,
    287, 347, *358,* 391, *566,* 568, 583
    abolition and, 445
    African-Americans in, 575
    creation of, 249
    in election of 1824, 364
    Johnson's impeachment and,
      569–70
Houston, Sam (1793–1863), 462
Houston, Ulysses S. (b. 1825), 551
Howard, Merrimon (b. 1821), 554
Howard, O. O. (1830–1909), 557, 558,
    562
Howard University, 553
Howe, Julia Ward (1819–1910), 520
Howe, Samuel Gridley (1801–1876),
    454
Howe, Timothy (1816–1883), 574
Howe, William (1729–1814), 185,
    194–95, *195*
Hudson, Henry (d. 1611), 39, 49
Hudson River, 114, 307, 309
Hudson River school, *331*
Hudson Valley, 43, 44, 123, 135, 257
Huexotzinco, 27
Huexotzinco Codex, 27
Hughes, John (1797–1864), 326, 432
Huguenots, *16,* 32, 38, 41, *110*
    see also Christianity
Hume, David (1711–1776), 178
Hunt, Thomas, 66
Hunter, Robert (1666–1734), 145

hunting, 57, 114, 154
Hurons, 17, 39, 159
Hutchinson, Anne (1591–1643), 71–73, 74, 78, 81
Hutchinson, Thomas (1711–1780), 171, 173, 176

Iberian Peninsula, 18, 21
IBM, 1063
Ibo people, 136
Ice Age, 6
Ickes, Peter, 207
Illinois, 312, 316
    Black Hawk War in, 374
    black rights in, 353
    blacks barred from, 339
    Lincoln-Douglas campaign in, 486–89
    38th Infantry of, 506
Illinois Central Railroad, 480
Illustrated London News, 532
"Immediate Emancipation Illustrated," 444
immigrants, immigration, 2, 3, 5, 106–7, 107, 324–26, 325, 326, 482
    Abraham Lincoln and, 494
    African-Americans vs., 482
    from England, 49–50, 53–55, 61, 65–67, 107
    from France, 38
    from Germany, 157, 324–26, 432
    growth of, 324–26
    from Ireland, 324–26, 432
    numbers of, 324–25, 325
    population of, 324–25
    from Scandinavia, 326
    of Scotch-Irish, 109, 157
    to South Carolina, 134–35
    from Spain, 25–27
    from Sweden, 326
    see also specific nationalities
impeachment, of Andrew Johnson, 569–70
impressment, 141, 276, 296–97, 300
    in Civil War, 535
Inauguration of Mr. Lincoln, 499
Incas, 8, 23–24, 31
income taxes, see taxes, income
indentured servitude, 6, 35–38, 54–55, 55, 61–62, 62, 64, 96–97, 228
    American Revolution and, 167, 193, 205, 215–16, 234
    in Carolina, 92
    decline of, 215–16
    in New England, 77, 136
    in Pennsylvania, 136
    slavery compared with, 94
    in Virginia, 97–98, 99, 100, 133
Independence Day Celebration in Centre Square (Krimmel), 350
Independence Hall, 249
Independent Monitor, 580
Independent Treasury, 381
India, 18, 20, 20, 24, 158, 174, 181
Indiana, 9, 312, 316
    blacks barred from, 339
    in election of 1858, 489
"Indian country," 114
Indian removal, 374–77, 375

Missouri and, 374
    slavery as motive for, 374
    see also Native Americans
Indian Removal Act (1830), 374
indigo, 128, 134
individualism, 330–34
    education and, 434
    freedom and, 331, 336
    market revolution and, 329
    reform and, 432
    Second Great Awakening and, 335
    in Utopian societies, 430
Indonesia, 20
industrial revolution, 316, 321–23, 322, 390, 480, 503
Industrious Man, The, 339
industry, 459, 529, 529
    in Civil War, 524, 529
    factory system and, 321–23
    law and, 327–29
    workers' life and, 324, 325
    see also market revolution; specific industries
Infant Liberty Nursed by Mother Mob, 277
inflation, 217
influenza, 24
information revolution, 350–51
In Side of the Old Lutheran Church in 1800, York, Pa., 213
Intolerable Acts (1774), 181–82, 185
Iowa, blacks barred from, 339
Iraq War, 506
Ireland, 3, 50–51, 52, 60, 94, 109
    conquered by England, 50–51
    emigration to North America from, 55
    English control over, 83
    English immigration to, 54
Ireton, Henry (1611–1651), 143
Irish, Irish immigrants, 324–26, 432, 432
Irish-Americans, 3, 324–26, 370, 482, 484
Iron Act (1750), 172
ironclads, 504
Iroquois, 12, 15, 15, 38, 39, 87, 156–57, 157, 222–23, 298
    relations with New York colony, 87
Iroquois Confederacy, 44, 90–91, 222
Isabella, queen of Spain (1451–1504), 21
Islam, 20, 150
    in American colonies, 137
Israel Hill, 406
Is This a Republican Form of Government? (Nast), 585
Ives, James (1824–1895), 567, 581

Jackson, Andres (1767–1845), and Panic of, 1837, 380
Jackson, Andrew (1767–1845), 210, 307, 365, 366, 372, 444, 463, 476
    American Colonization Society and, 435
    annexation of Texas and, 463
    in battle with Bank of the United States, 378–80, 378
    defies Supreme Court, 375
    dubbed "King Andrew," 347, 349
    in election of 1824, 361–64

in election of 1828, 366, 366
    inauguration of, 347
    Indians and, 347, 367, 374–76
    Indian wars of, 315
    Kitchen Cabinet of, 369
    nickname of, 367
    in nullification crisis, 374
    "pet banks" and, 379
    rise of democracy and, 347, 351
    as slaveholder (1767–1845), 300
    state banks and, 379
    veto power and, 379, 567–68
    views of blacks of, 367
    in War of 1812, 300–302, 303–4
Jackson, Rachel (1767–1828), 366
Jackson, Thomas "Stonewall" (1824–1863), 505, 538
Jacksonville, Fla., 32
Jacobin clubs, 280
Jacobs, Jane, 989
Jamaica, 36, 119, 138, 139, 415, 790
    free blacks in, 406
    seizure by England of, 83
    slave uprisings in, 139
James, duke of York (1633–1701), see James II, king of England
James, Thomas, 176
James I, king of England (1566–1625), 49–50, 52, 60, 61, 80
James II, king of England (1633–1701), 90, 91, 93, 102–3, 104
James River, 49
Jamestown, Va., 31, 49, 57, 58–61, 58, 100
    death rate at, 58
    difficult beginnings of, 58
    founding of, 49–50
    Indian conflicts in, 59–61
    Indian relations with, 60–61
    Indian uprising of 1622, 60–61, 61
    typhoid fever in, 58
Japan, 471–72
Japanese immigrants, World War II internment of, 258
Jarvis, John Wesley (1780–1840), 373
Jay, John (1745–1829), 200, 228, 252, 254, 267, 274, 276–77
Jay, William (1792–1837), 445
Jay's Treaty (1795), 276–77
Jefferson, Thomas (1743–1826), 118, 144, 247, 278, 279, 361, 364, 365, 448
    on African-Americans, 268–69
    on Alien and Sedition Acts, 286
    Bible version by, 212
    campaign portrait of, 287
    Declaration of Independence and, 187–92, 190, 206, 213–14, 222, 234, 259
    in election of 1796, 284
    in election of 1800, 286–87
    in election of 1804, 296
    and elimination of Federalist Party, 303
    embargo of, 296
    "empire of liberty" and, 239, 245
    foreign policy of, 294
    freedom and, 217
    French Revolution and, 276
    Haiti and, 289

inauguration of, 290
    Indian policies of, 297
    Louisiana Purchase and, 291–92
    on Missouri Compromise, 358
    national bank opposed by, 275
    on Native Americans, 222–23, 266
    Ordinance of 1784 and, 243
    public schools and, 215
    religion and, 149, 211–12
    selected secretary of state, 273–74
    on Shays's rebellion, 246
    as slaveholder, 225, 227, 251, 269
    slavery and, 225, 269
    strong local self-government sought by, 290–91
    trade as viewed by, 296
    western land speculation of, 222
    writings of, 184, 212
Jemison, Edwin Francis (d. 1862), 506
Jennings, Samuel (1755?–1834?), 205, 224, 229
jeremiads, 78
Jerry (slave), 476
Jesuits, 15, 39, 91
Jesus, 27, 34, 35, 37, 82–83, 93, 215, 413, 420, 427
    Jefferson's life of, 212
    Mormons and, 336–37
Jewett, William S., 470
Jews, 41, 116, 135, 140
    in American colonies, 110, 143, 210
    in colonial Maryland, 83
    in colonial Pennsylvania, 93, 110
    in colonial Rhode Island, 71
    Hasidic, 150
    in New Amsterdam, 42
    in Spain, 21, 26, 27
    voting rights and, 212
Jim Crow, 352
John, king of England (1166–1216), 79
John Quincy Adams, 354
Johnson, Andrew (1808–1875), 386, 394, 562
    background of, 564–65
    emancipation and, 565
    impeachment of, 569–70
    Reconstruction policies of, 558, 562, 564–69, 567, 571
Johnson, Anthony (d. 1670), 98
Johnson, Richard M., 300
Johnson, Samuel (1709–1784), 159, 224
Johnson, William (1715–1774), 406
Johnston, Joseph E. (1807–1891), 509
"Join, or Die," 164
joint stock company, 40
Joliet, Louis (1645–1700), 35
Jones, Charles C., 396, 413
Josephe, 37
Journal of Commerce, 370
Jubilee of Liberty, 307
judicial review, 291
Judiciary Act of 1789, 291
Julius Caesar (Shakespeare), 205
Junto (club), 146

Kansas, 478, 487, 493
    violence in, 484–85
Kansas-Nebraska Act (1854), 478–79, 479, 482, 485, 486, 487

Kaufmann, Theodore (1910–1986), *577*
Kearney, Stephen W. (1794–1848), 466
Keep Within Compass, 232
Kelley, Abby (1810–1887), 425, 426, 449, 454, 573
Kemmelmayer, Frederick (ca. 1760–ca. 1821), *278*
Kendall, Amos (1789–1869), 444
Kentucky, 221–22, 242
  creation of, 284
  in Panic of 1819, 356
  resolution in legislature of, 286, 372
  slavery in, 315–16
  voting rights in, 352
Key, David M. (1824–1900), 585
Key, Francis Scott (1779–1843), 299
Key of Liberty, The (Manning), 279–80
Kieft, William (1597–1647), 43–44
King, Charles Bird (1785–1862), *298*
King, Martin Luther, Jr. (1929–1968), 465
King, Rufus (1755–1827), 278, 356
"King Andrew," 347, *349*
King George's War, 157
King Philip's War, 87, 101, *102*
Kiowas, 525
Kitchen Ball at White Sulphur Springs, Virginia (Mayr), *410*
Kitchen Cabinet, 368
kivas, 34
Kleindeutschland, 326
Know-Nothing (American) Party, 480–83, 485, 494
Knox, Fort, 355
Knox, Henry (1750–1806), 185, 232, 266
Knox, Lucy (1754–1824), 232
Kongo, 139
Korea, 87–90
Krans, Olof, *326*
Krimmel, John Lewis (1786–1821), *350*
Ku Klux Klan, 580, *580*, *581*, 584

La Bahia, N.Mex., 154
Labor:
  agricultural, 325
  costs, 321
  demand for, 324
  free blacks as skilled, 406
  gang, 407–9
  Philadelphia Mechanic's Advocate newspaper for, 351
  Republican Party (modern) and free, 483
  rise of free, 215–16
  unemployment and, 380
  as wage earners, 215, 323
  in West, 330
  women and, 339–41, 452
  and work hours, 323–24, *323*, 342
  see also unions
"Laboring Classes, The" (Brownson), 343
labor movement, 343, 434, 439, 474, 531
  early nineteenth century, 341–42, *342*
  in Panic of 1837, 380
  see also unions

Ladies' Association, 232
Lady's Magazine and Repository of Entertaining Knowledge, 280
Lafayette, Marquis de (1757–1834), 200, 307–8
Lagonda Agricultural Works, *482*
La Isabella, 21
Lakin, A. S. (1810–1890), *580*
Lancaster, Pa., massacre of Indians at, 161
Land Commission, 577
land grants, 2, 145, 178
L'Anse aux Meadows, 21
Larcom, Lucy (1824–1893), 324
La Salle, René-Robert Cavelier, Sieur de (1643–1687), 35
Las Casas, Bartolomé de (1474–1566), 29–30, 36, 52, 59
"Las Siete Partidas," 98
Latané, William, *536*
Latrobe, Benjamin (1764–1820), *127*
Laurens, Henry (1724–1792), 228
Laurens, John (1754–1782), 228
law, corporate, 328
Lecompton Constitution, 493
Lee, Ann (1736–1784), 427
Lee, Richard Henry (1732–1794), 182
Lee, Robert E. (1807–1870), 489, 508, 509, 510, 538, *538*, *544*, 545
Lee family, 118, 157
Leisler, Jacob (ca. 1640–1691), 104–5, 143
Lely, Peter (1618–1680), *83*, *100*
Le Monde Illustré, *516*
L'Enfant, Pierre Charles (1754–1825), 275, 290, *290*
Lenni Lanapes, 111
Leopard, *296*
Letters from a Farmer in Pennsylvania (Dickinson), 178, 187
Letters from an American Farmer (Crèvecoeur), 267
Letters on the Equality of the Sexes (Sarah Grimké), 447
Levellers, 80–81, *82*, 147
Leviathan (Hobbes), *81*
Lewis, Meriwether (1774–1809), 293–94, *294*
Lewis and Clark expedition, 293–94, *294*
  Native-Americans and, 293–94
Lexington, Battle of, 184, *185*, *196*, 216
Libby Prison, 536
libel, 147–48
liberalism, 142–43
Liberal Republican Party, 581–82
Liberator, 351, 421, 437, *437*, 439, 441, 450, *453*, *455*
Liberia, 435, *435*
Liberty, 179
Liberty and Washington, *275*
Liberty Bell, *436*, 441
Liberty Displaying the Arts and Sciences (Jennings), *205*, 224, 229
Liberty Hall, 175
Liberty in the Form of the Goddess of Youth, *281*
Liberty Party, 440, 454–55, *455*, 464
Liberty Pole, 175, 278, 286

Liberty Tree, 175, *181*, 185, *185*
libraries, public, 146–47, 148
Library Company of Philadelphia, 146
Lieber, Francis (ca. 1798–1872), 370
Life and Age of Man, 340
Life and Age of Women, 340
Life in California (Robinson), 461
Lima, *130*
Lima, Peru, 25
Lincoln, Abraham (1809–1865), 263, 386, 389, 400, 402, *487*, *488*, 490–91, *498*, 508, 512, *520*, 543–46, 564, *578*
  Address at Sanitary Fair of, 527
  assassination of, 545, *546*
  in Black Hawk War, 374
  and black suffrage, 519
  Civil War message to Congress, 512
  in 1858 Senate campaign, 487–89
  elected president, 494–95, *497*
  in election of 1860, 494–95
  in election of 1864, 540
  emergence of, 485–95
  inaugural address of, 497–98
  and Jefferson Davis compared, 532, 534
  market revolution and, 308
  and Mexican War, 465
  and Native Americans, 524–25
  parents of, 242
  plans for reconstruction of, 542–43
  second inaugural address, 543–45
  slavery as viewed by, 487–88
  Southern secession and, 497
  and suspension of habeas corpus, 523
  war planning and, 507
  see also Emancipation Proclamation
Lincoln, Benjamin (1733–1810), 246
Lincoln, James (d. 1791), 256
Lincoln administration, 495, 514, 517, 523, 531, 533
Lincoln and the Female Slave (Bowser), *520*
Lincoln penny, *275*
"Literacy, Land, and Liberation," 574
Little Turtle (1752–1812), 265
Livermore, Mary (1820–1905), 531, 572
Liverpool, 129
livestock, 6, 25, 43, 57, 129, 134, 266, 319
Livingston, Robert (1746–1814), 90, 219
Livingston family, 118, 144, 176, 177, 207, 219
Locke, John (1632–1704), 142, *143*, 149, 184, 191, 225, 268
Locomotive DeWitt Clinton, *312*
Logan, James (1674–1751), 111
London, *53*, 140
Long, Joseph, 404
Longfellow, Henry Wadsworth (1807–1882), 498–99
Long Island, N.Y., 42, 91
Long Walk, Navajo's, *see* Trail of Tears
Lord Dunmore's proclamation, 185
"Lords of the Lash," 392
"Lords of the Loom," 392
Lords of Trade, 103, 133
Los Adaes, N.Mex., 154
Los Angeles, Calif., 154, 155

Lossing, Benson, 427
Louisa (slave), *395*
Louisbourg, Fort, 158
Louisiana, 152, 292, *292*, 312, 542
  obtained by Spanish, 152
  2nd Regiment of, *506*
  slave trade in, *395*
Louisiana Purchase (1803), *273*, 291–92, *293*, 297, 354, 356, 357, *357*, 365, 472, 478
  Texas and, 464
Louisiana Territory, 158, 294
  population of, 156
  slave uprising in, 139
Louis XIV, king of France, *110*
Louis XVI, king of France (1754–1793), 276
Lovejoy, Elijah P. (1802–1837), 444, 445
Lowell, Mass., 321, 322, 324, *324*, 325, 333, 343
Loyalists, 199, 200, 207, 218–21, *219*, *220*, 233, 234, 303
  black, 227
Loyal Nine, 171
loyalty, oaths, 219
Luke, William (1831–1870), 580
Luther, Martin (1483–1546), 28
Lutherans, 109, 110
Lynch, James D. (1839–1872), 551, 574
Lyon, Matthew (1749–1822), 286, *286*
Lyon, Pat, *337*

Mackintosh, Ebenezer (1737–1816), 171
Macon's Bill No. 2, 296
Madame Butterfly (Puccini), 472
Madeira, 20
Madison, James (1751–1836), 191, 246, *247*, *278*, 279, 299, 365
  Alien and Sedition Acts as viewed by, 286
  American System plan of, 354
  Bank of the United States opposed by, 275
  Bill of Rights and, 257–58, 259
  church-state separation and, 214
  colonization and, 435
  at Constitutional Convention, 248–50
  elected president, 296
  elimination of Federalist Party and, 303
  Federalist and, 254–56
  in *Marbury v. Madison*, 291
  religion and, 212, 214
  as slaveholder, 227, 251
  trade policy of, 296–97
  Virginia Plan and, 248
  on war, 298
Magellan, Ferdinand (1480–1521), 22, 23
Magna Carta (1215), 79–80
Mahoney, James, *55*
Maine, 312
  entrance into union of, 357
  voting rights in, 352
Maine Bank of Portland, 379
malaria, 134
Mali, 19

Malvern Hill, Battle of, *506*
Manhattan Island, 39
manifest destiny, 329–30, 459–72, *461*, 524
Manigault, Louis, *513*
Manila, 24
Mann, Horace (1796–1859), 434
Manning, William (1747–1814), 279–80
Manon, 156
Mansfield, Lord, *182*
manufactures, American system of, 322–23
manufacturing:
    in early nineteenth century, 321–23, *321*
    J. Q. Adams's promotion of, 365
    see also industry
Marbury, William, 291
Marbury v. Madison, 291
March to the Sea, 543, *544*
Marine Corps, U.S., 295
Marion, Francis (1732?–1795), 199
market revolution, 303, *310*, *313*, 348, 351, 369, 394
    abolition and, 439
    Abraham Lincoln and, 308
    African-Americans and, 338–39
    agriculture and, 307, 318–19
    canals and, 168, 309–11, *310*, 354
    cotton and, 312, *317*
    freedom and, 336, 341
    individual and, 329
    manufacturing and, 321–23
    middle class created by, 338, 341
    prosperity and, 337–43, *337*
    railroads and, 168, 308, 311, 321
    Republicans and, 480
    rise of banks in, 355, 378
    roads and, 308, *310*
    rural areas and, 318–19
    Second Great Awakening and, 336
    society and, 318–29
    technology and, 316, 321–23, *322*, *482*
    textile mills and, 321–24, *322*, *323*, *324*
    transportation and, 307, 308, 321, 328
    urban areas and, *320*, 321
    water power and, 322, *322*
    women and, 339–41
"maroons," 139
Marquette, Jacques (1637–1675), 35
Marshall, John (1755–1835), 247, 328, 356, 371
    American Colonization Society and, 435
    death of, 379
    French Revolution as viewed by, 276
    Missouri Controversy and, 356
    nationalism and, 356
    Native Americans and, 374–75
    strong Supreme Court favored by, 291
    see also Supreme Court, U.S.
Marshall Court, 291, 328, 371
Martha's Vineyard, Mass., *66*
Martin, James (b. 1753), 233
Martin, Luther (1748–1826), 251

Martin (slave), 289
Martineau, Harriet (1802–1876), 329, 435
Martinique, 106, 158
Marx, Karl (1818–1883), 517
Mary, wife of William III, *116*
Mary I, queen of England (1516–1568), 50, *51*
Mary II, queen of England (1662–1694), 102
Maryland, 275
    constitution of, 209, 213
    free blacks in, 406–7
    settlement of, *58*
    slavery in, *136*
    slave trade in, 318
    uprising in, 103–4
    voting rights in, 209, 352
Maryland colony, 2, 54, 63, 91, 103–4, 118, *133*
    close ties to Britain of, 133
    as feudal domain, 63
    free blacks in, 98
    government of, 63, 144
    indentured servitude in, 64
    "plundering time" in, 82
    religion in, 63–64, 82–83
    tobacco in, 63
Mashpees, 223
Mason, George (1725–1792), 133, 248
Mason-Dixon Line, 390
Massachusett language, *73*
Massachusetts, 233, 342, 364
    constitution of, 210, 212–13, 223
    government in, 209
    legislature, 328
    Shays's rebellion in, 246
    U.S. Constitution and, 257
    war debt and, 275
Massachusetts Bay Company, 67, 68
Massachusetts Charter (1629), 82, 181
Massachusetts colony, 56, *65*, 66–70, 71–73, 77, 104–5, *119*, 173, *173*, 211
    assembly in, 145
    General Court of, 68, 69, 77, 78, 103
    government of, 68–70
    and King Philips War, 87
    in Pequot War, 76
    population of, 67
    Quakers in, 81–82
    repeals economic regulations, 78
    seal of, *67*
    self-governing towns in, 68–69
    slave trade in, 128
    uprising in, 171
    views on independence of, 185
Massachusetts Magazine, 281
Massachusetts Spy, The, 226
Massasoit (ca. 1590–1661), 66
mass production, 321
"masterless men," 53–54, 107
Mather, Cotton (1663–1728), 140
Mather, Increase (1639–1723), 106
Matlack, Timothy (1736?–1829), 207
Mayflower, 66
Mayflower Compact (1620), 66
Mayr, Christian (ca. 1805–1851), *410*
May Session of the Woman's Rights Convention, The, 448

Mazzini, Giuseppe (1805–1872), 520
McCarthy era, 258
McClellan, George B. (1826–1885), *503*, 509, 540, *540*
McCormick, Cyrus (1809–1884), 319
McCulloch v. Maryland, 356
McHenry, Fort, 299
McIlvaine, Samuel (1824–1863), *503*
McIntosh, Fort, 242
McKim, J. Miller, *417*
Meade, George G. (1815–1872), 538
measles, 24, 131
medicine men, 12
Mediterranean Sea, 20
Meeting of the General Council of the Army at Putney, 82
"melting pot", U.S. as, 267
Melville, Herman (1819–1891), 335, 352, 355, 465
Memphis, Tenn., Reconstruction riot in, 569
Menéndez de Avilés, Pedro (1519–1574), 32
Mennonites, 109, 110, 219
    as immigrants to Pennsylvania, 113
Men of Color to Arms (Douglass), 526
mercantilism, 77–78, 88, 90, 133
Meridian, Miss., 580
Merrimac, 504
Merrimack River, 321
Merritt, Susan Torrey, *440*
Merryman, John (1824–1881), 523
Meschianza, 197
message to Congress, 354, 365, 512
    see also State of the Union Address
mestizos, 26, *26*, 33, 106
Metacom (King Philip; d. 1676), 87, 377
Methodism, 150, *151*
Methodists, 110, 377, 412
    African-American, 412, 553
    Gabriel's Rebellion and, 289
    in Great Awakening, 150, 151
    in Second Great Awakening, 335, 412
    slavery and, 472
metis (French-Indian children), 39
Mexican Cession, 466
Mexican War, 386, 463, 465–67, *465*, *467*, 475
Mexico, 8, 10, 23, 24, *25*, *26*, 27, *28*, 30, *31*, 32, 33, 106, 365, 466–67, 492, 493, 497
    abolition of slavery in, 461, 469
    conquering of, 24
    Cortés's exploration of, *23*
    frontier of, 460–61
    independence of, 155, 359, 460, 461
    invention of agriculture in, 6
    as obstacle to westward expansion, 329
    population decline of, 24
    slaves bound for, 98
    Texas revolt and, 461–62
Mexico City, Mexico, 25, 27, 33, 34, 37, 146, 152, 153, 466
    population of, 115
Miami, Fla., 32
Miami Confederacy, 265
Michigan, 312

Microcosm of London, The, 79
Middle Ages, 17, 20
Middle Atlantic States, in election of 1800, 287
    created by market revolution, 338, 341
    market revolution and, 341
Middle Colonies, 54, 114, 118, 120, 128–29
    elections in, *144*
    slavery in, 135, 138
middle ground, 156–57
Middle Passage, *132*
Middle States, 275
    construction of roads in, 309
"midnight judges," 291
militias:
    blacks in, 353
    Connecticut colony and, 185
Miller, Lewis (1796–1882), *318*
Mill on the Brandywine, 323
Milton, John (1608–1674), 80, *119*
Minerva, *175*
Minnesota, 9
minstrel shows, 352
missionaries, 33–34, 57, 156, 266, 460, 468
    Jesuit, 39
    Spanish, 28, *28*, 29–30, *30*, 32, 146, *152*, 154–55, *155*
Mission Carmel, *30*
Mission Dolores, 191
Mission of San Javier, *152*
Mission San José del Cabo, *155*
Mississippi, 156, 292, 312, 374
    Senate, *576*
Mississippi River, 35, 49, 156, *160*, 222, 292, 302, 307, 309, 312, *313*, 316, 354
Mississippi Valley, 9, 154, 155, 298, 311, 542
Missouri, 312
    constitution of, 357
    entrance into union of, 356–57, 435
    legislature, *367*
    slave trade in, *400*
Missouri Compromise (1820), 356–58, *357*, 366, 371, 419, 473, 478, *479*, 485–86, 496
Missouri Territory, slave population of, 356
Mitred Minuet, The, *182*
Mobile, Ala., 155, 318, *535*
Moby Dick (Melville), 352
Modern Times, N.Y., 430
Mohawks, 12, 223, 266
Mohicans, 298
Molasses Act (1733), 172, 173
monarchy, U.S. rejection of, 206, 208
Monitor, 504
Monrme, James (1758–1831), Era of Good Feelings under, 356
Monroe, James (1758–1831), 289, 356
    Monrovia named for, 435
Monroe Doctrine, 360–61, 364
    American foreign policy and, 360–61
    nationalism and, 361
    neutrality and, 361

Monrovia, Liberia, 435
Monterey, Calif., 154
Montesquieu, Baron (1689–1755), 140,
  178
Montreal, surrender of, 158
Moore, Joshua B., 535
Moors, 21, 26, 51
Mor, Antonis, *51*
moral suasion, slavery and, 439, 442
Moravian Brethren, 109, 110, 214, 219
Moravian Indians, 164
More, Thomas (1478–1535), 53, 426
Morgan, Daniel (1736–1802), 199
Morgan, J. P. (1837–1913), 529
Morgues, Jacques Le Moyne de (d.
  1588), *16*
Mormons, 336–37, *336*, *462*
  and Jesus, 336–37
  polygamy and, 337
  see also Christianity
Morrill, Justin S., 524
Morrill Land Grant College Act (1862),
  524
Morris, Gouverneur (1752–1816), 251,
  253
Morrison, Toni (1931–), 476
Morse, Samuel F. B. (1791–1872), 311–12,
  358
Morton, Sarah W., 281
*Mother and Daughter Reading, Mt. Meigs,
  Alabama* (Eickemeyer), *553*
Mott, Lucretia (1793–1880), 448, 573
"mound builders," 9, 13
mulattos, 138
Murray, Judith Sargent (1751–1820),
  281, 282
music, *137*, *524*
Muslims, 19, 20, 21, 27, *136*, 150, 295,
  295
  in Pennsylvania colony, 110
"mustee," *139*
Myers, Myer, 116
Mystic, Conn., 76
Mystic River, *76*

Napoleon I, emperor of France (1769–
  1821), 291, 292, 296, 299, 303
Napoleon III, emperor of France, 475
Narragansett Indians, *57*, 76, 298
Nast, Thomas (1840–1902), *571*, *582*,
  585
Natchez, Miss., 318
Natchez Indians, 13, 139
Nation, The, 581
National Anti-Slavery Bazaar (Boston),
  438
National Anti-Slavery Standard, *478*
national debt, 274, 370
nationalists, nationalism, 247, *248*, 297,
  303, 353–58
  Civil War and, 520–21
  John C. Calhoun and, 371–72
  Monroe Doctrine and, 361
  South and rise of, 490–91
National Woman Suffrage Association,
  573
Native Americans, 2, 3, 8, *12*, *15*, *16*, *21*,
  30, *56*, 106, 111, *114*, 121, 134, 139,
  154, 155, 162, 263–66, 315, *377*, *468*

in alliance with French, 38–39,
  104, 127
American Revolution and, 205,
  221–23, 234
in attempted conversion to
  Catholicism, 3, 28–29, *28*, 33–35,
  39
in battles with Spanish, 30, 32–33,
  152–54
California gold rush and, 471
in Carolina, 92
Cherokee Phoenix newspaper for, 351
Christianity and, 12, 32, 36, 37, 52,
  87, 154–55
and Civil War, 524–29
cliff dwellings of, *10*
coastal tribes of, 76
colonial assemblies and, 147
conflicts with colonists, 56
conflict with Jamestown of, 59–61
Declaration of Independence and,
  222
displacing of, 56
diverse societies of, 10–13
of eastern North America, 10–12
economy of, 12–13
English relations with, 54, 55–57,
  299
epidemics and, 2, 3, 5, 23, 26, 30, 32,
  39, 54, 57, 73, 76, 87, 97, 106, 155
Europeans' negative views of, 15, 38
European trade with, 57, 66, 92,
  156–57
execution of, 525, *525*
forced labor of, 6, 16, 25, 28–30,
  32–33, 52, 92, 134, 155
freedom and, 15–16, 221–23, 266
gender relations of, 14
George Washington and, 222
government of, 10, 12, 16, *17*
intermixing with Europeans by,
  26, *26*, 55
Irish compared with, 51
Jackson and, 315, 347, 367, 374–76
Jamestown and, 59–61
Jefferson's policies on, 297
John Adams and, 377
lack of technologies of, 33–34
land as viewed by, 12–13, *13*
land lost by, 615
Lewis and Clark expedition and,
  293–94
loss of Southern land of, 316
maps of tribes of, *11*, *264*
matrilineal societies of, 14
in Mexican Cession, 466–67, 469
of New England, 13
New England and, *57*
New France and, 38–39
New York colony and, 90–91
as "noble savages," 14
origins of, 6
pan-Indian identity of, 159
and Pennsylvania colony, 161
Pilgrims and, 66
Puritans and, 73–76, 87
railroads and, 524
religions of, 12, *12*, 14, *15*, 137
removal of, 374–77, *375*, 459

Seven Years' War and, 157–58
sexual division of labor of, 14, 15
slavery and, 6, 16, 25, 29–30, 87,
  94–98, 471
societies of, 2, 6
Spanish and, 106
trade among, 9–10, 13, *13*
uprisings of, 34, 87, 92, 154, 159, 191,
  221–23
U.S. treaties with, 242, 265
in Virginia, 99–100, 111
voting rights and, 144
war atrocities against, 222–23
War of 1812 and, 299–300
of western North America, 9–10
westward expansion of U.S. and,
  242–43, 297–98, 329, 459
women's roles among, 14
  see also Indian removal
Native Americans, population of, 8,
  242, 374
  in California, 154, 471
  decline of, 10, 24, 25, 28–29, 33
  in Florida, 154
  in New England, 73
nativism, 326–27, *327*, 482
Nat Turner's Rebellion, 419–21, *421*
Naturalization Act (1790), 268
Naturalization Act (1798), 285
Nauvoo, Ill., *336*, 337
Navajos, 34, 460, 529
Navajos' Long Walk, *see* Trail of Tears
Navigation Acts, 83, 88, 103, 116, *117*,
  172, 173, 186, 218
Navy, U.S.:
  African-Americans in, 353, 517
  in Mexican War, 466
  at Tripoli, 295, *295*
Nebraska, 478
Necessity, Fort, 158
"Negro Church," 413
Netherlands, 38, 39–41, 83, 88, 364
  in Anglo-Dutch war, 88
  colonization and, 2, 15, 35, 66
  freedom in, 41
  see also Dutch Empire
Neue Jerusalem, Das, *335*
Nevada, 466
Nevis, Spanish attack on, 97
New Amsterdam, 41–42, *42*, 90
  role of women in, 90
New Brunswick, Canada, Loyalists
  exiled in, 219–21
Newcastle, duke of, 144, 157
New Deal, 557
New Display of the United States, A
  (Doolittle), *285*
New England, 275, 322, 392
  building of roads in, 309
  Dominion of, 103
  in election of 1796, 284
  in election of 1800, 287
  in election of 1804, 296
  in election of 1824, 361, 364
  Indian of, *57*
  inducement to settle, 53–54
  industrialization of, 321–23
  Puritan emigration to, 66
  shipbuilding in, 88

1675 map of, *102*
  trade with West Indies, 77
  voting rights in, 353
New England colonies, 2, 54, 64–70,
  103, 104, 110, 123, 156, 164, 194,
  226
  Atlantic trade of, 128–29, *129*
  division in, 70–78
  economy of, 76–78
  elections in, 144
  hierarchical society of, 69
  map of, *72*
  Native Americans in, 13
  population growth of, 120
  population of, 87
  slavery in, 135–36
  social equality in, 77
  triangular trade of, 130–31
New England Courant, 147
Newfoundland, 21, 23, 35, 51, 158
New France, 35, 38–39, *40*, 44, 106, 146
  Indians and, 38–39
  population of, 38
New Hampshire colony, 116, 178
  chartering of, 78
New Harmony, Ind., 429
New Haven, Conn., 71
New Jersey:
  constitution of, 209–10, 228
  election of 1796 and, 284
  slaves in, 228
  voting rights in, 351
New Jersey colony, 54, 93, 110, 114–15
  slaves in, 136
  Washington's army in, 195, *196*
New Jersey Dutch Reformed, 150
New Jersey Plan, 249
New Lanark, Scotland, 429
New Laws, 29
New Lights, 150
New Mexico, 10, *10*, 33–35, *35*, 37, 39,
  49, 146, 152, 154, *154*, 466, 469
  population of, 153, 460
  Texas invasion of, 524
New Netherland, 35, *40*, 49, 88, 90
  freedom in, 41–45
  population of, 41–42
  religious freedom in, 41
  seal of, *43*
  slavery in, 41
  uprisings in, 43
New Orleans, La., 155–56, 292, 294,
  350, 353, *394*, 577
  battle of, 300, *350*, 361
  black community in, 406, 417, 543
  Caribbean heritage of, 393
  in Civil War, 511, *512*
  cotton trade in, 393, *394*
  French heritage of, 393
  population of, 294, 393
  Reconstruction riot in, 569
  slave auctions in, 391
  slave rebellion in, 419
  slave trade in, 318, *395*
  sugar trade in, 393
News from America, 76
New Spain, *31*, 152
newspapers, *see* press
New Sweden, 43

New Testament, 16, 17
Newton, Isaac (1642–1727), 149, 217–18
New World, 4–47, 51
  commerce in, 83, 88
  conquering of, 23–24
  dangers of, 54
  education in, 25
  peoples of, 8–16, 23–24
  settling of, 7
  slavery in, 3, 5, 25, 94–98, 130–32
  women and, 26, 38, 39
New York, 10, 12, 39, 158, 242, 287
  constitution of, 212
  demands return of slaves, 227
  election of 1796 and, 284
  legislature, 328
  map of, 157
  Mormons in, 336, 337
  population of, 358
  religious liberty in, 212
  slavery in, 228
  U.S. Constitution and, 257, 259
  voting rights in, 209, 352
New York, N.Y., 39, 73, 90–91, 114, 116, 139, 176, 211, 228, 281, 309, 311, 321, 326, 392
  African-Americans in, 339
  boycotts of Britain in, 179
  as capital of U.S., 273
  as country's financial center, 480
  population of, 115
  population of slaves in, 135–36, 228
  religious diversity in, 211
  slave uprising in, 138–39
New York colony, 2, 54, 87, 90–91, 103, 104, 109, 144, 156, 171
  African-Americans lose jobs in, 90
  American Revolution and, 207
  anti-British rebellion in, 104
  assembly in, 145
  British boycott in, 183
  growth of, 114–15
  Howe's army occupies, 195
  Loyalists in, 218–19, 220
  Native Americans and, 87, 90–91
  politics in, 143
  population of, 90
  slavery in, 135, 138–39
  slave trade in, 129
  Stamp Act Congress and, 175
  Vermont split from, 178
  views on independence of, 185–86
  Washington's army in, 194–95, 196
New York Evening Post, 445
New York Harbor, 39, 129
New York Herald, 350, 351, 352
New York House of Refuge, The, 433
New York Illustrated, 535
New York State militia for service in the Civil War, 509
New York Sun, 350
New York Times, 325, 523
New York Tribune, 449, 581
New Zealand, 347
Nicaragua, 493
Nicholas I, czar of Russia, 300–302
Ninety-Five Theses (Luther), 28
Ninigret II, 57
Ninth Amendment, 259

Noble, Harriet L., 332
No More Grinding the Poor–But Liberty and the Rights of Man, 342
"Non-Freeholders," 348
Non-Intercourse Act (1809), 296
Norfolk, Va., 187
Norman's Chart of the Lower Mississippi River (1858), 396
North, in election of 1824, 361
North, Frederick (1732–1792), 181, 182
North America, 2, 6, 7, 8, 9, 44, 51, 89, 201
  Dutch in, 43
  early population of, 24, 32
  English colonization of, 48–85
  exploration of, 30–32
  Indians of, 9–14, 11
  Irish emigration to, 55
  map of east coast of, 108
  map of, 153
  shifting borderlands and boundaries in, 44–45
Northampton County, Pa., 183
North Briton, 180
North Carolina, 51, 240, 288, 374
  U.S. Constitution and, 257, 259
  voting rights in, 210, 348, 352, 362
  women and, 232
North Carolina colony, 114, 134
  in American Revolution, 199
  French in, 156
  Loyalists in, 218–19, 220
  Moravian Brethren in, 214
  Regulators in, 177
Northup, Solomon (1808–1863?), 407–8, 414, 417
Northwest Ordinance (1787), 245, 315, 358, 473, 485
Northwest Passage, 35, 39, 293
Notes on the State of Virginia (Jefferson), 212, 268
Nott, Josiah C. (1804–1873), 442
Nova Scotia, Canada, 35, 158
  as haven for former slaves, 227, 227, 228, 302
  Loyalists exiled to, 219–21
Nueces River, 465, 468
nullification crisis, 371–74, 371, 372, 375, 381
nurses, in Civil war, 530, 530

Oath of a Freeman, 70
Of Course He Wants to Vote the Democratic Ticket, 584
Oglethorpe, James (1696–1785), 135
O-Grab-Me, or, the American Snapping-Turtle, 296
Ohio, 242, 312, 315–16
  120th Infantry of, 503
  population of, 315
Ohio Company (1750s), 157–58
Ohio Company (1780s), 245
Ohio River, 35, 156–57, 307, 315–16, 319, 354
Ohio River Valley, 9, 91, 156–57, 157, 222–23, 245, 265, 293, 311
  Indians of, 159
Ohio Valley Indians, 221–22
Old Lights, 150

Old Northwest, 302, 314, 315, 319, 374
Old Plantation, The (Rose), 137
Old Plantation Home, The (Currier and Ives), 581
Old Southwest, 313
Old State House Bell, 436, 441
Olive Branch Petition (1775), 186
Oliver, Andrew (1706–1774), 171, 175
Oliver family, 118
Olmsted, Frederick Law (1822–1903), 415
Oñate, Juan de (ca. 1551–ca. 1626), 33
"On Civil Disobedience" (Thoreau), 465
Oneida community, 427–28
Oneida County, New York, 334
Oneida people, 162
Oneidas, 12, 222
Onondagas, 12
Ontario, 39
"On the Equality of the Sexes" (Murray), 281, 282
Opechancanough, 60
Orange, Fort, 39
Oration on the Beauties of Liberty (Allen), 183
Ordinance of 1784, 243
Ordnance Bureau, Confederate, 508
Oregon Territory, 294, 314
  blacks barred from, 339
  Great Britain and, 459, 462
  migration to, 459, 462
  U.S.-British dispute over, 464–65
Osceola, 376
Ostend Manifesto, 492
O'Sullivan, John L. (1813–1895), 329, 469
Otis, Harrison Gray (1725–1783), 286
Otis, Harrison James (1725–1783), 173
Otis, James (1725–1783), 175, 224, 232
Ottawa Indians, 159
Outer Banks, N.C., 12
"outwork" system, 321
Ovando, Nicolás de (ca. 1451–ca. 1511), 21
Overseer Doing His Duty, An, 127
Owen, Robert (1771–1858), 429, 429, 447
Owen, Robert Dale (1801–1877), 429
Owenites, 429–30

Pacific islands, and Native Americans, 6
Pacific Northwest, 803
Pacific Ocean, 23, 24, 35, 294
pacifism:
  abolitionists and, 439
  Quaker, 93
Paine, Thomas (1737–1809), 167, 186, 191, 195, 206, 207, 208, 209, 225, 280
  Common Sense and, 186–87, 189, 191
Pale, 51
Palmerston, Henry John Temple, Viscount, 533
Panama, 23
Panic of 1819, 355
Panic of 1837, 380
Papacy, 50, 52

Papists, 113
Paradise Lost (Milton), 119
Paraguay, 152, 506
Paris, Treaty of (1763), 158
Paris, Treaty of (1783), 200, 200, 219–21, 223
Paris Commune, 506
Parliament, British, 49, 80, 103, 109, 140, 147, 192, 263
  army of, 81
  Bill of Rights and, 103
  Charles I's conflict with, 80
  colonists' desire for representation in, 173, 224
  first Navigation Act and, 83
  forces in Maryland colony, 82–83
  taxation on America by, 171, 172–76, 174, 187–90
parties, political, 366, 367–69, 478–79
  newspapers and, 368, 369
  origins of U.S., 273, 277–78
  patronage and, 368
  spoils system and, 368
  views of Van Buren of, 365–66
  see also specific parties
Paterson, N.J.:
  industrial city planned for, 274
  Thomas Rodgers and, 338
Pat Lyon at the Forge, 337
patronage, political parties and, 368
"patroons," 43
Patuxet Indians, 66
Paul III, Pope (1468–1549), 29
Pawtucket, R.I., 321, 322
Paxton Boys, march on Philadelphia by, 161
Peace of Paris (1763), 159, 160
Peale, Charles Willson (1741–1827), 233, 247
Pearl Harbor, 510
Pemberton, John C. (1814–1881), 539
peninsulares, 26
Penn, Thomas, 114
Penn, William (1644–1718), 92–94, 92, 93, 111, 114, 161
Penn family, 114, 118, 145
Penn school, 541–42
Pennsylvania, 12, 228
  black disenfranchisement in, 363
  coat of arms of, 210
  constitution of, 208, 208, 209, 209, 215
  and election of 1796, 284
  in election of 1858, 489
  religious laws in, 371
  voting rights in, 352
  Whiskey Rebellion and, 278
Pennsylvania, University of, 441
Pennsylvania Abolition Society, 288
Pennsylvania Assembly, 149
Pennsylvania colony, 2, 110, 110, 111, 112, 114, 118, 121, 135, 138, 156, 157, 158, 161, 162
  American Revolution and, 207–8, 219
  assembly in, 145
  elections in, 144
  establishment of, 93
  freemen in, 94

Pennsylvania colony (*continued*)
  government in, 93–94, 144
  Holy Experiment of, 161
  immigration to, 54, 109
  Loyalists in, 219
  Mennonite emigration to, 113
  Native Americans and, 161
  population of, 111
  religious freedom in, 103, 110, 210
  social order in, 93
  standard of living in, 115
  views on independence of, 185–86
Pennsylvania Gazette, 147
Pennsylvania Magazine, 191
"penny press," 350
People's Convention, 348
People the Best Governors, The (anon.), 208
Pequot Indians, 76, *76*, 222, 298
Pequot War, 76
perfectionism, 433
Perry, Matthew (1794–1858), 472
Perry, Oliver H. (1785–1819), 299
Peru, 8, 23–24, *29*, 30, 32, *130*, 359
"pet banks," 379, 381
Petersburg, Battle of, 540, 545
Petitions of Slaves to the Massachusetts Legislature, 231
Petley, Robert, 227
Philadelphia, Pa., 10, 115–16, *115*, 146, 158, *207*, 217, 322, 342, *368*, *522*
  in American Revolution, 195–97
  boycott of Britain in, 179, 183
  Constitutional celebrations in, 239
  Constitution ratified in, 239
  population of, 115–16
  shipbuilding in, 239
  skilled workers of, 115
  slaves in, 136
  trade with West Indies, 116
Philadelphia Mechanic's Advocate, 351
Philadelphia Society for the Promotion of Agriculture, *278*
Philadelphia State House, *249*
Philip, King (Wampanoag chief; d. 1676), 87, 377
Philip II, king of Spain (1556–1598), 32
Philippines, 23, 24
  returned to Spain, 158
Philipse, Frederick (1626–1702), 90
Philipse family, 177
Phillips, Wendell (1811–1884), 445, 546
Phillipsburgh Proclamation, 227
photography, in Civil War, 507
Pickett, George E. (1825–1875), 539
Pickett's Charge, 539
Pic-Nic Party, A (Cole), *331*
Piedmont, 133
Pierce, Franklin (1804–1869), 477–78, 479, 484, 493
Pierce, George (1811–1884), 521
Pietists, 110
Pike, James, *185*
Pike, James S. (1811–1882), 582
Pilgrims, 41, 66, *66*
Pillow, Fort, 519, 547
Pinchback, Pinckney B. S. (1837–1921), 575
Pinckney, Charles C. (1746–1825), 252, 296

Pinckney, Thomas (1750–1823), 284
Pinckney's Treaty (Treaty of San Lorenzo) (1795), 292
pirates, 32, 35
  Barbary Coast, 95
  British, 98
Pitt, William (1708–1778), 158, 159
Pius IX, Pope (1792–1878), *483*
Pizarro, Francisco (ca. 1475–1541), 23–24
Plains of Abraham, 158
Plantation Burial (Antrobus), *414*
Planter, 576
planter class, 395–96
planters, plantations, 51, 82, 118, *137*, 139, *292*, 316–18, 347, 395–96, 407, 408, 475, 542, 574, 577, *581*
  American slavery based on, 95–96
  cotton, 316–18, *409*, 463–64
  as dominating South, 393, 394
  emancipated slaves and, *555*
  and national affairs, 385
  post-Civil War, 556, 557, 558–60
  Protestants and, 82
  rice, 132, 408
  slavery on, 6, 20, 92–93, 118, 134–35
  sugar, 96–97, *96*, 132, 408, 419, 473
  tobacco, 118, 133
  of the West Indies, 106
Planters Bank of Savannah, 379
Pleasants, John H. (1797–1846), 396
Plumer, William (1759–1850), 356
"plundering time", in Maryland colony, 82
Plymouth Colony, 66, 68, 104
Pocahontas (ca. 1596–1617), 56, 59–60, *59*
Pocanets, 298
Poems on Slavery (Longfellow), 498
Polk, James K. (1795–1849), 381, 414, 463–65, 485
  as slaveholder, 463
Polling, The (Hogarth), *142*
Ponce de León, Juan (1460–1521), 31
Pontiac (ca. 1720–1769), 159, 163
Pontiac's Rebellion, 159, 161, 163
Poor Richard's Almanack, 148
Pope, John (1822–1892), 509
Popé (d. 1688), 34
"popery," *see* Catholics, Catholicism
"Popery Truly Displayed" (Las Casas), 52
popular sovereignty, 473, 478, 488, 493
population:
  of African-Americans, 229, *267*
  in American colonies, 2–3, 61, 106–7, 132–33
  of Barbados, 97
  black, of English Caribbean, 97
  of Boston, 115
  of California, 154–55, 460, 469, 471
  of Civil War border states, 513
  of Confederacy, 504
  of early South America, 24
  of England, 52, 54
  of Florida, 154
  of France compared with England, 54
  of free blacks, *403*, 406, *406*

of immigrants, 325
of Indians, 23, 25, 111
of Indians, decline in, 10, 24, 28–29, 33
of Jews in America, 503
of London, 140
of Los Angeles, 155, 768
of Louisiana, 156
of Massachusetts, 67
of Mexican Cession, 466
of Mexico, 24
of Mexico City, Mexico, 115
of New England, 87, 121
of New England Indians, 73
of New France, 38
of New Mexico, 33, 34, 154, 460
of New Netherland, 43
of New Orleans, 294, 393
of New York, 90, 358
of New York City, 115
of Pennsylvania, 114
of Philadelphia, 116
of San Francisco, 470
of slaves, 101, 132–33, 135, *135*, 154, 223, 228, 229, 239, 289, 294, 356, 372, 385, 390, *392*, *393*, 516
of Southern Indians, 374
of Spanish America, 26
of Texas, 154, 461
of Union, 504
of United States, 239, 307, *316*
of urban centers, 321
of Virginia, 61, 358
of West, 297
in Western states, *316*
West Indies English, 96
west of Appalachian Mountains, 315
world, *25*
Populist movement, 257,
Porter, James (b. 1828), 551
Portia (Abigail Adams), 205
Portrait of John and Elizabeth Lloyd Cadwalader and Their Daughter Anne (Peale), *233*
Port Royal, S.C., 32, *139*
Port Royal Island, *541*
Portsmouth, N.H., 78
Portugal, *19*, *20*, 22, 27, 49, 97, 949
  loses Brazil to Dutch, 41
  navigation of, 18–19, *19*
  and West Africa, 19–20
Poverty Point, 9
Powhatan (ca. 1550–1618), 59, *60*, 76
Presbyterians, 109, 110, 211
  American Revolution and, 214
  in Great Awakening, 150
Presidential Reconstruction, 565
presidents, presidency, U.S., 248, 249–50
  veto power of, 379, 567–68
  see also specific presidents
presidios, 154
press, 279, *466*, 469, 556
  "alternative," 350–51
  attack on Washington by, 280
  circulation of, 350
  in Civil War, 506–7, 509, 523
  colonial, 146–48
  Democratic, 369, 382, 523

in election of 1830, 368
growth of, 279, 350
politics and, 368, 369
during Reconstruction, 581–82
Republican (Jeffersonian), 280, 285
Republican (modern), 509, 523
rise of, 350
and Sea Islands, 541
sensationalism in, 350
slavery and antislavery, 400, 419, 420, 441–42, 443, 444, *452*, 473
women's rights and, 449, 452
prices, control of, 217, *217*
primogeniture, 122, 217
printing press, *64*, 68
prisons, 433
  debt and, 342
private property, 426
  shunned by Shakers, 427
  in Utopian societies, 429
Problem We All Live With, The (Rockwell), *299*
Procession of Victuallers, *368*
Proclamation of 1763, 159–61, 173, 221
progressivism, 387
Prohibition, 633, 734–35, *734*, *735*, 760, 764, 766, 774, 782–83, *782*, *783*, 789, 793, 805, 814, 835
Promised Land, The–The Grayson Family (Jewett), *470*
propaganda, in World War I, 731–32, *742*
Propagation Society, The - More Free than Welcome, *483*
Prophetstown, 298
Proposition 13 (California), 1038
Proposition 14 (California), 980
Proposition 187 (California), 1080
proprietorship, 2, 69, 92, 103, 104, 118, 135
  Maryland as, 63
Prospective Scene in the City of Oaks, A, *580*
Prostrate State, The (Pike), 582
Protestant Association, 104
Protestant-Catholic-Jew (Herberg), 941
Protestants, *51*, 149, 164, 370, 429, 432, 446, 468, 469, 633, 710, 742, 784, 788, 827, 914, 940, *941*, 965, 1034, 1036
  and Al Smith, 793
  in American colonies, 101, 104, 109, 110, *110*
  in Amsterdam, 41
  Dissenters, and, 102–3
  Dissenters and, 71
  in England, 50–51, 80, 83, 140
  evangelical, 483, 1034, 1036
  French, 32, 38
  fundamentalist, 782–83
  immigration to South Carolina of, 134
  Indians and, 3, 28
  and Irish immigrants, 326
  in Maryland colony, 64, 82, 101, 104
  modernism and, 782–83
  in New York colony, 42, 91
  planter class, 82
  Prohibition and, 734

slavery and, 137
social reform and, 632–33
and spread of Protestantism, 51–52
tax support of, 213
voting rights and, 210–11
women preachers allowed by, *338*
see also Christianity; *specific denominations*
protests, against Vietnam War, 926
Providence, R.I., 683
Prussia, 158, 364
public housing, 939, *939*
Publick Occurrences, Both Foreign and Domestick, 147
public opinion, opinion polls, 1020, 1036, 1084, 1085, 1096, 1107, 1108, 1111–12
public relations and, 773, 863, 878, 879
Public Opinion (Lippmann), 773
public relations, 732, 739, 770
and public opinion, 773, 863, 878, 879
see also Bernays, Edward
Public Utilities Act, California, 702
Public Whipping of Slaves in Lexington, Missouri, in 1856, A, 410
Public Works Administration (PWA), 810–11, *810*
"Publius," 254
Puccini, Giacomo (1858–1924), 472
Puck, *595, 599, 620, 665, 697*
Pueblo Bonita, 10, *10*
Pueblo Indians, 10, 14, 33–35, 102, 123, 152, 460
Pueblo Revolt, 33–35, *34*, 37
pueblos, 10
Puerto Rico, 31, 667, 671, 672, 674, 743–44, 1003–4
as commonwealth, 673
migration from, 939, *940*, 1072
U.S. acquisition of, 640, 665, 668, 669, *669*, 719
Pujo, Arsène (1861–1939), 768–69
Pulitzer, Joseph (1847–1911), 666
Pulitzer Prize, *1018*
Pullman, Ill., strike in, 644, *645*, 662, 691
Punch, *514*
Pure Food and Drug Act (1906), 682, 710
Puritans, Puritanism, 43, 53, 65–67, 104–5, 172, 432
beliefs of, 64–65, 67–70
emigration to New England, 65
families of, 67–68, *68*
Indians and, 73–76, 87, 1079
intolerance in, 70, 81–82
liberties of, 70
rise of, 64–66
sermons of, 65
slavery and, 69, 1079
women's role in, 67–68, 77
worldly success as viewed by, 65, 78
Putting the Screws on Him, 710
PWA, *see* Public Works Administration
pyramids, Egyptian, 9

quadrant, 18
Quaker Meeting, A, 94
Quaker Oats Company, 594, *988*
Quakers, 42, 81–82, 92–94, *94*, 105, 110, 129–30, 143, 161, 219, 225, 233
Gabriel's Rebellion and, 289
liberty of, 93–94
as pacifists, 93
in Pennsylvania Assembly, 145
slavery repudiated by, 93, 435, 446, 447
Quayle, Dan (1947–), 1049
Quebec, 35, 49, 158, 174, *174*
Quebec, Canada, 221
Quebec Act (1774), 181, *182*, 211
Queen Anne's War, 157
Quicksilver Messenger Service, *997*
Quito, Ecuador, 25
"quitrents," 63

Rabelais, François (ca. 1494–1553?), 779
race, racism, 839, 870, 871, 878, 880–81, 903, 906, 910, 913, *974*, 975, 982, 988, 1000, 1049, 1081
Americanism vs., 839, 870, 983
Andrew Johnson and, 565
and class, 352–53
Hollywood and, 903
and Japanese-Americans, 761, 874–77, *874*, 875–77
lack of opportunities and, 338–39
law and, 787–88
Nixon and, 1017–18
as pillar of slavery, 398
and post–World War II civil rights, 909–10
progressivism and, 738
as "race problem," 738, 744
Reconstruction and, 579
riots and, 338, *658*, 871, 877, 985–86, *985*, 1078, 1122
social construction of, 788
in South Africa, 902
theories of, 469
by U.S. government, 835
see also segregation
Races and Racism (Benedict), 870
radar, 859, 930
radiation, 884, 912, *912*, 949
Radical Division, Justice Department, 751
Radical Reconstruction, 564–78
Radical Republicans, 514, 540, 543, 566–67, *566*, 568, 581, 642
radio, 760, 764, 766, 767, 783, 863, 864
FDR and, 823, *823*
fundamentalism on, 819
religion and, 819, *819*, 940
railroad, transcontinental, 472, 610
Railroad Administration, 731
railroads, 168, 308, 311–12, *312*, 321, 325, 379, 407, *459*, *480*, *481*, 561, 593, 596, 604, 620, 685, 688, 691, 701–3, 713, 714, 775
agriculture and, 605, 640
in Civil War, 504, 507, 524, 533
Great Depression and, 797
Indians and, 614–16

labor and, 644–45
land granted to, 592, 603, *603*, *604*
lobbyists of, 620
and mileage built, *593*
network of, *594*
in Northwest, 480
Populists and, 642
prison labor and, 648
protests against, 622, 623
rate discrimination and, 627
rates regulated, 710
in Reconstruction, 577
segregation and, 652
Socialist party and, 713
Southern, 393, 395
strikes, 628–29, *629*, 633, 773, 908
transcontinental, 478, 494, 524, 585, 593
trusts, 596, 709
westward expansion and, 606, 614–15
Rainey, Joseph H., *575*
Rainsborough, Thomas (ca. 1610–1648), 80
Raleigh, N.C., 971, *973*
Raleigh, Walter (1554–1618), *12*, 51, 52
Ramsay, David (1749–1815), 260
Randolph, A. Philip (1889–1979), 878, *921*, 974, 986, *986*
Randolph, Edmund (1753–1813), 267
Randolph, John (1773–1833), 187, 297, 396
Randolph, Richard, 228, 406
Rankin, Jeanette (1880–1973), 706, 733, 853
Rapp, George (1757–1847), 429
Rapp-Coudert Committee, 841
Rauschenberg, Robert, *1011*
Rauschenbusch, Walter (1861–1918), 633
Raynal, Guillaume Thomas, 30
RCA Victor, 766
Readjustor movement, 651
"re-Africanization," 136
Reagan, Nancy (1921–2016), *981*, 1042, *1046*
Reagan, Ronald (1911–2004), 870, 914, *981*, *1015*, 1033, 1038, 1039–49, *1039*, *1042*, 1056, 1062, 1092, 1104, 1116
background of, 1039
Cold War and, 1046–47, 1049
conservatives and, 1045–46
in election of 1980, 926, 1039
Gorbachev and, 1048–49, *1049*
as host of *General Electric Theater*, 935
inequality under, 1044–45, 1049
Iran-Contra affair and, 1048, 1049
labor and, 1043–44
legacy of, 1049
Reaganomics, 1042–44
Reagan Revolution, 1039–49
real estate:
deals, 1044
speculation, 1044
reaper, 319, *482*
Reason, Charles L. (1818–1893), 443
Reasonableness of Christianity, The (Locke), 149

Rebel without a Cause (movie), 953
recall, 702
recessions:
of 1974–75, 1028
of 1991, 1055, 1064
of 2001, 1100
of 2007, 1107, 1111, *1112*, 1119–20
of 2008–9, 1119
African-Americans and, 1120–21
recessions, economic, of, 1990–1991, 1062
recessions, Reaganomics and, 1044
Recollections of Harriet L. Noble, 332
reconquista, 21
Reconstruction, 386–87, 389, 415, 518, 542–43, 547, 550–87, *553*, *554*, *564*, *583*, 588, 614, 625, 642, *744*, 1083, 1084
African-Americans in, 386–87, 552–60, 561, 567–68, *568*, 570–72, *571*, 574–76, 648, 649, 650–51, 652–54, *744*, 761, 848, 908
battle over, 565–66
black officeholders during, 575–76, *576*
"black supremacy" during, 579
Johnson's policies in, 558, 564–69, *567*, 568–69
Ku Klux Klan in, 652, 745, *785*
overthrow of, 579–85
public schools in, 577, *578*, 579
radical, 564–78
railroads built in, 578
Redeemers and, 648
segregation in, 652–54
violence in, 579–80
white farmers in, 560–61, *560*
women's rights and, 572
see also Presidential Reconstruction; Radical Reconstruction; Second Reconstruction
Reconstruction Act (1867), 568–69, 574
Reconstruction Finance Corporation, 797
Red Cross, 877, *877*
Red Dawn (movie), *1047*
Redeemers, 584, 648
redemptioners, 109
see also indentured servitude
Red Jacket (1750–1830), *263*
Red Line Agreement, 778
red-lining, *835*
Red Menace, The (movie), *902*, 903
Red Monday, 1006
Red Power, 1004
Red Scare, 258, 751–52, 763, 793
Red Square, *1049*
Red Sticks (Creeks), 300, 376
Reed, Esther (1746–1780), 232
Reed, Joseph (1741–1785), 232
Reed, Philip, 459
Reeder, Andrew H. (1807–1864), 484
Reedy, William M., 698
referendum, initiative and, 702
reform, 424–57, 566, 705, 713–14, 841–42
freedom and, 432–33
in Gilded Age, 622–26, 632–33
and immigrants, 739–40, *743*

reform (*continued*)
  maternalist, 707–8, 822
  middle class and, 630
  and Prohibition, 734–35, *734*
  Protestants and, 632–33
  religion and, 430–31, 632–33
  segregation and, 745
  sexual freedom and, 771
  temperance and, 431, 633
  utopian communities and, 426–30
  World War I and, 727
Reform Act (1884), 620
Reformation, 28, 50, 51, 64
Reform Bureau, 632
reform schools, *433*
Refregier, Anton, *910*
Regents of the University of California v. Bakke, 1019, 1105
Regulators, 177
regulatory power, 773
  rise of U.S. government, 710, 808, 828, 841, 983, 984
Rehnquist, William (1924–2005), 1106
Reid, Wallace (1892–1923), 779
religion, 719, 760, 1080–81, 1086–87
  African, 137
  of African-Americans, rise in, 553, *555*
  and attempted conversions of Indians, 3, 12, 28–30, *28*, 32, 33–35, 39
  Bible and, 28, 64, 68, 70
  Bible Commonwealth and, 69, 70, 77, 104
  Civil War and, 521–22, *522*
  Cold War and, 940–41
  as conflict source, 1105, *1106*
  counterculture and, 998–99, *999*
  divisiveness of, 1105, *1106*
  Enlightenment and, 148–50
  and founding of Connecticut, 71
  fundamentalist, 782–84
  in Maryland, 63–64, 82
  media and, 819, *819*
  missionaries and, 28–29, *28*, *30*, 32, 34, 39, 57, 146, 154–55, 156, 266
  nationalism and, 1129
  Native American, 12, 14, *15*, 137
  and Prohibition, 734
  radio and, 819, *819*
  reform and, 430–31
  Salem witch trials and, 105–6
  and separation of church and state, 110, 167, 212–15
  social reform and, 632–33
  temperance and, 633
  Thomas Jefferson and, 149, 211–12, 213–14
  witchcraft and, 70, 105–6, *106*
  see also Great Awakening, Great Awakening, Second; *specific denominations*
religious freedom, 883
  in American colonies, 2, 3, 103, 109
  in Carolina, 92
  communism and, 940–41
  in early U.S., 149, 210–15, 325
  in England, 80–81
  First Amendment and, 258, 259

Four Freedoms and, 847, 862, 887
Fourteenth Amendment and, 789
fundamentalism vs., 783
in Maryland colony, 63–64, 104
Muslims and, *1106*
in New England colonies, 2, 104
in New Netherland, 41–43
in New York City, *211*
in New York colony, 90, 91
in Pennsylvania, 208
in Pennsylvania colony, 93
in Rhode Island, 71
September 11 terrorist attacks and, 1092
Universal Declaration of Human Rights and, 905
voting rights and, 211–14
see also diversity; pluralism
religious right, 1034–35, 1039
  see also Christian Right
"Remember the Maine," *666*
Remington, Frederic (1861–1909), *618*, *668*
rendition, Bush administration and, 1100
Reno, Janet (1938–), 1056
Reno, Milo, 796
repartimiento system, 29
"Report on Economic Conditions in the South," 841
Report on Manufactures (Hamilton), 274
reproductive rights, 1002, 1008, 1010, 1116
republicanism, 141–42, 143
Republicanism, Christian, 214–15
republican motherhood, 233–34, 339
Republican Party (Jeffersonian), 277, 280, 284, 287, 299, 353, 356–57, 366
  in election of, 1824, 364
  in Missouri Compromise, 358
  and national bank, 169
  platform of, 279
  press of, 280, 285
Republican Party (modern), 386–87, 486–92, 515, 531, 532, 533, 620, 621, *623*, *624*, 631, 643, 646–47, 773–74, 787, 835, 838, 841, 852, 860, 897, 911, 912, 915, 917, 918, 944, 946–47, 978, 981, 992, 994, 996, 1016, 1030, 1038, 1049, 1058, 1061, 1065, 1101, 1107, 1114, 1115, 1117, 1125–26, *1126*
  as anti-immigrant, 1080, 1091
  as antislavery, 483–84, *495*
  black members of, 651
  black voters and, 574
  in campaign of 1960, 964, 965
  Christianity aligned with, 1015, 1080–81
  Clinton and, 1055
  conservatives in, 948
  Contract with America, 1057
  corruption in, 621
  Eisenhower and, 944–47
  in election of 1896, 646–47, *647*
  in election of 1928, 793
  in election of 1936, 827

in election of 1946, 908
in election of 1952, 944, 945–46, *945*
in election of 1968, 1011
in election of 1972, 1024
in election of 1992, 1055
in election of 2000, 1084
and Equal Rights Amendment, 1039
high tariff supported by, 622
Indians and, 615
industrialists and, 629
Johnson's impeachment and, 569–70
Liberal, 581–82, 625
liberal reformers' split from, 625
and Lincoln's nomination, 494
in 1916 elections, 727
in 1920s, 773–74
1964 convention of, 980, 1039
1984 convention of, *1015*, *1039*
1992 convention of, 1055, 1080
North and, 647
press of, 509, 523
in Reconstruction, 556, 564–70, 574, 577, 579, 581, 582–84
rise of, 479, 480–85, 635
South and, 651
Soviet Union and, 848
and Supreme Court, 815
Taft and, 712
Truman Doctrine and, 894
YAF and, 981
  see also Radical Republicans; *specific elections and campaigns*
Republic Steel, 818
Rerum Novarum, 689
reservations, Indian, 614–17, *616*, *618*, 700, 786, 832, 874, 1004
Resettlement Administration, 812–13, *814*
Residence of David Twining, The (Hicks), *121*
Resolution of Regret (2012), 657
Return from Toil, The (Sloan), *687*
Revels, Hiram (1822–1901), 575, *575*, *577*
Revenue Act (1767), 173
Revere, Paul (1735–1818), *141*, 179, *180*, 184
reverse discrimination, 985, 1019
"Revolution of 1800," 288, 289
Rhineland, 752, 849
Rhine River, 109, 882
Rhode Island, 247, *349*
  Dorr War in, 348
  Narragansetts of, *57*
  U.S. Constitution and, 257, *259*
  voting rights in, 348, 362
Rhode Island colony, 71, 73, 81, 103, 110, 194, 210, 216
  government in, 144
  religious freedom in, 71
  slave trade in, 128
Rhodes Scholar, *1020*
rice, 128, *408*, 649
  slavery and, 134–35, 138
  in Southern colonies, 92, 118, 132, 134–35
Rice, Thomas D., *352*
Rice Culture on the Ogeechee, *409*
Richardson, Elliot (1920–1999), 1025

Richmond, Va., 289, 362, 508, 509, 536, *544*, 545
  population of slaves in, 289
Richmond *Enquirer*, 400
Richmond Times-Dispatch, 827
Richmond Whig, 396
Rickey, Branch (1881–1965), 909–10
Ridge, Major (ca. 1771–1839), 297
Ridgely, Fort, 525
Riesman, David (1909–2002), 952
rifles, in Civil War, 505
"rights of Englishmen," 79–80
Rights of Man (Paine), 280
right to work laws, 908
Riis, Jacob (1849–1914), *601*, 602, 1102
Rincon Center, *910*
Rindisbacher, Peter (1806–1834), *298*
Rio Grande, 106, 152, 465, 468
Riot in Philadelphia, 327
riots:
  draft, *532*
  food, 535
  race, 338, *658*, 748, *748*, 871, 877, 985–86, *985*, 1078, 1122
  Reconstruction, 569
  zoot suit, 874
Riots in New York, The: The Mob Lynching a Negro in Clarkson Street, 532
Ritchie, Thomas (1778–1854), 366
"River, The," 1028
River Rouge auto plant, 765, 935
River Rouge Plant (Sheeler), 769
Riverside Church, 782
R.J. Reynolds Tobacco Company, 1045
roads, 309, *310*, 353–54, 764, 810, *810*, 811, 819, 821
  toll, 309
Road to Serfdom, The (Hayek), 869
Roanoke Island, Va., 51
Roaring Twenties, 764
robber barons, 599, 942
Roberts, Bishop, *117*
Roberts, John (1955–), 1106
Roberts, Lemuel (b. 1751), 184–85
Robertson, Pat (1930–), 1080
Robeson, Paul (1898–1976), 839, 881–82, *882*, 920
Robin Hood, 916
Robinson, Alfred (1806–1895), 461
Robinson, Bill, 791
Robinson, Earl (1910–1991), 838
Robinson, Jackie (1919–1972), 909–10, *909*
Robinson, Jo Ann (1912–1992), 960, 974
Rochester, N.Y., 309, *696*
rock-and-roll, 953, 998
Rockefeller, John D. (1839–1937), 529, 599, 664, 682, 696, 712, 768, 782
Rockefeller, Nelson (1908–1979), 849, 1029
Rockwell, Norman (1894–1978), 847, 848, *849*, 863, 865, 866, 871, 904, *910*, 929
Rocky Mountains, 152
Rocky Mountains, Lander's Peak (Bierstadt), *610*
Rödel, Peter, 343
Rodgers, Thomas (1792–1856), 338
Roe v. Wade, 1008, 1036, *1037*
Rogers, Will (1879–1935), 774–75

Rolfe, John (1585–1622), 56, 60, 61
"Roll on, Columbia" (Guthrie), 803
Romania, 893
Rome, ancient, 25, *91*
  slavery in, 95, 398, 459, *460*
Rommel, Erwin (1891–1944), 856
Romney, Mitt (1947–):
  "47 percent" remark by, 1127
  Bain Capital and, 1126
  Massachusetts health-care plan and, 1126
  in 2012 election and campaign, 1126–28
Romney campaign spending, 1128
Roosevelt, Eleanor (1884–1962), 829, *829*, 834, 905, 906, *906*
Roosevelt, Franklin D. (1882–1945), 649, 679, 751, 761, *806*, *807*, 819, *823*, 824, 830, 835, 837, 848–49, 853, 858, 859, *868*, 878, 881, 884–85, *885*, 892, 894, 910, 917, 926, 984, 1015, 1042, 1058, 1084, 1092
  antilynching law and, 834, 835
  Atlantic Charter and, 887
  background of, 804–5
  black voters and, 827
  "court packing" by, *827*, 828, 841
  death of, 882, *887*
  Economic Bill of Rights and, 868–69
  First New Deal and, 807–15
  Four Freedoms and, 761, 847, *849*, 862–63, 887, 941
  freedom and, 823–27, 847, *849*, 877, 891
  Hitler and, 850, 851, 871
  on housing, 814
  Japanese American internment and, 875
  pluralism and, 870
  and polio, 805–6
  Second New Deal and, 820–23
  and South, 841
  U.S.-Soviet relations and, 893
  and West, 803, *803*
  World War II strategy of, 855–56
  see also New Deal
Roosevelt, Theodore (1858–1919), 635, 703, *709*, *723*, 731, 804, 827, 1056
  African-Americans and, 745
  Asian-Americans and, 744
  as conservationist, *711*, 712
  and corporations, 709
  Panama Canal and, 721–22
  as Progressive candidate, 712, 807
  as Progressive president, 589, 709–15, *710*
  as Rough Rider, 668, *668*
  U.S. government regulatory power and, 710
  World War I and, 726
Roosevelt Corollary, 722–23
Rose, Ernestine (1810–1892), 453
Rose, John (1752/1753–1820), *137*
rosemary, 19
Rosenberg, Ethel (1915–1953), 914–15, *914*
Rosenberg, James N. (1874–1970), *794*

Rosenberg, Julius (1918–1953), 914–15, *914*
Rosie the Riveter, 865
Ross, Fort, 154
Ross, Frederick (1796–1883), 400
Ross, John (1790–1866), 297, 375
Ross, Martha Jackson, *982*
Ross, Nellie Taylor, 706
Ross, Thomas J., 563
Rossiter, Thomas Pritchard (1818–1871), *253*
Rothko, Mark, *904*
Rough Riders, 668, *668*
Rowlandson, Mary (1637?–1711), 73
Royal Africa Company, 88, 101
Royal Air Force, 851
Royal Army, 194
Royal Navy, 117, 127, 141
Royal Society, *149*
Royal University of Mexico, 68
rubber, 662, 765, 859, 936
Ruef, Abraham (1864–1936), 702
Rugendas, Johann Moritz, *97*
Ruins of the Pittsburgh Round House, *629*
"Rule Britannia," 140
Rumsfeld, Donald, 1094
Rural Electrification Agency, 820
Rush, Benjamin (1745–1813), 186, 207, 225, 234, 239, 253
  public schools and, 215
Russia, 158, 361, 364, 685, *754*
  Alaskan fur traders from, 154, 191
  immigrants in, *684*
  Iran and, 1124
  Iraq War and, 1095
  U.S. acquires Alaska from, 466
  in World War I, 725, 726
  see also Soviet Union
Russian immigrants, 656, 682
Russian Revolution, 728, 737, 749, 750, 751, 752, *780*
Russo-Japanese War, 721
Russwurm, John B. (1799–1851), 443
Rustin, Bayard (1910–1987), 986
Ruth, Babe (1895–1948), 766
Rwanda, genocide in, 1059, 1060
Ryan, John A. (1869–1945), 689, 823
Ryan, Martha, *232*
Ryan, Paul D. (1970–), 1127

Saar, Betye (1926–), *988*
Saar Basin, 752
Sacajawea (ca. 1786–ca. 1812), 294
Sacco, Nicola (1891–1927), 763, *765*
Sacred Experiment, 154
Sadat, Anwar (1918–1981), *1032*
Saddam Hussein (1937–2006), 927, 1054, 1094, 1096
  and weapons of mass destruction, 1094–95, 1096
Sagard, Gabriel, *17*
Sagebrush Rebellion, 1038, 1041
Saginaw, Mich., 840
Sahara Desert, 19
St. Anthony and the Infant Jesus, *34*
St. Augustine, Fla., 31, 32, 139, 152
St. Clair, Arthur (1736–1818), 265
Saint Domingue, 97, 106, 288, *289*, 291, 292

St. Helena Island, 541–42, *542*
St. John Baker, Anthony (1784–1854), *361*
St. Lawrence River, 35, 49, 158
St. Lawrence valley, 106, 155–56
St. Louis, Mo., 9, 223, 319, *673*
St. Louis Post-Dispatch, 639, *745*
St. Simons Island, 32
Salem, Mass., 105–6
Salinger, J. D. (1919–), 953
SALT (Strategic Arms Limitations Talks), 1021, 1032
Salt Lake City, Utah, *462*
"salutary neglect," 145
Sambo (slave), 400
Sampson, Deborah (1760–1827), 229–32
San Antonio, N.Mex., 154
San Antonio, Tex., 152, *464*, *469*
San Antonio Independent School District v. Rodriguez, 1019
San Bernardino, Calif., terrorist attack in, 1125
San Bernardino Valley, Calif, 934
San Diego, Calif., 154, 191, *1070*, *1073*
Sandinistas, 778, *779*, 1032, 1047
Sandino, Augusto César (1895–1934), 778, *779*
Sandy (Jefferson's slave), *269*
Sandy Hook Elementary School, 1129
San Fernando Valley, Calif., 934
Sanford, Maine, *325*
San Francisco, Calif., 154, 191, 470, 601, 702, 860, 879, *997*, 998, 1003, 1063, 1078–79
  Beats in, 953, 954
  bread lines in, *795*
  immigration to, 683
  manufacturing and trading in, 606
  population of, 470
  strike in, 816, *816*
  U.N. conference in, 886
  water needs of, 711
San Francisco Bay, 1004, *1004*
San Francisco Chronicle, 895
Sanger, Margaret (1883–1966), 699, 700, 734
Sanitary Fairs, 527, 530–31, *530*, 531
San Jacinto, Battle of, 462, *463*
San Jose, Calif., 1028
San Juan, Calif., *609*
San Juan, P.R., 36, 939
San Juan Hill, 668, *668*
San Juan Pueblo, 34
Sankore University, 20
San Lorenzo, Treaty of (Pinckney's Treaty) (1795), 292
San Salvador, 21
Santa Anna, Antonio López de, 461–62, 466
Santa Barbara, Calif., 154
Santa Elena settlement, 32
Santa Fe, N.Mex., 33–34, 49, 152
Santa Fe Trail, 460
Santiago, Cuba, 667
Sarajevo, Serbia, 725
Saratoga, Battle of, 195–97, *196*
Sargent, John Singer, *719*
Saturday Evening Post, 847, 863

Saturday Night Massacre, 1025
Saudi Arabia, 987, 1054, 1078, 1086–87, 1106, 1124
Sauk Indians, 374
Savage, Edward (1761–1817), *68*
Savage Family, The (Savage), *68*
Savannah, Ga., 135, 138, 223, *497*
  demands return of slaves, 227
savings and loans associations, 1045
Savio, Mario (1942–1996), *990*, 991
scabs, *691*
scalawags, 577
Scalia, Antonin (1936–), 1106
Scandinavia, 851
  socialism in, 692–93
Scandinavian immigrants, 326, 604, 655, *706*
Scarouyady (Oneida leader), 162
Schaff, Philip (1819–1893), 432
Schechter Poultry Company, 815
Schenck, Charles T., 780
Schlafly, Phyllis (1924–), *1035*, 1036
school prayer, 1007, *1007*
school prayer, proposed amendment regarding, 1046
schools, public, 1019, 1076
school shootings, *1128*, 1129
Schultz, George (1920–), 1018
Schurz, Carl (1829–1906), 557, 570
Schuylkill River, *110*
Schwerner, Michael (1939–1964), 979
scientific management, 690
Scopes, John (1900–1970), 783–84
Scopes Trial, 783–84, *784*
Scotch-Irish, 109, 111, 157, 161, 211
  as immigrants to America, 109, 111, 157, 161
Scotland, 3, 109, 127
Scott, Dred (ca. 1800–1858), 485–86, *485*, 488, 494
Scott, Harriet (d. ca. 1859), 486
Scott, Thomas A. (1823–1881), 596
Scott, Winfield (1786–1866), 466, 478, 725
Scottish immigrants, 218
Scottsboro, Ala., trial in, 839, *839*, 960
Scourge of Aristocracy, The (Lyon), 286
Scowcroft, Brent (1925–), 1095
Screen Actors Guild, 1039
Scribner's Magazine, 629
SDS, *see* Students for a Democratic Society
Seabury, Samuel, 188
Sea Islands, 32, *139*, 517, 541–42, *541*, 558, 576
  Special Field Order 15 and, 551
Seale, Bobby (1936–), 1009
Sears, Roebuck & Co., 594
SEATO, 901
Seattle, Wash., 770, *798*, 860, *1053*, *1062*, 1063, 1069
  anti-Chinese riot in, *658*
  government contracts and, 930
  Ku Klux Klan in, *785*
  strike in, 750
  WTO meeting in, *1053*, 1060–61
Seattle Post-Intelligencer, 875
secession, 495–97, *505*
  see also South

Second Amendment, 258, 1129
"Second American Revolution," 519–32
Second Confiscation Act, 514
Second Continental Congress, 184, 185, 186, 187, 195, 205, 207, 211, 230
Second Emancipation, 747
Second Great Awakening, see Great Awakening, Second
"second industrial revolution," see industrial revolution, "second"
Second New Deal, see New Deal, Second
Second Reconstruction, 643–44, 663
    civil rights movement as, 585
Second Seminole War, 376–77, 376
Second Vatican Council, social activism and, 999
sectionalism:
    Calhoun and, 372
    fear of political, 366
    post–Civil War, 642
Securities and Exchange Commission (SEC), 814, 1112
Security Council, U.N., 886, 897, 899
Sedgwick, Catharine Maria (1789–1867), 351
Sedition Act (1798), 285–86, 286, 291, 736, 1006, 1099
Sedition Act (1918), 736, 780
seditious libel, 147–48
segregation, 352, 577, 652–54, 674, 744, 746, 791, 834, 835, 863, 870, 871, 874, 877, 878, 879, 880–81, 883, 891–92, 909, 910, 913, 921, 938, 955–61, 963, 963, 972, 986, 1017–19, 1042, 1073, 1076
    Birmingham campaign and, 974
    Booker T. Washington on, 659
    Brown v. Board of Education and, 925
    courts and, 929, 955–58, 962–63, 964
    dismantling of, 925, 929, 957, 957, 959, 964, 982, 986, 1017–19
    diversity vs., 838–39
    education and, 658, 1017–19
    federal government and, 975
    in federal housing, 834, 835
    in Greensboro, N.C., 971
    labor and, 649–50
    laws, 652–53
    railroads and, 652
    reformers and, 745
    "separate but equal" principle and, 652–53, 653, 957, 958–59
    in South, 836
    South and, 648–56
    in Southwest, 743
    in Spanish-American War, 668
    suburbia and, 938–40, 939
    in U.S. military, 747, 878
    see also race, racism; South, segregation in
Seguín, Juan, 468, 469
Seidel, Emil (1864–1947), 691
Seine River, 309
Selective Service Act (1917), 731
"self-made" man, 337, 338, 389
    Andrew Jackson as, 347
    Frederick Douglass as, 389

Selling a Freeman to Pay His Fine at Monticello, Florida, 566
Selling of Joseph, The, (Sewall), 225
Selma, Ala., 955, 982, 982
Seminoles, 315, 361, 374, 376
    fugitive slaves and, 376
Seminole War:
    First, 376
    Second, 376–77, 376
Senate, U.S., 249, 347, 621, 664, 665, 818, 819, 821, 886, 957, 1083, 1091, 1097, 1100, 1101, 1126
    African-Americans in, 575, 576
    comic book hearings of, 953
    creation of, 249
    and Johnson's impeachment, 569–70
    LBJ in, 978
    McCarthy and, 915–16
    popular vote and, 703
    Smith's speech in, 915, 918
    World War I and, 728
Seneca Falls Convention, 425, 448, 452, 896
Seneca Falls Convention of, 1848, 425
Seneca Falls Declaration of Sentiments, 448, 449
Seneca Indians, 12, 263, 298
Senegal, 136, 964
Seoul, South Korea, 901
"separate but equal" principle, 652–53, 653, 957, 958–59
separation of powers, in U.S. Constitution, 250
separatists, 66
September 11, 2001, terrorist attacks of, 510, 735, 927, 977, 1028, 1085–87, 1085, 1086, 1087, 1091, 1092, 1093, 1094, 1097, 1105, 1113, 1131
    Cold War and, 1087
Sequoia, 374
Serbia, 725, 1039, 1059, 1060
serfs, 92
Serra, Father Junípero, 30
Serra, Junípero (1713–1784), 154–55, 155
Servicemen's Readjustment Act, 868
settlement houses, 704, 704, 713
settler societies, 618
Seven Days' Campaign, 509
Seventeenth Amendment, 489, 703
Seventh Day Baptists, 110
Seven Years' War, 127, 157–58, 160, 162, 163, 185, 193, 197, 221, 222, 267, 292
    effects of, 159, 161, 164, 171–72, 173
Sewall, Samuel (1652–1730), 225
Seward, William H. (1801–1872), 473, 475–76, 484, 494, 515, 664
"Seward's icebox," 664
sex:
    Beats and, 954
    censorship and, 779, 781
    and public officials, 1083–84
    women's rights and, 453, 698–99, 760, 770–72, 938, 1000, 1002
sexism, 1002
Sex Side of Life, The (Dennett), 781
sexual harassment, 1083
sexual politics, 1002

sexual revolution, 926, 998, 1008, 1019–20, 1019, 1020, 1034, 1080
Seymour, Horatio (1810–1886), 569, 570
Shackle Broken-by the Genius of Freedom, The, 551
Shahn, Ben (1898–1969), 814, 868
Shahn, Bernarda, 814
Shakers, 426–27, 427, 429
Shakespeare, William (1564–1616), 119, 178
shamans, 12
Shame of the Cities, The (Steffens), 682
"shape up" system, 816
sharecroppers, 831
    in Great Depression, 812, 813
    New Deal and, 820
sharecropping, 387, 559, 560, 563, 577, 640, 748, 823, 835, 838, 838, 929, 931
Share Our Wealth, 819, 820
Sharon, Conn., 981
Sharon Statement, 980–81
Shaw, Lemuel (1781–1861), 329
Shaw, Robert Gould (1837–1863), 518, 526
Shawnees, 156, 298
Shays, Daniel (1747?–1825), 246
Shays's Rebellion, 246, 254, 274
Sheeler, Charles (1883–1965), 768, 769
Sheen, Fulton J. (1895–1979), 940
sheep farming, 608–9
Shenandoah Valley, 114, 120
Sheppard-Towner Act (1921), 771
Sheridan, Philip H. (1831–1888), 611
Sherman, William T. (1820–1891), 535, 540, 543, 551, 557, 574, 975
    March to the Sea of, 543, 544
Sherman Antitrust Act (1890), 623, 627–28, 709, 712
    see also monopolies; trusts, business
Shiite Muslims, 927, 1095–96
Shiloh, Battle of, 511, 512
shipbuilding:
    European, 946
    in New England, 88
    in Philadelphia, 239
    in South, 931
    in World War II, 865
Shoemakers' Strike in Lynn-Procession in the Midst of a Snow-Storm, of Eight Hundred Women Operatives, The, 343
shopping, 934
Shoshones, 294
"shunpikes," 309
Siam, see Thailand
Sicily, invasion of, 856
Sickles, Daniel E. (1819–1914), 513
Siegfried, André (1875–1959), 766
Sierra Blanca, Battle of, 154
Sierra Club, 710, 1005
Sierra Leone, as haven for former slaves, 227, 228
"Significance of the Frontier in American History, The" (F.J. Turner), 602
Signing of the Constitution, The (Rossiter), 253
Signs (Rauschenberg), 1011

Silent Protest Parade, 748–49
Silent Spring (Carson), 989, 1005
Silicon Valley, 1063
silver, 24, 29, 32, 53–54, 58, 88, 97, 106, 380
    coinage, 145
    corporate mining of, 608
    as currency, 646
    currency and, 355, 378, 379
Simmons, Isaac (d. 1944), 877
Sinclair, Upton (1878–1968), 682, 730, 779, 818
Singer Sewing Machines, 664
Singleton, Benjamin "Pap" (1809–1892), 650
Sinners in the Hands of an Angry God (Edwards), 150
Sioux, 525, 610, 614, 618
    in Buffalo Bill's Wild West Show, 619
Sioux Dakotas, execution of, 525, 525
Sirica, John J. (1904–1992), 1024
Sister Carrie (Dreiser), 682
Sisterhood is Powerful!, 1002
Sisters of Charity, 522
sit-down strike, 817, 817
sit-ins, 971, 972, 973, 986
Sitting Bull (ca. 1831–1890), 611, 614
    in Buffalo Bill's Wild West Show, 619
Six-Day War, 1059
Sixteenth Amendment, 712
Sixth Avenue and Thirtieth Street (Sloan), 679
"Sixties, The," 989, 1002, 1003, 1005, 1008, 1008
    activism in, 1000–1002
    legacy of, 1011
Skilling, Jeffrey, 1065
slacker raids, 737
Slater, Samuel (1768–1835), 321
Slaughterhouse Cases (1873), 583
Slave Auction, The (Crowe), 389
Slave Market of America, 439
Slave Power, 483, 631
slavery, 6, 94–101, 205, 234–35, 268, 269, 281, 366, 388–423, 429, 581, 880, 881, 905, 1073, 1109
    abolished in Mexico, 461, 469
    American, origins of, 94–101
    American Revolution and, 167, 205, 223–29, 231, 234, 413, 435
    in ancient Greece, 398
    in ancient Rome, 95, 398, 459, 460
    arguments in favor of, 397–98, 625
    bank financing of, 355
    Biblical passages as justification for, 398, 405
    in Brazil, see Brazil, slavery in
    and Catholic Church, 98, 137
    in Chesapeake region, 132–33, 134, 138
    Christianity and, 99, 137, 151, 412–13, 446, 472
    in cities, 409
    Civil War and, 511
    Congress and, 473
    Constitution and, 251–52, 251, 263
    cotton gin and, 316

in Cuba, 137
Democratic Party and, 369
divisiveness of, 288–89
Dred Scott decision and, 485–86
English Liberty vs., 141
in Europe, 20, 95
expansion of, 127, 169
federal government and, 372
Free Soil position and, 474
gender roles in, 412
in Georgia, 252
in Georgia colony, 135, 138
growth of, 134–35
history of, 95–96
indentured servitude vs., 94
Indian, abolition of, 29
Indians and, 6, 16, 25, 29–30, 87, 94,
    471, 1079
law and, 420
Levellers opposed to, 80–81
in Lincoln-Douglas campaign,
    488–89
Lincoln's views of, 487–88
Locke and, 143
in Louisiana, 294
in Maryland, *136*
in Maryland colony, *133*
in Mediterranean, 95
in Middle Colonies, 133, 135
in Missouri Territory, 356–57
in New England, 76, 77, 133, 135
in New Netherland, 41
newspapers and, 400, 419, 420,
    441–42, 443, 444, 452, 473
in New World, 3, 5, 25, 29–30,
    94–98, *129*, 132
in New York, *228*
North as affected by, 393
in Northern colonies, 135–36
Northern vs. Southern, 135
Northwest Ordinance and, 245, 315
party politics and, 478–79
paternalist ethos and, 396, *398*
perceived advantages of, 94
planter class and, 395–96
Puritanism and, 69
Quaker repudiation of, 93
racism as justification for, 396
Republican Party (modern) opposed
    to, 483–84
on rice plantations, 118, 134–35
Seward's views on, 484
slave resistance to, 138–39, 415–21,
    416
South as affected by, 393, 655
in Southern colonies, 132–33, 215–16
strengthening of, 493
in Texas, 462
on tobacco plantations, 118, 133
United States as center of, 390
in Virginia colony, 59, 98, 101,
    133–34
after War of 1812, 307
in West, 602
in West Indies, 25, 30, 87, 92, 96–98,
    129, *131*, 132, 134
and westward expansion, 524
westward expansion and, 243, 316,
    358, 374, 385, 386, 390, 471, 472,

473–74, 483–84
Wilmot proviso and, 473, 474
see also abolition movement
Slavery As It Is (Weld), 438
slaves, 54, 59, *63*, *97*, 120, 121, *134*, 143,
    227, *228*, *408*, *409*, *410*, *496*
in Antigua, *96*
barred from education, 401
bound for Mexico, 98
in Carolina colony, 92
and Christianity, 412–13
Civil War and, 538
colonization of, 435–36, 514, 517
culture of, 136–39, *137*, 385, 410–15
death rate of, 101, 132
diet and health of, 401
disciplining of, 409–10
emancipated, 227–28, 511–19, 546
family life of, 410
folk tales of, 414
freedom desired by, 101, 138–39, 226,
    231, 413–15, 435
fugitive, 288, 376, 415–17, *415*, *417*,
    475, 476–77, 487, 495, 513, *513*,
    514, 516
gang labor and, 407–9
harbored by Seminoles, 376
holdings, *397*
importation from Africa of, 96–97,
    252
labor of, 407
law and, 400–401
Native Americans as, 87, 471
New York uprising of, 138–39
population of, 134–35, *135*, 289, 356,
    385, 516
prices of, 395
prohibition on importation of, 390
religion and, 412–13, *413*
revolts, 288–90, 418–19, 439
rights of, 98
runaway, advertisement for, *415*, *417*
in South Carolina, *402*
tax on importation of, 135
women as, *98*
slaves, emancipated, 551–60, *553*, *575*
    Andrew Johnson and, 565
    Second New Deal and, 821
    suffrage and, 551, 553, 568, 570
slaves, population of:
    in British colonies, 132–33
    in colonies, 224–25
    in Florida, 154
    in Missouri Territory, 356
    in New York City, 135–36, 228
    in 1776, 223
    in South Carolina, 371
    in U.S., 239, 390, *392*, *393*
slave ships, *132*
slave trade, 20, *20*, 41, 88, 94, 116,
    127–35, *130*, 132, *136*, 223, *223*,
    389, 391–92, *393*, 492, 881
    abolished in Washington, D.C., 475
    advertisement for, *411*
    and Africa, 5, 20
    Atlantic, 128–30
    auctions in, 391, *395*
    Carolina colony and, 134
    in Charleston, S.C., 92

Congressional prohibition on, 391
Constitution and, 251–52, *251*
cotton plantations and, 316–18
families and, 411
Middle Passage of, 130–32, 136
in Missouri, *400*
in New Orleans, 318, 391
in original Declaration of
    Independence, 187
prohibition of, 251, 316
reopening of, 316
statistics on, 391
within U.S., 316–17
Slave Trader, Sold to Tennessee (Miller),
    318
"slavocracy", Southern planters as, 394
Slavs, Nazi extermination of, 858
Sloan, John (1871–1951), *679*, 682, *687*,
    689
smallpox, 23, *24*, 39, 66, 131
Smalls, Robert (1837–1915), 576
Smith, Adam (1723–1790), 5, 18, 218,
    234
Smith, Adams (1723–1790), 1111
Smith, Alfred E. (1873–1974), 793
    Protestants and, 793
Smith, John (1580–1631), 49–50, 53,
    58, *59*, *60*
Smith, Joseph (1805–1844), 336
Smith, Margaret Chase, McCarthy
    and, 915, 919
Smith, Matthew (1810–1879), 601, *602*
Smith, Melancton (1744–1798), 256
Smith, Thomas, 77
Smith Act (1940), 841
Smithfield, R.I., *1059*
Smithsonian Institution, 611
Smith v. Allwright, 880
Smoot-Hawley Tariff (1930), 797
SNCC, *see* Student Non-Violent
    Coordinating Committee
Snowden, Edward, 1125
social contract, 142
Social Darwinism, 625–26, 630, 635
Social Gospel, 633, 646, 999
socialism, 426, 691, 692–93, 696, 699,
    775, 778, 781, 783, 795, 806, 815,
    819, 906, 917, 949, 990, 1010,
    1033, 1067
    capitalism vs., 713, 836
    in Chicago, 634
    Communist Party and, 836
    Espionage Act and, 736
    European vs. American view of, 632
    Friedrich Hayek and, 869
    in Gilded Age, 629, 632
    Henry Wallace and, 911
    immigrants and, 742, 770
    middle class and, 632
    as nationalism, 632
    woman suffrage and, 705
    World War I and, 726, 737
Socialist Party, 691, *692*, 699, 713, *713*,
    731, 741, 752, 770
    capitalism vs., 713, 836
"social legislation," 700
social media:
    Black Lives Matter and, 1122
    ISIS and, 1124

social rights, in U.S., 1129
Social Security, *822*, 827, 830, 842, 881,
    943, 980, 1016, 1045, 1128
    African-Americans and, 831, 834,
        984
    creation of, 822
    Eisenhower and, 946
    freedom and, 829
    NRPB and, 867
    taxes support for, 822, 830, 831
    Truman and, 907, 911, 920
    in World War II, 860
Social Security Act (1935), 804, 822,
    831, 832
Social Security Bill, 822
Society in America (Martineau), 435
Society of American Indians, 699–700
Society of Friends, *see* Quakers
Society of Patriotic Ladies, A, 232
Society of Pennsylvania, 283
Soiling of Old Glory, The (Forman), *1018*
Solomon (slave), 289
Solomon Islands, 854
Somalia, 1076
    war on terror in, 1124
Somerset case, 252
Somoza, Anastasio (1925–1980), 778,
    779, 849, 1032, 1047
Son of the Forest, A, 377
Sonoma, Calif., 154
Sons of Italy, 763
Sons of Liberty, 176, 177, 179, 207, 223
Sorel, Edward (1929–), *1057*
Sorry Day, 618
Sotomayor, Sonia (1954–), 1116
Soule, George (1887–1970), 827
Soulé, Pierre (1801–1870), 492
Souls of Black Folk, The (Du Bois), 661
Souls of Black Folks, The (Du Bois), 745,
    755
Souter, David (1939–), 1116
South, 275, 622, *735*, 746, 767, 847, *861*,
    878, 972–73, 1015, 1024, 1085,
    1115
    African-Americans in, 649–50, 746,
        747, 770, 790, *790*, 871, 878, 883,
        921, 978, 985
    agriculture in, 931
    black migration from, 939, 955
    convict labor in, 648
    cotton crop in, 316–18
    Democratic Party and, 648, 793
    desegregation in, 880, *929*, 957, 959,
        962, 964, 986
    economy of, 393–96
    election of 1796 and, 284
    in election of 1824, 364
    in election of 1948, 911–12
    in election of 1964, 980
    factory production in, 323
    family life in antebellum, *395*
    Freedom Rides in, 972
    fundamentalists in, 783
    illiteracy in, 394
    industry in, 830–31, 860, 930–31,
        947
    Jim Crow and, 955
    libertarianism in, 942
    New, *see* New South

South (*continued*)
New Deal and, 830–31
Nixon and, 1017–18
Operation Dixie in, 907
People's Party in, 641
political influence of, 358
population growth and, 1028
poverty in, 841, 1102
religion in, 760
secession of, 495–97
segregation in, 640, 648–56, *836*, 871, 883, 958, *958*, *963*, 971, 972–73, 1017–19
sit-ins in, 971, *973*
slavery and, 391, 393
slave trade in, 316–18
society in, 395–96
strikes in, 816
urban areas of, 561
voting in, 773, 909, 978
see also Confederate States of America
South Africa, 754, 902, 1021, 1047, 1053
apartheid in, 997
South America, 2, 6, 7, 8, 21, 25–26, *31*, 106, 155, 849
early population of, 24
immigrants from, 1072, 1075
immigrants in, *684*
South Asia, Islam in, 1105
South Braintree, Mass., Sacco and Vanzetti in, 763
South Carolina, 219, 240, 288, 347, 366, 367, 376, 562, 649, 701, 1106
Confederate flag and, 963
at Constitutional Convention, 251
constitution of, 209, 210
in nullification crisis, 371–74, *372*
Reconstruction in, 577, 582
secession of, 495
slavery in, 132, 252, 372, 399–400
slaves in, *402*
slave trade in, 316, 318
textiles in, 648
upcountry of, 316
voting rights in, 352, 366
South Carolina Canal and Railroad, 311
South Carolina colony, 32, 33, 111, 114, *117*, *139*, 143, 144, 156, 182
in American Revolution, 194, 199, 222
assembly in, 145
Declaration of Independence and, 187
elite class in, 119–20
Indians in, 111
Loyalists in, 218, *220*
planters in, 119
population of slaves in, 134
Regulators in, 177
rice plantations in, 134
slavery in, 134, *137*, 139, 187, 224, 226, 227, 228, 252
task system, 134
South Carolina Gazette, 139
South Carolina Senate, 1109
South Dakota, 604
corporate mining in, 608

population of, 681
Wounded Knee massacre in, 616–17
South Dakota territory, 603
Southern Christian Leadership Conference, 962
Southern Conference for Human Welfare, 841, 920
Southern Manifesto, 957, 962
Southern Pacific Railroad, *604*, 606, 702
Southern Tenant Farmers Union, 839–40
Southern veto, 830–31
South Gate, Calif., 1044
South Korea, 1026, 1032
and BP oil rig, 1117
creation of, 897–99
immigrants from, 1070
South Vietnam, 991, 992, 996, *996*, 1008, 1022
Southwest, 1103
Sovereignty and Goodness of God, The (Rowlandson), 73
Soviet Exhibition, 929
Soviet Unino, *1024*
Soviet Union, 749, 760, 761, 795, 806, 836, 848, 850, 851, 856, 884–85, *891*, 892–93, 894, 904, 906, 911, 914, 920, 944, 952, 988, 1016, 1021, 1030, 1032, 1048–49
Afghanistan invasion by, 1033
American National Exhibition and, 929, *931*
atomic bomb of, 897
Berlin occupation by, 896–97
breakup of, 1053, 1054
Cold War and, 901–2
collapse of communism in, 924, 1053
Cuban Missile Crisis and, 976
Czechoslovakia invasion by, 1010
Eastern Europe occupation by, 885, 886, 892, 896, 897
Eisenhower and, 948–49
European empires and, 949
German invasion of, 852, 856, *857*, 892
Gulf War and, 1054
hydrogen bomb and, 947
invasion of Germany by, 882
Korean War and, 897–901
Lend-Lease and, 852
Manchuria invasion by, 884
Reagan and, 1046
space exploration and, 947, *947*, 965, 975
spying of, 916
support of the arts by, 903
in U.N., 886
Universal Declaration of Human Rights and, 906
Vietnam and, 991, 1021
weapons tests of, 912
see also Cold War
soybean, 931
Spain, *16*, 21–27, *22*, *23*, 27–30, *44*, 49, 51–52, 53, 54, 111, 157, 158, 186, 191, 239, 365, 492, 666–69, 749, 916
American Revolution and, 197

and Catholicism, 51–52
Columbus sponsored by, 21
loses Jamaica to England, 83
Louisiana Territory and, 292
as refuge for Huguenots, 38
rise of Franco in, 850
slavery in, 20
in War of Jenkins' Ear, 139
Spanish America, 3, 21–35, *28*, 36, *44*, 49, 51, 52, 55, 134, 152–54, 314–15
beginnings of, 21
boundaries of, 152
in Florida, 25, 31–32, 91, 146, 152
government of, 25
immigrants to, 25–27
independence of, 359, *360*
Indians and, 30–37, 92, 106
interracial mixing in, 26, *26*
justification for conquest of, 3, 15, 27, 29
in Louisiana, 294
map of, *153*
in New Mexico, 33–35, 49, 152
in North America, 151–55, 287
as obstacle to westward expansion, 329
population of, 25
Pueblo Indians and, 10, 33–35, 102
size of, 25
in Texas, 152
women in, 26
Spanish-American War, 588, *639*, 665, 666–67, *667*, *668*, 669, *669*, *670*, 672, 673, *674*, 711, 787
acquisition of empire and, 719
Battle of San Juan Hill in, 668
casualties in, 667
causes of, 666–67
naval battle at Manila Bay in, 667
see also Philippine War
Spanish Armada, *51*, 52
Spanish Civil War, 850–51, 916
Spanish Inquisition, 34
Sparkman, John (1899–1985), 921
speakeasies, 764, 783, 790
Special Field Order 15, 551
Special Forces, U.S., 1124
special interests, 711
lobbying by, 620, 773, 868–69
specie, 355
Specie Circular, 380
Spencer, Lilly M. (1822–1902), *507*
Spiegel, Marcus M. (1829–1864), 503
Spirit of the New Deal, The, 808
spoils system, 368
see also parties, political; patronage
Spokane, Wash., 697
Spotswood, Alexander (1676–1740), 101
Spotsylvania, Battle of, 539
Spotsylvania, Va., *539*
Sprigs, Elizabeth, 54–55
Springfield, Mo., *745*
Springsteen, Bruce (1949–), 1028
Sputnik, 946–47, 965
Squanto (d. 1622), 66
Square Deal, 709
squatters, 314, *315*
stagflation, 1026–27, 1039

Stalin, Joseph (1879–1953), 806, 836, 851, 884–85, *885*, 892, 894, 897, 901, 911, 917, 948
death of, 948
and nonaggression pact, 851
Stalin, Joseph, World War II strategy of, 855–56
Stalingrad, 856
Stamp Act (1765), 171, 223
repeal of, *176*, 177
resistance to, 173–76, 177, 178, 226
teapot, *175*
Stamp Act Congress (1765), 175
Standard Oil Company, 596, 599, *599*, 664, 682, 712
Stanford University, 742
Stanton, Edwin M. (1814–1869), 551, 569
Stanton, Elizabeth Cady (1815–1902), 448, 452, 453, 572, 573, *573*, *663*, 741, 770
Stanton, Frederick (1794–1859), 395
Stanwix, Fort, 242
Starbucks, *1062*
Star of Empire, 461
Starr, Kenneth (1947–), 1083–84
"Star-Spangled Banner, The" (Key), 299, 666
"starving time," 58
state-church separation, 212–15, 783, 1007
State Department, U.S., 893, 904, 914, 948, 963, 991, 1030, 1047, 1094, 1096
McCarthy and, 914, 915, 918
Staten Island, N.Y., 1121
State of the Union Address (1815), 354
State of the Union Address (1825), 365
State of the Union Address (1941), 847
State of the Union Address (1996), 1058
State of the Union Address (2002), 1093
states' rights, 370, 372, 910, 1039
Andrew Johnson's views of, 565
Calhoun and, 371–73
Confederacy and, 534
in Constitution, 259
nullification and, 371, *371*
States' Rights Democratic Party, 910–11, 912
Statue of Freedom, 459, *460*
Statue of Liberty, 591, 613, 633, 635, 688, *689*, 726, 731, 732, 737, 739, 745, *745*, 862, *916*, 941, *981*, *1002*, *1006*, *1055*, *1067*, *1129*
Stead, W. T. (1849–1912), 719
steamboats, 168, 307, 309, *319*, 328
steamships, 596
steel industry, 597, *599*, 639, 649, 662, 688, 690, 719, 750–51, 764, 773, 815, 817–18, 860, 907, 930, 936, 946, 947, 1027, 1043–44, *1043*, 1100
Steel Workers Organizing Committee, 816, 817
Steffens, Lincoln (1866–1936), 682, 766
Stegner, Wallace (1913–1993), 330
Steichen, Edward (1879–1973), 682

Stein, Gertrude (1874–1946), 779
Steinbeck, John (1902–1968), 812, 825
Stennis, John C. (1901–1995), 1024
Stephens, Alexander (1812–1883), 497
sterilization, involuntary, 743
Stettheimer, Florine, 737
Stevens, Thaddeus (1792–1868), 352–53, 514, *566*, 567, 568, 581
Stevenson, Adlai (1900–1965), 921, 945, *945*, *946*
Stewart, Alexander T. (1803–1876), 601
Stewart, Maria (1803–1879), 447, 448
Stewart, William (1827–1909), 566
Stieglitz, Alfred (1864–1946), 682, *682*
Stiles, Ezra (1727–1795), *210*, 234
Still, William, *417*
Stimson, Henry (1867–1950), 859, 880, 883
Stockbridge Indians, 222
stock market, 764, 769, *770*, 793, *794*, 808, 1044, 1064, 1111, 1113, 1120
New Deal and, 761
Stone, Lucy (1818–1893), 425, 453, 454, 573
Stonewall Inn, police raid on, 1003
Stono, S.C., 139
Stono Rebellion, 139
Story, Joseph (1779–1845), 347
Stowe, Harriet Beecher (1811–1896), 327, *351*, *441*, 442
Strategic Arms Limitations Talks (SALT), 1021
Strategic Bombing Survey, 883
Strategic Defense Initiative, 1046
Straus, Jack (1900–1985), 934
strict constructionism, 275, 354, 356, **365**
Stride Toward Freedom (King), 961
Strike, The (Koehler), 629
strikes, 328–29, 342, *343*, 380, 574, 623, 628–29, 691, 693–97, 749, 750, 770, 907–8, 1009, *1009*, 1043
of air traffic controllers, 1043
in Arizona, 737, *738*
in Boston, Mass., 750, 774
in colleges, 1022
of cowboys, 606
in Depression, 816–18, *816*, *817*
in Detroit, Mich., 877
in France, 1010
in Homestead, Pa., 639–40, 659–62
in Idaho, 691
in Lawrence, Mass., 693–96
in Ludlow, Colo., 696–97
McCormick Company and, 634
in Memphis, Tenn., 871
mining and, 645, 737, *738*
in New Orleans, La., 696
in New York, N.Y., 679, 693–97, *696*
in 1934, 816, *816*
in Paterson, N.J., 696
in Pennsylvania, 710
Pullman, 644–45, 662
railroad, 628–29, *629*, 633, 773
rights and, 714
in Rochester, N.Y., *696*
scabs and, *691*
in Seattle, Wash., 750
sit-down, *813*, 817

steel, 750–51, *751*, 947
suppression of, 773
wildcat, 947
women and, *343*
in World War II, 860, 861
in W.Va., 710
Strong, Josiah (1847–1916), 665
Stuart, Gilbert (1755–1828), *206*, *268*
Stuart kings, 80
Student Non-Violent Coordinating Committee (SNCC), 972, 974, 978, 984, 987, 988, 996, 1001, 1004, *1008*
students, as activists, 972
Students for a Democratic Society (SDS), *989*, 990–91, 996, 1001–2, 1003, 1004, 1009
Student Volunteer Movement for Foreign Missions, 665
Stump Speaking (Bingham), 367
Stuyvesant, Petrus (1610?–1672), 42–43
submarines:
    construction of, 931
    in World War I, 726, 727–28, *727*
    in World War II, 854, 856
"subprime" mortgages, 1110, 1111
    minorities and, 1111
subtreasury plan, 641, 645
Suburban Gardens, *791*
suburbs, 952, *952*, 967, 1000, 1019, 1034, 1039, 1070, 1115, 1129
    "blockbusting" and, 940
    highways and, *936*, 946
    Latinos in, 1070
    rise of, 764, 925, 932–33, *932*, 936, *936*
    as segregated, 938–40, *939*, 955
Sudan, 1076
Sudbury, Mass., 77
Sudetenland, 850
Suez Canal, 950
Suffolk Resolves (1775), 182
suffrage, *see* voting rights
sugar, 20, 77, 83, 88, *96*, *97*, 116, 128, 308, *408*
    in Caribbean, 717
    in Cuba, 976
    in Hawaii, 665
    as most profitable crop, 97
    plantations, *see* planters, plantations, sugar
    in Puerto Rico, 939
    trade in New Orleans, 393
Sugar Act (1764), 173, 174, 175
suicide rate, Great Depression and, 795
Sullivan, John (1741–1795), 222
Sullivan, Timothy "Big Tim," *701*
Summary View of the Rights of British America, A (Jefferson), 184
Sumner, Charles (1811–1874), 484, *484*, 567, 571, 572, 741
Sumner, William Graham (1840–1910), 626
Sumter, Fort, 386, 498, 507, 520
Sunday, Billy (1862–1935), *781*, 782
Sunni Muslims, 927, 1095–96
Sun of Liberty, 286
Sunshine and Shadow in New York (Smith), 601, *602*

Sun Yat-Sen, 700
Superman, 953
supply and demand, law of, 218, 625
supply-side economics, 1030, 1044, 1045, 1092
Suppressed Book about Slavery, The, 410
Supreme Court, U.S., 249, 274, 291, 347, 356, 371, 374–75, 571, 573, 583, 584–85, 615, 627, 645, 652, 658, 672, 691, 707, 710, 711–12, 763, 773, 774, 777, 780, 788, 789, *789*, 916, *1007*, 1025, 1035, 1038, 1042, 1046, 1078, 1105–6
    abortion and, 927, 1008, 1036, *1037*, 1081
    affirmative action and, 1019
    African-American rights and, 746, 880
    Amistad and, 418
    Brown v. Board of Education and, 925, 957, 958–60, *959*, 962
    and campaign contributions, 1128
    civil liberties and, 780–81, 840, 925, 962–63
    civil rights and, 1006–7, *1007*, 1010, 1017–19
    in Civil War, 523
    Clinton's appointments to, 1056
    "court packing" and, *827*, 828
    Defense of Marriage Act and, 1081
    Dred Scott decision of, 485–86, *485*, 570
    FDR and, 807, 827–28, *827*, 841
    First Amendment and, 862
    G. W. Bush and, 1106–7
    homosexuals and, 1045
    housing segregation and, 938
    Jackson's defiance of, 375
    Japanese-American internment and, 876–77
    and judicial review power, 291
    New Deal and, 815
    Obama and, 1116
    Pentagon Papers and, 1023
    Plessy v. Ferguson and, 652–53, *653*, 957, 958
    right to privacy and, 1008
    sanctions involuntary sterilization, 743
    Scottsboro case and, 839
    "separate but equal" ruling of, 652–53, *653*
    and 2000 election, 1084, *1084*
    as undemocratic, 349
    Voting Rights Act repealed by, 1121
    see also Burger Court; Marshall Court; Warren Court
surgeon's kit, Civil War, *508*
Suriname, 1130
surveillance, government, 1125, *1125*
Susquehanna Indians, 111
Susquehanna River, 113
Sutherland, George (1862–1942), 773
Sutter, Johann A. (1803–1880), 469
Swann v. Charlotte-Mecklenburg Board of Education, 1018
Swanson, *935*
sweatshops, 679, 705
Sweatt, Heman (1912–1982), 958

Swedish immigrants, *326*
Sweet, Henry O. (ca. 1905–1940), 792
Sweet, Ossian, 792
Sweetwater, Tex., *866*
Swift, Jonathan (1667–1745), *826*
Switzer, Katharine, *1001*
Switzerland, male suffrage in, 620
Syria, 754, 1026, 1100
    ISIS in, 1124

Taft, Robert (1889–1953), 826, 876
Taft, Robert A. (1889–1953), 944
Taft, William Howard (1857–1930), 589, 671, *672*, 709, 711–12, 714, 774
    inaugural address of, 711
    Latin America and, 723
Taft-Hartley Act (1947), 908, 910, 920, 947
Taiping Rebellion, 506
Taiwan, 897, 1021, 1026
Tajikistan, 1093
Taliban, 1033, 1093, 1123
Tallmadge, James (1778–1853), 356–57
Tammany Hall, 793
Taney, Roger B. (1777–1864), 328, 379, 486, 523
tanks (military), 858, *860*
Tanzania, 949
    terrorist attack in, 1087
Tape, Joseph and Mary, 658
Taper, Joseph, 404, 414–15
Tape v. Hurley, 658
Tappan, Arthur (1786–1865), 437
Tappan, Lewis (1788–1873), 437
Tarbell, Ida (1857–1944), 682
"tariff of abominations," 371
tariffs, 169, 247, 275, 354, 369, 382, 529, 592, 622, *623*, 646, 647, 665, 712, 714, 773, 797
    in Constitution, 253
    of 1828, 371
    of 1832, 373
    J. Q. Adams and, 365
    lowered by Democrats, 370
    Polk and, 464
Tarkington, Booth (1869–1946), 863
Tarleton, Banastre (1754–1833), 199
tarrifs, *624*
tax, single, 702
taxes, 61, 103, 179, *254*, 355, 713, 778, 819, 908, 942, 943, 1034, 1042, 1045, 1057, 1076, *1126*
    under Articles of Confederation, 240
    in Civil War, 529, 534
    corporate, 861
    on corporations, 820
    demands for lowering, 1037–38
    dispute over, 167, 205
    Gingrich and, 1057
    in Great Britain, 80, 1039
    Great Depression and, 797
    G. W. Bush's cuts in, 1091–92, 1107, 1116
    on imported slaves, 135, 139
    imposed by British Parliament, 171, 172–76, *174*, 187–90
    income, 529, 642, 710, 712, 714, 731, 773, 858, 980, 983

taxes (continued)
  inheritance, 710
  Jefferson's abolition of, 291
  John Adams and, 205
  in Massachusetts colony, 70
  New Deal and, 830, 831
  poll, 98, 651, 745, 910, 982
  property, 701, 1018
  Reagan's cuts in, 926
  and representation, 174–75
  right to consent to, 91
  single, 631
  Social Security, 822, 830, 831
  to support churches, 110, 151, 211, 213
  on tea, 181
  in Virginia colony, 99, 100
  on whiskey, 274, 275
  on women, 98
  World War I and, 731
  World War II and, 858
Tax Reform Act (1986), 1042
Taylor, Frederick W. (1856–1915), 690
Taylor, Zachary (1784–1850), 473, 476
  as Mexican War general, 465
tea, 115, 181, 308
Tea Act (1773), 181
Teacher, Frank, Jr., 803
Tea Party, 1126
  agenda of, 1125–26
  Paul D. Ryan and, 1127
  U.S., 1126
Teapot Dome scandal, 774
technology, 57
  agriculture and, 316, 319, 482
  in Civil War, 504–6, 507
  effects of, on exploration, 18–20
  innovations in, 594–95
  manufacturing and, 321–23
  market revolution and, 316, 321–23, 322, 482
  Native American, 33–34
  in World War I, 726
Tecumseh (1768–1813), 298, 299, 300
teenagers, 952–53, 953
Tehran, 884, 885, 1033
Tejanos, 461–62, 468
telegraph, 309, 311–12
  in Civil War, 504
  transatlantic, 594
telephones, 594, 765–66, 767
television, 925, 929, 930, 932, 934, 935, 935, 1010, 1047, 1063, 1073, 1100, 1122
  civil rights movement and, 973, 974, 982
  family life on, 935, 937
  Iran hostage crisis and, 1033
  in 1960 campaign, 965
  politics and, 945, 1049
  religion and, 819, 940
  religious programing and, 1035
  Vietnam War and, 1008
Teller, Henry (1830–1914), 667
Teller Amendment, 667
temperance, 370, 426, 430, 431, 431
"Temperance diagram" (Franklin), 146
Tenant uprising, 177–78
Tennent, Gilbert (1703–1764), 150

Tennent, William (1673–1746), 150
Tennessee, 242, 316, 367
  creation of, 284
  Ku Klux Klan founded in, 580
Tenochtitlán, 8, 9, 23, 23, 25
Ten-Percent Plan of Reconstruction, 542–43
Tenskwatawa (1775–1836), 298, 298
Tenth Amendment, 259
Tenure of Office Act (1867), 569
Ten Views in Antigua, 96
Terry, Eli (1772–1852), 323
Terry, Luther, 496
Texas, 152, 154, 314, 461
  annexation of, 466, 469
  borderlands of, 468
  independence from Mexico of, 462
  New Mexico invaded by, 524
  population of, 460
  Republic of, 462
  revolt in, 461–62
  slavery in, 462–63
  U.S. annexation of, 464
Texas and Pacific Railroad, 585
Texas Revolution, 469
textile industry, 130
  during Civil War, 523
  and cotton, 385
  and immigration, 325
  and market revolution, 321–24, 322, 323, 324
Thames, Battle of, 299
Thanksgiving, 66
third parties, in U.S. elections, 623
Thirteenth Amendment, 543, 567
Thomas, Jesse (1777–1853), 357
Thomas, Lorenzo (1804–1875), 518
Thoreau, Henry David (1817–1862), 330, 331, 331, 465, 489
Thoughts on African Colonization, 437
Thoughts on Government (J. Adams), 208
three-fifths clause of U.S. Constitution, 251, 252, 288, 303
Ticonderoga, Fort, 158, 185
Tidewater, Va., 133
Tilden, Samuel J. (1814–1886), 584
Tillman, Juliann Jane, 338
Timbuktu, Mali, 20
Times, The, 380
Tippecanoe, Battle of, 298
Tituba, 106
Tlaxcala Codex, 25
tobacco, 88, 128, 172, 275, 316, 406, 408, 559
  in the backcountry, 114
  in Chesapeake region, 54, 58, 60–61, 61, 62, 63, 94, 98, 99, 107, 116, 123, 132–33
  health effects of, 61
  in New England, 77
  plantations, 118, 132–33
  as substitute for gold, 61
  and workers' death rate, 97
Tobacco Belt, 559
"tobacco brides," 61
Tocqueville, Alexis de (1805–1859), 307, 309, 329, 331, 335, 349, 351, 352, 395, 425, 446
Tokyo Harbor, 472

Toleration Act (1689), 103
Toleration Act, as repealed, 83
tolls, 309
Torrey, Jesse, 299
Toussaint L'Ouverture, François Dominique (1744–1803), 288, 289
Towne, Laura M. (1825–1901), 541–42
Townshend, Charles (1725–1767), 178
Townshend Acts, 178
Townshend Acts, repeal of, 180
Townshend crisis, 178
trade, 20–21, 35, 38–39, 63, 114–15, 294
  in British-French war, 296
  in Constitution, 253
  of Dutch Empire, 35
  in early U.S., 308
  English mercantilism and, 88
  European, with Africa, 19, 20
  European, with Asia, 18, 19, 19
  European, with Indians, 57, 66, 92, 156–57, 158
  free, 217
  fur, 35, 38, 39, 43, 57, 76, 91, 116, 123, 154, 156, 159
  among Indians, 9–10, 13, 13
  in Jefferson's inaugural address, 290
  Navigation Acts and, 88
  New England and, 77
  regulations of, 104
  of Rhode Island, 247
  routes of, 18, 19
  transatlantic, 2, 5, 115–17, 127
  see also free trade; slave trade
Trail of Tears, 376, 529
transcendentalism, 330, 429, 449
transportation, 168, 239, 307, 308, 311, 312, 314, 328, 353–54
  market revolution and, 307, 308, 318, 328
  in Northwest, 319
  in South, 318
  see also canals; railroads
Transportation of Cargo by Westerners at the Port of Yokohama (Utagawa), 472
Trapper and His Family, The (Deas), 376
Travis, James W., 506
Treasury Department, U.S., 381
Treaty of Ghent (1814), 300
Treaty of Greenville (1795), 265, 265, 298
Treaty of Guadalupe Hidalgo (1848), 466–67
Treaty of Paris (1763), 158, 159
Treaty of Paris (1783), 200, 200, 210, 219–21, 223
Treaty of San Lorenzo (Pinckney's Treaty) (1795), 292
Treaty of Utrecht (1713), 128
treaty system, 265
Tree of Liberty, 286
Trelawny, Edward (1792–1881), 138
Trenchard, John (1662–1723), 141–42, 148
Trenton, Battle of, 195
triangular trade, of New England colonies, 130–31
Tripoli, 295, 295

Triumphant Entry of the Royal Troops into New York, 195
Trumbull, John, 247
Trumbull, Lyman (1813–1896), 567, 581
Truth, Sojourner (1799–1883), 449–52
Tryon, William (1729–1788), 157
Tubman, Harriet (1820–1913), 417
Tucker, George (1775–1861), 289–90
Tufts, Joshua, 150
Turner, Benjamin S., 575
Turner, Nat (1800–1831), 419–21, 420, 439
Twain, Mark (1835–1910), 572
Twelfth Amendment, 287
"twenty-negro" provision, in Civil War, 534
Two Treatises on Government (Locke), 142, 143
Tyler, John (1790–1862), 348, 382, 418, 463
Tyler administration, 418, 463
Types of Mankind (Nott and Gliddon), 442
typhoid fever, in Jamestown, 58

Uncle Sam, 571
Uncle Sam's Thanksgiving Dinner (Nast), 571
Uncle Tom's Cabin (Stowe), 441, 442
Underground Railroad, 417–18, 476–77
Underhill, John (1609–1672), 76
Underwood Tariff (1913), 714
unemployment, 380
Union League, 574–75, 576
Union Pacific Railroad, 524
unions, 342, 426
  emergence of, 380
  see also labor; labor movement; specific unions
United States, Great Seal of, 242
United States Magazine and Democratic Review, 351
United States Sanitary Commission, 530
  see also nurses
United States v. Cruikshank, 584
Universalists, 214
universal suffrage, 571, 573
Ursuline Convent, 328
Uruguay, 506
Usefull Arts and Sciences, 496
Utagawa Sadahide (1807–1873), 472
Utah, 337, 466
Utes, 460
Utopia, Ohio, 430
Utopia (More), 53, 426
utopian communities, 426–30, 428
Utrecht, Treaty of (1713), 128

"vagrants," 53
Vallandigham, Clement C. (1820–1871), 523
Valley Forge, Pa., 197
Valley of Mexico, 26
Van Buren, Martin (1782–1862), 375–76, 378, 462
  Amistad and, 418
  and annexation of Texas, 463–64
  background of, 365–66

and depression of 1837, 381
and election of 1828, 366
Free Soil Party and, 473
as Jackson's Secretary of State, 372
nickname of, 367
sectionalism and, 366
van de Passe, Simon, *59*
Van Lew, Elizabeth (1818–1900), 536
Van Rensselaer, Kiliaen, 43
Van Rensselaer family, 118
Vassa, Gustavus, *see* Equiano, Olaudah
Venerate the Plough, 278
Venezuela, 359
Vera Cruz, Mexico, 466
Vermont:
   colony of, 178
   constitution of, 209, 228
   creation of, 284
   government in, 209
   2nd Vermont Volunteers of, *511*
Verrazano, Giovanni da (ca. 1480–1527?), 14, 16, 66
Veteran in a New Field, The (Homer), *546*
veto, presidential, 379, 567–68
vice presidency, U.S., 250
Vicksburg, Battle of, *507, 537,* 539, 542
View from Bushongo Tavern, 216
Vikings, 20–21, 50
Village of Secoton, The (White), *12*
Vindication of the Rights of Woman, A (Wollstonecraft), 280, *280,* 453
Vinland, 21
Virginia, 217, 225, 240, 275
   domination of federal government by, 303
   Gabriel's Rebellion in, 289–90
   government of, 209, 214
   population of, 358
   religious freedom in, 211
   resolution in legislature of, 286, 372
   slavery in, 391, *412*
   slave trade in, 318, *393*
   U.S. Constitution ratified by, 257
   voting rights in, 209, 348, 352, 362
Virginia, University of, 214
Virginia Bill for Establishing Religious Freedom, 213
Virginia colony, *13,* 49–50, 52, *52,* 53, 54, *54,* 56, 58–59, *59,* 60–61, *61,* 64, 66, 103, 111, 118, 127, 143, 144, 157, 178, 194
   assembly in, 145
   Bacon's rebellion and, 99–101
   black population of, 101
   Britain's close ties to, 133
   Dissenter persecution in, 82
   elite class in, 118
   as first royal colony, 60
   free blacks in, 98, 99, 133–34, 143–44
   independence as viewed by, 185
   Indians in, 99–100, 111
   population of, 61
   poverty in, 99, 120
   settlement of, *58*

sides with Charles I, 82
slavery in, 98, 101, 133–34, *251*
Stamp Act and, 175
status of children in, 99
white society of, 61
women's role in, 61–62
Virginia Company, 2, 49–50, 58–59, 60
Virginia Luxuries, 412
Virginia Plan, 248
Virgin Islands, slave uprising in, 139
Virgin Mary, 27, *27,* 34, 37
Virgin of Guadalupe, 27, *28*
"virtual representation", in British Parliament, 173, *174*
Visit from the Old Mistress, A (Homer), *556*
voting rights, 211–14, 349–50, 351–52, 482–83
   for African-Americans, 402, 519, 568, 570, 571, 572
   in American colonies, 143–44, 207–8
   and black disenfranchisement in Pennsylvania, 363
   emancipated slaves and, 551, 553, 568, 570
   freeholder requirements and, 362
   property qualifications and, 168, 208, 209, 348, 349
   religious freedom and, 210
   universal, *571,* 573
   in U.S., 169, 207–8
   for women, 143, 351, 448–49, 570, 571, 572
Voting Rights Act (1965), 351

Wade, Benjamin F., 569
Wade-Davis Bill, 543
wages, 215, 217, 325, 342, 343, 439, 474
   African-Americans and, 339, 542
   decline in real, 380
   equal pay for equal work and, 447
   family, 341
   hourly, 323
   and right to vote, 348
   slavery compared with working for, 343, *343,* 439
   strike for higher, 328–29, 342, 574
   and wage-earning poor, 330
   women and, 340, 449, 453
Wagner, Fort, 518
Wahhabbism, 150
Wahunsonacock, 59
Walden (Thoreau), 331
   title page of, *331*
Waldseemüller, Martin (1475–1522), *8*
Walker, David (1796?–1830), 436–37, *436,* 442
Walker, William (1824–1860), 492–93
Walking Purchase (1737), 111
Walls, Josiah T., *575*
Waltham, Mass., 321, 322
Wampanoag Indians, *66*
Wampanoags, 87
wampum, *91*
War Hawks, 297
War News from Mexico (Woodville), *466*

War of 1812, 221, 295, 298–303, *298, 299, 303,* 321, *350,* 353, 354, 355, 376, 382, 554
   Canadian border and, 302–3
   causes of, 296–97, 298
   map of, *301*
War of Independence, *see* American Revolution
War of Jenkins' Ear, 139, 157
War of the Spanish Succession, 157
War of Triple Alliance, 506
War Party at Fort Douglas (Rindisbacher), *298*
Warren, James (1726–1808), 232
Warren, Josiah, 430
Warren, Mercy Otis (1728–1814), 232
War Spirit at Home (Spencer), *507*
Washington, D.C., 290, *290*
   British invasion of, 299, *299*
Washington, Fort, 195
Washington, George (1732–1799), 118, 119, 157, 161, 179, 185, 194, 246, *276,* 289, 307, *350,* 356, 485
   in battle against French and Indians, 157–58
   cabinet of, 273
   Constitutional Convention and, 247
   at Constitution signing, *253*
   in Continental Congress, 182
   death of, *268, 269, 275*
   Delaware crossing of, 195
   and exclusion of blacks from military, 194, 517
   executes mutineers, 199
   Farewell Address of, 284
   inauguration of, 273
   Native Americans and, 222, 265, 266
   re-election of, 284
   Republican press abuse of, 280
   and return of slaves, 227
   as slaveholder, 227, *228, 268,* 269
   war strategy of, 194
   western land speculation of, 222
   Whiskey Rebellion and, 278, *278*
   at Yorktown, 200
Washington, Harry, 227
Washington, Lund (1737–1796), 194
Washington, Madison, 418
Washington, Martha (1732–1802), 269
Washington, William D., *536*
Washington Society, 431
water power, 322, *322,* 323, 328
Watertown, Conn., 212
Watling Island, 21
Waud, William (1832–1878), *540*
Wayne, Anthony (1745–1796), 265, *265*
Wealth of Nations, The (Smith), 5, 218, 234
Webster, Daniel (1782–1852), 368, *378*
   American Colonization Society and, 435
   Compromise of 1850 and, 475, *476*
   death of, 478
   nullification crisis and, 372
Webster, Noah (1758–1843), 216, 343, 349
Webster-Hayne debate, 372
Weekly Journal, 148, *148*
Weld, Theodore (1803–1895), 437–38, 444, 445

Welles, Gideon (1802–1878), 517
West, *326*
   in election of 1824, 364
   manifest destiny and, 329–30
   population growth in, 297
   rise of, 312–15
West, Benjamin (1730–1813), *114*
Western Hemisphere, *44*
Western Ordinances, *244*
West India Company, 41, 42–43, *43*
West Indies, 5, 24, 41, 51, *95,* 106, *115,* 116, 139, 173, 174, 245, 246, *247,* 276, 492
   American embargo of, 182
   in American Revolution, 197
   economy of, 96–98
   English population of, 96
   European owners of, 96
   immigration to, 38, 54, 219
   New England trade with, 77
   Philadelphia's trade with, 116
   slavery in, 25, 30, 87, 92, 96–98, 129, *131,* 132, 134, 227, 396, 401, 402–6, 411, 415, 443
   tobacco in, 61
West Jersey Concessions (1677), 93
Westo Indians, 102
West Point, N.Y., 199
westward expansion of U.S., 167, 221–22, 240–45, *241,* 355, *474*
   African-Americans and, 317–18
   Civil War and, 510–11, *512,* 524–29
   Confederation government and, 242
   Douglas's views on, 478–79
   free homesteads in, 495
   Jefferson's views on, 274
   Madison's views on, 255–56, 274
   market revolution and, 168, 308, 312–15, *313,* 329, *329,* 348
   Mexican War and, 386
   Native Americans and, 242, 263, 297–98
   of the North, 319
   numbers of people in, 459
   Ordinance of 1784 and, 243
   slavery and, 243, 316–18, 374, 385, 386, 390, 471, 472, 473–74, 483–84, 524
   of the South, 316–18
   women and, 332
wheat, 319
Wheatley, Phillis (1753?–1784), 226, *226*
Whig Party, 367, 368–69, 373, 381–82, *381,* 434, 463, 464, 465, 485, 582
   Abraham Lincoln as member of, 487
   beliefs of, 369, 370–71
   collapse of, 479
   creation of, 364
   division between Democrats and, 169, 369
   in election of 1836, 381
   in election of 1840, 381–82
   in election of 1848, 473
   freedom as viewed by, 370
   origin of name of, 347
   presidential veto and, 379
   and westward expansion of slavery, 386

Whirling Thunder, *373*

Whiskey Rebellion, 278, *278*, 280, 284

Whiskey Ring, 579

White, Garland H. (1829–1894), 545

White, John (1540–1593), *12*, *14*, *56*

Whitefield, Edwin, *315*

Whitefield, George (1714–1770), 150–51, *150*

White Hall Plantation, *292*

White House, The, *361*

White-Jacket (Melville), 465

Whitman, Walt (1819–1892), 307

Whitney, Asa (1791–1874), 471–72, 524

Whitney, Eli (1765–1825), 316, 323

Whittier, John Greenleaf (1807–1892), 454

Whole Book of Psalms Faithfully Translated into English Metre, The, *64*

Wichita, Kans., 606

Wilder, L. Douglas (b. 1931), 575

Wilderness, Battle of the, 540

Wilkes, John (1727–1797), 180–81, *180*

Will, William, *207*

William III, king of England (1650–1702), 102, *103*, 104, *116*

William Penn's Treaty with the Indians, *114*

Williams, Roger (1820–1910), 13, 70–71, 73, 81

Williamsburg, Va., *120*

Wilmington, Del., 43

Wilmot, David (1814–1868), 473, 474

Wilmot Proviso, 473, 474, 475

Wilson, Henry, in election of 1868, *569*

Wilson, James (1742–1798), *253*

Winstanley, Gerard (1609?–1660), 81

Winthrop, John (1588–1649), 53, *65*, 68, 69, 75, 432

    Anne Hutchinson and, 72, 74

    liberty as viewed by, 65, 68

    Roger Williams and, 71

    Speech to Massachusetts General Court of, 75

Winthrop, John, II (1606–1676), *57*

Wirz, Henry (1823–1865), 566

Wisconsin, 312

Wisconsin Territory, 485

Wise, Henry A. (1806–1876), 489

witchcraft, 70

    in New England, 105–6, *105*

"witch doctors," 15

Wolfe, James (1727–1759), 127

Wollaston, John (ca. 1642–1749), *150*

Wollstonecraft, Mary (1759–1797), 280–81, *280*, 453

Woman in the Nineteenth Century, 449

Woman's Emancipation, 452

Woman's Rights Quilt, A, *425*

women:

    agriculture and, 14, 15, 122–23

    and American Revolution, 179, 229–35, *232*

    capitalism and, 341

    and Civil War, 530–31, *530*

    colonial roles of, 122–23

    Confederacy and, 536–37

    and "cult of domesticity," 339, 454

    Daughters of Liberty, 179, 229–35

    and decline in birthrate, 340

    education and, 281, 282

    free speech and, 447

    in gold rush, 470

    industrialization and, 324, *324*, *325*

    labor and, 340–41

    market revolution and, 339–41, *343*

    middle class, *351*

    Native American, 14

    in New Amsterdam, 90

    in New Netherland, 41

    in New World, 26, 38, 39

    in New York colony, 90

    of planter class, 395

    politics and, 232–33

    poll tax on, 98

    as Protestant preachers, *338*

    in Puritanism, 67–68

    and "republican motherhood," 339

    role of, 232

    as slaves, *98*

    strikes and, *343*

    subservience of European, 15, 17

    in Virginia colony, 61–62

    and wages, 449, 453

    in westward expansion, 332

    in the work force, 339–41, 449–53

    see also gender relations; women's rights

women's rights, 17, 169, 210, 280–84, *280*, 340, 385, 425, *425*, 426, 446–55, *448*

    Abigail Adams and, 205

    American Revolution and, 167, 205, 229–35

    antislavery movement and, 385

    Declaration of Sentiments and, 448, 449

    and education, 281, 282

    equal pay for equal work and, 447

    families and, 453–54

    Frederick Douglass and, 389

    John Locke and, 142

    in Louisiana, 294

    Lydia Maria Child and, 341

    newspapers and, 449, 452

    Owenites and, 429

    in Quaker society, 93, *94*

    quilt, *425*

    Reconstruction and, 570, 572

    Seneca Falls Convention and, *425*, 448, 452

    sex and, 453

    and suffrage, 143, 351, 448–49, 531, 570, 573, *573*

    in Utopian societies, 426, 430

    see also gender relations; women

Woodbury, Levi (1789–1851), 379

Woodside, John Archibald (1781–1853), *303*

Woodville, Richard D. (1825–1855), *466*

Wool Act (1699), 172

Woolman, John (1720–1772), 129–30

Worcester, Mass., *281*

Worcester v. Georgia, 375

Workingman's Advocate, 341

Workingmen's Parties, 342

World Anti-Slavery Convention, 448

Wright, Frances (1795–1852), 447, 448

Wright, Jonathan (1840–1887), 576

Wyatt, Francis (c. 1575–1644), 60

Wyoming territory, woman suffrage in, 572–73

XYZ affair, 285, *285*

Yamasee Indians, 92

York, Pa., *213*, *216*

Yorktown, Battle of, *198*, *199*, 200

Yoruba people, 136

Young, Brigham (1801–1877), 337

Young, Thomas, 207

Young Lady's Book, 340

Young Woman with a Harpsichord, *26*

Zenger, John Peter (1697–1746), 148, *148*

Zheng, Admiral, 18

Zoar, 426

Zuni Indians, 10